S0-BZE-192

CYBERLAW

CYBERLAW

National and International Perspectives

Roy J. Girasa

Lubin School of Business
Pace University

Upper Saddle River, New Jersey 07458

Library of Congress Cataloging-in-Publication Data

Girasa, Roy J.
Cyberlaw: national and international perspectives / Roy J. Girasa
p. cm.
Includes bibliographical references and index.
ISBN 0-13-065564-3
1. Internet—Law and legislation—United States. 2. Computers—Law and legislation—United States. 3. Internet—Law and legislation. 4. Computers—Law and legislation. I. Title.

KF390.5C6 G57 2001
343.7309'944—dc21 2001036590

Acquisitions Editor: Melissa Steffens
Editor-in-Chief: Jeff Shelstad
Executive Editor (Editorial): David Shafer
Assistant Editor: Jennifer Surich
Editorial Assistant: Virginia Sheridan
Media Project Manager: Michele Faranda
Marketing Manager: Debbie Clare
Managing Editor (Production): John Roberts
Production Editor: Renata Butera
Production Assistant: Diane Falcone
Permissions Coordinator: Suzanne Grappi
Associate Director, Manufacturing: Vincent Scelta
Production Manager: Arnold Vila
Manufacturing Buyer: Diane Peirano
Design Manager: Jayne Conte
Cover Design: Bruce Kenselaar
Manager, Print Production: Christina Mahon
Composition: Impressions Book and Journal Services, Inc.
Full-Service Project Management: Impressions Book and Journal Services, Inc.
Printer/Binder: Maple Vail, Binghamton

Credits and acknowledgments borrowed from other sources and reproduced, with permission, in this textbook appear on appropriate page within text.

10 9 8 7 6 5 4 3 2 1
ISBN 0-13-065564-3

To my wife, Eleanor, and our children
George, James, Roy, Stacy, Kristin, Thomas

And to CG

Brief Contents

APPENDICES

Contents

APPENDICES

Preface

We are all inundated with materials advising of the necessity of becoming acquainted with computers and, more particularly, with the Internet. After much resistance by many older members of the scholastic community, the mastery of the new technology became a matter of survival. Having taken a series of seminars at the School of Computer Sciences and Information Systems at Pace University, this author was called upon by Daniel Farkas, chairperson at the said school, to prepare and deliver a course on the legal aspects affecting technology. Thus, I began an intense investigation of the field. Internet Law, or *cyberlaw* as it is more popularly named, has developed as rapidly and as extensively as the new technology.

After a year of researching, downloading, and analyzing almost innumerable Web sites, law review articles, statutes, cases, and general materials concerning the Internet, the need for a cyberlaw text became apparent. From course outlines at other universities, one was able to gauge the topics deemed important by the legal community. In so doing, I determined the main issues with which the business community and users at large were concerned. The problem is that any text, upon publication, is somewhat out of date due to the rapid statutory and case law developments taking place on an almost daily basis. Rather than preparing a standard text with annual or biannual editions, it is the intention of this author to update the text monthly or more frequently at the Prentice Hall Web site, *www.prenhall.com/girasa.* The subject matter will be amended as new legal issues, cases, and statutes arise. I also intend to develop more fully certain topics that may arise periodically. Students reading the text will be able to access the said author's Web site and gain the latest information that this author is able to locate and prepare.

Computer or cyberspace law is on the cusp of the law. Thus, few persons feel competent to say confidently what the status of such law is and, especially, what the law's trend will be in the forthcoming years of the new millennium. Building upon the enormous output of scholarly works, judicial decisions, and the explosion of available collateral information, I offer the following overview of cyberspace law.

It is important for the reader to read and analyze closely the cases set forth in the text. The cases are not simply examples of the principles of law presented in the main text; they also present the best explanation of current law as found by this author, especially those cases set forth at length in the text. Most cases are the leading cases appearing to date and are vital to an understanding of the present state of Internet law. The cases were chosen for the discussion of the area of law under study. In reading the cases closely, the student begins to have a *feel* of how judges and courts are engaged in the decision-making process and which issues most concern them.

Inasmuch as the materials were researched, written, and typed by the author alone, all errors are to be attributed solely to him. Suggestions and corrections by readers are desired greatly. In addition to those stated in the text, there are a number of persons and Web sites that were utilized in the preparation for this text. The obvious source for the examination of cases and articles is LEXIS-NEXIS. Other less known but important sources, at least initially, were the course outlines and hypertext materials in connection therewith used at other law schools. I was guided by the excellent summaries and reviews of the latest Internet cases prepared by Martin H. Samson, Esq., of the law firm of Phillips Nizer Benjamin Krim & Ballon LLP.

I am deeply indebted to my family members who have condoned my lack of attention to their needs, especially during "vacation" periods. I also wish to thank the following persons: the said Daniel Farkas, who caused me to investigate and become enormously interested in the field of cyberlaw; members of my Department of Legal Studies and Taxation, especially Dr. Richard J. Kraus, who assisted in editing the text, Professors Peter Edelstein, Arthur Magaldi, Ivan Fox, Saul LeVine, Robert Wiener, and Martin Zern, and Professors Martin Topol and Karen Berger from the Marketing Department. Thanks also to Diana D'Amico Juettner of Mercy College, with whom I collaborated on past articles on subjects covered in the text; to Professor Carolyn Perricone of Westchester Community College; to my former law partners, N.Y.S. Supreme Court Justice Michael DeMarco, Thomas Sassone, and George Pappas; to Deans Arthur Centonze and James Russell for the encouragement; and to my son Roy Girasa for his many suggestions. Kudos also to Darren and Richard Fabbri, Susanne Marolda, and Connie Petruzziello of Tufts University, who gave insightful comments.

Much thanks to the Prentice Hall personnel, particularly Kate Moore, who is the finest representative I have encountered from any company; Debbie Clare, who initially suggested the writing of a text as well as introducing me to Virginia Sheridan, who discussed the proposed text with the author and gave early drafts to reviewers; Melissa Steffens for helping me to understand the process of publishing a text and speeding the process of publication; Renata Butera for her editorial assistance and warm words of encouragement; Jennifer Surich, for her assistance in preparation of the Instructor's Manual; David Palmer, for his aid and advice; Jim Boyd, who directed my efforts to a previously not experienced maze of submitting a book for publication; Jeri Lambert, Susan Ryan, and Paul O'Mara from Impressions Book and Journal Services for their editing suggestions and changes; to anonymous reviewers who gave wonderful suggestions that were adopted in great part; and to many other persons who rooted for me and assisted in so many ways.

Thanks also to our departmental secretaries, Geraldine Seiter and Thomas Vail, and to Patrice Moriarty, who took my class on cyberlaw both to learn and to critique the text from a student's point of view.

I can be reached at the following address:

Dr. Roy J. Girasa
Lubin School of Business
Pace University
Goldstein Center
861 Bedford Road
Pleasantville, New York 10570-2799

Telephone: (914) 773-3518
FAX: (914) 773-3908
E-mail: rgirasa@pace.edu

PART

I

INTRODUCTION AND JURISDICTION

CHAPTER

1 INTRODUCTION TO CYBERLAW

Chapter Outline

Few areas of the law have developed so rapidly in so short a time span as Internet (cyberspace)[1] law, or *cyberlaw*. National and international law-making bodies are struggling to keep pace with the latest technological developments that render existing laws and regulations obsolete or require significant amendments. Legislative and judicial attempts to establish rules for overseeing and protecting legitimate concerns of national inhabitants have been frustrated by the incredible pace of technological advances.

The benefits brought about by computer technology are obvious. Anyone seeking to gain information over the superhighway is inundated by the degree and quality of the data made readily available and immediately accessible. Within a very short time span, an individual can become quite knowledgeable about subjects that were previously barely known. For example, several television talk shows called upon this writer to render his views about certain aspects of immigration law and policy, with only several hours of advanced notice. A quick review of Internet sources permitted him to view and comprehend a large volume of accurate, technical data downloaded within a few minutes in preparation for the said programs. Previously, one had to go to the library, attempt to find the subjects in the card catalogs, go to the bookshelves on different floors, and try to locate the data in books that often were either not appropriate or missing entirely. At the annual meeting of the American Business Law Association in August 2000, more than one-half of the papers presented concerned cyberlaw. In the past, the dominant themes concerned employment law topics. Cyberlaw is the hot area of law today. The reason, in addition to the growing influence of the technology on everyone's life, is the unsettled nature of the field.

The statistics are familiar to everyone exploring this new arena. The growth of computer-related commercial and personal activities is almost beyond comprehension. There were over 90 million Internet users as of early 2000 and a projected growth of ten times that within five years thereof. Two-thirds of the users shopped online as of the third quarter of 1999. Fifty-four percent of Internet users purchased products online. Online retail sales in the United States constituted $3.5 billion in March and $4.3 billion in April, 2001. Online advertising expenditures were $4.6 billion in 1999, some tenfold greater than in 1996 and are proportionately greater for 2000 and 2001.[2]

The political, social, and economic consequences of Internet use can only dimly be seen "through a glass darkly." Countries that seek to insulate themselves from the global community today, either are unable to prevent outside access or do so with significantly negative economic results. In past decades, inhabitants of remote countries did have limited knowledge of the outside world, fostered by reading or television viewing. Such access, however, could be restricted with relative ease by dictatorial governments. Such attempts today to restrict access may be futile.

Even in the midst of recent military confrontations such as in the former Yugoslavia, communications took place via the Internet by use of e-mail and other resources. The global society, yearned for by thinkers of old, is coming to fruition. With such expanse of the human endeavor, problems also emanate. Pornography, invasion of secret computer banks, loss of privacy, and so-called viruses implanted by hackers have now become almost daily news. Where such exponential growth of knowledge will lead can only be speculated. The one clear message is that life as it was known before the Internet has been altered greatly and will continue to change dramatically. Those persons, especially entrepreneurs, who ignore the new technology will be left behind. In the past, changes took place gradually, thereby allowing some transitional period of adjustment. No such grace period exists today.

COMPUTER BASICS

The basis for cyberspace and cyberlaw is the computer. Before we proceed with an explanation of cyberspace, it is important to define the nature of a computer from a legal point of view. A *computer* is defined by statute as:

> an electronic, magnetic, optical, electrochemical, or other high speed processing device performing logical, arithmetic, or storage functions, and includes any data storage facility or communications facility directly related to or operating in conjunction with such device, but such term does not include an automated typewriter or typesetter, a portable held calculator, or other similar device.[3]

The definition is important because the computer-related statutes only apply to hardware and software coming within the definition.

Computers may be *personal* in nature, that is, operated by one person at a time, or they may be *servers* that permit multiple users to access data, services, and other uses. Computers contain *operating systems* that consist of a software program that permits users to perform tasks, as well as allocating disk space, main memory space, and other functions. The most popular operating system is Microsoft Windows, which is issued in a number of versions, including Windows 2000 and Windows NT.[4]

Computers operate by a series of on and off switches, using the digit *0* for the off switch and *1* for the on switch. The 0 or 1 is called a *bit,* which is the smallest unit of memory in the computer. A *byte* is a group of eight bits that represents a character, that is, a letter or a number. A *kilobyte* consists of 1,024 bytes, and a *gigabyte* consists of 1,024 megabytes. Through the collection of bytes, persons using the computer can accomplish many tasks. The difficulty is that most persons would be unable or lack the desire to input commands without the assistance of programming languages that facilitate the entry of data and commands. These programming languages translate sets of instruction into machine-readable strings of 1s and 0s.

WHAT IS *CYBERSPACE*?

The most comprehensive overview of the Internet, cited thereafter in numerous federal and state appellate decisions,[5] was set forth in the Findings of Fact in *ACLU* [American Civil Liberties Union] *v. Reno,* wherein the parties stipulated to the history and basic technology of the Internet. The background of the two consolidated actions concerned the filing of motions for a preliminary injunction by the plaintiffs challenging the constitutionality of Title V of the Telecommunications Act of 1996. The contention was that certain sections of the statute, making it a crime to transmit by interactive computers any communications with patently offensive materials to persons under the age of 18 years, were unconstitutionally vague. The claim therein is that such statutory provision would include the criminalization of speech about abortions or abortifacient drugs and devices, which would violate the right of free speech protected by the First Amendment of the Constitution. The issues are less relevant for our discussion herein than the agreed upon definitions and explanations by all of the parties to the litigation that formed the first 48 paragraphs of the Findings of Fact. The court, in granting the motion, stated the nature of cyberspace as follows.

ACLU V. RENO

929 F. Supp. 824 (E.D.Pa. 1996)

II. FINDINGS OF FACT

The Nature of Cyberspace

The Creation of the Internet and the Development of Cyberspace **1.** The Internet is not a physical or tangible entity, but rather a giant network, which interconnects innumerable smaller groups of linked computer networks. It is thus a network of networks. This is best understood if one considers what a linked group of computers—referred to here as a "network"—is, and what it does. Small networks are now ubiquitous (and are often called "local area networks"). For example, in many United States Courthouses, computers are linked to each other for the purpose of exchanging files and messages (and to share equipment such as printers). These are networks.

2. Some networks are "closed" networks, not linked to other computers or networks. Many networks, however, are connected to other networks, which are in turn connected to other networks in a manner, which permits each computer in any network to communicate with computers on any other network in the system. This global Web of linked networks and computers is referred to as the Internet.

3. The nature of the Internet is such that it is very difficult, if not impossible, to determine its size at a given moment. It is indisputable, however, that the Internet has experienced extraordinary growth in recent years. In 1981, fewer than 300 computers were linked to the Internet, and by 1989, the number stood at fewer than 90,000 computers. By 1993, over 1,000,000 computers were linked. Today [1996], over 9,400,000 host computers worldwide, of which approximately 60 percent located within the United States, are estimated to be linked to the Internet. This count does not include the personal computers people use to access the Internet using modems. In all, reasonable estimates are that as many as 40 million people around the world can and do access an enormously flexible communication Internet medium. That figure is expected to grow to 200 million Internet users by the year 1999.

4. Some of the computers and computer networks that make up the Internet are owned by governmental and public institutions, some are owned by non-profit organizations, and some are privately owned. The resulting whole is a decentralized, global medium of communications—or "cyberspace"—that links people, institutions, corporations, and governments around the world. The Internet is an international system. This communication medium allows any of the literally tens of millions of people with access to the Internet to exchange information. These communications can occur almost instantaneously, and can be directed either to specific individuals, to a broader group of people interested in a particular subject, or to the world as a whole.

5. The Internet had its origins in 1969 as an experimental project of the Advanced Research Project Agency ("ARPA"), and was called ARPANET. This network linked computers and computer networks owned by the military, defense contractors, and university laboratories conducting defense-related research. The network later allowed researchers across the country to access directly and to use extremely powerful supercomputers located at a few key universities and laboratories. As it evolved far beyond its research origins in the United States to encompass universities, corporations, and people around the world, the ARPANET came to be called the "DARPA Internet," and finally just the "Internet."

6. From its inception, the network was designed to be a decentralized, self-maintaining series of redundant links between computers and computer networks, capable of rapidly transmitting communications without direct human involvement or control, and with the automatic ability to re-route communications if one or more individual links were damaged or otherwise unavailable. Among other goals, this redundant system of linked computers was designed to allow vital research and communications to continue even if portions of the network were damaged, say, in a war.

7. To achieve this resilient nationwide (and ultimately global) communications medium, the ARPANET encouraged the creation of multiple links to and from each computer (or computer network) on the network. Thus, a computer located in Washington, D.C., might be linked (usually using dedicated telephone lines) to other computers in neighboring states or on the Eastern seaboard. Each of those computers could in turn be linked to other computers, which themselves would be linked to other computers.

8. A communication sent over this redundant series of linked computers could travel any of a number of routes to its destination. Thus, a message sent from a computer in Washington, D.C., to a computer in Palo Alto, California, might first be sent to a computer in Philadelphia, and then be forwarded to a computer in Pittsburgh, and then to Chicago, Denver, and Salt Lake City, before finally reaching Palo Alto. If the message could not travel along that path (because of military attack, simple technical malfunction, or other reason), the message would automatically (without human intervention or even knowledge) be re-routed, perhaps, from Washington, D.C. to Richmond, and then to Atlanta, New Orleans, Dallas, Albuquerque, Los Angeles, and finally to Palo Alto. This type of transmission, and re-routing, would likely occur in a matter of seconds.

9. Messages between computers on the Internet do not necessarily travel entirely along the same path. The Internet uses "packet switching" communication protocols that allow individual messages to be subdivided into smaller "packets" that are then sent independently to the destination, and are then automatically reassembled by the receiving computer. While all packets of a given message often travel along the same path to the destination, if computers along the route become overloaded, then packets can be re-routed to less loaded computers.

10. At the same time that ARPANET was maturing (it subsequently ceased to exist), similar networks developed to link universities, research facilities, businesses, and individuals around the world. These other formal or loose networks included BITNET, CSNET, FIDONET, and USENET. Eventually, each of these networks (many of which overlapped) were themselves linked together, allowing users of any computers linked to any one of the networks to transmit communications to users of computers on other networks. It is this series of linked networks (themselves linking computers and computer networks) that is today commonly known as the Internet.

11. No single entity—academic, corporate, governmental, or non-profit—administers the Internet. It exists and functions as a result of the fact that hundreds of thousands of separate operators of computers and computer networks independently decided to use common data transfer protocols to exchange communications and information with other computers (which in turn exchange communications and information with still other computers). There is no centralized storage location, control point, or communications channel for the Internet, and it would not be technically feasible for a single entity to control all of the information conveyed on the Internet.

How Individuals Access the Internet

12. Individuals have a wide variety of avenues to access cyberspace in general, and the Internet in particular. In terms of physical access, there are two common methods to establish an actual link to the Internet. First, one can use a computer or computer terminal that is directly (and usually permanently) connected to a computer network that is itself directly or indirectly connected to the Internet. Second, one can use a "personal computer" with a "modem" to connect over a telephone line to a large computer or computer network that is itself directly or indirectly connected to the Internet. As detailed below, both direct and modem connections are made available to people by a wide variety of academic, governmental, or commercial entities.

13. Students, faculty, researchers, and others affiliated with the vast majority of colleges and universities in the United States can access the Internet through their educational institutions. Such access is often via direct connections using computers located in campus libraries, offices, or computer centers, or may be through telephone access using a modem from a student's or professor's campus or off-campus location. Some colleges and universities install "ports" or outlets for direct network connections in each dormitory room or provide access via computers located in common areas in dormitories. Such access enables students and professors to use information and content provided by the college or university itself, and to use the vast amount of research resources and other information available on the Internet worldwide.

14. Similarly, Internet resources and access are sufficiently important to many corporations and other employers that those employers link their office computer networks to the Internet and provide employees with direct or modem access to the office network (and thus to the Internet). Such access might be used by, for example, a corporation involved in scientific or medical research or manufacturing to enable corporate employees to exchange information and ideas with academic researchers in their fields.

15. Those who lack access to the Internet through their schools or employers still have a variety of ways they can access to the Internet. Many communities across the country have established "free-nets" or community networks to provide their citizens with a local link to the Internet (and to provide local-oriented content and discussion groups). The first such community network, the Cleveland Free-Net Community Computer System, was established in 1986, and free-nets now exist in scores of communities as diverse as Richmond, Virginia, Tallahassee, Florida, Seattle, Washington, and San Diego, California. Individuals typically can access free-nets at little or no cost via modem connection or by using computers available in community buildings. Free-nets are often operated by a local library, educational institution, or non-profit community group.

16. Individuals can also access the Internet through many local libraries. Libraries often offer patrons use of computers that are linked to the Internet. In addition, some libraries offer telephone modem access to the libraries' computers, which are themselves connected to the Internet. Increasingly, patrons now use library services and resources without ever physically entering the library itself. Libraries typically provide such direct or modem access at no cost to the individual user.

17. Individuals can also access the Internet by patronizing an increasing number of storefront "computer coffee shops," where customers—while they drink their coffee—can use computers provided by the shop to access the Internet. The shop typically provides such Internet access for a small hourly fee.

18. Individuals can also access the Internet through commercial and non-commercial "Internet service providers" that typically offer modem telephone access to a computer or computer network linked to the Internet. Many such providers—including the members of plaintiff Commercial Internet Exchange Association—are commercial entities offering Internet access for a monthly or hourly fee. Some Internet service providers, however, are non-profit organizations that offer free or very low cost access to the Internet. For example, the International Internet Association offers free modem access to the Internet upon request. Also, a number of trade or other non-profit associations offer Internet access as a service to members.

19. Another common way for individuals to access the Internet is through one of the major national commercial "online services" such as America Online, CompuServe, the Microsoft Network, or Prodigy. These online services offer nationwide computer networks (so that subscribers can dial-in to a local telephone number), and the services provide extensive and well-organized content within their own proprietary computer networks. In addition to allowing access to the extensive content available within each online service, the services also allow subscribers to link to the much larger resources of the Internet. Full access to the online services (including access to the Internet) can be obtained for modest monthly or hourly fees. The major commercial online services have almost twelve million individual subscribers across the United States.

20. In addition to using the national commercial online services, individuals can also access the Internet using some (but not all) of the thousands of local dial-in computer services, often called "bulletin board systems" or "BBSs." With an investment of as little as $2,000.00 and the cost of a telephone line, individuals, non-profit organizations, advocacy groups, and businesses can offer their own dial-in computer "bulletin board" service where friends, members, subscribers, or customers can exchange ideas and information. BBSs range from single computers with only one telephone line into the computer (allowing only one user at a time), to single computers with many telephone lines into the computer (allowing multiple simultaneous users), to multiple linked computers each servicing multiple dial-in telephone lines (allowing multiple simultaneous users). Some (but not all) of these BBS systems offer direct or indirect links to the Internet. Some BBS systems charge users a nominal fee for access, while many others are free to the individual users.

21. Although commercial access to the Internet is growing rapidly, many users of the Internet—such as college students and staff—do not individually pay for access (except to the extent, for example, that the cost of computer services is a component of college tuition). These and Internet users can access the Internet without paying for such access with a credit card or other form of payment.

Methods to Communicate over the Internet

22. Once one has access to the Internet, there are a wide variety of different methods of communication and information exchange over the network. These many methods of communication and information retrieval are constantly evolving and are therefore difficult to categorize concisely. The most common methods of communications on the Internet (as well as within the major online services) can be roughly grouped into six categories:

1. one-to-one messaging (such as "e-mail"),
2. one-to-many messaging (such as "listserv"),
3. distributed message databases (such as "USENET newsgroups"),
4. real time communication (such as "Internet Relay Chat"),
5. real time remote computer utilization (such as "telnet"), and
6. remote information retrieval (such as "ftp," "gopher," and the "World Wide Web").

Most of these methods of communication can be used to transmit text, data, computer programs, sound, visual images (i.e., pictures), and moving video images.

23. One-to-one messaging. One method of communication on the Internet is via electronic mail, or "e-mail," comparable in principle to sending a first class letter. One can address and transmit a message to one or more other people. E-mail on the Internet is not routed through a central control point, and can take many and varying paths to the recipients. Unlike postal mail, simple e-mail generally is not "sealed" or secure, and can be accessed or viewed on intermediate computers between the sender and recipient (unless the message is encrypted).

24. One-to-many messaging. The Internet also contains automatic mailing list services (such as "listservs"), [also referred to by witnesses as "mail exploders"] that allow communications about particular subjects of interest to a group of people. For example, people can subscribe to a "listserv" mailing list on a particular topic of interest to them. The subscriber can submit messages on the topic to the listserv that are forwarded (via e-mail), either automatically or through a human moderator overseeing the listserv, to anyone who has subscribed to the mailing list. A recipient of such a message can reply to the message and have the reply also distributed to everyone on the mailing list. This service provides the capability to keep abreast of developments or events in a particular subject area. Most listserv-type mailing lists automatically forward all incoming messages to all mailing list subscribers. There are thousands of such mailing list services on the Internet, collectively with hundreds of thousands of subscribers. Users of "open" listservs typically can add or remove their names from the mailing list automatically, with no direct human involvement. Listservs may also be "closed," i.e., only allowing for one's acceptance into the listservs by a human moderator.

25. Distributed message databases. Similar in function to listservs—but quite different in how communications are transmitted—are distributed message databases such as "USENET newsgroups." User-sponsored newsgroups are among the most popular and widespread applications of Internet services, and cover all imaginable topics of interest to users. Like listservs, newsgroups are open discussions and exchanges on particular topics. Users, however, need not subscribe to the discussion mailing list in advance, but can instead access the database at any time. Some USENET newsgroups are "moderated" but most are open access. For the moderated newsgroups, all messages to the newsgroup are forwarded to one person who can screen them for relevance to the topics under discussion. USENET newsgroups are disseminated using ad hoc, peer to peer connections between approximately 200,000 computers (called USENET "servers") around the world. For unmoderated newsgroups, when an individual user with access to a USENET server posts a message to a newsgroup, the message is automatically forwarded to all adjacent USENET servers that furnish access to the newsgroup, and it is then propagated to the servers adjacent to those servers, etc. The messages are temporarily stored on each receiving server, where they are available for review and response by individual users. The messages are automatically and periodically purged from each system after a time to make room for new messages. Responses to messages, like the original messages, are automatically distributed to all other computers receiving the newsgroup or forwarded to a moderator in the case of a moderated newsgroup. The dissemination of messages to USENET servers around the world is an automated process that does not require direct human intervention or review.

26. There are newsgroups on more than fifteen thousand different subjects. In 1994, approximately 70,000 messages were posted to newsgroups each day, and those messages were distributed to the approximately 190,000 computers or computer networks that participate in the USENET newsgroup system. Once the messages reach the approximately 190,000 receiving computers or computer networks, they are available to individual users of those computers or computer networks. Collectively, almost 100,000 new messages (or "articles") are posted to newsgroups each day.

27. Real time communication. In addition to transmitting messages that can be later read or accessed, individuals on the Internet can engage in an intermediate dialog, in "real time," with other people on the Internet. In its simplest forms, "talk" allows one-to-one communications and "Internet Relay Chat" (or IRC) allows two or more to type messages to each other that almost immediately appear on the others' computer screens. IRC is analogous to a telephone party line, using a computer and keyboard rather than a telephone. With IRC, however, at any one time there are thousands of different party lines available, in which collectively tens of thousands of users are engaging in conversations on a huge range of subjects. Moreover, one can create a new party line to discuss a different topic at any time. Some IRC conversations are "moderated" or include "channel operators."

28. In addition, commercial online services such as America Online, CompuServe, the Microsoft Network, and Prodigy have their own "chat" systems allowing their members to converse.

29. Real time remote computer utilization. Another method to use information on the Internet is to access and control remote computers in "real time" using "telnet." For example, using telnet, a researcher at a university would be able to use the computing power of a supercomputer located at a different university. A student can use telnet to connect to a remote library to access the library's online card catalog program.

30. Remote information retrieval. The final category of communication may be the most well known use of the Internet—the search for and retrieval of information located on remote computers. There are three primary methods to locate and retrieve information on the Internet.

31. A simple method uses "ftp" (or file transfer protocol) to list the names of computer files available on a remote computer, and to transfer one or more of those files to an individual's local computer.

32. Another approach uses a program and format named "gopher" to guide an individual's search through the resources available on a remote computer.

The World Wide Web

33. A third approach, and fast becoming the most well-known on the Internet, is the "World Wide Web." The Web utilizes a "hypertext" formatting language called hypertext markup language (HTML), and programs that "browse" the Web can display HTML documents containing text, images, sound, animation and moving video. Any HTML document includes links to other types of information or resources, so that while viewing an HTML document that, for example, describes resources available on the Internet, one can "click" using a computer mouse on the description of the resource and be immediately connected to the resource itself. Such "hyperlinks" allow information to be accessed and organized in very flexible ways, and allow people to locate and efficiently view related information even if the information is stored on numerous computers all around the world.

34. Purpose. The World Wide Web (W3C) was created to serve as the platform for a global, online store of knowledge, containing information from a diversity of sources and accessible to Internet users around the world. Though information on the Web is contained in individual computers, the fact that each of these computers is connected to the Internet through W3C protocols allows all of the information to become part of a single body of knowledge. It is currently the most advanced information system developed on the Internet, and embraces within its data model most information in previous networked information systems such as ftp, gopher, wais [wide area information servers], and USENET.

35. History. W3C was originally developed at CERN, the European Particle Physics Laboratory, and was initially used to allow information sharing within internationally dispersed teams of researchers and engineers. Originally aimed at the High Energy Physics community, it has spread to other areas and attracted much interest in user support, resource recovery, and many other areas, which depend on collaborative and information sharing. The Web has extended beyond the scientific and academic community to include communications by individuals, non-profit organizations, and businesses.

36. Basic Operation. The World Wide Web is a series of documents stored in different computers all over the Internet. Documents contain information stored in a variety of formats, including text, still images, sounds, and video. An essential element of the Web is that any document has an address (rather like a telephone number). Most Web documents contain "links." These are short sections of text or image, which refer to another document. Typically the linked text is blue or underlined when displayed, and when selected by the user, the referenced document is automatically displayed, wherever in the world it actually is stored. Links for example are used to lead from overview documents to more detailed documents, from tables of contents to particular pages, but also as cross-references, footnotes, and new forms of information structure.

37. Many organizations now have "home pages" on the Web. These are documents which provide a set of links designed to represent the organization, and through links from the home page, guide the user directly or indirectly to information about or relevant to that organization.

38. As an example of the use of links, if these Findings were to be put on a World Wide Web site, its home page might contain links such as these:

- The nature of cyberspace
- Creation of the Internet and the development of cyberspace
- How people access the Internet
- Methods to communicate over the Internet

39. Each of these links takes the user of the site from the beginning of the Findings to the appropriate section within this Adjudication. Links may also take the user from the original Web site to another Web site on another computer connected to the Internet. These links from one computer to another, from one document to another across the Internet, are what unify the Web into a single body of knowledge, and what makes the Web unique. The Web was designed with a maximum target time to follow a link of one tenth of a second.

40. Publishing. The World Wide Web exists fundamentally as a platform through which people and organizations can communicate through shared information. When information is made available, it is said to be "published" on the Web. Publishing on the Web simply requires that the "publisher" has a computer connected to the Internet and that the computer is running W3C server software. The computer can be as simple as a personal computer costing less than $1500 dollars or as complex as a multi-million dollar mainframe computer. Many Web publishers choose instead to lease disk storage space from someone else who has the necessary computer facilities, eliminating the need for actually owning any equipment oneself.

41. The Web, as a universe of network accessible information, contains a variety of documents prepared with quite varying degrees of care, from the hastily typed idea, to the professionally executed corporate profile. The power of the Web stems from the ability of a link to point to any document regardless of its status or physical location.

42. Information to be published on the Web must also be formatted according to the rules of the Web standards. These standardized formats assure that all Web users who want to read the material will be able to view it. Web standards are sophisticated and flexible enough that they have grown to meet the publishing needs of many large corporations, banks, brokerage houses, newspapers and magazines which now publish "online" editions of their material, as well as government agencies, and even courts, which use the

Web to disseminate information to the public. At the same time, Web publishing is simple enough that thousands of individual users and small community organizations are using the Web to publish their own personal "home pages," the equivalent of individualized newsletters about that person or organization, which are available to everyone on the Web.

43. Web publishers have a choice to make their Web sites open to the general pool of all Internet users, or close them, thus making the information accessible only to those with advance authorization. Many publishers choose to keep their sites open to all in order to give their information the widest potential audience. In the event that the publishers choose to maintain restrictions on access, this may be accomplished by assigning specific user names and passwords as a prerequisite to access to the site. Or, in the case of Web sites maintained for internal use of one organization, access will only be allowed from other computers within that organization's local network.

44. Searching the Web. A variety of systems have developed that allow users of the Web to search particular information among all of the public sites that are part of the Web. Services such as Yahoo!, Magellan, Altavista, Webcrawler, and Lycos are all services known as "search engines" which allow users to search for Web sites that contain certain categories of information, or to search for key words. For example, a Web user looking for the text of Supreme Court opinions would type the words "Supreme Court" into a search engine, and then be presented with a list of World Wide Web sites that contain Supreme Court information. This list would actually be a series of links to those sites. Having searched out a number of sites that might contain the desired information, the user would then follow individual links, browsing through the information on each site, until the desired material is found. For many content providers on the Web, the ability to be found by these search engines is very important.

45. Common standards. The Web links together disparate information on an ever-growing number of Internet-linked computers by setting common information storage formats (HTML) and a common language for the exchange of Web documents (HTTP [i.e., hypertext transfer protocol]). Although the information may be in many different formats, and stored on computers which are not otherwise compatible, the basic Web standards provide a basic set of standards which allow communication and exchange of information. Despite the fact that many types of computers are used on the Web, and the fact that many of these machines are otherwise incompatible, those who "publish" information on the Web are able to communicate with those who seek to access information with little difficulty because of these basic technical standards.

46. A distributed system with no centralized control. Running on tens of thousands of individual computers on the Internet, the Web is what is known as a distributed system. The Web was designed so that organizations with computers containing information can become part of the Web simply by attaching their computers to the Internet and running appropriate Worldwide Web software. No single organization controls any membership in the Web, nor is there any centralized point from which individual Web sites or services can be blocked from the Web. From a user's perspective, it may appear to be a single, integrated system, but in reality it has no centralized control point.

47. Contrast to closed databases. The Web's open, distributed, and decentralized nature stands in sharp contrast to most information systems that have come before it. Private information services such as Westlaw, Lexis/Nexis, and Dialog, have contained large storehouses of knowledge, and can be accessed from the Internet with the appropriate passwords and access software. However, these databases are not linked together into a single whole, as is the World Wide Web.

48. Success of the Web in research, education, and political activities. The World Wide Web has become so popular because of its open, distributed, and easy-to-use nature. Rather than requiring those who seek information to purchase new software or hardware, and to learn a new kind of system for each new database of information they seek to access, the Web environment makes it easy for users to jump from one set of information to another. By the same token, the open nature of the Web makes it easy for publishers to reach their intended audiences without having to know in advance what kind of computer each potential reader has, and what kind of software they will be using.

In Chapter 8, we will discuss how a person is able to access the Internet, that is, to connect from one's Internet address to that of the destination. The discussion will focus on domain names, their registration, and limitations on them. The changes brought about by the Internet have occupied the attention of all nations of the world. It has become a matter of national urgency and security to initiate policies safeguarding governmental, economic, and social institutions. In the United States, President Clinton took the lead in proposing an agenda for future development of the new technologies.

A FRAMEWORK FOR GLOBAL ELECTRONIC COMMERCE

On July 1, 1997, the president of the United States issued a report entitled "A Framework for Global Electronic Commerce."[6] The underlying principles of governmental policy in the foreseeable future were set forth, and they will be discussed where relevant throughout this book. The report recognizes the enormous changes that the new media, especially the Internet, will cause in almost all facets of the global community. From telemedicine to new outlets for political and personal expressions, electronic media have necessitated new models for commercial interaction and will continue to do so.

The Global Information Infrastructure (GII) will change the way business is conducted, how entertainment products are conveyed, the manner in which information and professional services are conducted, and other transformations. These occurrences will require new rules to bring order and protection of rights in the new economy. The issues that have to be resolved are mind numbing. Issues involving taxes, customs duties, licensing, standards development, consumer protection, security, privacy, and other matters will have to be addressed.

The president outlined a number of principles and policies to foster the development of the GII. They are as follows:

1. The private sector should lead.
2. Governments should avoid undue restrictions on electronic commerce.
3. Where governmental involvement is needed, its aim should be to support and enforce a predictable, minimalist, consistent, and simple legal environment for commerce.
4. Governments should recognize the unique qualities of the Internet.
5. Electronic commerce over the Internet should be facilitated on a global basis.

The report also presents issues to be addressed in order "to preserve the Internet as a non-regulatory medium, one in which competition and consumer choice will shape the marketplace." The issues are divided into three categories: financial issues, which encompass customs and taxation, and electronic payments; legal issues, which address intellectual property protection, privacy, security, and a Uniform Commercial Code (UCC) for electronic commerce; and market access issues, to wit, telecommunication infrastructure and information technology, content, and technical standards. The legal issues will be addressed later in this text. The report thus lays out a blueprint for minimal governmental intrusion while ensuring the safety and development of the Internet.

THE AMERICAN LEGAL SYSTEM

Before commencing the procedural and substantive aspects of our text, it would be useful for readers not familiar with the U.S. legal system to have a brief overview of its structure. There are two major divisions of the U.S. legal system, namely the federal courts and the state courts. Superficially, they all possess the same three-tier structure of a trial court, a first appeals court, and a highest appeals court. A more incisive view of these 51 court systems will reveal substantial dissimilarities. The federal system, which we are most concerned with, is composed of a trial court, known as the district court; the first level of appeals, known as the U.S. Court of Appeals; and the highest court of the land, the U.S. Supreme Court.

The District Court. All trials take place at the district court level.[7] Although it appears to be at the lowest level, in practical terms, it is the most important court for most litigants. It is where evidence is presented before one presiding judge who determines what law is applicable to the facts of the case, and the judge or the jury, if there is a jury, decides the facts and outcome of the case. To institute a civil lawsuit, the plaintiff files a summons (generally with a complaint) with the court, and the party being sued (the defendant) is served with the papers. Thereafter, the defendant files and serves an answer to the complaint and may also serve a counterclaim alleging facts that, if proven, would render the plaintiff liable to the defendant. In the interim before the actual trial takes place, legal counsel to each party generally conducts examinations of the other party and of witnesses to ascertain the nature of the claims and defenses to the lawsuit. After the depositions and other discovery take place, the case is then made ready for trial. At a trial, the presiding judge and the jury (if there is a jury) listen to the evidence, determine the alleged true facts amidst often contradictory testimony, and apply the law to the facts at hand. In the end, a verdict is rendered in favor of one or the other party, and that verdict is reduced to a judgment of the court. Upon entry of the judgment, the prevailing party will have the right to the relief granted by the court (usually, a money judgment plus interest and costs).

Every state must have at least one federal district court, although some states have more than one district court due to their larger populations and geographical distances. Thus, Wyoming has one federal district court, located in Cheyenne (Wyoming has a population of only one-half million), but California has district courts in San Diego, Los Angeles, San Francisco, and Sacramento.

U.S. Courts of Appeals. The losing or dissatisfied party in a district court case may appeal to the U.S. Court of Appeals. There are 11 circuit courts of appeals; the territory of each encompasses a number of states from whose district courts appeals may be taken. A 12th court of appeals, known as the District of Columbia Circuit, sits in Washington, D.C., and resolves appeals from within the District. An additional court of appeals, known as the Court of Appeals for the Federal Circuit, resolves appeals in specialized cases, such as appeals from the Court of Federal Claims, the Patent and Trademark Office, and the Court of International Trade (customs cases). The right to appeal is absolute to any party to litigation who files a timely notice of appeal, with the sole exception that a prosecutor in a criminal case may not appeal a not-guilty verdict in a criminal case. The appeals court does not hear or accept new evidence. It renders its decision based on the stenographic record of a transcript of the trial, the written briefs of the attorneys, and the oral presentations by said attorneys to the presiding judges. Generally, three judges sit in an appeals case; in an en banc proceeding, which occurs in unusual or important cases and with permission of the court, all of the judges of the court of appeals for the particular circuit listen and determine the merits of the appeal. A decision by a majority of two, or of more than half of the judges in an en banc proceeding, finally ends the litigation unless the U.S. Supreme Court, in very rare circumstances, grants permission for a further appeal to its Court (such permission is called a *writ of certiorari*).

The U.S. Supreme Court. The highest court of the land, the U.S. Supreme Court, is composed of nine justices whose majority decision renders finality to the issue or case at hand. Its decision is binding upon all persons—including the president and the Congress—and courts within the United States. It hears only a very limited number of cases (usually about 200 cases annually, not including the many writs of habeas corpus brought on by prisoners confined to prison facilities). The cases taken for review are usually cases in which two or more lower courts of appeals have rendered contradictory decisions in similar cases and cases wherein the Court wishes to set a bright-line policy (specific guidelines) for courts to follow. To ensure impartiality in their decision making, the Constitution mandates that all federally appointed judges are appointed for life terms, and their compensation may not be diminished during their tenure.

DECIPHERING COURT CITATIONS

Throughout the text, we will use citations after a case. Whenever one sees a citation containing *U.S.,* as in 471 U.S. 462 (1985), it refers to U.S. Supreme Court decisions reported in United States Reports. Thus, the citation means "Volume 471 United States Reports page 462, decided in 1985." If one sees *F.2d* or *F.3d,* it is a U.S. court of appeals decision. The particular court of appeals is stated in parenthesis as well as the year. Thus, 89 F.2d 1257 (6th Cir. 1996) means that the decision made in 1996 is by the U.S. Court of Appeals for the 6th Circuit and is found in Volume 89 Federal Reports Second Series page 1257. *D.C. Cir.* refers to the court of appeals for the District of Columbia. If one sees *F. Supp.,* as in 937 F. Supp. 295 (S.D.N.Y. 1996), this is a decision of the U.S. district court found in a series of law volumes known as the Federal Supplement. Therefore, the case may be found in Volume 937 Federal Supplement page 295, and the decision was made in 1996 by the single judge sitting in the U.S. district court located in the Southern District of New York. *S.D.Ca.* refers to the Southern District of California, *D.Md.* to the district court sitting in Maryland, and *D.D.C.* to the district court of the District of Columbia.

TEXT STRUCTURE

The extensive scope of cyberlaw may be divided into a number of areas generally agreed upon by scholars to encompass the major topics in the discipline. We begin in Chapter 2 with the subject of jurisdiction. This topic is highly controversial because it involves global activities to a degree never experienced previously in intergovernmental relations. Unlike prior law topics, which were almost exclusively domestic in nature, the Internet knows no boundaries. Communications, through the World Wide Web to anyone with a computer and modem, are immediate and at nominal cost. Crimes may be committed at one's convenience and in almost total privacy. Criminals have been able to take advantage of the lack of legislation and clear rules in less developed nations whose legal systems and laws lack the sophistication of more developed countries. The issues of who may hear a case, which laws are applicable, and where trials are to take place become critical to enforcement.

In Part II, we discuss the major basic commercial topics of contracts, torts, and crimes in connection with the Internet. Chapters 3 and 4 cover the law of Internet contracts. We begin with a basic review of the law of contracts, integrate electronic contracts with past legal principles, and discuss current legislative initiatives, particularly the Uniform Computer Information Transactions Act. We also review the controversial area of shrink-wrap licenses and click-wrap agreements. We will also discuss a number of issues arising from tortious conduct, as Internet transactions often cause the law of torts to become applicable. Included in the discussion are the topics of spam, defamation, and cases related thereto. Litigation involving the law of torts is not confined to Chapter 4. Other topics with tort aspects are included in later substantive law chapters, particularly in Chapter 8, "Trademarks, Domain Names, and Cybersquatting." We devote much of Chapter 4 to the constitutional and legal issues applicable to those subjects.

In Chapter 5, we examine the dark side of the Internet, namely the manifold criminal issues that have arisen caused by perpetrators seeking to take advantage of the lack of knowledge and security prevalent around the globe. There are many local, national, and international developments in this area. Of particular importance are the ongoing problems of child pornography and obscenity.

In Part III, we review the numerous legal developments in the protection of intellectual property rights. Possessors of such rights have never been exposed to piracy to the degree that it exists today. The new technological advances occurring almost daily allow owners to duplicate almost all forms of such rights. There are many cases emanating from the courts especially in the protection of trademarks and the problem of domain names. We review the basic legal principles, the latest legislative additions, and the efforts by courts to grant judicial relief to holders of such rights.

In Part IV, we review an issue that has dominated media attention, that of privacy and the major inroads made by commercial entities to ascertain the public's most protected secrets. The telephone number of almost anyone in the country can be obtained by a click of a computer mouse. Companies routinely request and derive information concerning our buying habits, our medical problems, and other formerly little known data about consumers. Employment law implications are included not only in the discussion of the law of privacy but in other chapters where issues concerning it are relevant.

In Part V, we examine three areas of the law directly concerning governmental intervention: antitrust, securities regulation, and Internet taxation. In Chapter 11, we discuss the antitrust implications of companies engaged in electronic commerce. In particular, the *Microsoft* case created a great deal of controversy among legal scholars and the public. We also review antitrust law and the application of the law to the current technology. In Chapter 12, we follow with a discussion of securities regulation and include the application of the Foreign Corrupt Practices Act. In the final chapter, the very important and hotly debated topic of sales tax on Internet transactions is explored. Both state and local governments fear greatly the loss of necessary revenues from the exclusion of such sales from taxation. In the past, interstate purchases constituted a relatively small percentage of consumer purchases. Today, such sales are becoming much more significant. Owners of stores that are compelled to charge sales taxes face competitive problems because Internet sales may be made at a lower cost, not only due to the nontaxable aspect but also because of the lesser need for physical facilities. The ramifications and future trends are also examined.

In each chapter we include international implications and initiatives. Rather than stating a brief synopsis of such developments, we include lengthy discussions of the interplay of international and national rules. Often, European countries have been most aggressive in protecting privacy and other rights. Their programs have served as models for the rest of the globe, including the United States.

We trust that this review, based on numerous cases, law review articles, legislative data, and many other sources, will assist the reader to have an awareness of the legal problems and the governmental and private attempts to adapt to the new human endeavor.

Endnotes

1. The science fiction writer William Gibson created the term *cyberspace* in his book *Neuromancer* (Ace Science Fiction Books, 1984). The term appears to have been first used in the context of global electronic space by John Perry Barlow in an "online gathering place" known as The Well. Tim Berners-Lee is credited for inventing what he termed the *WorldDwidEweb* when he proposed in 1989 that a global hypertext be created accessing network information by use of a Universal Document Identifier. See *www.w3.org/People/Berners-Lee/Short History .html.*
2. See Federal Trade Commission, *Privacy Online: Fair Information Practices in the Electronic Marketplace: A Report to Congress* (May 2000), p. 1; and Forester Research, *www.forester.com/ER/Marketing/ 0,1503,218,FF.html.*
3. 18 U.S.C.A. Section 1030(e)(2) (Supp. 1998).
4. For a discussion of computer basics from which part of this discussion emanates, see *Universal City Studios, Inc. v. Reimerdes,* No. 00 Civ. 0277 (LAK), 2000 U.S. Dist. LEXIS 11696 (S.D.N.Y. Aug. 17, 2000).
5. For example, see *Apollomedia Corp. v. Reno,* No. C-97–346 MMC (N.D.Ca. 1998); *Zeran v. America Online, Inc.,* 129 F.3d 327 (4th Cir. 1997); *Blumenthal v. Drudge,* 992 F. Supp. 44 (D.D.C. 1998); *PSINet, Inc. v. Chapman,* 108 F. Supp. 2d 611 (W.D.Va. 2000).
6. The report can be found at *www.ecommerce.gov/framewrk.htm.*
7. In practical terms, the statement is correct. Article 3, Section 2(2) of the Constitution does grant original jurisdiction to the U.S. Supreme Court "in all cases affecting ambassadors, other public ministers, and consuls, and those in which a State shall be party . . . ." Such trials actually take place before a Master appointed by the Court, who renders a report recommending a particular result, which report almost always becomes the decision of the Court.

CHAPTER

2 JURISDICTION IN CYBERSPACE

Chapter Outline

Jurisdiction is based on the concept of boundaries. An astronaut allegedly said that, when viewing earth from outer space, there were no boundaries separating humanity. Nevertheless, from time immemorial, human beings have created artificial borders separating themselves from one another from city to city and, eventually, from nation to nation. Wars have been fought over claims of territory. Neighbors build fences to delineate their small plot of land from that of adjoining property owners. Countries have border-crossing stations to prevent people or contraband from entering without their consent. Laws are based on the territorial sovereignty of a state or central governing authority. When we speak of cyberspace, however, by definition we enter into a realm where there are no borders. Nations have been perplexed as to determining how to enforce local laws with respect to activity that is global in nature. The Internet has entered homes and businesses and has dominated much of the activity taking place therein. Courts have tried to apply old laws to the new technology. In many of the cases being adjudicated, however, the results have been less than satisfactory.

A number of authors have summarized the difficulty facing nations by noting that cyberspace has radically undermined the relationship between activity and physical location.[1] In the past, torts, crimes, and contracts have taken place at specific locales. Courts within those areas could assert power and authority over the activity and the persons responsible. Cyberspace has greatly modified the link connecting geographical location and the power of governments over activities taking place within their borders. It has transformed (1) the *power* of governments to control online behavior; (2) the *effects* that the Internet has on individuals or things; (3) the *legitimacy* of local governments to enforce rules respecting the Internet; and (4) the ability of a specific location to give *notice* of the rules applicable to the given activity. Borders are as irrelevant to cyberspace as they are to outer space. Nevertheless, nations continue to assert authority over the Internet, using old legal concepts, applying analogies to existing laws, passing new legislation, and entering into international agreements.

The problem to be discussed is whether a particular court in a given state or the federal courts of the United States or other governmental entities may try litigation involving parties from other states or countries. Courts, with rare exceptions, have substantial limitations imposed on them as to the types of cases they may adjudicate. For example, a New York court could not try an automobile accident that takes place in Los Angeles involving California residents, absent some nexus with New York. A nation's courts may not be able to hear a case affecting foreign persons, absent some legal justification, which may include an agreement by the parties to adjudicate all disputes in a certain country or a locality therein.

Much of our discussion will focus on parties residing outside of the jurisdiction of a given court. A *foreign party* may be either an out-of-state person or a person in a foreign country. A *person* may include individuals, partnerships, corporations, or other recognized legal entities. Constitutional issues arise in both domestic and international arenas. Initially, the focus will be on U.S. domestic jurisdiction, that is, whether a person in one state may be sued in the courts of another state. Thereafter, we will review international jurisdiction. The emphasis for both interstate and foreign country jurisdictions will be on cases involving the Internet.

In this chapter, we will review the concept of jurisdiction to explore the difficulties facing governmental entities and the efforts made to resolve disputes. In addition, we will review the concepts of venue and choice of law, both of which are related to jurisdiction.

JURISDICTION OVER ACTIVITIES IN CYBERSPACE

Jurisdiction is of crucial importance in Internet cases. In the recent past, a computer virus referred to as the "I love you" virus was allegedly transmitted by persons in the Philippines, causing worldwide disruptions. The estimated damage to computers exceeded $7 billion. The threats to life and safety to affected persons can only be speculated. Which of the numerous affected countries has jurisdiction over the perpetrators? Can they be tried in all of the affected countries? An additional problem posed in that particular scenario was that such action was not illegal within the Philippines due to the absence of legislation regarding that cybercrime. Thus, the transgressors, according to Philippine law, could not be extradited to the United States or any other country, because the activity would have had to violate the laws of both the home country and the foreign state seeking extradition. What about an activity such as gambling, which may be legal in Nevada or in another state or country but is made available to Internet users in different states, where such activities are not legal? Can these states prosecute criminally or sue civilly within their borders those persons responsible for conducting gambling operations that are lawful in the state where the Web sites emanate but unlawful where the gamblers reside?

At the close of the millennium, the so-called Y2K problem caused much concern, anguish, and large preventive expenditures of money. Were Microsoft and other companies liable to all affected persons using computers with the alleged defect? If so, the potential liability could easily have bankrupted the companies allegedly involved. Thus, jurisdictional issues are very important in determining who may be sued in civil cases or face criminal charges.

U.S. DOMESTIC JURISDICTION

As discussed in Chapter 1, there are 51 governmental entities in the United States, namely, the federal government and the 50 state governments. Each entity is sovereign unto itself, limited only by constitutional restrictions. The federal government and each state have their own judicial systems unique unto themselves. Both the federal and state judicial systems have two major divisions of jurisdiction: *subject-matter jurisdiction* and *in personam jurisdiction* (jurisdiction over the parties).

Subject-Matter Jurisdiction

Federal subject-matter jurisdiction is found in Article 3, Section 2 of the U.S. Constitution, which states:

The judicial Power shall extend to all Cases, in Law and Equity, arising under this Constitution, the Laws of the United States, and Treaties made . . . to Controversies to which the United States shall be a Party;—to controversies between two or more States;—between a State and Citizens of another State;—between Citizens of different States; . . . and between a State, or the Citizens thereof, and foreign States, Citizens or Subjects.

Federal jurisdiction is very broad, extending to all laws passed by Congress, to cases involving citizens of different states, to cases involving ambassadors and other foreign diplomatic personnel, to disputes between states, and other related areas. Such jurisdiction may be *exclusive* or *concurrent.* Laws passed by Congress expressly or implicitly provide federal courts with exclusive or concurrent jurisdiction. Exclusive jurisdiction exists in certain areas of federal law, such as bankruptcy, federal crimes, and international treaties. Federal courts may share jurisdiction with state courts in cases concerning *diversity of citizenship,* that is, lawsuits in which a party is from a state different from the opposing litigant, when a U.S. citizen is sued by a foreign country, or when the lawsuit is between a U.S. citizen and a foreign citizen, and the sum sued for is over $75,000. Federal courts may also share jurisdiction (concurrent jurisdiction) with state courts in matters arising from the U.S. Constitution or from laws or treaties wherein Congress did not reserve exclusive jurisdiction for the federal courts. Federal courts may also determine cases or controversies without monetary limitations when there is a *federal question.* A federal question arises when the court has to determine issues involving federal statutes, matters of constitutional interpretation, or treaties entered into by the United States.

States have exclusive jurisdiction over all cases not granted to the federal government and concurrent jurisdiction over cases wherein the federal government has the power to determine a case or controversy but elects not to exercise it exclusively. Cases involving diversity of citizenship wherein the sum sued for is $75,000 or less are reserved to the states. State crimes, issues concerning property within a state, torts, and other domestic matters are within the province of the state courts. Recently, in *United States v. Morrison,* 529 U.S. 598 (2000), the U.S. Supreme Court overturned a key part of the 1994 Violence Against Women Act (42 U.S.C. Section 13981) by holding that victims of rape and domestic violence could not seek damages in a federal court because rape was a state rather than a federal matter.

Jurisdiction over the Parties

Courts also have jurisdiction over the parties. They may obtain jurisdiction over the person (in personam jurisdiction) by service of process within a state or outside of a state if constitutional rules concerning *long-arm statutes* are adhered to. Jurisdiction may be obtained *in rem,* that is, by asserting authority over property located within the state. For example, mortgage foreclosure proceedings are almost always commenced in the locality of the property, irrespective of the parties' residence. A court may also assert *attachment jurisdiction* by permitting the seizure of in-state property belonging to out-of-state persons.

Long-Arm Statutes. A state may attempt to exercise jurisdiction over a case by use of a long-arm statute. Every state possesses a long-arm statute. The law allows a court to hear a case in which one of the parties is a resident and the party being sued either committed a tort or engaged in business within the state, although having no actual presence therein. In order for a court to hear and determine such action, it is necessary that there be a long-arm statute giving the court such authority. A long-arm statute is exemplified by the following Texas enactment:

Section 3. Any foreign corporation . . . that engages in business in this State, irrespective of any Statute or law respecting designation or maintenance of resident agents, and does not maintain a place of regular business in this State or a designated agent upon whom service may be made upon causes of action arising out of such business done in this State, the act or acts of engaging in such business within this State shall be deemed equivalent to an appointment by such foreign corporation . . . of the Secretary of State of Texas as agent upon whom service of process may be made in any action, suit or proceedings arising out of such business done in this State, wherein such corporation . . . is a party or is to be made a party.

Section 4. For the purpose of this Act, and without including other acts that may constitute business, any foreign corporation . . . shall be deemed doing business in this State by entering into contract by mail or otherwise with a resident of Texas to be performed in whole or in part by either party in this State, or the committing of any tort in whole or in part in this State. The act of recruiting Texas residents, directly or through an intermediary located in Texas, for employment inside or outside of Texas shall be deemed doing business in this State.

Lawsuits may be instituted against any out-of-state person who transacted business with an in-state person, committed a tort upon such person, or possesses property within the state. The issue that arises, when a long-arm statute is exercised, is whether the constitutional rights of an out-of-state person are being violated. The issue becomes more pertinent when use of the Internet gives rise to litigation. Federal courts may use the state's long-arm statute to assert jurisdiction over nonresidents in cases where there is subject-matter jurisdiction and when there is diversity of citizenship.

The Internet has created enormous problems in the determination of jurisdiction. In the past, courts have had to resolve relatively simple issues as to whether there was a sufficient connection in one state by an out-of-state person to permit a court to hear a dispute between these parties. Such connection referred mainly to physical presence within the state seeking to assert jurisdiction. The Internet, by its availability to all persons in possession of a computer and a telephone connection, has exacerbated the jurisdictional problems facing courts. There have been many conflicting decisions in the courts leaving the issue in a state of flux. An example of the problems faced by courts is illustrated by the following state court case that has an extensive discussion of the jurisdictional issues presented by out-of-state activities.

STATE OF MINNESOTA V. GRANITE GATE RESORTS, INC.

No. C6-95-7227, 1996 WL 747431 (Minn. Ramsey County, 1996)

FACTS: This is an action for consumer protection instituted by the Minnesota Attorney General against a computer services company. The complaint alleged deceptive trade practices, false advertising, and consumer fraud in violation of Minnesota law. The defendant moved to dismiss the action for lack of personal jurisdiction.

The Minnesota Attorney General alleged that Kerry Rogers, a Nevada resident, formed a corporation known as Granite Gate Resorts, Inc. to purchase a repossessed hotel in Prescott, Arizona. After the deal fell through, Rogers used the Corporation to commence a computer services business under the name of "On Ramp Internet Computer Services." On Ramp is Nevada based. Rogers advertised a gambling site on the World Wide Web requiring hardware and software to access a server located in Belize (Central America). The user had to pay a $100 setup fee for the hardware and software. Thereafter, s/he would be issued a card system linked to their personal computer that allowed access to a WagerNetTM On-Line betting site. Bets are matched against other betters. The service company charged a 2.5% transaction fee, which allegedly was much less than other Nevada bookmakers' fees.

The advertised site was accessible to all potential users thereof worldwide, including potentially numerous Minnesota residents. In addition, the defendant Rogers, through On Ramp, owned the "Vegas.Com" network that was a site providing tourist information about Las Vegas and Reno as well as gambling information. Two gambling businesses in Nevada advertised on Vegas.Com including All Star Sports, Inc., later identified as being part of Granite, and On Ramp, that accepted bets for sports picks.

A consumer investigator from the Minnesota Attorney General's office telephoned Rogers, said he was from Minnesota, and asked how the betting service worked. The said defendant said the service would be running shortly and that the betting over the Internet did not violate federal law. The investigator placed bets with All Star. Thereafter, the Attorney General brought a civil suit [presumably, he could not bring a criminal action because the defendant's activities were not illegal from where they emanated] alleging that federal law prohibited the interstate or foreign transmission of betting information and bets using wire communication facilities. The State of Minnesota also forbade such bets. The defendant, Rogers, refused to obey a Court order for limited discovery of mailing lists.

ISSUES: (1) Did the Minnesota courts have jurisdiction over the defendants as a result of the Internet advertisements?

(2) Did the defendants purposefully avail themselves of the market in Minnesota by their Internet advertisement activities so as to give this Court personal jurisdiction?

DECISION: (1) The Court found in favor of the Attorney General holding that the Minnesota Court did have jurisdiction.

(2) The defendants did purposefully avail themselves of the Minnesota market.

REASONING: Judge Connolly

MINIMUM CONTACTS

Due process requires that a nonresident defendant have "minimum contacts" with the forum state such that it would reasonably anticipate being hailed into Court there. *World-Wide Volkswagen Corp. v. Woodson,* 444 U.S. 286, 297 (1980). Furthermore, maintenance of the suit in the forum state cannot offend traditional notions of fair play and substantial justice. . . .

FIVE FACTOR TEST

Minnesota uses a five-factor analysis to evaluate due process in the context of personal jurisdiction:

1. The quantity of contacts with the forum.
2. The nature and quality of those contacts.
3. The connection of the cause of action with the contacts.
4. Interest of the state in providing a forum.
5. Convenience of the parties.

QUANTITY OF ADVERTISING ACTS AND CONTACTS WITH MINNESOTA

If the Defendants in this case had advertised in any type of national publication such as *U.S.A. Today,* the *New York Times, Time* magazine, *Sports Illustrated,* etc., their argument that they had not purposefully availed themselves of the jurisdiction of Minnesota would have no validity. The Defendants attempt to hide behind the Internet and claim that they mailed nothing to Minnesota, sent nothing to Minnesota, and never advertised to Minnesota. This argument is not sound in the age of cyberspace. Once the Defendants place an advertisement on the Internet, that advertisement is available 24 hours a day, seven days a week, 365 days a year to any Internet user until the Defendants take it off the Internet . . .

Here, Defendant knew that once he put the WagerNet ad on the Internet, the ad would be continuously on the Internet and that it had to reach national markets that included Minnesota . . .

As we prepare to enter into the 21st century, those arguments or analogies have no relevancy whatsoever. Here, the computer hits on Defendants' Web sites and the fact that the advertisements give consumers phone numbers to call, along with the fact that the Court has determined that WagerNet's mailing list includes Minnesota residents, are more than sufficient evidence that Defendants have made a direct marketing campaign to the State of Minnesota. Therefore, it is not unforeseen nor unreasonable to Defendants to be required to come to Minnesota to defend themselves particularly when the Defendants have said that they have the option for any of the customers of WagerNet with whom they have a dispute to sue them in Minnesota. The Minnesota Attorney General's office has a valid right to attempt to get injunctive relief if it is later determined that the Defendants had committed illegal conduct herein . . .

Likewise, in the case at hand Defendants knew that 1.5 million consumers view their advertisement a month. Logic dictates that the WagerNet mailing list contains the names of many Minnesota residents (that Defendants refuse to turn over).

Contacts with Minnesota

Defendants keep track of who is accessing their website, and therefore know that Minnesota computers are accessing them. Defendants' websites are set up so that they can record all of the Internet protocol numbers or URL addresses of the computers accessing them . . .

THE NATURE AND QUALITY OF DEFENDANTS' PURPOSEFUL ADVERTISING CONTACTS WITH MINNESOTA REGARDING THE SECOND FACTOR

In matters of consumer protection, courts routinely hold that out of state defendants soliciting in-state residents have purposely availed themselves of the privilege of conducting business within the State . . .

Here, Rogers and WagerNet maintain a Website which can be accessed by any Internet user, and which logically appears to be maintained for the purpose and in anticipation of being accessed and used by any and all Internet users, including Minnesota residents. This activity certainly arises to the type of promotional activity or active solicitation to provide the minimum contacts necessary for exercising personal jurisdiction over non-residents . . .

WagerNet, when it posts information about its new, up-coming service through a Web site, seeks to develop a potential customer list of users who will be essential to the success of its service. Clearly, WagerNet obtained the Website for the purpose of and in anticipation that Internet users who search the Internet for Websites will access WagerNet's Website and eventually fill out the forms and become part of WagerNet's customer list.

THE CONNECTION OF CAUSE OF ACTION WITH CONTACTS

The Minnesota Attorney General brings this lawsuit in an attempt to enforce Minnesota's gambling laws and consumer protection law. The primary relief the Attorney General seeks is an injunction. They ask for Defendant to either stop sending advertisements to Minnesota computer users or to state in the advertisement that their services are void in Minnesota . . .

FOURTH FACTOR: INTEREST OF STATE IN PROVIDING A FORUM

Minnesota Is the Right Forum for This Action

Here, the Defendants crossed the Minnesota borders through Internet advertisements and solicited business for their gambling venture. If our Attorney General cannot hail them into our court, then the citizens of Minnesota will not have an adequate consumer Protection remedy.

FIFTH FACTOR: INCONVENIENCE?

In *Hanson v. Denckla,* 357 U.S. 251 (1958), the [U.S.] Supreme Court stated, "Progress in communications and transportation has made defense of a suit in a foreign tribunal less burdensome." Here, Defendants tell their prospective customers, "We will either sue you in your State or Belize." Defendants are "hard put" to argue it would be inconvenient to come to Minnesota. Minnesota certainly is much more convenient to both parties than Belize.

REASONABLY ANTICIPATE

In order to reasonably anticipate being hailed into court under the doctrine of Minimum contacts, there must be some acts by which the Defendant purposefully avails itself of the privileges of conducting activities within the forum State, thus involving the benefits and protections of its laws . . . . In this case, the acts of WagerNet consisted of placing its ads on the Internet 24 hours, seven days a week, 365 days a year . . .

[On appeal, an equally divided Minnesota Court of Appeals affirmed the decision.]

CASE QUESTIONS

1. Was the action taken by Granite illegal in Nevada from where it emanated?
2. Was there sufficient nexus (connection) between the residents of Minnesota and the Web site?
3. Do you agree with the court in its statement that advertising in the *New York Times, Time* magazine, and *Sports Illustrated* opens one up to liability wherever the magazines were sold?
4. What if a small company purchased a quarter-inch advertisement in a national magazine? Is that a sufficient nexus to require it to defend itself in any part of the U.S. or the world, even if only one person therein purchased the product?

The Due Process Clause and Jurisdiction

The Minnesota case presents a major jurisdictional issue in Internet cases, namely, the power of a court to hear a case in which the party sued is out of state, has not physically set up an office within the state, and all transactions are accomplished by electronic means. Another issue is whether prior precedents have relevance in cyberspace litigation. The constitutional problem raised by such cases is the alleged inherent unfairness of the assertion of jurisdiction in violation of the due process clause of the Fifth and the Fourteenth Amendments of the Constitution. The due process clause of the Fifth Amendment states: "No person shall . . . be deprived of life, liberty, or property, without due process of law . . . ." The Fourteenth Amendment extended the protection to persons as state citizens.

What is meant by *due process?* The essence is the requirement of *fairness*—fairness in the substance of the law and fairness in the procedure utilized in the prosecution and enforcement of the law. Historically, fairness substantively has been extended to prohibit states from imposing unreasonable regulations that prevent the right to marry, travel, vote, and other such rights. Fairness in procedure extends to rights a person has in a lawsuit. It is concerned with, for example, how a person may be sued, which courts have authority to hear a case, the manner in which a trial may be conducted, and numerous other aspects of procedural rights. Critical to our discussion is whether the out-of-state person referred to previously may be sued in a state court.

Early Precedents. The U.S. Supreme Court has been concerned about the extension of a state court's power over nonresident parties. In an 1877 case, *Pennoyer v. Neff,* 95 U.S. 714, it stated that due process requirement arises whenever a government seeks to deprive a person of an interest in real or personal property. Included in due process is the question of fairness in compelling persons to defend themselves in a lawsuit whenever and wherever a court may determine, irrespective of the court's limited connection to the parties. There was little dispute that a court has jurisdiction to hear and determine *in personam* actions, that is, litigation based on a court's power over persons served with process within the state. It also could exercise jurisdiction over its citizens, over property located within the state, and where the defendant consents to jurisdiction. In most cases, a person's presence within a state was essential in order for a court to exercise such power. Later decisions, however, expanded a court's power to try cases involving nonresidents who had a certain number of "minimum contacts" with the state.

In the 1940s, the U.S. Supreme Court discussed the applicability of the due process clause to issues of jurisdiction in *International Shoe Co. v. Washington,* 326 U.S. 310 (1945). International Shoe, a Delaware corporation, sued the state of Washington to recover contributions paid to the state's unemployment compensation fund, alleging that the state had violated the due process clause of the Constitution in exacting such payments. The claimant had no office in Washington, no contracts for the sale or purchase of merchandise therein, no stock of merchandise, and made no deliveries in interstate commerce. Its only connection with the state of Washington was the employment of 7 to 13 salesmen who resided in the state under the supervision of sales managers located in Missouri. The salesmen operated in the state of Washington and were compensated by commissions earned from their sales. The salesmen received supplies of samples and, on occasion, rented samples and other rooms in the state.

The Court held there was sufficient nexus (connection) by International Shoe with the state of Washington to permit the state court to adjudicate the action. Due process depended upon the "quality and nature of the activity in relation to the fair and orderly administration of the laws which it was the purpose of the due process clause to insure." The corporation exercised the privilege of conducting activities within the state, enjoyed the benefits provided by the state, and therefore, had obligations to it. The activities took place over a number of years, were not sporadic but were systematic and consistent, and resulted in a large volume of business.

Evolving Constitutional Standard. In the *Minnesota v. Granite* case discussed previously, the state court relied mainly on two prior U.S. Supreme Court precedents for its decision. It cited *World-Wide Volkswagen Corp. v. Woodson,* 444 U.S. 286 (1980) and *Hanson v. Denckla,* 357 U.S. 235 (1958). In *World-Wide,* New York residents had purchased an automobile from a New York dealer and were involved in an automobile accident in Oklahoma while on their way to their new home in Arizona; the issue presented was whether they could sue in the state of Oklahoma. The action was a products liability suit (the claim was that the automobile that was in a fiery accident was defective) against the New York dealership that sold the automobile, the manufacturer of the automobile in Germany, the importer of the vehicle, and the regional distributor, World-Wide. The only connection that the defendants had with Oklahoma was that the accident occurred there. The U.S. Supreme Court held the exercise of jurisdiction in Oklahoma against the retailer and regional distributor violated the due process clause of the Constitution. There had to exist at least some minimum contacts for a lawsuit to take place in the state, but in *World-Wide,* there was no connection with Oklahoma other than the accident having taken place therein. The sale and service of the vehicle, residence of the parties, and all other connections with the vehicle were outside of Oklahoma. Thus, it would have been unfair to compel the vehicle's dealer, distributor, manufacturer, and importer to go to Oklahoma to defend the lawsuit.

The Minnesota court also cited *Hanson v. Denckla,* wherein the U.S. Supreme Court noted that technological progress had increased greatly the interstate flow of goods, thereby making it necessary to revisit the boundaries of jurisdiction. The Court does not require a physical presence per se wherein the defendant is served with process but rather looks to the extent "by which the defendant purposefully avails itself of the privilege of conducting activities within the forum State, thus invoking the benefits and protections of its laws."

Lack of Physical Presence. Whereas previously the need for a physical presence within a state at some point in time was necessary for a court to exercise jurisdiction, the Court said in *Burger King Corp. v. Rudzewicz,* 471 U.S. 462 (1985) at 476: "It is an inescapable fact of modern commercial life that a substantial amount of commercial business is transacted solely by mail and wire communications across state lines, thus obviating the need for physical presence within a State in which business is conducted." In *McGee v. International Life Ins. Co.,* 355 U.S. 220 (1957), an insurance company had to defend a lawsuit in a state wherein it had only one policyholder. The Court noted that in today's world, it is much less of a burden for a person engaged in economic activity to defend a lawsuit. If one conducts business in a state, it may have to defend itself in the courts of that state.

Thus, the constitutional standard for jurisdiction has evolved from: (1) requiring a physical presence and service of process within a state; (2) some past presence in the state; and (3), as presently, a standard requiring certain minimum activities with the forum even though the defendant may never have physically entered the state.

It should be noted that a party's inability to sue in a particular court does not deprive a person from suing. It simply means that a party cannot pick and choose any court or state that seems most attractive even if the court has little or no connection with the claims asserted against a defendant. There are many reasons why a person may wish to select a particular court over another. Some local courts are well known as sites of high jury awards. For example, jury awards in New York City tend to be much greater than awards in other localities. Other courts have the reputation for being more liberal, more restrictive, more profarmer, or for favoring some other interest group. Nevertheless, the right to select a court may be denied unless the court is one in which it is reasonable for the parties to have their dispute adjudicated.

Cyberjurisdiction. In Internet-related cases, the prior rules concerning jurisdiction do not blend well with the new technology. Commercial activities occur over a time–space continuum. Offers are made through a computer from persons around the globe. Middlepersons (for example, stores) facilitating such transactions are no longer needed. Consumers are contacted in accordance with predisposition characteristics stored in computer banks based on prior purchases and exhibitions of preferences. Criminal and tortious behavior has taken place involving persons often unknown to the receivers of the communications. Courts have grappled with the difficulties inherent in exercising jurisdiction over persons who have no physical presence within a state or who have not directed the sued-upon activity to the plaintiff.

In an endeavor to fit old rules to the current technologies, courts have devised analogous concepts. In the following 1997 case, the U.S. district court, in a well-cited opinion by other courts, reviewed the current state of the law of jurisdiction. Note the discussion of general and specific jurisdiction and the sliding-scale, active-passive analysis.

ZIPPO MANUFACTURING COMPANY V. ZIPPO DOT COM, INC.

952 F. Supp. 1119 (W.D.Pa. 1997)

FACTS: Plaintiff sued defendant for alleged trademark dilution, infringement, and false designation under the Federal Trademark Act and for trademark dilution under Pennsylvania State law [Trademark law is discussed in Chapter 8.]. Plaintiff is a Pennsylvania corporation that manufactures the popular "Zippo" tobacco lighters. The defendant is a California corporation that operates an Internet Web Site and an Internet news service not in competition with the plaintiff. Defendant registered and received the right to use the domain names of "zippo.com," "zippo.net," and "zipponews.com" on the Internet. It operates an on-line news service to subscribers for a fee. Defendant has no offices, employees, or agents within Pennsylvania. It advertises its service on its Web page that is accessible to Pennsylvania residents and others through the Internet. Defendant has 140,000 subscribers, two percent of whom are from Pennsylvania. The plaintiff holds the trademark to the name "zippo" and says that defendant's use of the trademark was wrongful.
ISSUE: Did the Federal Court located in Pennsylvania have personal jurisdiction over the defendant?
DECISION: The Court held it did have jurisdiction.
REASONING: [The court recited Pennsylvania's long-arm statute, which authorized a court to "exercise jurisdiction over non-resident defendants upon . . . (2) contracting to supply services or things in this Commonwealth." Dot Com supplied services to some 3,000 Pennsylvania residents through seven Internet access providers and came within the statutory provision for long-arm jurisdiction. The issue then arises as to constitutional limitations on such service.]

Judge McLaughlin:

1. THE TRADITIONAL FRAMEWORK

The Constitutional limitations on the exercise of personal jurisdiction differ depending upon whether a court seeks to exercise general or specific jurisdiction over a non-resident defendant . . . General jurisdiction permits a court to exercise personal jurisdiction over a non-resident defendant for non-forum related activities when the defendant has engaged in "systematic and continuous" activities in the forum state. *Helicopteros Nacionales de Columbia, S.A. v. Hall,* 466 U.S. 408, 414–16 (1984). In the absence of general jurisdiction, specific jurisdiction permits a court to exercise personal jurisdiction over a non-resident defendant for forum-related activities where the "relationship between the defendant and the forum falls within the 'minimum contacts' framework" of *International Shoe Co. v. Washington,* 326 U.S. 310 (1945) and its progeny, *Mellon* [*Bank PSFS. v. Farino,* 960 F.2d 1217 (3d Cir. 1992)], 960 F.2d at 1221." Manufacturing does not contend that we should exercise general personal jurisdiction over Dot Com. Manufacturing concedes that if personal jurisdiction exists in this case, it must be specific.

A three-pronged test has emerged for determining whether the exercise of specific personal jurisdiction over a non-resident defendant is appropriate: (1) the defendant must have sufficient "minimum contacts" with the forum state, (2) the claim asserted against the defendant must arise out of those contacts, and (3) the exercise of jurisdiction must be reasonable. *Id.* The "Constitutional touchstone" of the minimum contacts analysis is embodied in the first prong, "whether the defendant purposefully established" contacts with the forum state. *Burger King Corp. v. Rudzewicz,* 471 U.S. 462, 475 (1985) [citing *International Shoe Co. v. Washington,* 326 U.S. 310, 319 (1945)]. Defendants who "reach out beyond one state and create continuing relationships and obligations and obligations with the citizens of another state are subject to regulation and sanctions in the other State for consequences of their actions." *Id.* [citing *Travelers Health Assn. v. Virginia,* 339 U.S. 643, 647 (1950)] . . . "[T]he foreseeability that is critical to the due process analysis is . . . that the defendant's conduct and connection with the forum State are such that he should reasonably expect to be haled into court there." *World-Wide Volkswagen Corp. v. Woodson,* 444 U.S. 286, 295 (1980). This protects defendants from being forced to answer for their actions in a foreign jurisdiction based on "random, fortuitous or attenuated" contacts. *Keeton v. Hustler Magazine, Inc.,* 465 U.S. 770, 774 (1984). "Jurisdiction is proper, however, where contacts proximately result from actions by the defendant himself that create a 'substantial connection' with the forum State." *Burger King,* 471 U.S. at 475.

[The court found that the three-prong test was met. The defendant, Dot Com, not only posted information accessible to out-of-state residents on its Web site, but also sold passwords to the site to some 3,000 subscribers in Pennsylvania and entered into seven contracts with Internet service providers in Pennsylvania. The contacts were not fortuitous as in *World-Wide Volkswagen,* but were repeatedly and consciously chosen to process applications from the state and to assign passwords. It could have refused to do business with persons in Pennsylvania. The contacts were numerous in nature. The infringement and dilution of plaintiff's trademark was significant and the damage substantial.]

2. THE INTERNET AND JURISDICTION

[The court reviewed the use of the Internet in commercial activities using a sliding-scale analysis.] [O]ur review of the available cases and materials . . . reveals that the likelihood that personal jurisdiction can be constitutionally exercised is directly proportionate to the nature and quality of commercial activity that an entity conducts over the Internet. This sliding scale is consistent with well developed personal jurisdiction principles. At one end of the spectrum are situations where a defendant clearly does business over the Internet. If the defendant enters into contracts with residents of a foreign jurisdiction that involve the knowing and repeated transmission of computer files over the Internet, personal jurisdiction is proper. E.g. *CompuServe, Inc. v. Patterson,* 89 F.2d 1257 (6th Cir. 1996) . . . . At the opposite end are situations where a defendant has simply posted information on an Internet Web site which is accessible to users in foreign jurisdictions. A passive Web site that does little more than make information available to those who are interested in it is not grounds for the exercise of personal jurisdiction. E.g. *Bensusan Restaurant Corp. v. King,* 937 F. Supp. 295 (S.D.N.Y. 1996). The middle ground is occupied by interactive Web sites where a user can exchange information with the host computer. In these cases, the exercise of jurisdiction is determined by examining the level of interactivity and commercial nature of the exchange of information that occurs on the Web site. E.g. *Maritz, Inc. v. Cybergold, Inc.,* 947 F. Supp. 1328 (E.D.Mo. 1996).

CASE QUESTIONS

1. Compare and contrast general jurisdiction and specific jurisdiction.
2. Compare *Zippo* and *Minnesota.* How do you believe Judge McLaughlin would have decided the *Minnesota* case?

General Jurisdiction Versus Specific Jurisdiction

In *Zippo,* the court distinguished between general and specific jurisdiction citing *Helicopteros.* In *Helicopteros,* a 1984 U.S. Supreme Court case, four U.S. citizens died when a helicopter owned by a Colombian corporation crashed in Peru. The corporation did not conduct business nor was it licensed to do business in Texas where the lawsuit took place. Its only connection with Texas was that it sent its chief executive officer to Houston to negotiate a contract to provide helicopter service for a Peruvian consortium during the latter's construction of a pipeline in Peru. The petitioner, Helicopteros, had purchased helicopters from Bell Helicopter in Texas, sent prospective pilots for training in Texas, and sent management and maintenance personnel there for consultations. It also accepted checks drawn on a Texas account into its New York bank account.

The Court held there was insufficient connection with Texas to permit a lawsuit to take place therein. The long-arm statute of Texas allowed such a lawsuit against persons engaging in business within the state irrespective of the failure of the defendant to maintain a place of business or local agents therein. The due process clause of the Fourteenth Amendment was violated by such assertion of jurisdiction due to the lack of minimum contacts with the forum state that would not violate the traditional notions of fair play and substantial justice.

The Court said in a footnote: "When a State exercises personal jurisdiction over a defendant in a suit not arising out of or related to the defendant's contacts with the forum, the State has been said to be exercising 'general jurisdiction.'" A state may always assert jurisdiction over one of its inhabitants, even if a tort or contract takes place outside of the state. It may also exercise general jurisdiction if an out-of-state resident defendant has been present continuously within a state or is engaged in activities in a systematic fashion within the state.

When a state court exercises personal jurisdiction in a lawsuit relating to an out-of-state person based on contacts with the forum, then it is exercising *specific jurisdiction.* In *Helicopteros,* the claims did not arise nor were related to *Helicopteros*'s activities within Texas and, therefore, there was no specific jurisdiction. There also was no general jurisdiction because of the lack of minimum contacts with the state. One visit by the defendant to negotiate a contract, acceptance of checks drawn on a Texas bank, and the training trips were insufficient to constitute a minimum nexus.

Thus, *general jurisdiction* exists when the defendant engages in significant activities within a given state but the lawsuit is not about those activities. Rather, the facts concerned some other grievance the defendant allegedly caused the plaintiff. The court, however, may exert specific jurisdiction when the harm was caused in the forum state, provided the minimum-contacts prong exists.

The distinction between general and specific jurisdiction was discussed at length in *Panavision International, L.P. v. Toeppen.*

PANAVISION INT'L, L.P. V. TOEPPEN

938 F. Supp. 616 (S.D.Ca. 1996)

FACTS: The plaintiff, a Delaware corporation, owned a number of registered trademarks, including "Panavision" and "Panaflex." The defendant, Toeppen, a resident of Illinois, owned a number of web sites, including "panavision.com" and "panaflex.com" that it acquired from the defendant Network Solutions, Inc., a District of Columbia corporation with a principal place of business in Virginia. NSI required of applicants representations and warranties that the domain names did not interfere or infringe with the rights of any third party with respect to intellectual property rights. Toeppen did not use the domain names in connection with goods and services. When plaintiff tried to register the domain names for which it had registered trademarks, it could not do so because of the prior Toeppen registrations. Toeppen was willing to sell the domain names to the plaintiff for $13,000 but plaintiff refused to purchase them. Plaintiff sued for dilution of its trademark, trademark infringement, unfair competition, and other theories. Defendant made a motion to quash the pleadings for lack of jurisdiction due to its residence in Illinois and that all of its actions occurred in Illinois.
ISSUE: Did the California Federal Court possess jurisdiction on the basis of the facts stated above?

DECISION: It did possess jurisdiction.
REASONING: [The court discussed at length the distinction between general and specific jurisdiction. As said in *Zippo,* a court with general jurisdiction may exercise personal jurisdiction over a defendant as to any cause of action arising between the parties. Such jurisdiction arises when the defendant is domiciled within the particular jurisdiction or the activities of a nonresident within the forum state are substantial, continuous, or systematic. Where there is no general jurisdiction, the court may exercise specific jurisdiction. The Court of Appeals for the Ninth Circuit uses the following three-prong test for assertion of specific jurisdiction: "(1) the nonresident defendant must do some act or consummate some transaction with the forum or perform some act by which he purposefully avails himself of the privilege of conducting activities in the forum, thereby invoking the benefits and protections of its laws; (2) the claim must be one which arises out of or results from the defendant's forum-related activities; and (3) the exercise of jurisdiction must be reasonable."]

Judge Pregerson:

1. THE "PURPOSEFUL AVAILMENT" PRONG

The "purposeful availment" prong assures that a nonresident defendant will be aware that it could be sued in the forum state [citing *World-Wide*]. In other words, this requirement protects a nonresident from being haled before a court solely because of "random, fortuitous or attenuated" contacts over which it has no control [citing *Burger King*]. To pass this part of the test, it must be foreseeable that the defendant's conduct and connection with the forum state are such that the defendant should reasonably anticipate being haled into court there. The "purposeful availment" test differs depending upon the underlying cause of action. . . . For example, in cases arising from contract disputes, merely contracting with a resident of the forum state is insufficient to confer specific jurisdiction . . . in the tort setting, however, jurisdiction "can be predicated on (1) intentional actions (2) expressly aimed at the forum state (3) causing harm, the brunt of which is suffered—and which the defendant knows is likely to be suffered—in the forum state. . . . This doctrine is known as the "effects test." . . .

[The court discussed the test in connection with the case at hand. It found that the plaintiff had valuable trademarks that the defendant knew were valuable and that there would be a time when the plaintiff would want to use the trademarks in a Web site. Thus, defendant deliberately registered the trademarks as his domain names with the expectation that the plaintiff would then be compelled to purchase them from the defendant. Though the defendant was not acting in a competing business, nevertheless, the defendant's business was to act as a so-called spoiler, preventing the plaintiff from registering its trademarks as domain names. The plaintiff's claim then is in the nature of a tort action having an effect on the California resident. Jurisdiction was, therefore, proper in California because the state was the focal point of the tortious conduct. Under the "effects doctrine," the defendant harmed the plaintiff by conduct expressly aimed at the plaintiff in the state of California.]

2. THE "ARISES OUT OF OR RESULTS FROM" PRONG

Courts in the Ninth Circuit follow a "but for" analysis of this prong of the test. . . . That is, if the plaintiff would not have suffered loss "but for" the defendant's forum-related activities, courts hold that the claim arises out of the defendant's forum-related activities . . . Here, "but for" Toeppen's conduct in registering Panavision's trademarks as domain names, Panavision would be able to establish an easily located web site and thus would not have been injured.

3. THE "REASONABLENESS" PRONG

This prong requires that the court's exercise of jurisdiction comport with "fair play and substantial justice" [citing *Burger King*]. The factors that the court must consider are: (1) the extent of defendant's "purposeful" interjection; (2) the burden on defendant in defending in the forum; (3) the extent of conflict with the sovereignty of the defendant's state; (4) the forum state's interest in adjudicating the dispute; (5) the most efficient judicial resolution of the controversy; (6) the importance of the forum to plaintiff's interest in convenient and effective relief; and (7) the existence of an alternative forum . . . No one factor is dispositive: the court must balance all seven. . . .

In the tort setting, "if a nonresident acting outside the state, intentionally causes injuries within the state, local jurisdiction is presumptively not unreasonable." "Where a defendant who purposely has directed his activities at forum resident seeks to defeat jurisdiction, he must present a compelling case that . . . would render jurisdiction unreasonable."

[The court found that the defendant failed to establish that the exercise of jurisdiction was unreasonable. It said that requiring a party to litigate in an era of fax machines is not constitutionally unreasonable.]

CASE QUESTIONS

1. Using the "reasonableness" prong and the factors cited therein by the court, do you believe that the burden placed on the defendant to defend itself in the particular forum to be unfair?
2. Was the upholding of jurisdiction "the most efficient judicial resolution of the controversy"?
3. Compare the results of this case with *Maritz* and *American Home* in the following discussion.

Active Web Sites Versus Passive Web Sites

Increasingly, courts in Internet cases have distinguished between so-called active Web sites and passive Web sites in determining whether jurisdiction exists. Although there are significant exceptions, the more passive one's Internet site is, the less likely courts will find the minimal connections required by the due process clause. The more that a site is interactive and affords communication possibilities, the more likely courts will assume jurisdiction over disputes. An additional element is the accessibility of the site to out-of state persons. A number of courts have emphasized that the Internet site was available on a 24-hour basis, rather than being a mere blip of activity, thereby allowing assertion of activity.

In *Cybersell Inc. v. Cybersell Inc.,* 130 F.3d 414 (9th Cir. 1997), the "purposeful availment" test was applied by the Arizona Federal District Court with respect to a lawsuit between an Arizona corporation and a Florida corporation with the same name. The Arizona company alleged infringement of its registered trademark "Cybersell." Both entities offered consultation services for advertising on the Internet. The Arizona statute permitted the long-arm jurisdiction "to the maximum extent permitted by the Constitution of this state and the Constitution of the United States." The defendant claimed lack of jurisdiction. The plaintiff argued that the court had specific jurisdiction. The lower court dismissed the action and the dismissal was upheld on appeal by the U.S. court of appeals.

Using the test, the court distinguished between *active* and *passive* Web sites. A passive Web site conveys information but is not specially directed at any territory. In order for purposeful availment to take place and become active, additional steps have to be taken, such as interaction with users. Interaction is demonstrated, for example, by allowing a person to register a user name or to be placed on a mailing list, having toll-free telephone availability, showing a significant number of hits, or providing an e-mail address for further communication. The Arizona District Court held that the defendant's tortious actions directed to the state gave it specific jurisdiction. On appeal, the court of appeals said the site was passive, merely advertised its services, did not specifically transact business through the Internet, and did not otherwise sell its products or services online. There were no hits by residents of Arizona, no contracts, and no sales or telephone calls between the defendant and Arizona residents. The "effects" test also did not pass muster. The court rejected the claim that the tort committed had effects within Arizona. The court said for the tort to give rise to jurisdiction, it had to be intentionally aimed at the state coupled with knowledge that its conduct would likely cause harm therein. Therefore, the action was dismissed.

In *Maritz, Inc. v. Cybergold, Inc.* 947 F. Supp. 1328 (E.D.Mo. 1996), the plaintiff, a Missouri corporation, sued defendant, a California corporation, for trademark infringement and unfair competition alleging wrongful use of plaintiff's registered trademark for defendant's domain name. The defendant raised the defense of operating a passive Web site. The court rejected the defense and upheld jurisdiction by reasoning that the defendant's actions amounted to active solicitations and promotional activities. The Web site, accessed by over 100 users at least 311 times in Missouri, solicited them to sign onto its advertising mailing list.

The defendant had "indiscriminately responded to every user" who had accessed the Web site. The court used a two-prong process. It first looked at the Missouri long-arm statute that extended jurisdiction "as to any cause of action arising from the doing of any of such acts: (1) The transaction of any business within this State; . . . (3) The commission of a tortious act within this State." The court found that, if the facts were proven, there was a tortious act. It then discussed whether the due process clause of the Constitution would be violated if jurisdiction extended to the facts of the within case. It found that the defendant's conduct was such that he could reasonably anticipate being haled into court and, therefore, met the constitutional requirements.

Subject-matter jurisdiction applied inasmuch as the claim was for breach of the Lanham Act, which provides a remedy against persons wrongfully using the registered trademark of the holder thereof. The court rejected the defendant's claim that its Web site with the offending trademark usage was not yet operational and, therefore, did not give rise to a cause of action because no commercial activity had taken place. "A Lanham Act claim can exist even before a defendant actually opens the business, so long as the acts of defendant are imminent and impending."

In *American Home Care v. Paragon Scientific Corp.* No. CV-893 (WWE), 1998 U.S. Dist. LEXIS 17962 (D.Conn. 1998), the court held that a Web site with an 800 telephone number that solicited participation in an essay contest for children was a passive Web site. Therefore, the Connecticut long-arm statute did not confer jurisdiction upon the court. In another Connecticut case, *Cody v. Ward,* 954 F. Supp. 43 (D.Conn. 1997), 15 e-mail messages and 4 telephone calls from California containing misrepresentations to Connecticut residents sufficed to subject the out-of-state person to Connecticut jurisdiction under the long-arm statute.

JURISDICTION IN INTELLECTUAL PROPERTY CYBERSPACE DISPUTES

Trademark

Many of the leading jurisdictional cases have concerned trademark issues. In *Zippo,* a trademark infringement case, the court referred to a three-prong test for determining whether there was specific personal jurisdiction. It determined that each of the prongs had been met. In *Bensusan Restaurant Corp. v. King,* 937 F. Supp. 295 (S.D.N.Y. 1996), the federal district court in New York dismissed the complaint against the defendant, a Missouri resident. Plaintiff had a trademark for cabaret services known as The Blue Note, which was a successful jazz club in New York City. Defendant operated a club in Columbia, Missouri, using the same name. The problem arose when the defendant allowed a company to create a Web site on the Internet with the name of The Blue Note. Suit was brought for violation of the Lanham Act and the Federal Trademark Dilution Act of 1995. The Internet site did state that the Missouri club was not to be confused with the New York club. The disclaimer was followed by a hyperlink whereby users could link up to plaintiff's site.

The court said that its ruling was based on the New York long-arm statute, which provides in essence that to assert jurisdiction for a tort claim as stated herein, the tort had to be committed within the state of New York. All acts committed by the defendant were done in Missouri and, thus, did not meet the requirements of New York for the assertion of jurisdiction.

Does *Bensusan* conflict with the opinion in *Zippo?* As stated by Judge McLaughlin, it appears that the cases are distinguishable. The New York long-arm statute appears to be somewhat more restrictive than the Pennsylvania statute, and the conduct of the defendant was more passive than the conduct in *Zippo.* The court in *Zippo* distinguished *Bensusan,* stating that the defendant's conduct was passive in that he "simply posted information on an Internet Web site which is accessible to users in a foreign [out-of-state] jurisdiction. A passive Web site that does little more than make information available to those who are interested in it is not grounds for the exercise of personal jurisdiction."

In *Inset Systems, Inc. v. Instruction Set, Inc.,* 937 F. Supp. 161 (D.Conn. 1996), the U.S. district court decided that the defendant, a Massachusetts corporation, that allegedly infringed upon the trademark of the plaintiff, could be sued in Connecticut based on a Connecticut long-arm statute that permits an action against a foreign corporation arising from repeated solicitation of business within the state. The basis for the court's finding of compliance with due process requirements was that the defendant continuously advertised over the Internet, including over 10,000 access sites in Connecticut; that such advertisements were on-going rather than sporadic; and that the travel time between the defendant's place of business was less than two hours from the court in Hartford, Connecticut. Therefore, the fairness and minimum-contacts requirements of the due process clause would appear to have been satisfied in the action.

In *Desktop Technologies, Inc. v. Colorworks Reproduction & Design, Inc.,* No. 98-5029 (E.D.Pa. 1999), plaintiff, a Pennsylvania corporation, sued a Canadian corporation whose principal place of business was in British Columbia. The defendant did not transact any business, provide or contract for services, nor enter into contracts in Pennsylvania. It did business solely in British Columbia, Alberta, and Yukon. Both the plaintiff and the defendant prepared and printed color reproductions. Plaintiff owned the U.S. trademark Colorworks and registered it in the United States on June 4, 1996. Defendant owned the trademark ColorWorks, which was registered in Canada on March 25, 1997. The defendant had a Web site on the Internet using the domain name colorworks.com, which was accessible to all Internet users, including sites in Pennsylvania.

The suit was for infringement of plaintiff's trademark rights and for unfair competition. Defendant's Web site had advertisements about the company and employment opportunities. It also said it serviced clients in British Columbia, and allowed the reader to send e-mail messages and exchange files. The site did say it did not conduct sales, accept orders, or receive payments through the Web site.

The court held in favor of the defendant, dismissing the action for want of jurisdiction. Discussing the constitutional need for minimum-contacts requirements, the court noted that the site was passive in nature. The interactivity with defendant's Web site consisted solely of exchanging files by e-mail, or Internet FTP. To transact business, a fax order had to be completed and sent to the defendant. There were no "systematic or continuous contacts necessary to establish general jurisdiction." There was no specific jurisdiction either; minimum contacts are needed to so establish.

The court elaborated:

> The likelihood that personal jurisdiction can be constitutionally exercised is directly proportionate to the nature and quality of commercial activity that an entity conducts over the Internet. . . . [citing *Zippo*] . . . This sliding scale approach is similar to the approach used to determine whether general jurisdiction can be exercised. At the end of the spectrum are situations where a defendant clearly does business over the Internet. If the defendant enters into contracts with residents of a foreign jurisdiction that involve the knowing and repeated transmission of computer files over the Internet, personal jurisdiction is proper. . . . At the opposite end are situations where a defendant has simply posted information on a web site which is accessible to users in foreign jurisdictions. Thus, "[a] passive Web site that does little more than make information available to those who are interested in it is not grounds for the exercise [of] personal jurisdiction." . . . The middle ground is occupied by interactive web sites where a user can exchange information with the host computer. . . . In these cases, the exercise of jurisdiction is determined by examining the level of interactivity and the commercial nature of the exchange of information that occurs on the web site.

The court held that merely registering someone else's trademark as a domain name and posting a Web site over the Internet did not suffice to invoke jurisdiction. Additional activity was needed. In this case, unlike *Zippo,* the only contacts were an Internet presence and an e-mail link. No contracts were entered into through the Internet. The Web site specifically stated that it serviced clients in British Columbia, Alberta, and Yukon. It never entered Pennsylvania, made no sales or received income, nor sent messages to users in Pennsylvania.

Copyright

The U.S. Court of Appeals for the Sixth Circuit had occasion to consider the jurisdictional aspects of a copyright action. In *CompuServe, Inc. v. Patterson,* 89 F.2d 1257 (6th Cir. 1996), plaintiff is a computer information service located in Columbus, Ohio, that contracted with individual subscribers to allow access computing software products and information services on the Internet known as "shareware." It receives a percentage of the fees charged for the shareware placed on the Internet by its creator. Defendant is an attorney, residing in Texas, who placed shareware items on CompuServe after signing a Shareware Registration Agreement with the plaintiff. He uploaded 32 master software files onto CompuServe's server in Ohio via the Internet. A dispute arose concerning CompuServe's marketing of a software product allegedly similar to the one uploaded by the defendant. On a motion for a declaratory judgment to determine the legitimacy of the defendant's claims, the court of appeals reversed the lower court's dismissal of the claim for lack of jurisdiction.

The court cited the U.S. Supreme Court's opinion in *World-Wide Volkswagen* wherein the Supreme Court noted the "increasing nationalization of commerce," the "modern transportation and communication," and the relaxation of rules mandated by the due process clause. The Ohio long-arm jurisdiction requirements permit out-of state service upon persons transacting business within Ohio. There was specific personal jurisdiction herein because of Patterson's act of sending his computer software to Ohio for sale on its service. The court held that the defendant met the criteria for upholding jurisdiction, namely, that the defendant purposely availed itself of the privilege of doing business in the forum state, that the cause of action arose from the defendant's activities therein, and that the acts of the defendant had a substantial enough connection with the forum to make the exercise of jurisdiction over the defendant reasonable.

U.S. ASSERTION OF JURISDICTION OVER PARTIES IN A FOREIGN COUNTRY

The due process requirement that the assertion of jurisdiction be based on minimum contacts and that it be otherwise fair and substantial justice afforded becomes particularly important when the defendant is in a foreign country. The U.S. Supreme Court, in a product liability case, had occasion to discuss the applicability of the due process requirements to a Japanese defendant who was sued as a third party.

ASAHI METAL INC. V. SUPERIOR COURT OF CALIFORNIA, SOLANO

480 U.S. 102 (1987)

FACTS: This case arose out of a product liability case instituted by a motorcyclist whose wife was killed and who was injured allegedly as result of a defective tire manufactured by a Taiwanese company (Cheng Shin). A cross-complaint was instituted by Cheng Shin against Asahi Metal, a Japanese company that manufactured valve assemblies sold to Cheng Shin. The action with the motorcyclist had been settled between Cheng Shin and the injured party. The action between the Taiwanese and Japanese companies survived.
ISSUE: Did the California courts have jurisdiction in the within action between the two foreign parties?
DECISION: The U.S. Supreme Court reversed the decision of the California Supreme Court and determined that there was no jurisdiction.
REASONING: Justice O'Connor
[T]he Due Process Clause of the Fourteenth Amendment limits the power of a state court to exert personal jurisdiction over a nonresident defendant. "[T]he constitutional touchstone" of the determination whether an exercise of personal jurisdiction comports with due process "remains whether the defendant purposefully established 'minimum contacts' in the forum State" [citing *Burger King, International Shoe* and *Hanson*]. . . . [M]inimum contacts must have a basis in "some act by which the defendant purposefully avails itself of the privilege of conducting activities within the forum State, thus invoking the benefits and proportions of its laws." . . . Jurisdiction is proper . . . where the contacts proximately result from actions by the defendant *himself* that create a substantial connection with the forum State. . . .

The placement of a product into the stream of commerce, without more, is not an act of the defendant purposefully directed toward the forum State. Additional conduct of the defendant may indicate an intent or purpose to serve the market in the forum State, for example, designing the product for the market in the forum State, advertising in the forum State, . . .

[R]espondents have not demonstrated any action by Asahi to purposefully avail itself of the California market. It has no office, agents, employees, or property in California. It does not advertise or otherwise solicit business in California. It did not create, control, or employ the distribution system that brought valves to California. . . . There is no evidence that Asahi designed its product in anticipation of sales in California. . . . On the basis of these facts, the exertion of personal jurisdiction over Asahi by the Superior Court of California exceeds the limits of Due Process.

The strictures of the Due Process Clause forbid a state court from exercising personal jurisdiction over Asahi under circumstances that would offend "traditional notions of fair play and substantial justice" [citing *International Shoe*]. . . .

Certainly the burden on the defendant in this case is severe. Asahi has been commanded by the Supreme Court of California, not only to traverse the distance between Asahi's headquarters in Japan and the Superior Court of California in and for the County of Solano, but also to submit its dispute with Cheng Shin to a foreign nation's judicial system. The unique burdens placed upon one who must defend oneself in a foreign legal system should have significant weight in assessing the reasonableness of stretching the long arm of personal jurisdiction over national borders. . . .

Moreover, it is not at all clear at this point that California law should govern the question whether a Japanese corporation should indemnify a Taiwanese corporation on the basis of a sale made in Taiwan and a shipment of goods from Japan to Taiwan.

Considering the international context, the heavy burden on the alien defendant, and the slight interests of the plaintiff and the forum State, the exercise of personal jurisdiction by a California court over Asahi in this instance would be unreasonable and unfair.

When a person in a foreign country is a potential party, it appears that the Due Process Clause would impose a greater burden upon litigants and courts asserting jurisdiction. "Minimum contacts" require more than incidental connection with the forum State. A mere sale of a product that ultimately arrives into the U.S. would appear to lack Due Process strictures.

CASE QUESTIONS

1. Is there a difference between foreign defendants defending themselves in a lawsuit in a U.S. court and defendants from one U.S. state compelled to defend themselves in another U.S. state?
2. What additional elements were present that influenced the Court's decision?

Whether the U.S. courts will give greater deference to foreign parties because of their lack of easy accessibility and familiarity to U.S. courts remains to be determined in future cases. It would appear that a defendant's distance from a forum and lack of such familiarity, among other aspects of the case, will be factors in rendering a decision.

VENUE

When a court does possess jurisdiction, it may nevertheless refuse to exercise its right to hear a case. Courts often do so for a variety of reasons. The following case discusses the factors that courts consider in making such a determination.

THOMPSON V. HANDA-LOPEZ, INC.

998 F. Supp. 738 (W.D.Tex. 1998)

FACTS: Plaintiff sued defendant for fraud, breach of contract and violation of the Texas Deceptive Practices Act. Defendant operated a gambling Website out of California. Plaintiff, in Texas, played games on defendant's Internet casino and allegedly won certain prizes. When he attempted to redeem the offered prizes, defendant refused to pay. The Web site allowed all users of the Internet to access it. Buried in the contract between the casino and the user was a clause that stated that disputes were governed by the laws of California and resolvable by arbitration in San Jose, California.

ISSUE: (1) Did the Texas Court have jurisdiction over the litigation?

(2) Should the Texas Court refuse to exercise jurisdiction because of improper venue?

DECISION: (1) The Court held in favor of the plaintiff, holding that it did possess jurisdiction.

(2) The Court decided that venue was proper in the within case.

REASONING: Judge Prado

[The court reviewed the *Zippo, Bensusan, CompuServe, World-Wide Volkswagen, and Inset* cases in its discussion of jurisdiction. It found the minimum jurisdiction requirements necessary to satisfy the due process requirements of the Fourteenth Amendment of the U.S. Constitution. The court noted that the defendant advertised itself as the "World's Largest" Internet casino, and its advertisements were designed to communicate with people from every state, including thousands of users within Texas.] Defendant Handa-Lopez did more than advertise and maintain a toll-free telephone number—it continuously interacted with the casino players, entering into contracts with them as they played the various games. Defendant Handa-Lopez did not exchange information with residents of various states *hoping* to use that information for commercial gain in the *future.* In the instant case, Defendant Handa-Lopez entered into contracts with the residents of various states *knowing* that it would receive commercial gain at the *present time.* Furthermore, in the instant case, the Texas Plaintiff played the casino games while in Texas, as if they were physically located in Texas, and if the Plaintiff won cash or prizes, the Defendant would send the winnings to the Plaintiff in Texas. . . .

[With respect to Defendant's claim that the Plaintiff accepted the forum selection clause in the contract:]

First, this clause is not a forum selection clause because it does not mandate that disputes arising from this contract be litigated in California; it merely states that disputes shall be governed by the laws of the State of California and shall be resolved exclusively by final and binding arbitration in California. This clause by no means requires, nor does it even suggest, that a lawsuit must be filed in California.

In addition, Texas clearly has a strong interest in protecting its citizens by adjudicating disputes involving the alleged breach of contract, fraud, and violations of the Texas Deceptive Practices Act by an Internet casino on Texas residents.... These concerns outweigh the burden created by requiring the Defendant to defend the suit in Texas.

VENUE

Defendant also moves this Court to dismiss this case for improper venue, or to transfer this case for improper venue, pursuant to 28 U.S.C. Section 1406(a), "on the basis that Texas Courts are improper venue for this case based upon a forum selection clause found in Defendant's Official Rules and Regulations."

Section 1406(a) provides:

The district court of a district in which is filed a case laying venue in the wrong division or district shall dismiss, or if it be in the interest of justice, transfer such case to any district or division in which it could have been brought.

This argument is meritless because this case was not brought in an improper venue. As previously stated, the clause at issue does not prohibit a lawsuit from being brought in Texas.

Defendant also argues that this case should be transferred to the Northern District of California pursuant to 28 U.S.C. Section 1404(a). which provides that "for the convenience of the parties and witnesses, in the interests of justice, a district court may transfer any civil action to any other district or division where it might have been brought." The purpose of this statute is to prevent the waste of time, energy, and money and to protect litigants, witnesses, and the public against unnecessary inconvenience and expense.... To prevail, the moving party must show that the balance of convenience and justice weighs heavily in favor of the transfer.... Therefore, when assessing the merits of a Section 1404(a) motion, a court must determine if a transfer would make it substantially more convenient for the parties to litigate the case....

The decision to transfer a pending case is committed to the sound discretion of the district court.... The criteria weighed by a court in a Section 1404(a) motion include:

(1) the convenience of the parties; (2) the convenience of material witnesses; (3) the availability of process to compel the presence of unwilling witnesses; (4) the cost of obtaining the presence of witnesses; (5) the relative ease of access to sources of proof; (6) calendar congestion; (7) where the events in issue took place; and (8) the interests of justice in general....

In the instant case, a review of the relevant factors indicates that a transfer is not warranted. The Defendant claims that all of its witnesses and evidence are located in California. While this may be true, the same applies to the Plaintiff with regard to Texas—all of his witnesses and evidence are located in Texas. The Defendant also claims that it would be very burdensome for it to travel to Texas to defend this lawsuit. However, it would be at least as burdensome, if not more so, for the Texas Plaintiff to travel to California as it would be for the "World's Largest" Internet casino to come to Texas.

Defendant further argues that this case should be transferred to California because Plaintiff, to the extent he receives a judgment against Defendant, "would be required to enforce the judgment in California." This argument is meritless because if Plaintiff receives a judgment against Defendant, he will be able to enforce the judgment in California; California certainly gives full faith and credit to judgments received in Texas.

Finally, Defendant claims that in the interest of justice this case should be transferred since "Plaintiff agreed that the forum for any dispute regarding Defendant would be in California." As previously mentioned, this clause clearly neither compels nor suggests that a lawsuit be brought in California. Furthermore, this clause did not give Plaintiff notice that California was a possible forum, since the clause was inconspicuously buried within the several page contract—Plaintiff did not notice it, nor would a reasonable person have noticed it. Plaintiff entered into a contract with Defendant and played on Defendant's casinos without ever contemplating that he may be compelled to fight a potential lawsuit in California.

CASE QUESTIONS

1. Compare the meaning of *jurisdiction* with the meaning of *venue*.
2. What are the elements a court will consider in determining the proper venue?
3. Which elements do you believe are the most important?

CHOICE OF LAW

In the preparation of contracts, particularly international contracts, parties often insert clauses specifying the forum to be used in the event of a dispute (generally, arbitration before a specific tribunal) and the choice of law applicable to the dispute. Laws differ from country to country and from locality to locality within a country. When a tort or breach of contract has been committed, which jurisdiction's laws apply? If the parties do insert a choice-of-law provision in their contract, must a court be bound by such provision? In the following litigation, the court summarized the law concerning this very important issue in national and international disputes.

BROWN V. SAP AMERICA, INC.

C.A. No. 98-507-SLR, 1999 U.S. Dist. LEXIS 15525 (D.Del. 1999)

FACTS: The trustee in bankruptcy for FoxMeyer in Delaware sued the defendant, a German software designer, and its U.S. subsidiary. He alleged that the defendants sold defective software to plaintiff, FoxMeyer, which crippled its business, thereby causing it to become bankrupt. Defendants claimed its software would operate all aspects of plaintiff's business, handle its demands, absorb high processing volumes than its existing computer system, interface with the other plaintiff's software, and save plaintiff up to $10 million in operating costs. Relying on the promises and demonstrations of the defendants, the plaintiff purchased the software.

The agreement warranted the software would be in good working order for twelve months after date of delivery and perform in substantial compliance with the specifications set forth in the documentation provided. The agreement disclaimed all other express or implied warranties, including those of merchantability and fitness for a particular purpose. Thereafter, plaintiff contracted to distribute pharmaceuticals to the University Health System Consortium, a network of teaching hospitals. After the installation of the software on behalf of FoxMeyer, it did not perform as promised. Plaintiff claimed breach of express warranties, fraud, concealment of material facts, gross negligence, and other claims.

All but one of the five debtor plaintiffs were incorporated in Delaware and all of them have their principal places of business in Carrollton, Texas. The agreement between the parties specified that disputed contract claims were to be governed by Pennsylvania law.

ISSUE: Whether federal or state law applies and, if the latter, which state law is applicable?

DECISION: The Court decided that the law of the State of Texas was applicable to the tort claims made in the within proceeding.

REASONING: Judge Robinson

[Contract claims.] Both parties agree that Pennsylvania law shall govern plaintiff's contract claims. The choice of law provision contained in the Agreement signed by the parties provides that it "shall be governed by and construed under Pennsylvania law." Delaware courts honor such choice of law provisions in contracts, so long as some material connection links the chosen jurisdiction to the transaction. . . . Because SAP America has its principal place of business in Pennsylvania, that essential connection is present. . . . Therefore, the court shall apply Pennsylvania law in reviewing plaintiff's contract claims.

[Tort claims.] The parties disagree as to the law applicable to plaintiff's tort claims. Plaintiff's tort claims consist of fraudulent misrepresentation and concealment (count four), negligent misrepresentation (count five), and negligence and gross negligence (count six). Plaintiff contends that, under Delaware's "most significant relationship" test, Texas law governs. . . . Defendants, on the other hand, seem to deny that the "most significant relationship" test applies and argue instead that Pennsylvania law governs plaintiff's tort claims. Defendants rely on Section 201 of the Restatement, which states that "the effect of misrepresentation . . . upon a contract is determined by the law selected by application of the rules of Sections 187–188." Section 187 of the Restatement provides, in pertinent part, that courts should apply a party's choice of law provision unless,

- **a.** the chosen state has no substantial relationship to the parties or the transaction and there is no other reasonable basis for the parties' choice, or
- **b.** application of the law of the chosen state would be contrary to a fundamental policy of a state which has a materially greater interest than the chosen state in the determination of the particular issue and which, under the [most significant relationship test of Section 188 of the Restatement], would be the state of the applicable law in the absence of an effective choice of law by the parties. . . .

Neither Delaware courts nor federal courts applying Delaware law have employed Section 202 to determine the state law applicable to tort claims arising out of a contract dispute. Instead, Delaware courts have applied the Restatement's "most significant relationship" test to tort claims associated with contract disputes. . . . Indeed, courts have recognized that a contract's choice of law provision does not necessarily govern fraud, misrepresentation, and other tort claims related to the contract. . . .

In the present case, it is not evident that the Agreement's choice of law provision "embraces all aspects" of FoxMeyer and SAP America's legal relationship. . . . Although the Agreement provides that FoxMeyer "consents to the jurisdiction of any federal or state court sitting in Delaware County, Pennsylvania for all claims, suits, or actions arising under this Agreement," the fact that FoxMeyer consented to venue in Pennsylvania does not compel the conclusion that Pennsylvania law must govern all non-contract claims. Because of the fair import of the Agreement's choice of law provision does not embrace plaintiff's tort claims, the court shall employ Delaware's "most significant relationship" test to determine the law applicable to plaintiff's tort claims.

Delaware courts have adopted Section 145(1) of the Second Restatement of Conflicts, which contains the general principles of the "most significant relationship" test. It provides that "the rights and liabilities of the parties with respect to an issue in tort are determined by the local law of the state which, with respect to that issue, has the most significant relationship to the occurrence and the parties under the principles stated in Section 6." . . . Section 145(1). This rule applies generally to all torts, while other related sections of the Restatement provide more detailed factors to assess the significance of a state's relationship to particular torts. . . . In this case, section 148 of the Second Restatement of Conflicts is particularly relevant to plaintiff's tort claims. That section provides a more detailed choice of law analysis for the torts of fraud and misrepresentation. Section 148(2) sets forth six factors to assess which state has the most significant relationship to the tort and to the parties. Those factors are:

1. the place, or places, where the [injured party] acted in reliance upon defendant[s'] representations,
2. the place where the [injured party] received the representations,
3. the place where the defendant[s] made the representations,
4. the domicile . . . place of incorporation and place of business of the parties,
5. the place where a tangible thing which is the subject of the transaction between the parties was situated at the time, and
6. the place where the [injured party] is to render performance under a contract which [it] has been induced to enter by the false representations of the defendant[s].

Although no "definite rules as to the selection of the applicable law can be stated[,] . . . if any two of the above-mentioned contracts . . . are located wholly in a single state, this will usually be the state of the applicable law with respect to most issues." . . .

[The court then examined each of the factors in connection with the litigation and found that the place of the alleged misrepresentations was in Texas, the installation of the software was in Texas, the domicile of the parties and place of incorporation was in Texas, the copy of the software was in Texas, and the place where performance was to be made was also in Texas. Therefore, the court held that Texas law was applicable to the alleged torts.]

CASE QUESTIONS

1. Do parties have the right to determine which court may decide a dispute between them?
2. Why wasn't Pennsylvania law made applicable to the dispute?
3. What do you believe is the difference between a *tort* and a *contract?* (We will discuss both topics in subsequent chapters).

In *Bibeault v. Advanced Health Corp.*, 1999 U.S. Dist. LEXIS 7173 (S.D.N.Y. 1999), the plaintiff sued in a securities litigation claiming that the defendants committed fraud in violation of the Securities Exchange Act of 1934, common law fraud, and other claims. The subscription agreement governing the transaction contained a choice-of-law provision that stated that the laws of the state of New York would be applicable to "any dispute which may arise between them arising out of or in connection with this Subscription Agreement. . . ." The issue arose whether tort-based allegations were subject to the choice-of-law limitation. The court cited New York case law that said "a contractual choice of law provision will not bind the parties with respect to tort claims arising incident to the contract unless 'the express language of the provision [is] sufficiently broad' as to encompass the entire relationship between the parties." In this particular case, the court decided that the language was broad enough to make New York law applicable to the plaintiff's claims.

An example of the confusion that can arise under choice-of-law and conflict-of-laws analysis is the case of *Itar-Tass v. Russian Kurier, Inc.*

ITAR-TASS V. RUSSIAN KURIER, INC.

153 F.3d 82 (2d Cir. 1998)

FACTS: The defendant, Kurier, is a Russian language weekly newspaper published in New York, having a 20,000 circulation. Some of the plaintiffs consisted of corporations that publish daily and weekly Russian language newspapers in Russia and Russian magazines in Russia or Israel. Itar-Tass is a Russian News Agency that has a wire service and news gathering company with its principal location in Moscow. Plaintiff, Union of Journalists, is a professional writers union of journalists of the Russian Federation. The defendants copied, without permission, some 500 articles that had previously appeared in plaintiffs' publications or were distributed by Itar-Tass. The copied material was a small part of Kurier's publications and consisted of pictures, bylines, headlines, pasted cut out text, and other material of the plaintiffs. The Federal District Court issued a preliminary injunction barring the defendant, Kurier, from copying the works of four Russian publications. Russia acceded to the Berne Convention [protecting copyrighted works] in March 1995.

ISSUE: Does Russian or U.S. law apply to the dispute at hand?

DECISION: The Court of Appeals affirmed the District Court's opinion granting the temporary injunction in favor of Itar-Tass, but reversed its decision concerning the remaining plaintiffs.

REASONING: Judge Newman

We start our analysis with the Copyright Act itself, which contains no provision relevant to the pending case concerning conflicts issues. We therefore fill in the interstices of the Act by developing federal common law on the conflicts issue. . . .

The choice of law applicable to the pending case is a form of property, and the usual rule is that the interests of the parties in property are determined by the law of the state with "the most significant relationship" to the property and the parties. . . . The Restatement [(Second) of Conflict of Laws] recognizes the applicability of this principle to intangibles such as "a literary idea." . . . Since the works were created by Russian nationals and first published in Russia, Russian law is the appropriate source of law to determine issues of ownership of rights. In terms of the United States Copyrights Act and its reference to the Berne Convention, Russia is the "country of origin" of these works. . . .

Selection of Russian law to determine copyright ownership is, however, subject to one procedural qualification. Under United States law, an owner (including one determined according to foreign law) may sue for infringement in a United States court only if it meets the standing test of 17 U.S.C. Section 501(b), which accords standing only to the legal or beneficial owner of an "exclusive right."

Conflicts rule for infringement issues. On infringement issues, the governing conflicts principle is usually lex loci delicti, the doctrine generally applicable to torts. . . . We have implicitly adopted that approach to infringement claims, applying United States copyright law to a work that was unprotected in its country of origin. . . . In the pending case, the place of the tort is plainly the United States. To whatever extent lex loci is to be considered only one part of a broader "interest" approach, . . . United States law would still apply to infringement issues, since not only is this country the place of the tort, but also the defendant is a United States corporation.

The division of issues, for conflicts purposes, between ownership and infringement issues, will not always be as easily made as the above discussion applies. If the issue is the relatively straightforward one of which two contending parties owns a copyright, the issue is unquestionably an ownership issue, and the law of the country with the closest relationship to the work will apply to settle the ownership dispute. But in some cases, including the pending one, the issue is not simply who owns the copyright but also what is the nature of the ownership interest. Yet as a court considers the nature of an ownership interest, there is some risk that it will too readily shift the inquiry over to the issue of whether an alleged copy has infringed the asserted copyright. Whether a copy infringes depends in part on the scope of the interest of the copyright owner. Nevertheless, though the issues are related, the nature of a copyright interest is an issue distinct from the issue of whether the copyright has been infringed. . . . The pending case is one that requires consideration not simply of who owns an interest, but, as to the newspapers, the nature of the interest that is owned.

[The court decided that Russian Copyright Law denies newspapers the right to individual articles written by their employees. Authors of newspaper articles can sue for infringement concerning the text of their articles, and newspaper publishers can sue for wholesale copying of all of the newspaper or portions thereof that embody the selection, arrangement, and presentation of the articles.]

II. DETERMINATION OF OWNERSHIP RIGHTS UNDER RUSSIAN LAW

Since United States law permits suit only by owners of "an exclusive right under a copyright," 17 U.S.C. 501(b), we must first determine whether any of the plaintiffs own an exclusive right. That issue of ownership, as we have indicated, is to be determined by Russian law.

CASE QUESTIONS

1. What is meant by *federal common law*?
2. Why did the court refuse to exercise jurisdiction with respect to the determination of ownership of the copyright?
3. Distinguish between *ownership* and *infringement* of a copyright. Should a distinction be made between the two concepts?

STANDING

A subsidiary issue to the determination of jurisdiction is the right of a person to sue. In order to do so, one must be somehow connected with the lawsuit or in a circumstance in which the statute sued under specifically allows a person to sue. In *Cyberspace, Communications, Inc. v. Engler,* 55 F. Supp. 2d 737 (E.D.Mich. 1999), the court quoted the U.S. Supreme Court's decision in *Lujan v. Defenders of Wildlife,* 504 U.S. 555 (1992), that stated there were at least three requirements for a party to have standing in a lawsuit:

1. an injury in fact—i.e., an injury which is concrete and actual or immanent, not merely speculative or hypothetical;
2. a causal relationship between the injury and the challenged conduct; and
3. a likelihood that the injury will be addressed by a favorable decision.

The concept is based on Article 3 of the U.S. Constitution that extends the judicial power "to all Cases, in Law and Equity . . . [and] to Controversies. . . ." A person must have some interest in the outcome of the litigation, "allege personal injury fairly traceable to the . . . allegedly unlawful conduct and likely to be redressed by the requested relief," *Allen v. Wright,* 468 U.S. 737, 751 (1984). One must allege more than merely being a U.S. citizen affected by a particular law. Something in addition to a highly generalized remote injury is necessary. Unless a person is able to demonstrate such an injury, the lawsuit, almost assuredly, will be dismissed on the basis of lack of standing or as *moot,* where the outcome will have no affect on the desired result.

Ripeness

A case is moot if the result being sought will have no effect upon the relief sought in the particular case. For example, if a person were suing for permission to use banned drugs to alleviate pain associated with terminal cancer and the person dies during the pendency of the litigation, a court may deem the case to be moot because no relief could now assist the claimant. The injury claimed must in fact be pending, that is, likely to occur or is occurring at the time of judicial determination.[2] *Ripeness* requires that a controversy that is premature because the injury is speculative, or where the controversy is no longer an issue, be dismissed.[3] A court may not give an advisory opinion or decide a case that has lost its character. For example, if a person sues alleging a law applicable to his or her case to be unconstitutional, but the law is changed during the pendency of the case so as to remove its objectionable provisions, then the case may be dismissed for want of a case or controversy.

REFUSAL TO ASSERT JURISDICTION OVER FOREIGN ENTITIES

Comity in International Litigation

Comity is a concept of international law holding that courts of one country will extend the privilege of courtesy and deference to the judgments and private rights accorded to persons under the laws of foreign countries. The principle is not a rule of law but rather is a discretionary grant that courts may ignore if such grant is contrary to the policies and mores of the local jurisdiction. A court may deny jurisdiction over a case if a party is another country or is a company owned by a foreign state, particularly if litigation affecting it has taken place in the foreign state. The issue arose in the following case on appeal wherein the U.S. district court dismissed a lawsuit against a French telecommunications company wholly owned by the government of France.

FILETECH S.A. V. FRANCE TELECOM S.A.

157 F.3d 922 (2d Cir. 1998)

FACTS: Plaintiffs, Filetech S.A., a French corporation with its principal place of business in France, and its U.S. subsidiary, Filetech U.S.A., sued France Telecom S.A., a French corporation with its principal place of business in France and which is wholly owned by the Republic of France, and its U.S. subsidiary, France Telecom Inc. Plaintiffs alleged that the defendants were engaged in anticompetitive conduct in violation of the Sherman Antitrust Act [discussed in Chapter 11]. The U.S. District Court dismissed the complaint for lack of subject matter jurisdiction.

Filetech is in the business of selling marketing lists of French residents designed to meet the distinctive criteria required by purchasers of the lists. Under French law, residents of France may block inclusion of their names on commercial mailing lists. France Telecom, publishes an electronic directory, a database of its yellow and white pages. It is required to maintain a list of telephone subscribers who do not want their names used for marketing purposes. It also claims that it is precluded under French law from disclosing the names of individuals seeking exclusion for marketing purposes. Without knowledge of the database other companies seeking to market to French customers would violate French law if it communicates telephonically for marketing purposes to the excluded persons. The plaintiff sued in France unsuccessfully to require the defendant to furnish the excluded list. The Commercial Court of France issued a judgment denying plaintiff's request. Suits are now pending in French courts concerning whether the restrictions violate European Union antitrust policy. Filetech sued in the U.S. District Court alleging violation of the U.S. antitrust laws.

ISSUE: Whether the District Court's dismissal for reason of international comity was proper under the facts of the case?

DECISION: The Court of Appeals reversed the lower Court's decision and remanded the case for further inquiry as to the conduct of the defendants.

REASONING: Judge Miner

[T]he district court addressed the arguments in the order presented and therefore began its analysis by examining the issue of international comity. The court determined, on the basis of Supreme Court precedent and earlier cases in this Circuit, that (1) "a party seeking the dismissal of a Sherman Act case on the ground of international comity must first demonstrate that a true conflict exists between the Sherman Act and relevant foreign law"; and (2) "that, once the threshold barrier of conflict of law is passed, comity analysis in this Circuit looks to the same factors described by the Ninth Circuit in Timberlane cases and in the Restatement." . . . *Timberlane Lumber Co. v. Bank of America,* 749 F.2d 1378 (9th Cir. 1984) and the Restatement (Third) of the Foreign Relations Law of the United States Section 403(2), adopted a seven-factor analysis to be applied in deciding whether international comity dictates that a court decline to exercise jurisdiction. [In a footnote to the decision, the court listed the factors stated in *Timberlane* as follows:]

The degree of conflict with foreign law or policy, the nationality or allegiance of the parties and the locations or principal places of business of corporations, the extent to which enforcement by either state can be expected to achieve compliance, the relative significance of effects on the United States as compared with those elsewhere, the extent to which there is explicit purpose to harm or affect American commerce, the foreseeability of such effect, and the relative importance to the violations charged of conduct within the United States as compared with conduct abroad.

In concluding that a true conflict is present in this case, the district court determined that "the most that can be said in the case at bar is that France Telecom has asserted a substantial claim that its conduct gives rise to a conflict between the requirements of the Sherman Act and of French law." . . . The court gave two reasons for this determination: (1) any conflict between the Sherman Act and French law "goes to the heart of the case, including, significantly, the propriety of this Court's enjoining France Telecom's conduct in ways that may violate French law and regulations," . . . and (2) it is more appropriate that the French courts declare the French law in the course of litigation being pursued in France. The district court then proceeded to apply the seven Timberlane factors, concluding that the first factor alone required dismissal on the ground of comity, and further noting that "if that factor alone does not require that conclusion, it surely does when viewed in conjunction with other Timberlane factors." . . .

[W]e do not, approve or disapprove of the district court's analysis or application of the doctrine of international comity, except to the limited extent that follows. We here note our disagreement with the court's conclusion that there is a true conflict between French law and United States law. There is as yet no basis for such a conclusion in the record. "What is required to establish a true conflict is an allegation that compliance with the regulatory laws of both countries would be impossible. . . ."

In the first place, the district court found only that French Telecom had "asserted a substantial claim" of true conflict. A "substantial claim" is insufficient: a conflict must be clearly demonstrated. Secondly, the court's true conflict determination was grounded in findings: (1) that if there were a conflict, it would "go to the heart of the case" including the propriety of an injunction violative of French laws; and (2) that it would be "more appropriate" for French law to be declared by French courts. These findings are insufficient to demonstrate any apparent conflict of laws.

CASE QUESTIONS

1. Is the court of appeals' reversal of the district court's decision a final determination of the merits of the case?
2. Should the court have deferred to the French court to render a decision in the case? What are the arguments for and against such deference?

Sovereign Immunity

When a party to a lawsuit or arbitration proceeding is a country, the defense of *sovereign immunity* may preclude the other party from proceeding with litigation to make the state responsible for its conduct. The proponents of the doctrine believe that a foreign country as sovereign is immune from all lawsuits arising in another country and cannot be compelled to litigate without its permission. The extreme view of sovereign immunity, *absolute sovereign immunity,* had many proponents, including the United States until 1952 and the former Soviet Union. Today, almost all countries subscribe to the doctrine of *restrictive immunity,* which permits a person to sue a foreign country or entity in his or her court for private commercial disputes. A foreign country still retains sovereign immunity for its public acts, such as a decision to deploy military forces to a particular country or other political actions; however, a government that enters into a commercial agreement, such as purchasing wheat from other countries, may subject the state to the jurisdiction of the courts of the seller's state.

As a result of decisions that upset Congress concerning nationalization of the property of U.S. nationals, Congress passed the Foreign Sovereign Immunities Act of 1976 (28 U.S.C. Sections 1602–1611). The act codified the restrictive view of sovereign immunity. The key provision provides:

> A foreign state will be immune from the jurisdiction of U.S. courts except in cases (1) in which the foreign state has waived its immunity, either explicitly or implied; (2) in cases involving commercial activity, either carried on or performed in the U.S. or having a direct effect in the U.S.; (3) in cases where property is taken in violation of international law or is present in the U.S. as a result of commercial activity carried on by the foreign state in the U.S.; (4) real property in the U.S. or other property acquired by succession or gift; (5) non-discretionary tortious acts in the U.S. by the foreign state with some exceptions; and (6) maritime liens based upon a commercial activity. In addition to the above, a foreign state will waive its immunity if it institutes an action in the U.S. courts and the party being sued interposes a counterclaim which either is exempt from immunity as previously stated or arises out of the same transaction or occurrence of the foreign state's action or is for a sum not exceeding the amount demanded by the foreign state in its complaint.

The act defines commercial activity as one

> [i]n which the action is based upon a commercial activity carried on in the United States by the foreign state; or upon an act performed in the United States in connection with a commercial activity of the foreign state elsewhere, or upon an act outside the territory of the United States in connection with a commercial activity of the foreign state elsewhere and that act causes a direct effect in the United States.

In the *Filetech* case, the court observed that France Telecom S.A. would not be immune from suit in the United States if it were established that it was engaged in commercial conduct having a substantial effect in the United States. As stated by the court, it is conclusively established "that civil antitrust actions predicated on wholly foreign conduct which has intended and substantial effect in the United States come within [the Sherman Act's] Section One's jurisdiction."

INTERNATIONAL BASES FOR ASSERTION OF JURISDICTION

Jurisdiction with respect to judicial proceedings is defined as the power of a court, granted by law, in a given territory to exercise authority over a case. Principles of jurisdiction have been the focus of international law from its inception.[4] The theories of jurisdiction upon which nations have asserted their authority are (1) territoriality, (2) nationality, (3) the effects upon the territory by outside activity, (4) protection from outside activity, (5) universality, and (6) the passive personality principle. Internally, nations assert jurisdiction based upon a variety of statutory and common-law principles.

The *territorial principle* provides that every country has a right to make rules concerning persons and property within its territory and to enforce those rules therein. It is the leading principle governing the exercise of jurisdiction over domestic and foreign parties. It is illustrated by a quote of Chief Justice John Marshall of the U.S. Supreme Court, who stated in *The Schooner Exchange v. M'Faddon,* 11 U.S. (7 Cranch) 116, at 136 (1812):

> The jurisdiction of the nation within its own territory is necessarily exclusive and absolute. It is susceptible of no limitation not imposed by it. Any restriction upon it, deriving validity from an external source, would imply a diminution of its sovereignty to the extent of the restriction, and an investment of that sovereignty to the same extent in that power which could impose such restriction.

The *nationality principle* is premised on the concept that a nation may apply its laws over its inhabitants wherever they may be located. In the oft-cited taxation case of *Cook v. Tait,* 265 U.S. 47 (1924), the U.S. Supreme Court upheld the power of Congress to impose a tax upon the income of a U.S. citizen permanently residing and domiciled in Mexico from real and personal property located in Mexico. The Court stated that "government, by its very nature, benefits the citizen and his property wherever found" and, therefore, the power to tax is not dependent upon the site of the property or where the national is residing but rather is found in the relation of a citizen to his or her country irrespective of where he or she may live.

The *effects principle* has been very controversial. It refers to jurisdiction based on the effect outside conduct has within a nation. Such exercise of jurisdiction is one area of the law that has caused much antagonism between the United States and otherwise friendly countries, such as Great Britain, France, and other Western nations. In the past, U.S. courts have exercised their power to hear and adjudicate cases that other countries believe the United States had no right to entertain. An example is the trial of antitrust cases and the imposition of penalties involving overseas companies that engaged in acts legal within their respective countries. A leading case establishing the right of U.S. courts to determine the legality of conduct by foreign companies having a substantial effect within the United States is *United States v. Aluminum Co. of America,* 148 F.2d 416 (2d Cir. 1945). In that action, Alcoa, through its Canadian subsidiary, entered into a cartel with foreign manufacturers of aluminum, dividing territories for its sales and thereby restricting imports into the United States

The court of appeals asserted that the United States government had the right to exercise authority over foreign transactions that have a substantial effect upon the United States. Accordingly, the court imposed sanctions against the cartel composed entirely of foreign companies entering into an agreement that was legal where it took place. Congress did attempt to ameliorate the antagonism caused abroad by such assertion of jurisdiction by providing in the Foreign Trade Antitrust Improvements Act that U.S. antitrust law will not apply to foreign conduct unless it had a "direct, substantial, and reasonably foreseeable effect on United States commerce." Although western European countries strenuously objected to such assertion of jurisdiction,[5] nevertheless, they appear to be using similar principles to uphold jurisdiction against foreign companies. In *A. Ahlstrom Osakeyhtio v. E. C. Commission,* 1987–88 Tfr. Binder Common Mkt. Rep. (CCH) 14,491 (E.U. Ct. of Jus. 1988), the European Union's Court of Justice held that the European Commission could impose fines against foreign producers engaged in anticompetitive activity with respect to sales to the European Union (E.U.) notwithstanding that their actions, where taken, were legal within their own countries.

The *protective principle* is premised on the theory that a state has the power to make a rule of law governing conduct from without that threatens its security or the operation of its governmental functions. The examples given by *Restatement, Second, Foreign Relations Law of the United States* (1965), Section 33(2), are counterfeit of a country's seals and currency and the falsification of official documents. The *universality principle* permits a country to assert jurisdiction over conduct such as piracy, the slave trade, trafficking in prostitution, trafficking in narcotics, and war crimes. All such conduct is universally condemned and may be tried by any nation. The *passive personality principle* permits a government to assert jurisdiction over foreign persons whose actions injured the nation's subjects. Most countries have rejected this principle as a basis for jurisdiction, but the onslaught of terrorism has caused dissenting nations to reexamine the principle's validity.

INTERNATIONAL VIEWS CONCERNING JURISDICTION

Jurisdictional issues become even more complex when one examines the multiplicity of jurisdictions worldwide. Each country has its own set of mores, norms, values, and cultural variations. When translated into legal precepts, the variety of such laws creates a great deal of uncertainty.[6] Countries such as India object strenuously to the perceived attempts by Western industrial powers to foster a new imperialism.

The difficulty inherent in determining international jurisdiction, as illustrated by the *Braintech* case, is to determine which country's law will apply. Confusion exists because cyberspace contradicts the former simpler analysis of determining, for example, where the contract came into existence or where the dominant aspects of the contract or incident occurred (*siege social* in France). Such analysis in cyberspace is almost useless. Common-law jurisdictions, like Canada, tend to apply a due process type of analysis to the case at hand. The *Braintech* case is illustrative of the analysis used to adjudicate conflict of law basis.

Like all other countries, Canada has had to wrestle with the jurisdictional problems presented by the Internet. In the following case, the plaintiff, a domiciliary of Nevada, with its principal office in British Columbia, sought to enforce a default judgment rendered in Texas against a person domiciled in British Columbia whose activities emanated from British Columbia but were accessible to Texas residents.

BRAINTECH, INC. V. KOSTIUK

Court of Appeal for British Columbia (1999 BCCA 0169)

FACTS: On May 7, 1997, Braintech, Inc. sued the defendant, John Kostiuk, for defamation and disparagement of its business before a local court in Texas. It recovered a default judgment against Kostiuk due to his failure to appear in the proceeding. The claim made was that the defendant allegedly used the Internet to publish defamatory material about the plaintiff. A year later, the plaintiff commenced an action against the defendant seeking a judgment based on the Texas judgment before the Supreme Court of British Columbia, Canada. After judgment was awarded in favor of Braintech, an appeal was taken by Kostiuk. He alleged that he was never served with process in the Texas action. Kostiuk was not a resident of Texas nor did he appoint an agent to act on his behalf in Texas. Texas long-arm statute permits jurisdiction over nonresidents who commit a tort within the State. In such an event, the Texas Secretary of State is authorized to accept process on behalf of the alleged tortfeasor who then mails a copy of the pleadings to the defendant.

Braintech has its corporate offices in Vancouver, British Columbia, with research and development facilities in Austin, Texas. It appears that the pleadings were mailed to defendant's father at the address indicated by the plaintiff. Believing he was not properly served, the defendant failed to appear.

ISSUES: (1) Under the facts of the within action, did the Texas Court have a real and substantial connection with the subject matter of the action thereby giving it jurisdiction?

(2) What is the standard of review to be followed by the courts of Canada under the circumstances of the case at bar?

DECISION: (1) The Canadian Court of Appeal refused to enforce the judgment of the Texas Court stating that the Texas Court had no jurisdiction to enter a default judgment.

(2) The Court set forth the standard of review as recited below.

REASONING: Justice Goldie

[36] I am of the view that under the principles alluded to in *DeSavoye v. Morguard Investments Limited,* [1990] 3 S.C.R. 1077 ("Morguard") and enlarged on in *Amchem Products Inc. v. British Columbia (Workers Compensation Board),* [1993] 1 S.C.R. 897 ("Amchem") the issue of service is to be looked at in terms of its relationship to the obligations of the British Columbia courts to recognize the foreign judgment in accordance with the principles of comity. The minimum standard of service to be observed by the American courts is that mandated under the due process clause of the 14th Amendment to the Constitution of the United States.

[39] This brings me to a consideration of Issue 3. . . . The standard of review of a foreign judgment by a Canadian Court.

[40] The starting point is the judgment of the Supreme Court of Canada in Morguard.

[42] Mr. Justice La Forest, speaking for the Court, concluded that considerations which reflected modern requirements of commerce and the reality of modern means of communication justified a departure from 19th century standards. At 1079 he said:

> These concerns, however, must be weighed against fairness to the defendant. The taking of jurisdiction by a court in one province and its recognition in another must be viewed as correlatives and recognition in other provinces should be dependent on the fact that the court giving judgment "properly" and "appropriately" exercised jurisdiction. It may meet the demands of order and fairness to recognize a judgment given in a jurisdiction that had the greatest or at least significant contacts with the subject matter of the action. But it hardly accords with principles of order and fairness to permit a person to sue another in any jurisdiction, without regard to the contacts that jurisdiction may have to the defendant or the subject matter of the suit. If the courts of one province are to be expected to give effect to judgments given in another province, there must be some limit to the exercise of jurisdiction against persons outside the province. If it is reasonable to support the exercise of jurisdiction in one province, it is reasonable that the judgment be recognized in other provinces.
>
> The approach of permitting suit where there is real and substantial connection with the action provides a reasonable balance between the rights of the parties. It affords some protection against being pursued in jurisdictions having little or no connection with the transaction or the parties.

[The court then recited the three-pronged test in *Zippo,* namely, the necessity of showing minimum contacts with the forum, the claim asserted must arise from those contacts, and the exercise of jurisdiction must be reasonable.]

[62] In these circumstances the complainant must offer better proof that the defendant has entered Texas than the mere possibility that someone in that jurisdiction might have reached out to cyberspace to bring the defamatory material to a screen in Texas. There is no allegation or evidence Kostiuk had a commercial purpose that utilized the highway provided by the Internet to enter any particular jurisdiction.

[63] It would create a crippling effect on freedom of expression if, in every jurisdiction the world over in which access to Internet could be achieved, a person who posts fair comment on a bulletin board could be haled before the courts of each of those countries where access to this bulletin could be obtained.

[66] The record demonstrates British Columbia was the natural forum for the resolution of a dispute between two residents. For the following reasons (which are not exhaustive) the connections in the case at bar show that Texas was not even an appropriate forum:

1. Kostiuk is a non-resident of Texas who has neither done business nor maintained a place of business nor appointed an agent for service there. His only connection is "deemed" by virtue of the allegations of having committed a tort in Texas.
2. Braintech is a Nevada corporation domiciled in British Columbia. . . . As of 31 December 1996 its transfer agent was located in Salt

Lake City; its office in North Vancouver, British Columbia; . . . its principal officers . . . were located in North or West Vancouver.

3. Braintech has had no presence in Texas since 31 December 1996. . . . [I]ts head office was located in Arizona. In the fall of 1995, it was moved to Vancouver.
4. No person in Texas is alleged to have seen the alleged defamatory material and the witnesses required to prove its damages are acknowledged to be citizens of Canada. . . .
5. No judicial advantage is alleged to accrue in Texas which is not available if a defamation action was brought in British Columbia.
6. The mode of service in the case at bar falls below the minimum constitutional standards for an American court.

[69] . . . In the circumstances revealed by record before this court, British Columbia is the only natural forum and Texas is not an appropriate forum. That being so, comity does not require the courts of this province to recognize the default judgment in question.

CASE QUESTIONS

1. Does Canada have the right to ignore the decisions of a U.S. court?
2. On what bases would such a court uphold the decisions of a U.S. court?
3. Are U.S. court decisions precedents to be followed by a Canadian court? Why did the Canadian court cite U.S. cases in its decisions?

Canadian courts are wrestling with the same difficulties found by American courts, namely, which jurisdiction is more appropriate and fair in determining issues concerning Internet contracts, intellectual property matters, and tort and criminal behavior. Canada appears to arrive at a conclusion similar to that enunciated by the U.S. Supreme Court in *Asahi.* At the bases of its decision are the concepts of fairness and substantial justice to the person being sued. Such concepts underlie the due process requirement enunciated by American courts.

Personal jurisdiction under Canadian law, like U.S. states, differs from province to province. Nevertheless, there are common threads linking all courts. They are based on the necessity of finding a "real and substantial connection" to the adjudicating court. Statutorily, the grounds used by Canadian courts to assert jurisdiction include: (1) the litigated business activity occurred in the province; (2) the tort or breach of contract took place in the province; (3) the duty to perform the contract was to take place in the province; (4) the parties to the contract state in the contract which jurisdiction and which laws are to be used in the event of a dispute; (5) in a marital dispute, one of the parties or children are domiciled or reside within the province; or (6) the basis of the dispute concerns real property or goods situated within the province.[7]

In a tort case, it appears that Canada may take jurisdiction when the activity takes place therein. In *Pindling v. National Broadcasting Corp.,* 49 O.R. 2d 58 (1984), the court assumed jurisdiction in a libel case wherein the alleged libelous statement was made in the United States against a Canadian.

Canada apparently also recognizes the doctrine for *forum non conveniens,* that is, a court may refuse to hear a case if it can be shown that another forum would be more suitable for adjudication of the dispute at hand. The *Braintech* case cited the leading Canadian case of *Amchem Products Inc. v. British Columbia,* (1993) 1 S.C.R. 897 that so held. As in the United States, Canadian courts will examine a number of factors including the availability and locality of the evidence and key witnesses to the forthcoming trial.[8]

In Germany, the general manager for an online service, CompuServe Deutschland, was indicted for trafficking in pornography and for neo-Nazi propaganda. The materials appeared over the Internet but were not produced by the Internet service provider. CompuServe, as it is in the United States, was simply the medium for the transmission of materials. Whether such service companies can be held accountable for forbidden transmissions remains to be seen.[9]

United Nations Recommendations

In its *Manual on the Prevention and Control of Computer-Related Crime,* the United Nations (U.N.)

reviewed the various principles for the assertion of jurisdiction by nations.[10] With respect to the territoriality principle, it recommended:

254. States should, therefore, endeavour to negotiate agreements on the positive conflicts issue. These agreements should address the following issues:

   1. An explicit priority of jurisdictional criteria: for example, of location of act over location of effect, of the place of physical detainment of the suspect over in absentia proceedings or extradition;
   2. A mechanism for consultation between the States concerned in order to agree upon either the priority of jurisdiction over the offence or the division of the offence into separate acts;
   3. Cooperation in the investigation, prosecution and punishment of international computer offences, including the admissibility of evidence lawfully gathered in other countries, and the recognition of punishment effectively served in other jurisdictions. This would prevent unreasonable hardship to the accused, otherwise possible by an inflexible interpretation of the territoriality principle.

The U.N. also discussed the other principles for the assertion of jurisdiction. With respect to the nationality principle, it expressed the concern that basing the assertion of jurisdiction on the nationality of the accused may result in parallel concurrent jurisdictions leading to possible double jeopardy. Therefore, it recommended that such application be limited to serious offenses. The passive personality assertion of jurisdiction, based on the nationality of the victims, should seldom be used. It could subject a national of one country to prosecution in another country for committing acts lawful in the national's state but that affect a national of another state in which those acts are illegal. The protective principle raises concern because it is based on "the vital interests of a State." If the state interprets *security* too broadly, there is a potential for abuse over the nationals of the other state. The universality principle should be applied only in serious cases where the country that normally would have jurisdiction over the offense is unable or unwilling to prosecute.

The U.N., therefore, encourages "a spirit of moderation" in the exercise of these principles, and it cautions states to engage in international cooperation to avoid significant conflicts of jurisdiction. It fosters harmonized legislation (presumably uniform laws such as the U.N. Convention on the International Sale of Goods), the settlement of jurisdictional claims where two or more countries assert jurisdiction, and the development of agreements on mutual cooperation and transfer of criminal proceedings.

CONCLUSION

The reader is left understandably in a state of some confusion. Federal and state courts are attempting to find their way in determining when jurisdiction exists in cyberspace actions. A variety of theories have been proposed, none of which satisfies totally the myriad of cases and events that have transformed the lives of a majority of the people globally. It is clear that some type of national and international consensus will have to take place to clarify the issue of when a court may hear and dispose of a particular action. Some cases are clearly within and just as clearly beyond the scope of courts to adjudicate. Internationally, many cases may not be adjudicated due to the lack of consensus and laws governing Internet activities. Nationally, the U.S. Supreme Court and Congress will have to enter the field and establish bright-line guidelines. The Supreme Court has to date refused to establish such guidelines due to the many, almost day-to-day changes in the new technology. Courts have been compelled to fit old, square legal concepts into the round holes of cyberspace. At some juncture, however, decisions and policies will have to be established to clarify the rights of litigants both here and abroad.

The results of the cases show major splits among the various federal and state courts. Jurisdiction is more likely to be found by state courts than by federal courts. Among the federal courts, decisions are dependent on the degree of contacts an out-of-forum defendant has with the state seeking jurisdiction. It appears, however, that something more than a Web site is needed to find jurisdiction. Some additional factors are necessary beyond a mere passive posting on the Web. The added factors include interactivity with the forum state, including e-mails; contracts with the forum state; provision of services; money derived from the forum state; closeness of the out-of-state forum to the forum state; violation of federal or state statutes; and other bases.[11]

Does cyberspace require a rethinking of due process requirements for assertion of jurisdiction? Some scholars have argued that the present rules should not be operable on cyberspace issues.[12] The Internet, according to the argument, is a voluntary, contractual arrangement for commercial information service or Internet access. A user may refuse to access a particular service provider and use other, more friendly providers. Cyberspace, by definition, is beyond the spatial boundaries of states and nations. It is potentially accessible to all persons globally.

The problem that will confront nations is how to regulate that which may not be readily subject to regulation. National borders serve to regulate those persons and activities within its boundaries but also act to protect nationals from prosecution and lawsuits from abroad. Unless there is a global consensus, any maverick nation-state can create chaos by permitting its inhabitants to evade global restraints in its cyberactivities. A significant degree of harmonization of laws and regulations can be accomplished if countries deem it in their best interest to do so. The promulgation of the United Nations Convention on the International Sale of Goods is an excellent example of international cooperation. Jurisdictional issues can also be resolved if the nation-states are willing to harmonize their laws to the extent of dealing with international disputes.

Pending the ultimate clarification of jurisdictional issues by the U.S. Supreme Court, there are steps that a person can take to make litigation in an inconvenient forum less likely. In contractual matters, especially in international trade, it is customary to insert in a contract the forum for resolution of disputes and which country's law is to govern the transaction. Similarly, in an Internet contract, the agreement should make clear which jurisdiction should govern the transaction and which state's, province's, or country's law is to be applied. It would be advisable to require that any dispute be submitted to arbitration. It might also be wise to form a separate, subsidiary corporation for Internet sales so as to insulate the parent company from liability. Keep in mind that one should do business with persons from areas in which one is prepared to litigate. If one does not intend to sell to certain states or foreign countries over the Internet, such refusal should be clearly stated in offers communicated in cyberspace. Contracts online should be accomplished by secure means. Care should be taken not to misappropriate the intellectual property of others. This is particularly important in Internet transactions. Courts worldwide will take jurisdiction over such alleged tortious acts. Ultimately, there is insurance coverage for many forms of possible liability. Insurance companies are much more familiar than most business concerns with litigation in a variety of jurisdictions.

Internet disputes may lend themselves well to alternative dispute mechanisms, such as arbitration and mediation. By selecting specific arbitral bodies, the jurisdictional issue may be avoided. The problem is that the parties must agree in advance to resort to such resolutions. Nonjudicial dispute resolution methodologies are being established online, for example, the *Virtual Magistrate Project,* a voluntary online arbitration system in cooperation with the American Arbitration Association and other organizations.

Questions and Problems

1. What are the basic principles that countries use as bases for the assertion of jurisdiction?
2. What are the bases for the assertion of U.S. domestic jurisdiction?
3. Distinguish between *active Web sites* and *passive Web sites.*
4. Explain the meaning of *long-arm jurisdiction.* What are the factors that courts weigh in determining whether they may exercise such jurisdiction?
5. Explain the difference between *jurisdiction* and *venue.* What are the factors that courts will use in determining whether venue is appropriate?
6. In 1967, Tattilo began publishing a men's magazine in the Italian language with the name *Playmen.* In 1979, it sought to publish an English version with the same title in the United States. Playboy Enterprises, Inc. (PEI), which publishes the well-known *Playboy* magazine, sued to enjoin Tattilo's use of the name *Playmen* alleging violation of its trademark, false designation of origin, unfair competition, and violation of New York's antidilution statute. A permanent injunction was issued in 1981, barring Tattilo from using the name *Playmen* in the United States on its magazine or any products connected therewith. Although the courts of England, France, and West Germany also barred the use of the name *Playmen,* the Italian courts refused to grant such protection. In 1996, Tattilo created an

Internet site with the *Playmen* name, featuring sexually explicit photographic images and sale of products. The site is available worldwide, including the U.S. market. PEI sued for contempt of the prior order of the court. Decide whether Tattilo should be held in contempt. Does commencing a Web site in Italy that is available worldwide violate the injunction? Does it matter that the injunction was issued well before the availability of the Internet? *Playboy Enterprises, Inc. v. Chuckleberry Publishing, Inc.,* 939 F. Supp. 1032 (S.D.N.Y. 1996).

7. Plaintiff is a well-known professional sports photographer residing in California. His photographs regularly appear in *Sports Illustrated, Time,* and other magazines. Defendant, Fallon, is a Minnesota advertising agency. Plaintiff claims that the defendant created an original photograph depicting basketball player Charles Barkley. The photo was subject to copyright registration issued to Time, Inc., and to the plaintiff. The defendant allegedly reproduced the photo for a Nikon camera advertisement without permission. Plaintiff sued for copyright infringement, unfair competition, violation of privacy, and publicity rights. The defendant had no clients, no office, no permanent employees, no bank accounts, and pays no taxes in California. Defendant did purchase advertising space from California-based entities and placed advertisements that appeared in California. The plaintiff claims that the court did not have jurisdiction in the within action. Decide who should prevail and state the reasons for your opinion. *McDonough v. McElligott, Inc.,* No. 95-4037, 1996 U.S. LEXIS 15139 (S.D.Ca. 1996).
8. GTE sued BellSouth, U.S. West, and other companies for violation of the Sherman Antitrust Act, alleging that the defendants engaged in a conspiracy with an illicit purpose to dominate the Internet business directories' market. Defendants moved to dismiss the complaint for lack of jurisdiction, alleging that "the mere ability of District [of Columbia] residents to access the defendants' Internet Yellow Pages from locations within the city is insufficient to establish personal jurisdiction." GTE contends that the lawsuit is based on tortious injury, which thus falls within the District of Columbia's long-arm statute. It alleged that the conspiracy caused Internet users with access to GTE links, to be diverted to the defendants' links, thereby depriving GTE of advertising revenue. The lower court stated there was sufficient evidence to support personal jurisdiction, noting, however, that the defendants' sole connection with the District of Columbia was its interactive Web site without any other contacts therein. The decision was appealed. Decide. *GTE New Media Services Inc. v. BellSouth Corp.,* 199 F.3d 1343 (D.C. Cir. 2000).
9. Plaintiff is a business incorporated and with its principle place of business in Oregon. It opened its first retail outlet using the name Music Millennium in 1969, has two retail music stores in Portland, Oregon, and sells products through the mail and telephone orders and through its Internet Web site. Defendants are South Carolina corporations that operate retail stores under the name Millennium Music and also sell products through retail outlets and through their Web site. Defendants sell the vast majority of products through their retail stores. Through the Internet, they sold only 15 compact discs for a total of $225 to nine customers in six states and in one foreign country. Defendants purchased a small amount of supplies from a distributor in Oregon. An Oregon resident purchased one compact disc from the defendants, and that person was related to plaintiff's attorney. No other merchandise was sold to Oregon residents. Plaintiff sued for damages and for an injunction for trademark infringement and trademark dilution. Decision? *Millennium Enterprises, Inc. v. Millennium Music,* 33 F. Supp. 2d 907 (D.Or. 1999).
10. Plaintiff, Gianino, sued Jones and Negri, cofounders of a software company called Panacya, Inc., and the corporation to enforce a preincorporation agreement. The claim is that the plaintiff, together with the two individual defendants, agreed to start a new business to develop and market a software-based security system and antivirus software to protect computers and computer networks. Initial contacts were made in New York. Negri is a Georgia resident who traveled to

New York to meet Jones and Gianino concerning the development. A patent application was developed in New York, and the three persons retained New York counsel as their patent attorneys. Gianino performed other services for the prospective business from his home in New York. The three parties solicited capital and sales in New York and had diverse meetings therein. Jones and Negri claim that for the past year no business was conducted in New York, and the corporation later formed had not done business in New York nor in any state. The New York statute authorizes jurisdiction where a defendant transacted business in New York, as long as the defendant's activities were purposeful and substantially related to plaintiff's claim. Does the court have jurisdiction over the two individual defendants? Does it have jurisdiction over the corporation formed after the said alleged acts had taken place? *Gianino v. Jones,* No. 00 CIV. 1584 (SHS), 2000 U.S. Dist. LEXIS 12338 (S.D.N.Y. 2000).

Endnotes

1. See, for example, David R. Johnson and David G. Post, *Law and Borders: The Rise of Law in Cyberspace, www.cli.org/X0025_LBFIN.html,* at p. 3.
2. *National Treasury Employees Union v. United States,* 101 F.3d 1413 (D.C. Cir. 1996).
3. *Akella v. Michigan Department of State,* 67 F. Supp. 2d 716, 726 (E.D.Mich. 1999), citing *Abbott Lab. v. Gardner,* 387 U.S. 136, 148 (1967).
4. For a discussion of the theories of the principles of jurisdiction, see any standard text on international law. This discussion is based partly on examples from Mark W. Janis, *An Introduction to International Law,* 2d ed., (Boston: Little, Brown, 1993), Ch. 10; and Louis Henkin, *International Law: Cases and Materials* (St. Paul, MN: West, 1980), Ch. 7.
5. For the European Union's position, see its *Comments on the U.S. Regulations Concerning Trade with the U.S.S.R.* 21 Intl. Legal Materials 891 at 893–99 (1982).
6. For a discussion of the difficulties inherent in the creation and enforcement of legal norms, see Dan L. Burk, *Muddy Rules for Cyberspace,* 21 Cardozo L. Rev. 121 (October 1999), especially the discussion of jurisdictional uncertainties at p. 160 et seq.
7. See Ogilvy Renault, *Jurisdiction and the Internet: Are Traditional Rules Enough?* Uniform Law Conference of Canada, 1998, especially p. 4 thereof. *www.law.ualberta.ca/alri/ulc/current/ejurisd.htm.*
8. Ibid.
9. Stuart Biegel, *Indictment of CompuServe Official in Germany Brings Volatile Issues of CyberJurisdiction into Focus,* The UCLA Online Institute for Cyberspace Law and Policy, *www.gseis.ucla.edu/iclp/apr97.html.*
10. International Review of Criminal Policy—Nos. 43 and 44, *International Review of Criminal Policy—United Nations Manual on the Prevention and Control of Computer-Related Crime, www.ifs.univie.ac.at/~pr2gqi/rev4344.html.*
11. For an excellent discussion of long-arm issues affecting the Internet, see Roger J. Johns Jr. and Anne Keath, *Caught in the Web: Websites and Classic Principles of Long Arm Jurisdiction in Trademark Infringement Cases,* 10 Alb. L.J. Sci. & Tech. 65 (1999).
12. See Johnson and Post, *Law and Borders;* and David R. Johnson, *Due Process and Cyberjurisdiction, www.ascusc.org/jcmc/vol2/issue1/due.html.*

PART

II

CONTRACTS, TORTS, AND CRIMINAL ASPECTS OF CYBERLAW

CHAPTER

3 INTERNET CONTRACTS

Section 1: Basic Concepts and Recent Developments

Chapter Outline

- Growth of Use of Electronic Contracts
- Fundamental Principles of Contract Law
- The Uniform Commercial Code
- Requirements of a Writing: The Statute of Frauds Under the Common Law and the UCC
- Electronic Commerce Contracts: The Uniform Computer Information Transactions Act
- Digital Signatures
- The Uniform Electronic Transfers Act
- Shrink-Wrap Licenses and Click-Wrap Agreements
- Conclusion

The Internet has increased greatly the sale of goods and services not only among global business concerns but also between merchants and individual consumers who are located in other countries. In the early 1990s, there were virtually no direct international consumer transactions except in the European Union. Today, the Internet has made such transactions more common and will increase geometrically as each year passes. Sales involve contracts. Laws pertaining to contracts contain rules that operate as severe impediments to international transactions. For centuries, there has been a bias in Anglo-Saxon countries towards the necessity of putting agreements in writing. Commencing in 1677 with the enactment of the Statute of Frauds, the law has favored a written contract for types of contracts in which the occurrence of fraud by perjured testimony was rampant. The Statute of Frauds has been a part of U.S. state and federal law from the inception of the nation.

The technological advances that gave rise to the Internet have compelled rethinking of existing law to cope with the new reality of the marketplace. Laws must follow technological developments so as to protect nationals who are parties to transactions in each of the localities or countries of habitation. We will discuss some of the major issues raised by the Internet and the legal developments occurring to date. We will commence with an examination of the increasing use of the Internet for the purchase and sale of goods. Thereafter, we will review the Statute of Frauds and the latest statutes in connection with

Internet transactions and discuss other issues, such as the validity of electronic signatures and shrink-wrap licenses.

GROWTH IN USE OF ELECTRONIC CONTRACTS

There has been an enormous growth in shopping online, with purchases made by 36.1 million people (16.6 percent of U.S. population age 14 or over) from December 1998 to December 1999. Revenues in the United States from business to consumer totaled $5.3 billion for the fourth quarter of 1999 and were projected to rise to $15 billion in 2000 and to $35.3 billion by 2003. Globally, the projection is $3.2 trillion by 2003. U.S. business-to-business e-commerce is expected to generate $2.7 trillion by 2004.[1] The major segments of the world's economy in this regard have been mainly in automobiles, housewares, clothing, and consumer electronics.

With the proliferation of Internet sales, it is important to understand the laws, both nationally and internationally, pertaining to such contracts. There have been major attempts to unify the law of sales. In the United States, the passage of the Uniform Commercial Code, especially Article 2 thereof, clarified considerably the legal rights and obligations of parties to sale-of-goods contracts. Article 2A, pertaining to leases of goods; the Uniform Computer Information Transactions Act (UCITA), governing computer information transactions; and the Uniform Electronic Transactions Act (UETA), concerning electronic contracting, have been additional attempts to unify state laws in their respective areas of concern. Subsequently, other proposals have been enacted as statutes concerning the changes necessary for computer-generated sales.

Internationally, the adoption of the United Nations Convention on Contracts for the International Sales of Goods has unified the laws of those nations ratifying the Convention regarding international commercial sales. There are efforts by the United Nations, the Organization for Economic Cooperation and Development, and the European Union to modernize their laws, particularly as to the new technologies. Before we review the recent developments, we will examine basic principles affecting the law of contracts. Thereafter, we will discuss new legislation and proposals for adapting old law to computer-related transactions.

FUNDAMENTAL PRINCIPLES OF CONTRACT LAW

Elements of a Contract

A contract is an agreement between two or more parties that the law will enforce. Not all agreements give rise to legal sanctions. For example, an unfulfilled promise to meet someone for dinner ordinarily will not result in legal liability. A contract generally has four elements: (1) an *offer* and an *acceptance;* (2) the parties must have the *capacity* to enter into an agreement; (3) the basis of the agreement must be *lawful* in nature; and (4) there must be *consideration*.

Offer and Acceptance. In the ordinary course of dealing, a person makes an offer, such as a proposal to sell a house, perform services, employ someone, or other such offers. To have legal effect, the offer must be communicated by the person making the offer (the *offeror*) to the receiver of the offer (the *offeree*). The offer must not be made in jest but must be one intended to convey a desire to engage into a binding agreement. The offer generally must contain all of the essential elements of a contract, such as making clear who are the parties to the transaction, the subject matter, the price, and other terms depending on the nature of the transaction. The offer may be made to a specific person or to a larger number of persons. Offers that call for an act, such as an offer for a reward, may result in a *unilateral* contract, that is, a promise made in exchange for an act. For example, if a person fulfills the terms of the offer for a reward, then a unilateral contract is formed. The offeror must perform as agreed once the act called for has been completed. If a promise is made in exchange for another promise (for example, a promise to sell a specified object in exchange for a promise to purchase the object), then the result will be a *bilateral* contract. Unless otherwise agreed, each party must perform as stated in the agreement.

An acceptance of an offer may be made by the accomplishment of the act in a unilateral offer situation or by a return promise. The return promise, unless the contract falls under the Uniform Commercial Code, must be in exact accordance (a *mirror image*) with the terms of the offer. Any deviation, such as agreeing to a lesser price, is a counteroffer and not an acceptance.

Capacity. The parties have to have the capacity to enter into an agreement. If a party to the contract is a minor, the agreement may be *voidable,* that is, the minor may be able to avoid obligations that an adult party could not. States vary widely as to the obligations of a minor. In all states, unless the contract is one of a *necessary* (the contract concerns subject matter necessary for the health and welfare of the minor such as food, clothing, housing, auto insurance, schooling, etc.), the minor may opt out of accomplishing the terms of the agreement. States vary as to the liability of a minor who fails to return the subject matter of the contract as initially received or who committed a tort such as lying about one's age. For example, if a minor buys a new car, wrecks it, and then seeks to return the automobile for a full refund, states have differing results ranging from denial of the refund to the extent of the diminished value of the auto to a full refund. The lesson to be derived is that one deals with a minor contractually at one's own peril.

Also included among persons lacking capacity are persons who were so intoxicated or so mentally lacking as to disable them from understanding the nature and terms of the contract. If a person has been declared by a court to be mentally incapacitated, then any agreement entered into by that person will be *void,* that is, of no force and effect. Otherwise, the agreement is *voidable,* that is, the person with the disability may elect to avoid the agreement. The concept herein is that, in an enforceable contract, the parties knowingly and willfully entered into an agreement. A person without such capacity should not be taken advantage of to his or her detriment.

Legality. The agreement must be one that is legal in nature. For example, a "contract" to perform an illegal act is not a contract. These agreements are *unenforceable,* or as courts have said, "We will leave the parties as we find them!" A so-called contract to perform an illegal act is not really a contract but an unenforceable agreement between the parties thereto. Included among unenforceable contracts are those performed by persons who fail to have the requisite licenses for services rendered, such as unlicensed attorneys, accountants, and other professionals. Any performance, irrespective of how well accomplished, does not give rise to liability by the recipient of the act.

Another aspect of legality is the issue of whether members of the bar in one state may engage in the practice of law in another state by means of the Internet. A Texas federal court decided in the negative. In *Unauthorized Practice of Law Committee v. Parsons Technology,* No. 3:97-CV-2859-H, 1999 U.S. Dist. LEXIS 813 (N.D.Tex. 1999), the defendant is a California corporation with its principal place of business in Iowa. It publishes and markets well-known software, such as *Quicken Financial Software* and *Turbo Tax.* It also published and sold *Quicken Family Lawyer,* which offered over 100 legal forms, including wills, real estate leases, prenuptial agreements, and other legal instruments. It claims its forms were valid in 49 states and the District of Columbia. A person using the software is asked a series of questions, which is followed by explanations of legal considerations.

The "practice of law" is defined by the Texas statute as including the preparation of pleadings and practice before a judge and "the giving of advice or the rendering of any service requiring the use of legal skills or knowledge, such as preparing a will, contract or other instrument, the legal effect of which under the facts and conclusions involved must be carefully determined." The court determined that the program did violate Texas law, having gone well beyond merely providing forms to giving false and misleading advice.

With respect to First Amendment considerations, the court stated "there is no right of unlicensed laymen to represent another under the First Amendment's guarantees of freedom of association and freedom to petition one's government, nor is there a violation of freedom of speech." The Texas law is *content-neutral,* that is, the government did not regulate this form of speech because of a disagreement with the message conveyed. The statute is aimed at preventing the unauthorized practice of law and "has nothing to do with suppressing speech."

The court then used the four-part "intermediate scrutiny" test of *U.S. v. O'Brien,* 391 U.S. 367 (1968) to determine its constitutional validity. The court found: (1) The statute is within the constitutional power of the state of Texas to prohibit the unauthorized practice of law; (2) The statute did further an important government interest in protecting its citizens from being mislead; (3) The government's interest herein was unrelated to the suppression of freedom of expression; and (4) The incidental restriction of speech in the within case was no greater than necessary for the furtherance of the governmental interest.

Consideration. The final requirement is that there be *consideration,* that is something of legal value given in exchange of the other person's promise or performance. A promise to give someone an automobile without a return promise to pay or perform some other act is a promise to make a gift and is not ordinarily an enforceable promise. If the person fails to give the vehicle as promised, no liability ensues. There are exceptions based mainly on substantial promises made to charities. The consideration need not be of equal value. For example, a promise to sell an almost new Mercedes automobile for $1,000 will be enforced absent a showing that the offeror was incapacitated or subject to some other extraneous disability.

Conduct Invalidating Agreements

Voidable agreements may arise if either or both of the parties to the alleged contract were subject to undue influence, duress, or fraud, or if the parties operated under a mutual mistake of fact concerning the essence of the agreement.

Undue Influence. A person may be subjected to undue influence where there is a close relationship between the parties such as parent–child, clergy–member of the congregation, attorney–client, and so on. In essence, if a court determines that a person lacked free will in making a decision to enter into an agreement, then the judge may prevent its enforcement. This may occur especially when one of the parties is feeble, has little or no ability to make a decision, is subject to a physical or mental infirmity, or there are other disabling factors. It is very common for elderly persons to become subject to the will and directions of someone who is physically or emotionally close to them. The mere fact that a contract is one-sided is not a ground in and of itself for overturning the agreement. A contract, by definition, is a legally enforceable agreement between two or more parties. If one of the parties did not possess the ability to understand the nature and extent of the agreement, then the court may permit dissolution of the contract by the person suffering from the disability.

Duress. Duress involves two basic scenarios. If a party is subject to immediate physical harm unless a contract is signed or enforced (e.g., one party putting a gun to the head of the other party), then such agreement is void. If there are other forms of duress, such as threatening to have one's child arrested for embezzlement unless the parent pay the full sum to the victim, such agreements may be voidable and unenforceable even though agreed to by the persons receiving the threats.

Fraud. Fraud also may render an agreement void or voidable. For example, asking for an autograph from a celebrity who unknowingly signs a contract or commercial instrument would not make the celebrity liable. The law says it is *fraud in the execution* and such alleged agreement is *void.* On the other hand, *fraud in the inducement* is a voidable agreement wherein the victim may refuse to perform and may sue for damages, including for punitive damages (damages over and above the damages actually sustained to punish the wrongdoer). *Fraud in the inducement* is defined as making an intentional, false representation of material fact by one party to the other in order to induce the other party to enter into an agreement that the other party would not have entered into but who did so in reliance upon the misrepresentation to that person's injury. For example, a merchant lying about the value of a diamond to a prospective buyer ("The diamond is valued at $10,000 on the open market," whereas it was a poor-quality diamond having much less value) may give rise to liability.

Fraud is a tort that may arise out of circumstances evidencing a contract. Depending on state law, a party who is the victim of a fraud may sue using a variety of theories, including breach of contract based on warranty theory, a suit in tort for fraud, rescission (setting aside the contract and restoring all parties to their position before the contract was entered into), innocent misrepresentation, and other theories. A person suing must look to the state to determine whether it is necessary to choose among alternative theories upon which to sue or whether he or she may utilize a variety of theories. Often, an attorney will use the theory of an alleged intentional tort in place of a contract theory in order to coerce a merchant to settle disputes in fear of an adverse tort decision.

The difference in recovery using a tort theory rather than a contract theory can be significant. If one sues in contract, the recovery is based on what the innocent party would have received had the contract been fulfilled. For example, if a person contracted to purchase goods having a total cost of $5,000 and the seller defaults, thereby causing the buyer to go elsewhere for the same or comparable goods at a cost of $6,000, the recovery would be $1,000 plus applicable interest and court costs. Using an intentional tort theory, if the same person alleges and convinces a jury that the seller lied or misled the buyer about a transaction, the recovery may include *punitive* damages (to be discussed), which can be considerably more than the amount of loss incurred.

The courts in the state of Wisconsin, Illinois, Michigan, Florida, and elsewhere have formulated an *economic loss doctrine,* which provides that "a commercial purchaser of a product cannot recover from a manufacturer, under tort theories, damages that are solely economic losses." The basis for the doctrine was the desire to accomplish three fundamental policies: "(1) to maintain the fundamental distinction between tort law and contract law; (2) to protect commercial parties' freedom to allocate economic risk by contract; and (3) to encourage the party best situated to assess the risk [of] economic loss, the commercial purchaser, to assume, allocate, or insure against that risk. *Daanen & Janssen, Inc. v. Cedarapids, Inc.,* 216 Wis. 2d 395, 400 (1998) . . . cited in *Budgetel Inns, Inc. v. Micros Systems, Inc.,* 8 F. Supp. 2d 1137 (E.D.Wis. 1998)."

There appears to be a state of confusion as to the interpretation of the doctrine as applied by the courts when the claim is one for fraud in the inducement. Breach of contract assumes that there is an underlying contract the fulfillment of which has not taken place. Fraud in the inducement states that the contract purportedly entered into was based on lies or other misrepresentation or on concealment of material facts that caused an innocent party to enter into a contract that he or she would not have entered into had the true facts been known. The contract is of full force and effect if the innocent party elects not to disavow the agreement, but such party may elect to nullify the agreement. Discussion of these issues may be found in the following action.

BUDGETEL INNS, INC. V. MICROS SYSTEMS, INC.

8 F. Supp. 2d 1137 (E.D.Wis. 1998)

FACTS: Budgetel, which operates a chain of hotels, sought to purchase a new software system that was designed to handle a complex property management system. The defendant, Micros, proclaimed to Budgetel that its 8500 system was new and able to meet Budgetel's needs. As a result, a contract was entered into between the parties wherein Micros was to supply Budgetel with property management system software, system support, and maintenance, in exchange for a license fee of $250,000 and ongoing maintenance and support fees of $150,000 annually. Three months later, Budgetel learned that Micros acquired an interest in another software company and was no longer marketing the 8500 software and shifted most of its personnel to the new company. Budgetel sued alleging that the defendant knew of the future plans prior to contract and fraudulently induced Budgetel to buy its 8500 system.

ISSUE: Whether Budgetel's fraud claim is barred by the economic loss doctrine?

DECISION: The Court decided in favor of Budgetel, holding that its fraud claim is not barred by the doctrine.

REASONING: Judge Adelman

"Economic loss" is "defined generally as 'the diminution in the value of the product because it is inferior in quality and does not work for the general purposes for which it was manufactured and sold.' " . . . "Economic loss" encompasses direct economic loss, based upon the difference in value between what was received as compared to what was represented, together with costs of replacement and repair. It also includes consequential, or indirect, economic losses attributable to the product defect, such as loss profits resulting from the inability to make use of the product. . . .

The doctrine does not bar claims involving physical injury or physical harm to property, however, as those are considered proper tort claims. . . .

The United States Supreme Court's decision in *East River S.S.Corp. v. Transamerica Delaval Inc.,*

476 U.S. 858 . . . (1986) encouraged acceptance of the doctrine and the perceived need to separate tort claims from contract claims. *East River* involved supertankers that malfunctioned at sea because of manufacturing defects in the turbines. The plaintiffs, who had chartered the supertankers, sued the turbine manufacturer in negligence and strict liability for economic losses. The Supreme Court rejected the tort claims, holding that a manufacturer in a commercial relationship has no duty outside of contract "to prevent a product from injuring itself." . . . According to the Court, "loss due to repair costs, decreased value, and lost profits is essentially the failure of the purchaser to receive the benefit of its bargain—traditionally the core concern of contract law." . . . The Court justified its decision as necessary to protect contract law from "drowning in a sea of tort." . . .

In regard to the tort versus contract distinction, the [Supreme Court of Wisconsin] said that while contract law rests on obligations imposed by bargain, the law of torts rests on obligations imposed by law. While contract law seeks to hold commercial parties to their promises, ensuring that each party receives the benefit of their bargain, tort law protects society's interest in human life, health, and safety. . . .

In regard to protecting the parties' allocation of risk, the court stated that if a commercial purchaser is given a direct cause of action in tort against a manufacturer, the entire risk of economic loss is borne by the manufacturer. Limitations in warranties would be meaningless. . . .

Without the economic loss doctrine, a purchaser would be encouraged to purchase goods "as is" in exchange for a lower price. If the product failed down the road and the purchaser could nevertheless reach back to the manufacturer for tort damages, the purchaser would obtain more than the benefit of the bargain to which it agreed and for which it paid. The law of contracts would be emasculated in the process. . . .

THE FRAUD IN THE INDUCEMENT EXCEPTION

[The court cited a number of Florida cases that decided that the economic loss doctrine did not bar causes of action based on tort because "it requires proof of facts separate and distinct from the breach of contract." It cited approvingly the statement in another action that: "Fraud in the inducement presents a special situation where parties to a contract appear to negotiate freely—which normally would constitute grounds for invoking the economic loss doctrine—but where in fact the ability of one party to negotiate fair terms and make an informed decision is undermined by the other part's fraudulent behavior."]

But while in one sense the tort of fraud in the inducement is always "interwoven" with a contract, in another sense the tort is always independent of the contract. That is, the duty out of which the tort arises is always based in common law and never in the contract. This is exactly the independence that is required. . . . Even though a duty of good faith and fair dealing exists both with respect to the creation and performance of a contract, . . . fraud in the inducement by definition occurs prior to the formation of the contract itself, thus, it never constitutes a breach of contract. . . . On the other hand, fraud in the performance of a contract is not an independent tort because the duty giving rise to the tort is established by the contract. . . .

There is considerable difference between a promise never intended to be performed (fraud in the inducement) and a promise intended to be performed but which ultimately is not (breach of contract).

CASE QUESTIONS

1. Compare the *Budgetel* case with the *Ice Bowl* case discussed next. With which decision are you in agreement?
2. Contrast a tort with a contract. What are the essential differences between the two theories of recovery?

In *Ice Bowl L.L.C. v. Weigel Broadcasting Co.*, 14 F. Supp. 2d 1080 (E.D.Wis. 1998), in a decision a month later than *Budgetel,* another judge in the same U.S. district court came to a different conclusion in a fraud in the inducement action. Ice Bowl, a Wisconsin company in the business of sports marketing, sued Weigel, an Illinois corporation that owns a television station in Milwaukee. The underlying agreement between the parties called for Ice Bowl to make a local sports celebrity available for Weigel's use in creating a number of television programs and related materials. Weigel was to pay Ice Bowl and the celebrity for the appearances. Weigel allegedly failed to live up to its bargain and was sued by Ice Bowl for, among other things, intentional misrepresentation and fraud in the inducement. The court dismissed the tort claims based on the economic loss doctrine. It stated that the claim was one sounding in contract and, therefore, the doctrine that "commercial parties to a contract must resolve disputes arising from such contract according to principles of contract and warranty law and the text of their agreement. . . . Having bargained a contract, the parties cannot reallocate bargained for risk by pleading in tort, economic losses."

After the *Ice Bowl* decision, the attorneys for Budgetel asked for reconsideration of the earlier decision based on the reasoning in *Ice Bowl.* The court declined using the same reasoning as in the prior decision. The judge in *Budgetel,* Lynn Adelman, said: "The fact that I disagree with other judges in this district regarding the correct interpretation of Wisconsin case law does not create any unacceptable problem in the courts. It means only that the issue is debatable among reasonable jurists. Until guidance from the Wisconsin appellate courts or the Seventh Circuit comes along, each judge in this district is entitled to add his own interpretation to the mix." *Budgetel Inns, Inc. v. Micros Systems, Inc.,* 34 F. Supp. 2d 720 (E.D.Wis. 1999).

Mutual Mistake of Fact. Mutual mistake of a material fact may allow a party to rescind a contract. For example, if a person were to purchase a painting that was mistakenly believed to be a Rembrandt but that was, unknown to the seller, a forgery, the buyer could rescind the sale and receive the return of the amount paid upon returning the painting to the former owner. A one-sided mistake rarely permits a person to rescind the agreement if no fraud has been committed.

Assignments and Third-Party Beneficiary Contracts

Assignments. Contracts may involve third parties who either become parties to the agreement at a later date by way of assignment or are parties to the agreement initially by having been named therein. An assignment is the transfer of rights under a prior contract to a third party. Often the one who receives the assignment also agrees to perform the duty under the contract. For example, a person having a lease of an apartment may assign the lease to a third party who then receives the right to the occupancy of the apartment and further agrees to be responsible for the rental expenses thereafter. The right to assign the right and delegate the duty is subject to the terms of the agreement between the original parties and whether such rights or duties involve personal services. For example, a person cannot assign the right to an automobile insurance policy to another person, because such right changes the risk assumed under the contract by the insurance company. On the other hand, if a loss takes place, a person may assign the proceeds of the loss to a third party inasmuch as it does not affect materially the duty of the insurance company to pay the sums due and owing under the policy.

Third-Party Beneficiary Contracts. Third-party beneficiary contracts are contracts that name a third party to be the recipient of rights thereunder. The most common example is a life-insurance policy. The insured agrees to purchase a policy of life insurance from an insurance company naming a third person as a beneficiary. The third party has the right to make claim for the money due under the contract even if that person was not aware of being named under the policy until long after the agreement was entered into.

Remedies

Common-Law Remedies. The law gives a number of remedies for breach of a contract. In summary, the victim of a breach is entitled to be placed, insofar as the law is able, where he or she would have been had the contract been fulfilled. For example, if one party agrees to sell a quantity of oil but then defaults, the aggrieved party would be entitled to recover the additional costs, if any, to purchase the goods elsewhere (*compensatory* damages). Furthermore, a person may incur additional damages over and above the money involved in the contract. For example, if a person purchases a defective tire, the buyer is entitled not only to the return of the amount paid for the tire but also for reasonably foreseeable injuries occurring as a result of the defect (*consequential* damages). An injured person may also be entitled to *incidental* damages as a result of the defective performance, such as storage and advertising costs, and loss of profits.

Punitive damages may also be awarded when a person commits an intentional tort, that is, an intentional wrong causing injury to the other party. Punitive damages, as stated previously, are moneys awarded over and above the actual damages awarded for injury incurred. The purpose of such an award is to punish the offending party. Such damages may be awarded, for example, in a contract situation for the commission of fraud. For example, a seller of a vehicle who substantially lessens the mileage reading on the odometer and sells the vehicle without advising the buyer of the lower mileage, may be held liable for punitive damages. *Liquidated* damages are sums of money that the parties to a contract agree in advance to pay in the event of a breach of contract. For example, it is very common in real estate contracts for the buyer to make a down payment of 10 percent of the purchase price. If the buyer willfully defaults, the buyer may lose the said sum irrespective of whether the seller later sells the premises for an equal or even higher sum. *Nominal* damages are awarded to a person who has a legitimate claim but was not monetarily injured. In such cases the court will award the sum of $1.00 or some similar amount.

Equitable Remedies. Sometimes, money is not the desired or satisfactory result. For example, if a person entered into an agreement to buy a house or an item of personal property that is unique, such as a painting, the court may order the seller who refuses to perform to transfer the subject matter of the contract. A court may order a receiver be appointed to transfer the deed to a house or title to the painting to a buyer under the contract. Such a remedy given in lieu of money is called *specific performance.* Other unusual remedies when an award of money is not a satisfactory option include an *injunction,* which is a court order barring a person from doing something such as a strike or violating the trademark, patent, or copyright of the holder thereof, and *reformation,* wherein a court, on rare occasions, modifies a contract entered into by the parties in the best interest of justice.

THE UNIFORM COMMERCIAL CODE

Article 2: Law of Sales

The law of contracts has been with us for a number of centuries, having originated in England, whose common-law roots include Roman law. After World War II, it became increasingly evident that the rigid rules that had developed over the centuries did not fit well in the modern era of interstate and foreign commercial activities. As a result, a group of legal scholars, practitioners, judges, and others came together with a view toward gathering diverse state uniform laws governing a variety of commercial subjects into one unified code. The code that was proposed and eventually adopted in the 1960s is the Uniform Commercial Code. It contained 10 articles, the most pertinent of which for our discussion is Article 2, governing "sales," although the statute reads "transactions in goods" (Section 2–102). In essence, the law of contracts as it pertains to goods (not services) was greatly modified to conform to actual commercial practice.

Merchant/Non-Merchant Distinction. The article distinguishes *merchants* from *non-merchants.*[2] With respect to merchants, many requirements of the common law of contracts were relaxed or changed substantially. For example, under the common law, an acceptance of an offer had to be a mirror image of the terms of the offer. Any deviation would not constitute an acceptance but was rather a *counteroffer.* Under Article 2, if a party sends an acceptance within a reasonable time which states terms that are additional to or different from the original offer, the agreement will be effective unless the acceptance is made conditional upon the assent to the added or differing terms. As between merchants, the additional terms will become part of the contract unless they offer limited acceptance to the exact terms of the offer, or they materially change the offer, or the offeror objects to the added terms within a reasonable time (Section 2–207(1)(2)).

Lack of Essential Terms. Unlike the common law, wherein courts will not enforce contracts that do not meet the strict requirements of the law, the UCC seeks to save the contract if the court is satisfied that the parties had intended to enter into a binding agreement. Under the common law, if any essential part of the contract had not been agreed to, such as the nature of the parties, price, quantity, or other essential terms, the court will hold that the agreement is not enforceable. The theory is that the parties did not have a meeting of the minds as to all essential terms. Under Article 2 of the UCC, if the court believes that the parties had intended to enter into a contract, it has the right to complete the contract by filling in the missing terms, such as the price, place of delivery, and other terms except quantity.

Good Faith and Fair Dealing. The UCC also imposed the duty of good faith ("honesty in fact in the conduct or transaction concerned" [Article 1-201(19)]) and the avoidance of unconscionability in the agreement. For a merchant, *good faith* means "honesty in fact and the observance of reasonable commercial standards of fair dealing in the trade" (Article 2-103(1)(b)). The requirement of the avoidance of unconscionability allows a court to refuse to enforce all or part of a contract that it deems to be *unconscionable* (an agreement that in all or part shocks the conscience of the court). In cases interpreting the statute, courts have refused to enforce contracts between merchants and non-merchants that have small-print disclaimers and other denial or limitations of reasonable rights of consumers.

Warranties. If an agreement comes within Article 2, then a panoply of warranties may apply to the transaction. Section 2-213 gives legal protection to *express warranties,* which are affirmations of fact or promises by sellers to buyers that are part of the basis of the bargaining process. They also include descriptions of goods and uses of samples or models in the discussions of the purported transaction. The law also grants *implied warranties,* which include, unless the parties agree otherwise, the warranty of merchantability and fitness for a particular purpose. The *warranty of merchantability* is a warranty that the law will imply in a sale of goods to include the characteristics that they be fit for the ordinary purpose for which such goods are sold; that they conform to the contract description; that they are adequately contained, packaged, and labeled as the agreement between the parties may require; and that, in the case of fungible goods (such as oil, coal, corn, and the like), they be of fair average quality for such goods. The implied *warranty of fitness for a particular purpose* is a warranty wherein a buyer tells a seller of particular needs and relies upon the seller to select the goods that satisfies the buyer's needs. If the goods are not in conformity of such purpose, the buyer may seek legal remedies. For example, if a buyer tells a seller of a need for an air conditioner that will cool a room of certain dimensions and relies on the seller to pick the right size air conditioner, then the seller who complies with the request is obligated to fulfill the need properly. In addition, the seller also warrants that good title be passed without any liens on the goods and that they do not infringe the intellectual property rights of a third person.

To what extent may a seller exclude or modify warranties made to a consumer or to a commercial buyer? Courts have been troubled by the apparent contradiction between the making of an express promise and the attempt thereafter to prevent claims based on such promises. In most instances, courts will ignore disclaimers, particularly against consumers, on the theories that the merchant-seller acted in bad faith, that the exclusion was unconscionable, or that a seller cannot lie and then claim that it is not responsible for the lie. The UCC, Article 2-316(1), states that "the negation or limitation [of an express warranty] is inoperative to the extent that such construction is unreasonable."

More troubling is the attempted exclusion of implied warranties of merchantability or fitness for a particular purpose. Article 316(2) states that "to exclude or modify the implied warranty of merchantability or any part of it the language must mention merchantability and in case of a writing must be conspicuous [such as a different color or size print]." To exclude or modify the implied warranty of fitness for a particular purpose, such exclusion must be in writing and must be conspicuous. Nevertheless, Section 316(3) provides that all implied warranties may be excluded by expressions such as "as is," "with all faults," or other comparable language.

Irrespective of the language of the statute, courts have sided quite often with the consumer in cases concerning implied warranties with the said exclusionary language. If the language is placed after the signature of the consumer or on the opposite side of the contract, courts will generally ignore the disclaimer. Even if the language is in bold print above the consumer's signature, courts will often take the view that such exclusion, under the circumstances of the case, is unconscionable. Courts feel less protective of commercial buyers and less prone to find the disclaimer to be unconscionable because such buyers are presumably more able to understand and refuse to accept such disclaimers. This aspect of the law will become pertinent when we discuss shrink-wrap agreements and click-wrap agreements later in the chapter. In the following case, the issue arose whether a disclaimer of liability between commercial parties was effective.

BROWN V. SAP AMERICA, INC.

C.A. No. 98-507-SLR, 1999 U.S. Dist. LEXIS 15525 (D.Del. 1999)

FACTS: [The facts of the within case previously reviewed in Chapter 2 are repeated herein.] The trustee in bankruptcy for FoxMeyer in Delaware sued the defendant, a German software designer, and its U.S. subsidiary. He alleged that the defendants sold defective software to plaintiff, FoxMeyer, which crippled its business, thereby causing it to become bankrupt. Defendants claimed its software would operate all aspects of plaintiff's business, handle its demands, absorb high processing volumes than its existing computer system, interface with the other plaintiff's software, and save plaintiff up to $10 million in operating costs. Relying on the promises and demonstrations of the defendants, the plaintiff purchased the software.

The agreement warranted the software would be in good working order for twelve months after date of delivery and perform in substantial compliance with the specifications set forth in the documentation provided. The agreement disclaimed all other express or implied warranties, including those of merchantability and fitness for a particular purpose. Thereafter, plaintiff contracted to distribute pharmaceuticals to the University Health System Consortium, a network of teaching hospitals. After the installation of the software on behalf of FoxMeyer, it did not perform as promised. Plaintiff claimed breach of express warranties, fraud, concealment of material facts, gross negligence, and other claims.

ISSUE: Whether the defendant's disclaimer of liability and damages is effective against the plaintiff?

DECISION: The Court stated that the limitation of liability clause was effective against the plaintiff.

REASONING: Judge Robinson

In count one of the complaint, plaintiff claims that FoxMeyer and SAP America entered into an enforceable contract that SAP America unilaterally and materially breached. . . . Count two alleges that SAP America breached the Agreement's express warranty that "the Software, when delivered, will be in good working order . . . and will perform in substantial compliance with [the Software's] specifications . . ." Plaintiff [claims breaches of express and implied warranties and seeks consequential damages]. The following language of the Agreement, signed by FoxMeyer and SAP America, purports to limit SAP America's liability:

9. LIMITATION OF LIABILITY

9.1 . . . [FoxMeyer's] sole and exclusive remedy for any damages or loss in any way connected with any software . . . or services furnished by SAP whether by SAP's negligence, or any breach of any other duty, shall be, at SAP's option, (i) replacement of the [R/3] Software or performance of services or (ii) return or credit of an appropriate portion of any payment made or to be made by [FoxMeyer] with respect to such software or services.

9.3 ANYTHING TO THE CONTRARY HEREIN NOTWITHSTANDING, UNDER NO CIRCUMSTANCES SHALL SAP BE LIABLE TO [FOXMEYER] OR ANY OTHER PERSON OR ENTITY FOR SPECIAL, INCIDENTAL, CONSEQUENTIAL, OR INDIRECT DAMAGES, LOSS OF GOOD WILL, OR BUSINESS PROFITS, WORK STOPPAGE, DATA LOSS, THIRD PARTY CLAIMS, COMPUTER FAILURE OR MALFUNCTION, ANY AND ALL OTHER COMMERCIAL DAMAGES OR LOSS, AND EXEMPLARY OR PUNITIVE DAMAGES.

1. PLAINTIFF'S ATTEMPT TO RESCIND THE AGREEMENT'S LIMITATION OF LIABILITY PROVISIONS

In an effort to save his breach of contract and warranty claims from these limitation of liability provisions, plaintiff argues that these provisions are not enforceable because defendants procured the Agreement through fraud. Plaintiff does not argue that defendants procured the particular release provisions by fraud but, rather, that they fraudulently induced FoxMeyer to sign the entire agreement. . . . If plaintiff were only alleging fraud, the Agreement's limitation of liability provisions would not bar plaintiff's fraud and misrepresentation claims. . . . This is so because fraud renders the entire contract void, including the limitation of liability provisions. Here, however, plaintiff attempts to maintain a breach of contract and warranty action by using his fraud allegations to surgically remove only the Agreement's limitation of liability provisions. This he cannot do. If proven, fraud in the inducement would vitiate the entire Agreement, leaving plaintiff without a contract upon which to premise counts one through three. . . . Consequently, a party cannot both affirm the existence of a contract while, at the same time, seek rescission of the contract under a theory of fraudulent inducement. . . .

2. THE AGREEMENT'S LIMITED LIABILITY PROVISIONS BAR PLAINTIFF'S BREACH OF CONTRACT AND WARRANTY CLAIMS AGAINST SAP AMERICA.

Accordingly, the court must determine whether the Agreement's limitation of liability provisions bar plaintiff's breach of contract and warranty claims. . . . Pennsylvania's version of the Uniform Commercial Code ("UCC") permits parties to limit "the remedies of the buyer in return of the goods and repayment of the price or to repair and replacement of nonconforming goods or parts." . . . Moreover, contracts may limit or exclude damages unless the limitation or exclusion would be unconscionable. . . . There is no dispute that the UCC governs the Agreement. Where the limitation is not unconscionable, courts routinely enforce limitation of liability clauses negotiated between sophisticated parties. . . .

In the present case, plaintiff does not contend that the Agreement's preclusion of consequential damages was unconscionable. . . . Because Pennsylvania courts routinely enforce limitation of liability clauses in the absence of unconscionability the court must uphold the parties' Agreement and dismiss counts one, two, and three, insofar as count three relates to SAP America. [The defendant, SAP AG, was not absolved by reason of the limitation of liability provision because it was not a party to the agreement containing the limitations clause.]

CASE QUESTIONS

1. Would the result be different if this were a consumer transaction?
2. Should a corporation be treated differently than consumers with respect to a disclaimer clause?
3. Was the clause unconscionable under the circumstances of the case?

Article 2A: Leases

Article 2A was added to the UCC to cover lease agreements. Many of the provisions contained therein are analogous to Article 2: Sales. The provision concerning express warranties is identical in both articles.

REQUIREMENTS OF A WRITING: THE STATUTE OF FRAUDS UNDER THE COMMON LAW AND THE UCC

Common Law

Historically, oral contracts were enforceable under English law until 1677 when the Statute of Frauds and Perjuries was enacted by the British Parliament.[3] In essence, the statute provided that certain agreements had to be in writing, to wit: (1) promise to answer for the debt of another; (2) agreements that by their tenor cannot be performed within one year from the making thereof; (3) agreements made in consideration of marriage; (4) agreements concerning the sale of realty; (5) promise by an executor or administrator of a decedent's estate to pay estate indebtedness from his or her personal funds; (6) sale of goods whose price is $500 or more [as modified in the UCC]; and (7) miscellaneous other agreements as provided by state law.

Uniform Commercial Code

The section of the Statute of Frauds that most pertains to electronic commerce is the requirement of a writing for sale of goods whose price is $500 or more. Unlike other transactions that have to be in writing, the sale of goods provision has very important exceptions. It is governed by the UCC, Article 2,

Section 2-201. It provides that the sale of goods is not enforceable absent a writing indicating that a contract for sale had been entered into by the parties thereto *and signed by the party against whom enforcement is sought or by his authorized agent or broker.*

The exceptions to the requirement of such a writing and signature are: (1) in a contract of sale between merchants, a written confirmation sent within a reasonable time by one merchant to the other will bind the latter unless a written objection is made within 10 days of receipt of the confirmation; (2) specially manufactured goods, not otherwise suitable for sale in the ordinary course of business, wherein a substantial beginning of their manufacture or commitments for their procurement before notice of repudiation; (3) admission in a pleading, testimony, or comparable statements made in court by the party against whom enforcement of the contract is sought but only to the extent of the quantity admitted; and (4) goods for which payment has been made and accepted or for goods received and accepted.

Signature Requirement

The difficulty presented by the Statute of Frauds is that a writing is required for all of the contracts mentioned, unless otherwise excepted, thus rendering unenforceable agreements not in accordance therewith. The writing must include the signature signed by the party to be charged. Does a digital signature conform to the Statute of Frauds? The fear of courts and other observers, prior to changes in the law, was that the use of an electronic signature could be easily forged or altered so as to permit the fraud that the Statute of Frauds was intended to prevent. The Statute of Frauds says that the agreement, promise, or undertaking must be subscribed by the party to be charged therewith, or by his lawful agent.[4]

In general, a signature serves a number of purposes: (1) as *evidence* in a court of law to establish the authenticity of the document and the fact that the subscriber did agree to the contents therein; (2) as *ceremony* to remind the person signing the document of the importance of the act of subscription and the obligation contained therein; (3) *approval* of the document; and (4) *efficiency and logistics,* that is, the document and the signatures convey a finality that often prevents a court from looking beyond the four corners of the instrument.[5] The Statute of Frauds requires a signature, but the issue as to what is a signature has been broadly interpreted. The test generally is whether the person seeking to enforce the contract reasonably believed that the other party intended to authenticate the writing. Thus, initials or other symbols may be sufficient. The sign or symbol can be anywhere on the document and not necessarily at the end thereto. The signature may be typed, stamped, or printed.[6] The UCC 1-201(39) states that *signed* includes "any symbol, executed or adopted by a party with present intention to authenticate a writing."

It appears from the exceptions created by the enactment of the UCC three centuries later, that scholars are uneasy about rendering unenforceable contracts lacking the requirements of a writing. Historically, prior to the 1677 statute, writings were unnecessary because most inhabitants were illiterate. With the post–World War II enactment of the Uniform Commercial Code, the addition of several major exceptions to the requirement of a writing indicated a desire by the drafters to be more in accord with the customs of the marketplace. The new realities of cyberspace and the multitude of contracts of purchase and sales now taking place illustrate the need to create a new regime for Internet contracts. One may seriously question whether, today, the statute protects against fraud or permits fraud by allowing a person wishing to avoid a contract to raise the lack-of-writing defense.[7]

Electronic-type messages weren't created recently. Telegraph messages, use of cable, telex transmissions, and other such communications have been with us for a long time. Digital signatures are but one type of electronic signatures. The issue is whether such communications have the reliability required by the Statute of Frauds for the authentication of signatures.

It can be argued that electronic signatures may be more reliable than traditional signatures rather than encompassing an impediment to the fulfillment of the Statute of Frauds. The use of encryption software may provide *greater* security than one's written signature. Such software would permit both the sender and receiver of a transmission to possess private numeric keys known only to them. Thus, they would be able to authenticate the transmission without fear of a third-party intrusion.[8]

The use of such means comes within the United Nations Commission on International Trade Law (UNCITRAL)'s *Model Law on Electronic Commerce with Guide to Enactment.*[9] The pertinent provision, Article 7: Signature states:

(1) Where the law requires a signature of a person, that requirement is met in relation to a data message if:
   (a) a method is used to identify that person and to indicate that person's approval of the information contained in the data message; and
   (b) that method is as reliable as was appropriate for the purpose for which the data message was generated or communicated, in the light of all the circumstances, including any relevant agreement.

(2) Paragraph (1) applies whether the requirement therein is in the form of an obligation or whether the law simply provides consequences for the absence of a signature.

Electronic Contracts and the UCC

Do Internet contracts come within the purview of Article 2: Sales, of the Uniform Commercial Code, or are they subject to common-law rules? The applicable sections of the UCC are as follows:

Article 2. Sales. Section 2-102. Scope; Certain Security and Other Transactions Excluded from This Article

Unless the context otherwise requires, this Article applies to *transactions in goods* [emphasis added]; it does not apply to any transaction which although in the form of an unconditional contract to sell or present sale is intended to operate only as a security transaction nor does this Article impair or repeal any statute regulating sales to consumers, farmers or other specified classes of buyers.

Article 2A. Leases. Section 2-105. Definitions: Transferability; "Goods"; "Future" Goods; "Lot"; "Commercial Unit".

(1) "Goods" means all things (including specially manufactured goods) which are movable at the time of identification to the contract for sale other than the money in which the price is to be paid, investment securities (Article 8) and things in action. "Goods" also includes the unborn young of animals and growing crops and other identified things attached to realty as described in the section on goods to be severed from realty. (Section 2-107)

Section 2A-103. Definitions and Index of Definitions.

(1) In this article unless the context otherwise requires:

(h) "Goods" means all things that are movable at the time of identification to the lease contract, or are fixtures (Section 2A-309) but the term does not include money, documents, instruments, accounts, chattel paper, general intangibles, or mineral or the like, including oil and gas, before extraction. The term also includes the unborn young of animals.

(j) "Lease" means a transfer of the right to possession and use of goods for a term in return for consideration, but a sale, including a sale on approval or a sale or return, or retention or creation of a security interest is not a lease. Unless the context clearly indicates otherwise, the term includes a sublease.

Computer Software as Goods

There is little doubt that computer hardware does constitute "goods" under the previously discussed UCC provisions. It has physical attributes that the senses can detect—it can be seen, touched, felt, and so on. Software, however, has mixed attributes of sensation and electronic and digital characteristics. The following two cases illustrate the difficulties courts have had in rendering decisions as to whether computer software constitutes "goods" under the UCC.

In *Neilson Business Equipment Center, Inc. v. Monteleone,* 524 A. 2d 1172 (Sup. Del. 1987), the plaintiff, Dr. Monteleone, a neurologist, sued defendant, Neilson, for breach of the warranties of merchantability and fitness for a particular purpose arising out of a lease contract for computer hardware, software, and related services. Ultimately, he prevailed and was awarded the sum of $34,983.42. Defendant had been called upon to survey the needs of the plaintiff concerning programs for billing and record keeping. A lease was entered into between the parties for hardware and software with an option to purchase. There were significant problems with the program that caused the plaintiff to cease using the hardware and software. The issue in the case was whether the objects of the lease, namely, computer hardware, software programs, and services, constituted "goods" under the UCC and were therefore subject to the warranty provisions of the statute.

The court decided that they did constitute goods under the within contract. The court held that the turnkey computer system was a package constituting goods. It was a mixed contract and not separable into the component parts. Thus, even though the hardware was without defect, the court treated the objects of the contract as a whole. Plaintiff purchased a whole system using a lease/purchase format for tax purposes. The consulting services were ancillary to the contract.

There was a clear breach or warranty of merchantability because the system failed to pass without objection in the trade under the contract description and to be fit for the ordinary purposes for which it was intended as required by the UCC. The five elements were present for such breach, namely, (1) the goods were sold by a merchant; (2) the goods were not merchantable at the time of sale; (3) the plaintiff was damaged; (4) the damage was caused by the breach of warranty of merchantability; and (5) the seller had notice of the damage.

There was breach of fitness for a particular purpose. Defendant selected the system after being told of plaintiff's needs. Plaintiff relied on defendant's expertise in the computer industry to select and deliver the appropriate system suited to plaintiff's needs. There was clear reliance by the plaintiff.

In *Communications Groups, Inc. v. Warner Communications Inc.*, 138 Misc. 2d 80 (N.Y. Civ. Ct. 1988), the plaintiff sued for breach of written agreement for licensing, installation, and servicing of a certain computer software package. Thereafter, two subcontracts for added software and related hardware were entered into. Defendant paid 50 percent on signing and was to pay the balance upon installation of the software. It refused to do so, alleging breach of express warranty, the implied warranties of fitness and merchantability, express warranty, and breach of contract. Plaintiff sought to have the defenses dismissed under Article 2 of the UCC, alleging that the transaction was a software system. Accordingly, it was neither for a tangible product or goods, nor was it a sale or lease of devices or goods. Rather, the claim is that it was a license for limited use of copyrightable information.

The court reiterated the issues of (1) Whether the software computer package or system involved "goods" under the UCC, and (2) Was the transaction a sale or lease or merely a license to use and service the software and therefore not subject to UCC or common-law implied warranties of fitness and/or merchantability?

The court decided that: (1) The items under the contract were "goods"; and (2) The transaction was a lease even though it said "license to use" the software. The court stated that computer software is a tangible, movable item and not merely an intangible idea or thought. It is clear that the installation of specially designed software equipment was done for defendant's particular telephone and computer system, needs, and purposes.

The contract was clearly analogous to a lease of chattel or goods and, therefore, was subject to common-law defenses of implied warranties of fitness and/or merchantability. Moreover, the said defenses may arise also under the UCC, Article 2, because the definition of *goods* has been liberally construed as provided for under Section 1-102 and under 2-105(1). The definition states that "transaction in goods" refer to "all things (including specially manufactured goods) which are movable at the time of identification to the contract." The word *transaction* has also been liberally applied and does not mean merely a sale of goods. The exclusionary clauses in the agreement fail to state the words "merchantability," "fitness," "as is," "warranty," or "all faults" and, thus, do not exclude such warranties.

Apparently Article 2 would apply to actions involving computer hardware and software programs.[10] There is a service component to computers and software programs, but it would appear that the dominant component is the sales aspect rather than the services provided.[11] Customized software may be considered as a service, thereby relegating claimants to a state's common law for alleged breach of contracts.[12] The issue of whether computer contracts are subject to the UCC provisions has significant consequences; this became particularly evident when the issue of potential Y2K liability loomed on the horizon. The problem arises, however, that courts need clarification of the status of Internet transactions. Contracts under Articles 2 and 2A require a "good" to exist to apply to the transaction and not be incidental thereto.

ELECTRONIC COMMERCE CONTRACTS: THE UNIFORM COMPUTER INFORMATION TRANSACTIONS ACT

Historical Background

The need for clarification of the status of electronic contracts led to the undertaking by the American Law Institute and the National Conference of Commissioners on Uniform State Laws (NCCUSL) to clarify the law concerning the new technologies. A draft of an Article 2B of the Uniform Commercial Code was initially prepared, called *Software Contracts and Licenses of Information.*[13] It recognized that many, if not most, of the transactions occurring over the Internet consist of services. It is especially true in recent days in the purchase of securities, airline and other transportation reservations, and banks, which have tried for years to have customers use their computer programs for most transactions. The purpose of Article 2B was to clarify the law pertaining to computer-related agreements.

Article 2B was not approved due to intense opposition of a variety of groups, including those in the entertainment industry, many states' attorneys general, bar associations, libraries, and consumer groups. The result was the removal of Article 2B as a part of the Uniform Commercial Code. It underwent substantial changes and became known as the Uniform Computer Information Transactions Act. Though similar to Article 2B, it is a proposed uniform law that remains outside the overall umbrella of the Uniform Commercial Code and awaits adoption by the states.[14] It is also the first entrée into the legal aspects of contract affecting computer technology. A comparison of UCC Article 2 with UCITA will reveal substantial similarity between the two enactments (see Table 3.1).

General Provisions

Scope of UCITA. UCITA applies to a contract relating to a computer information transaction. It is not a sale of goods; rather, it is in the nature of a licensing of computer information. A *computer information transaction* is defined as:

> an agreement or the performance of it to create, modify, transfer, or license computer information or informational rights in computer information. The term includes a support contract under Section 612.[15] The term does not include a transaction merely because the parties' agreement provides that their communications about the transaction will be in the form of computer information.

Computer information refers to information rendered in electronic form obtained from or from the use of a computer or is in a form that is capable of being processed through a computer. It includes a copy of the information as well as any documentation or packaging that comes with the copy.[16]

Exclusions. UCITA does not apply to:

(1) Financial services transactions;
(2) Agreements concerning audio or visual programming by broadcast, satellite, or cable;
(3) Motion pictures, sound recordings, musical works, or phonorecords;
(4) A compulsory license;
(5) Contract of employment of an individual unless such person is an independent contractor furnishing computer information; or
(6) Matters coming within the scope of Articles 3–8 of the Uniform Commercial Code.[17]

Opting Out of the Act. If the agreement contains a material part of the covered subject matter, the parties have the choice of having the act apply in whole or in part, or they may opt out of the act's provisions. If they decide affirmatively to exclude the act's provisions, nevertheless, consumer protection statutes will still be applicable. Furthermore, in a mass-market transaction (a consumer transaction or license contract directed to the general public as a whole wherein the licensee acquires information or in a retail transaction), the licensor will continue to be subject to consumer protection statutes and to the doctrines of unconscionability and good faith.[18]

Formation of Contract. UCITA's Statute of Frauds is found in Section 201. A contract calling for the payment of $5,000 or more is not enforceable unless:

(1) the party against which enforcement is sought authenticated a record sufficient to indicate that a contract has been formed and which reasonably identifies the copy or subject matter to which the contract refers; or
(2) the agreement is a license for an agreed duration of one year or less or which may be terminated at will by the party against which the contract is asserted.

The record will suffice even if a term is missing but is enforceable only up to the number of copies or subject matter stated in the record.

The agreement will nevertheless be enforceable in the absence of the prescribed record if the performance was tendered or the information was made available and accepted by the party to be charged. Also, the agreement will be enforced to the extent that the said party admits under oath in court, in the pleadings of the case, or by testimony that such a contract was formed. As between merchants, a record sent in confirmation of the contract within a reasonable time will make the agreement enforceable unless objection is made by the receiver within 10 days of receipt.

Offer and Acceptance. A contract may be formed in any manner that signifies that the parties have entered into an agreement. As in Article 2 of the UCC, a contract may be formed even if one or more terms have been left open or a party reserves the right to modify the agreement if the parties so intended. The open terms will not cause a contract to be unenforceable provided that it is reasonable for a court to render a remedy. A major disagreement regarding a material term will ordinarily nullify the existence of a contract.

Warranties

UCITA's provisions on warranties are similar to those proconsumer warranties found in the UCC's Article 2 warranties. They include warranties against infringement, express warranties, and a number of implied warranties.

Warranty Regarding Infringement. A merchant licensor warrants that the information delivered under an agreement subject to the statute will be delivered free from a rightful claim of infringement or misappropriation. The exception is if the licensee furnishes to the licensor detailed specifications and the method for complying with them. The warranty includes noninterference with the licensee's rightful enjoyment of the information and that any licensed patent rights conveyed under the agreement are valid and exclusive. There are exclusions for conspicuous disclaimer of such warranty and rights subject to privileged use, collective administration, or compulsory licensing. The warranty covers only informational rights arising under U.S. law unless specified otherwise.[19]

Express Warranties. An express warranty is created by (1) an affirmation of fact or promise by the licensor to the licensee, including advertising, that is part of the basis of the bargain between the parties; (2) a description of the information in the bargaining process; and (3) reasonable conformity to any sample, model, or demonstration of a final product. Exclusions to liability of the licensor for predictions of the value of the subject matter, a display or description for aesthetic or similar purpose, or a statement of opinion.[20]

Implied Warranties. There are three implied warranties under the act: (1) merchantability of computer program; (2) informational content; and (3) licensee's purpose.

The first, the implied warranty of merchantability, is very similar to the UCC Article 2 warranty of merchantability. Unless disclaimed or modified, the merchant licensor warrants to the end user that the computer program is fit for the ordinary use of such program; to the distributor that the program is adequately packaged and labeled as per agreement and, if there are multiple copies, that they are of even kind, quality, and quantity except for minor variations; that the program conforms to promises or affirmations of fact stated therein; and any other implied warranties arising from course of dealing or usage of trade.[21]

Second, a merchant, using reasonable care, warrants to a licensee that informational content compiled, collected, processed, or transmitted is accurate. Exceptions to responsibility are given to published informational content and where the person conveying the information is merely acting as a conduit, providing no more than editorial services in the compilations and transmission of the information.[22]

Third, when the licensor is made aware of the licensee's particular purpose for the requested computer information and that the licensee is relying upon the licensor's skill to select, develop, or furnish the information, then an implied warranty arises that the information given is fit for such purpose. If the licensor is paid for the time or effort regardless of the fitness of the information to be conveyed, then the warranty is that the information will not fail to meet such purpose by reason of the licensor's lack of reasonable effort. Exceptions to liability are for aesthetics, suitability to taste, subjective quality of informational content, or published informational content unless the selection was negligently made on behalf of the licensee.[23]

Disclaimers. Express warranties may not be unreasonably disclaimed or modified. In order to disclaim the implied warranty of merchantability, the language used must be conspicuous and must specifically mention "merchantability," "quality," or similar words. To disclaim the warranty of informational content, the language in a record must mention "accuracy" or similar wording. To disclaim the implied warranty of licensee's purpose, the language must be conspicuous and state to the effect that there is no warranty that the information, the licensor's efforts, or the system will fulfill the particular purposes of the licensee. Except for the warranty of infringement, language such as "as is," "with all faults," and similar language will suffice to disclaim implied warranties. A licensee who has examined a model or sample before entering into a contract receives no implied warranty as to any deficiencies apparent upon inspection. An implied warranty can be disclaimed by a course of dealing, course of performance, or usage of trade. Remedies can be expressly limited concerning liquidation or limitation of damages.[24]

Warranties are cumulative unless such construction is unreasonable. A licensee who modifies a computer program will forfeit the warranties as to the portion of the program that has undergone modification. The warranties also extend to the licensee's immediate family and to foreseeable users.[25]

Breach of Contract. UCITA provides a number of remedies for a breach of contract. The act provides them in the absence of an agreement setting forth in what manner damages will be assessed. A material breach is one that the contract so states, or where there is substantial failure to perform or there is substantial likelihood of injury or deprivation of what was reasonably expected under the contract.[26] The aggrieved party may waive the breach and accept the performance as rendered. There is no waiver if the acceptance of the performance was made on the presumption that the breach would be cured or if notice is given to the party at fault. If a party refuses a performance, notice should be given of the specific defect if readily ascertainable and the defect could have been seasonably cured. As between merchants, failure to comply with a request concerning the nature of the defect may operate as a waiver.[27]

The party who breaches the agreement may cure the defect if time for performance remains and there is seasonable notification to the other party. A person receiving a defective tender of performance may reject the tender, accept it, or accept the portion that is not defective and reject the remaining performance. Refusal of tender must be done before acceptance or within a reasonable time after tender or completion of time to cure, and there must be notification of refusal to the tendering party. The contract may be canceled only if there is a material breach of the contract. In a mass-market transaction calling for only a single tender of a copy, a licensee may refuse a defective tender if there is a lack of conformity to the contract.[28]

A *mass market transaction* is treated differently by UCITA. It is defined as:

(A) a consumer contract; or
(B) any other transaction with an end-user licensee if:
   (i) the transaction is for information or informational rights directed to the general public as a whole, including consumers, under substantially the same terms for the same information;
   (ii) the licensee acquires the information or informational rights in a retail transaction under terms and in a quantity consistent with an ordinary transaction in a retail market; and
   (iii) the transaction is not
      (I) a contract for redistribution or for public performance or public display of a copyrighted work;
      (II) a transaction in which the information is customized or otherwise specially prepared by the licensor for the licensee, other than minor customization using a capability of the information intended for that purpose;
      (III) a site license;
      (IV) or an access contract.[29]

A party receiving a nonconforming tender of a copy may revoke acceptance for a material breach only if the other party is notified, there was acceptance on the reasonable assumption that the defect would be cured, or the acceptance was induced by the other party's assurances. Revocation will be precluded if there was a substantial alteration of the information by the accepting party, or there was a failure to notify seasonably. If a party reasonably believes that performance will not be made by the other party, a demand for adequate assurance of due performance may be sought. Until such adequacy of performance is accomplished, the party making the demand may suspend its performance.[30]

Remedies

Remedies are cumulative so that it is possible for an aggrieved party to have several forms of relief. They are (1) *cancellation* of the contract for material breach upon notification to the other party; (2) remedies as provided for in the agreement between the parties if such remedies are not unconscionable; (3) *liquidated damages* (wherein the parties agree at the outset what money will be due and owing in the event of a breach); (4) *compensatory damages* as determined by a court based on market value as of the date of breach of contract, but a party may not recover *consequential damages* for losses of published informational content unless otherwise provided for in the contract, nor are speculative damages recoverable. Consequential damages will be allowed for disclosure or misuse of trade secrets.[31]

A licensor may recover no more than the contract fee and the market value of other consideration required under the contract. Damages include the accrued and unpaid contract fees, the market value of other consideration earned but not received for performance accomplished or for a reasonably hypothetical substituted performance, plus consequential and incidental damages. A licensee may recover damages no more than the market value of the performance, plus restitution of amounts paid for performance not received, plus incidental and consequential damages, less fees paid for performance that has been accepted by the licensee.[32] In addition, the aggrieved party may deduct the sum from money due and owing to the other party for the deficient performance and may request specific performance if the aggrieved party is not seeking money but rather the unique agreed-upon performance.[33]

The annexed Table 3.1 illustrates the many similarities between the UCC and UCITA. The earlier proposed Article 2B had many provisions comparable to those reflected throughout UCITA that was finally chosen for submission to the states.

TABLE 3.1 Comparative Provisions of UCITA and UCC

UCITA	*UCC*
102 "Authentication": (A) To sign, or (B) Adopt electronic means for signature	1-201(39) "Signed": Any symbol with intention to authenticate
103 "Exclusions" Financial services transactions Audio or visual programming Motion pictures, musical works, compulsory license, contract of employment, non-computer information	2-102 Exclusions Security transaction Statutes regulating sales to consumers, farmers
105 "Public Policy" Exclusions Term violates public policy Contract conflicting consumer protection law	2-102 Exclusions Statute regulating sales to consumer laws
106 "Rules of Construction" Liberal construction Realize full potential of computer information transactions Promote uniformity of law Expand commercial practice by commercial usage & agreement by the parties	1-102 "Rules of Construction" Liberal construction Simplify, clarify & modernize the law Make uniformity of law Expand commercial practice through custom, usage & agreement of parties
107 Electronic Record	
109 Choice of Law Parties may choose applicable law except some consumer contracts If no agreement, in access contract, state of licensor; else, need significant relationship	1-105 Choice of Law Parties may choose applicable law with reasonable relation to the selected state If no agreement, need relation to state
110 Choice of Forum Parties choose unless unreasonable; must say "exclusive" to be sole jurisdiction	

TABLE 3.1 *(continued)*

UCITA	*UCC*
111 Unconscionable Contract or Term Court may refuse to enforce Parties have right to present evidence of setting, purpose & effect	2-302 Unconscionable Contract or Clause Court may refuse to enforce Parties have right to present evidence of setting, purpose & effect
113–114 Variations by Agreement, Good Faith Obligations of good faith, diligence, reasonableness, and care Extensive list of exceptions	1-203 Obligation of Good Faith Obligation of good faith in its performance or enforcement
201 Formal Requirements Contract for fee of $5,000 or more, need authenticated record Exceptions: license—one year or less; performance tendered & accepted; admission in testimony or pleading; merchants—record in confirmation	1-206 Statute of Frauds for Personal Property (not sale of goods, etc.) Not enforceable w/o writing beyond $5,000 2-201 Statute of Frauds for Sale of Goods w/price of $500 or more Need writing signed by party to be charged Exceptions: Specially manufactured goods; performance accepted; admission in pleading or testimony; between merchants, confirmation w/i reasonable time
202 Formation in General Contract may be formed in any manner showing agreement including by electronic agents Can be contract with missing terms if can ascertain reasonably No contract if material disagreement re material term	2-204 Formation in General Contract may be formed in any manner showing agreement Can be contract with missing terms if can ascertain reasonably Court has power to fill in missing price, time, delivery terms
203 Offer and Acceptance in General Offer invites acceptance in any manner or reasonable medium Order for prompt delivery invites acceptance by promise to ship or by shipment	2-206 Offer and Acceptance Offer invites acceptance in any manner or reasonable medium Order for prompt delivery invites acceptance by promise to ship or by shipment
204 Acceptance with Varying Terms If material, no contract unless assent or agrees by conduct If contract formed by conduct, added or varying terms are not part of contract Between merchants, added nonmaterial terms becomes part of contract unless objected to w/i reasonable time	2-207 Additional Terms in Acceptance If acceptance with added or different terms, there is contract Between merchants, varying terms become part of contract unless offer precludes, or is material change, or objected to w/i reasonable time
303 Modification and Rescission Agreement to modify needs no consideration Authenticated record precluding modification or rescission except by authenticated record cannot be changed without it	2-209 Modification, Rescission, & Waiver Agreement to modify needs no consideration Written agreement precluding modification or rescission except by a writing cannot be changed without it
401 Warranty Concerning Noninterference and Noninfringement Merchant licensor warrants information is free from rightful claim of infringement. Exception where licensee gives detailed specifications and method to be followed	2-312 Warranty of Title and Against Infringement Seller warrants that title conveyed is good and is free from liens. Exception—full disclosure. Merchant seller warrants free of rightful claim of infringement. Exception—buyer furnishing specs
402 Express Warranty Affirmation of fact or promise by licensor to licensee, including advertising, that is part of basis of bargain; sample; model; demonstration No need for formal words	2-313 Express Warranties by Affirmation; Promise; description; sample; affirmation of fact or promise re: goods that is part of basis of bargain No need for formal words

TABLE 3.1 (*continued*)

UCITA	*UCC*
403 Implied Warranty of Merchantability of Computer Program Merchant warrants to end user that computer program is fit for ordinary purpose of program Merchant to distributor that program is adequately packaged and labeled conforms to promises or affirmations	2-314 Implied Warranty of Merchantability Merchant warrants goods pass w/o objection in trade; are fit for ordinary purpose; adequately packaged and contained; conforms to promises or affirmations of fact
404 Implied Warranty of Licensee's Purpose Licensor gives implied warranty when knows of particular purpose of information and that licensor knows of reliance on licensor's skill or judgment to select computer information	2-315 Implied Warranty of Fitness for Particular Purpose Seller knowing of particular reason for contracted goods and of buyer's reliance on seller to choose product
406 Disclaimer or Modification of Warranty Express warranty—not excludable if unreasonable Implied warranty—must be conspicuous Must use wording showing exclusion Can be disclaimed by course of dealing or usage of trade	2-316 Exclusion or Modification of Warranties Express warranty—not excludable if unreasonable Implied warranty—must be conspicuous Can be disclaimed by course of dealing or usage of trade
409 Third-Party Beneficiaries of Warranty Warranty extends to licensee and intended beneficiaries; if to consumer, extends to family	2-318 Third-Party Beneficiaries of Warranties States are given 3 choices—family, guests; any natural person who may use; or any person affected
702 Waiver of Remedy for Breach of Contract Aggrieved party may waive breach; waive by failure to notify of defect; bet. merchants, refusal to state defects	2-602 Manner and Effect of Rightful Rejection Reject w/i reasonable time; after rejection, buyer does not exercise ownership; exercise reasonable care of goods
704 Refusal of Defective Tender For *material* breach, party may refuse the tender, accept the tender, or accept commercially reasonable units and refuse the rest	2-601 Buyer's Rights on Improper Delivery For *any* lack of conformity, buyer may reject the whole, accept commercial unit and reject rest
707 Revocation of Acceptance Can revoke acceptance if reasonably believes there will be cure Done w/i reasonable time and w/o substantial change to copy	2-608 Revocation of Acceptance Can revoke acceptance if reasonable belief of cure Done w/i reasonable time after discovery of defect
708 Adequate Assurance of Performance If reasonable grounds for insecurity of performance, can demand adequate assurance be given	2-609 Right to Adequate Assurance of Performance If reasonable grounds for insecurity, can demand adequate assurance of performance
709 Anticipatory Repudiation Can await performance if other party says will not perform; suspend own performance	2-610 Anticipatory Repudiation If party repudiates performance, other party can wait reasonable time for performance, resort to any remedy for breach, suspend own performance

DIGITAL SIGNATURES

Irrespective of whether states adopt UCITA, all states are bound by the latest federal legislation governing digital signatures. The authentication of digital signatures becomes vital in assuring the enforceability of contracts and the true identification of customers. Contracts under the Statute of Frauds require signatures of the party to be charged. E-mail offers would be binding once accepted if they can be transmitted without tampering. The problem is that many Americans do falsify information given online.

Under American Bar Association guidelines, enforceable digital signatures should at least be able to "indicate who signed a document, message or record, and should be difficult for another person to produce without authorization."

Nature of Digital Signatures

Digital signatures permit the verification of the authenticity of a document sent through the Internet. Digital signatures operate in electronic commerce the way written signatures operate on typed documents. Neither party to an agreement can disown the signature absence proof of forgery. Digital signatures require use of two keys, one private and one public. The keys are issued by a certification authority (CA). The private key is for the sender, and messages are decrypted with the public key. A sender who signs a document with the private key can have his or her signature confirmed by use of the public key.

A document is initially created, for example, as a word document, which is sent to digital-signature software to be processed. The processing or coding is done by means of a sender performing a mathematical computation on his or her document *(hash function),* which generates a string of code called a *message digest.* The message digest is based on the specific content of the original document so that any changes would give a different message digest. The algorithm may, for example, create or count the number of letters or characters between two specific letters in the document. The hash function or result is exhibited as a series of numbers.

The sender encrypts the message digest with his private key, which is a password or number known by the sender only; attaches his or her signature to the end of the documents, thereby signing it by means of a second algorithm; and sends it to the receiver. The receiver, having access to the public key, may now verify the sender's identity and the integrity of the document. The signature is decrypted with the sender's public key, and the original message digest is revealed. The receiver performs the hash function by typing in a public key on his or her copy of the message digest. The public key performs its own algorithm on both the hash function and the signature. If they are identical, the receiver knows the message was not altered and knows that it could only have been encrypted with the sender's private key.[34] There are also other methodologies being developed for ensuring the safety of signatures; among them are use of electronic fingerprinting, full inscription of the signature, and other forms of coding.

Thus, under the guidelines, there are three participating parties: the sender, the receiver, and the certification authority. The sender or subscriber to the certification process creates a private and public key. A copy of the public key is given to the certification authority. The private key is kept secret by the subscriber. The certification authority acts as an intermediary between the sender/subscriber and the receiver. The certification authority confirms the sender's identity and the validity of the key pair. Upon verification, the certification authority issues a certificate with the subscriber's name, identifying information, and the subscriber's public key. Once accepted by the subscriber, the party may then use the key pair to digitally sign the documents. All certificates issued by the authority are placed online for receivers so that they can access the subscriber.[35]

Digital Signatures and Electronic Commerce

Digital signatures allow parties to authenticate and bind parties rendering enforceable online contracts and agreements. Signatures are valuable in furnishing evidence of agreement; they are hard to forge; the document is original and authentic; they constitute affirmation of the person signing to be bound; and they are efficient in indicating authorization of a transaction.

Furthermore, they satisfy the Statute of Frauds, according to which, agreements required to be in writing but that contain no signatures are unenforceable. Companies and customers would feel more secure in doing business online knowing whom they are dealing with. Stock traders would feel more comfortable in selling to clients who may not be able to disclaim the purchase.

Problems Raised by the Use of Digital Signatures

The first problem is that digital-signature capabilities are not free. It is costly to train representatives, create new institutions, establish accreditation procedures, and determine how to license and audit. There are costs of purchasing the software and keys. The second problem is the many differing laws governing the area. Unless all state and global authorities agree upon a uniform system, the use of such a system may have limited application.[36]

Federal Digital-Signature Legislation

Essential Provisions. It became apparent that federal legislation was necessary to overcome the multiplicity of state laws. Some laws give wide credence to digital-signature use, while others are very restrictive. There is a need for a singular standard.

Such legislation should allow nonfinancial institutions to use electronic authentication services and should allow use of electronic signatures online. Accordingly, Congress passed the Electronic Signatures in Global and National Commerce Act, and President Clinton signed it into law on June 30, 2000. The act is in keeping with the president's "Framework for Global Electronic Commerce." As stated by the president in signing the legislation, the act is simple and nonregulatory, does not favor one technology over another, and allows private parties maximum freedom to form electronic contracts as they see fit.[37]

The law became effective on October 1, 2000. The key provision is the opening Section 101, General Rule of Validity, that states:

(a) GENERAL RULE—With respect to any contract, agreement, or record entered into or provided in, or affecting, interstate or foreign commerce, notwithstanding any statute, regulation, or other rule of law, the legal effect, validity, or enforceability of such contract, agreement, or record shall not be denied—
 (1) on the ground that the contract, agreement, or record is not in writing if the contract, agreement, or record is an electronic record; or
 (2) on the ground that the contract, agreement, or record is not signed or is not affirmed by a signature of the contract, agreement, or record is signed or affirmed by an electronic signature.

Right of Parties to Determine Electronic Validity. No party to an agreement is required to use or accept electronic records or signatures. The parties to an electronic contract may establish among themselves the procedures or requirements concerning such records and electronic signatures. The legal effect of such record or agreement does not depend on the type or method of electronic record or signature used.[38] If a statute or regulation requires that a written record be given to a consumer, an electronic record will suffice if the consumer assents to the terms, which terms have to be conspicuous and set apart from other provisions of the agreement between the consumer and the merchant. The merchant has to advise the consumer prior to assenting of the hardware and software requirements for access to and retention of electronic records. If a record, contract, or agreement is required by law to be kept in writing, this may be done by electronic means provided that it accurately reflects the writing and is accessible. This provision applies also to checks and situations in which originals are required. The validity of signatures and other parts of the document can be contested.[39]

Exceptions. A state may alter or supersede the requirements of the act provided it does so due to the enactment of the Uniform Electronic Transactions Act, specifies alternative procedures for use or acceptance of electronic records or signatures, and, if enacted on or after this federal statute, specifically refers to the federal statute as being superseded. No state law or regulation shall supersede the act if it discriminates against or in favor of a specific technology, or a specific process or techniques for storing or authenticating, or if it is otherwise inconsistent with the federal statute.[40]

Exclusions. The act does not apply to laws governing wills or trusts; domestic relations matters; the Uniform Commercial Code, except for Sections 1-107 and 1-206 and Articles 2 and 2A; federal regulatory agency regulations; the Uniform Anatomical Gift Act; and the Uniform Health-Care Decisions Act. The act also does not apply to intrastate commerce, nonmarket agreements, court orders or other court documents, notices for cancellations of utilities, foreclosures, and termination of health and life insurance benefits.[41]

Future Studies. The act provides for a 5-year study by the secretary of commerce concerning state laws enacted after the act and an 18-month study of the act's effectiveness as compared with the use of ordinary and express mail services. The secretary has the further duty within 180 days to identify domestic and foreign impediments to electronic signature products and services. He also must identify the nations and international organizations complying with the principles of electronic commerce as they pertain to the marketplace, neutrality and nondiscrimination of electronic commerce, the right of parties to use electronic commerce, and the legal recognition of the validity of electronic records and signatures.[42] Title 3 of the act concerns electronic records under Federal Securities Law and is discussed in Chapter 12, concerning securities.

THE UNIFORM ELECTRONIC TRANSFERS ACT

In July of 1999, the NCCUSL approved the Uniform Electronic Transfers Act for submission to the states for adoption. This process was underway for 3 years—compared with more than 10 years spent on the revisions to the UCC—concluding with the adoption of UCITA about the same time.

The importance of the UETA is that Congress specifically refers to the Electronic Signatures in Global and National Commerce Act as an exception to the UETA's mandate. The key provision of the act is Section 7: Legal Recognition of Electronic Records, Electronic Signatures, and Electronic Contracts, which states:

(a) A record or signature may not be denied legal effect or enforceability solely because it is in electronic form.
(b) A contract may not be denied legal effect or enforceability solely because an electronic record was used in its formation.
(c) If a law requires a record to be in writing, an electronic record satisfies the law.
(d) If a law requires a signature, an electronic signature satisfies the law.

The act applies to electronic records and signatures relating to a transaction connected to a business, commercial, and governmental affairs. It is broader than Article 2B and UCITA inasmuch as it is not limited to licensing agreements and it covers the transactions in Article 2 of the UCC. By adopting UETA, states need not be concerned with an expansive definition of a writing nor need they adopt the controversial Article 2B. Thus, it appears that states have a variety of choices in the legislative scheme they wish to adopt. The clear mandate is that an electronic record may no longer be denied legal effect.

SHRINK-WRAP LICENSES AND CLICK-WRAP AGREEMENTS

Shrink-Wrap Licenses

An on-going issue on which courts have decided in opposition to each other is the legality of shrink-wrap licenses. We are all familiar with the packages ensconced in clear plastic containing a notice such as:

> Before you open this package: Carefully read the following legal agreement regarding your use of the enclosed product. By the act of opening the sealed package, using the software or permitting its use, you will indicate your full consent to the terms and conditions of this agreement. If you don't agree with what it says, you may return the software package within 7 days of your receipt for a full refund.

An extensive, small-print restrictive notice follows the warning. Such notice constitutes what is euphemistically called a shrink-wrap license or agreement.[43] It is on most software packages. The difficulty is that most consumers who purchase the products are unaware of the restrictions being imposed upon them. How legal is it to compel purchasers and users of goods containing such notices to comply with the postpurchase restrictions?

At first blush, such notices may be superfluous inasmuch as software programs are protected by the copyright laws that restrict users from unlawful copying or distribution of the programs. The leading cases discussing the issue are: *ProCD, Inc. v. Zeidenberg*[44] and *Step-Saver Data Systems, Inc. v. Wyse Technology and The Software Link, Inc.*[45]

PROCD, INC. V. ZEIDENBERG

86 F.3d 1447 (7th Cir. 1996)

FACTS: The plaintiff, ProCD, compiled a computer database containing some 3,000 telephone directories. The database is sold under the trademark label "SelectPhone" to users on CD-ROM discs. The license agreement is seen as soon as the packaging is unwrapped. A copyrighted application program permits the user to search the database for the telephone number of the person named by the user. The plaintiff spent some $10 million to compile and keep current the database. The database costs about $150 to purchasers thereof. The resale or other dissemination of the product was thus restricted by the licensing agreement when the package was opened as well as set forth on initial application of the software.

The defendant, Zeidenberg, bought the software and decided to ignore the restrictive notice by reselling the information under his corporation, Silken Mountain Web Services, Inc. The price charged was less than that charged by the plaintiff. When the plaintiff sued for an injunction and other relief, the trial court decided that the license was not enforceable because the terms were not displayed on the outside of the package.

ISSUE: (1)Are buyers of computer software subject to the terms of the shrink-wrap license stated within the packaging?

(2) Does the Copyright Act prevent enforcement of shrink-wrap licenses?

DECISION: The Court of Appeals decided in favor of the plaintiff, reversing the decision of the trial court and holding (1) buyers are subject to the license terms and (2) the Copyright Act did not prevent enforcement thereof.

REASONING: Judge Easterbrook

Shrinkwrap licenses are enforceable unless the terms are objectionable on grounds applicable to contracts in general (for example, if they violate a rule of positive law, or if they are unconscionable).

... Zeidenberg does argue, and the district court held, that placing the package of software on the shelf is an "offer," which the customer "accepts" by paying the asking price and leaving the store with the goods.... [B]ut one of the terms to which Zeidenberg agreed by purchasing the software is that the transaction was subject to a license.... Vendors can put the entire terms of a contract on the outside of a box only by using microscopic type, removing other information that buyers might find more useful....

Transactions in which the exchange of money precedes the communication of detailed terms are common. Consider the purchase of insurance. The buyer goes to an agent, who explains the essentials (amount of coverage, number of years) and remits to the home office, which sends back a policy.... Or consider the purchase of an airline ticket. The traveler calls the carrier or an agent, is quoted a price, reserves a seat, pays, and gets a ticket, in that order. The ticket contains elaborate terms, which the traveler can reject by canceling the reservation.... Just so with a ticket to a concert....

Consumer goods work the same way. Someone who wants to buy a radio set visits a store, pays, and walks out with a box. Inside the box is a leaflet containing some terms, the most important of which usually is the warranty, read for the first time, in the comfort of home.... Drugs come with a list of ingredients on the outside and an elaborate package insert on the inside. The package insert describes drug interaction, contraindications, and other vital information....

Next consider the software industry itself. Only a minority of sales takes place over the counter, where there are boxes to peruse. A customer may place an order by phone in response to a line item in a catalog or a review in a magazine. Much software is ordered over the Internet by purchasers who have never seen a box. Increasingly, software arrives by wire....

According to the district court, the UCC does not countenance the sequence of money now, terms later. One of the court's reasons—that by proposing as part of the draft Article 2B a new UCC sec. 2-2203 that would explicitly validate standard-form user licenses, the American Law Institute and the National Conference of Commissioners have concede the invalidity of shrink-wrap licenses under current law ... depends on a faulty inference. To propose a change in a law's text is not necessarily to propose a change in the law's effect. New words may be designed to fortify the current rule with a more precise text that curtails uncertainty....

What then does the current version of the UCC have to say? We think that the place to start is sec. 2-204(1): "A contract for sale of goods may be made in any manner sufficient to show agreement, including conduct by both parties which recognizes the existence of such a contract." A vendor, as master of the offer, may invite acceptance by conduct, and may propose limitations on the kind of conduct that constitutes acceptance. A buyer may accept by performing the acts the vendor proposes to treat as acceptance. And that is what happened. ProCD proposed a contract that a buyer would accept by using the software after having an opportunity to read the license at leisure. This Zeidenberg did. He had no choice, because the software splashed the license on the screen and would not let him proceed without indicating acceptance....

Section 2-606, which defines "acceptance of goods," reinforces this understanding. A buyer accepts goods under sec. 2-606(1)(b) when, after an opportunity to inspect, he fails to make an effective rejection under sec. 2-602(1). ProCD extended an opportunity to reject if a buyer should find the license terms unsatisfactory; Zeidenberg inspected the package, tried out the software, learned of the license, and did not reject the goods. . . .

[With respect to the claim that the Copyright Act provided an exclusive remedy for copyright infringements, the court stated that the defendant was precluded by contract if not by copyright law from duplicating the information contained in the CD-ROM.]

CASE QUESTIONS

1. The UCC allows a court to set aside a clause or agreement that is unconscionable. Is a shrink-wrap clause unconscionable?
2. Does the average person read or understand a shrink-wrap clause?

In a state of Washington case, *A. Mortenson Co., Inc. v. Timberline Software Corp.,* 970 P.2d 803 (1999), citing the *ProCD* decision, an appeals court upheld a license agreement that was enclosed in a sealed envelope and on the inside cover of the manual accompanying the program. Whenever a user opened the program, reference to the agreement appeared on the screen. The agreement also limited the damages for which the company could be held liable. The user was advised that if the user did not agree with the contents of the license, the program could be returned for a full refund. The license agreement was held to be a permissible accept-or-return license.

In the *Step-Saver* action, the Court of Appeals for the Third Circuit came to a different conclusion with respect to shrink-wrap licenses. In 1981, Step-Saver developed a program combining hardware and software to satisfy word processing and other purposes for use by physicians and attorneys based on the IBM personal computer system. It selected a program created by the defendant, The Software Link (TSL), as the operating system and terminals manufactured by the other defendant, Wyse, to accomplish its purposes. Having done so, the plaintiff received many complaints from customers and sued Wyse and TSL, seeking indemnity with respect to lawsuits instituted against Step-Saver by its customers. The plaintiff alleged breach of warranties by Wyse and TSL. The trial court dismissed the complaint against TSL, holding that the box-top license disclaimed all express and implied warranties. The court of appeals reversed the decision, holding in favor of Step-Saver.

The court noted that the box-top license states that the customer did not purchase the software but only a personal, nontransferable license to use the program; that all expressed and implied warranties were disclaimed; that the sole remedy was to return the defective disk for replacement and that all damages were disclaimed; that the license was the final and complete expression of the parties' agreement and that opening the package indicated an acceptance of those terms and conditions. If the user did not agree, the software could be returned within 15 days of purchase and all moneys would be returned.

With respect to the effect of the box-top license, the plaintiff alleged that it did not become a part of the contract because it was a material term and that the license was not intended to be a final and complete expression of the terms of the agreement. The court stated that UCC Section 2-207 was applicable. The section provides:

Additional Terms in Acceptance or Confirmation.

(1) A definite and seasonable expression of acceptance or a written confirmation which is sent within a reasonable time operates as an acceptance even though it contains terms additional or different from those offered or agreed upon, unless acceptance is expressly made conditional on assent to the additional or different terms.

(2) The additional terms are to be construed as proposals for addition to the contract. Between merchants such terms become part of the contract unless:
   (a) the offer expressly limits acceptance to the terms of the offer,
   (b) they materially alter it, or
   (c) notification of objection to them has already been given or is given within a reasonable time after notice of them is received.

(3) Conduct by both parties which recognizes the existence of a contract is sufficient to establish a contract for sale although the writings of the parties do not otherwise establish a contract. In such a case the terms of the particular contract consist of those terms on which the writings of the parties agree, together with any supplementary terms incorporated under any other provision of the Act.

The court stated that Section 2-207 attempts to distinguish between standard terms in a form confirmation that a party wishes the court to incorporate in the event of a dispute and the actual terms understood by the parties as governing the agreement. The burden is upon the party asking the court to enforce its form to determine that a particular clause was part of the contract. In applying this test, the court said that the consent by opening provision did not make Step-Saver's acceptance conditional. When a person has gone through the effort of making a purchase, "the purchaser has made a decision to buy a particular product and has actually obtained the product, the purchaser may use it despite the refund offer, regardless of the additional terms specified after the contract formed" [at p. 34]. There was no evidence to show that TSL would have refused to sell if Step-Saver had not consented to the restrictive terms. The court thus held that the box-top license did not contain the complete and final expression of the terms of the parties' agreement.

The difference in the two decisions may lie in the refusal of both courts to become parties to actions by a defendant to evade responsibility for errant actions. In the *ProCD* case, the defendant converted the effort of the plaintiff in amassing data that required the expenditure of millions of dollars and significant time to integrate telephone listings from many hundreds of sources. In the *Step-Saver* case, the defendant sought to prevent liability accruing to it for defective performances as to leave the plaintiff in the position of bearing the loss for its unsatisfactory performance. It would appear, however, that shrink-wrap licenses would be enforceable provided that they are not unreasonable, particularly in consumer transactions.

The Gateway 2000 Cases. In *Hill v. Gateway 2000,* 105 F.3d 1147 (7th Cir. 1997), the action concerns a typical consumer who purchases a computer by telephone and uses a credit card for the purchase. The customer then receives the box containing the purchase, with terms stating that they will govern the transaction unless the box is returned within 30 days. The customer almost never reads the terms. One such term is an arbitration clause that was not prominently set forth but was one of many paragraphs in the terms of the agreement.

The court referred to Section 2 of the Federal Arbitration Act, that makes no provision that an arbitration term had to be prominently set forth in an agreement. The court said, "an agreement to arbitrate must be enforced 'save upon such grounds as exist at law or in equity for the revocation of any contract.' . . . A contract need not be read to be effective; people who accept take the risk that the unread terms may in retrospect prove unwelcome. . . . Terms in Gateway's box stand or fall together. If they constitute the parties' contract because the Hills had an opportunity to return the computer after reading them, then all must be enforced." The court refused to modify the holding in the *ProCD* case, repeating the statements that such terms are common in many agreements, such as air transportation and the like. The court further indicated that the result in *ProCD* was not limited to merchants but also applied to consumers. It was not relevant that the terms and conditions in the Gateway box did not make reference of such terms on the outside box. The court also determined that claims under the Racketeer Influenced and Corrupt Organizations Act (RICO) may be determined by arbitration.

In *Brower v. Gateway 2000,* 676 N.Y.S. 2d 569 (1998), a New York appeals court was also called upon to determine the validity of the Standard Terms and Conditions Agreement contained in the Gateway 2000 computer box purchased by the plaintiffs. In slightly larger print than the remaining terms, one of the terms, entitled Dispute Resolution, stated: "Any dispute or controversy arising out of or relating to this Agreement or its interpretation shall be settled exclusively and finally by arbitration. The arbitration shall be conducted in accordance with the Rules of Conciliation and Arbitration of the International Chamber of Commerce. The arbitration shall be conducted in Chicago, Illinois, U.S.A. before a sole arbitrator. Any award rendered in any such arbitration proceeding shall be final and binding on each of the parties, and judgment may be entered thereon in a court of competent jurisdiction."

Brower sued alleging deceptive sales, breach of warranty, breach of contract, fraud, and unfair trade practices. The basis for the claim is Gateway's promise of around-the-clock free technical support, free software, and other related promises. Plaintiffs claimed that it was almost impossible to connect to such technician as allegedly promised. Gateway moved to dismiss the case and to enforce the arbitration clause. Plaintiffs claimed that the contract was one of adhesion and that the said clause was unconscionable under UCC 2-302 for the reason that it was almost impossible to contact the arbitration tribunal; that the cost of such arbitration was prohibitive requiring application fees of $4,000 of which $2,000 was not refundable even if the plaintiff prevailed; that the travel costs were high relative to the amount at issue, to wit, about $1,000; that the loser would have to bear the legal expenses of the victorious party; and all correspondence had to be sent to the International Chamber of Commerce (ICC) headquarters in France.

The New York Appellate Division cited the *Hill v. Gateway 2000* and *ProCD* cases and, though stating they did not constitute precedents, agreed with the rationale of the decisions. "[T]here is no agreement or contract upon the placement of the order or even upon the receipt of the goods. By the terms of the Agreement at issue, it is only after the consumer has affirmatively retained the merchandise for more than 30 days—within which the consumer has presumably examined and even used the product(s) and read the agreement—that the contract has been effectuated." The court rejected the claim of contract unenforceability as a contract of adhesion, which means that the consumer had no choice or negotiation but was in a take-it-or-leave-it position with unequal bargaining power. The court said that the customer had the right to return the merchandise within 30 days and purchase similar merchandise from a competitor, of which there were many.

The clause was not unconscionable inasmuch as it was not stated in fine print or hidden and tucked away; the purchasers were not subject to high-pressure sales; and the purchasers had 30 days to read and decide whether to accept the merchandise. Nevertheless, the court did agree that the cost of arbitration was excessive under the circumstances and ordered that the parties have leave to seek appointment under 9 U.S.C. Section 9 (the Federal Arbitration Act). The court cited yet another Gateway 2000 action (*Filias v. Gateway 2000* (No. 97C 2523, ND Ill, Jan. 15, 1998), wherein the federal district court appointed the American Arbitration Association (AAA) to conduct the arbitration. Due to the nonrefundable cost to the AAA of $500, the New York court said it would designate an arbitrator upon application of either party if one is not otherwise designated.

In the following more recent Gateway case, the U.S. district court in Kansas had the benefit not only of the prior cited cases for reference but also of the commentaries of legal scholars.

KLOCEK V. GATEWAY, INC.

104 F. Supp. 2d 1332 (D.Kan. 2000)

FACTS: Klocek sued Gateway and Hewlett-Packard concerning the purchase of a H-P scanner. Gateway was sued for allegedly inducing him and other consumers to purchase computers and support packages by making false promises of technical support, as well as for breach of contract and warranties. As in the other cited cases, Gateway claims that the plaintiff must arbitrate his claims under Gateway's Standard Terms and Conditions Agreement located in the box containing the computer power cables and instruction manuals. At the top of the first page, the Standard Terms include the following notice:

NOTE TO THE CUSTOMER:

This document contains Gateway 2000's Standard Terms and Conditions. By keeping your Gateway 2000 computer system beyond five (5) days after the date of delivery, you accept these Terms and Conditions.

The notice was inside the printed box, in larger print than the other printed materials and was set apart from other provisions of the document. The Standard Terms are four pages in length, paragraph 10 of which contained the following arbitration clause:

DISPUTE RESOLUTION. Any dispute or controversy arising out of or relating to this Agreement or its interpretation shall be settled exclusively and finally by arbitration. The arbitration shall be conducted in accordance with the Rules of Conciliation and Arbitration of the International Chamber of Commerce. The arbitration shall be conducted in Chicago, Illinois, U.S.A. before a sole arbitrator. Any award rendered in any such arbitration proceeding shall be final and binding on each of the parties, and judgment may be entered thereon in a court of competent jurisdiction.

Gateway alleges that after the sale of the computer, it mailed to all customers in the U.S. a copy of its quarterly magazine with a notice of change permitting customers the option of choosing either the International Chamber of Commerce, the American Arbitration Association, or the National Arbitration Forum in Chicago, Illinois for the site of arbitration [presumably due to the *Hill* decision]. Gateway requested the Court to dismiss the case under the Federal Arbitration Act, 9 U.S.C. Section 1 that provides

If any suit or proceeding be brought in any of the courts of the United States upon any issue referable to arbitration under an agreement in writing for such arbitration, the court in which such suit is pending, upon being satisfied that the issue involved in such suit or proceeding is referable to arbitration under such agreement, shall on application of one of the parties stay the trial of the action until such arbitration has been had in accordance with the terms of the agreement, providing the applicant for the stay is not in default in proceeding with such arbitration.

ISSUE: Whether the contract of sale between Gateway and the plaintiff included the Standard Terms as part of the agreement?

DECISION: The Court denied Gateway's motion to dismiss the action holding that the Standard Terms were not part of the agreement.

REASONING: Judge Vratil

The Uniform Commercial Code ("UCC") governs the parties' transaction under both Kansas and Missouri law . . . [2-102] (UCC applies to "transactions in goods."); Kansas Comment 1 (main thrust of Article 2 is limited to sales) . . . ("'Goods' means all things . . . which are movable at the time of identification to the contract of sale . . . "). Regardless whether plaintiff purchased the computer in person or placed an order and received shipment of the computer, the parties agree that plaintiff paid for and received a computer from Gateway. This conduct clearly demonstrates a contract for the sale of a computer. . . .

State courts in Kansas and Missouri apparently have not decided whether terms received with a product become part of the parties' agreement. Authority from other courts is split. [The court cited the *Step-Saver, ProCD, Hill,* and other cases.] . . .

Gateway urges the Court to follow the Seventh Circuit decision in *Hill.* That case involved the shipment of a Gateway computer with terms similar to the Standard Terms in this case, except that Gateway gave the customer 30 days—instead of 5 days—to return the computer. In enforcing the arbitration clause, the Seventh Circuit relied on its decision in *ProCD,* where it enforced a software license which was contained inside a product box. . . . In *ProCD,* the Seventh Circuit noted that the exchange of money frequently precedes the communication of detailed terms in a commercial transaction. . . . Citing UCC Section 2-204, the court reasoned that by including the license with the software, the vendor proposed a contract that the buyer could accept by using the software after having an opportunity to read the license. . . . Specifically, the court stated:

A vendor, as master of the offer, may invite acceptance by conduct, and may propose limitations on the kind of conduct that constitutes. A buyer may accept by performing the acts the vendor proposes to treat as acceptance.

. . . The *Hill* court followed the *ProCD* analysis, noting that "practical considerations support allowing vendors to enclose the full legal terms with their products." . . .

[In its footnote, the court noted:] Legal commentators have criticized the reasoning of the Seventh Circuit in this regard . . . (outcome in Gateway is questionable on federal statutory, common law and constitutional grounds as a matter of contract law and is unwise as a matter of policy because it unreasonably shifts to consumers search costs of ascertaining existence of arbitration clause and return cost to avoid such clause). . . .

(1) The Court is not persuaded that Kansas or Missouri courts would follow the Seventh Circuit reasoning in *Hill* and *ProCD.* In each case the Seventh Circuit concluded without support that UCC Section 2-207 was irrelevant because the cases involved only one written form. . . . This conclusion is not supported by the statute or by Kansas or Missouri law. Disputes under Section 2-207 often arise in the context of a "battle of forms," . . . but nothing in its language precludes application in a case which involves only one form [see the Section 2-207 recited previously].

. . . By its terms, Section 2-207 applies to an acceptance or written confirmation. It states nothing which requires another form before the provision becomes effective. In fact, the official comment to the section specifically provides that Sections 207(1) and (2) apply "where an agreement has been reached orally . . . and is followed by one or both of the parties sending formal memoranda embodying the terms so far agreed and adding terms not discussed. . . . Thus, the Court concludes that Kansas and Missouri courts would apply Section 2-207 to the facts in this case. . . .

In addition, the Seventh Circuit provided no explanation for its conclusion that "the vendor is the master of the offer." . . . In typical transactions, the purchaser is the offeror, and the vendor is the offeree. . . . While it is possible for the vendor to be the offeror, . . . Gateway provides no factual evidence which would support such a finding in this case. The Court therefore assumes for purposes of the motion to dismiss that plaintiff offered to purchase the computer (either in person or through catalog order) and that Gateway accepted plaintiff's offer (either by completing the sales transaction in person or by agreeing to ship and/or shipping the computer to plaintiff). . . .

Under Section 2-207, the Standard Terms constitute either an expression of acceptance or written confirmation. As an expression of acceptance, the Standard Terms would constitute a counter-offer only if Gateway expressly made its acceptance conditional on plaintiff's assent to the additional or different terms. . . ." The conditional nature of the acceptance must be clearly expressed in a manner sufficient to notify the offeror that the offeree is unwilling to proceed with the transaction unless the additional or different terms are included in the contract." . . . Gateway provides no evidence that at the time of the sales transaction, it informed plaintiff that the transaction was conditioned on plaintiff's acceptance of the Standard Terms. Moreover, the mere fact that Gateway shipped the goods with the terms attached did not communicate to plaintiff any willingness to proceed without plaintiff's agreement to the Standard Terms. . . .

Because plaintiff is not a merchant, additional or different terms contained in the Standard Terms did not become part of the parties' agreement unless plaintiff expressly agreed to them. . . . Gateway argues that plaintiff demonstrated acceptance of the arbitration provision by keeping the computer more than five days after the date of delivery. Although the Standard Terms purport to work that result, Gateway has not presented any evidence that plaintiff expressly agreed to those Standard Terms. Gateway states only that it enclosed the Standard Terms inside the computer box for plaintiff to read afterwards. It provides no evidence that it informed plaintiff of the five-day review-and-return period as a condition of the sales transaction, or that the parties contemplated additional terms to the agreement. . . . The Court finds that the act of keeping the computer past five days was not sufficient to demonstrate that plaintiff expressly agreed to the Standard Terms. . . . Thus, because Gateway has not provided evidence sufficient to support a finding under Kansas or Missouri law that plaintiff agreed to the arbitration provision contained in Gateway's Standard Terms, the Court overrules Gateway's motion to dismiss.

CASE QUESTIONS

1. Compare *Klocek* with *ProCD.* With which result are you in agreement? Why?
2. If you agree with *Klocek,* would you then set aside all agreements wherein the customers had no opportunity to view them in advance? What about airline tickets and other such agreements?

UCITA does not apply to the facts of the within case because it is a sale of goods rather than a computer information transaction, which is defined as an agreement "to create, modify, transfer, or license computer information or informational rights in computer information" (Sections 102(11) and 103).

The reasoning in *Klocek* appears to be persuasive. The UCC, Article 2, has "good faith" dealing as a fundamental premise, which is defined as "honesty in fact in the conduct or transaction concerned" (UCC 2-201(19)). Gateway's position that a consumer purchasing its computer may institute dispute resolution only in Illinois before the International Chamber of Commerce (and, later, as a result of judicial decisions, the American Arbitration Association) for a purchase that may be under $1,000, without recovery of legal expenses, appears to be manifestly lacking in the good faith requirement. The consumer, who at least had 30 days to read and return a computer if he or she did not agree with the terms, now has only 5 days. Especially in holiday purchases or purchases for students about to travel to campuses in other states, consumers often do not open the box containing the computer until after the 5-day period. Gateway has offices throughout the country and can resolve disputes in the state where purchases are made. It is in a far better position to absorb such legal and other expenses as a result of its transactions than consumers in distant states.

Click-Wrap Agreements

Click-wrap agreements are similar to shrink-wrap licenses. When setting up a new computer or when installing a new program, the user generally is faced with an agreement to which the user is given the choice of agreeing or not agreeing with the contents. The program will not open unless consent by clicking on the box containing the words "I agree" or similar wording to the terms on the agreement is given. The question again is whether such agreements are valid and enforceable against the user.

In *Crispi v. The Microsoft Network, L.L.C.*, 323 N.J. Super. 118 (N.J. App. Div. 1999), the New Jersey appellate court upheld the trial court's determination that such consent by a user becomes a binding contract. The court also upheld the forum selection clause contained in the agreement that compels all lawsuits arising out of the contract to take place in Kings County, in the state of Washington. Thus, the result of the case is that a person purchasing and using Microsoft programs may have to travel to the state of Washington to sue or defend a lawsuit for an alleged breach of an agreement, consent to which agreement becomes known only after the person opens the program.

A similar result took place in *Geoff v. America Online, Inc.*, No. C.A. No. PC 97-0331, 1998 (R.I. Super. Ct. 1998) wherein the court upheld an agreement wherein a subscriber to America Online's Internet service had to consent to the posted agreement before the service could be accessed. The court said that a person who signs an agreement by clicking onto the "I agree" button cannot later complain that the agreement was not read or understood. Also, like the *Microsoft* case, the court upheld the validity of the forum selection clause requiring all litigation take place in Virginia.

CONCLUSION

The world of technology is transforming the marketplace so as to make global purchases as easy as going to a nearby shopping mall. To enable buyers and sellers of goods using the ever-improving electronic marketing technology to engage in global purchases, the rules of the game have to keep pace. Contracts over the Internet are but one area of law that has to be greatly modified. Because the technology is changing at such a rapid rate, legal protections must be rapidly updated to keep current with the technology. Congressional enactments in diverse areas concerning the Internet have taken place as to intellectual property rights, cybercrime, and the like. Similar developments in cybercontracts are now taking shape at both the federal and state levels. The future is here. Legal enactments generally take years to formulate. Such delay can no longer be tolerated. Technological advances are occurring so rapidly as to compel governmental authorities to address issues on an almost daily basis.

The efforts to create uniform laws are major steps toward achieving free and open access to cyberspace as well as the recognition that written agreements sent through the mail are becoming as obsolete as the use of checks for supermarket purchases. Whether states will adopt UETA, UCITA, amendment to definitions in the UCC, added articles to the UCC, or other statutory enactments will be left to the states to decide. It is clear, however, that there is no choice concerning the recognition of electronic contracts and signatures.

Questions and Problems

1. Compare the common law of contracts with Article 2 of the Uniform Commercial Code.
2. What is a *signature* for purposes of fulfilling the requirements of the Statute of Frauds? How did the Electronic Signatures in Global and National Commerce Act affect the signature requirement?
3. Compare UCITA with the UCC.
4. Are the warranties under UCITA and the UCC, Article 2, comparable? Discuss.
5. Are shrink-wrap and click-wrap provisions valid? Explain.
6. Plaintiff, Dendrite International, is a major global supplier of products and services for the pharmaceutical industry and consumer products for purchasers thereof. Two of the defendants, known as John Doe 3 and John Doe 4, posted alleged derogatory comments about plaintiff's products as well as allegedly posting trade secrets belonging to the company. The statements were posted on Yahoo!'s financial boards. The plaintiff sued the unknown defendants and requested that the New Jersey Chancery Court issue a subpoena to Yahoo! Inc. (not a party to the lawsuit) to compel it to reveal the identities of the two John Does. Yahoo! opposed plaintiff's request. Decide. *Dendrite International v. John Does,* Docket No. MRS C-129-00 (Sup. Ct. N.J. Chancery Div. Nov. 28, 2000).
7. Plaintiff is a manufacturer of colored art glass. It sued Schmid for damages for breach of contract, alleging the defendant failed to deliver goods consisting of a glass-rolling machine within the six-month period designated by the agreement. Defendant counterclaimed, alleging money was due and owing for work performed and that it did not violate the time of delivery clause. On January 15, 1962, defendant contracted with plaintiff to deliver a double rolling machine, and the contract contained a delivery clause that read: "Maximum approximately six (6) months after receipt by seller of accepted proposal and down payment." After defendant made the proposal but before plaintiff returned acceptance of the agreement, defendant wrote to the plaintiff, "We may make some minor changes. . . ." Plaintiff responded on January 15, 1962: "We are returning a signed contract with check in separate mail for $7000 to cover our down payment with the understanding that several changes may yet be made in our final design of the machine." When the machine arrived on September 29, 1962, many parts did not fit the machine sold. After a number of attempts to correct defects, the machine was finally made operable on January 2, 1963. Defendant claims that plaintiff's initial acceptance letter concerning the minor changes waived the delivery date. Decide. *Kokomo Opalescent Glass Co., Inc. v. Arthur W. Schmid Intn'l, Inc.,* 371 F.2d 208 (7th Cir. 1966).
8. Ingram Micro, Inc. is a wholesale distributor of microcomputer products. As a result of a power outage at its facility, its computers ceased working, thereby losing custom programming configurations in their random access memory and therefore were unable to function. The company made a claim against its insurer, alleging damage as a "direct physical loss or damage" arising from the eight hours of lack of functioning. The policy insured "[a]ll risks of direct physical loss or damage from any cause howsoever and wheresoever occurring. . . ." The insurance company refused to pay, claiming the loss was not covered under the policy inasmuch as the loss was not a physical loss. Decide. *American Guarantee & Liability Ins. Co. v. Ingram Micro, Inc.,* Civ. 99-185 TUC ACM (D. Ariz. April 19, 2000).
9. Apollo purchased software from Oracle that included a database system and Oracle Financials, an accounting software package. Apollo then attempted to purchase the computer system to run the software from Avnet. After representatives from the three companies discussed the needs and prospective purchases, Avnet, by letter dated May 11 to Apollo, submitted a price quote to Apollo that included a statement indicating it had reviewed all system requirements with the Apollo representative and that a particular named computer "will meet your requirements." Apollo didn't accept the May 11 proposal, which then expired a month later. A second proposal several days later

from Avnet to Apollo included a warranty disclaimer in capital letters that disclaimed all warranties of merchantability or fitness for a particular purpose and that stated any damages would be limited to the purchase price of the product. Apollo accepted Avnet's proposal thereafter. After installation, it was found that the computer system was insufficient to run the Apollo system. The representatives again met. Apollo sought to replace the machine with a more powerful computer and asked Avnet to accept return of the first computer or to exchange it for a more powerful system. Avnet refused. Apollo sued Avnet for misrepresentation, negligence, breach of warranty, and breach of contract. The district court dismissed the case. Your decision on appeal? *Apollo Group, Inc. v. Avnet, Inc.*, 58 F.3d 477 (9th Cir. 1995).

10. NMP is in the business of manufacturing and designing large mechanical switchboards for the U.S. Navy. It contracted with Parametric to enter into a licensing agreement whereby Parametric would license its Pro/E software to NMP. The license agreement was entered into on September 17, 1993. Prior to the agreement, Parametric had performed a demonstration showing that its software would be suitable for NMP's switchboards. Initially, the program worked well for NMP's smaller assemblies but was found to be defective concerning its larger assemblies. The problems were ascertained sometime in August–September 1995. When Parametric refused to reimburse NMP for the costs of the money spent for the Pro/E software, a lawsuit was commenced. The licensing agreement stated that any lawsuit had to be commenced within a year and that all warranties were valid for 30 days after installation. The agreement also disclaimed warranties of merchantability and fitness for a particular purpose. Does the licensing agreement constitute a "sale of goods" that would be governed by the UCC? Does the limitation of time and damages apply in this case so as to bar the plaintiff from relief? *NMP Corp. v. Parametric Technology Corp.*, 958 F. Supp. 1536 (N.D.Ok. 1997).

Endnotes

1. Report of the U.S. Secretary of Commerce, *Digital Economy 2000, www.esa.doc.gov//de2k2.htm.* See also, Kalama M. Lui-Kwan, *VI. Business Law: 1. Electronic Commerce: a) Digital Signatures: Recent Developments in Digital Signature Legislation and Electronic Commerce,* 14 Berkeley Tech. L.J. 463 (1999); and Forester Research on eMarketplaces, *www.businessnewsnow.com/storydetail.asp?.storyid=2629.*
2. A *merchant* is defined in Article 2, Section 2-104(1) as "a person who deals in goods of the kind or otherwise by his occupation holds himself out as having knowledge or skill peculiar to the practices or goods involved in the transaction or to whom such knowledge or skill may be attributed by his employment of an agent or broker or other intermediary who by his occupation holds himself out as having such knowledge or skill."
3. For a discussion of the Statute of Frauds, see any standard basic business law text such as Henry R. Cheeseman, *Business Law: Ethical, International, & E-commerce Legal Environment,* 4th ed. (Upper Saddle River, NJ: Prentice-Hall, 2001). The Statute of Frauds in New York can be found in *General Obligations Law, McKinney's Consolidated Laws of New York Annotated,* Book 23 A, Sec. 5-701. See also, the Uniform Commercial Code, Sec. 2-201 for the sale of goods provision of the Statute of Frauds.
4. See *McKinney's,* 5-701(a).
5. American Bar Association, *Digital Signature Guidelines Tutorial, www.abanet.org/scitech/ec/isc /dsg-tutorial.html.*
6. See E. Allan Farnsworth, *Contracts,* 2d ed. (Boston: Little, Brown, 1990), pp. 434–35, citing *Southwest Engr. Co. v. Martin Tractor Co.,* 205 Kan. 684, 473 P.2d 18 (1970), where the seller's trademark on sales brochures was a signature. In *Merrill, Lynch, Pierce, Fenner & Smith v. Cole,* 189 Conn. 518, 547 A.2d 656 (1983), a letterhead or billhead was sufficient for statutory requirements under UCC 2-210.
7. For an in-depth discussion of the Statute of Frauds and its applicability in today's world, see Shawn Pompian, *Is the Statute of Frauds Ready for Electronic Contracting?,* 85 Va. L. Rev. 1447 (Oct. 1999).
8. Such transmissions may be made in accordance with the Digital Signature Guidelines: Legal Infrastructure for Certification Authorities and Secure Electronic Commerce.
9. General Assembly Resolution 51/162 of December 16, 1996.
10. See, for example, *Advent System Ltd. v. Unisys Corp.,* 925 F.2d 670 (3d Cir. 1991) and *Chatlos Sys.,*

Inc. v. Nat'l Cash Register Corp., 635 F.2d 1081 (3d Cir. 1980).

11. See Bonna Lynn Horovitz, *Computer Software as a Good Under the Uniform Commercial Code: Taking a Byte Out of the Intangibility Myth,* 65 B.U.L.Rev. 129 (1985).
12. See *Computer Servicenters, Inc. v. Beacon Mfg. Co.,* 328 F. Supp. 653, 655 (D.S.C. 1970), discussed in Jennifer B. Cannata, *Time is Running Out for Customized Software: Resolving the Goods Versus Service Controversy for Year 2000 Contractual Disputes,* 21 Cardozo L. Rev. 283 (October 1999) at 285.
13. For a lengthy examination of Article 2B, see Jody Storm Gale, *Service Over the Internet: New Principles of Contract Law in Conflict,* 49 Case W. Res. 567 (Spring 1999).
14. To date, the states of Virginia (effective July 1, 2000) and Maryland (effective October 1, 2000) have adopted UCITA. A copy of the proposed act may be found at *www.law.upenn.edu/bil/ulc/ucita/ucita200.htm.*
15. A *support contract* is an agreement to correct performance problems in computer information other than an agreement to cure a defect amounting to a breach of contract.
16. The definitions are found in UCITA Section 102.
17. Id. Section 103.
18. Id. Section 104.
19. Id. Section 401.
20. Id. Section 402.
21. Id. Section 403.
22. Id. Section 404.
23. Id. Section 405.
24. Id. Section 406.
25. Id. Sections 407 and 409.
26. Id. Section 701.
27. Id. Section 702.
28. Id. Sections 703–704.
29. Id. Section 102(44).
30. Id. Sections 707–708.
31. Id. Section 808.
32. Id. Section 809.
33. Id. Sections 811–812.
34. For a visual illustration of the process, see Ron White, *How It Works: Digital Signatures,* PC Computing (March 2000), pp. 152–53.
35. For a detailed description of the process and the Guidelines, see Edward D. Kania, *The ABA's Digital Signature Guidelines: An Imperfect Solution to Digital Signatures on the Internet,* 7 CommLaw Conspectus 297, particularly pp. 301–2.
36. A number of states, such as Florida, Minnesota, Utah, and Washington, have adopted the Guidelines. There is a bill pending before Congress known as the Electronic Financial Services Efficiency Act of 1997, but there are a number of alleged flaws with the Guidelines that have caused the legislators to withhold a federally mandated statute. Such flaws include the possibility of fraud because it is the subscriber who creates the key pair and may attempt to act in bad faith by altering digitally signed documents after they have been transmitted. Id. p. 308.
37. The president's remarks can be found at *www.pub.whitehouse/uri-res/12R . . . :pdi://oma.eop .gov.us/2000/6/30/18.text.1.* It is also in accord with the principles set forth in "A Framework for Global Electronic Commerce." The principles as applied to contracts are:

    - parties should be free to order the contractual relationship between themselves as they see fit;
    - rules should be technology neutral (i.e., the rules should neither require nor assume a particular technology) and forward looking (i.e., the rules should not hinder the use or development of technologies in the future);
    - existing rules should be modified and new rules should be adopted only as necessary or substantially desirable to support the use of electronic technologies; and
    - the process should involve the high-tech commercial sector as well as businesses that have not yet moved online.

38. *Electronic Signatures in Global and National Commerce Act* Section 101(b)(1).
39. Id. Section 101(c)(d).
40. Id. Section 102(a)(b).
41. Id. Section 103.
42. Id. Section 201.
43. For a more detailed discussion of this issue, see David A. Einhorn, *Shrink-Wrap Licenses: The Debate Continues,* IDEA: The Journal of Law and Technology, 38 IDEA 383–401.
44. 86 F.3d 1447 (7th Cir. 1996).
45. 939 F.2d 91 (3d Cir. 1991).

CHAPTER

4 INTERNET CONTRACTS AND TORTS

Section 2: International Regulation and Tort Issues

Chapter Outline

Before turning our attention to tort aspects of Internet law, we will begin this chapter with a discussion of the international aspects of commerce. As we have stated, commerce is now global. The trend took place for the United States after World War II, and increased exponentially in the past several decades. The advent of the European Union, the opening of China in 1979, and the end of Soviet domination have all served to foster increased internationalization of commerce, even among smaller companies that were previously content to serve domestic consumers only. As trade among corporations in different nations expanded, the multiplicity of laws affecting sales became major impediments to trade. The United Nations, aware of the need for greater uniformity of laws among the nations in areas of mutual concern, proposed a variety of conventions for adoption by member states so as to facilitate the globalization of such commerce and, as a corollary, to increase the cooperation and harmony among the participating countries. A major effort in this regard is the Convention on Contracts for the International Sale of Goods (CISG). The convention has been adopted by some 55 nations, including virtually all of the major trading states.

THE UNITED NATIONS CONVENTION ON CONTRACTS FOR THE INTERNATIONAL SALE OF GOODS

The sale of goods across national borders has always been fraught with numerous pitfalls for the unwary trader. Conversion of currency, receipt of payments, language differentiation, and transportation are among the difficulties that a trader must confront. In addition, each nation's legal system encompasses its unique religious, cultural, and historical traditions. In an endeavor to assist traders in exchange of goods in the global marketplace, the U.N. Commission on International Trade Law prepared for adoption a proposed Convention on Contracts for the International Sale of Goods.[1] The United States ratified the convention on December 11, 1986, thus making it a part of its federal statutes.

Application

The convention applies to the sale of goods between businesses in *different* countries that have adopted CISG or where private international laws permit the application of the convention. It is possible for the operation of the convention to apply to a dispute between two domestic corporations where one or both have places of business outside of the United States and the sale of goods (not services) is to its foreign place of business. The convention applies to a sale of *goods* that are not consumer in nature or are goods sold by auction, or consist of securities, or are for the sale of marine vessels or aircraft, or involve electricity (Article 2(1)). *Services* are specifically omitted. The UCC Article 2, which governs transactions between U.S. persons, differs by extending its scope to *transactions* in goods and includes all types of goods, both consumer and farm goods, and transactions between merchants (UCC Section 2-105(1)). Thus, some courts, by analogy, have extended the application of the UCC to services and also to realty. Under the UCC, a *sale* is defined as the transfer of title to goods for a price. The convention appears to concur (compare UCC 2-106(1) with CISG Articles 30 and 53).

The convention reaffirms the freedom of contract between the parties thereto by permitting them to exclude the application of the convention in whole or in part (Article 6). The convention is made applicable to the formation of the contract and to the rights and obligations of the parties flowing therefrom (Article 4). It is not concerned with the contact's validity or any provision thereof or the effect the contract may have on the property (title) of the goods sold. It does not apply in cases involving death or personal injury caused by the goods (Article 5). The UCC has no such exclusions. Countertrade (barter-type transactions), gifts, bailments, leases, and consignment appear to be excluded from both the convention and the UCC.

Like the UCC, the convention states that the parties are bound by any usages or practices to which they have agreed or established (compare UCC Section 1-205). Unlike the UCC, there is no Statute of Frauds. A contract of sale may be proven by any means, including the use of witnesses. Any country requiring a writing, however, may specifically provide for it.

Formation of the Contract

The convention states that a proposal is an *offer* if it is addressed to another party and is "sufficiently" definite, indicating an intention by the offeror to be bound. By *definite* it means that the goods being offered are stated and the quantity and price are explicitly or implicitly fixed (Article 14(1)). Any other proposal is merely an invitation to make an offer. It thus appears that an advertisement or similar communication would not satisfy this criteria, unlike the warranty provisions of the UCC. Recall that the convention excludes sales to consumers. Presumably, businesspersons are more sophisticated than consumers in this regard.

There are also differences in the manner in which irrevocable offers are treated. Under the UCC, a written offer signed by a merchant is a firm offer for a period up to three months when its terms indicate assurance that it will be held open. The convention defines an irrevocable offer more expansively as one which indicates that it is so by stating a fixed time for acceptance or it is reasonable for an offeree to believe it was irrevocable and acted accordingly (compare UCC Article 2-205 with the Convention Article 16). The convention does not state a time limit for an offer to remain open other than it must be reasonable, nor must it be in writing signed by the offeror. The merchant, therefore, should be very careful in specifying whether an offer is or is not irrevocable or else be subject to a possible implication that it is irrevocable.

The convention states that an acceptance is a statement or conduct by an offeror indicating assent. It is effective when *received* by the offeree. An acceptance may be withdrawn if the withdrawal is received by the offeror prior to or at the same time as the acceptance (Article 22). An offer, even if signified as "irrevocable," may be revoked by the offeror if the revocation is received by the offeree prior to or at the same time as the offer (Article 15). The convention permits late acceptance if the offeror so informs the offeree (Article 21(1)).

Obligations of the Parties

The convention sets forth the respective obligations of the seller and the buyer, after stating a number of general provisions.

Seller's Duties. The essence of a seller's obligation is to "deliver the goods, hand over any documents relating to them and transfer the property (title) in the goods 'as per contract.'" The UCC, or a country's basic law, determines when and whether title passes; whether a security interest has been created; whether necessity for a certificate of title exists; or whether a contract has been invalidated as, for example, for undue influence, fraud, or duress.

Delivery. A seller's obligation to deliver goods is similar to the UCC. If the contract does not specify delivery, the seller is required to deliver the goods to the carrier if carriage of goods is specified; otherwise, delivery is at the seller's place of business. If the parties were aware that the goods were to be produced from a specified stock or manufactured at a specified place, then delivery is to take place at that location (Article 31). The convention, like the UCC, seeks to maintain the integrity of the contract even though certain essential terms are missing (Articles 31–34; compare with UCC Sections 2-305 to 2-310).

With respect to goods that are shipped but are not clearly identified to the contract by markings or by documentation, the seller must give notice to the buyer of the consignment of the specific goods that are being sent to it so that the buyer can retrieve them. A seller, who is bound to arrange for the transportation of goods, must use appropriate means for their shipment. If insurance is not provided for, the seller, at the buyer's request, must provide all information necessary so as to enable the buyer to procure such insurance if it deems it suitable (Article 32). The convention implicitly adopts the terms and obligations accruing therefrom with respect to terms such as "F.O.B." (free on board), "F.A.S." (free alongside), and "C.I.F." (costs, insurance, and freight). Delivery is to take place at the date fixed by contract or within a reasonable time after the conclusion of the contract (Article 33).

Conformity of Goods. The seller is required under CISG to deliver goods containing the quantity, quality, and description specified in the contract and that are appropriately contained and packaged. The convention then summarizes and includes warranties of merchantability and fitness for a particular purpose, unless the buyer knew or should have known of the lack of conformity to the contract (Article 35). Thus, the goods must be fit for their ordinary purpose and use, be fit for the specific purpose if made known to the seller by the buyer, be like the model or sample if one is used, and be adequately packaged and contained. The seller is liable for any lack of conformity both at the time of delivery and for any guaranteed period thereafter (Article 36).The convention includes the implied warranties of title and against infringement of claims of industrial secrets and intellectual property (Articles 41–42). Excepted from the warranty are those situations where the seller infringed such intellectual property rights by having conformed with the "technical drawings, designs, formulae, or other specifications furnished by the buyer" (Article 42(2)(b)).

Remedies for Seller's Breach. One of the major changes brought about by the UCC was the extensive enhancement of remedies available to nondefaulting parties. The buyer has both prelitigation, as well as litigation, remedies. Among the prelawsuit remedies are: the right to reject a tender of nonconforming goods; revoke acceptance of the goods if they had a material defect; cover (purchase the goods elsewhere); recover goods upon seller's insolvency; and set off any damages from payments due and owing to the seller. In addition, the buyer is entitled to sue for damages consisting of the differences between the contract price and cover or market value, and for consequential damages and incidental damages, if any. The buyer cannot sue for specific performance unless the goods are unique or the buyer cannot cover in the exercise of reasonable efforts (UCC Section 2-716). The convention extends the latter right of a buyer by permitting it to require a seller's performance irrespective of whether the goods are unique (Article 46). The buyer may compel the seller to deliver substitute goods if there is a material breach of performance or to repair goods unless the remedy is unreasonable under the circumstances. Nevertheless, the convention permits individual countries to alter this right (Article 28).

Another variance from the UCC is the right of the buyer to fix an additional time period for the seller to perform. During such period, if the remedy is exercised, the buyer may not exercise any other remedy unless the seller notifies the buyer it will not perform. The buyer may later claim damages for any delay in seller's performance (Article 47). The seller is allowed to remedy its failure to perform if it can do so without unreasonable delay and without causing unreasonable inconvenience to the buyer (Article 48). This is analogous to the UCC's right to cure except that the seller may cure after the date of performance. If the seller inquires of the buyer whether the buyer will accept the cure of a failure to perform and the buyer does not respond, the seller may perform (Article 48).

A buyer may avoid a contract if there is a material breach or if the goods are not delivered by the seller during the extension of time to perform given by the buyer or seller or the seller states it will not perform (Article 49(1)). The UCC rule of *perfect tender* (a buyer may initially reject goods that have the slightest defect), applicable at time of delivery, is not followed (compare UCC Section 2-601 with the Convention Article 49(1)(a)). If nonconforming goods are accepted by a buyer, the convention permits the acceptance and reduces the price in direct proportion as the difference in value of the nonconformity unless the seller has cured its performance (Article 50). This is comparable to UCC Section 2-717, which permits a buyer on notification to a seller to deduct any damages to the extent of the latter's breach.

Obligations of the Buyer. Both the UCC and CISG require the buyer to take delivery and pay for the goods received (UCC Section 2-301; Convention Article 53). Upon receipt of the goods, the buyer must examine them as soon as practicable. The immediacy of the inspection may be deferred until delivery if a carrier is involved, particularly, if the goods have been rerouted in transit (Article 38).

Unless the buyer advises the seller of any lack of conformity to the contract within a reasonable time with some degree of specificity, the buyer may forfeit the right to reject the goods. The longest time a buyer may delay notification is two years from the date of delivery, unless the parties agree otherwise. The seller has no right to take advantage of the buyer's failure to notify if it knew or should have known of the lack of conformity (Article 51). The convention also allows the buyer to claim damages excluding loss of profit if it has a reasonable excuse for failure to give the required notice of nonconformity (Article 44). The convention thus differs from the UCC with its two-year notice provision and the denial of profits even if the buyer had a reasonable excuse for failure to notify seller of nonconformity. A defect that is not noticed, because of its hidden nature, until more than two years after purchase, will prevent the buyer from suing for loss of profits, even though the product may be warranted beyond the two-year time frame. The UCC would have permitted the buyer to recover such damages, provided the late notification was reasonable.

The convention is somewhat more liberal than the UCC with respect to delivery if only a portion of the goods is shipped or if only some of the goods are in conformity with the terms of the agreement. The buyer may not avoid the contract under such circumstances unless the failure to fully deliver conformed goods constitutes a fundamental breach of contract (Article 51). Moreover, if delivery is early, the buyer may reject the goods until the time of delivery has arrived. If a greater quantity of goods is delivered to the buyer, the excess quantity can either be rejected or paid for at the contract rate (Article 52).

The buyer's obligation to pay the price includes the obligation of taking all steps necessary to enable payment to be made. Presumably, it includes the obligation of complying with the requirements for the use of a letter of credit and complying with government regulations for the conversion and transfer of funds (Article 54). Like the UCC, the convention makes a provision for missing-price terms. It summarily provides that the price, in the absence of a fixed sum, is the price generally for such goods under comparable circumstances (Article 55; UCC Section

2-305). If the price is fixed by the weight of goods, the convention deems it to be based on net weight (Article 56). The price is to be paid, in the absence of agreement, at the seller's place of business or simultaneous with the transfer of goods or documents where such event takes place (Article 57). The convention allows a seller to insist upon payment prior to handing over the goods or documents. Nevertheless, the buyer need not pay the price until it has a reasonable opportunity of inspection. Of course, the parties may always agree upon some other course of dealing (Article 58).

The second major obligation of the buyer is to take delivery of the goods, which involves the performance of all acts reasonably necessary to enable the seller to make delivery. Presumably, it includes a place to accept delivery, obtaining appropriate licenses, payment of fees, and so on (Article 60).

Remedies for Buyer's Breach. The convention gives the seller remedies similar to those of the buyer in case of breach. The seller can force the buyer to pay the price, take delivery of the goods, or perform other contractual obligations. The seller may fix an additional period of time for the buyer to perform its obligations. Again, the seller, like the buyer in the reverse scenario, may not resort to other remedies unless the buyer advises it will not perform within the fixed time frame. The seller may make claim for damages incurred for delay of performance. The seller may avoid the contract if the buyer has substantially breached the agreement or has not performed within the additional time allotted. Payment of the price by the buyer will prevent the seller from avoiding the contract unless it was avoided prior to the late payment or the agreement was terminated within a reasonable time after the breach or after the additional time given for performance (Articles 61–64).

Damages. The UCC and CISG both emphasize the essential goal of contractual damages, namely, to make the nondefaulting party whole. Damages under the convention are equal to the loss sustained, including loss of profit, not to exceed the foreseeable sum at the time of concluding the contract (Article 74). A nondefaulting seller or buyer may receive the difference between the contract price and the resale or cover price. If resale or cover does not take place, then the damages are the difference between the contract price and the market price for the goods at the time of breach at the place where the goods or their reasonable substitute were to be delivered (Articles 75–76).

The convention recognizes the common law necessity of mitigation of damages. A party that fails to exercise such duty may find itself receiving substantially less damages. Interest on damages accrues on any damages received (Articles 77–78).

Miscellaneous Provisions

Anticipatory Breach. The UCC and the convention make specific provisions for anticipatory breach (UCC Section 2-610 and CISG Articles 71–72). The convention permits a party to suspend its obligations when it becomes evident that the other party will materially breach its duties because of inability to perform, diminution of credit worthiness, or conduct of performance. A seller has a right to exercise stoppage in transit even though the buyer has documents authorizing it to acquire the goods. The convention requires, however, that a party suspending performance before or after shipment of the goods give prompt notice to the other party with a pledge to continue performance upon receipt of adequate assurances (Article 71). The UCC is less explicit with respect to anticipatory breach. No notice is apparently required.

Exemptions. Traditionally, non–Anglo-Saxon courts have been much more liberal in recognizing excuses for nonperformance. U.S. courts do recognize the defense of impossibility of performance, but the defense is rarely allowed unless there was objective impossibility, to wit, no one similarly situated could have performed. Examples include the death or incapacity of a person required to give personal services, the destruction of the subject matter essential to performance, the contract's subsequent illegality, or commercial frustration. Other countries have traditionally recognized the concept of *force majeure,* which essentially connotes the idea that performance could not be accomplished as anticipated by the parties for reasons beyond their control. Circumstances such as fire, war, acts of God, strikes, and even labor slowdowns have been recognized.

The UCC apparently did attempt to liberalize the common-law interpretations by permitting excuse for nonperformance when performance is commercially impracticable due to events not anticipated in good faith at the time of contracting (UCC Section 2-615). The convention continued the civil-law approach by excusing performance if it can be proven that the failure was due to an impediment beyond the performer's control, which was not reasonably anticipated at the time of contract. It also applies to situations in which the failure to perform was due to a third party who experienced such difficulties. Notice to the other contracting party must be given within a reasonable time. Failure to perform caused by one's own act or omission is not excused (Articles 79–80).

Effects of Avoidance. If a contract is avoided, both parties are released, but the obligation to pay damages by a defaulting party nevertheless remains. Restitution is permitted to the party that performed in whole or in part, less any damages due for nonperformance. If a buyer seeks to avoid the contract, it may not do so unless it can return the goods to the seller in substantially the same condition as received. Exceptions allowed include the impossibility of restoration not due to the buyer's act or omission, as when the goods are perishable or deteriorated or the goods had been resold before discovery of their nonconformity (Articles 81–82). In any event, the buyer still retains all other remedies previously discussed. If a seller is obliged to return the price, it must do so with interest. A buyer returning the goods must account for all benefits derived from their use (Articles 83–84).

Preservation of Goods. A seller who retains possession of the goods sold because of a buyer's delay in taking delivery due to failure to pay the price due, must make a reasonable effort to preserve the goods. Reimbursement for reasonable expenses for their preservation is allowed. The buyer has a reciprocal duty for goods rightfully rejected, provided the buyer is not unreasonably inconvenienced or caused to incur unreasonable expense. Either party may warehouse the goods with a third person and cause the party at fault to pay reasonable expenses. If the party required to preserve the goods is caused to hold them for an unreasonably long period of time, then it may sell them upon notice to the other party. If the goods are perishable, the other party must take reasonable steps to sell them and give reasonable notice to the other party of such intent (Articles 85–88).

The stated provisions are quite comparable to the UCC. Unlike the convention, the UCC permits the buyer who sells goods on behalf of the seller to deduct all reasonable expenses plus a commission comparable to the customary rate or, if there is no set rate, then a sum not exceeding ten percent of the gross proceeds (UCC Section 2-603).

The adoption of CISG is part of a continuing process of unifying the laws applicable to world trade. The process is as necessary to world trade as the UCC has been to unifying commercial laws of the 50 United States. Disparate laws among several hundred countries pose significant barriers to the efficient transfer of goods and services among each other. The convention, when adopted by almost all states, will remove a major impediment to the flow of goods.

EUROPEAN UNION DIRECTIVE CONCERNING E-COMMERCE

The European Union has issued a proposed directive entitled "Proposal for a European Parliament and Council Directive on Certain Legal Aspects of Electronic Commerce in the Internal Market."[2] The difficulty addressed is the desire of merchants for cross-border commercial activities by use of the Internet and the inherent legal problems presented by such activity.[3] The E.U. is very cognizant of its failure to keep up with U.S. developments, noting that 80 percent of electronic commerce is U.S. generated while Europe is "trailing behind the dynamic performance of the United States."[4] Such activity involves a multiplicity of national laws, potential liability in several countries, taxation, inability of consumers to utilize e-commerce, and other matters. Like the United States, and more particularly the rest of the globe, there is a lack of substance clarity in the legal framework governing e-commerce. The aim of the E.U. "is to remove legal barriers which could impede the spread of electronic services across Europe" with consumer-protection measures.[5]

The directive concerns five areas of e-commerce. They are (1) establishment of providers of information society services; (2) commercial communications; (3) contracts; (4) liability of intermediaries; and (5) implementation. The first area concerns the country-of-origin of the Internet services providers. Article 3(1) of the proposed directive states that each member state is to ensure the service providers over the Internet are to comply with national provisions of the member state falling within the domain of the directive. The essence of the provision is that the member state's rules and regulations will apply wherein the service provider has the most or essential contacts. The problem arises that member states have differing laws concerning distance purchasing, so that some laws are relatively mild and least intrusive while others are more protective of consumer purchasers.[6] The proposed directive leaves open the need for cross-border networks so that consumers can have inexpensive protection against e-commerce vendors in other member states. In addition, the laws of the consumer's country may apply rather than those of the vendor's, although the wording of the directive appears to favor the country having the most contacts with the service provider.

The second issue is commercial communications (Article 6 of the proposed directive). In making an e-commerce offering, the service provider is to give, at a minimum, details of the service including the law applicable to the contract as provided for in another directive as well as offering a right of withdrawal.[7] Unsolicited advertising by e-mail must be so identified so that the recipient can opt out of the message. Privacy is partly assured by mandating that data received by service providers be fairly and accurately processed and that it be shared in a manner that would be minimally invasive of the recipient's privacy. In addition, the communication is to distinguish between editorial content and advertising.

With respect to electronic contracts, the directive (Article 9) requires member states to remove legal obstacles preventing the effective use of such contracts or that would deny validity or effect to such agreements. Exceptions include contracts requiring a notary, those needing government approval, and contracts associated with family law or wills and trusts.[8] Member states remain free to require encryption features in certain contracts and exclude certain contracts from the directive governing electronic signatures. In order for an electronic contract to have legal effect, the service provider must issue an acknowledgment of receipt.[9] The acceptance of the offer and the acknowledgment of receipt are considered legally received when the parties to the agreement are able to access them electronically.[10] The Economic and Social Committee cited the query of whether final consumers are aware of the need to examine their electronic terminals frequently for such documents.[11]

As to liability of intermediaries (Articles 12–15) of the proposed directive (service providers such as America Online (AOL) in the United States), they will not be held either strictly liable or for their negligence for transmissions provided that they do not commence the transmission, do not select the receiver of the transmission, or do not select or modify the contents of the transmission. The protection assumes that such providers are merely go-betweens who neither know nor have the reasonable capability of preventing the transmission.[12] They are akin to postal services that merely deliver the mail without knowing the contents in the communications. They are subject to court injunctions that must be obeyed when directed to them.

Service providers are also exempt from liability for automatic, intermediate, temporary storing of the information for later transmission to recipients. Such exemption is subject to similar provisos that they do not modify the information, comply with conditions of access to the information and rules of updating the information, do not interfere with the technology used to update the data, and act forthwith to remove the information when made known of its illegality or order compelling removal from a competent authority.[13]

With respect to dispute resolution, Article 17 of the proposed directive encourages the use of alternatives to overburdened court proceedings, which would include mediation, conciliation, and arbitration. As to distance contracts entered into by consumers, the European Union issued a directive, "On the Protection of Consumers in Respect of Distance Contracts." This directive prevents consumers from waiving rights conferred by the enactment of laws pursuant to the directive, and it further mandates: "Member States shall take the measures needed to ensure that the consumer does not lose the protection granted by this Directive by virtue of the choice of the law of a non-member country as the law applicable to the contract if the latter has close connection with the territory of one or more Member States."[14]

UNCITRAL MODEL LAW ON ELECTRONIC COMMERCE

The United Nations Commission on International Trade Law enacted the UNCITRAL Model Law on Electronic Commerce with Guide to Enactment in 1996, which discusses and attempts to resolve the issues discussed previously when applied in domestic and international trade.[15] Article 5 states: "Information shall not be denied legal effect, validity or enforceability solely on the grounds that it is in the form of a data message." If state law requires a writing, such law is complied with by a data message.[16] With respect to the requirement of a signature, it is complied with by use of a method identifying the person signifying approval of the information in the data message and by a showing that the method was reliable for the purpose intended.[17] The originality of the message is met by establishing that there was reasonable assurance concerning the integrity of the message. The program used by the parties will show if the message was altered in any manner.[18]

In a legal proceeding, the rules of evidence are not to deny the admissibility of a data message in evidence solely because it is a data message or that it is not in original form if it is the best evidence. The weight to be given to the data message is dependent on the manner in which the evidence was generated, stored, or communicated, the integrity of the message, the manner in which the originator of the message was identified, and other relevant factors.[19] An offer and the acceptance thereof may be expressed by data messages unless the agreement provides otherwise. Such agreement shall be enforceable as a contract.[20]

The originator of a message may request the acknowledgment of a data message. Unless the originator makes a particular form of the acknowledgment, such acknowledgment may be given by any means of communication by the addressee or by conduct sufficient to indicate the receipt of the message. If the receipt of acknowledgment is a condition of the data message, then no data message is deemed sent without such receipt of acknowledgment.[21] The time and place of sending and receipt of the message is determined by ascertaining if the addressee has designated an information system. If the addressee does so designate, then receipt occurs when the data message enters the said information system; or, if the designated information system is not used, then receipt occurs when the data message is retrieved by the addressee. If no information system is designated by the addressee, then receipt takes place when the data enters the addressee's information system.[22]

DEFINITION AND TYPES OF TORTS

For the remainder of this chapter, we will direct our discussion toward tort aspects of Internet law. A tort is wrongful conduct for which the law provides a remedy. All of us, in a sense, are bundles of rights and duties. We have a right to be free from harm due to the acts or omissions of others. We also have the legal duty to refrain from acting in a way that may cause injury to others. Statutes and case law define these rights and duties. There are three major divisions of tort law, namely, *intentional* torts, *negligent* torts, and *strict liability* torts. An intentional tort is a tort wherein a person, owing a duty to act or refrain from acting in a particular way, intentionally or with gross carelessness breaches a duty that the law imposes, causing injury to the person or property of another. Often, an intentional tort is the civil side of a criminal act. For example, hitting a person without just cause is a battery that may constitute a misdemeanor or a felony, depending on the extent of the injury. The state punishes the person criminally for breach of the peace. The victim may sue the perpetrator in a civil court to recover compensation for the injury. False arrest, defamation, and almost all forms of criminal behavior causing injury to a victim are examples of intentional torts.

A negligent tort occurs when a person breaches the legally imposed duty to act or refrain from acting, causing injury to another. It differs from an intentional tort because the act or omission involves carelessness (rather than commission with intent) in accordance with the standard of how a reasonable person would act under similar circumstances. Examples include when a driver of a motor vehicle exceeds the speed limit or does not pay attention to the act of driving, thereby causing an accident. Malpractice cases involve negligence in most instances.

A strict liability tort is conduct that is unrelated to intent or carelessness but that is punishable by law. Product-liability cases impose liability upon a manufacturer of a product that is defective and causes injury to the consumer or user. It is not necessary to prove that the manufacturer was careless in its conduct; rather, a showing of a defect in the manufacture or design of a product, or the failure to post warnings of danger with respect to the product may give rise to liability.

In most cases involving the Internet, the conduct sued upon concerns deliberate acts by the person being sued. Examples of Internet torts include breach of intellectual property rights and other unlawful activity such as wrongful conversion, theft, and trespass. Tort issues concerned with intellectual property rights are discussed in Chapters 6 through 9 hereafter. Another example of an intentional tort is that of *spam*.

SPAM

All users of the Internet are aware of the inundation of Web sites with unsolicited commercial bulk e-mail that is similar to junk mail received in the regular mail. By virtue of *cookies,* many of the advertisements are directed by commercial sites to identifiable potential customers. That marketers are able to ascertain and direct advertisements raises a number of issues that permeate many areas of the Internet. The problem of advertising and the invasion of privacy are discussed in Chapter 10. In this chapter, we will review some of the pertinent issues and court opinions concerning the use of spam.

Spam and the First Amendment

Does a private person have the right under the U.S. Constitution to use the facilities of a private Internet service provider to send unsolicited commercial messages to users of the service? In the following well-cited case, the court discusses First Amendment application to the attempts of a company to utilize such service without consent of the service provider.

CYBER PROMOTIONS INC. V. AMERICA ONLINE INC.

948 F. Supp. 436 (E.D.Pa. 1996)

FACTS: Cyber is an advertising agency incorporated in the same year as the lawsuit. It provides advertising services for companies and other persons wishing to use e-mails to potential customers. It sends millions of e-mail messages utilizing a number of Internet service providers (ISPs), including AOL, without paying for the use of the services. In January 1996, AOL advised Cyber of its unhappiness with Cyber's dissemination and, subsequently, sent a number of "e-mail bombs" to Cyber's ISPs to disable the ISPs. Cyber sued AOL because other ISPs no longer wished to serve Cyber's advertising efforts. It claimed that AOL had violated the Computer Fraud and Abuse Act, intentional interfered with its contractual relations, and other grounds. AOL countersued alleging service and trade name infringement and dilution and other claims.
ISSUE: Whether a private company (Cyber) has the right under the First Amendment of the U.S. Constitution to send unsolicited e-mail advertisements to subscribers of an Internet service provider, such as America Online, without interference by the provider?
DECISION: The Court held that Cyber did not have such First Amendment privilege.
REASONING: Judge Weiner
The First Amendment to the United States Constitution states that "Congress shall make no law respecting an establishment of religion, or prohibiting the free exercise thereof; or abridging the freedom of speech, or of the press." The United States Supreme Court has recognized that "the constitutional guarantee of free speech is a guarantee only against abridgment by government federal or state. . . . Only recently, the Supreme Court has stated that "the guarantees of free speech . . . guard only against encroachment by the government and 'erec[t] no shield against merely private conduct.'"

[T]he parties have stipulated that AOL is a private online company that is not owned in whole or in part by the government. . . . The parties have further stipulated that "AOL is not a government entity or political subdivision." . . . They have also stipulated that there has been no government involvement in AOL's business decision to institute or reinstitute a block directed to Internet e-mail sent by Cyber to AOL members or subscribers . . .

Despite these stipulations, Cyber argues that AOL's conduct has the character of state action. As a general matter, private action can only be considered state action when "there is a sufficiently close nexus between the State and the challenged action of [the private entity] so that the action of the latter may be fairly treated as that of the State itself." . . . [T]he

Supreme Court appears to utilize three distinct tests in determining whether there has been state action. . . . First, we must consider whether "the private entity has exercised powers that are traditionally the *exclusive* prerogative of the state." . . . This test is known as the exclusive public function test. If the private entity does not exercise such powers, we must consider whether "the private entity has acted with the help of or in concert with state officials." . . . The final test is whether "[t]he State has so far insinuated itself into a position of interdependence with . . . [the acting party] that it must be recognized as a joint participant in the challenged activity."

With regard to the first test, AOL exercises absolutely no powers which are in any way the prerogative, let alone the *exclusive* prerogative, of the State. . . . [T]he Court previously found that no single entity, including the State, administers the Internet. . . . Rather, the Court found that the Internet is a "global Web of linked networks and computers" which exist and functions as the result of the desire of hundreds of thousands of computer operators and networks to use common data transfer data protocol to exchange communications and information. . . .

By providing its members with access to the Internet through its e-mail system so that its members can exchange information with those members of the public who are also connected to the Internet, AOL is not exercising *any* of the municipal powers or public services traditionally exercised by the State. . . . Although AOL has technically opened its e-mail system to the public by connecting with the Internet, AOL has not opened its property to the public by performing any municipal power or essential public service and, therefore, does not stand in the shoes of the State. . . .

Having found that AOL is not a state actor under the exclusive public function test, we evaluate whether AOL is a state actor under the remaining two tests. . . . [The court then stated it found no state action by AOL's activities in its efforts to seek injunctive relief or damages.]

CASE QUESTIONS

1. Should the Internet be available to all persons, both commercial and private persons?
2. Do commercial establishments and individuals have the same constitutional rights of free speech? Is there a difference between advertising commercial messages having a social message, such as environmental issues, and the garden variety of pure commercialism, such as selling pots and pans or detergents?
3. Should Internet service providers be the sole arbiters of what messages may not be sent through their servers?

In *Hotmail Corp. v. Van$ Money Pie,* No. C-98-20064, 1998 U.S. Dist. LEXIS 10720 (N.D.Ca. 1998), the court enjoined defendants from using the plaintiff's e-mail on the World Wide Web that it provides free to millions of registered subscribers. The defendants sent spam e-mails to thousands of subscribers that contained false return addresses bearing Hotmail's account return addresses. The messages advertised get-rich-quick schemes, pornography, and other advertisements. Hotmail was swamped with hundreds of thousands misdirected responses to defendants' spam, thereby bringing about numerous complaints from subscribers, and significant increased costs to the company to handle the complaints.

The court found that there was a likelihood of success that the plaintiff would prevail in its claim of trademark dilution, violation of the Computer Fraud and Abuse Act, breach of contract due to defendants' failure to comply with Hotmail's Terms of Service to customers, fraud and misrepresentation, and trespass (intentional interference with the possession of personal property causing injury).

In *127623 Ontario Inc. v. Nexx Online Inc.* (No. C20546/99 Ontario Superior Court of Justice 1999), the court ruled in favor of the defendant ISP that deactivated plaintiff's Web site due to plaintiff's sending of unsolicited e-mails advertising its business and Web site. The court said the plaintiff violated the so-called Netiquette that the plaintiff agreed to abide with in accessing the defendant's service.

Spam and Trespass

In *Hotmail,* the court found a likelihood that the defendant committed trespass upon the plaintiff's site. In the following case, the issue of trespass was prominently discussed in connection with defendant's spamming activities using plaintiff's online computer services.

COMPUSERVE INC. V. CYBER PROMOTIONS

972 F. Supp. 1015 (S.D.Oh. 1997)

FACTS: CompuServe is a major online computer service provider. It operates a computer communication service and allows access to extensive content material within its proprietary network and linkages to other Internet resources. Defendant Cyber wanted to send unsolicited email advertisements to hundreds of thousands of Internet users, many of whom were CompuServe customers. When CompuServe advised defendants of the prohibition to use its service, defendants continued to do so.

ISSUE: Whether an online computer service company has the right to prevent a commercial enterprise from sending unsolicited electronic mail advertising to its subscribers?

DECISION: The Court held in favor of CompuServe enjoining the defendant and its president from sending the unsolicited advertisements to electronic mailing addresses maintained by CompuServe.

REASONING: Judge Graham

CompuServe predicates . . . its motion for a preliminary injunction on the common law theory of trespass to personal property or to chattels, asserting that defendants' continued transmission of electronic messages to its computer equipment constitutes an actionable tort.

Trespass to chattels has evolved from its common law application, concerning primarily the asportation of another's tangible property, to include the unauthorized use of personal property.

Its chief importance now, is that there may be recovery . . . for interferences with the possession of chattels which are not sufficiently important to be classified as conversion, and so to compel the defendant to pay the full value of the thing with which he has interfered. Trespass to chattels survives today, in other words, largely as a little brother of conversion.

[I]n order to constitute a conversion, it was not necessary that there should have been an actual appropriation of the property by the defendant to its own use and benefit. It might arise from the exercise of dominion over it in exclusion of the rights of the owner, or withholding it from his possession under a claim inconsistent with his rights. If one takes the property of another, for a temporary purpose only, in disregard of the owner's right, it is a conversion. Either a wrongful taking, an assumption of ownership, an illegal use or misuse, or a wrongful detention of chattels will constitute a conversion. . . .

The Restatement Section 217(b) states that a trespass to chattel may be committed by intentionally using or intermeddling with the chattel in possession of another. Restatement Section 217, Comment e defines physical "intermeddling" as follows:

> intentionally bringing about a physical contact with the chattel. The actor may commit a trespass by an act which brings him into an intended physical contact with a chattel in the possession of another.

Electronic signals generated and sent by a computer have been held to be sufficiently physically tangible to support a trespass cause of action. . . . It is undisputed that plaintiff has a possessory interest in its computer systems. Further, defendants' contact with plaintiff's computers is clearly intentional. Although electronic messages may travel through the Internet over various routes, the messages are affirmatively directed to their destination.

. . . [T]he Restatement (Second) of Torts Section 218 defines the circumstances under which a trespass to chattels may be actionable:

> One who commits a trespass to a chattel is subject to liability to the possessor of the chattel if, but only if,
> (a) he dispossesses the other of the chattel, or
> (b) the chattel is impaired as to its condition, quality, or value, or
> (c) the possessor is deprived of the use of the chattel for a substantial time, or
> (d) bodily harm is caused to the possessor, or harm is caused to some person or thing in which the possessor has a legally protected interest. . . .

A plaintiff can sustain an action for trespass to chattels, as opposed to an action for conversion, without showing a substantial interference with its right to possession of that chattel. . . . Harm to the personal property or diminution of its quality, condition, or value as a result of defendants' use can also be the predicate for liability. Restatement Section 218(b).

An unprivileged use or other intermeddling with a chattel which results in actual impairment of its physical condition, quality, or value to the possessor makes the actor liable for the loss thus caused. In the great majority of cases, the actor's intermeddling with the chattel impairs the value of it to the possessor, as distinguished from the mere affront to his dignity as possessor, only be some impairment of the physical condition of the chattel. There may, however, be situations in which the value to the owner of a particular type of chattel may be impaired by dealing with it in a manner that does not affect its physical condition. . . . In such a case, the intermeddling is actionable, even though the physical condition of the chattel is not impaired.

. . . [H]andling the enormous volume of mass mailings that CompuServe receives places a tremendous burden on its equipment. . . . Defendants' more recent practice of evading CompuServe's filters by disguising the origin of their messages commandeers even more computer resources because CompuServe's computers are forced to store undeliverable e-mail messages and labor in vain to return the messages to an address that does not exist. . . . To the extent that defendants' multitudinous electronic mailings demand the disk space and drain the processing power of plaintiff's computer equipment, those resources are not available to serve CompuServe subscribers. Therefore, the value of that equipment to CompuServe is diminished even though it is not physically damaged by defendants' conduct. . . .

Many subscribers have terminated their accounts specifically because of the unwanted receipt of bulk e-mail messages. . . . Defendants' intrusions into CompuServe's computer systems, insofar as they harm plaintiff's business reputation and goodwill with it's customers, are actionable under Restatement Section 218(d).

CASE QUESTIONS

1. Compare the reasoning in *Cyber Promotions* and *CompuServe.* How do they differ?
2. Did the earlier *Cyber Promotions* case serve as a precedent for *CompuServe?* Why or why not?
3. Is the service provided by an ISP a *chattel* as to come within the purview of the Restatement's definition of *trespass*?

In *America Online, Inc. v. IMS,* No. 98-0011-A, 1998 U.S. Dist. LEXIS 20448 (E.D.Va. 1998), the defendants sent over 60 million unsolicited and unauthorized e-mail messages to AOL subscribers over a course of 10 months. They continued to do so after receiving a written notice to cease and desist by AOL. The messages resulted in AOL's receipt of over 50,000 member complaints. The court granted summary judgment in favor of AOL. Citing *CompuServe,* the court upheld the claim of trespass. The unauthorized contact with AOL's computer network injured its goodwill and diminished the value of AOL's possessory interest in its computer network. In addition, the defendant was found to have diluted AOL's trademark and service mark in violation of the Lanham Act (discussed in Chapter 8).

In *eBay, Inc. v. Bidder's Edge, Inc.,* 100 F. Supp. 2d 1058 (N.D.Ca. 2000), the plaintiff is a well-known person-to-person trading site that permits sellers the ability to list items for sale and buyers the ability to bid and purchase the posted items. Persons using the site must register and agree to the eBay User Agreement that contained a prohibition of the use of any robot, spider, other automatic device, or manual process to monitor or copy Web pages or their content without eBay's consent. The defendant, Bidder's Edge (BE) is an auction aggregation site offering online auction buyers the ability to search for items across numerous online auction sites without the need to search each of the sites individually. Its site had information about over five million items on over one hundred auction sites. In early 1998, eBay gave permission to BE to include information concerning eBay's auctions for Beanie Babies and Furbies in the BE database. The permission was temporary in contemplation of a forthcoming licensing agreement. A dispute arose concerning the method to be used for the search of the eBay site. BE continued to use eBay's site after eBay told them not to do so. Its web crawlers constituted between 1.11 percent and 1.53 percent of the total load on eBay's listing servers.

The court issued an injunction preventing BE from using any automated query program, robot, Web crawler, or similar device in connection with eBay. *Trespass,* historically, referred to a person who wrongfully was on someone's land. In recent years, *trespass as to chattels* is the intentional interference with the possession of personal property proximately causing injury. The court noted that in the within case, the plaintiff was required and did show that "(1) defendant intentionally and without authorization interfered with plaintiff's possessory interest in [eBay's] computer system; and (2) defendant's unauthorized use proximately resulted in damage to plaintiff."

Proof of Damages

How does one prove damages in spam cases? In the *eBay* case, was plaintiff damaged by the defendant's wrongful use of eBay? The court cited the *CompuServe* litigation in stating, "A trespasser is liable when the trespass diminishes the condition, quality, or value of personal property." The quality or value of such conduct may take place even if the plaintiff cannot establish physical damage. The Restatement (Second) of Torts Section 218, Comment e (1977), states:

> The interest of a possessor of a chattel in its inviolability, unlike the similar interest of a possessor of land, is not given legal protection by an action for nominal damages for harmless intermeddlings with the chattel. In order that an actor who interferes with another's chattel may be liable, his conduct must affect some other and more important interest of the possessor. Therefore, one who intentionally intermeddles with another's chattel is subject to liability only if his intermeddling is harmful to the possessor's materially valuable interest in the physical condition, quality, or value of the chattel, or if the possessor is deprived of the use of the chattel for a substantial time, or some other legally protected interest of the possessor is affected.... Sufficient legal protection of the possessor's interest in the mere inviolability of his chattel is afforded by his privilege to use reasonable force to protect his possession against even harmless interference.

In the *eBay* litigation, the sending of 80,000 to 100,000 requests by BE to eBay wrongfully appropriated eBay's valuable bandwidth and capacity, albeit without causing physical damage.

CIVIL ENFORCEMENT OF THE COMPUTER FRAUD AND ABUSE ACT OF 1986

In an endeavor to protect Web sites from unwarranted interruption and other tortious and criminal activities, Congress passed the Computer Fraud and Abuse Act (CFAA), 18 U.S.C. Section 1030. The relevant portions of the act prohibits a person from doing the following:

> (A) knowingly causing the transmission of a program, information, code, or command, and as a result of such conduct, intentionally causing damage without authorization, to a protected computer;
> (B) intentionally accessing a protected computer without authorization, and as a result of such conduct, recklessly causing damage; or
> (C) intentionally accessing a protected computer without authorization, and as a result of such conduct, causing damage. (18 U.S.C. Section 1030(a)(5))

A *protected computer* is defined by the statute as any computer "which is used in interstate or foreign commerce or communication." *Damage* under the act is defined as "any impairment to the integrity or availability of data, a program, a system or information that ... causes loss aggregating at least $5,000 in value during any 1-year period to one or more individuals. ..."

Although violation of the statute is criminal in nature, the act also creates a private right of enforcement against persons who violate it. It states:

> Any person who suffers damage or loss by reason of a violation of this section may maintain a civil action against the violator to obtain compensatory damages and injunctive relief or other equitable relief. (18 U.S.C. Section 1030(g))

Civil penalties for violation of the act include compensatory damages, injunctive and other equitable relief.

In the following case, AOL sought to hold the defendant liable for spamming under CFAA. The relevant provisions and issues are discussed in the following AOL litigation.

AMERICA ONLINE, INC. V. NATIONAL HEALTH CARE DISCOUNT, INC.

2000 U.S. Dist. LEXIS 17055 (N.D.Ia. 2000)

FACTS: AOL is a well-known Internet service provider. The defendant, NHCD, is an Iowa corporation with sales offices in a number of states. It is engaged in the sale of discount optical and dental service plans to consumers from participating dentists and optical care providers. The defendant sent a large-volume of unsolicited, commercial e-mail messages to Internet users using AOL facilities without permission. Although AOL had filtering programs to prevent spamming, the defendant was able to circumvent such efforts. AOL had posted a number of statements regarding use of its facilities advising of its prohibitions. It advised the defendant to cease and desist in its AOL usage.

ISSUE: Did the defendant violate the CFAA by using AOL to send unsolicited email messages without authorization?

DECISION: The Court decided that it was unclear whether the defendant did violate the statute and set the matter down for trial of all the issues.

REASONING: Judge Zoss

The elements of a civil claim under section 1030(a)(5)(C) are as follows: (1) the person or entity must intentionally access a computer; (2) the computer must be a "protected computer"; (3) the access must be without authorization; and (4) the access must cause damage. There is no question that AOL's computers are "protected computers." However, it remains for the court to determine whether NHCD's contract e-mailers intentionally accessed AOL's computers, whether any such access was "without authorization," and whether such access caused damage to AOL.

The CFAA does not define "access," but the general definition of the word, as a transitive verb, is to "gain access to." . . . As a noun, "access," in this context means to exercise the "freedom to . . . make use of" something. . . . The question here, therefore, is whether NHCD's e-mailers, by harvesting e-mail addressees of AOL members and then sending the members UBE [unsolicited e-mail] messages, exercised the freedom or ability to make use of AOL's computers. The court finds they did. . . .

The next disputed element of AOL's claim under section 1030(a)(5)(C) is whether the access was "without authorization." Again, the CFAA gives no direct guidance on the meaning of the phrase "without authorization." [The court said it was unclear whether AOL members, by violating the terms and conditions of membership, are considered to have unauthorized access.]

[Concerning damages], the Court said "it can be concluded that when a large volume of UBE causes slowdowns or diminishes the capacity of AOL to serve its customers, an 'impairment' has occurred to the 'availability' of AOL's 'system.'" . . . [The court then stated that it had to be proven at a trial whether AOL in fact did sustain the minimal damages required by statute.]

CASE QUESTIONS

1. Examine the Computer Fraud and Abuse Act. Do you agree with the court that it was unclear whether there was intentional access to the computer? Whether it was without authorization?
2. Did not AOL's warning to the defendant to cease and desist from using its Web site for commercial purposes constitute *without authorization*?

In *Shaw v. Toshiba America Information Systems, Inc.*, 91 F. Supp. 2d 926 (E.D.Tex. 1999), the issue arose as to the meaning of *transmission* under CFAA. Shaw and others commenced a class-action lawsuit against Toshiba and NEC Electronics, alleging that the defendants manufactured, sold, and marketed faulty floppy-diskette controllers that are supposed to detect data errors and allow the control program to rewrite the affected data correctly. Such failures were claimed to result in the storage of corrupt data or to destroy data without knowledge to the control program or without the knowledge of the operator.

In denying defendants' motions for dismissal of the case, the court took an expansive approach to the meaning of *transmission.* The word "includes the design, manufacture, creation, distribution, sale, transmission, and marketing of floppy-diskette controllers allegedly made faulty by defective microcode." The court refused to accept Toshiba's claim that the CFAA was never intended to apply to manufacturers but applied instead to computer hacking. It stated that the act did not have a blanket exemption for manufacturers nor did the word *hacking* appear anywhere in the statute. Transmission includes both a marketplace transfer of data from outside the computer as well as intercomputer communication. Therefore, subject to proof at a trial, the design specifications tainted by faulty floppy-disk controllers guided by defective microcode could give rise to liability under the statute.

CIVIL RICO

The Racketeer Influenced and Corrupt Organizations Act will be discussed in the following chapter, on Internet crime. In essence, the statute makes it a crime for a person to be involved in a pattern of racketeering activity. In addition to criminal penalties of up to 20 years of imprisonment and a life term if the crimes alleged carry a life sentence, the statute permits civil lawsuits for persons injured by the activity. In the following case, the chief executives of the major tobacco companies falsely testified before Congress concerning the effects of tobacco on health and other deleterious aspects. In addition, the tobacco companies allegedly lied and misled the public for decades concerning the deleterious effects of their products. The claim is that the defendants violated the mail fraud and wire fraud statutes, to be discussed, thereby forming the necessary predicate acts underlying the RICO racketeering activity.

FALISE, KLEIN, MACCHIAROLA, AND MARKETY AS TRUSTEES V. AMERICAN TOBACCO COMPANY

99 F. Supp. 2d 316 (E.D.N.Y. 2000)

FACTS: Plaintiffs, as trustees of a Trust that arose from the bankruptcy of the Johns-Manville Corporation due to the company's inability to pay for asbestos claims, filed a multibillion dollar civil-RICO action against tobacco companies seeking money for their contribution to the claimants' asbestos-related injuries. The claim was that the defendant tobacco companies misled the public and the Trust's beneficiaries through decades of misrepresentations and intentional omissions and misinformation concerning the addictive and harmful effects of their products. The alleged racketeering consisted of tobacco's fraudulent scheme of misinformation directed at the plaintiff Trust to cover-up its share of the liability for the injuries of claimants against the Trust, the encouragement to asbestos workers to smoke knowing that such usage would cause workers to become ill or exacerbate the asbestos' injuries; and causing the Trust to pay more for claims than the extent of their liability.
ISSUE: Whether the plaintiffs established that the defendants were liable under RICO.
DECISION: The Court denied the defendant tobacco companies' motion to dismiss the lawsuit and set the matter down for trial.
REASONING: Judge Weinstein
To recover under civil RICO, a plaintiff must establish an injury to his business or property "by reason of" the alleged racketeering activity. . . . At a minimum, the injury must have been caused in fact by the racketeering activity. . . . It must have been a *"substantial factor in the sequence of responsible causation"* leading to the injury at issue. . . . "Although detrimental reliance is not an element of mail or wire fraud claims generally, a plaintiff seeking to base

RICO liability on these predicate acts must prove that its injuries are the result of reliance on the fraud." . . .

A RICO plaintiff may establish reliance sufficient to prove injury causation deriving from the predicate acts of mail or wire fraud in one of two ways . . . First, a plaintiff may "claim that he was the direct target of the fraudulent scheme. In that case, to plead causation, [the] plaintiff would have to allege that he himself relied on the underlying misrepresentations to his detriment." . . . As a second possibility, a plaintiff may allege that "his injuries were indirectly but proximately caused by a fraudulent scheme directed at third parties, that is to say, the third parties' reliance on the underlying misrepresentations." . . . [The court held that both categories were satisfied by the plaintiffs.]

[As to the claim that the plaintiffs failed to identify specific misrepresentations relied upon by the Trust and the asbestos claimants], a plaintiff in order to establish reliance for injury causation need only establish (1) that the RICO defendants intentionally engaged in a scheme to distort the body of public knowledge, (2) that the defendants were successful in doing so (e.g., a substantial factor causing the distortion), (3) that there was detrimental reliance on this distorted knowledge by an intended and foreseeable class of victims, (4) that such reliance was reasonable in the totality of the circumstances, and (5) that the plaintiff was proximately injured by this reliance. [The court determined that the plaintiffs did state a claim for which compensation would be awarded if proven at a trial. Therefore, the court found in favor of the plaintiffs in refusing to dismiss the lawsuit.]

CASE QUESTIONS

1. Some observers, including the author of the statute, have said that RICO was designed to attack gangster-type activities and was never intended to go after legitimate businesses. Do you believe RICO should have been used under the circumstances of the case?
2. If so, how do you justify Congress's continued grant of money for tobacco farmers and its refusal to prohibit the sale of tobacco?
3. Should RICO be used to condemn the sale of food products that may cause long-term harm to consumers, such as that sold by fast food service establishments?

MAIL AND WIRE FRAUD AS A TORT

Mail or wire fraud is a crime and is an intentional tort to those persons victimized by the act. The elements of the tort are (1) a scheme to defraud whose object is the attainment of (2) money or property, and (3) the use of the mails or wires to conduct the scheme. In order to sue, one must plead specifically the alleged false or misleading statements that were made by the perpetrator, with particulars as to when and where they were made, who made the statements, and the purpose of the mailing with respect to the fraudulent scheme. The mail or wire communication must be an integral part of the scheme. In the following action, the plaintiff sought to combine a RICO claim with mail and wire fraud.

SCHNELL V. CONSECO, INC.

43 F. Supp. 2d 438 (S.D.N.Y. 1999)

FACTS: Schnell sued Conseco and Sands Brothers, Inc. on behalf of a purported class of public investors alleging fraud in violation of the Racketeer Influenced and Corrupt Organizations Act ("RICO"). The claim is that the defendants effectuated a series of transactions through the sale of debentures in the NAL Financial Group in order to gain control of the company by the purchase of common stock at artificially low prices to the detriment of the other public shareholders. Conseco had loaned $5 million to NAL in exchange for which he was given a note and warrants to purchase 275,000 shares at a price of $.15 per share. Thereafter, Conseco agreed with NAL to purchase five million shares for $5 million and agreed not to cause NAL to file for bankruptcy prior to October 1, 1997. The transactions were filed with the SEC [Securities and Exchange Commission] and shareholders were advised of the transactions and were sent a proxy proposing the doubling of the number of authorized shares. The mail or wire communications contained no false information, and no showing of a scheme to fraud other than the acquisition of shares at a discount and an attempt to acquire remaining shares by less than adequate consideration.

ISSUE: Has the plaintiff made a prima facie case warranting a trial on the merits?

DECISION: The Court held in favor of the defendant, Conseco, stating that the complaint failed to state a cause of action.

REASONING: Judge Parker

Conseco's challenges to the complaint's RICO allegations are essentially that they do not adequately allege a scheme to defraud, a pattern of racketeering activity, or causation. In relevant part, RICO prohibits

> Any person employed by or associated with any enterprise engaged in, or the activities of which affect, interstate or foreign commerce, to conduct or participate, directly or indirectly, in the conduct of such enterprise's affairs through a pattern of racketeering activity or collection of unlawful debt.

18 U.S.C. Section 1962(c). A "pattern of racketeering activity" requires at least two acts of racketeering activity within the past ten years. 18 U.S.C. Section 1961(5). Mail and wire fraud are included within the definition of "racketeering activity." 18 U.S.C. Section 1961(1).

[The court recited the elements of mail or wire fraud.] In this case, plaintiff does not contend that the wire and mail communications that allegedly formed the RICO predicate acts contained false and misleading information. Rather, plaintiff claims that the mails and wires were used in furtherance of the scheme to defraud. . . .

In fact, a scheme to defraud "requires 'fraudulent or deceptive means, such as material misrepresentation or concealment.' . . ." Here, however, plaintiff's complaint contains no allegations that Conseco employed fraudulent or deceptive means. While plaintiff alleges that Conseco moved to acquire a controlling interest by arranging to acquire NALF shares at a discount and attempting to acquire the remaining interest without paying adequate consideration, no fraudulent or deceptive actions are alleged with respect to Conseco. In addition, while plaintiff claims that Conseco caused NALF to file for bankruptcy on the first day it could contractually do so, this allegation is also insufficient to support the existence of a scheme to defraud. And while plaintiff contends that Conseco's actions were "coercive," coercion alone does not constitute a scheme to defraud. . . .

Even if plaintiff's mail and wire fraud allegations were sufficient, plaintiff has failed to properly allege a pattern of racketeering activity. In order to plead a pattern of racketeering activity, plaintiff must allege two or more predicate acts by defendant that are sufficiently related and amount to, or pose a threat of, continued criminal activity. . . . Showing the threat of continuing activity requires the allegation of either an "open-ended" (i.e., past criminal conduct with a threat of future criminal conduct) or "closed-ended" (i.e., past criminal activity extending over a substantial period of time) pattern of racketeering activity. . . .

With respect to an open-ended pattern of racketeering activity, our Circuit has noted:

> In cases in which the acts of the defendant or the enterprise were inherently unlawful, such as murder or obstruction of justice, and were in pursuit of inherently unlawful goals, such as narcotics trafficking or embezzlement, the courts generally have concluded that the requisite threat of continuity was adequately established by the nature of the activity, even though the period spanned by the racketeering acts was short. In contrast, in cases concerning alleged racketeering activity in furtherance of endeavors that are not inherently unlawful, such as frauds in the sale of property, the courts generally have found no threat of continuing criminal activity arising from conduct that extended over even longer periods.

[The court found Conseco's activity not to be inherently unlawful or false and deceptive.]

Whether a closed-ended pattern of racketeering activity exists depends on analysis of a number of non-dispositive factors, including the length of time over which the alleged predicate acts took place, the number and variety of acts, the number of participants, the number of victims, and the presence of separate schemes. . . .

[The court found the acts by Conseco over a period of 23 months not to be closed-ended because they were in themselves innocuous and not alleged to be false and misleading.]

An additional deficiency in plaintiff's RICO allegations is his failure adequately to allege that his injury was both caused in fact, and proximately caused, by the conduct alleged to constitute the predicate acts under RICO. . . .

[The court found that the allegations of injury were speculative and merely conclusory and were insufficient to merit a plenary trial on the merits of the case.]

CASE QUESTIONS

1. The decision was made denying the plaintiff the right to have a trial on the merits of the case. Were there sufficient facts to warrant a full trial?
2. Does the fact that Conseco purchased shares of stock below their value and then compelled the company to file for bankruptcy protection shortly thereafter establish a scheme to defraud?

DEFAMATION

Defamation is a tort consisting of the making of a false statement about a person that injures that person's reputation in the community. The elements generally required for defamation are: (1) a statement either in writing or oral; (2) that is false; (3) tending to hurt a person's reputation in the estimation of others; and (4) communicated to a third person (It is not defamation to falsely accuse someone to that person alone). Additional elements may include the following: (1) to collect damages, the injured party should establish a monetary loss or establish injury to one's reputation (for example, this author represented an employee who falsely accused her employer of misdeeds in front of coworkers. In a lawsuit that transpired, the employer recovered $.06 due to lack of proof of monetary damages and was not compensated his attorney's fees for the litigation); and (2) proof of fault especially as to newspaper accounts. The person sued must be shown to have known or should have known that the statement was not true, although some statements are so defamatory as to be "per se" libelous, as calling a person a "whore" or other untrue comparable statements.

Libel is written defamation and includes all forms of the media including magazines, radio and television, and, computer transmissions.[23] *Slander* is oral defamation, that is, spoken words made to a third person.

Defenses to defamation actions with some exceptions are: (1) truth (defamation by definition is the utterance of a false statement); (2) fair comment (statement of opinion rather than of fact about another person); and (3) privilege. With respect to privilege, there are various types the law has evolved. Political figures have both fewer and greater rights than the individual citizen with respect to defamation. A statement made in the chambers of a legislature (such as in Congress, by a legislator or other public figure), no matter how outrageously false and done with malice, cannot be the basis of litigation for defamation. The same statement made on the Capitol steps to the media, however, may be libelous. A public official and, generally, a public figure (person often in the news or prominently known, such as a famous actor) accused of misdeeds with respect to voting or other legislative activities usually cannot sue successfully the person making the statement in the absence of proof of malice. Newspapers and, to a lesser degree, other forms of media have a conditional privilege that protects them from liability as to public figures in the absence of malice. Non-public figures have greater rights in regard to such news accounts.

Libel and the Right of Freedom of Speech

The right of a person to be free from injury to one's person or reputation inevitably runs afoul of the right of another to speak freely. Absent a recognized defense, courts will grant protection from such statements when the evidence at a plenary trial establishes the falsity of the statements.

May a court issue a preliminary injunction prior to a plenary trial, barring alleged libel statements made in a defendant's Web site? The following action contains a detailed statement of the First Amendment's protection against such court orders.

BIHARI V. GROSS

No. 00 Civ. 1664 (SAS), 2000 U.S. Dist. LEXIS 14180 (S.D.N.Y. Sept. 28, 2000)

FACTS: The District Court was called upon to determine, among other issues, whether a preliminary injunction should be granted against defendants to stop them from using domain names or metatags containing alleged libel statements of the plaintiff's person and business. Bihari is an interior designer having provided interior design services in New York City and elsewhere for a period in excess of 15 years. The name is well known in the high-end residential interior market and is reliant upon referrals for business. Gross was a former client of Bihari who became engaged in a state court case as a plaintiff alleging fraud and breach of contract. Gross procured the domain names, "designscam.com" and "manhattaninteriordesign.com" that contained statements as metatags about Bihari including that she committed fraud and deceit; she had an arrest record [the arrest was based on defendant's allegations but was later dismissed]; and other negative comments.

ISSUE: May a Court issue a preliminary injunction against the defendants barring alleged libelous statements about the plaintiffs prior to a plenary trial?

DECISION: The Court held in favor of the defendants in its refusal to grant such an injunction.

REASONING: Judge Scheindlin

A preliminary injunction is a prior restraint, and as such, "bear[s] a heavy presumption against its constitutional validity. . . . Nearly thirty years ago . . . the Supreme Court struck as unconstitutional a state court's order enjoining distribution of leaflets critical of the respondent's business practices. The Supreme Court emphasized: "It is elementary, of course, that in a case of this kind the courts do not concern themselves with the truth or validity of the publication. . . . [T]he injunction, so far as it imposes prior restraint on speech and publication, constitutes an impermissible restraint on First Amendment rights. . . ." This is consistent with Supreme Court decisions holding prior restraints to be presumptively invalid, even when the potential harm was much greater than injury to reputation . . . (even during wartime, newspapers [were] not enjoined from publishing papers that the government feared could threaten national security).

Our Court of Appeals [Second Circuit] has longed warned against enjoining libel: "Equity will not restrain by injunction the threatened publication of a libel, as such, however great the injury to property may be. This is the universal rule in the United States and was formerly the rule in England." . . .

The rule against preliminarily enjoining libel rests on two grounds. First, a preliminary injunction would be unconstitutional as a prior restraint on freedom of expression. "The special vice of a prior restraint is that communication will be suppressed . . . before an adequate determination that it is unprotected by the First Amendment." . . . Prior restraints of future speech are particularly dangerous because of the difficulty courts face in designing an order that does not chill protected speech. . . . Second, injunctive relief is unnecessary because plaintiffs have an adequate remedy at law. . . .

The Gross websites concern the business practices and alleged fraud of a well-known interior designer. Such speech is "arguably within the sphere of legitimate public concern," which imbues the speech with a heavy presumption of constitutional protection. . . . Similarly, New York law places a heavy burden on the plaintiff to prove that the disparaging statements are not opinion, which is granted absolute protection. . . .

[The issues concerning alleged trademark violations are discussed in Chapter 8.]

CASE QUESTIONS

1. The court states that the First Amendment prevents the imposition of prior restraint of speech. Do you agree that a person must await highly defamatory statements to be made and possibly destroy one's business reputation before applying for an order to restrain such speech?
2. What are the limits of prior restraint, if any? What if a person is about to publish accurately the method to produce an atomic bomb or other such destructive device? Can such speech be prevented before publication?

Note: This author represented a political figure who had served an extended time in the legislature. Shortly before the election was to take place, his opponent prepared a brochure alleging that the political figure had committed many crimes, including murder and fixing of races at a racetrack, that he was gay, that he took bribes, and other such claims. None of the statements had any factual basis. The said opponent later said she believed (wrongfully) that a person could say anything about a political figure without being subject to litigation. She had no monetary assets that could be taken if a successful defamation lawsuit were to take place. Assuming that the said statements were to be believed by the public, was it fair to prevent such literature from being circulated, thereby causing the possible loss of reputation and career?

Defamation and Internet Service Provider Liability

Internet service providers potentially face numerous lawsuits for libel and for other torts due to statements and illegal activities that may take place for messages made over the Internet. The question then arises: What is the liability of a company such as AOL or CompuServe for defamatory materials made over the Internet through its medium? Similarly, do ISPs have potential liability for pornographic or other materials shown over the network?

Fortunately for ISPs, Congress came to their rescue. In essence, the Communications Decency Act (CDA) of 1996 exempted ISPs from any liability for unlawful or tortious acts committed over the Internet unless they were directly involved in the activity.[24] The purpose of the statute was set forth in the Policy that Congress wanted to establish. After reciting a number of Findings[25] that reiterated the development of the Internet, the extraordinary opportunities the Internet offers in its provision of educational and informational resources, its forum for discourse, and services in diverse areas, the statute states:

[Sec. 230] (b) POLICY—It is the policy of the United States—

(1) to promote the continued development of the Internet and other interactive computer services and other interactive media;
(2) to preserve the vibrant and competitive free market that presently exists for the Internet and other interactive computer services, unfettered by Federal or State regulation;
(3) to encourage the development of technologies which maximize user control over what information is received by individuals, families, and schools who use the Internet and other interactive computer services;
(4) to remove disincentives for the development and utilization of blocking and filtering technologies that empower parents to restrict their children's access to objectionable or inappropriate online material; and
(5) to ensure vigorous enforcement of Federal criminal laws to deter and punish trafficking in obscenity, stalking, and harassment by means of computer.

Congress analogized ISPs as postal or express-mail deliverers who merely convey to receivers what was given to them by senders of the letters or packages. Just as mail carriers are not responsible for the content of the material delivered, ISPs have similar exemption from responsibility unless they directly engage in tortious or criminal conduct. The key statutory provision states:

[Sec. 230(c)] (1) TREATMENT OF PUBLISHER OR SPEAKER—No provider or user of an interactive computer service shall be treated as the publisher or speaker of any information provided by another information content provider.

In the following case, which was instituted after passage of the statute, the court was presented with an ISP that was more than a mere passive conduit of defamatory statements.[26] In it, the court discusses an additional section of the statute relevant to the case at hand.

BLUMENTHAL V. DRUDGE

992 F. Supp. 44 (D.D.C. 1998)

FACTS: Matt Drudge, a gossip columnist, alleged on the Internet in his electronic publication called the "Drudge Report" that the plaintiff, Sidney Blumenthal, an assistant to the President, had a history of spousal abuse. The report was not true. The Drudge web site was available to users worldwide at no cost. Drudge earned income by entering into licensing agreements with "Hotwired," an electronic Internet publication, and thereafter with AOL. The agreement with AOL was made available to all AOL subscribers for a one-year period for which Drudge received a royalty of $3,000 a month. The licensing agreement provided that Drudge was to create, edit, update, and manage the content of the report. AOL had the right to remove content of the report that violated its standard terms of service. Drudge later retracted the defamatory statements, apologized to Blumenthal. AOL removed the said report and printed the retraction.

ISSUE: Whether AOL was liable for the defamatory statements in light of the exemption from liability given to Internet service providers in the Communications Decency Act of 1996?

DECISION: The Court said that AOL was not liable.

REASONING: Judge Friedman

In February of 1996, Congress made an effort to deal with some of these challenges in enacting the Communications Decency Act of 1996. While various policy options were open to the Congress, it chose to "promote the continued development of the Internet and other interactive computer services and other interactive media" and "to preserve the vibrant and competitive free market" for such services, largely "unfettered by Federal or State regulation . . ." 47 U.S.C. [Section] 230(b)(1) and (2). Whether wisely or not, it made the legislative judgment to effectively immunize providers of interactive computer services from civil liability in tort with respect to material disseminated by them but created by others. In recognition of the speed with which information may be disseminated and the near impossibility of regulating information content, Congress decided not to treat providers of interactive computer services like other information providers such as newspapers, magazines or television and radio stations, all of which may be held liable for publishing or distributing obscene or defamatory material written or prepared by others. While Congress could have made a different policy choice, it opted not to hold interactive computer services liable for their failure to edit, withhold or restrict access to offensive material disseminated through their medium.

Section 230(c) of the Communications Decency Act of 1996 provides: No provider or user of an interactive computer service shall be treated as the publisher or speaker of any information provided by another information content provider." . . .

Plaintiffs make the additional argument, however, that Section 230 of the Communications Decency Act does not provide immunity to AOL in this case because Drudge was not just an anonymous person who sent a message over the Internet through AOL. He is a person with whom AOL contracted, whom AOL paid $3,000 a month. . . . Furthermore, the license agreement between AOL and Drudge by its terms contemplates more than a passive role for AOL; in it, AOL reserves the "right to remove, or direct [Drudge] to remove, any content which, as reasonably determined by AOL . . . violates AOL's then-standard Terms of Service. . . ." Because it has the right to exercise editorial content over those with whom it contracts and whose words it disseminates, it would seem only fair to hold AOL to the liability standards applied to a publisher or, at least, like a book store owner or library, to the liability standards applied to a distributor. But Congress has made a different policy choice by providing immunity even where the interactive service provider has an active, even aggressive role in making available content prepared by others. In some sort of tacit *quid pro quo* arrangement with the service provider community, Congress has conferred immunity from tort liability as an incentive to Internet service providers to self-police the Internet for obscenity and other offensive material, even where the self-policing is unsuccessful or not even attempted.

In Section 230(c)(2) of the Communications Decency Act, Congress provided:

> No provider or user of an interactive computer service shall be held liable on account of—
>
> (A) Any action voluntarily taken in good faith to restrict access to or availability of material that the provider or user considers to be obscene, lewd, lascivious, filthy, excessively violent, harassing, or otherwise objectionable, whether or not such material is constitutionally protected.

As the Fourth Circuit stated in *Zeran:* "Congress enacted section 230 to remove . . . disincentives to self-regulation. . . . Fearing that the specter of liability would . . . deter service providers from blocking and screening offensive material . . . forbids the imposition of publisher liability on a service provider for the exercise of its editorial and self-regulatory functions. . . ."

. . . While it appears clear to this Court that AOL in this case has taken advantage of all the benefits conferred by Congress in the Communications Decency Act, and then some, without accepting any of the burdens that Congress intended, the statutory language is clear: AOL is immune from suit. . . .

CASE QUESTIONS

1. What added facts, if any, may make AOL liable after the passage of the Communications Decency Act?
2. Should AOL be allowed near-total exemption from liability? Compare the *Somm* case decided in Germany that is discussed in Chapter 5.
3. Do you agree with the analogy of AOL and other ISPs to mail delivery services?

The *Blumenthal* court discussed the decision in another AOL case, *Zeran v. America Online, Inc.*[27] In *Zeran,* AOL was sued for alleged unreasonable delay in removing defamatory messages posted on AOL by an unidentified third person, for its failure to post retractions of the defamatory messages, and for failing to screen similar messages. An unidentified person posted a message on an AOL bulletin board advertising the sale of shirts with offensive slogans, with instructions to call Zeran at his stated home telephone number. Zeran received numerous calls, death threats, and other messages. AOL was notified but delayed in removing the account and refused to post retractions. The district court dismissed the action. The dismissal was affirmed by the court of appeals based on Section 230 of the Communications Decency Act of 1996, cited earlier, which exempts ISPs from liability.[28] The court applied the statute to the *Zeran* case even though the alleged negligence took place prior to the enactment of the statute. The court stated that the statute applied to all actions commenced after the effective date of the statute as in *Zeran.* The claimant filed the lawsuit on April 23, 1996. The effective date of the statute is February 8, 1996, some two and one-half months prior to the filing. The court noted that the injured party retained the right to sue the party causing the libel.

Zeran claimed that AOL was liable as a "distributor" rather than as a "publisher." The statute exonerated only publisher liability. He claimed that AOL was given notice of the libelous statements and chose not to act expeditiously in removing the statements. The court held, however, that distributor liability was "merely a subset, or a species, of publisher liability, and is therefore also foreclosed." As a publisher, the law grants immunity from liability. AOL is not in the same category as the party who posted the offensive statement. The court indicated that if ISPs were subject to distributor liability, then every time a defamatory statement is made on the Internet, the ISP had potential liability. Clearly, it was the intent of Congress to forbid such liability.

With respect to the claim that AOL received notice of the offending material, the court said that such liability would create "a no-cost means" to plaintiffs. "Whenever one was displeased with the speech of another party conducted over an interactive computer service, the offended party could simply 'notify' the relevant service provider, claiming the information to be legally defamatory." In view of the very extensive traffic over the Internet, such a burden on ISPs would be intolerable.

The passage of CDA was based in part on an earlier decision by a state of New York trial court judge who held Prodigy liable for defamatory statements made about a securities investment by an unidentified bulletin board user on Prodigy's "Money Talk" computer bulletin board.[29] The statements indicated that the plaintiffs had committed criminal and fraudulent acts in connection with a stock offering. The court distinguished Prodigy from other ISPs in that it held itself as controlling the content of its bulletin boards and implemented the control by automatic software-screening software. The CDA clearly now exempts Prodigy from liability in such a case.

Prodigy cited an early case, *Cubby, Inc. v. CompuServe, Inc.*,[30] as precedent before the New York court for dismissal of the action. In *Cubby,* CompuServe was sued for libel and other grounds for defamatory statements made against it by a newsletter that was part of an electronic library that subscribers to CompuServe could access. The U.S. district court dismissed the action on the ground that it was a distributor rather than a publisher of the alleged defamatory materials. The court also discussed the First Amendment application, stating that a distributor must have knowledge of the contents of the publication before liability can be imposed for distribution of the defamatory materials.

In *Doe v. America Online, Inc.,* CL 97-631AE (Fla. Cir. Ct. June 26, 1997), one of the defendants sued had committed sexual battery on an 11-year-old boy ("John Doe") and two other minor male children. The said defendant communicated with minors and others through a chat room service provided by AOL. The plaintiff alleged AOL was responsible for distributing obscene materials, was negligent per se, and breached its duty of reasonable care to prevent such communications. The Florida trial court dismissed the action against AOL citing Section 230(c)(1) that prevents treatment of ISPs as publishers or speakers and (d)(3) "STATE LAW . . . No cause of action may be brought and no liability may be imposed under any State of local law that is inconsistent with this section." Thus, states are precluded from holding ISPs responsible under the statute.

Based upon the CDA and the *Blumenthal* case, it appears that ISPs have an almost unlimited exemption from liability. In order for an ISP to incur possible liability it would have to directly post the defamatory material of its own making, rather than merely being the transmitter of such material or exercise limited editorial or supervisory control over the data. Paying a transmitter a fee to post information will not suffice to make the ISP liable. Whether or not other courts of appeals and, ultimately, the U.S. Supreme Court will take such an expansive view of the CDA remains for future determination.

Defamation of Business Entity

The tort of defamation is not limited to individuals. Disparaging a business or product may result in tort liability, particularly if it results in the inducement of a breach of contract. If a businessperson deliberately or carelessly tells potential customers falsely that a competitor acts fraudulently or manufactures products that are poor in quality, such statements may give rise to liability. For example, if the Ford Motor Company says that its Lincoln Continental is superior to a particular Mercedes in certain, specific ways, then it must be able to prove the claims made by independent means. Failure to do so could result in significant liability. In the following case, the peril of counseling a person to breach a contract is made evident.

J. D. EDWARDS & CO. V. PODANY

168 F.3d 1020 (7th Cir. 1999)

FACTS: Plaintiff entered into a contract to sell computer services to a buyer, SNE. It broke the contract. A lawsuit was commenced against the business consultant, Podany, and also against his consulting firm, Mercer Management Consulting, Inc. The claim was that the defendants had advised the buyer to breach the contract with J. D. Edwards and, thus, was responsible for SNE's decision to comply with the advice. The consulting firm was allegedly a specialist in the field of business and computer systems. The jury awarded the plaintiff the sum of $2.3 million in damages against the consultant and his firm.
ISSUE: Whether the jury wrongfully rejected the consulting firm's defenses of "consultant's privilege" or privilege of rendering "honest advice"?
DECISION: The U.S. Court of Appeals affirmed the jury award against the defendants.
REASONING: Judge Posner
[The "consultant's privilege"] is the privilege of a consultant, or other advisor, to offer good-faith advice to a client without fear of liability should the client act on that advice to the harm of a third person, in this case the plaintiff. . . . The privilege resembles the rule in defamation law that where there is a duty to speak, a defamatory utterance, if made in good faith and not disseminated any further than necessary, is privileged. . . . A consultant is hired to give advice. Often the advice is painful, because firms frequently turn to consultants when they are in trouble or when they want to do something that hurts and want to spread the blame a bit. The consultant's advice may lead to downsizing, layoffs, outsourcing, and countless other perturbations, including, as here, contractual terminations. It would cast quite a large, dark cloud over the consulting business if consultants could be hauled into court for having given advice that in hindsight could be characterized as having been ill-advised, ill-informed, or otherwise negligent. The consultant's privilege cuts off this possibility. But it is not absolute. It is a qualified immunity as distinct from absolute immunity in the law of public officers' tort.

It is qualified in two ways. First, it is limited to advice given within the scope of the consultant's engagement. . . . Second, if the consultant does not give honest advice, if he uses his engagement to hurt other people exclusively for his own benefit (or out of dislike of his victim) rather than for the benefit of his client—he forfeits the privilege.

Both limitations on the consultant's privilege, scope and good faith, are in issue here. . . . [SNE manufactures windows and had contracted with the plaintiff to supply software that would streamline SNE's business. The defendant, Podany, was called in as a consultant. After reviewing the services to be performed by the plaintiff, he advised that the project with the plaintiff was unsound.] Podany is not a software expert and neither he nor his company had been retained to select software or offer a critique of the contract with J. D. Edwards. . . . Podany also advised Massel [SNE's officer] to stop installing J. D. Edwards' software. . . .

Podany, however, went further than merely advising Massell to stop installing J. D. Edwards' software. He ordered the SNE executive in charge of the implementation of the contract with J. D. Edwards to stop paying Edwards. This went well beyond his original engagement, but the engagement had been enlarged by Massel, who had directed everyone in his company to "have all computer related purchases approved by Randy [Podany]." . . .

The problem with the defendants' assertion of the consultant's privilege is not that Podany exceeded the scope of their engagement; it is that a reasonable jury could find that he acted in bad faith. Podany knew very little about the software that was being supplied by J. D. Edwards. The only software program he was familiar with was [that of a competing company]. . . . [H]e did all of this in order to land himself a lucrative job with SNE's parent as director of information services. And having done so he procured further engagements of his former employer, Mercer. [The court then stated that the consultant's privilege is forfeited if Podany's only object was to enrich himself.] It is when a consultant decides to make money by rendering dishonest advice (or going outside the terms of his engagement) that he loses the protection of privilege and assumes the usual liabilities. . . . He pronounced the J. D. Edwards software a "piece of shit" without knowing enough about it to have an opinion. Of course all these things could have been innocent mistakes. But the more egregious a consultant's mistakes, the less innocent they are likely to be. . . .

CASE QUESTIONS

1. What objections could you raise to the court's decision?
2. Does the decision create a climate whereby consultants would be fearful of giving advice to a client that includes making truthful but unsubstantiated derogatory statements about third parties who deal with the consultant's customer?
3. Compare this case with *Bihari.* What are the differences in the statements of opinion in the cases?

In an allied intentional tort, that of interference with business relations, a person who causes another entity to breach a contract or refusal to deal with a third party may be liable for harm arising from such conduct. In *Wine and Spirits Wholesalers of Mass., Inc. v. Net Contents, Inc.,* 10 F. Supp. 2d 84 (D.Mass. 1998), the plaintiff corporation, composed of 10 Massachusetts wine and spirits wholesalers and others, sued the defendant, Net Contents, Inc., a California corporation that sold wine and spirits to Massachusetts residents through its Internet site. The defendant was not licensed under state law either to sell its products directly to consumers or to licensed retailers within the state. Plaintiff sued for interference with plaintiff's business relations with its customers and sought an injunction preventing defendants from filling or delivering any order for alcoholic beverages for delivery to customers in Massachusetts. Defendants moved to dismiss the action.

The court dismissed the action stating that the plaintiff as a private party had no private right of enforcement under Massachusetts's law. The court stated: "It is, however, a well-settled rule in Massachusetts that a statute for the benefit and protection of the public at large, which authorizes criminal penalties for its violation, cannot be enforced in equity absent express statutory authority to do so." Presumably, the state could have sued to bar such sales. A similar holding took place in a lawsuit brought by a trade association that sought an injunction against an unlicensed seller of optometry services. Licensing statutes are not enacted to protect the professionals who provide licensed services but rather they are for the protection of the public.

AMERICANS WITH DISABILITY ACT OF 1990 AND REASONABLE ACCOMMODATION IN CYBERSPACE

In November, 1999, the National Federation for the Blind commenced a lawsuit against America Online in the federal district court in Massachusetts. The suit, later withdrawn, alleged that AOL violated the Americans with Disability Act by denying access to its service to blind users because the software needed to access the site differed from the text-reading software used by blind users. The case was resolved because AOL agreed to try to modify its software to accommodate blind persons. The issue raised by the lawsuit is whether AOL and other cyberspace companies were liable under the act. Before discussing the claim, it would be helpful to set forth the basic provisions of the law.

Purposes of the Act. After extensive hearings, Congress found that some 43 million Americans possessed physical or mental disabilities. As a result, many of them have been discriminated against in areas of employment, housing, recreation, and many other areas of daily life. Accordingly, Congress sought to provide a comprehensive mandate to eliminate such discrimination, set forth standards addressing the biases, and to address the problems faced by the victims of such prejudices (Section 2).

General Provisions. The term *disability* is defined as "(A) a physical or mental impairment that substantially limits one or more of the major life activities of such individual; (B) a record of such an impairment; or (C) being regarded as having such an impairment." The act forbids an employer having 15 or more employees (25 until July 26, 1994) from discriminating against a person having a disability with respect to the hiring, discharge, compensation, advancement, job training, and other aspects of employment unless the said person cannot, with reasonable accommodation, perform the duties required for the job. Exempted are corporations owned by the U.S. government and bona fide, tax-exempt, private-membership clubs (Section 101 (5)).

Qualified Persons Having a Disability. The statute defines such person as "an individual with a disability who, with or without reasonable accommodation, can perform the essential functions of the employment position that such individual holds or desires."

Reasonable Accommodation. "'Reasonable accommodation' may include—(A) making existing facilities used by employees readily accessible to and usable by individuals with disabilities; and (B) job restructuring, part-time or modified work schedules, reassignment to a vacant position, acquisition or modification of equipment or devices, appropriate adjustment or modifications of examinations, training materials or policies, the provision of qualified readers or interpreters, and other similar accommodations for individuals with disabilities" (Section 101(8)).

Title 3: Public Accommodations and Services Operated by Private Entities. Title 3 of the act is applicable to the private sector. Section 302 provides, in part, that "[n]o individual shall be discriminated against on the basis of disability in the full and equal enjoyment of the goods, services, facilities, privileges, advantages, or accommodations of any place of public accommodation by any person who owns, leases (or leases to), or operates a place of public accommodation." *Discrimination* includes criteria set up to screen out individuals with a disability unless such crate is necessary for the goods, services, and facilities, being offered. The term *public accommodations* is very broad. It includes inns, motels, restaurants, movie houses, bakeries, grocery stores, shopping centers and other such facilities, professional offices of a health care provider, bus and other such terminals, museums, libraries, parks, zoos, sports facilities, and places of education (Section 301).

Reasonable modifications must be made to accommodate individuals with disabilities unless such accommodation would fundamentally alter the nature of such goods, services, and so on. Physical barriers, such as those architectural in nature, are to be modified to permit persons with disabilities to access the facilities. A person having a handicap with respect to accessing a computer needed for employment can be accommodated in a variety of ways. A wheelchair-bound person can easily perform computer-related activities with relatively minor additions or changes in the work environment, such as additional space for the wheelchair, voice-activated computers for those lacking one or more limbs, larger screens for persons with poor eyesight, and so on if such accommodation does permit the individual to perform the assigned tasks.

Is the Internet a *Place* for Purposes of the Act? The cited AOL case raised the issue of the definition of a place of accommodation. Unfortunately, judicial decisions have gone both ways on this issue. On the one hand, the Seventh Circuit Court of Appeals, in *Doe v. Mutual of Omaha Ins. Co.,* 179 F.3d 557 (7th Cir. 1999), stated that Title 3 of the act in Section 302(a) prohibits discrimination on the basis of disability in "any place of public accommodation . . . (whether in physical space or in *electronic* space)" [emphasis added]; other courts of appeals in the third, sixth, and ninth circuits have refused to expand the definition to go beyond physical places. Regulations to the Americans with Disabilities Act defines a *place of accommodation* as a "facility operated by a private entity, whose operations affect commerce and fall within at least one of the following categories. . . ." The *facility* is then defined as "all or any portion of buildings, structures, sites, complexes, equipment, rolling stock or other conveyances, roads, walks, passageways, parking lots and other real or personal property, including the site where the building, property, structure or equipment is located." We will have to await a modification of the statute or a bright-line U.S. Supreme Court decision before the issue is resolved for the nation as a whole.

Remedies. Remedies include hiring, back pay, reinstatement, promotion, and reasonable attorneys' fees.

DISPUTE RESOLUTION

In the context of cyberspace, the methodology of resolving disputes that inevitably arise requires global consideration and response. Consider the growing trend of purchasing goods from the Internet. Two decades ago, purchases from other countries between a merchant and a consumer were extremely rare. Today, through services such as eBay, it is common for international purchases to be made by nonmerchants. The ramifications of such sales are enormous. In a relatively simple sale between a seller and a consumer buyer in adjoining states, if problems arise, there may be no practical remedy. Suing in federal court is not available because the amount in dispute is under the $75,000 jurisdictional amount. There is also the problem of legal fees, collecting against the judgment debtor if one is successful, the inconvenience of calling witnesses, travel, normal court delays, and the like. Brought onto the international stage, there are additional difficulties including language barriers, differences in legal systems, local biases especially in poorer countries that prevent effective remedies to foreign persons, significant travel inconvenience, cultural and social factors, collection on a judgment, legal fees, and other barriers. Thus, the present difficulty is the lack of mechanisms wherein potential purchasers and sellers can address their complaints and responses for alleged defective merchandise, fraudulent practices, and other legal issues.

Solutions in past global commercial transactions were rather straightforward. Merchants entered into a variety of arrangements to assure compliance by the respective parties. The key was the financing mechanism utilized for the payment of such goods. Letters of credit arrangements were made that placed the onus of payment upon the buyer's bank, which may be confirmed by the seller's bank once the seller had delivered all of the required documents evidencing proof that the merchandise was shipped in good order. Insurance policies covered casualty losses and the buyer generally was able to look to the carrier for reimbursement for failure to deliver the goods in apparent good condition. The conditions of the sale were governed usually by terminology in accordance with the rules promulgated by the International Chamber of Commerce (Incoterms). Customs brokers and freight forward agents took care of the customs duties and other regulatory requirements in the respective countries. Such arrangements are unavailable, in a practical sense, to the consumer purchaser.

In the event of a dispute wherein the financing mechanisms did not suffice to warrant a resolution, the parties were relegated to the judicial systems of their respective countries. In a practical sense, almost all disputes were resolved by means of an arbitration clause in the agreement between the parties. The clause almost always provided that in the event of a dispute, the parties agree to arbitration before a particular arbitral tribunal that shall base its decision on the laws of a particular country or subunit within the country (e.g., the laws of the state of New York). Such a clause is enforceable by federal and state law. The Federal Arbitration Act, Section 2, mandates the relegation of a contractual dispute to arbitration if the parties so agreed. It provides:

> [A] written provision in any maritime transaction of a contract evidencing a transaction involving commerce to settle by arbitration a controversy thereafter arising out of such contract or transaction . . . shall be valid, irrevocable, and enforceable, save upon such grounds as exist in law or in equity for the revocation of any contract. (9 U.S.C. Section 2)

Arbitration was deemed better for commercial dispute resolution. It had the format of a trial but there were distinct advantages that accrued with an arbitration. The hearing (trial) took place within the confines of a closed office thereby giving parties privacy (vs. an open court trial); the arbitrator was experienced in the general field of the dispute (unlike many judicial trials where the judge may be unfamiliar with the subject matter in dispute); there was no appeal (a court's decision may always be appealed); the case was heard within a short time frame (unlike a court trial where the calendar congestion may be years); the rules of evidence was relaxed (in court, there are formal rules of evidence that must be strictly complied with); the parties choose the place, arbitration tribunal, and the law to be applied (in court, the judge makes such determination); the cost in saved attorneys' fees could be considerable (as distinguished from the trial and possible appeals); and other advantages.

In the U.S. Supreme Court case of *Allied Bruce Terminix Companies, Inc. v. Dobson,* 513 U.S. 265 (1995), the Court said that an arbitration clause preempted state law (no state law could override it) and was to be interpreted broadly. The purpose of the Federal Arbitration Act was to prevent federal and state courts from reaching "different outcomes about the validity of arbitration in similar cases [citing the lead case of *Southland Corp. v. Keating,* 465 U.S. 1]." Arbitration provisions in a contract were to be obeyed in the same manner as other major provisions. So long as the parties contemplated at the time they entered into the contract that there would be substantial interstate activity, then the arbitration clause is to be obeyed and comes within the purview of the federal Arbitration Act.

Who decides if an arbitration clause in a commercial contract is to be followed? In *First Options of Chicago, Inc. v. Kaplan,* 514 U.S. 938 (1995), the U.S. Supreme Court said a court must defer to the arbitrator in making the decision whether a particular dispute must be arbitrated. In reviewing the arbitrator's decision on appeal, state courts are to apply their laws in determining whether the parties intended to submit an arbitrability issue to arbitration. The agreement to arbitrate disputes must be clear and unmistakable.

Employment Discrimination Cases. Arbitration clauses have been found to apply even where there is a claim of age discrimination under federal law. In the seminal case of *Gilmer v. Johnson/Lane Corporation,* 500 U.S. 20 (1991), the U.S. Supreme Court upheld an arbitration clause in a dispute between a securities broker and the employer. The clause was contained in the application by Gilmer with the New York Stock Exchange and was a part of the agreement permitting the broker to become employed. Thus, unless Congress explicitly relegates disputes coming under a variety of employment statutes to judicial determination only, it appears that the distinction in the validity of such clauses between private, commercial type agreements and public employment statutes may be eliminated.

Internet Dispute Resolution Mechanisms

Either the arbitration mechanism may be unavailable or a seller may be abusive in requiring in a standard form agreement, or shrink-wrap or click-wrap agreements, that all disputes be resolved by arbitration in its city (see the *Gateway 2000* litigation discussed in Chapter 3). Almost no purchaser of goods having a value less than $1,000 will travel abroad to arbitrate a claim. Thus, the consumer's dilemma. Goods that are desirable and unavailable locally may be purchased through the Internet, often from dealers whose reliability is unknown. The consumer may simply trust the merchant to send the goods as promised, and rely upon the use of a credit card and the card company's ability and legal requirement to withhold or cancel reimbursement in the event of a dispute. Some service provider companies that act as intermediaries, such as eBay, publish the reliability of sellers and buyers as reported by parties to prior transactions.

Other problems affecting the Internet are those of privacy and security. Consumers are hesitant rightfully to give out their credit card information to an open network that may be accessible by others. Privacy issues also arise by the sharing of often highly personal data by sellers of the goods. Reputable sellers have to be wary of defamatory comments by dissatisfied customers who often are judgment proof and who could seriously injure a company's reputation. The *Bihari* litigation is an example of the type of incident that can befall a merchant, rightfully or wrongfully, when a consumer becomes incensed.

A possible solution is the variety of online alternative dispute resolution (ADR) mechanisms that have been proposed and, to a limited degree, have been promulgated.[31] Some of the ways in which online dispute resolution (ODR) may take place are mediation, arbitration, cybertribunal, virtual magistrate, and online ombudsman. In the United States, in order to avoid litigation, the parties will have to agree on alternative dispute mechanisms. One party cannot unilaterally compel another party to agree to arbitration or other alternative formats.

Court Adjudication Online. Using the litigation approach, one way to handle matters coming within the monetary limits of small claims courts, a procedure could be instituted whereby the parties could submit their respective positions to a judge's law clerk for his or her recommended resolution. If such procedure is not successful, the presiding judge could then listen to the parties and their evidentiary submissions and make a determination. There may be constitutional issues relating to the procedure, but given the minimal sum at stake, an appellate court may very well find the procedure to be in accordance with due process requirements. Evidentiary documents could be deemed marked into evidence. Parties could cross-examine online. Such a procedure would become more feasible as Internet connections allow parties to be seen. Obviously, there is some sacrifice of the safeguards present at a courtroom proceeding, but the benefits would appear to outweigh the negative aspects. A problem with online discussion is the inability of the third party to see the contestants in person.

ALTERNATIVE DISPUTE RESOLUTION OR ONLINE DISPUTE RESOLUTION

Ombudsman

Many cities and localities have elected officials who act as ombudsman. An ombudsman may act as an intermediary between persons and may act as an advocate for persons who generally are unable to afford attorneys. They may investigate the allegations of a complaint, call in the disputing parties to discuss, mediate, and other such services. They may also serve to intervene with governmental bureaucracies to resolve complaints.

Online Mediation: Difficulties and Advantages

Assuming the parties wish to avoid going to a court, they may opt for a neutral third party to assist in having the parties come to an agreement or such party may make a determination. Mediation appears to be an almost ideal method of having the parties agree to a solution to their claims and defenses. As any experienced trial lawyer can verify, parties to a dispute very often cannot talk to one another. The trust that may have been present at the time of an agreement or prior to the incident in question is no longer present. A calm, experienced person, who is able to find merit in the various expressed points of view, can offer a reasonable solution that takes into account such views and is able to avoid extreme remedies.

The problem, however, is that mediation has assumed, in most instances, that a live, neutral third party could be spoken to directly by the antagonists. It was verbal communication whereby one or both parties had a sounding board, and they could see whether their arguments were persuasive. Often, a person acknowledges that an indebtedness is due and owing but wants the opportunity to explain why a portion of the debt should be forgiven, or that the debtor had mitigating circumstances for not paying, or that the creditor acted immorally, albeit legally, in the circumstances. Online mediation substantially negates such contact and venting of emotion.

Online mediation, by definition, does not involve face-to-face contact with the mediator and the opposing party. The process is generally one of e-mails that may take place within a short time frame or over a more extended period. Trial attorneys find that truthful or false testimony can often be gauged by a party's immediate, direct response to a question or comment. In online communication, the person's facial, hand, or other bodily reaction cannot be seen and weighed in determining who is telling the truth.

Other problems include the lack of experience of mediators online, who were trained to listen to the two or more parties making their comments and responses. Listening differs from e-mailing suggestions. The former is a live, direct, face-to-face experience while the online scenario is a correspondent, print version of a person's story. Consider the difference between trying a case in open court versus the appellate court's use of the bare pages of a transcript and briefs.

On the other hand, mediation electronically would allow reasoned arguments by a multitude of parties who can make their positions known at diverse times at their convenience. Time and expense of appearing at a distant office becomes unnecessary; e-mail allows time to compose a more rational response to an opponent's contentions; one has greater privacy of discussion from one's home or place of business; and cooler emotions emanate from familiar surroundings. All of these factors mitigate the negative aspects of ODR.[32]

Online Arbitration

Mediation and arbitration may take many forms. Mediation is not binding on the parties but rather consists of a neutral third party proposing a possible resolution of the conflict that the parties may or may not accept. Arbitration is quite varied. Although most arbitrations consist of a binding determination by a single arbitrator or a three-member panel, arbitrations may be advisory, conditionally binding, as med/arb (mediation that ends up as arbitration after unsuccessful mediation), as final offer arbitration, or mini-trials (resolving one or more specific issues only).[33]

Advantages. Like mediation, the advantages of alternative online arbitrations are fairly obvious. There may be considerable cost savings in the avoidance of travel; the comfort of using one's computer; time savings associated with remaining in one's office or home; diminished billable hours of lawyers if they have been retained; the capability to be heard from remote locations; the ability of different parties and witnesses to come online at diverse times; the option to go beyond the typical 9:00 A.M.–5:00 P.M., Monday–Friday time schedule; the privacy afforded to the parties; the cross-border capabilities (especially in consumer transactions in the European Union, whereby a customer makes a purchase from any one of a number of member states); and the ability to induce otherwise very busy practitioners to act as a neutral arbiter.

Disadvantages. On the other hand, like mediation, there are substantial difficulties. Often, visual clues and perceived reactions enable the mediator or arbitrator to propose meaningful suggestions. The mediator or arbitrator would not be able to receive such clues online. Another difficulty is that the experienced computer user may be much more able to transmit a convincing claim or defense than an inexperienced user. Ideally, the dispute is between two parties. If there are multiparties, the ability to speak to each of the parties in concert with each other may be compromised. A litigant who has lost a trial may be more prone to accept the loss having had his or her day in court. The same person may be more hesitant to resolve a problem with an unseen third party. Also, a person hearing a dispute is better able to control the admission of material and evidentiary data; receiving material online would lessen the opportunity to prevent irrelevant or inadmissible data from clogging the record or discussion. In addition, if the parties are from different countries, or there are differences in culture, language, and other variables, such factors may impede ODR.

Consumer interest groups have posed other difficulties arising out of compulsory arbitration clauses in agreements between commercial enterprises and consumers. Some of the problems posed by such groups and directed to non-Internet disputes are:

1. The mandatory arbitration clauses are often sprung upon unwitting consumers who do not read the fine print of the sales agreement. The latter do not realize they are giving up a constitutional right to a civil trial by jury. Juries tend to be more sympathetic to the complaints of consumers than are arbitrators, who often are beholden to corporate defendants for future business. In a typical arbitration, the parties are given the choice of a number of arbitrators to select from a list. Corporate litigators tend to know well the persons displayed on the list and to select those who tend to be more defendant friendly. Consumers, usually having their first experience, will not have the benefit of such knowledge.
2. There may be very sizable arbitration fees that may thwart consumers from pursuing their rights inasmuch as the cost of arbitration may outweigh any benefit derived from a favorable result (see the *Gateway* cases).
3. Consumers may have to travel a great distance to have their complaint aired.
4. The arbitration clause may limit the time in which to file a complaint. A 60-day period in which to file a complaint for arbitration is far shorter than a state's statutory period in which to sue (e.g., the state of New York allows a person six years to sue for breach of contract).

Other possible abuses include clauses that make the loser pay (a consumer is far less able to withstand the payment of corporate attorneys fees than the reverse), and some arbitration clauses allow only the corporation to choose arbitration or judicial remedies.[34]

It is obvious that any ODR would have to distinguish commercial parties from consumers. The latter must have some reasonable means of having their complaints resolved by some inexpensive, speedy process, whose resolution is determined by a neutral third party. Businesses should be willing to sacrifice some financial consideration in assuring customer satisfaction. It is when such online sales are deemed by consumers to be as safe as purchases from local stores that Internet transactions will be commonplace. All too many Internet sites have terminated because consumers fear loss of their money to unscrupulous vendors.

Other ODR Processes

In addition to the efforts to resolve disputes online just discussed, other, varied methodologies have been attempted.

The Virtual Magistrate Program. The now-defunct Virtual Magistrate program was an early attempt at online arbitration. The complaint, remedy asked, and supporting documentation were filed electronically. Thereafter, the American Arbitration Association undertook a consent agreement to arbitrate, assigned an online experienced magistrate to examine the documents, and rendered a decision. All communications were by e-mail and accomplished on a password-protected listserv. The site was discontinued for lack of interest.

Miscellaneous Sites. Such sites as CyberSettle.com, SettleSmart.com, and clickNsettle.com acted as mediation-type sites, using e-mail to seek bids for resolution by both parties and attempts to resolve. BBB*Online* and other consumer organizations have their own online facilities for the resolution of disputes.

INTERNATIONAL VIEWS OF ALTERNATIVE ONLINE DISPUTE RESOLUTION

Organization for Economic Cooperation and Development Guidelines

The Organization for Economic Cooperation and Development (OECD),[35] encompassing most of the major states in global trade, issued its recommendations concerning guidelines to be adopted by member states. The guidelines are to be disseminated to all governmental departments and agencies, as well as to business sectors involved in electronic commerce, to consumer representatives, the media, educational institutions, and other public-interest groups. They include detailed obligations of businesses to act in a manner that omits deceptive and fraudulent practices; to post clear and accurate information; to act with fairness in contractual terms; and to post online disclosures that state accurate information concerning their businesses and their goods and services, the nature of the transaction, a confirmation process, and mechanism for payment.

Dispute Resolution and Redress. Cross-border business-to-consumer transactions that take place electronically or by other means, are to be subject to the laws and jurisdictions where they take place. Inasmuch as electronic commerce creates a number of difficulties due to its multicountry extension, the guidelines call for governments to ensure fairness to consumers and to businesses. "Consumers should be provided meaningful access to fair and timely alternative dispute resolution and redress without undue cost or burden" (Article VI. B). The major actors are to work together to use a "fair, effective and transparent self-regulatory and other policies and procedures," including ADR procedures. Consumer complaints and problems are to be addressed fairly and in a timely manner. Businesses and consumer representatives are to continue to establish cooperative self-regulatory programs to address consumer complaints; and if such procedures do not resolve the conflict, then the ADR is to take place at minimal cost or burden to the consumer.

Canada

Canadian ADR and ODR is similar to that of the United States. In addition, it has tried the Cyber Tribunal, a University of Montreal–based initiative that is a bilingual, voluntary mediation process that attempts to resolve disputes by parties agreeing to be bound by its determinations. It is an online project that seeks to initially mediate a dispute and follows it with an arbitration-type decision making. It also seeks to create a voluntary code of conduct for businesses to adopt for the resolution of disputes.[36]

International Enforcement of Arbitration Awards

Arbitration awards are recognized and enforced in over one hundred countries by reason of their adherence to the 1958 New York Convention on the Recognition and Enforcement of Foreign Arbitral Awards. This convention makes an arbitration award between parties of member states enforceable in all of the member states. Latin American arbitration awards are also enforceable by reason of the Inter-

American Convention on International Commercial Arbitration.

CONCLUSION

Internationally, the president's Framework for Global Electronic Commerce suggests that UNCITRAL, the United Nations International Institute for the Unification of Private Law (UNIDROIT), and the International Chamber of Commerce develop model provisions that will do the following:

eliminate administrative and regulatory barriers and to facilitate electronic commerce by:

- encouraging governmental recognition, acceptance and facilitation of electronic communications (i.e., contracts, notarized documents, etc.);
- encouraging consistent international rules to support the acceptance of electronic signatures and other authentication procedures; and
- promoting the development of adequate, efficient, and effective alternate dispute resolution mechanisms for global commercial transactions.

It is clear that international prosperity will be dependent upon the formation and implementation of a global framework that will facilitate commercial activity. The joint efforts of the various international bodies are required to accomplish such goal.

The internationalization of the economy has led to the promulgation of agreements and conventions to harmonize the laws and regulations governing commercial activity. Without such harmonization, almost insuperable difficulties would arise in the import and export of goods and services. The European Union, the U.N., OECD, the Association of Southeast Asian Nations (ASEAN), and other regional organizations are all preparing and issuing reports, recommendations, and regulations to make the free flow of trade a reality.

Coupled with contractual expansion are activities by persons seeking to act in a manner that is violative of the rights and obligations of participants. It is even more important for global cooperation to prevent and prosecute criminal and tortious activities. Nations that formally refused to extend cooperation to major nations, particularly to the United States, have come to the realization that cooperation is necessary to prevent unlawful and highly detrimental intrusions upon the Internet.

Questions and Problems

1. How does the U.N. Convention for the International Sale of Goods differ from the UCC Article 2?
2. Compare and contrast the three types of torts. Give examples of each type.
3. Does a person who subscribes to AOL or other ISPs have absolute right to say anything he or she desires on the Web? What restrictions may the ISP impose? Can the ISP impose prior restraint so as to prevent information from being transmitted over the Internet?
4. What is meant by *trespass?* What type of tort does it constitute?
5. Are all persons entitled to the same rights and protections against defamatory remarks?
6. Discuss the various types of online dispute-resolution mechanisms.
7. Robert Konop was a pilot for Hawaiian Airlines, Inc. He maintained a Web site wherein he posted bulletins that criticized the airlines, its officers, and the Air Line Pilots Association (a pilots' union) for its concessions to management. Access to the personal Web site was restricted to employees of the airline and forbidden to management and the union. To access the site, an employee had to obtain a password, view the site, register, and consent to the nondisclosure agreement contained at the Web site. In December 1995, a vice president of the airline received from an eligible employee permission to access the Web site, although the said employee had never created an account with the site and had not consented to the restrictive covenant. The said vice president accessed the site and clicked agreement to its restrictive terms. Konop was later called by the union representative and told that management had been upset by the contents of the site. Konop sued claiming violation of Electronic Communications Privacy Act. The federal district court dismissed the action. Konop appealed. Decide.
8. Ford Motor Company, a Delaware corporation with its principal place of

business in Michigan, is licensed by the Texas Motor Vehicle Commission Code to operate as an auto manufacturer in Texas. From May 1998, Ford began operating a Web site wherein consumers could view preowned vehicles that were offered for sale or lease. The vehicles were sold on a no-haggle basis, whereby the consumer can hold a vehicle until they are able to view it at a dealership of their choice. By telephone, the hold is confirmed by Ford and is sent to the dealership after the consumer places a refundable deposit on their vehicle by Internet or by telephone. After a test drive, the consumer may decide to purchase the vehicle from the dealership. The terms of the agreement are between the dealer and the consumer. The dealership is not allowed to show any other vehicle at the dealership until the consumer has rejected the held vehicle. Ford holds title to the vehicle, which is assigned to the dealer for sale to the consumer or for purchase at a wholesale price by the dealer. The director of the Texas Department of Transportation filed a complaint against Ford, alleging that Ford violated Texas law by selling preowned vehicles directly or indirectly to consumers through the Internet without a dealer's license. Ford alleges that the Texas statute violates the First Amendment, the commerce clause, and the due process clause of the Constitution. Decide. *Ford Motor Company v. Texas Dept. of Transportation,* 106 F. Supp. 2d 905 (2000).

9. Register.com is a registrar of Internet domain names. Verio developed an automated software program consisting of a search robot that enabled it to access the WHOIS database maintained by accredited registrars, including Register.com. Verio was able to collect information about customers who recently registered domain names from the database. Register.com's terms of use expressly prohibits the retrieval and use of such information for marketing purposes. Verio proceeded to contact and solicit Register.com's customers by e-mail, regular mail, and by telephone. Register.com sues to enjoin Verio from accessing such database for marketing purposes, alleging breach of contract by Verio, trespass and violation of the Computer Fraud and Abuse Act. The act requires that the complainant be damaged. Did the acts by Verio constitute breach of contract? Trespass? Violation of the Computer Fraud and Abuse Act? *Register.com, Inc. v. Verio, Inc.,* No. 00 Civ. 5747 (BSJ), 2000 U.S. Dist. LEXIS (S.D.N.Y. 2000).

10. Computer Associates creates and licenses computer software. It licensed its programs to National Car Rental. The license agreement stated that the license program could only be used for National's internal operations and for the processing of its own data. A later agreement allowed National to permit Electronic Data Systems to provide the services for National subject to the same licensing restrictions. Computer Associates ascertained that other leasing companies were using the program. When it sued National for its refusal to abide by the license, National claimed that inasmuch as the claim was one for copyright violations, the Copyright Act preempted all claims for breach of contract. The district court found in favor of National, finding that the claim was one for "exclusive copyright of distribution of copies of the work" and, therefore, came under the Copyright Act. Computer Associates claimed that this was simply a breach of contract concerning a licensing agreement. Decide. *National Car Rental System, Inc. v. Computer Associates Intn'l, Inc.,* 991 F.2d 426 (8th Cir. 1993).

Endnotes

1. Adopted on April 11, 1980, Final Act, A/CONF 97/18, Annex (April 10, 1980).
2. The directive was proposed on November 18, 1998, and was approved by the E.U. Parliament subject to amendments on April 23, 1999.
3. For a discussion of this topic see Nigel Howard, Karen Opp, and Erika Takeuchi, *Proposed Directive is an Important Step,* New York Law Journal (supplement entitled *Intellectual Property* July 26, 1999), pp. S1, S8-S9; and *Opinion of the Economic and Social Committee* on the said proposal, dated April 29, 1999, *Lexis-Nexis.com/universe.*
4. *Opinion* at 1.1.2.
5. Id. at 3.2 and 3.3.
6. For example, some places have laws that prohibit advertising to children or that restrict medicinal

products sold by mail, while other countries have few regulations in many areas of marketing. See *Opinion,* 3.4.

7. Directive 97/7/EC on distance contracts.
8. Article 9(2).
9. Article 11(1).
10. Howard, Opp, and Takeuchi, *Opposed Directive,* p. S9, citing Explanatory Report, Article 11(1).
11. *Opinion,* 4.10.2.
12. Article 12(1) of the proposed directive.
13. Id. Articles 13 and 14.
14. Article 12. For a discussion, see Trevor Cox, *Information and the Internet: Understanding the Emerging Legal Framework for Contract and Copyright Law and Problems with International Enforcement,* 11 Transnat'l Law 23 (Spring 1998).
15. General Assembly Resolution, 51/162, *Model Law on Electronic Commerce,* December 16, 1996.
16. *Data message* is defined in Article 2 as "information generated, sent, received or stored by electronic, optical or similar means including but not limited to, electronic data interchange (EDI), electronic mail, telegram, telex or copy."
17. Article 7.
18. Article 8(1).
19. Article 9 of the model law.
20. Id. Article 11.
21. Id. Article 14.
22. Id. Article 15.
23. It is unclear whether defamation through the Internet is libel or slander, but it appears that it is most akin to libel inasmuch as it can be downloaded, viewed as reading material, and printed out.
24. 47 U.S.C. Section 230. *Protection for Private Blocking and Screening of Offensive Material.*
25. Section 230(a).
26. For an excellent review of issues concerning defamation and the Internet, see *III. The Long Arm of Cyber-reach,* 112 Harv. L. Rev. 1610 (1999).
27. 129 F.3d 327 (4th Cir. 1997).
28. For a discussion of *Blumenthal,* see Michelle J. Kane, *VI. Business Law: 11. Electronic Commerce: b) Internet Service Provider Liability: Blumenthal v. Drudge,* 14 Berkeley Tech. L.J. 483 (1999). The reader should note that, although parts of the CDA were declared to be unconstitutional with respect to the obscenity aspects of the law, the ISP exemption was not invalidated.
29. *Stratton Oakmont, Inc. v. Prodigy Servs. Co.,* 1995 WL 323710 (N.Y. Sup. Ct. May 24, 1995).
30. 776 F. Supp. 135 (S.D.N.Y. 1991).
31. For a discussion of online dispute resolution, see Lucille M. Ponte, *Throwing Bad Money after Bad: Can Online Dispute Resolution (ODR) Really Deliver the Goods for the Unhappy Internet Shopper?* unpublished paper delivered to the American Business Law Association (August 2000); Christine Hart, *Online Dispute Resolution and Avoidance in Electronic Commerce,* Uniform Law Conference of Canada, *www.law.ualberta.ca/alri/ulc/current/hart.htm;* Catherine Kessedjian, *Internet Dispute Resolution Mechanisms and Applicable Law, www.cetp.ipsl.fr/~porteneu/inet98/2e/2e_1.htm;* and Joel B. Eisen, *Are We Ready for Mediation in Cyberspace?* 1998 B.Y.U.L. Rev. 1305 (1998).
32. See Eisen, *Are We Ready.*
33. Council of Better Business Bureaus BBB*Online,* Letter dated March 21, 2000, to the Federal Trade Commission, *www.ftc.gov/bcp/altdisresolution/comments/cfa.htm,* p. 3.
34. Letter of March 20, 2000, from the Trial Lawyers for Public Justice to the Federal Trade Commission, *www.ftc.gov/bcp/altdisresolution/comments/cfa.htm.*
35. Organization for Economic Cooperation and Development, *Recommendation of the OECD Council Concerning Guidelines for Consumer Protection in the Context of Electronic Commerce* (April 1998).
36. Christine Hart, *Online Dispute Resolution and Avoidance in Electronic Commerce, www.law.ualberta.ca/alri/ulc/current/hart.htm.*

CHAPTER

5

CRIMINAL ASPECTS OF CYBERSPACE

Chapter Outline

CYBERCRIME

The negative side of computer technology is its susceptibility to criminal behavior. In any given month, there are news accounts of the implantation of a virus affecting computers worldwide. Some of the viruses are mere nuisances, while other viruses may cause significant destruction to data, programs, and hard drives. Banks and other financial institutions have lost large sums of money, and most of these instances either have not been reported or have been kept confidential with investigative authorities. National security data and company trade secrets, unlawfully downloaded by skilled trespassers, have been sold to foreign spy organizations. Perhaps the greatest losses have been incurred by owners of intellectual property, who see their protected works spring up on computer screens, accessed by users free from payments of royalties. In addition to property destruction, theft offenses, and misappropriation of intellectual property, pornographers have avoided prosecution by a variety of technological devices and by causing their conduct to emanate from countries whose laws have not kept up with the latest developments. We will examine both national and international efforts to curb cybercrime.

Problems and Issues Raised by Cybercrime

***Cybercrime* Defined.** There is no uniform definition of cybercrime, either nationally or globally. Nevertheless, we can identify certain characteristics and formulate a definition. Cybercrime is a generic term covering, generally, the multiplicity of crimes found in penal codes or in legislation having the use of computer technology as a central component. A crime requires proof of the act or omission forbidden by law *(actus reus)* coupled with criminal intent *(mens rea)* in the commission of the act or omission of a required duty. There are almost as many types of cybercrimes as there are non-computer-related offenses. Thus, cybercrime includes criminal trespass, willful destruction of property, theft of intellectual property, forgery, obscenity, child pornography, larceny, and other offenses. In this chapter, we will review some of the multiplicity of criminal legislation enacted to address criminal behavior as it affects cyberspace.

Jurisdiction. We discuss the problem of ascertaining jurisdiction in Chapter 2. The issue is more complex when criminal statutes are applicable. All countries have basic laws forbidding the commission of common criminal acts, but the Internet is so relatively new that less-developed and, to a lesser degree, developed countries lack statutory enactments making cybercrime illegal within these countries. Many countries have passed legislation forbidding certain cybercrimes, but it contains loopholes that allow perpetrators to be exonerated. Also, many countries either forbid or are very reluctant to permit the extradition of their citizens to countries affected by the criminal acts of their inhabitants. The United States is not an exception. Until recently, the downloading and uploading of programs were not unlawful unless there was a profit motive. Thus, persons lacking such motive were able to have their cases dismissed.

Certain activities, such as gambling, are not forbidden in certain countries, thereby permitting these venues to be safe havens for otherwise unlawful activity. The United States often demands the extradition of foreign nationals for alleged crimes affecting U.S. persons. It complains strenuously when such demands are not met. Nevertheless, the United States also would be reluctant to extradite a U.S. national, on constitutional grounds, who engages in speech protected by the First Amendment but that may impinge on the legal rights of a foreign person. An example is the protection given to extremist groups in the United States, which may preach Nazi propaganda or transact business in Nazi paraphernalia in violation of foreign laws.

Countries have very different views as to direct and vicarious liability of legal persons (corporations, partnerships, joint ventures, etc.) concerning content of transmissions. Issues of jurisdiction and criminal liability of a director of a foreign subsidiary for the service provided by a parent were discussed in a very controversial German case that had global ramifications.

PEOPLE V. SOMM

Local Court Munich, File No. 8340 Ds 465 Js 173158/95

FACTS: The defendant was employed as Managing Director of CompuServe Information Services GmbH located in Munich. CompuServe is an Internet Service Provider whose parent company is located in Virginia, U.S.A. Newsgroups posted on the service contained pornographic images of sex pedophilia of boys and girls with photographs and offers of swaps. The defendant did advise CompuServe to block or delete the newsgroups. Although some deletions took place, the police gave CompuServe in Munich a lengthy list of sites containing pedophilia, which it demanded that CompuServe remove. CompuServe USA took the position that providing "parental control" tools to users to block access sufficed to limit access to such sites and took no further steps to cease display of the pornography. The Court then recited the numerous sites that violated Germany's anti-pornography statutes. The defendant, who was the Director of CompuServe in Germany, was arrested for violation of German law.

ISSUE: Whether the defendant was liable criminally for failure of the Internet Service Provider, in which he was the Director, to block access to the said pornographic sites?

DECISION: The defendant was found guilty of assisting in the dissemination of pornographic writings. He was sentenced to two years probation and compelled to pay the costs of the proceeding.

REASONING: Judge Hubbert

The accused is found guilty of having assisted in the dissemination of pornographic writings. . . .

He made publicly accessible pornographic writings containing acts of violence, sexual abuse of children and sex acts between human beings and animals.

Pursuant to [German law] . . . offenses relating to the business of CompuServe Germany are attributable to him as Managing director. . . .

[The court recited the elements of the crime, namely, the pornographic writings, the representations, the content stored on data-storage devices, the public accessibility of the writings, the defendant's complicity by connection to CompuServe USA, and other related elements.]

The violent, child, or animal pornographic representations stored on and accessible from the newsserver constitute a source of risk, because they present the danger of misrepresentation of children or youths and of the abuse of children. Moreover, adults could become victims of offenders having an inclination to violent pornography. . . .

CompuServe USA exercises the actual physical control over its newsserver. They are in a position to block or deblock both newsgroups specifically indicating hard pornography and news articles assigned to such newsgroups. . . .

Therefore, CompuServe USA was under a duty to block access to said pornographic content. This duty also exists if the risk can be attributed to a third party . . . if the corresponding news articles are contributed by third parties as in the present case.

CompuServe had the opportunity to block access by blocking newsgroups which clearly indicated violent, child, or animal pornography. If CompuServe USA had removed the relevant newsgroups from its data storage device, said newsgroups would not have been made accessible to the customers of CompuServe USA via the data storage device of CompuServe USA. . . . CompuServe USA's criminal liability based on failure to act is unaffected by the fact that other persons also made hard pornography publicly accessible through their newsservers. . . .

The contribution to the offense made by CompuServe USA must be imputed to the accused, since the contributions of both were performed due to a joint decision. [The court recited the notifications given by the police to CompuServe Germany, the correspondence that took place, and the refusal of CompuServe to block access to the sites given to it by the police.] . . .

Liability is excluded under the . . . Teleservices Act for providers who make available for use third-party content. . . .

1. The conditions for an exemption from liability [under the act] are not met, since CompuServe Germany is not an access provider.

An access provider provides his customers with direct access to computer networks, in particular the Internet. CompuServe Germany, however, neither has its own customers nor provides access to the network. Access to the network is provided only by the parent company, which also makes third-party content available for use. CompuServe Germany is only responsible for connecting the customers of CompuServe USA in Germany via a local dial-in node and a dedicated line with the parent company. This dedicated line between parent company and subsidiary does not make the subsidiary into an access provider.

[The court recited the evidence and factual issues in question in great detail and found the evidence supported the court's finding of deliberate criminal and negligent conduct of the ISP and the director.]

CASE QUESTIONS

1. Should CompuServe, as an Internet service provider, be responsible for the multitude of messages and data sent through it as a medium?
2. Is the CompuServe-postman analogy used by U.S. courts appropriate in this case?
3. Is an officer of a corporation responsible for the actions of its employer?

Other Issues

The problems faced by the United States and the international community were succinctly stated in a United Nations Manual on cybercrime.[1] They are:

1. The lack of global consensus on what types of conduct should constitute a computer-related crime;

2. The lack of global consensus on the legal definition of criminal conduct;
3. The lack of expertise on the part of police, prosecutors and the courts in this field;
4. The inadequacy of legal powers for investigation and access to computer systems, including the inapplicability of seizure powers to intangibles such as computerized data;
5. The lack of harmonization between the different national procedural laws concerning the investigation of computer-related crimes;
6. The transnational character of many computer crimes;
7. The lack of extradition and mutual assistance treaties and of synchronized law enforcement mechanisms that would permit international cooperation, or the inability of existing treaties to take into account the dynamics and special requirements of computer-crime investigation.

In addition to the problems addressed in the U.N. Manual, there are language barriers, lack of procedures concerning the preservation of data in response to a foreign country's request, and sovereignty issues.

U.S. CRIMINAL STATUTES AFFECTING THE INTERNET

Fraud Statutes

Countries, especially the United States, have enacted a number of statutes to regulate and set ground rules for civil and criminal conduct. Among the laws enacted in the United States that may pertain directly or indirectly to computer technology are statutes concerning fraud and, in particular, fraudulent activities affecting the Internet.

Access Device Fraud Act (18 U.S.C. Section 1029). The problem addressed by Congress was the lack of statutory authority to prosecute Internet crimes. A number of courts, such as the decision reflected in the *LaMacchia* case to be discussed, dismissed alleged Internet crimes for failure to strictly comply with the provisions of the respective statutes.[2] Accordingly, Congress passed the Access Device Fraud Act of 1984 and the Computer Fraud and Abuse Act of 1986.

The Access Device Fraud Act of 1984, as amended, makes it a crime by "whoever . . . knowingly and with intent to defraud produces, uses or traffics in one or more counterfeit access devices" in interstate commerce (18 U.S.C. Section 1029(a)(1)). The act also forbids production, trafficking in, control or custody of, or possession of device-making equipment with intent to defraud (18 U.S.C. Section 1029(a)(4)). The act protects computer passwords. Possession of counterfeit or unauthorized access devices or device-making equipment may violate the act.

An *access device* is defined as "any card, plate, code, account number or other means of account access that can be used, alone or in conjunction with another access device, to obtain money, goods, services, or anything of value, or that can be used to initiate a transfer of funds (other than a transfer originated solely by paper instrument)." A *counterfeit access device* is "any access device that is counterfeit, fictitious, altered, or forged, or an identifiable component of an access device or a counterfeit access device" (18 U.S.C. Section 1029(e)(1)(2)). Credit cards obtained from issuing companies by means of false applications with intent to defraud are subject to the statute. The following case illustrates the application of the act to cellular telephones.

UNITED STATES V. ASHE

47 F.3d 770 (6th Cir. 1995)

FACTS: Ashe was found guilty of producing and possessing altered cellular telephones that enabled users to access cellular telephone services without charge in violation of the Access Device Fraud Act. A second defendant pled guilty of trafficking in the altered telephones.

ISSUE: Whether "the possession, distribution, sale, and use of mobile cellular telephones which have been converted, by the insertion of a 'tumbling' microchip that counterfeits electronic codes that access the transmitting facilities operated by commercial cellular telephone companies, in a manner that converts the carrier's service monitoring procedures thereby permitting the user to avoid charges resulting from the illicit invasion of the cellular telephone company's property" violated the Access Device Fraud Act?

DECISION: The Court of Appeals upheld the lower Court's determination that the statute was violated by the defendant.

REASONING: Judge Krupansky

. . . Cellular telephone service is available from commercially owned and operated communication networks that utilize individual cellular telephone units which have wireless radio transmission capabilities, operating among a series of geographic cells. Each geographic cell is served by a radio transmission tower and antenna, and as the cellular telephone user moves from one cell to another, the telephone call is automatically relayed from one transmission tower to the other, thus maintaining consistent signal quality. . . .

Another feature provided by cellular carriers permits a cellular telephone customer to "roam" placing calls from a foreign geographic cell, that is a geographic cell owned and operated by a carrier with whom the customer has no subscription account, i.e. a foreign carrier. This permits a caller to place a local or long distance call anywhere in the United States while outside the geographical area serviced by his/her home carrier with whom he has a subscription contract. When a "roamer" places a call from a foreign geographical service area the cellular telephone automatically transmits the caller's assigned MIN [mobile identification number] and ESN [electronic serial number]. By design, the MIN transmitted by a "tumbling" cellular telephone will identify an ostensible home carrier located outside of the geographical region from which the user placed the illegitimate call; accordingly, all calls made on the "tumbling" cellular telephone are treated as "roamer" calls by the servicing carrier.

In processing a "roamer" call, a foreign carrier immediately recognizes the MIN as belonging to another existing carrier. To provide effective customer service, "roamer" calls are, by internetwork agreement, practice, and procedure, immediately transmitted by a foreign carrier before validation of the identifying MIN/ESN combination has been completed by a central data bank clearing house located in San Angelo, Texas. Because the clearing house is incapable of instant validation, a time lag occurs while its computers seek to match the automatically transmitted identifying MIN/ESN with an existing home carrier-subscriber combination recorded in its data bank of national internetwork listings. In the absence of a valid match all subsequent calls using the same MIN/ESN combination will be rejected. Although service charges resulting from unmatched MIN/ESN combinations are listed together with all pertinent information related to the call in the foreign carrier's billing computer, the illicit "roaming" customer cannot be identified; consequently the charges cannot be collected from any individual. The illicit "roaming" caller may use the same combination of counterfeit MIN/ESN numbers until it is invalidated, at which time the user merely "re-tumbles" the numbers by entering a new, randomly selected combination into the key board of the cellular telephone, and may continue to "free ride" indefinitely. . . .

[T]he invasion of an identifiable customer's account is not a necessary element of proof to support a conviction under the statute here in issue. To prevail, the government need only prove by the appropriate weight of the evidence that the defendant possessed, produced, trafficked, had control over, or had custody of an instrument or device (or device-making equipment) that permits a theft of services. Because preexisting agreements and practices within the inter-telephone carrier network require an MIN-identified home carrier to reimburse a foreign carrier for the air time incurred by either a valid subscriber or an illicit "roamer" identified by a transmitted MIN and ESN combination that actuated access to the inter-cellular telephone network, a fraudulently identified ostensible home carrier ultimately assumes the loss of the unidentified "free-rider" call which was debited to its account as a result of the counterfeit MIN/ESN identification combination. In 1992, the losses charged to cellular telephone carriers resulting from "free-riding" amounted to over $100 million.

This court accordingly concludes that a converted "tumbling" cellular telephone is a device which is capable of accessing cellular telephone carrier accounts by transmitting counterfeit MIN and ESN signals that permit illicit "roamers" to fraudulently obtain free air time. In sum, the instruments here in issue are devices that permit and facilitate the theft of "air time" from the individual cellular telephone carriers comprising the national inter-cellular telephone network of companies that are engaged in the commerce of providing cellular telephone services to subscribers, and is accordingly in violation of 18 U.S.C. Section 1029. . . .

CASE QUESTIONS

1. Assuming the telephone service, the caller, and the activity all took place within one state, does the federal statute apply?
2. For a defendant to be convicted of a crime, the statute must inform a potential defendant clearly of the alleged crime. Does the statute make the potential defendant realize that an altered mobile cellular telephone comes within the statute's prohibitions?

In *United States v. Bailey,* 41 F.3d 413 (9th Cir. 1994), the U.S. court of appeals upheld a jury verdict of guilt against the defendant who modified cellular telephones "to fool the local network into permitting calls placed by those phones to be completed in roaming code," which could not be billed to the defendant. The defendant read the phone's program and rewrote it so that it randomly changed the electronic serial number. He then sold five modified chips to undercover government agents who proceeded to arrest him. The court decided that unassigned but functioning long distance access codes were "access devices" under the statute.

In *United States v. Scartz,* 838 F.2d 876 (6th Cir. 1988), the defendant and three other persons were indicted for conspiracy to use counterfeit credit cards to defraud banks and merchants. The defendant claimed that, inasmuch as no one suffered a loss because the banks ultimately did not honor the credit cards proffered to them, he could not be charged under the statute and that the alleged crime was not in interstate commerce. The court of appeals affirmed the jury conviction, stating that the government only had to demonstrate that the defendant used a counterfeit credit card with knowledge and intent to defraud and that there was some connection with interstate commerce. That there was no ensuing loss to the banks or merchants did not negate the elements of the crime nor did it detract from the interstate element of the activity. The statute does not appear to apply to satellite television descramblers. *United States v. McNutt,* 908 F.2d 561 (10th Cir. 1990).[3]

Computer Fraud and Abuse Act of 1986 (18 U.S.C. Section 1030). The Computer Fraud and Abuse Act of 1986 is the leading statute governing computer crime. Its basic provisions are set forth in the endnotes.[4] In essence, this act provides that it is a crime punishable up to 20 years in prison to unlawfully access a computer to obtain secret or restricted data from the government or financial institutions, or to use data wrongfully obtained to perpetrate fraud or for other unlawful purposes.

The application of the statute was questioned in the following case wherein a first-year graduate student at Cornell University was found guilty of releasing a so-called worm, or virus, into a computer program.

UNITED STATES V. MORRIS

928 F.2d 504 (2d Cir. 1991)

FACTS: The defendant, Robert Tappan Morris, was convicted of releasing a "worm" or virus onto the Internet thereby causing computers at educational institutions and military sites to crash. Morris had been given a computer account at Cornell's Computer Science Division permitting him to use its computers. In October 1988, Morris began work on a computer program known as the INTERNET "worm." The purpose of the program was to reveal the deficiencies of the current security measures on computer networks by revealing the security defects Morris discovered in his research. He then released the worm that was designed to spread widely without revealing its source. It also was designed to occupy little computer operation time and not interfere with the normal use of the computers. He released the worm from a computer at M.I.T. [Massachusetts Institute of Technology] to disguise the Cornell source. Due to a miscalculation, the worm duplicated itself well beyond Morris' intent, thereby causing computers throughout the country to crash. He attempted to kill the worm but it was too late to prevent the extensive damage.

ISSUES: (1) Whether the Government must prove both that the defendant intended to access a federal interest computer and that he intended to prevent authorized use of the computer's information and thereby cause loss?

(2) What elements of proof are necessary to satisfy the statutory requirement of "access without authorization?"

DECISION: (1) The Court decided that the applicable section of the Act (1030(a)(5)(A)) did not require that the Government prove that the defendant intentionally prevented authorized use and thereby caused loss.

(2) The elements of proof are recited in the Court's reasoning below.

REASONING: Judge Newman

. . . Section 2(d) of the Computer Fraud and Abuse Act of 1986 . . . punishes anyone who intentionally accesses without authorization a category of computers known as "federal interest computers" and damages or prevents authorized use of information in such computers, causing loss of $1,000 [now $5,000] or more. . . .

I. THE INTENT REQUIREMENT IN SECTION 1030(a)(5)(A)

[Section 1030(a)(5) provides that it is unlawful for a person to:

(A) knowingly causes the transmission of a program, information, code, or command, and as a result of such conduct, intentionally causes damage without authorization, to a protected computer;
(B) intentionally access a protected computer without authorization, and as a result of such conduct, recklessly causes damage; or
(C) intentionally accesses a protected computer without authorization, and as a result of such conduct, causes damage.]

Morris argues that the Government had to prove not only that he intended the unauthorized access of a federal interest computer, but also that he intended to prevent others from using it, and thus cause a loss. The adverb, "intentionally," he contends, modifies both verb phrases of the section. The Government urges that since punctuation sets the "accesses" phrase off from the subsequent "damages" phrase, the provision unambiguously shows that "intentionally" modifies only "accesses." . . .

There is a problem, however, with applying Morris's explanation to section 1030(a)(5)(A). As noted earlier, the predecessor of subsection (a)(5)(A) explicitly placed the same mental state requirement before both the "accesses" phrase and the "damages" phrase. In relevant part, that predecessor in the 1984 statute covered anyone who "*knowingly accesses* a computer without authorization . . . *and* by means of such conduct *knowingly uses,* modifies, destroys, or discloses information in, or prevents authorized use of, such computer. . . . This earlier provision demonstrates that Congress has on occasion chosen to repeat the same scienter standard in the "accesses" phrase and the subsequent phrase of a subsequent subsection of the Computer Fraud Statute. More pertinently, it shows that the 1986 amendments adding subsection (a)(5)(A) placed the scienter requirement adjacent only to the "accesses" phrase in contrast to a predecessor provision that had placed the same standard before both the phrase and the subsequent phrase. . . .

II. THE UNAUTHORIZED ACCESS REQUIREMENTS IN SECTION 1030(a)(5)(A)

Section 1030(a)(5)(A) penalizes the conduct of an individual who "intentionally accesses a Federal interest computer without authorization." Morris contends that his conduct constituted, at most, "exceeding authorized access" rather than "unauthorized access," and that even if the evidence sufficed, he was entitled to have the jury instructed on his "theory of defense."

We assess the sufficiency of the evidence under the traditional standard. Morris was authorized to use computers at Cornell, Harvard, and Berkeley, all of which were on INTERNET. As a result, Morris was authorized to communicate with other computers on the network to send electronic mail (SEND MAIL), and to find out certain information about the users of other computers (finger demon). The question is whether Morris' transmission of his worm constituted authorized access or accessing without authorization. . . .

The evidence permitted the jury to conclude that Morris's use of the SEND MAIL and finger demon features constituted access without authorization. . . .

CASE QUESTIONS

1. One of two elements of a crime is that of criminal intent. Do you believe that Morris intended to commit the crime for which he was prosecuted?
2. Does the fact that he had an innocent motive—to show the deficiencies of the current computer system—rather than the intention to cause harm or gain profit negate the commission of the crime?
3. Should Morris receive the same or similar sentence that would be imposed upon a person having the intent to cause serious harm to computer systems in cyberspace?

Other Fraud Statutes

Wire Fraud (18 U.S.C. Section 1343). The statute reads as follows:

> Whoever, having devised or intending to devise any scheme or artifice to defraud, or for obtaining money or property by means of false or fraudulent pretenses, representations, or promises, transmits or causes to be transmitted by means of wire, radio, or television communication in interstate or foreign commerce, any writings, signs, signals, pictures, or sounds for the purpose of executing such scheme or artifice, shall be fined not more than $1,000 or imprisoned not more than five years, or both. If the violation affects a financial institution, such person shall be fined not more than $1,000,000 or imprisoned not more than 30 years, or both.

To prove wire or mail fraud, it is necessary for the prosecution to show "(1) a scheme to defraud by means of false pretenses; (2) the defendant's knowing and willing participation in the scheme with the intent to defraud; and (3) the use of interstate wire or mail communications in furtherance of the scheme."[5] The Wire Fraud Statute of 1952 contained a major loophole that compelled the court, in the notorious *LaMacchia* criminal proceeding, to dismiss the action. Is *confidential information* considered to be property under the statute? At least one court has stated, "Where such information is obtained—thus depriving the rightful owner of its property rights—through dishonest or deceitful means, the wire and mail fraud statutes may be violated. . . . [M]ere access to the confidential information is insufficient. . . . "[6]

UNITED STATES V. LAMACCHIA

871 F. Supp. 535 (D.Mass. 1994)

FACTS: David LaMacchia was a 21-year-old M.I.T. student who used the school's computer network to gain access to the Internet. Using pseudonyms and an encrypted address, he set up an electronic bulletin board named "Cynosure" on which he requested correspondents to upload popular software such as Excel 5.0, WordPerfect 6.0, and computer games. He then transferred the programs to another encrypted address where users having the Cynosure password could download them without cost. LaMacchia was indicted for conspiracy to violate the wire fraud statute (18 U.S.C. 1343) in that he with others caused the illegal copying and distribution of copyrighted software without payment of royalties. Citing the U.S. Supreme Court case of *Dowling v. United States,* 473 U.S. 207 (1985), LaMacchia claimed that the government had wrongfully used the wire fraud statute to enforce the copyright laws.

ISSUE: Whether defendant's conduct of causing the uploading and downloading of software programs without fee violated the wire fraud statute?

DECISION: The Court held such conduct did not violate the statue and the action was dismissed.

REASONING: Judge Stearns

[The court extensively discussed the *Dowling* decision (to be summarized) as well as the history of copyright legislation. It discussed the Copyright Act of 1909, which made it a crime to knowingly and willfully aid and abet another's infringing activities. Congress passed the Sound Recording Act of 1971 to extend copyright protection to sound recordings and included criminal penalties.] In 1992 . . . Congress passed the Copyright Felony Act. . . . The Act . . . extend[ed] its felony provision to the criminal provision to the criminal infringement of all copyrighted works including computer software. . . . The *mens rea* for criminal infringement remained unchanged, requiring prosecutors to prove that the defendant infringed a copyright "willfully and for purpose of commercial advantage or private financial gain." . . .

[The court recited the Wire Fraud Statute, set forth previously.]

As the legislative history makes clear, the wire fraud statute was intended to complement the mail fraud statute by giving federal prosecutors jurisdiction over frauds involving the use of interstate (or foreign) wire transmissions. . . .

Unlike the criminal copyright statute, 17 U.S.C. Sec. 506(a), the mail and wire fraud statutes do not require that a defendant be shown to have sought to personally profit from the scheme to defraud. . . .

LaMacchia is not alleged to have violated section 506(a) [the law requires a profit motive] . . . the copyright holder owns only a bundle of intangible rights which can be infringed, but not stolen or converted. The owner of confidential, proprietary business information, in contrast, possesses something which has clearly been recognized as an item of *property*. . . .

The issue thus is whether the "bundle of rights" conferred by copyright is unique and distinguishable from the indisputably broad range of property interests protected by the mail and wire fraud statutes. I find it difficult, if not impossible, to read Dowling as saying anything but that it is. . . .

I agree with Professor Nimmer that:

> The *Dowling* decision establishes that Congress has finely calibrated the reach of criminal liability [in the Copyright Act], and therefore absent clear indication of Congressional intent, the criminal laws of the United States do not reach copyright-related conduct. Thus copyright prosecutions should be limited to Section 506 of the Act, and other incidental statutes that explicitly refer to copyright and copyrighted works.

Accordingly, I rule that the decision of the Supreme Court in *Dowling v. United States* precludes LaMacchia's prosecution for criminal copyright infringement under the wire fraud statute. . . .

CASE QUESTIONS

1. Should the court have read the statute so narrowly so as to excuse the defendant's conduct?
2. Could LaMacchia have been convicted of some other criminal statute? [See copyright infringement statute, to be discussed.]

After the *LaMacchia* decision, Congress passed the No Electronic Theft Act of 1997. The act removed the requirement of financial gain from 18 U.S.C. Section 506(a) as a mandatory requirement for electronic misuse and specifically includes conduct involving copyright infringement by electronic means.

Criminal Infringement of a Copyright (18 U.S.C. Section 506(a)). The act makes it a criminal offense as follows:

> (a) CRIMINAL INFRINGEMENT—Any person who infringes a copyright either—
> (1) for purposes of commercial advantage or private financial gain, or
> (2) by the reproduction or distribution, *including by electronic means* [emphasis added], during any 180-day period, of 1 or more copies or phonorecords of 1 or more copyrighted works, which have a total retail value of more than $1,000 shall be punished as provided under section 2319 of title 18, United States Code. For purposes of this subsection, evidence of reproduction or distribution of a copyrighted work, by itself, shall not be sufficient to establish willful infringement.

The Copyright Act of 1976 made it a crime to willfully infringe a copyright for profit. The 1982 amendment to Section 506 of the Copyright Act raised the level of the crime to a felony.

In *Dowling v. United States,* 473 U.S. 207 (1985), the defendant, Dowling, was convicted of conspiracy, interstate transportation of stolen property, copyright violations, and mail fraud by virtue of his sale of bootleg copies of Elvis Presley recordings by soliciting catalog orders from a post office box in California. The U.S. Supreme Court decided that bootleg copyrighted materials on a phonorecord were not property within the meaning of the Stolen Property Act that made a perpetrator punishable for property that was stolen, converted, or taken by fraud. The Court said that a copyright, unlike other types of property, does not permit a holder to acquire exclusive dominion over the thing owned. For example, copyrights are subject to fair use limitations and other exemptions. Stealing an object does not lend itself to such limitations. To allow such conduct to be subject to the stolen property statutes would criminalize a broad range of conduct involving intellectual property laws that were regulated historically by civil laws.

In *United States v. Mullins,* 992 F.2d 1472 (9th Cir. 1993), three travel agents were convicted of mail and wire fraud for conspiring to defraud an airline by electronically transferring frequent flyer miles to fictitious accounts and using the accounts to acquire free airline tickets. The defendants claimed that they did not violate the statute, because the airline was not deprived of anything of value. They claimed that the credit for miles flown on an airline was the property of the passenger who does the flying, and a passenger who elects not to join the frequent flyer mile program abandons such property (ordinarily, anyone may legally take abandoned property of another). The court of appeals rejected the argument, stating that the defendants did receive value, to wit, convertible miles for free airline tickets by misuse of confidential information provided by the airline.

Counterfeit Trademarks (18 U.S.C. Section 2320). The Trademark Counterfeit Act of 1984 states:

> Whoever intentionally traffics or attempts to traffic in goods or services and knowingly uses a counterfeit mark on or in connection with such goods or services shall, in an individual, be fined not more that $2,000,000 or imprisoned not more than 10 years, or both, and, if a person other than an individual, be fined not more than $5,000,000. In the case of an offense by a person under this section that occurs after that person is convicted of another offense under this section, the person con-

victed, if an individual, shall be fined not more than $5,000,000 or imprisoned not more than 20 years, or both, and if other than an individual, shall be fined not more than $15,000,000.

Civil infringement is discussed in Chapter 8 and is much broader than the criminal statute. Civil liability is predicated on the avoidance of confusion by consumers seeking to purchase goods having identical or confusingly similar marks. Also, civil liability may ensue for dilution of a famous mark even if a consumer would not be confused by the similarity of the marks.

Mail Fraud (18 U.S.C. Section 1341). It is unlawful to use the mail to devise a scheme to commit or attempt to commit a fraud to obtain money or other tangible or intangible property. The statute includes counterfeit coins, obligations, securities, or other articles. Under this statute, the same provisions apply to a remote terminal or microcomputer to perpetrate a computer fraud, or when one telephones an accomplice in another state in furtherance of a fraud scheme.

Conspiracy to Defraud the U.S. Government (18 U.S.C. 371). It is a felony punishable by up to five years for two or more persons to conspire to commit an offense against the United States, or any of its agencies, or to defraud the United States coupled with the commission of an act to effect the object of the conspiracy. The exception to the statute concerns the maximum punishment for an offense where the parties conspire to commit a misdemeanor—in such cases the maximum punishment is limited to the punishment that could have been imposed for the lesser crime.

False Statements (18 U.S.C. Section 1001). Allied to Section 371 is the statute that prohibits the making of a false, fictitious, or fraudulent statement to a department or agency concerning a "matter within the jurisdiction" of that department or agency. It does not require that a thing of value be involved, only that the statement was knowingly and willfully made.

Identity Theft and Assumption Deterrence Act (18 U.S.C. Section 1028). This act, passed in 1998, makes it a felony for a person who "(7) knowingly transfers or uses, without lawful authority, a means of identification of another person with the intent to commit, or to aid or abet, any unlawful activity that constitutes a violation of Federal law, or that constitutes a felony under any applicable State or local law." Imprisonment up to 20 years may be imposed for serious offenses, such as facilitating a drug-trafficking offense or if the offense is done in connection with a crime of violence. *Means of identification* refers to any name or number used to identify an individual, including a name, social security number, driver's license, unique electronic identification number, telecommunication-identifying information or access device, and other such identifying manifestations (Section 28(d)). Interestingly, the attempt or conspiracy to commit the crime is made subject to the same penalties as the commission of the act.

The Racketeer Influenced and Corrupt Organizations Act (RICO) (18 U.S.C. Section 1961). The congressional purpose of the statute is "to seek the eradication of organized crime in the United States by strengthening the legal tools in the evidence-gathering process, by establishing new penal prohibitions, and by providing enhanced sanctions and new remedies to deal with the unlawful activities of those in organized crime." Few laws are as controversial as RICO. Originally aimed at prosecuting members of organized crime, the statute has been used and abused, especially civilly, to prosecute or sue otherwise legitimate organizations.

It is unlawful for any person to receive or conspire to receive income, directly or indirectly, derived from a pattern of racketeering activity or through the collection of an unlawful debt. In order for the statute to be applicable, a pattern of racketeering activity must be alleged and proven. To constitute a *pattern,* at least two acts of racketeering activity within 10 years must be established. *Racketeering activity* has a very lengthy definition that includes violent offenses, dealing in obscene matter, many types of fraud, transmission of gambling information, criminal infringement of intellectual property, and numerous other offenses affecting interstate commerce (Section 1961).

The criminal penalties include fines, imprisonment of up to 20 years (life if the racketeering activity has a maximum penalty of life imprisonment), temporary restraining orders and injunctions, and forfeiture of profits and property derived from the racketeering activity. Forfeiture of property includes real and personal, tangible and intangible property. Civil remedies that can be imposed include divestiture of any interest in the forbidden enterprise, reasonable restrictions on the future activities and investments in the same or similar enterprise, and the dissolution of the enterprise (Section 1963). What gives the statute greater enforceability is the provision that any person who is injured as a result of the prohibited activities may sue the offending persons and recover triple damages plus costs and reasonable attorney's fees. It is this latter provision that may be seriously abused inasmuch as many lawful enterprises have engaged in conduct (often unwittingly through overly aggressive agents and employees) that come within the act's prohibitions.

Other Applicable Statutes

Wire and Electronic Communications Interception and Interception of Oral Communications (18 U.S.C. Section 2511). The statute prohibits the interception of any wire, oral, or electronic communication; the interference with radio transmissions; the use of devices to intercept oral communications without consent, and the disclosure thereof. There are numerous exceptions including: the interception of radio communications available to the general public; persons affiliated with the Federal Communications Commission in the normal course of employment; where the person is a party to the communication or has given prior consent, unless the interception is to commit a criminal or tortious act; electronic surveillance for foreign intelligence operations; and other such purposes. Also applicable is the prohibition of *unlawful access to stored communications* (18 U.S.C. Section 2701). According to the congressional findings annexed to the statute, the act seeks both to permit interception, under court order and supervision, of wire or oral communications made in the commission of crimes and also to protect the privacy of innocent persons from unwarranted intrusions.

Unlawful Access to Stored Communications (18 U.S.C. 2701). The statute provides:

(a) Offense. . . . [W]hoever—
  (1) intentionally accesses without authorization a facility through which an electronic communication service is provided; or
  (2) intentionally exceeds an authorization to access that facility; and thereby obtains, alters, or prevents authorized access to a wire or electronic communication while it is in electronic storage in such system shall be punished as provided in subsection (b) of this section.

Exceptions to liability are given to providers of a wire or electronic communication service, the user of the service with respect to a communication of or intended for that user; and law enforcement officers who have obtained authorization. Under the statute, a governmental entity may require a provider of electronic communication service to disclose the contents of an electronic communication in electronic storage for a period of up to 180 days pursuant to a warrant issued by a federal or state court (Section 2703). Punishment ranges from a maximum of only six months to two years, depending on whether the offense was committed for a commercial advantage and whether the offense was a first or subsequent offense.

Transportation of Stolen Goods, Securities, Moneys (18 U.S.C. Section 2314). It is a criminal offense to transport goods in interstate commerce that are known to be stolen or fraudulently obtained and that have a value of more than $5000.[7] The statute is also a fraud statute, providing that it is violative of the act to devise any scheme to obtain money by false pretenses or promises inducing a person to travel interstate in pursuance of the scheme, wherein the value of the fraud is $5000 or more. The statute clearly applies to stolen hardware. Does software stored on tape or disk constitute *goods* within the meaning of the statute? The act was found to apply to the fraudulent diversion of funds by computer. *United States v. Jones,* 553 F.2d 351, 356 (4th Cir. 1977). The *LaMacchia* case holding was that the copying of computer software without a profit motive was not a physical taking that violated the act. Taking computer programs were found not to be in violation of the act in at least two other cases. *United States v. Brown,* 925 F.2d 1301, 1308 (10th Cir. 1991) and *United States v. Wang,* 898 F. Supp. 758, 760 (D.Colo. 1995).[8] It is certainly arguable, as stated in Chapter 3, that software does appear to be *goods* and, thus, come within the statute's prohibition.

In *U.S. v. Martin,* 228 F.3d 1 (1st Cir. 2000), the defendants, Dr. Martin and Caryn Camp, were found guilty of conspiring to transport stolen goods from Maine to California. *Conspiracy* requires that there be an agreement between two or more people to commit a crime and that at least one coconspirator commits some act in furtherance of the conspiracy. Camp was employed as a chemist for IDEXX, a manufacturer of veterinary products located in Maine. She signed a nondisclosure and noncompete agreement with the company. Martin was a California scientist and chief executive officer of Wyoming DNA Vaccine. He proposed to IDEXX to collaborate on research into human immunodeficiency virus (HIV) and feline immunodeficiency virus. Although the proposal was later rejected, Martin signed a confidentiality agreement not to disclose secret data shared during the negotiations. Thereafter, through a prolonged series of correspondence, Martin caused Camp to send him a series of e-mails containing confidential data as well as test kits.

The issue was whether there was a violation of the Transportation of Stolen Goods Statute (both Martin and Camp were found guilty of violating the Economic Espionage Act). The court said that a reasonable jury could have found (as it did in this case) that Martin's request for a copy of IDEXX's software from Camp and his receipt of test kits did constitute a conspiracy to violate the statute. With respect to the $5,000 value requirement, the court said that although the e-mails containing the secret data did not constitute *goods* under the statute, the $5,000 sum could include both the value of goods covered by the statute and the value of the information conveyed by the e-mails.

Trafficking in Counterfeit Goods and Services (18 U.S.C. Section 2320). This act makes it a felony punishable by a fine up to $2 million ($5 million if not an individual) and imprisonment up to 10 years if such person intentionally traffics or attempts to traffic in goods or services knowingly using a counterfeit mark.

Extortion and Threats (18 U.S.C. Section 875). Use of a computer or other means of communication in interstate or foreign commerce, for the purpose of demanding or requesting a ransom or reward for the purpose of releasing a kidnapped person or to restrain from kidnapping or injuring another person is subject to criminal prosecution and a maximum sentence of a fine and imprisonment of up to 20 years. There are lesser penalties for the threat to kidnap without demand for monetary or other value and for the threat to injure the property or reputation of another live or deceased person.

INTERNET GAMBLING

Gambling over the Internet presents a panoply of issues that the federal government will have to resolve. Among the issues gambling raises are jurisdictional problems, enforcement of local and national laws, money laundering, and social issues including that of addiction. The bettor is able to gamble from a desktop in relative obscurity, most often in violation of local laws. The chances of being caught are minuscule, due mainly to the U.S. Constitution's Fourth Amendment right to be free from unreasonable search and seizure in one's home. Even if a person is prosecuted, such crimes rarely result in a bettor serving jail time. The betting establishment also has legal protection. Where a site emanates from protected areas whose laws permit gambling (for example, in states such as Nevada or on Native-American Indian reservations), there can be no prosecution within those jurisdictions. Even if Internet gambling becomes subject to federal control, there is nothing to prevent such establishments from proceeding offshore in jurisdictions that not only permit but also encourage such sites. Gambling revenues rival those of major casinos. It is estimated that 1998 revenues by the some 14 million online gamblers approached $1 billion.

Statutory Regulation. Almost all states regulate gambling. Indian reservations are exempt from state and federal legislation concerning gambling. There are a number of federal statutes that may be applicable. Among them are the Wire Act (18 U.S.C. Section 1084), the Travel Act (18 U.S.C. Section 1952), the Professional and Amateur Sports Protection Act (28 U.S.C. Section 3702), and the Interstate Transportation of Wagering Paraphernalia Act (18 U.S.C. Section 1953). There are a number of proposed statutes pending in Congress that, with exceptions, would prohibit such gambling. Even if Congress does act to prohibit Internet gambling, the enforcement of such laws if made applicable to offshore betting would be spurious.

Judicial Interpretations. As reviewed in Chapter 2, in *State of Minnesota v. Granite Gate Resorts, Inc.* (568 N.W. 2d 715), the state of Minnesota took the position that a Nevada-based gambling site could be sued civilly in Minnesota because the defendant advertised its activities over the Internet, including to consumers in Minnesota. A judgment in a civil proceeding would be entitled to enforcement in another state under the full faith and credit clause of the U.S. Constitution. In *Thompson v. Handa-Lopez,* 998 F. Supp. 738 (W.D.Tex. 1998), the Texas Federal District Court also found that jurisdiction would be proper against a California corporation that maintained a gambling Web site accessible by any Internet user. In *Thompson,* the California defendant was alleged to have refused to honor substantial winnings of the Texas resident who had placed bets on the defendant's Internet casino site.

Whether Congress will act to curb interstate gambling remains in doubt. In the June 18, 1999, *Report of United States National Gambling Impact Study Commission,* the commission recommended that Internet gambling be banned, although casinos and resorts would continue to provide such services where legal within their state borders. Opponents to the ban present a variety of arguments, including the specter of privacy rights violations and the difficulty and cost of enforcing such a ban.

INTERNATIONAL EFFORTS TO COMBAT CYBERCRIME

Although the United States has led efforts to prosecute and punish individuals committing unlawful activity, there has been substantial investigation and recommendations made by international organizations for cooperation among nations in the global community concerning cybercrime. The G-8, the Council of Europe, the United Nations, and the OECD have all explored the problems and proposed solutions for combating cybercrime.[9]

The G-8

In a "Communiqué," dated December 9–10, 1997, of the Meeting of Justice and Interior Ministers of the Eight, a 10-point plan of Principles and Actions was proposed. The Statement of Principles is as follows:

I. There must be no safe havens for those who abuse information technologies.

II. Investigation and prosecution of international high-tech crimes must be coordinated among all concerned States, regardless of where harm has occurred.

III. Law enforcement personnel must be trained and equipped to address high-tech crimes.

IV. Legal systems must protect the confidentiality, integrity, and availability of data and systems from unauthorized impairment and ensure that serious abuse is penalized.

V. Legal systems should permit the preservation of and quick access to electronic data, which are often critical to the successful investigation of crime.

VI. Mutual assistance regimes must ensure the timely gathering and exchange of evidence in cases involving international high-tech crime.

VII. Transborder electronic access by law enforcement to publicly available (open source) information does not require authorization from the State where the data resides.

VIII. Forensic standards for retrieving and authenticating electronic data for use in criminal investigations and prosecutions must be developed and employed.

IX. To the extent practicable, information and telecommunications systems should be designed to help prevent and detect network abuse, and should also facilitate the tracing of criminals and the collection of evidence.

X. Work in this area should be coordinated with the work of other relevant information fora to ensure against duplication of efforts.

The Action Plan is:

1. Use our established network of knowledgeable personnel to ensure a timely, effective response to transnational high-tech cases and designate a point-of-contact who is available on a twenty-four hour basis.
2. Take appropriate steps to ensure that a sufficient number of trained and equipped law enforcement personnel are allocated to the task of combating high-tech crime and assisting law enforcement agencies of other States.
3. Review our legal systems to ensure that they appropriately criminalize abuse of telecommunications and computer systems and promote the investigation of high-tech crimes.
4. Consider issues raised by high-tech crimes, where relevant, when negotiating mutual assistance agreements or arrangements.
5. Continue to examine and develop workable solutions regarding the preservation of evidence prior to the execution of a request for mutual assistance; transborder searches; and computer

searches of data where the location of that data is unknown.

6. Develop expedited procedures for obtaining traffic data from all communications carriers in the chain of a communication and to study ways to expedite the passing of this data internationally.
7. Work jointly with industry to insure that new technologies facilitate our effort to combat high-tech crime by preserving and collecting critical evidence.
8. Ensure that we can, in urgent and appropriate cases, accept and respond to mutual assistance, requests relating to high-tech crime by expedited but reliable means of communications, including voice, fax, or e-mail, with written confirmation to follow where required.
9. Encourage internationally-recognized standards-making bodies in the fields of telecommunications and information technologies to continue providing the public and private sectors with standards for reliable and secure telecommunications and data processing technologies.
10. Develop and employ compatible forensic standards for retrieving and authenticating electronic data for use in criminal investigations and prosecutions.

Council of Europe

The Committee of Ministers of the Council of Europe issued a number of recommendations concerning procedural issues affecting cyberlaw.[10] Its recommendations are as follows:

1. *Search and seizure*—The council emphasized that a distinction be made between the search of computer systems and seizure of stored data and the interception of data. Criminal procedure laws should permit governmental authorities to search and seize such data as permitted by the nation's laws and that the owner thereof be so advised. The right to do so would extend also to networks. All such searches and seizures would be subject to "appropriate safeguards."
2. *Technical surveillance*—It was recommended that laws concerning technical surveillance be reviewed and that they permit investigators to take such measures to enable them to collect traffic data in investigating crimes.
3. *Obligations to cooperate with the investigating authorities*—Internet service providers are to be required to provide investigators with information concerning the identity of users; persons in charge of computer systems are to deliver evidentiary data under their control; and telecommunications networks are to avail themselves of all necessary technical measures to enable interception of such telecommunications.
4. *Electronic evidence*—Procedures for the collection, preservation, and presentation of electronic evidence are to be set forth in criminal procedure laws.
5. *Use of encryption*—The council emphasized the need to minimize the illegitimate use of cryptography concerning the investigation of criminal offenses.
6. *Research, statistics, and training*—Governmental authorities are to conduct research, compile statistics, and provide appropriate training.
7. *International cooperation*—The council urged nations to enter into agreements "as to how, when and to what extent such search and seizure" of foreign computer systems may be accomplished. Cooperation should be expedited to exchange evidence when requested by foreign authorities.

The United States, although encouraged that the recommendations would overcome the previous refusal of foreign authorities to cooperate in civil and criminal matters, may have its own difficulties in complying with the suggested changes. For example, the Fourth Amendment search and seizure clause and the Fifth Amendment right of an individual to remain silent may prevent the seizure of evidence from an individual.

Organization for Economic Cooperation and Development Guidelines

The OECD commenced a study as early as 1983 to harmonize criminal laws. In 1986, it published a report, *Computer-Related Crime: Analysis of Legal*

Policy, that examined laws dealing with the Internet and recommended that member countries enact certain minimal criminal laws and regulations governing particular cyberabuses. In 1992, it adopted "Guidelines for the Security of Information Systems." On March 27, 1997, it addressed the problem of security in the field of communications by its issuance of the "Guidelines for Cryptography Policy."

United Nations Recommendations

In its manual on the prevention and control of computer-related crime, the U.N. emphasized the need for international efforts in both developed and developing nations. It recited studies that alleged computer crime has been much covered up by victims, especially by corporations not wishing to reveal their vulnerability to cyberhackers. The major types of computer crimes referred to in the report are fraud, computer forgery, damage to or modifications of computer data or programs, unauthorized access to computer systems and service, and unauthorized reproduction of legally protected computer programs.

OBSCENITY AND CHILD PORNOGRAPHY

Historically, an area of criminal law that has brought about extensive litigation and constitutional interpretations has been that of obscenity and related topics, especially child pornography. The most difficult areas of the law are not issues of right versus perceived wrongs but a weighing of rights as against opposing rights. The increased use and popularity of the Internet has exacerbated the issue of what may be communicated over the Internet. Even a casual user most likely has been inundated by unwelcomed pornographic offerings. Accessing as innocent a topic in past years as *chemistry* or *whitehouse.com* (the White House site is *whitehouse.gov*) can expose the viewer to pornographic sites and invitations. The ethical and legal difficulty is whether the government should be involved in the regulation of the Internet so as to prevent or greatly diminish such sites, especially because they are accessible to minors.

Defendants in obscenity proceedings invariably raise the defense of First Amendment freedom of speech, freedom of the press, and freedom of association. The first hurdle to be crossed by prosecutors is the determination that the act was unlawfully obscene.

What Is Obscenity?

Defining *obscenity* has been a most difficult task for courts. Especially in the 1960s, there were numerous judicial decisions that attempted to define it and, at the same time, place limitations as to what was constitutionally protected. The present test used by courts was announced by the U.S. Supreme Court in *Miller v. California,* 413 U.S. 15 (1973). In *Miller,* the Court set forth a three-prong bright-line test for determining what obscenity is. A court has to inquire whether: (1) "the average person applying 'contemporary community standards' would find the work, taken as a whole, appeals to the prurient interest"; (2) it "depicts or describes, in a patently offensive way, sexual conduct specifically defined by applicable state law"; and (3) "the work, taken as a whole, lacks serious literary, artistic, political, or scientific value." An oft-cited case in which the defendants were convicted for violating the federal obscenity laws is the *Thomas* case. The statute in question is 18 U.S.C. Section 1465, Transportation of Obscene Matters for Sale or Distribution. It states:

> Whoever knowingly transports or travels in, or uses a facility or means of, interstate or foreign commerce or an interactive computer service (as defined in section 230(e)(2) of the Communications Act of 1934) in or affecting such commerce for the purpose of sale or distribution of any obscene, lewd, lascivious, or filthy book, pamphlet, picture, film, paper, letter, writing, print, silhouette, drawing, figure, image, cast, phonograph recording, electrical transcription or other article capable of producing sound or any other matter of indecent or immoral character, shall be fined under this article or imprisoned not more than five years, or both.
>
> The transportation as aforesaid of two or more copies of any publication or two or more copies of any article of the character described above, or a combined total of five such publications and articles, shall create a presumption that such publications or articles are intended for sale or distribution, but such presumption shall be rebuttable.

UNITED STATES V. THOMAS

74 F.3d 701 (6th Cir. 1996)

FACTS: Defendants, Robert and Carleen Thomas, were convicted of: (1) conspiracy to violate federal obscenity laws; (2) using their computer/telephone system for transporting obscene, computer-generated material in interstate commerce; and (3) shipping obscene videotapes. The Thomas' operated a bulletin board system that used telephones, modems, and personal computers in which they scanned and converted sexually explicit magazines into some 14,000 Graphic Interchange Format (GIF) files. They also purchased and sold sexually-explicit videotapes to bulletin board members. The files were accessed through the computer modem by use of a password for which members paid a membership fee.

ISSUES: (1) Whether the aforesaid conduct constitutes a violation of federal law?

(2) Whether the convictions violated the defendants' First Amendment rights of freedom of speech?

DECISION: The U.S. Court of Appeals upheld the convictions on appeal from the U.S. District Court holding: (1) The conduct did violate federal law; and (2) The First Amendment rights were not violated by the statute and the convictions thereunder.

REASONING: Judge Edmunds

[Defendants contend that their conduct does not constitute a violation of 18 U.S.C. Section 1465 because the section does not apply to intangible objects like computer files and that Congress did not intend to regulate the computer transmissions involved herein.]

Defendants focus on the means by which the GIF files were transferred rather than the fact that the transmissions began with computer-generated images in California and ended with the same computer-generated images in Tennessee. The manner in which the images moved does not affect their ability to be viewed on a computer screen in Tennessee or their ability to be printed out in hard copy in that distant location.

The record does not support Defendants' argument that they had no knowledge, intent or expectation that members of their [bulletin board] would download and print the images contained in their GIF files. They ran a business that advertised and promised its members the availability and transportation of the sexually-explicit GIF files they selected. In light of the overwhelming evidence produced at trial, it is spurious for Defendants to claim now that they did not intend to sell, disseminate, or share the obscene GIF files they advertised on the [bulletin board] with members outside their home and in other states. . . .

Likewise, we conclude that Defendants' conduct here falls within the plain language of Section 1465. Moreover, our interpretation of Section 1465 is consistent with Congress' intent to legislate comprehensively the interstate distribution of obscene materials. . . .

1. DEFENDANTS' RIGHT TO POSSESS THE GIF FILES IN THEIR HOME

Defendants . . . argue they have a constitutionally protected right to possess obscene materials in the privacy of their home. They insist that the GIF files containing sexually-explicit material never left their home. . . .

[T]he right to possess obscene materials in the privacy of one's home does not create "a correlative right to receive it, transport it, or distribute it" in interstate commerce even if it is for private use only. Nor does it create "some zone of constitutionally protected privacy [that] follows such material when it is moved outside the home area."

Defendants went beyond merely possessing obscene GIF files in their home. They ran a business that advertised and promised its members the availability and transportation of the sexually-explicit GIF files they selected. . . .

2. THE COMMUNITY STANDARDS TO BE APPLIED WHEN DETERMINING WHETHER THE GIF FILES ARE OBSCENE

[The court set forth the *Miller* three-prong test for obscenity.]

Under the first prong of the *Miller* obscenity test, the jury is to apply "contemporary community standards." . . . The computer-generated images . . . were electronically transferred from Defendants' home in California to the Western District of Tennessee. Accordingly, the community standards of that judicial district were proper in this case. . . . Prosecutions may be brought either in the district of dispatch or the district of receipt, . . . and obscenity is determined by the standards of the community where the trial takes place. . . . Moreover, the federal courts have consistently recognized that it is not unconstitutional to subject interstate distributors of obscenity to varying community standards.

3. THE IMPLICATIONS OF COMPUTER TECHNOLOGY ON THE DEFINITION OF "COMMUNITY"

Defendants . . . argue that the computer technology used here requires a new definition of community, i.e., one that is based on the broad-ranging connections among people in cyberspace rather than the geographic locale of the federal judicial district of the criminal trial. Without a more flexible definition, they argue, there will be an impermissible chill on protected speech because [bulletin board] operators cannot select who gets the material they make available on their bulletin boards. . . .

Defendants' First Amendment issue, however, is not implicated by the facts of this case. This is not a situation where the bulletin board operator had no knowledge or control over the jurisdictions where materials were distributed for downloading or printing. Access to Defendants' [bulletin board] was limited. Membership was necessary and applications were submitted and screened before passwords were issued and materials were distributed. Thus, Defendants had in place methods to limit user access in jurisdictions where the risk of a finding of obscenity was greater than that in California. They knew they had a member in Memphis; the member's address and local phone number were provided on his application form. If Defendants did not wish to subject themselves to liability in jurisdictions with less tolerant standards for determining obscenity, they could have refused to give passwords to members in those districts, thus precluding the risk of liability. . . .

We next address the Defendants' argument that the district court erred when it instructed the jury that the government was not required to present expert testimony regarding the prurient appeal of the materials at issue here. Under the first prong of the *Miller* obscenity test, the jury must consider whether the allegedly obscene material "appeals to the prurient interest."

The computer-generated images and videotapes involved here portrayed bestiality, incest, rape, and sex scenes involving defecation, urination, and sadomasochistic abuse. Defendants argue that the Government is required to present expert testimony when sexually-explicit material is directed at a deviant group. We disagree. Neither the United States Supreme Court nor this court has adopted any such *per se* rule.

CASE QUESTIONS

1. Review the statute. Is it unconstitutionally vague?
2. What do the words *obscene, lewd,* and *filthy* mean to you?
3. *Obscenity* in a rural Georgia or West Virginia village may have a very different meaning than to a supposedly sophisticated dweller of a major city. Is it fair to judge the latter by rural standards? Does it violate the constitutional right of equal protection under the laws?

Protecting the Minor

Federal computer-related statutes governing obscenity are directed mainly at protecting minor against the onslaught of pornographic materials. Among the statutes that have been enacted are 18 U.S.C. Section 2256 and 18 U.S.C. Section 1401 (the Child Online Protection Act), which amended the Communication Act of 1934 (47 U.S.C. Section 201). Section 1401 provides:

Whoever knowingly and with knowledge of the character of the material, in interstate of foreign commerce by means of the World Wide Web, makes any communication for commercial purposes that is available to any minor and that includes any material that is harmful to minors shall be fined not more than $50,000, and/or imprisonment of not more than six months.

The statute excludes liability to Internet service providers, telecommunications carriers, and similar type providers. It is also an affirmative defense to criminal liability that there was good faith effort to restrict access by minors by requiring use of a credit card, adult access code, or adult personal identification number and other reasonable measures to restrict access. For purposes of this statute, a minor is a person under 17 years of age.

The types of material deemed harmful to minors are any communication, picture, image, graphic image file, article, recording, writing, or other matter that the average person, by applying contemporary community standards, would consider to pander to the prurient interest, or material that depicts, describes, or represents sexual acts or conduct, sexual perversion, or other lewd exhibition of the body, and that lacks serious artistic, political, or scientific value for minors.

The most controversial enactment, that was later found to be unconstitutional in part, was Title V of the Telecommunications Act of 1996, known as the Communications Decency Act of 1996.[11] We will discuss the statute in detail because the litigation that arose from the statute detailed the parameters within which statutes must abide to sustain constitutionality. The relevant provisions of Title V are as follows:

(a) Whoever
- (1) in interstate or foreign communications
  - (B) by means of a telecommunications device knowingly
    - (i) makes, creates, or solicits, and
    - (ii) initiates the transmission of,

      any comment, request, suggestion, proposal, image, or other communication which is obscene knowing that the recipient of the communication is under 18 years of age, regardless of whether the maker of such communication placed the call or initiated the communication;
- (2) knowingly permits any telecommunications facility under his control to be used for any activity prohibited by paragraph (1) with the intent that it be used for such activity, shall be fined under Title 18, or imprisoned not more than two years, or both.[12]

(d) Whoever
- (1) in interstate or foreign communications knowingly
  - (A) uses an interactive computer service to send to a specific person or persons under 18 years of age, or
  - (B) uses any interactive computer service to display in a manner available to a person under 18 years of age,

  any comment, request, suggestion, proposal, image, or other communication that, in context, depicts or describes, in terms patently offensive as measured by contemporary community standards, sexual or excretory activities or organs, regardless of whether the user of such services placed the call or initiated the communication; or
- (2) knowingly permits any telecommunications facility under such person's control to be used for an activity prohibited in paragraph (1) with the intent that it be used for such activity, shall be fined under Title 18, or imprisoned not more than two years, or both.[13]

There are two affirmative defenses that may be raised against imposition of liability: (1) the taking of good faith, reasonable, effective, and appropriate actions to restrict access by minors to the prohibited communications; and (2) restricting access by requiring certain specified forms of age proof, such as a verified credit card or an adult identification number or code.[14]

There were a number of precedents in cases previously decided that upheld the constitutionality of antiobscenity legislation. These precedents were discussed at length by the U.S. Supreme Court in *Reno v. ACLU* (to follow) that upheld the decision of a lower court determining that the law was unconstitutional. The precedents upholding the constitutionality of laws and regulations that still apply to obscenity cases are: *Ginsberg v. New York,* 390 U.S. 629 (1968); *FCC v. Pacifica Foundation,* 438 U.S. 726 (1978); *Renton v. Playtime Theatres, Inc.,* 475 U.S. 41 (1986); and *Sable Communications of Cal. Inc. v. FCC,* 492 U.S. 115 (1989).

In *Ginsberg,* the constitutionality of a New York State statute was in question. The law prohibited the sale to minors under 17 years of age of material considered obscene to them although not necessarily to adults. The defendant had sold so-called girlie magazines to a minor. The statute was upheld on several grounds: (1) the prohibition of sales to minors did not prevent their parents from purchasing the magazines for their children; (2) the statute applied only to commercial transactions; (3) the statute said that the material had to be "utterly without redeeming social importance to minors"; and (4) the statute defined a minor to be 17 years of age, rather than 18 as in the CDA. The Court held that the First Amendment did not prevent states from enacting legislation restricting access of pornographic images to children, even though the display of such images is constitutionally permissible for viewing by adults. The Court noted:

> Obscenity is not protected expression and may be suppressed without a showing of the circumstances which lie beyond the phrase "clear and present danger" in its application to protected speech. . . . To sustain state power to exclude material defined as obscenity by [the New York statute] requires only that we be able to say that it was not irrational for the legislature to find the exposure to material condemned by the statute is harmful to minors. . . . We therefore cannot say that [the New York statute], in defining the obscenity of material on the basis of its appeal to minors under 17, has no rational relation to the objective of safeguarding such minors from harm.

In *Pacifica,* the Court upheld an order of the Federal Communications Commission (FCC) that imposed administrative sanctions against a radio station for airing the recording of a 12-minute monologue by George Carlin titled—and composed of—"Filthy Words." The use of words referring to excretory functions, in an afternoon broadcast when children could be exposed to the monologue, was patently offensive and indecent although not obscene. The Supreme Court held that not all government regulation of speech is prohibited by the First Amendment. The Court stated that children having easy access to the broadcast, together with the *Ginsberg* concerns, justified upholding the FCC. It appears that such speech would be constitutionally protected if it were made to an adult audience wherein the presence of children would be barred or restricted. Nevertheless, the government does have an interest in protecting the "well-being of its youth."

In *Renton,* a zoning ordinance was upheld that kept adult theaters out of residential neighborhoods. The purpose of the ordinance was to prevent secondary effects; it was not the content of the speech that was being regulated but rather the potential secondary effects.

In *Sable,* the Court distinguished "obscene" from "indecent" speech. Sable challenged the constitutionality of an amendment to the Communications Act that prohibited indecent and obscene speech in interstate commercial telephone messages. The company was engaged in a dial-a-porn enterprise, which engaged in sending sexually oriented prerecorded telephone messages. The Court decided that the statute was constitutional only insofar as it regulated obscene, as distinguished from indecent, messages. Although the government has a vested right in protecting the well-being of children that includes preventing the receipt of indecent messages, nevertheless, the telephone messages were not the same as a radio broadcast. The broadcast was sent out into the airwaves to be received by anyone tuning into the frequency, whereas the telephone messages required that the listener take affirmative steps to receive the communication.

Therefore, government can regulate obscene speech, particularly if minors are exposed freely to the contents thereof. If speech is deemed to be indecent, then the court will examine the context in which it is given to determine its constitutionality.

The U.S. Supreme Court, in the following action, for the first time decided a matter involving regulation of the Internet.[15] The cases just mentioned were cited, discussed in detail, and distinguished from the case at hand.

ACLU V. RENO

521 U.S. 844 (1997)

FACTS: This action is an appeal from a decision of the District Court holding that the above-cited sections of the Communications Decency Act of 1996 were unconstitutional. Immediately after the law was passed, the ACLU and 19 other plaintiffs sued claiming the law violated the First Amendment of the U.S. Constitution.

ISSUE: Whether the two cited provisions of the statute are constitutional?

DECISION: The Supreme Court decided in favor of the ACLU and other plaintiffs, holding that the said provisions abridged the freedom of speech under the First Amendment of the U.S. Constitution.

REASONING: Justice Stevens

[The Court initially summarized the nature of the Internet (see Findings of Fact recited in Chapter 1), set forth the relevant provisions of the CDA, reviewed the precedents, and proceeded to discuss the constitutionality of the cited text.]

The vagueness of the CDA is a matter of special concern for two reasons. First, the CDA is a content-based regulation of speech. The vagueness of such a regulation raises special First Amendment concerns because of its obvious chilling effect on free speech.... Second, the CDA is a criminal statute. In addition to the opprobrium and stigma of a criminal conviction, the CDA threatens violators with penalties including up to two years in prison for each violation. The severity of criminal sanctions may well cause speakers to remain silent rather than communicate even arguably unlawful words, ideas and images....

[The Court discussed the three-prong test set forth in *Miller*.]

In contrast to *Miller* and our other previous cases, the CDA thus presents a greater threat of censoring speech that, in fact falls outside the statute's scope. Given the vague contours of the coverage of the statute, it unquestionably silences some speakers whose messages would be entitled to constitutional protection. That danger provides further reason for insisting that the statute not be overly broad. The CDA's burden on protected speech cannot be justified if a more carefully drafted statute could avoid it.

We are persuaded that the CDA lacks the precision that the First Amendment requires when a statute regulates the content of speech. In order to deny minors access to potentially harmful speech, the CDA effectively suppresses a large amount of speech that adults have a constitutional right to receive and to address to one another. That burden on adult speech is unacceptable if less restrictive alternatives would be at least as effective in achieving the legitimate purpose that the statute was enacted to serve. In evaluating the free speech rights of adults, we have made it perfectly clear that "[s]exual expression which is indecent but not obscene is protected by the First Amendment." . . . "[W]here obscenity is not involved, we have consistently held that the fact that protected speech may be offensive to some does not justify its suppression." . . .

It is true that we have repeatedly recognized the governmental interest in protecting children from harmful materials. . . . But that interest does not justify an unnecessarily broad suppression of speech addressed to adults. As we have explained, the Government may not "reduc[e] the adult population . . . to . . . only what is fit for children." . . .

The breadth of the CDA's coverage is wholly unprecedented. Unlike the regulations upheld in *Ginsberg* and *Pacifica,* the scope of the CDA is not limited to commercial speech or commercial entities. Its open-ended prohibitions embrace all nonprofit entities and individuals posting indecent messages or displaying them on their own computers in the presence of minors. The general, undefined terms "indecent" and "patently offensive" cover large amounts of nonpornographic material with serious educational or other value. Moreover, the "community standards" criterion as applied to the Internet means that any communication available to a nation-wide audience will be judged by the standards of the community most likely to be offended by the message. The regulated subject matter includes any of the seven "dirty words" used in the *Pacifica* monologue, the use of which the Government's expert acknowledged could constitute a felony. . . . It may also extend to discussions about prison rape or safe sexual practices, artistic images that include nude subjects, and arguably the card catalogue of the Carnegie Library.

... Under the CDA, a parent allowing her 17-year-old to use the family computer to obtain information on the Internet that she, in her parental judgment, deems appropriate could face a lengthy prison term. . . . Similarly, a parent who sent his 17-year-old college freshman information on birth control via e-mail could be incarcerated even though neither he, his child, nor anyone in their home community, found the material "indecent" or "patently offensive," if the college town's community thought otherwise. . . .

The Government's three remaining arguments focus on the defenses provided in section 223(e)(5). First, relying on the "good faith, reasonable, effective, and appropriate" provision, the Government suggests that "tagging" provides a defense that saves the constitutionality of the Act. The suggestion assumes that transmitters may encode their indecent communications in a way that would indicate their contents, thus permitting recipients to block their reception with appropriate software. It is the requirement that the good faith action must be "effective" that makes this defense illusory. The Government recognizes that its proposed screening software does not currently exist. Even if it did, there is no way to know whether a potential recipient will actually block the encoded material. Without the impossible knowledge that every guardian in America is screening for the "tag," the transmitter could not reasonably rely on its action to be "effective."

For its second and third arguments concerning defenses which we can consider together the Government relies on the latter half of section 223(e)(5) which applies when the transmitter has restricted access by requiring use of a verified credit card or adult identification. Such verification is not only technologically available but actually is used by commercial providers of sexually explicit material. These providers, therefore, would be protected by the defense. Under the findings of the District Court, however, it is not economically feasible for most noncommercial speakers to employ such verification. Accordingly, this defense would not significantly narrow the statute's burden on noncommercial speech. Even with respect to commercial pornographers that would be protected by the defenses, the Government has failed to adduce any evidence that these verification techniques actually preclude minors from posing as adults. . . .

CASE QUESTIONS

1. Compare the *Thomas* case with *ACLU v. Reno.* Are the cases consistent with each other?
2. What are your views concerning obscenity? To what extent are they influenced by your cultural background?

It appears that the decision was not unexpected. The Supreme Court, historically, has indicated that when the government attempts to restrict the *content* of speech, it faces a *strict scrutiny* standard. Such restriction will not be upheld absent a showing either of a clear and present danger that may occur as a result of the speech or that it is defamatory. Moreover, speech by commercial interests has limited constitutional protection, unlike other forms of speech. Commercial speech will be protected in those cases "where the public has a right to know." Examples are posting of prices for drugs that the state has forbidden and advertisements by abortion clinics. Where the regulation is other than content, then the Court will engage in a balancing exercise weighing the competing interests. In *Reno,* the Court emphasized that the statute regulated content and, thus, in the absence of a showing of a clear necessity for the restriction, it will not pass constitutional muster. The Court emphasized the criminal nature of the prohibition. Being subject to a felony and its enhanced concomitant of imprisonment subjects such a law to greater scrutiny than an administrative regulation, such as those imposed by the FCC, that carries no penalty of incarceration.

In *Apollomedia Corp. v. Reno,*[16] the federal district court was confronted with the application of the "telecommunications device" as recited in the CDA.

Apollomedia is a media technology company that openly acknowledged that some of its online databases contained material that was sexually explicit and had vulgar language that some communities would consider to be indecent. The court, after reciting the *ACLU v. Reno* case presented in this chapter, as well as the precedents contained therein, nevertheless held that that portion of section 223(a)(1)(A) not declared unconstitutional by the Supreme Court was valid. Thus, the section that prohibits the use of a telecommunications device to initiate a transmission that is "obscene, lewd, lascivious, filthy, or indecent, with intent to annoy, abuse, threaten, or harass another person" is valid inasmuch as it applies only to communications between nonconsenting parties. It differed from the following provision of the act, which prohibits such communication between consenting persons at least one of whom is a person under 18 years of age.

In *People v. Foley,* Case No. 98-2083 (N.Y. App. Div., 4th Dept., 1999), the Appellate Division of the New York State Supreme Court decided that New York Penal Law, Section 235.22, making it a crime to use a computer system to "disseminate graphic images to [a] minor depicting nudity, sexual conduct or sadomasochistic abuse that is 'harmful to minors'" and that "importunes, invites or induces a minor to engage in sexual activity" did not violate the First Amendment of the U.S. Constitution.

In the following case, a federal district court was called upon to determine the constitutional merits of a Michigan statute that sought to protect minors from sexually explicit materials emanating from the Internet.

CYBERSPACE, COMMUNICATIONS, INC. V. ENGLER

55 F. Supp. 2d 737 (E.D.Mich. 1999)

FACTS: In 1978, the State of Michigan enacted a statute to prohibit the distribution of obscene materials to children. The statute was amended in 1999 to make it applicable to computers and to the Internet. The statute was also amended to extend the statute to prohibit "sexually explicit" materials to minors. Plaintiffs, consisting of organizations and individuals who use the Internet for communication, dissemination and other purposes, sued the Governor of Michigan and the Attorney General alleging that the statute violated their First Amendment freedom of speech rights. The prohibition stated as follows:

A person is guilty of disseminating sexually explicit matter to a minor if that person does either of the following:

(a) Knowingly disseminates to a minor sexually explicit visual or verbal material that is harmful to minors;
(b) Knowingly exhibits to a minor sexually explicit performance that is harmful to minors.

The Act makes it unlawful to communicate, transmit, display, or otherwise make available sexually explicit material by means of the Internet or a computer, computer program, computer system, or computer network.

ISSUE: Whether the aforesaid Act violated the First Amendment freedom of speech rights of the plaintiffs?

DECISION: The Court held in favor of the plaintiffs stating that it did violate their constitutional rights.

REASONING: Judge Tarnow

[The court recited the Findings of Fact stated in *ACLU v. Reno* set forth in Chapter 1.]

IV. FIRST AMENDMENT CHALLENGE

. . . Defendants argue that the Act comports to the specifications of *Ginsberg* and *Miller;* therefore the Act is constitutional. Yet in these cases, the "materials" referenced were magazines and brochures, respectively. Magazines or brochures can be brown bagged or hidden in the backroom of purveyors. With the Internet, you would have to "close the bookstore" because the disseminator and the recipient are not face to face. A magazine can be regulated or censored by the county in which it is located. A person's age can be verified because that person is physically there, and the disseminator can logically be held responsible for conveying "sexually explicit matter" to a minor. The Internet does not distinguish between minors and adults in their audience. To comply with the Act, a communicant must speak only in language suitable for children. Even under the guise of protecting minors, the government may not justify the complete suppression of constitutionally protected speech because to do so would "burn the house to roast the pig." *Butler v. Michigan,* 352 U.S. 380, 383 (1957). . . .

The Internet is cyberspace or an international network of computers. It is virtually impossible to prevent the content of messages from being read by someone under 18. The only way to ascertain an individual's age would be to require submission of a driver's license, birth certificate or some other form of identification. Considering a website may receive ten to a million plus "hits" a day, and many of these websites are established and maintained by even just one publisher; the impossibility of identification checking is understood. With the imposition of the government policing speech and deciding what is acceptable; a user, publisher, disseminator or communicant is faced with a Hobson's choice of shutting down their website (or whatever vehicle of information exchange), or risk prosecution for exercising protected speech.

The Act itself may in fact pass constitutional muster as a permitted regulation of obscenity, as it is quite similarly worded as those statutes upheld by the Supreme Court in *Miller* and *Ginsberg.* Defendant argues that a state does have the police power to regulate obscenity within their borders. This is true, but proper focus centers on this Public Act's impact on the Internet. The Internet is an international free flow of ideas and information. Enforcement of this Act would stifle one of the cornerstones of American society—what Thomas Jefferson called "The Marketplace of Ideas."

The amended statute at issue limits the receipt and communication of information through the Internet based on the content of that information. A content-based limitation on speech will be upheld where the state demonstrates that the limitation "is necessary to serve as compelling state interest and that it is narrowly drawn to achieve that end." . . .

This test involves three distinct inquiries: (1) whether the interests asserted by the state are compelling; (2) whether the limitation is necessary to further those interests; and (3) whether the limitation is narrowly drawn to achieve those interests [citing *Mainstream Loudoun,* which will be set forth in detail].

(1) Whether the Defendant's Interests Are Compelling

. . . The Court is quite sympathetic to the attempt of the Michigan legislature to protect minors. Society has a compelling interest in preserving the innocence of children. Although Defendants have failed to address this prong, there is arguably a compelling state interest to shelter our children from sexually explicit material until maturity. The Supreme Court has recognized such an interest: "We have recognized that there is a compelling interest in protecting the physical and psychological well-being of minors. This interest extends to shielding minors from the influence of literature that is not obscene by adult standards." *Sable Communications of California, Inc. v. FCC,* 492 U.S. 115, 126 (1989). . . .

(2) Whether the Act is Necessary to Further Those Interests

To satisfy strict scrutiny, defendants must do more than demonstrate that it has a compelling interest; they must also demonstrate that the Act is necessary to further that interest. Defendants "must demonstrate that the recited harms are real, not merely conjectural, and that the regulation will in fact alleviate these harms in a direct and material way." . . .

The Defendants failed to satisfy that the Act will further a compelling interest of the State. Plaintiffs though did submit testimony and documentation that such an Act could produce a result contrary to the desires of society. The free flow of information on the Internet enables a teenager to ask about premarital sex or sexually transmitted diseases with anonymity. . . . Sometimes words were used in [discussions concerning contraceptives and abstention] which could be construed as "sexually explicit" and "harmful to a minor," which theoretically could subject the disseminator to criminal prosecution.

This would have an adverse affect on public policy. With all Internet participants fearful of criminal prosecution if certain terminology is utilized, the discussions would be stifled to the point that a teenager seeking answers to curious questions concerning a subject foremost on their mind, could not find answers via this medium. Without open discussion of how to prevent being raped or birth control or abstention, there would quite possibly be greater numbers of teenage pregnancy or sexually transmitted diseases. This would be contrary to the interests of the State.

(3) Whether the Act is Narrowly Tailored to Achieve the Compelling Government Interests
Even if defendants could demonstrate that the Act was reasonably necessary to further compelling state interests, it would still have to show that the Act is narrowly tailored to achieve those interests. The government may effectuate even a compelling interest only "by narrowly drawn regulations designed to serve those interests without unnecessarily interfering with First Amendment freedoms." . . .

Many Internet Service Providers (ISPs) allow parents to regulate content with different levels of restriction. The ISP allows parents to establish separate accounts for their children depending on their ages restricting entry to only child-friendly, fun and educational places on the Internet. These areas are usually monitored by employees of the ISP and a communicant that shows offensive language will be blocked when discovered. . . .

Although it is difficult in today's society to constantly monitor the activities of children, it is still the right, and duty, of every parent to teach and mold children's concepts of good and bad, right and wrong. This right is no greater than in the confines of ones' own home. A family with values will supervise their children. This includes setting limits, and either being there to enforce those limits, or utilizing the available technology to do so. With such less restrictive means to monitor the online activities of children, the government need not restrict the right of free speech guaranteed to adults. . . .

CASE QUESTIONS

1. Compare the *Thomas, ACLU,* and *Cyberspace* cases. Are they consistent with each other? Apply the *Miller* prongs in your discussion of the issues therein.
2. What are the obligations of parents in preventing the influx of pornographic images onto their computers? Should it be their responsibility rather than that of the state to prevent the dissemination of the images?

In *PSINet, Inc. v. Chapman,* 108 F. Supp. 2d 611 (W.D.Va. 2000), the state of Virginia passed a law similar to that in the *Cyberspace* case just discussed. Like Michigan, Virginia amended its statute that prohibited the knowing display of materials for a commercial purpose that was harmful to juveniles to extend to "electronic files or messages." Internet service providers and electronic mail service providers were exempted under the act.

As in the *Cyberspace* case, the court cited the U.S. Supreme Court decision in *Sable Communications v. FCC,* 492 U.S. 115 (1989) and *Reno v. ACLU,* 521 U.S. 844 (1997), which applied the strict scrutiny standard to content-based regulation of Internet speech. The court said:

The 1998 Act is not narrowly tailored—it effects a total ban on the display of all "electronic file[s] or message[s]," containing "harmful" words, images or sound recordings, that juveniles may "examine and peruse." By prohibiting all such communications that juveniles could possibly examine or peruse, the Act necessarily eliminates access for adults as well. This conclusion follows from the nature of the Internet, as described previously. Most speakers on the Internet have no way to determine the age of those who "examine and peruse" their communications. . . . The majority of Web users also cannot segregate or label communications in a way that would block them from the screen for viewing by juveniles.

The court used much of the same reasoning of the *Cyberspace* case in its emphasis that (1) that the Internet is unlike traditional media in physical spaces wherein a bookstore owner can distinguish juveniles from adults; and (2) that the act is not the most effective means of regulating so-called harmful materials to juveniles (parental supervision and blocking software are preferable ways of regulating such materials). The court also found that the statute violated the commerce clause of the U.S. Constitution (Article 1, Section 8, clause 3) because it "unduly burdens interstate commerce by placing restrictions on electronic commercial materials that impede the communication of said materials in all states, not just Virginia."

Accordingly, the constitutionality of the Child Online Protection Act of 1998 may be called into question due to the reasoning set forth in the *Cyberspace* and *PSINet* cases.

First Amendment Issues and Restrictions Concerning Violent Video Games to Children

Although children's access to pornography may be prohibited by states constitutionally, the question arises whether such prohibition may extend to video games containing images of graphic violence. In the following case, a number of amusement companies and trade associations sued the city of Indianapolis, Indiana, and other defendants to prevent the enforcement of an ordinance against them, restricting the display and operation of coin-operated amusement machines deemed "harmful to minors" if such machines (consisting mainly of video games) contained either "strong sexual content" or "graphic violence." The case is discussed in considerable detail because of its recitation of the constitutional rights of minors, particularly under the First Amendment of the U.S. Constitution.

AMERICAN AMUSEMENT MACHINE ASSC. V. COTTEY

115 F. Supp. 2d 943 (S.D.Ind. 2000)

FACTS: Plaintiffs manufacture, distribute and display video games. On July 10, 2000, the City Council of Indianapolis and Marion County adopted an Ordinance that restricted children's access to video games containing strong sexual content or graphic violence (defined as "an amusement machine's visual depiction or representation of realistic serious injury to a human or human-like being where such serious injury includes amputation, decapitation, dismemberment, blood shed, mutilation, maiming or disfiguration"). The Ordinance made it unlawful for such amusement establishment to allow a minor access to such machines unless s/he is accompanied by a parent, and required the posting of a conspicuous sign on the machine restricting access to persons 18 years or older.

ISSUES: (1) Whether violent video games are forms of expression protected by the First Amendment?

(2) Whether a local government may restrict children's access to games with graphic violence?

DECISION: (1) The Court decided that at least some games are expressions entitled to First Amendment protection.

(2) A local government may restrict such access without violating the First Amendment's rights of the plaintiffs.

REASONING: Judge Hamilton

III. VIDEO GAMES AS PROTECTED EXPRESSION

. . . In the early 1980s, most courts examining the issue concluded that the video games of that era were not protected by the First Amendment. See, e.g., *America's Best Family Showplace Corp. v. City of New York,* 536 F. Supp. 170, 173–74 (E.D.N.Y. 1982) (finding that video games were "pure entertainment" not protected by the First Amendment because there was no "element of information or some idea being communicated"); . . .

However, these courts in the 1980s did not foreclose the possibility that further development of video games might transform them into a medium of protected expression. . . . As a general matter, video games will be protected under the First Amendment only if they include sufficient communicative, expressive, or informative elements to fall at least within the outer limits of constitutionally protected speech. The Supreme Court has never articulated a precise test for determining how the First Amendment protects a given form of expression. Instead, the Court has stated generally: "Each medium of expression . . . must be assessed for First Amendment purposes by standards suited to it, for each may present its own problems." . . .

[The court discussed the Gauntlet series of action-adventure video games, with its eight realms and an underworld, as an example of a video game that went beyond mere entertainment.]

Without any attempt to assess artistic merit, the court finds that the visual art and the description of the action-adventure games in the record support plaintiffs' contention that at least some video games contain protected expression. . . .

In finding that video games may contain at least some expressive content protected by the First Amendment, the court does not mean to suggest that video games are essential vehicles of political speech or fine art. Not all protected expression lies at the core of the First Amendment. For example, in *Barnes v. Glen Theatre, Inc.,* the Supreme Court found that several earlier cases supported the conclusion that the "nude dancing of the kind sought to be performed here is expressive conduct within the outer perimeters of the First Amendment, though we view it as only marginally so." 501 U.S. 560, 565–66. . . . Thus, even if, as the City suggests, video games can be labeled "low value" speech, they are entitled to protection under the expansive reach of the First Amendment. . . .

IV. REGULATING CHILDREN'S EXPOSURE TO "GRAPHIC VIOLENCE"

The conclusion that at least some video games are protected by the First Amendment does not mean the city is powerless to regulate "graphic violence" in the games offered to children. The Constitution permits the government to impose restrictions on speech in limited circumstances. Laws that arguably restrict speech are analyzed under a variety of First Amendment standards. Several can be rejected at the outset as inapplicable to the Indianapolis Ordinance.

First, the Ordinance does not regulate one of the categories of "unprotected speech that the government has broad power to regulate as to adults" . . . (obscenity, fighting words, and defamation . . .).

Second, the City's asserted purpose in passing the Ordinance—protecting children from exposure to games with graphic violence and strong sexual content—makes it clear that the City is directly regulating the dissemination of this material and not merely the "secondary effects" that result from having video games physically located in certain neighborhoods. . . .

Third, the Ordinance is not a content-neutral attempt to regulate solely the time, place, or manner of a minor's access to video games. . . .

A. The First Amendment Rights of Children

[The court discussed *Ginsberg* at some length, as recited earlier.]

Plaintiffs' First Amendment challenge to the Ordinance in this case is based ultimately on the premise that children have a First Amendment right to play video games, including those depicting graphic violence, without their parents' permission. Surely the plaintiffs have no *independent* First Amendment right to sell their entertainment services to children without the parents' permission. *Ginsberg* shows, however, that the Court examines regulation of material that is arguably "harmful to minors" under a standard less strict, at least as a practical matter, than the presumption of unconstitutionality applied to most content-based restrictions. . . . Under this standard, the government may restrict minors' access to some speech that is protected for adults.

Other Supreme Court decisions show that children have rights under the First Amendment, but that those rights are not as broad as those of adults. . . . In *Tinker* [*v. Des Moines Independent Sch. Dist.,* 393 U.S. 503 (1969)], the Supreme Court held that a school could not punish a student for expressing his political opposition to the Vietnam War by wearing a black armband in school . . . "Students in school as well as out of school are 'persons' under our Constitution. They are possessed of fundamental rights which the State must respect, just as they themselves must respect their obligations to the State." . . .

Similarly, in *Barnette* [*West Virginia State Bd. Of Educ. v. Barnette,* 319 U.S. 624 (1943)] the Court held that a student could not be punished for refusing to pledge allegiance to the flag and to the United States. . . . "If there is any fixed star in our constitutional constellation, it is that no official, high or petty, can prescribe what shall be orthodox in politics, nationalism, religion, or other matters of opinion." . . . *Board of Education of Island Trees v. Pico,* 457 U.S. 853 . . . (1982), also demonstrates the limits on children's First Amendment rights. The Court considered the First Amendment implications of a school board's decision to remove several controversial books from the school library. All the books remained available to children in bookstores and through other channels. The Court did not agree on a majority opinion. However, the Justices who found that the school board might have violated the First Amendment acknowledged that the school board was free to remove books because they were deemed "vulgar" or because they were deemed psychologically or intellectually inappropriate for the age group. . . . Similarly, all justices agreed that if the school board removed books because of the ideas expressed in them, that would violate the First Amendment. . . .

Indianapolis wrote its Ordinance with *Ginsberg* in mind, and there are several important similarities indicating that *Ginsberg* provides the proper standard of review here. First, as New York did in *Ginsberg,* the City relies on both its "independent interest in the well-being of its youth" and on "the principle that 'the parents' claim to authority in their own household to direct the rearing of their children is basic in the structure of our society." . . .

Second, just as the New York law in *Ginsberg* did not materially limit adults' access to the pornographic materials in question, the City's Ordinance also does not significantly limit adult access to video games containing graphic violence. . . .

Third, also like the New York law in *Ginsberg,* the Ordinance does not prevent parents who so desire from allowing their children to be exposed to the regulated material, either sexual material as in *Ginsberg* or sexual content or graphic violence in video games in this case. In other words, the Ordinance does not impose a total ban on access even as to children. . . .

Fourth, the Ordinance attempts to regulate only transactions in a commercial setting where it is reasonable to expect the seller to (1) physically separate games that are harmful to minors, (2) effectively monitor the regulated games, and (3) verify the customer's age. . . .

Fifth, the record demonstrates that many, perhaps most, video games contain only the barest minimum of protected speech, whereas magazines (at issue in *Ginsberg*) can lie much closer to the core of the First Amendment. . . .

E. Treating "Graphic Violence" as a Form of Obscenity as to Minors

Plaintiffs do not challenge the Ordinance's treatment of sexually explicit video games as "harmful to minors," but do contend that the First Amendment prohibits the City from taking these principles that apply to children's access to sexual pornography and extending them to video games that include "graphic violence." . . . The City also contends that no court has ever reached a holding that directly favors this step. However, the City also points out correctly that no court has rejected such a careful attempt to extend these principles to graphic violence. . . .

1. Drawing the "Obscenity" Line at Sexual Content in Prior Cases The Supreme Court has often said that the standard for obscenity with respect to adults is limited to sexual materials. In *Reno v. ACLU,* for example, the Court noted that the *Miller* definition of obscenity "is limited to 'sexual conduct,'" which the court distinguished from the Communications Decency Act, which also included "excretory activities" and "organs" of both a sexual and excretory nature. . . . In *Erznoznik* [*v. City of Jacksonville,* 422 U.S. 205 (1975)], the Court explained that the local ordinance ban on display of "nudity" in drive-in theaters in view of public streets was too broad because not all nudity was obscene even as to minors: "under any test of obscenity as to minors not all nudity would be proscribed. Rather to be obscene 'such expression must be, in some significant way, erotic.'" . . . In *Cohen v. California,* 403 U.S. 15 . . . (1971), the Court struck down a man's conviction for disturbing the peace based on his wearing of a jacket with the words "Fuck the Draft" in a courthouse. The Court held that the expression was not obscene within its First Amendment jurisprudence. The Court explained that a state could not prohibit expression as obscene unless it was "in some significant way, erotic." . . . Similarly, in *Cinecom Theaters Midwest States, Inc. v. City of Fort Wayne,* 473 F.2d 1297, 1301–02 (7th Cir. 1973), which was essentially a precursor to *Erznoznik,* the Seventh Circuit stated that a prohibition on nudity at drive-in theaters in view of public streets was too broad even as to children because not all nudity was obscene even as to minors. . . .

2. Extending "Obscenity as to Minors" to Graphic Violence The First Amendment allows the state to restrict children's access to sexually explicit material, but does it forbid any comparable effort to restrict access to the most extreme and graphic violence? This court believes the answer is no. The court bases this answer on the reasoning of *Ginsberg,* which is based on the protection of children and which remains viable today, and on the lack of any persuasive, principled basis for distinguishing between graphic violence and explicit sexual content in terms of potential harm to children . . . *Ginsberg* was based on the state's important and substantial interests in safeguarding the psychological well-being of children and enabling the exercise of parental responsibility. . . . Courts have repeatedly affirmed those interests as a legitimate foundation for laws regulating children's access to some forms of speech. . . . Justice Brennan's broad description of the state's interest for the Court in *Ginsberg* is not limited strictly to sexual material. A state's power to regulate indecent or harmful material for children, while still significantly limited by children's First Amendment rights, can extend beyond the regulation of sexual material upheld in that case. The focus was harm to the ethical and moral development of children. See *Ginsberg v. New York*, 390 U.S. at 640–41. . . .

CONCLUSION

It would be an odd conception of the First Amendment and "variable obscenity" that would allow a state to prevent a boy from purchasing a magazine containing pictures of topless women in provocative poses, as in *Ginsberg*, but give that same boy a constitutional right to train to become a sniper at the local arcade without his parent's permission. The plaintiffs have not shown they are reasonably likely to succeed on their claims that the Indianapolis Ordinance violates the First Amendment or is unconstitutionally vague. . . .

CASE QUESTIONS

1. Should video games be treated as pornography?
2. What guidelines should be used in determining what constitutes *violent* video games?
3. Most video games have some element of violence. Does the decision mean that all such games should be restricted to adults?
4. What are the responsibilities of a parent in this regard? Should government be acting as *parens patria* under the circumstances?

The First Amendment and Domain Names

Does a person have a constitutional right to demand that a registrar of Web site domain names register sexually oriented phrases? In *National A-1 Advertising, Inc. v. Network Solutions, Inc.*, Civ. No. 99-033-M (D.N.H. Sept. 28, 2000), the plaintiff corporation and an individual principal of the corporation sued Network Solutions, Inc. (NSI), alleging a violation of their First Amendment free speech privilege. NSI refused under its decency policy to register a number of domain names such as *www.tits.com* and *www.feelmytits.com* on behalf of the plaintiffs. NSI was the sole approved registrar at the time of attempted registration, but later other registrars were approved that would allow such registration.

The court said that the First Amendment proscribes government conduct, not those of private citizens. The issue then was whether NSI was a "state actor" in the performance of its duties. The court said that NSI is a private company that operated in accordance with a cooperative agreement with the National Science Foundation. The court said, "A private entity will be deemed a state actor if (1) it assumes a traditional public function when it undertakes to perform the challenged conduct or (2) an elaborate financial or regulatory nexus ties the challenged conduct to the State or (3) a symbiotic relationship exists between the private entity and the State." The court decided that NSI was not a government actor although the question was seriously in doubt. The court was persuaded that NSI's policy was its own and not dictated by the National Science Foundation or other government agency.

Restricting Internet Access in Libraries

A civil case that weighed the rights of adults and children with respect to Internet offerings in a public library is the *Loudoun* case.

MAINSTREAM LOUDOUN V. BOARD OF TRUSTEES OF LOUDOUN COUNTY LIBRARY

24 F. Supp. 2d 552 (E.D.Va. 1998)

FACTS: A number of adult members of the Loudoun County public libraries sued the Board of Trustees of the Library and certain individuals for their allegedly impermissible blocking of access to Internet sites. On October 20, 1997, the Library Board voted to adopt a policy requiring the installation of site-blocking software on all library computers so as to block "child pornography and obscene material" and material deemed to be harmful to juveniles under Virginia law. They alleged that the blocking devices prevented access to such non-pornographic sites as the Quaker Home Page, the American Association of University Women–Maryland, and other non-offensive sites.
ISSUE: Whether the Board's policy constituted an unconstitutional restriction on the right to access protected speech on the Internet?
DECISION: The Court held in favor of the plaintiffs to the extent that "the Library Board may not adopt and enforce content-based restrictions on access to protected Internet speech absent a compelling state interest and means narrowly drawn to achieve that end."
REASONING: Judge Brinkema
. . . [W]e conclude that . . . the First Amendment applies to, and limits, the discretion of a public library to place content-based restrictions on access to constitutionally protected materials within its collection. Consistent with the mandate of the First Amendment, a public library, "like other enterprises operated by the State, may not be run in such a manner as to 'prescribe what shall be orthodox in politics, . . . nationalism, religion, or other matters of opinion.'"

. . . The plaintiffs in this case are adults rather than children. Children, whose minds and values are still developing, have traditionally been afforded less First Amendment protection, particularly within the context of public high schools. . . . In contrast, adults are deemed to have acquired the maturity needed to participate fully in a democratic society, and their right to speak and receive speech is entitled to full First Amendment protection. . . .

Finally, the unique advantages of Internet speech eliminate any resource-related rationale libraries might otherwise have for engaging in content-based discrimination. The Supreme Court has analogized the Internet to a "vast library including millions of readily available and indexed publications," the content of which "is as diverse as human thought." . . . Unlike more traditional libraries, however, there is no marginal cost associated with acquiring Internet publications. Instead, all, or nearly all, Internet publications are jointly available for a single price. Indeed, it costs a library more to restrict the content of its collection by means of blocking software than it does for the library to offer unrestricted access to all Internet publications. Nor do Internet publications, which exist . . . only in "cyberspace," take up shelf space or require physical maintenance of any kind. Accordingly, considerations of cost or physical resources cannot justify a public library's decision to restrict access to Internet materials. . . .

In sum, there is "no basis for qualifying the level of First Amendment scrutiny" that must be applied to a public library's decision to restrict access to Internet publications. . . . We are therefore left with the First Amendment's central tenet that content-based restrictions on speech must be justified by a compelling governmental interest and must be narrowly tailored to achieve that end. . . .

[I]t is clear that defendants may not, in the interest of protecting children, limit the speech available to adults to what is fit for "juveniles." As plaintiffs point out, even when government regulation of content is undertaken for a legitimate purpose, whether it be to prevent the communication of obscene speech or materials harmful to children, the means it uses must be a "reasonable response to the threat" which will alleviate the harm "in a direct and material way." . . . Plaintiffs have adequately alleged a lack of such reasonable means here. As . . . such, plaintiffs have stated a valid First Amendment claim that can go forward.

CASE QUESTIONS

1. Would the placement of blocking software on computers restricted to children and the omission of such devices on alternate computers at the same library change the result of this case?
2. If software were developed to block out only pornographic images and other content, would the decision be the same?

International Regulation of Obscenity and Pornography

Germany enacted the Information and Communications Services Act of 1997.[17] The law was directed at censoring neo-Nazi propaganda, pornography, and violence. Unlike the protection given by U.S. law to service providers, the act explicitly makes ISPs liable for the content of the transmissions made available to users, with the proviso, however, that they "are only responsible . . . if they have knowledge of such content and blocking its use is both technically possible and can be reasonably expected." In addition, ISPs "are not responsible for third-party content to which they merely provide access for use."[18] The background to the act was an earlier prosecution of CompuServe (see *People v. Somm*).

The German statute applies to persons within Germany. Interestingly, had the statute sought to regulate ISPs outside of Germany, countries such as the United States would most likely refuse to extradite. ISPs within the United States have broader constitutional rights to relay neo-Nazi propaganda. A U.S. person wishing to espouse pro-Nazi views without instigating violent activities would have the constitutional right to do so. The German law would make such person liable criminally within the country.

Similarly, even if all U.S.-sourced pornographic sites were removed from the Internet, pornographers in countries with laws that do not restrict it or that are not enforced may continue to disgorge obscene materials on the medium. Unless there is a common international regime encompassing all nations, the endeavor may be without success. U.S. criminal laws end at the border unless other nations are willing to extradite violators of U.S. laws. Historically, countries are very uneasy about assisting in the enforcement of U.S. laws, particularly when the foreign state's laws are not as punitive as U.S. law.

CONCLUSION

As discussed at the beginning of this chapter, the Achilles heel of the Internet is the ability of hackers to invade the Internet, wreaking havoc globally. There is a need for all of the nations of the world to enact legislation and engage in a cooperative effort to suppress criminal violations, including the implantation of viruses, the commission of fraud, and other criminal activity. There are a number of efforts underway to combat computer crimes and other unethical and immoral activities. As nations become more adept at understanding the nature and capabilities of the new technology, laws will address societal needs in this regard. Such laws cannot be made in isolation. The threat is international, thereby requiring a global response. International conventions are necessary so that governmental response can be immediate and effective.

It is apparent, however, that governmental attempts to curb Internet excesses will engender much opposition from civil-liberties adherents. For example, the courts will continue to weigh the competing interests of the suppression of pornographic images and data to minors with the desire to leave the Internet an unfettered marketplace of unlimited and uncircumscribed ideas. There are strong arguments for both positions. If left unabated, pornographers will take advantage of their freedom to profit from the display of child pornography and other forms of illicit images. The perennial problem is how the public may be protected without surrendering the most cherished freedoms under the Constitution. Controlling the images and data emanating from the Internet will not be an easy task for those persons or officials inclined to so act. Such control ends at the national borders, however. As emphasized in this chapter, in time, there will be international efforts to arrive at reasonable, global solutions to the problems created by the new technology.

The difficulty in the given analysis is that the attempt to control obscenity on the Internet may be a fruitless endeavor. Pornographers who direct their activities to adult audiences have a great deal of latitude constitutionally under the First Amendment. Laws directed at protecting children have greater constitutional protection, but the *Reno* case defined the limits beyond which the Court will not permit. Courts emphasize the right of parents to control the activities of their children, particularly with respect to the Internet. The difficulty is that, unlike other media, parents are often technologically deficient and are unable to monitor sites that their more knowledgeable children are able to access. Although the Supreme Court has refrained from taking Internet cases because of its hesitancy to create bright-line rules, it was no accident that the Court selected *Reno* as its first venture into Internet issues.

Questions and Problems

1. What is a *crime?* How does *cybercrime* differ from or alter the definition of a crime?
2. Is an agent of a principal that commits a crime responsible for such acts, such as those by the parent company as in *People v. Somm*?
3. Review and detail some of the computer fraud statutes passed by Congress. Which statute(s) would be violated by a person using a stolen password to access the computer of another?
4. May a person who operates a gambling Web site that is legal in his or her own state but that is illegal in a second state where the site is accessed be extradited to that state for commission of the crime?
5. A computer programmer was ordered by his employer to decode a program he had prepared in an encoded state. As program manager for International Telephone and Telegraph Co. Courier Terminal Systems, the defendant undertook to develop a computer program concerning the depreciation of the company's assets. Defendant routinely encoded programs, as was customary at the company. When defendant asked for a period of personal leave, his supervisor asked him to disclose the code so that others could use the depreciation program in his absence. Defendant refused. He was suspended. The company had another programmer spend 10 hours to decode the defendant's program. The defendant was charged with violating an Arizona statute that provided

   A person commits computer fraud in the second degree by intentionally and without authorization accessing, altering, damaging or destroying any computer, computer system or computer network or any computer software, program or data contained on such computer, computer system or computer network.

   Defendant was acquitted under the said statute. The trial court found the acts did not amount to unauthorized alteration or impairment. He was convicted, however, of the more general charge of criminal damage. The statute stated: "A person commits criminal damage by recklessly: (2) Tampering with property of another person so as substantially to impair its function or value." *Tamper* means "any act of interference." The conviction was appealed. Decide. *State of Arizona v. Moran,* 162 Ariz. 524; 784 P.2d 730 (Ct. App. 1989).
6. Dickerson and others are wine consumers residing in Texas who tried to purchase wines from a winery in Arkansas, which wines were not available in Texas. They also want to tour wineries in other states and have desired wines, otherwise not available in Texas, shipped to them directly from the said wineries. Texas law prohibits the importation of more than three gallons of wine for personal use without a permit unless the resident of Texas personally accompanies the wine or liquor as it enters the state. Plaintiffs complain that, in violation of the commerce clause and their civil rights, the law deprives them of their constitutional right to participate in interstate commerce. Decide. *Dickerson v. Bailey,* 87 F. Supp. 2d 691 (S.D.Tex. 2000).
7. Wilson, of the state of Colorado, was tried and convicted for possession of three or more matters containing visual depictions of minors

engaged in explicitly sexual conduct. The Colorado resident had exchanged the computerized child pornography with a resident of Ohio. The depictions were produced and sent to Wilson in interstate commerce. The statute provides:

> any person who knowingly possesses 3 or more books, magazines, periodicals, video tapes, or other matter which contain any visual depiction . . . which was produced using materials which have been mailed or . . . shipped or transported in interstate or foreign commerce, by any means including by computer, if—(i) the producing of such visual depiction involves the use of a minor engaging in sexually explicit conduct; and (ii) such depiction is of such conduct; shall be punished . . .

The defendant claimed that the term *materials* as used but not defined in the statute refers to "ingredients of an object—here, the ingredients or components of a visual depiction." He claims that the definition "precludes any contention that 'materials' includes within its definitional scope tools or equipment or storage items (such as computers or floppy disks) used to hold, mold, or manipulate 'materials' into a visual depiction." Decide. *United States v. Wilson,* 182 F.3d 737 (10th Cir. 1999).

8. Defendant, an employee of Ellery Systems, Inc., copied and transmitted copyrighted computer files containing confidential source code to another person. The employee and the person receiving the files were arrested for violation of the Wire Fraud Statute, which states (18 U.S.C. Section 1343):

> Whoever, having devised or intending to devise any scheme or artifice to defraud, or for obtaining money or property by means of false or fraudulent pretenses, representations, or promises, transmits or causes to be transmitted by means of wire, radio, or television communication in interstate or foreign commerce, any writings, signs, signals, pictures, or sounds for the purpose of executing such scheme or artifice, shall be fined not more than $1,000 or imprisoned not more than five years, or both. . . .

The defendants allege that they cannot be prosecuted under the Wire Fraud Statute because the true nature of the prosecution is merely a copyright violation that cannot be prosecuted under the said statute. Further, they allege that copyright programs were not *property,* that is, "goods, wares, merchandise, securities or money" as defined in the National Stolen Property Act (18 U.S.C. Section 2314). Decide. *United States v. Wang,* 898 F. Supp. 758 (D.Col. 1995).

9. Middleton was employed as the personal computer administrator for Slip.net, an Internet service provider. He installed software and hardware on the company's computers and gave technical support to the company's employees. He knew detailed information about the company's internal system, including employee and computer program passwords. He became unhappy with his job and quit. Thereafter, he began sending threatening e-mails to his former employer. He was allowed to keep his e-mail account with Slip.net as a paying customer. He used his account to switch to another employee's account to enable him to make unauthorized use of the benefits and advantages given to company employees. When it was discovered, the company terminated his e-mail account. Thereafter, he again was able to access the system, causing considerable chaos by deleting the company's entire billing system and its registry and by other such activity. The company's president and two other employees were able to repair the damage after spending many hours over a weekend of effort. Middleton was arrested, charged, and convicted of violation of the Computer Fraud and Abuse Act. Middleton claims he was wrongfully convicted because the statute provides that to be convicted, he had to cause damage, which was defined by the statute (18 U.S.C. Section 1030(e)(8)(A)) as "any impairment to the integrity of data, a program, a system, or information, that causes loss aggregating at least $5,000 in value during any 1-year period to one or more *individuals* [emphasis added]." He claimed that *individuals* do not include corporations. Also, inasmuch as most of the time to repair the damage was by the company president and employees who were paid fixed salaries and received no additional sums, the company was not damaged to the

extent of $5,000 as required by the statute. Decide. *United States v. Middleton,* 231 F.3d 1207 (9th Cir. 2000).

10. Campos was convicted of transporting child pornography in interstate commerce by computer in violation of federal law. Campos claimed on appeal that the search of his residence violated the Fourth Amendment of the Constitution because it was overbroad. He further claimed that the jury should not have been shown two photographs that he had previously agreed and stipulated as constituting child pornography, and that testimony concerning his on-screen account should not have been admitted. The facts showed that a resident of Illinois had participated in a gay and lesbian chat room on AOL. He exchanged photographs and messages with several persons. Later, in early morning he was sent two images of child pornography from an AOL subscriber, known as "AMZEUS." He downloaded the images, notified the Federal Bureau of Investigation (FBI), and gave them the disk. Based on the information, a warrant was obtained to search Campos's home for items relating to child pornography, including the authority to seize computer equipment that may be used to visually depict child pornography or erotica. At the trial, even though Campos had stipulated that the photos were child pornography, the prosecutor showed the photos to the jury, thereby allegedly inflaming the jury. Campos also claimed that he lived with another individual in the apartment and that the said person was the culprit. Do any of the arguments have merit? Discuss and decide. *United States v. Campos,* 221 F.3d 1143 (10th Cir. 2000).

Endnotes

1. *International Review of Criminal Policy—United Nations Manual on the Prevention and Control of Computer-Related Crime, www.ifs.univie.ac.at/~pr2gq1/rev4344.html.*
2. See, for example, the refusal of a federal court to apply the statute forbidding interstate transportation of stolen property (18 U.S.C. Section 2314) to computer programs deemed by the court to be intangible property because the statute speaks of "goods, wares and merchandise," which the court found to be tangible property. For a discussion, especially of the Computer Fraud and Abuse Act, 18 U.S.C. Section 1030, see U.S. Department of Justice, Computer Crime and Intellectual Property Section, *The National Information Infrastructure Protection Act of 1996, www.usdoj.gov/criminal/cybercrime/1030_anal.html.*
3. For a listing of cases, see LEXIS-NEXIS statutory site.
4. Section 1030. Fraud and Related Activity in Connection with Computers states:

   (a) Whoever—
   (1) having knowingly accessed a computer without authorization or exceeding authorized access, and by means of such conduct having obtained information that has been determined by the United States Government pursuant to an Executive order or statute to require protection against unauthorized disclosure for reasons of national defense or foreign relations, or any restricted data . . . with reason to believe that such information so obtained could be used to the injury of the United States, or to the advantage of any foreign nation willfully communicates, delivers, transmits, or causes to be communicated, delivered, or transmitted, or attempts to communicate, deliver, transmit or cause to be communicated, delivered, or transmitted the same to any person not entitled to receive it, or willfully retains the same and fails to deliver it to the officer or employee of the United States entitled to receive it
   (2) intentionally accesses a computer without authorization or exceeds authorized access, and thereby obtains—
   (A) information contained in a financial record of a financial institution, or of a card issuer . . . or contained in a file of a consumer reporting agency on a consumer . . .
   (B) information from any department or agency of the United States; or
   (C) information from any protected computer if the conduct involved an interstate or foreign communication;
   (3) intentionally, without authorization to access any nonpublic computer of a department or agency of the United States, accesses such a computer of that department or agency that is used exclusively for the use of the government . . .

(4) knowingly and with intent to defraud, accesses a protected computer without authorization, or exceeds authorized access, and by means of such conduct furthers the intended fraud and obtains anything of value, unless the object of the fraud and the thing obtained consists only of the use of the computer and the value of such use is not more than $5,000 in any 1-year period;

(5) (A) knowingly causes the transmission of a program, information, code, or command, and as a result of such conduct, intentionally causes damage without authorization, to a protected computer;

(B) intentionally accesses a protected computer without authorization, and as a result of such conduct, recklessly causes damage; or

(C) intentionally accesses a protected computer without authorization, and as a result of such conduct, causes damage;

(6) knowingly and with intent to defraud traffics . . . in any password or similar information through which a computer may be accessed without authorization, if—

(A) such trafficking affects interstate of foreign commerce; or

(B) such computer is used by of for the Government of the United States;

(7) with intent to extort from any person, firm, association, educational institution, financial institution, government entity, or other legal entity, any money or other thing of value, transmits in interstate or foreign commerce any communication containing any threat to cause damage to a protected computer.

Punishments for conviction of any of the above offenses range from a fine to imprisonment of 1 to 20 years, depending on the offense.

5. *U.S. v. Martin,* 228 F.3d 1 (1st Cir. 2000); *U.S. v. Serrano,* 870 F.2d 1, 6 (1st Cir. 1989); and *U.S. v. Montminy,* 936 F.2d 626, 627 (1st Cir. 1991).
6. *U.S. v. Martin.*
7. 18 U.S.C. Section 2314 states:

   Whoever transports, transmits, or transfers in interstate or foreign commerce any goods, wares, merchandise, securities or money, of the value of $5,000 or more, knowing the same to have been stolen, converted or taken by fraud . . . shall be fined under this title or imprisoned not more than ten years, or both.

8. See Michael Hatcher, Jay McDannell, and Stacy Ostfeld, *Computer Crimes,* 36 Am. Crim. L. Rev. 397 (Summer 1999).
9. For a review of this subject, see David Goldstone and Betty-Ellen Shave, *International Dimensions of Crimes in Cyberspace,* 22 Fordham Int'l L.J. 1924 (June, 1999).
10. See Council of Europe, Recommendation No. R (95) 13 of the Committee of Ministers to Member States Concerning Problems of Criminal Procedure Law Connected with Information Technology, adopted on September 11, 1995, *www.usdoj.gov/criminal/cybercrime/crycoe.htm.*
11. Pub. L. 104–104, 110 Stat. 56 (1996).
12. 47 U.S.C. Section 223(a) (Supp. 1977).
13. Id. Section 223(d).
14. Id. Section 223(e)(5).
15. There are a number of articles that explored the findings of the *Reno v. ACLU* litigation. Among them are: April Bailey Cole, *Indecency on the Internet: RENO and the Communications Decency Act of 1996,* 27 Cap. U.L. Rev. 607 (1999); Kim L. Rappaport, *In the Wake of Reno v. ACLU: The Continued Struggle in Western Constitutional Democracies with Internet Censorship and Freedom of Speech Online,* 13 Am. U. Int'l Rev. 765 (1998); and Kelly M. Doherty, *www.obscenity.com: An Analysis of Obscenity and Indecency Regulation on the Internet,* 32 Akron L. Rev. 259 (1999).
16. No. C-97-346 MMC (N.D.Ca. 1998).
17. For a detailed discussion of the act, see Rappaport, *In the Wake.*
18. Article 1, Section 5(2) and (3) of the act.

PART III

INTELLECTUAL PROPERTY RIGHTS

CHAPTER

6 COPYRIGHT ISSUES RAISED BY THE INTERNET

Section 1: U.S. Copyright Law Provisions

Chapter Outline

The Internet, although bringing about remarkable changes globally, has created significant problems for governments and private persons seeking to protect intellectual property rights. Intellectual property rights are those rights that give legal protection to the output of creative energy. They include patents, trademarks, copyrights, and trade secrets. A *patent* is the legal protection given to persons who create an invention or process that is new, useful, and not obvious. A *trademark* is the protection given to names or symbols to designate a business, product, or service. A *copyright* is the protection given to a person for the expression of an idea, such as a book, poem, musical composition, dance movements, and other such creations. A *trade secret* consists of data, such as formulas, blueprints for future projects, and other secrets, on which a company has expended money and energy and that is known to only a select few major persons within an organization.

In this chapter and the following one, we will explore one aspect of intellectual property protection, namely, that of copyright and the Internet. We will review the nature of copyright law, recent statutory enactments, and the evolving legal architecture to protect such rights. We will also review the international efforts to afford worldwide and simplified copyright protection.

The difficulty inherent in the free dissemination of information concerns the conflict between legal protection given to owners of copyright material and the desire of users of the Internet to have unimpeded access to global data. In essence, those seeking protection argue that, unless potential copyright holders are protected in their endeavor to gain pecuniary rewards and other copyright protections, the incentive for creativity may diminish greatly. On the other hand, the pressure for unlimited access to data of whatever kind, from unlimited sources, has brought about conflict between the two opposing interests to a degree almost unimaginable a few years ago.

In 1997, copyright industries accounted for some $529.3 billion in value to the U.S. economy or 6.53 percent of the U.S. gross domestic product. Employment in the core copyright industries tripled in the two decades from 1977 through 1997. Over 6.9 million workers were employed in copyright-related industries, or 5.3 percent of the total U.S. workforce. Export sales of products and services affected by the said industries exceeded $71 billion. Thus, the financial impact of such industries is of major concern to the United States.[1]

The current intellectual rights regime has been inadequate to address the issues raised by the new technologies, due to the constant stream of innovative changes in the marketplace. Criminal and other tortious conduct occur often in countries with few legal restrictions or that have lax enforcement. Such laxity has plagued owners of protected works. Until recently, the People's Republic of China was accused of intellectual rights piracy and was on a watch list for possible imposition of sanctions. Prior thereto, other mainstream countries in Asia, such as South Korea and Taiwan, presented serious difficulties for copyright holders.

Internet service providers, educational institutions, computer hardware and software companies, and media organizations have been engaging intensively in a dialogue to set guidelines whereby users of the Internet, especially scholars and students, may advance their intellectual pursuits on the World Wide Web without infringing upon the rights of publishers and other media participants to protection given to owners of copyrighted creations. The issues raised are very significant; the resolution of which has to take place to prevent a great deal of litigation, lobbying efforts and other substantial costs, including legal fees, relating thereto. We will review the nature of copyright protection afforded in the United States and in international conventions and the interplay of the fair use exception and other defenses and exceptions to such protection.

CONSTITUTIONAL AND STATUTORY PROVISIONS

The legal protections afforded to works by authors have existed for several centuries. The invention of the printing press created both a desire by the monarchy to prevent the spread of subversive and heretical works and the demand by authors to protect the attribution and the integrity of their works. The English Statute of Anne, enacted in 1710, was the first law to give protection to authors and the works attributed to them. The American colonies followed English law by enacting their own protective measures.

Copyright law today has its legal basis in the U.S. Constitution and in the statutory enactments made in pursuance thereof. Article 1, Section 8 of the Constitution provides:

> The Congress shall have the power . . . [t]o promote the Progress of Science and the useful Arts, by securing for limited Times to authors and Inventors the exclusive Right to their respective Writings and Discoveries.

The first legislative enactment by Congress took place in 1790 and was quite limited in scope. Thereafter, there were a number of amendments and major changes, particularly the Copyright Act of 1909. Presently, the basic statutory U.S. enactment giving protection to copyright holders is the Copyright Act of 1976.[2] The act was amended on numerous occasions and includes the Semiconductor Chip Protection Act of 1984, the Audio Home Recording Act of 1992, and the Digital Millennium Copyright Act of 1998. Protection is also afforded by state law in the form of the right of publicity and tort concepts, such as misappropriation, but federal law preempts most state enactments concerning author's rights.

SUBJECT MATTER OF COPYRIGHTS

Fixation

Copyright protection is given to "original works of authorship fixed in any tangible medium of expression, now known or later developed, from which they can be perceived, reproduced, or otherwise communicated, either directly or with the aid of a machine or device."[3] It is not enough to have a creative thought or concept. It must be *fixed* in a tangible medium of expression, such as in a copy that may be seen, reproduced, or communicated in a somewhat permanent form. For example, there is no protection for a person singing a newly created song unless the song is reduced to a recording or other reproducible form.[4] A major exception in U.S. law to the fixation requirement brought about by the Agreement on Trade-Related Aspects of Intellectual Property Rights (TRIPS),[5] is the addition of a Chapter 11 to the Copyright Act, which became effective December 8, 1994. The addition prohibits anyone from making a copy or phonorecord of a live musical performance, as well as the transmission, distribution, or trafficking thereof, without the consent of the performer.

Original Works of Authorship

Works of authorship include but are not limited to:

1. literary works;
2. musical works, including the accompanying words;
3. dramatic works including any accompanying music;
4. pantomimes and choreographic works;
5. pictorial, graphic, and sculptural works;
6. motion pictures and other audiovisual works;
7. sound recordings; and
8. architectural works.[6]

Compilations and derivative works are also included within the subject matter of copyrights to the extent of the author's contribution to such works. "A *'compilation'* is a work formed by the collection and assembling of preexisting materials or of data that are selected, coordinated, or arranged in such a way that the resulting work as a whole constitutes an original work of authorship." It includes *collective works,* which are collections of separate works such as anthologies or encyclopedias. "A *derivative work* is a work based upon one or more preexisting works, such as a translation, musical arrangement, dramatization, fictionalization, motion picture version, sound recording, art reproduction, abridgment, condensation, or any other form in which a work may be recast, transformed, or adapted." It also includes editorial revisions, annotations, elaborations, or other such modifications that are original works of authorship.[7]

In *Ty, Inc. v. West Highland Publishing, Inc.,* 1998 U.S. Dist. LEXIS 15869 (N.D.Ill. 1998), the plaintiff manufactured Beanie Babies, which are very popular plush toys for children. It registered numerous copyrights of Beanie Babies characters, as well as registering trademarks for related products. The defendant produced and sold publications and products relating to Beanie Babies, without authorization, including trading cards, coloring books, and a newsletter. The defendant published some 900,000 copies of the *Beanie Baby Handbook.* In a suit for copyright and trademark infringement, the court found in favor of the plaintiff enjoining the defendant from manufacturing, selling, and distributing Beanie Baby trading cards, coloring books, and newsletters relating to the plush toys. The basis for the injunction was the infringement of plaintiff's exclusive rights to prepare derivative works.

Copyright protection is limited to the *expression* of an idea rather than to the idea, principle, system, concept, process, or method of operation.[8] Any person can use the ideas and concepts underlying the legal protection so long as he or she does not copy the manner in which the work has been set forth. Protection is not given to singular words or short expressions, although trademark law may protect them. For example, it is not uncommon for writers to use titles for their books that are identical to other similar works, such as *Business Law.* Many books, songs, and motion pictures, have identical or similar titles. Generally, such usage does not infringe upon the copyrights of owners of works having the same or similar title.

Computer Programs as Works of Authorship. TRIPS requires members of the World Trade Organization to comply with the provisions of the Berne Convention for the Protection of Literary and Artistic Works of 1971. Article 10 of TRIPS states that computer programs are to be protected as *literary works* under the Berne Convention whether such programs are in source or object code. It is in accordance with the U.S. Copyright Act, which includes computer programs as literary works. A *computer program* is defined by the Act (Section 101) as "a set of statements or instructions to be used directly or indirectly in a computer in order to bring about a certain result." *Literary works* are defined by the Act as:

> Works, other than audiovisual works, expressed in words, numbers, or other verbal or numerical symbols or indicia, regardless of the nature of the material objects, such as books, periodicals, manuscripts, phonorecords, film, tapes, disks, or cards, in which they are embodied.

Originality

The work to be protected must be *original,* that is, not a duplication from a prior work. It need not be useful (as for patents) or display artistry or creativity. For example, the protected work can be a poorly crafted poem or written work. Unpublished works are protected, as well as published works, emanating from countries that are parties to international copyright conventions or treaties, or where the U.S. president has determined such other countries offer copyright protection to U.S. persons.

What is an *original work?* We will review two cases, the first of which is the leading case discussing the issue. In *Feist Publications, Inc. v. Rural Tel. Service Co.,* the U.S. Supreme Court was called upon to decide whether the publisher of a telephone directory containing white and yellow pages was protected by the Copyright Act from the copying of telephone names and addresses therein by another publisher.

FEIST PUBLICATIONS, INC. V. RURAL TEL. SERVICE CO.

499 U.S. 340 (1991)

FACTS: Rural is a public utility company providing telephone service to a number of Kansas communities. It publishes a telephone directory composed of yellow and white pages. The data on the pages are supplied by customers who must furnish their names and addresses for telephone service. Feist is a publishing company that publishes telephone directories covering a larger geographic region than Rural. Feist requested Rural to license its white pages to Feist but it refused to do so. Feist then abstracted Rural's listings without the consent of Rural, thereby causing Rural to sue for copyright infringement.

ISSUE: Were the white pages consisting of telephone names and addresses entitled to copyright protection?

DECISION: The U.S. Supreme Court held that there was no protection under the Copyright Act, reversing the prior decision of the U.S. District Court that had been affirmed by the U.S. Court of Appeals.

REASONING: Justice O'Connor

This case concerns the interaction of two well-established propositions. The first is that facts are not copyrightable; the other, that compilations of facts generally are. Each of these propositions possesses an impeccable pedigree. That there can be no valid copyright in facts is universally understood. The most fundamental axiom of copyright law is that . . . "[n]o author may copyright his ideas or the facts he narrates. . . . At the same time, however, it is beyond dispute that compilations of facts are within the subject matter of copyright." Compilations were expressly mentioned in the Copyright Act of 1909, and again in the Copyright Act of 1976.

There is an undeniable tension between these two propositions. Many compilations consist of nothing but raw data—i.e., wholly factual information not accompanied by any original written expression. On what basis may one claim a copyright in such a work? Common sense tells us that 100 uncopyrightable facts do not magically change their status when gathered together in one place. Yet copyright law seems to contemplate that compilations that consist exclusively of facts are potentially within its scope.

The key to resolving the tension lies in understanding why facts are not copyrightable. The sine qua non of copyright is originality. To qualify for copyright protection, a work must be original to the author. . . . Original, as the term is used in copyright, means only that the work was independently created by the author (as opposed to copied from other works), and that it possesses at least some minimal degree of creativity. . . . To be sure, the degree of creativity is extremely low; even a slight amount "no matter how crude, humble or obvious" it might be. . . . Originality does not signify novelty; a work may be original even though it closely resembles other works, so long as the similarity is fortuitous, not the result of copying. . . .

Originality is a constitutional requirement. The source of Congress' power to enact copyright laws is Article I, 8, cl. 8, of the Constitution, which authorizes Congress to "secur[e] for limited Times to Authors . . . the exclusive Right to their respective Writings." . . .

It is this bedrock principle of copyright that mandates the law's seemingly disparate treatment of facts and factual compilations. "No one may claim originality as to facts." . . . This is because facts do not own their origin to an act of authorship. The distinction is one between creation and discovery: the first person to find and report a particular fact has not created the fact; he or she has merely discovered its existence. . . .

Factual compilations, on the other hand, may possess the requisite originality. The compilation author typically chooses which facts to include, in what order to place them, and how to arrange the collected data so that they may be used effectively by readers. These choices as to selection and arrangement, so long as they are made independently by the compiler and entail a minimal degree of creativity, are sufficiently original that Congress may protect such compilations through the copyright laws. . . .

This protection is subject to an important limitation. The mere fact that a work is copyrighted does not mean that every element of the work may be protected. Originality remains the sine qua non of copyright; accordingly, copyright protection may extend to those components of a work that are original to the author. . . .

This inevitably means that the copyright in a factual compilation is thin. Notwithstanding a valid copyright, a subsequent compiler remains free to use the facts contained in another's publication to aid in preparing a competing work, so long as the competing work does not feature the same selection and arrangement. . . .

The definition of "compilation" is found in 101 of the 1976 Act. It defines a "compilation" in the copyright sense as "a work formed by the collection and assembly of preexisting materials or of data that are selected. Coordinated, or arranged in such a way that the resulting work, as a whole, constitutes an original work of authorship." . . .

The purpose of the statutory definition is to emphasize that collections of facts are not copyrightable per se. It conveys this message through its tripartite structure. . . . The statute identifies three distinct elements, and requires each to be met for a work to qualify as a copyrightable compilation: (1) the collection and assembly of pre-existing material, facts, or data; (2) the selection, coordination, or arrangement of those materials; and (3) the creation, by virtue of the particular selection, coordination, or arrangement, of an "original" work of authorship. . . .

There is no doubt that Feist took from the white pages of Rural's directory a substantial amount of factual information. At a minimum, Feist copied the names, towns, and telephone numbers of 1,309 of Rural's subscribers. Not all copying, however, is copyright infringement. To establish infringement, two elements must be proven: (1) ownership of a valid copyright, and (2) copying of constituent elements of the work that are original. . . . The first element is not at issue here; Feist appears to concede that Rural's directory, considered as a whole, is subject to a valid copyright because it contains some forward text, as well as original material in its yellow pages advertisements. . . .

The question is whether Rural has proven the second element. In other words, did Feist, by taking 1,309 names, towns, and telephone numbers from Rural's white pages, copy anything that was "original" to Rural? Certainly, the raw data does not satisfy the originality requirement. . . . [T]hese bits of information are uncopyrightable facts; they existed before Rural reported them, and would have continued to exist if Rural had never published a telephone directory. . . .

The question that remains is whether Rural selected, coordinated, or arranged these uncopyrightable facts in an original way. . . .

The selection, coordination, and arrangement of Rural's white pages do not satisfy the minimum constitutional standards for copyright protection. As mentioned at the outset, Rural's white pages are entirely typical. Persons desiring telephone service in Rural's area takes the data provided by its subscribers and lists it alphabetically by surname. The end product is a garden-variety white pages directory, devoid of even the slightest trace of creativity. . . .

CASE QUESTIONS

1. What steps should Rural have taken to bring its work within the subject matter protected by the Copyright Act?
2. Should anyone be permitted to print identical data compiled through the significant efforts and expense by another?

In *CCC Info. Serv., Inc. v. Maclean Hunter Mkt. Reports,* Hunter published the *Red Book,* which was a compilation of car values in different regions of the country. It listed the editors' projections of the value of used cars for six weeks after publication. CCC used these values in compiling computer databases. Hunter sued for infringement. The court of appeals reversed the lower court's decision in favor of CCC. The court said that the *Red Book* valuations were not preexistent facts merely discovered by the *Red Book* editors. They represented predictions by the *Red Book* editors of future prices estimated to cover the various geographical regions. As such, copyright protection is merited. The prices were based not only on the many data sources but also represented professional judgment and expertise.

In *Nihon Keizai Shimbun, Inc. v. Comline Business Data, Inc.,* 166 F.3d 65 (2d Cir. 1999), Nihon, a Japanese corporation that publishes financial, business, and industry news, sued Comline, a company that gathers news articles from diverse sources, and sold substantial abstracts thereof to its customers. Comline selected the articles and gave them to translators and rewriters who then edited the abstracts, often using word-for-word excerpts of the news articles. A rewritten article contained approximately two-thirds of the original article on average, combining sentences, dividing a sentence, rearranging the facts, and adopting the same structure and organization of the facts reported by the plaintiff organization and other news organizations.

With respect to plaintiff's claim of copyright and trademark infringements, the court addressed the issue of whether the defendant had merely copied unprotectable facts and whether there was fair use of the material. The court restated the axiom that the law does not protect facts alone without some degree of originality. It stated the test to be used in determining whether the defendant had directly copied the plaintiff's articles.

> The standard test in determining substantial similarity is the "ordinary observer test": whether an average lay observer would overlook any dissimilarities between the works and would conclude that one was copied from another. . . . Where the work at issue contains both protectible and unprotectible elements, the test must be "more discerning," excluding the unprotectible elements from consideration. . . . Here, Comline had every right to republish the facts contained in Nikkei's articles; in determining substantial similarity, we must look only to the original elements in Nikkei's presentation of those facts. The appropriate inquiry is whether "the copying is quantitatively and qualitatively sufficient" to support a finding of infringement."

The court then analyzed the facts as presented, the degree of similarity, the verbatim use of the plaintiff's news articles by the defendant, and the originality of plaintiff's efforts in gathering and reporting the news in its newspapers. It found that the defendant did violate the plaintiff's copyright concerning the articles. It is an insufficient answer to say that the defendant infringed a total of 20 articles that the plaintiff published annually.

We are all familiar with color transparencies of art works sold in museum bookstores. Are the color transparencies of paintings and other works in the public domain that are in museums *original works* so as to qualify for copyright protection? The issue is discussed in the following case.

THE BRIDGEMAN ART LIBRARY, LTD. V. COREL CORPORATION

36 F. Supp. 2d 191 (S.D.N.Y. 1999)

FACTS: Plaintiff made transparencies of original works of museum art in the public domain that it sells through museums and elsewhere. It sued Corel for copyright infringement. Defendant, which had duplicated the content of the transparencies, requested the Court to dismiss the case on the ground that the transparencies were not original works and therefore were not copyrightable.

ISSUES: Whether the transparencies are copyrightable under either U.S. or U.K. law?

DECISION: Under both U.S. and U.K. law, the said transparencies were not original works that the law will protect. Accordingly, the Court dismissed the plaintiff's copyright infringement claim.

REASONING: Judge Kaplan

In *Burrow-Giles Lithographic Co. v. Sarony* [111 U.S. 53 (1884)], the Supreme Court held that photographs are "writings" within the meaning of the Copyright Clause [of the U.S. Constitution] and that the particular portrait at issue in that case was sufficiently original—by virtue of its pose, arrangement of accessories in the photograph, and lighting and the expression the photographer evoked—to be subject to copyright.... [T]here is broad scope for copyright in photographs because "a very modest expression of personality will constitute sufficient originality."

As the Nimmers [Melville B. Nimmer and David Nimmer, *Nimmer on Copyright*] have written, there "appears to be at least two situations in which a photograph should be denied copyright for lack of originality," one of which is directly relevant here: "where a photograph of a photograph or other printed matter is made that amounts to nothing more than slavish copying." The authors thus conclude that a slavish photographic copy of a painting would lack originality, although they suggest the possibility that protection in such a case might be claimed as a "reproduction of a work of art." ...

Baitlin involved the defendants claim to copyright in a plastic reproduction, with minor variations, of a mechanical cast-iron coin bank that had been sold in the United States for many years and that had passed into the public domain. The Court of Appeals affirmed a district court order compelling the defendants to cancel a recordation of copyright in the plastic reproduction on the ground that the reproduction was not "original" within the meaning of the 1909 Copyright Act, holding that the requirement of originality applies to reproductions of works of art. Only "a distinguishable variation"—something beyond technical skill—will render the reproduction original....

There is little doubt that many photographs, probably the overwhelming majority, reflect at least the modest amount of originality required for copyright protection. "Elements of originality ... may include posing the subjects, lighting, angle, selection of film and camera, evoking the desired expression, and almost any other variant involved." But "slavish copying," although doubtlessly requiring technical skill and effort, does not qualify. As the Supreme Court indicated in *Feist,* [discussed previously], "sweat of the brow" alone is not the "creative spark" which is the *sine qua non* of originality....

In this case, plaintiff by its own admission has labored to create "slavish copies" of public domain works of art. While it may be assumed that this required both skill and effort, there was no spark of originality—indeed, the point of the exercise was to reproduce the underlying works with absolute fidelity. Copyright is not available in these circumstances.

[The court analogized the case to making a photocopy of an original work in the public domain. Obviously such copy is not protectable. The court also discussed the law of the United Kingdom and determined that the result herein would most likely also take place in the U.K.]

CASE QUESTIONS

1. Would the decision be different if the plaintiff had altered the color, texture, or shading or made other changes in the copy of the works of art?
2. What is the dividing line between "slavish copies" of public domain works of art and works protected by the Copyright Act?

OWNERSHIP OF A COPYRIGHT PROTECTED WORK

Initial Ownership. The Copyright Act (Section 201(a)) states that copyright protection is initially vested in the author or authors of the work. Authors of a joint work are co-owners of the copyright. A *joint work* is defined (Section 101) as "a work prepared by two or more authors with the intention that their contributions be merged into inseparable or interdependent parts of a unitary whole."

Works Made for Hire. A *work made for hire* is "a work prepared by an employee within the scope of his or her employment." Thus, if one is paid for producing works eligible for copyright protection, while employed by another person, the latter will be deemed to be the author and owner of the copyright. A critical issue that must be resolved in each situation is whether a person is an employee or an independent producer or contractor—if an employee, then the employer under such circumstances prevails. If the person is an independent producer or contractor, then the law requires that certain conditions be met before the employer can prevail in a claim for copyright ownership, including a signed written agreement between the parties that the work is one made for hire.

Courts have looked at the rules of agency law to make the differentiation between an *employee* and an *independent contractor*.[9] The Restatement of the Law of Agency (Second), Section 220, lists a number of factors that a court will weigh in its determination. They are:

1. The extent of control which, by the agreement, the master [employer] may exercise over the details of the work;
2. Whether or not the one employed is engaged in a distinct occupation or business;
3. The kind of occupation, with reference to whether, in the locality, the work is usually done under the direction of the employer or by a specialist without supervision;
4. The skill required in the particular occupation;
5. Whether the employer or the workman supplies the instrumentalities, tools, and the place of work for the person doing the work;
6. The length of time for which the person is employed;
7. The method of payment, whether by the time or by the job;
8. Whether or not the work is a part of the regular business of the employer;
9. Whether or not the parties believe they are creating the relation of master and servant; and
10. Whether the principal is or is not in business.

In essence, the more control an employer has over a work in a work environment, the more likely courts will find an employer-employee relationship. A person working on an assembly line 40 hours a week, with specified vacation days, in a position where the employer deducts for FICA (Federal Insurance Contributions Act) and normal tax deductions and where the employer furnishes the place and equipment for the employment, will be deemed an employee rather than an independent contractor. The greater the independence of the person requested to perform a specific task, the greater the likelihood that such person is an independent producer. For example, calling upon someone to build a wing to an existing building would almost always establish a relationship of employer and independent contractor.

If the work is one that is the result of a request from an independent producer or contractor, then the issue arises of whether the creator of the work or the employer owns the copyright. The Copyright Act (Section 201(b)) states that to be considered as a "work made for hire" wherein the employer is deemed the author and owner of the copyright, it must be:

1. specially ordered or commissioned for use as (a) a contribution to a collective work; (b) as a part of a motion picture or other audiovisual work; (c) as a sound recording; (d) as a translation; (e) as a supplementary work [a work secondary to that of another author such as providing a forward, illustrating, commenting on, adding bibliography and so on]; (f) as a compilation; (g) as an instructional text; (h) as a test; (i) as answer material for a test; or (j) as an atlas; and
2. the parties agreed in a written instrument signed by them that the work is one made for hire.

In all other cases, the creator of the work is the author and owner of the work. In the following case, the U.S. Supreme Court discussed the distinction between a work made for hire and one wherein the creator may retain ownership of the copyright. In so doing the Court reviewed the common-law principles of the Restatement of Agency.

COMMUNITY FOR CREATIVE NON-VIOLENCE V. REID

490 U.S. 730 (1989)

FACTS: The plaintiff, CCNV, is a nonprofit unincorporated association dedicated to assist the homeless in the U.S. It conceived the idea of having a sculpture of a modern nativity scene wherein two homeless black parents and their newborn child are huddled over a steam gate. It commissioned a statue exemplifying the concept to be made by the defendant, Reid, called "Third World America." Reid agreed to create the statue without a fee other than the actual cost of materials and related expenses. The parties collaborated concerning the details of the project, including the nature of the sculpture, approval of sketches, the models to be used for the work, and other details. Thereafter, the parties disputed concerning who was entitled to claim copyright ownership.

ISSUE: Whether the work was one for hire thereby permitting CCNV to claim copyright ownership of the work?

DECISION: The Court stated that it was not a work for hire and remanded the case for a determination whether the work was jointly authored thereby permitting both parties to share copyright ownership.

REASONING: Justice Marshall

The Copyright Act of 1976 provides that copyright ownership "vests initially in the author or authors of the work." 17 U.S.C. Section 201(a). As a general rule, the author is the party who actually creates the work, that is, the person who translates an idea into a fixed, tangible expression entitled to copyright protection. The Act carves out an important exception, however, for "works made for hire." If the work is for hire, "the employer or other person for whom the work was prepared is considered the author" and owns the copyright, unless there is a written agreement to the contrary, Section 201(b). Classifying a work as "made for hire" determines not only the initial ownership of its copyright, but also the copyright's duration, Section 302(c), and the owners' renewal rights, Section 304(a), termination rights, Section 203(a), and right to import certain goods bearing the copyright, Section 601(b)(1). The contours of the work for hire doctrine therefore carry profound significance for freelance writers—including artists, writers, photographers, designers, composers, and computer programmers—and for the publishing, advertising, music, and other industries which commission their works. . . .

The petitioners do not claim that the statue satisfies the terms of Section 101(2). Quite clearly, it does not. Sculpture does not fit within any of the nine categories of "specially ordered or commissioned" works enumerated in that subsection, and no written agreement between the parties establishes "Third World America" as a work for hire.

The dispositive inquiry in this case therefore is whether "Third World America" is "a work prepared by an employee within the scope of his or her employment" under Section 101(1). The Act does not define these terms. In the absence of such guidance, four interpretations have emerged. The first holds that a work is prepared by an employee whenever the hiring party retains the right to control the product. . . . Petitioners take this view. A second, and closely related, view is that a work is prepared by an employee under Section 101(1) when the hiring party has actually wielded control with respect to the creation of a particular work. . . . A third view is that the term "employee" within Section 101(1) carries its common law agency law meaning. . . . Finally, respondent and numerous amici curiae [nonparty so-called friends of the court who file briefs on behalf of one party or another] contend that the term "employee" only refers to "formal, salaried" employees. . . .

The starting point for our interpretation of a statute is always its language. The Act nowhere defines the terms "employee" or "scope of employment." It is, however, well established that "[w]here Congress uses terms that have accumulated settled meaning under . . . the common law, a court must infer, unless the statute otherwise dictates, that Congress means to incorporate the established meaning of these terms." . . . In the past, when Congress has used the term "employee" without defining it, we have concluded that Congress intended to describe the conventional master-servant relationship as understood by common law agency doctrine. Nothing in the text of the work for hire provisions indicates that Congress used the words "employee" and "employment" to describe anything other than "the conventional relation of employer and employee." On the contrary, Congress' intent to incorporate the agency law definition is suggested by Section 101(1)'s use of the term, "scope of employment," a widely used term of art in agency law. See Restatement (Second) of Agency Section 228 (1958).... We ... agree with the Court of Appeals that the term "employee" should be understood in light of the general common law of agency.

[The Court set forth the factors stated in the Restatement of Agency given previously.] Examining the circumstances of this case in light of these factors, we agree with the Court of Appeals that Reid was not an employee of CCNV but an independent contractor. Thus, CCNV members directed enough of Reid's work to ensure that he produced a sculpture that met these specifications. But the extent of control the hiring party exercises over the details of the product is not dispositive. Indeed, all the other circumstances weigh heavily against finding an employment relationship. Reid is a sculptor, a skilled occupation. Reid supplied his own tools. He worked in his own studio in Baltimore, making daily supervision of his activities from Washington practically impossible. Reid was retained for less than two months, a relatively short period of time. During and after this time, CCNV had no right to assign additional projects to Reid. Apart from the deadline for completing the sculpture, Reid had absolute freedom to decide when and how long to work. CCNV paid Reid $15,000, a sum dependent on "completion of a specific job, a method by which independent contractors are often compensated." ... Reid had total discretion in hiring and paying assistants. "Creating sculptures was hardly 'regular business' for CCNV." ... Indeed, CCNV is not a business at all. Finally, CCNV did not pay payroll or social security taxes, provide any employee benefits, or contribute to unemployment insurance or workers' compensation funds.

Because Reid was an independent contractor, whether "Third World America" is a work for hire depends on whether it satisfies the terms of Section 101(2). This petitioners concede it cannot do. Thus, CCNV is not the author of "Third World America" by virtue of the work for hire provisions of the Act. However, as the Court of Appeals made clear, CCNV nevertheless may be a joint author of the sculpture if, on remand, the District Court so determines that CCNV and Reid prepared the work "with the intention that their contributions be merged into inseparable or interdependent parts of a unitary whole." 17 U.S.C. Section 101. In that case, CCNV and Reid would be co-owners of the copyright in the work. See Section 201(a)....

CASE QUESTIONS

1. What steps should CCNV have taken to assure itself ownership of the copyright?
2. On what basis did the Court believe that the work may have been jointly authored?

In *Kirk v. Harter,* 188 F.3d 1105 (8th Cir. 1999), the court of appeals discussed the issue as to who is entitled to claim ownership of a protected work. Plaintiffs consisted of a partnership known as Iowa Pedigree, which was engaged in the business of aiding dog breeders and brokers to comply with the licensing and registration requirements of the American Kennel Club and the U.S. Department of Agriculture. It retained the services of the defendant who had written a computer program that permitted owners to track information concerning dogs bred and sold by the kennel. Harter, at the request of the plaintiffs, wrote a computer program to assist owners to comply with the said requirements. Defendant developed a number of programs for the plaintiffs, maintained their computers, and serviced the software of plaintiff's clients. In 1996, a number of customers terminated their relationship with plaintiffs and received services directly from the defendant. In a suit for copyright infringement and other claims, a jury found in favor of the plaintiffs. The court of appeals reversed the decision.

The court stated that the issue was whether Iowa Pedigree was the sole owner of the copyrights to the computer programs. "The Copyright Act provides that an employer is the author when an item is considered a work made for hire.... See also 17 U.S.C. Section 101 (defining work made for hire as a 'work prepared by an employee within the scope of his or her employment'); ... Whether the computer programs in this case are works made for hire turns on the nature of the employment relationship between

Iowa Pedigree and Harter. . . . " The Court then reviewed the facts of the case and concluded that the defendant was an independent contractor and not an employee, and therefore the computer programs were not works made for hire. Thus, the plaintiff did not have exclusive right to the computer programs.

Joint Work. CCNV referred to a joint work. As mentioned previously, the Copyright Act (Section 101) defines a *joint work* as "a work prepared by two or more authors with the intention that their contributions be merged into inseparable or interdependent parts of a unitary whole." If a work is a joint work, then the parties share the ownership and the copyright protection. As co-owners they would have the right to use the work and license it subject to the rights of the co-owner.

Transfer of Ownership

The ownership of a copyright may be transferred in whole or in part by the copyright owner or it may descend to the owner's heirs upon death, or by involuntary court process. If there are multiple owners of a copyright, any one of such owners may commence litigation for infringement. The transferee receives all of the rights that the original owner possesses.

RIGHTS OF COPYRIGHT HOLDER

The possessor of a copyright is given a number of exclusive rights with respect to the protected work. They are:

1. *Reproduction* of copies or phonorecords
2. *Preparation* of derivative works[10]
3. *Distribution* of copies or phonorecords to the public by sale, rental, lease, lending or other transfers
4. *Performance*[11] publicly of a literary, musical, dramatic, or choreographic work or by pantomime or by making a motion picture or, in the case of sound recordings, by means of a digital audio transmission
5. *Display* of the said copyrighted work in public (other than motion pictures), including pictorial, graphic, sculptural works, or other audiovisual works.[12]

What Is a Copy?

The Copyright Act forbids the unauthorized reproduction of copies of the protected works. What is meant by a *copy,* particularly in the context of the digital environment? Is the downloading of protected works actionable against any computer user doing so? The leading case, *MAI Systems Corp. v. Peak Computer, Inc.,* is discussed hereafter.

Section 101 of the Copyright Act defines *copies* as:

Material objects, other than phonorecords, in which a work is fixed by any method now known or later developed, and from which the work can be perceived, reproduced, or otherwise communicated, either directly or with the aid of a machine or device.

A work is "fixed" in a tangible medium of expression when its embodiment in a copy or phonorecord, by and under the authority of the author, is sufficiently permanent or stable to permit it to be perceived, reproduced, or otherwise communicated for a period of more than transitory duration.

MAI SYSTEMS CORP. V. PEAK COMPUTER, INC.

991 F.2d 511 (9th Cir. 1993)

FACTS: Plaintiff sued the defendant, its president and another, for copyright infringement, misappropriation of trade secrets, trademark infringement, and other relief. The plaintiff manufactured and serviced computers and software. Defendant Peak maintains MAI computers for some 100 clients in Southern California, including routine maintenance and emergency repairs. The service manager for

MAI left his position at MAI and joined Peak. A number of businesses that had used MAI switched thereafter to Peak for servicing of their computers. MAI issued software licenses to MAI customers allowing them to use its software, subject to prohibitions against copying, disclosure, reconfiguration, and other specified wrongful acts. In addition, the Licensee was prohibited from giving access to or disclosing the diagnostic software without MAI's permission. Defendant, as individual licensee and without consent of the plaintiff, downloaded MAI's software in connection with its business.

ISSUE: Whether Peak's loading of the copyrighted software constituted a "copy" and is "fixed" so as to constitute a violation of the Copyright Act?

DECISION: The Court stated that it did constitute copying and upheld the District Court's injunction against the defendants.

REASONING: Judge Brunetti

The district court's grant of summary judgment on MAI's claims of copyright infringement reflects its conclusion that a "copying" for purposes of copyright law occurs when a computer program is transferred from a permanent storage device to a computer's RAM [random access memory]. This conclusion is consistent with its finding, in granting the preliminary injunction, that: "the loading of copyrighted computer software from a storage medium (hard disk, floppy disk, or read only memory) into the memory of a central processing unit ("CPU") causes a copy to be made. In the absence of ownership of the copyright or express permission by license, such acts constitute copyright infringement." We find that this conclusion is supported by the record and the law. . . .

Peak argues that this loading of copyrighted software does not constitute a copyright violation because the "copy" created in RAM is not fixed. . . . The law . . . supports the conclusion that Peak's loading of copyrighted software into RAM creates a "copy" of that software in violation of the Copyright Act. . . .

We have found no case which specifically holds that the copying of software into RAM creates a "copy" under the Copyright Act. However, it is generally accepted that the loading of software into a computer constitutes the creation of a copy under the Copyright Act. See e.g. *Vault Corp. v. Quaid Software Ltd.*, 847 F.2d 255, 260 (5th Cir. 1988) ("the act of loading a program from a medium of storage into a computer's memory creates a copy of the program"); 2 Nimmer on Copyright, Section 8.08 at 8–105 (1983) ("inputting a computer program entails the preparation of a copy"); Final Report of the National Commission on the New Technological Uses of Copyrighted Works, at 13 (1978) ("the placement of a work into a computer is the preparation of a copy").

CASE QUESTIONS

1. Does a person who downloads the almost innumerable sites make a *copy* of them?
2. If so, does a person who hyperlinks onto a copyright protected site violate the Copyright Act?

Moral Rights

Prior to 1990, the United States did not recognize *moral rights* in the author of a copyrighted work. With the passage of the Visual Arts Rights Act of 1990,[13] the Copyright Act was amended so as to add a new visual-art section (106A), which granted the author of a work the following additional rights heretofore recognized by most other countries.[14] These rights are as follows:

1. *Attribution,* that is, to claim authorship of the work and prevent use of one's name as author of a work or visual art not created by him or her
2. *Integrity,* that is, to prevent use of one's name of a work or visual art that was distorted, mutilated, or otherwise modified and that would injure his or her reputation
3. *Prevention* of intentional distortion, mutilation, destruction, or modification prejudicial to one's reputation and prevent destruction of any work of recognized statute. It is subject to modified exceptions concerning works that are part of a building structure.[15]

The rights are subject to prior consent or other waiver by the author.[16] Also, there are exceptions for works that become modified as a result of the passage of time, the inherent nature of the material, the result of conservation, or due to the lighting or placement of a publicly presented visual art work.[17]

Notice of Copyright

The use of the symbol © or the word *copyright* or *Copr* should be used, although it is not legally required to do so to receive copyright protection. By adding the word or symbol, a defendant is foreclosed from claiming that he or she did not know of the copyright in order to lessen the quantum of damages to be awarded to the plaintiff.[18]

Duration

For copyrighted works created on or after January 1, 1978, the protection is granted for a period of the life of the author plus 70 years. For joint works, the period is the life of the last surviving author plus 70 years. For anonymous and pseudonymous works and works for hire, the duration is 95 years from year of first publication or 120 years from the year of creation, whichever expires first.[19] Works created but not published or copyrighted before January 1, 1978 have the same terms but expire not sooner than December 31, 2002 and, if published on or before December 31, 2002, are protected until December 31, 2027.[20]

Previously, the act extended coverage to authors for a period of life plus 50 years. By virtue of the Sonny Bono Copyright Term Extension Act of 1998,[21] the statutory protection period was extended to life plus 70 years. The constitutionality of the extension was addressed in *Eldred v. Reno,* 74 F. Supp. 2d 1 (D.D.C. 1999). The court reviewed the constitutional authority and the history of the Copyright Act. The initial period of protection in the statute enacted in 1790 was 14 years and an additional 14 years if the author was a living U.S. citizen. With respect to the claim that the extensive copyright period violated the First Amendment rights of the plaintiffs, the court stated that there were no such rights. With respect to the claim that the statutory period exceeded the Constitutional protection to authors for "exclusive rights for limited times," the court cited prior U.S. Supreme Court decisions that Congress has the right to define the scope of the grant to authors or inventors (citing, e.g., *Sony Corporation of America v. Universal City Studios, Inc.,* 464 U.S. 417 (1984)).

Remedies

Anyone violating the rights of a copyright owner or author of a visual art or who imports copies or phonorecords in violation of the statute is an infringer and is subject to substantial criminal and civil penalties. The remedies available include the following:

1. Injunction, both temporary and final.[22]
2. The impounding of copies or phonorecords made in violation of the copyright owner's rights, including molds, plates, masters, tapes, matrices, film negatives, and other such articles. In addition, the court in its final judgment or decree may order the destruction or other disposition of the contraband.[23]
3. The infringer may be liable for the copyright owner's actual damages; the profits of the infringer attributable to the infringement; or statutory damages of a minimum of $500 to a maximum of $20,000. If the court finds the infringement to be willful, the court may order statutory damages of up to $100,000. If the court finds the infringement to be innocent, it may lower statutory damages to no less than $200, or to zero sum if the infringer believed the use was a fair use and, also, if the infringer was an employee of an educational institution or library or from a public broadcasting entity.[24]
4. Except as against the U.S. Government or its officers, the court may also allow, at its discretion, full costs and a reasonable attorney's fee to the prevailing party, including a successful defendant.[25]
5. A person who willfully infringes a copyright for commercial advantage or private financial gain may be subject to criminal penalties and so fined or imprisoned.[26] In addition, the court may order forfeiture and destruction of the copies, devices, and the like of the infringement. Imposition of criminal penalties is quite rare.

The act imposes greater penalties upon the infringer if the act was willful. Willfulness may be found when the court is satisfied that the infringer knows that its conduct is an infringement or if the infringer acts in a manner evidencing reckless disregard of the copyright owner's right. *Video Views, Inc. v. Studio 21, Ltd.,* 925 F.2d 1010, 1020 (7th Cir. 1991).

An interesting criminal case that resulted in a change of federal law was the *United States v. LaMacchia,* 871 F. Supp. 535 (D.Mass. 1994) (see Chapter 5 for detailed recitation). In a U.S. district court criminal action, the defendant, David LaMacchia, an MIT student, uploaded major software programs and transferred them to another site for downloading free of charge to anyone given a password. LaMacchia was acquitted of the charge of wire fraud because he did not personally profit from the scheme, as required by statute. The result of the ruling was the passage of the No Electronic Theft Act, signed into law on December 16, 1997, which amended Section 506(a) of the Copyright Act and made it a felony crime, irrespective of a profit motive, to reproduce or distribute copyrighted works with a value of over $1,000 without permission of the copyright owner. In addition to fines or imprisonment, forfeiture of property used in the commission of the crime is authorized. Forfeitures are especially important because Federal Sentencing Guidelines provide for relatively light prison sentences, while forfeitures in copyright infringement cases often encompass significant financial costs of expensive reproduction and other machinery.

A number of other federal statutes have either criminalized or extended the scope of their laws to include computer technological innovations. For example, statutory protections against trafficking in counterfeit labels now includes labels in computer programs. *Bootlegging,* defined as recording of live performances for commercial gain without performers' consent, is now a felony crime punishable up to five years in prison plus the possible imposition of fines or forfeiture.

The use of a fraudulent copyright notice subjects a person to a fine of up to $2,500. A similar penalty may be imposed for fraudulent removal of a copyright notice and for false representation of a material fact in an application for copyright registration.[27]

Comparable civil penalties also may be imposed against states, instrumentalities of states, and state officials for infringement of copyright.[28]

Attorney's Fees. Under Section 505 of the Copyright Act, reasonable attorneys' fees may be awarded to the prevailing party, including to a successful defendant. Is the award of such fees automatically awarded to a successful party under the Copyright Act? Should the ability to pay such fees be a sole factor in determining when and how much to assess a losing party? In *Mitek Holdings, Inc. v. Arce Eng'g Co.,* 198 F.3d 840 (11th Cir. 1999), the court of appeals cited the U.S. Supreme Court decision in *Fogarty v. Fantasy, Inc.,* 510 U.S. 517, 534 (1998), wherein the Court rejected the British rule of automatic recovery of attorney's fees by the prevailing party. It stated that such fees "are to be awarded to prevailing parties only as a matter of the court's discretion." The court of appeals recited that the factors to be considered in such an award include frivolousness, motivation, objective reasonableness, and the need to advance the considerations of compensation and deterrence.

Good faith is not determinative in the grant of attorneys' fees. The only precondition to the award of the fees is that they be reasonable. Differences in the wealth of the parties are irrelevant. "The touchstone of attorney's fees under Section 505 is whether raising of objectively reasonable claims and defenses, which may serve not only to deter infringement but also to ensure 'that the boundaries of copyright law [are] demarcated as clearly as possible' in order to maximize the public exposure to valuable works."[29]

Statute of Limitations. The Statute of Limitations for criminal and civil proceedings is three years from the commencement of the cause of action or claim.[30] In *Fisher v. United Feature Syndicate, Inc.,* 37 F. Supp. 2d 1213 (D.Col. 1999), the court dismissed the complaint for untimely filing. The plaintiff alleged that the reason he had filed beyond the statutory time period was because of the defendants "misleading conduct of repeated infringement violations." The court said, "A cause of action for copyright infringement under section 507(b) of the Copyright Act accrues 'when one has knowledge of a violation or is chargeable with such knowledge.'" The plaintiff relied on a precedent, *Herald Music Co. v. Living Music, Inc.,* 1978 U.S. Dist., LEXIS 14050 (S.D.N.Y. 1978), wherein the court invoked the doctrine of *estoppel* (to prevent a party from asserting an otherwise good defense due to misconduct or action that is highly prejudicial to the other party) to justify his late filing. The court said that in *Herald,* the defendant misled the plaintiff into believing that litigation was unnecessary in resolving their dispute. In the within case, the claim that the defendants should be estopped from asserting the defense was based upon the "inundation of alleged violations that delayed him." The court said such alleged conduct was not misleading behavior for purposes of invocation of the estoppel doctrine.

Exceptions

The Copyright Act lists a number of exceptions to the exclusive rights of copyright owners. They are:

1. Fair use;
2. Reproduction by libraries and archives;

3. Transfer by sale or otherwise to another person of a copy or phonorecord by the owner of the copy of phonorecord;
4. Certain performances and displays by instructors-pupils face-to-face teaching activities of a nonprofit educational teaching institution and related exemptions;
5. Certain secondary transmissions of a primary transmission not made by a cable system; and
6. Ephemeral recordings.[31]

Other Exceptions and Defenses

Copyright protection does not "extend to any idea, procedure, process, system, method of operation, concept, principle, or discovery, regardless of the form" it may take.[32] Names and titles of copyrighted works are not accorded protection.[33] U.S. government works have no protection, although the government may receive and hold copyrights by way of bequest, assignment, or other means.[34] Also, expired copyrights or works that are in the public domain (works for which the author may not have sought protection and the allowable statutory protection period has expired) receive no protection.[35] Other common defenses are innocent infringement, estoppel, and laches.

Innocent Infringement. 17 U.S.C. Section 405(b) provides that "[a]ny person who innocently infringes a copyright, in reliance upon an authorized copy . . . from which the copyright notice has been omitted and which was publicly distributed by authority of the copyright author . . . incurs no liability for actual or statutory damages . . . for any infringing acts committed before receiving actual notice that registration for the work has been made . . . if such person proves that he or she was misled by the omission of notice."

Innocent intent does not relieve a defendant of liability for copyright infringement, but if a person infringes innocently, as stated in the statute, then there is no liability. In *Marobie-FL, Inc. v. National Association of Fire Equipment Distributors* [NAFED], 983 F. Supp. 1167 (N.D.Ill. 1997), three volumes of software for producing clip art were developed and released for use by persons in the fire-service industry. Plaintiff owned the copyrights for each volume of the clip art software. NAFED has a Web site on which the files were available for downloading by users of the Web site. NAFED's agent had obtained the files containing plaintiff's clip art from an unknown source, copied the said files onto the hard drive of his computer, and transferred them to a host computer. NAFED claimed that it was an innocent infringer because its agent had obtained the clip art files without a copyright notice.

The court said that NAFED could not qualify as an innocent infringer "because the defense may be raised only when the infringer relied on an authorized copy that omitted the copyright notice. The agent relied on unauthorized copies of plaintiff's clip art files. Although the individual clip art images did not bear a copyright notice, notice should not be considered omitted because . . . the individual images are not the subject of the copyright; the volumes of clip art were copyrighted as compilations . . . [that] was accompanied by a single copy licensing agreement that prohibited use on a computer network and use on more than one computer or terminal at a time. . . . [E]ach individually packaged diskette sold by plaintiff contained a label containing a copyright notice."

Estoppel. The defense of *estoppel* may be applicable when the copyright or trademark owner becomes aware of an infringement of its rights yet acts in such a way as to induce, encourage, or mislead the infringer into believing that its actions were either proper or not violative of the owner's rights. An example is if the copyright owner enters into extensive negotiations with the infringer to license its copyrights and by its silence or inaction leads the other party to believe that there was no infringement.[36]

In the *Marobie* case, the court refused to accept the estoppel defense based on the failure of the plaintiff to affix copyright notices to any of the individual clip art images thereby causing defendant's agent to rely on its absence. The defense failed because no evidence was presented to show that plaintiff's conduct induced the defendant to reasonably rely on the absence of the notice to its detriment. Also, the suspicious manner in which defendant's agent acquired the clip art would make reliance on the absence of copyright notices on the individual images unreasonable.

Laches. The defense of *laches* is similar to that of estoppel. It prevents a party from suing successfully for copyright or trademark infringement when the person suing unreasonably and inexcusably delays pursuit of their claim to such an extent that the defendant is prejudiced by the delay. The defense rarely succeeds except in the most egregious cases. At the very least, a person holding a copyright or a trademark should notify the offending party to cease and desist from violation of the intellectual property rights as soon as such violations become known. For example, waiting for one or more years to act against a known infringer, at least by notification, may give rise to the defense.[37]

Unclean Hands. Courts will refuse to come to the aid of a litigant who has committed wrongful conduct against the other party and such conduct affects the subject matter of the lawsuit. Parties cannot ask a court to come to their assistance when they have committed some misconduct. The defense is rarely allowed inasmuch as the said conduct must go to the heart of the litigation.[38]

Method of Operation. In the following case, the court had to determine whether the alleged infringement was a *method of operation* that also would not be copyrightable.

LOTUS DEVELOPMENT CORPORATION V. BORLAND INTERNATIONAL, INC.

49 F.3d 807 (1st Cir. 1995)

FACTS: Lotus 1-2-3 is a spreadsheet program allowing users to perform electronic accounting functions on a computer. It uses a variety of commands known to all computer users such as "Copy," "Print," and "Quit." It also allows users to write "macros," whereby users can select a series of command choices by typing the first letter of the designated command. The defendant, Borland, released a "Quattro" program for public use with a spreadsheet that competed with Lotus and, allegedly, was superior thereto. In its program, Borland included the 1-2-3 menu of Lotus so as to make its program compatible with its competitor's program. Borland did not copy Lotus' underlying computer code; rather it copied only the words and structure of the plaintiff's menu command hierarchy.

ISSUE: Whether the copying of the plaintiff's computer menu command hierarchy is copyrightable subject matter?

DECISION: The Court of Appeals dismissed the lawsuit, reversing the lower Court's decision that had decided in favor of Lotus. It stated that the copying by Borland was not protected by the Copyright Act.

REASONING: Judge Stahl

To establish copyright infringement, a plaintiff must prove "(1) ownership of a valid copyright, and (2) copying of constituent elements of the work that are original." . . . To show ownership of a valid copyright . . . a plaintiff must prove that the work as a whole is original and that the plaintiff complied with applicable statutory formalities. "In judicial proceedings, a certificate of copyright registration constitutes prima facie evidence of copyrightability and shifts the burden to the defendant to demonstrate why the copyright is not valid." . . . To show actionable copying . . . a plaintiff must first prove that the alleged infringer copied plaintiff's copyrighted work as a factual matter; to do this, he or she may either present direct evidence of factual copying or, if that is unavailable, evidence that the alleged infringer had access to the copyrighted work and that the offending and copyrighted works are so similar that the court may infer that there was factual copying (i.e., probative similarity). . . . The plaintiff must then prove that the copying of copyrighted material was so extensive that it rendered the offending and copyrighted works substantially similar. . . . In this appeal, we are faced only with whether the Lotus menu command hierarchy is copyrightable subject matter in the first instance, for Borland concedes that Lotus has a valid copyright in Lotus 1-2-3 as a whole and admits to factually copying the Lotus menu command hierarchy.

As a result, this appeal is in a very different posture from most copyright-infringement cases, for copyright infringement generally turns on whether the defendant has copied protected expression as a factual matter. Because of this different posture, most copyright-infringement cases provide only limited help to us in deciding this appeal. This is true even with respect to those copyright-infringement cases that deal with computers and computer software.

The initial inquiry should not be whether individual components of a menu command hierarchy are expressive, but rather whether the menu command hierarchy as a whole can be copyrighted. . . .

THE LOTUS MENU COMMAND HIERARCHY: A "METHOD OF OPERATION"

Borland argues that the Lotus menu command hierarchy is uncopyrightable because it is a system, method of operation, process, or procedure foreclosed from copyright protection by 17 U.S.C. 102(b). Section 102(b) states: "In no case does copyright protection for an original work of authorship extend to any idea, procedure, process, system, method of operation, concept, principle, or discovery, regardless of the form in which it is described, explained, illustrated, or embodied in such work." Because we conclude that the Lotus menu command hierarchy is a method of operation, we do not consider whether it could also be a system, process, or procedure.

We think that "method of operation," as that term is used in 102(b), refers to the means by which a person operates something, whether it be a car, a food processor, or a computer. Thus a text describing how to operate something would not extend copyright protection to the method of operation itself; other people would be free to employ that method and to describe it in their own words. Similarly, if a new method of operation is used rather than described, other people would still be free to employ or describe that method.

We hold that the Lotus menu command hierarchy is an uncopyrightable "method of operation." The Lotus menu command hierarchy provides the means by which users control and operate Lotus 1-2-3. If users wish to copy material, for example, they use the "Copy" command. If users wish to print material, they use the "Print" command. Users must use the command terms to tell the computer what to do. Without the menu command hierarchy, users would not be able to access and control, or indeed make use of, Lotus 1-2-3 's functional capabilities.

The Lotus menu command hierarchy does not merely explain and present Lotus 1-2-3's functional capabilities to the user; it also serves as the method by which the program is operated and controlled. The Lotus menu command hierarchy is different from the Lotus long prompts, for the long prompts are not necessary to the operation of the program; users could operate Lotus 1-2-3 even if there were no long prompts. . . . The Lotus menu command hierarchy is also different from the Lotus screen displays, for users need not "use" any expressive aspects of the screen displays in order to operate Lotus 1-2-3; because the way the screens look has little bearing on how users control the program, the screen displays are not part of Lotus 1-2-3's "method of operation." . . . The Lotus menu command hierarchy is also different from the underlying computer code, because while code is necessary for the program to work, its precise formulation is not. In other words, to offer the same capabilities as Lotus 1-2-3, Borland did not have to copy Lotus's underlying code (and indeed it did not); to allow users to operate its programs in substantially the same way, however, Borland had to copy the Lotus menu command hierarchy. Thus the Lotus 1-2-3 code is not an uncopyrightable "method of operation." . . .

CASE QUESTIONS

1. What is the difference between a *process* that is protected by the Patent Act and a *method of operation*?
2. Is the creation of a menu command comparable to operating an automobile or a food processor?

FAIR USE

The fair use exception as stated in the Copyright Act is as follows:

> Notwithstanding the provisions of sections 106 [exclusive rights in copyrighted works] and 106A [rights of certain authors to attribution and integrity], use by reproduction in copies or phonorecords or by any other means specified by that section, for purposes such as criticism, comment, news reporting, teaching (including multiple copies for classroom use), scholarship, or research is not an infringement of copyright. In determining whether the use made of a work in any particular case is a fair use the factors to be considered shall include—
>
> 1. the purpose and character of the use, including whether such use is of a commercial nature or is for nonprofit educational purpose;
> 2. The nature of the copyrighted work;
> 3. The amount and substantiality of the portion used in relation to the copyrighted work as a whole; and
> 4. the effect of the use upon the potential market for or value of the copyrighted work.
>
> The fact that a work is unpublished shall not itself bar a finding of fair use if such finding is made upon consideration of all the above factors.[39]

Fair use, like many expressions, is pregnant with diverse meanings. To what extent may a person copy passages from a large work? What is the difference between commercial and noncommercial uses? Does the parody of a copyright work exempt it from copyright violation? Is there a difference whether the work is fictional or nonfictional? These issues are all relevant in determining fair use.[40] It is clear that noncommercial use, especially by educational institutions and libraries, will be given much more latitude in making use of copyrighted materials than commercial use of the same materials.[41] The problem arises of possible copyright infringement for educational institutions that are promulgating and expanding distance-learning courses. Distance learning differs from the traditional mode of teaching, which is interactive communication within a classroom setting, by its delivery and transmission of information to remote locations. What may be a fair use exception in a domestic classroom setting may run afoul of the statute when transmission is made to persons in other, more remote places.[42]

The basic test used by the federal courts interpreting the fair use doctrine is the determination of the applicability of the four elements in the statute that have been recited.[43] A leading case interpreting those factors is *Basic Books, Inc. v. Kinko's Graphics Corp.*,[44] wherein Kinko, which reproduced packets of copyrighted materials for professors and students, was held liable to the plaintiff publishing company because Kinko printed the materials for profit rather than doing so without such motive.

In a somewhat similar case, *Princeton University Press v. Michigan Document Services, Inc.*,[45] the U.S. Court of Appeals for the Sixth Circuit held, with a vigorous dissent, that the reproduction of substantial segments of copyrighted scholarly works bound into coursepacks and sold to students for use in courses given by University of Michigan professors, did not constitute fair use, thereby making the defendant, Michigan Document Services, liable to the plaintiffs under the Copyright Act. The court emphasized that the defendant did not request permission nor pay for any of the reproduced materials. Substantial portions of works ranging from 5 to 30 percent of a variety of copyrighted materials were reproduced without consent. The opinion noted that the defendant's owner was aware of the *Kinko* decision and determined that the decision of the New York court was incorrectly decided.

In the *Princeton* case, the court said that the fourth prong of the fair use test, namely, "the effect of the use upon the potential market for or value of the copyrighted work," was paramount herein. While it is true that, ordinarily, reproduction of works for purposes of criticism, comment, news reporting, teaching, and scholarship is not a copyright infringement, nevertheless, there is no blanket immunity from liability for such use. If the challenged use was of a noncommercial nature, liability would be questionable. However, the reproduction was accomplished by a for-profit corporation. Competing copyshops that sold coursepacks in the same area did pay permission fees for the privilege of copying from protected works. The court, discussing the fourth prong of the Supreme Court test, said:

> The three plaintiffs together have been collecting permission fees at a rate approaching $500,000 a year. If copyshops across the nation were to start doing what the defendants have been doing here, this revenue stream would shrivel and the potential value of the copyrighted works of scholarship published by the plaintiffs would be diminished accordingly.

MP3 Litigation

In recent years, Internet subscribers have utilized MP3 technology. As most such users are aware, thousands of recordings could be downloaded without cost by accessing a number of sites employing the technology. Litigation was commenced by record companies to prohibit the alleged theft of copyrighted materials. The litigation raised a number of issues that had to be addressed by the respective federal district courts. Among the issues presented were: Whether the conduct of MP3.com constituted fair use?; Whether it mattered if the defendants required proof of legal purchases of the recordings before permitting users of the site to exchange the recordings?; Whether merely providing a site for the music recordings interchange constituted actual, contributory, or vicarious liability?; Whether the technology could be restrained in light of the prior U.S. Supreme Court decision that permitted technologies that had both significant unlawful and lawful uses?; Whether the defendants providing the sites were protected by the First Amendment of the Constitution?; and other related issues.

Copyright owners live in dire fear that persons globally may be able to copy music, movies, and other protected works without payment of royalties. Such technology exists, including MP3, which permits enterprising persons to easily download music recordings without purchasing the recording. The process that is used was developed by the Moving Picture Experts Group in 1987, which set a standard file digital format for storage of audio recordings and was initially known as MPEG-3, now abbreviated to MP3. By a process called *ripping,* the software permits the user of a computer to copy an audio compact disk onto the computer's hard drive by the compression of the audio information on the CD into the MP3 format. Once that is accomplished, any person may use the format to transmit audio files electronically from one computer to another.[46]

The initial fundamental issue that courts had to resolve is whether the use of such technology could be forbidden. Courts have been reluctant to ban or limit use of technological advances due to a highly controversial but precedent-setting decision of the U.S. Supreme Court in 1984. The 1984 decision, decided by a 5–4 vote, was *Sony Corp. of America v. Universal City Studios, Inc.,* 464 U.S. 417 (1984). Sony manufactured the Betamax home video recorder (the rival technology of the current VHS recording devices), which could replicate copyright protected movies. Universal sued to bar the sale of such technology, claiming that Sony was liable for copyright infringement either directly or vicariously.

The Court decided in favor of Sony. In essence, it concluded that as long as the technology was capable of substantial noninfringing uses, it could not be barred from sale and distribution of the Betamax. In addition, a person making an unauthorized recording of a program for personal use does not violate the Copyright Act. The Court permitted such copy as a fair use under the Act. It assessed fair use by the application of the four factors of purpose and character of use, the nature of the protected work, the amount and substantiality of the portion used, and the effect on the market of the work. Inasmuch as the use of the Betamax was noncommercial and nonprofit, no liability would accrue. The companies using MP3 technology claimed the precedent applied to MP3 technology, namely, that it had substantial noninfringing use and, thus, the action should be dismissed. We will examine two major cases concerning MP3 technology. The first case is a New York district court decision, which is followed by the highly publicized Napster California federal court decision. The cases review the factors described by the Supreme Court and their application to MP3 technology.

UMG RECORDINGS, INC. V. MP3.COM, INC.

92 F. Supp. 2d 349 (S.D.N.Y. 2000)

FACTS: On January 12, 2000, the defendant launched its "My.MP3.com" service which it advertised as permitting subscribers to store, customize, and listen to the recordings contained in its CDs from wherever they have an Internet connection. The company bought some eighty thousand CDs and copied the recordings onto its computer servers without permission from their copyright owners. Users of the service could then download and replay the recordings from the site as they desired. In order to avoid copyright infringement MP3 allegedly required users to prove they owned a CD version of the recording by inserting a copy onto the CD-ROM drive or purchase the CD from MP3's online retailers. After doing so, the subscriber could then access a copy of the recording from anywhere in the world. The Recording Industry Association of America, together with Sony Music, Warner Music, and other recording companies, sued for damages arising out of the alleged infringements of copyrights.

ISSUES: (1) Did the defendant's service constitute infringement under the Copyright Act of 1976?

(2) Was the copying a "fair use" exception under the Act?

DECISION: (1) It did constitute infringement under the Act.

(2)The fair use exception was not applicable under the facts of the case.

REASONING: Judge Jed S. Rakoff

[The court recited the four factors that had to be present to establish a fair use defense.]

Regarding the first factor—"the purpose and character of the use"—defendant does not dispute that its purpose is commercial, for while subscribers to My.MP3.com are not currently charged a fee, defendant seeks to attract a sufficiently large subscription base to draw advertising and otherwise make a profit. Consideration of the first factor, however, also involves inquiring into whether the new use essentially repeats the old or whether, instead, it "transforms" it by infusing it with new meaning, new understandings, or the like. . . . Here, although defendant recites that My.MP3.com provides a transformative "space shift" by which subscribers can enjoy the sound recordings contained in their CDs without lugging around the physical discs themselves, this is simply another way of saying that the unauthorized copies are being retransmitted in another medium—an insufficient basis for any legitimate claim of transformation. . . . Here, defendant adds no "new aesthetics, new insights and understandings" to the original music recordings it copies . . . but simply repackages those recordings to facilitate their transmission through another medium. While such services may be innovative, they are not transformative.

Regarding the second factor—"the nature of the copyrighted work"—the creative recordings here being copied are "close to the core of intended copyright protection," . . . and, conversely, far removed from the more factual or descriptive work more amenable to "fair use," . . .

Regarding the third factor—"the amount and substantiality of the portion [of the copyrighted work] used [by the copier] in relation to the copyrighted work as a whole"—it is undisputed that defendant copies, and replays, the entirety of the copyrighted works here in issue, thus negating any claim of fair use. . . .

Regarding the fourth factor—"the effect of the use upon the potential market for or value of the copyrighted work"—defendant's activities on their face invade plaintiffs' statutory right to license their copyrighted sound recordings to others for reproduction. . . . [Defendant's arguments that such activities enhanced plaintiffs' sales] are unpersuasive. Any allegedly positive impact of defendant's activities on plaintiffs' prior market in no way frees defendant to usurp a further market that directly derives from reproduction of the plaintiffs' copyrighted works. . . . This would be so even if the copyrightholder had not yet entered the new market in issue, for a copyrightholder's "exclusive" rights, derived from the Constitution and the Copyright Act, include the right, within broad limits, to curb the development of such a derivative market by refusing to license a copyrighted work or by doing so only on terms the copyright owner finds acceptable. . . .

In sum, on any view, defendant's "fair use" defense is indefensible and must be denied as a matter of law. Defendant's other affirmative defenses, such as copyright misuse, abandonment, unclean hands, and estoppel, are essentially frivolous. . . ."

[In a later decision dated November 11, 2000, the court awarded a final judgment in favor of the plaintiffs in the sum of $53,400.00 in statutory damages, costs, and attorneys' fees.[47] The court also decided that statutory damages would be awarded based on each CD that was unlawfully infringed rather than each individual song, citing Section 505(c)(1) of the Copyright Act, which states that "all of the parts of a compilation or derivative work constitute one work."[48]]

CASE QUESTIONS

1. A person may make a copy for one's own use of any work that was legally acquired. Why did the court find a copyright violation when a person with an ostensible legal copy of a CD downloads a copy of another person's legally acquired CD?
2. If MP3 were to move offshore to an island that does not respect copyright laws, how would copyright owners protect themselves from infringement of their rights?
3. Are there First Amendment freedom of speech and assembly implications in the decision?
4. See *A&M Records, Inc. v. Napster, Inc.*, to follow. Should the difference in access methodology change the result?

In the following case, which was reported widely in the various media, the facts contained a different slant from the *UMG* case. Napster argued that it did not make copies of the recordings but acted only as the conduit for the sharing of recordings by users of its service. Such sharing, it believed, was a legitimate noncommercial use and, therefore, constituted fair use under the Copyright Act. Also, it claimed that the Digital Millennium Copyright Act gave the service an exemption.

The court decided that Napster was not entitled to the exemption given to Internet service providers under the Digital Millennium Copyright Act [discussed later in the chapter]. It issued an injunction barring such transmission as of July 28, 2000. The act limits liability where the ISP acts merely as a transmitting or routing service, much as a mailman delivering mail. Napster's role in transmitting MP3 files, the court decided, was much more active. It told the user's computer the location of MP3 files, allowed persons with computers to share directly each user's collections without payment of royalties, gave its permission to download the files, and engaged in other active roles in the transmission.

A&M RECORDS, INC. V. NAPSTER, INC.

239 F.3d 1004 (9th Cir. 2001)

FACTS: Plaintiffs, including Sony Music Entertainment, Motown Record Co., and Capitol Records, Inc., are major companies engaged in the commercial recording and distribution industries. Napster designed and operates a system that allows the transmission and retention of sound recordings using digital technology. The technology utilized is MP3. Napster facilitates the transfer of such files by allowing users to: make MP3 music files for storage unto one's computer for copying by other Napster users; search for MP3 music files stored in other Napster users' files; and transfer exact copies of other users' files onto one's computer. It is accomplished with Napster's free MusicShare software. Users use Napster's network servers and server-side software. It provides technical support for indexing and searching for MP3 files, and has a chat room for members to discuss music.

To access the Napster system, one has to go to its site, download the means to receive information, create a user library on the individual's hard drive that is uploaded unto Napster's servers, and thereafter locate a particular music file through Napster's search function and its hotlist function. The Napster server software obtains the Internet address of the user seeking the particular music file and the Internet address of the host user who has the file. A connection is then made between the host and the seeker of the file thereby permitting the downloading of the requested file. The problem is that these files are copyright protected.

ISSUES: (1) Did the district court employ the proper legal standards in its issuance of a preliminary injunction?

(2) Did Napster's conduct come within the fair use exception of the Copyright Act?

(3) Was Napster responsible for direct infringement of plaintiffs' copyrights? Contributory infringement?

DECISION: (1) The court of appeals sustained most of the decision of the district court but reversed in part stating that the injunction issued by the district court was overbroad.

(2) Napster's actions did not constitute fair use.

(3) The court of appeals sustained the district court's finding of direct and contributory infringement by Napster.

REASONING: Judge Beezer

... Preliminary injunctive relief is available to a party who demonstrates either: (1) a combination of probable success on the merits and the possibility of irreparable harm; or (2) that serious questions are raised and the balance of hardships tips in its favor.... "These two formulations represent two points on a sliding scale in which the required degree of irreparable harm increases as the probability of success decreases."...

[Direct infringement liability.] Plaintiffs claim Napster users are engaged in the wholesale reproduction and distribution of copyrighted works, all constituting direct infringement. Secondary liability for copyright infringement does not exist in the absence of direct infringement by a third party.... It follows that Napster does not facilitate infringement of the copyright laws in the absence of infringement by its users....

A. INFRINGEMENT

Plaintiffs must satisfy two requirements to present a prima facie case of direct infringement: (1) they must show ownership of the alleged infringed material and (2) they must demonstrate that the alleged infringers violate at least one exclusive right granted to copyright holders under 17 U.S.C. Section 106.... Plaintiffs have sufficiently demonstrated ownership. The record supports the district court's determination that "as much as eighty-seven percent of the files available on Napster may be copyrighted and more than seventy percent may be owned or administered by plaintiffs."... We agree that plaintiffs have shown that Napster users infringe at least two of the copyright holders' exclusive rights: the rights of reproduction, Section 106(1); and distribution, Section 106(3). Napster users who download files containing copyrighted music violate plaintiffs' reproduction rights.

Napster asserts an affirmative defense [of fair use] to the charge that its users directly infringe plaintiffs' copyrighted musical compositions and sound recordings.

B. FAIR USE

Napster contends that its users do not directly infringe plaintiffs' copyrights because the users are engaged in fair use of the material.... Napster identifies three specific alleged fair uses: sampling, where users make temporary copies of a work before purchasing; space-shifting, where users access a sound recording through the Napster system that they already own in audio CD format; and permissive distribution of recordings by both new and established artists.... We will address the [district] court's overall fair use analysis....

1. Purpose and Character of the Use

... This factor focuses on whether the new work merely replaces the object of the original creation or instead adds a further purpose or different character. In other words, this factor asks "whether and to what extent the new work is 'transformative.'" The district court first concluded that downloading MP3 files does not transform the copyrighted work.... This conclusion is supportable. Courts have been reluctant to find fair use when an original work is merely transmitted in a different medium....

This "purpose and character" element also requires the district court to determine whether the allegedly infringing use is commercial or noncommercial.... A commercial use weighs against a finding of fair use but it is not conclusive on the issue.... Direct economic benefit is not required to demonstrate a commercial use. Rather, repeated and exploitive copying of copyrighted works, even if copies are not offered for sale, may constitute a commercial use.... In the record before us, commercial use is demonstrated by a showing that repeated and exploitative unauthorized copies of copyrighted works were made to save the expense of purchasing authorized copies....

Works that are creative in nature are "closer to the core of intended copyright protection" than are more fact-based works.... The district court determined that plaintiffs' "copyrighted musical compositions and sound recordings are creative in nature . . . which cuts against a finding of fair use under the second factor." . . . We find no error in the district court's conclusion.

2. The Portion Used

. . . "While 'wholesale copying does not preclude fair use per se,' copying an entire work 'militates against a finding of fair use.'" . . . The district court determined that Napster users engage in "wholesale copying" of copyrighted work because file transfer necessarily "involves copying the entirety of the copyrighted work." . . . We agree. . . .

3. Effect of Use on Market

. . . "Fair use, when properly applied, is limited to copying by others which does not materially impair the marketability of the work which is copied." . . . The proof required to demonstrate present or future market harm varies with the purpose and character of the use: A challenge to a noncommercial use of a copyrighted work requires proof either that the particular use is harmful, or that if it should become widespread, it would adversely affect the potential market for the copyrighted work. . . . If the intended use is for commercial gain, that likelihood [of market harm] may be presumed. But if it is for a noncommercial purpose, the likelihood must be demonstrated.

Addressing this factor, the district court concluded that Napster harms the market in "at least" two ways: it reduces audio CD sales among college students and it "raises to plaintiffs' entry into the market for the digital downloading of music." . . . [The court reviewed the testimony of experts that purported to demonstrate that such students did make fewer purchases and not, as defendants' experts attempted to show, that MP3 encouraged rather than discouraged sales of CDs.] . . . We therefore conclude that the district court made sound findings related to Napster's deleterious effect on the present and future digital download market. Moreover, lack of harm to an established market cannot deprive the copyright holder of the right to develop alternative markets for the works. . . .

4. Identified Uses

. . . Napster maintains that its identified uses of sampling and space-shifting were wrongly excluded as fair uses by the district court.

a. Sampling . . . Napster contends that its users download MP3 files to "sample" the music in order to decide whether to purchase the recording. Napster argues that the district court: (1) erred in concluding that sampling is a commercial use because it conflated a noncommercial use with a personal use; (2) erred in determining that sampling adversely affects the market for plaintiffs' copyrighted music, a requirement if the use is noncommercial; and (3) erroneously concluded that sampling is not a fair use because it determined that samplers may also engage in other infringing activity.

The district court determined that sampling remains a commercial use even if some users eventually purchase the music. . . . Plaintiffs have established that they are likely to succeed in proving that even authorized temporary downloading of individual songs for sampling purposes is commercial in nature. . . . The record supports the district court's determinations that: (1) the more music that sampling users download, the less likely they are to eventually purchase the recordings on audio CD; and (2) even if the audio CD market is not harmed, Napster has adverse effects on the developing digital download market. . . .

b. Space-Shifting . . . Napster also maintains that space-shifting is a fair use. Space-shifting occurs when a Napster user downloads MP3 music files in order to listen to music he already owns on audio CD . . . [The claim here is that it is a fair use, for example, for a videotape recorder owner to record a television show for later viewing; or to make copies of files already on a user's hard drive. Such analogies are not appropriate in this case.] because the methods of shifting . . . did not also simultaneously involve distribution of the copyrighted material to the general public; the time or space-shifting of copyrighted material exposed the material only to the original user. . . . [I]t is obvious that once a user lists a copy of music he already owns on the Napster system in order to access the music from another location, the song becomes "available to millions of other individuals," not just the original CD owner. . . .

[The court goes on to discuss Napster's liability for contributory copyright infringement.] Traditionally, "one who, with knowledge of the infringing activity, induces, causes or materially contributes to the infringing conduct of another, may be held liable as a 'contributory' infringer." . . .

[L]iability exists if the defendant engages in "personal conduct that encourages or assists the infringement." . . .

KNOWLEDGE

. . . Contributory liability requires that the secondary infringer "know or have reason to know" of direct infringement. . . . It is apparent from the record that Napster has knowledge, both actual and constructive. The district court found actual knowledge because: (1) a document authored by Napster cofounder Sean Parker mentioned "the need to remain ignorant of users' real names and IP addresses 'since they are exchanging pirated music' "; and (2) the Recording Industry Association of America ("RIAA") informed Napster of more than 12,000 infringing files, some of which are still available. . . . The district court found constructive knowledge because: (a) Napster executives have recording industry experience; (b) they have enforced intellectual property rights in other instances; (c) Napster executives have downloaded copyrighted songs from the system; and (d) they have promoted the site with "screen shots listing infringing files." . . .

Under the facts as found by the district court, Napster materially contributes to the infringing activity. . . . [T]he district court concluded that "[w]ithout the support services defendant provides, Napster users could not find and download the music they want with the ease of which defendant boasts. . . ." We affirm the district court's conclusion. . . .

We turn to the question whether Napster engages in vicarious copyright infringement. Vicarious copyright liability is an "outgrowth" of respondeat superior. . . . In the context of copyright law, vicarious liability extends beyond an employer/employee relationship to cases in which a defendant "has the right and ability to supervise the infringing activity and also has a direct financial interest in such activities." . . .

A. FINANCIAL BENEFIT

. . . The district court determined that plaintiffs had demonstrated they would likely succeed in establishing that Napster has a direct financial interest in the infringing activity. . . . We agree. Financial benefit exists where the availability of infringing material "acts as a 'draw' for customers." . . . Ample evidence supports the district court's finding that Napster's future revenue is directly dependent upon "increases in userbase." More users register with the Napster system as the "quality and quantity of available music increases." . . .

B. SUPERVISION

. . . The ability to block infringers' access to a particular environment for any reason whatsoever is evidence of the right and ability to supervise. . . . Here, plaintiffs have demonstrated that Napster retains the right to control access to its system. To escape imposition of vicarious liability, the reserved right to police must be exercised to its fullest extent. Turning a blind eye to detectable acts of infringement for the sake of profit gives rise to liability. . . . The district court correctly determined that Napster had the right and ability to police its system and failed to exercise that right to prevent the exchange of copyrighted material. . . . As shown by the record, the Napster system does not "read" the content of indexed files, other than to check that they are in the proper MP3 format. Napster, however, has the ability to locate infringing material listed on its search indices, and the right to terminate users' access to the system.

[After the return of the action to the district court, the court, among other relief, granted anew a preliminary injunction enjoining Napster from "engaging in, or facilitating others in, copying, downloading, uploading, transmitting, or distributing copyrighted sound recordings." It also directed then plaintiffs to provide notice to Napster of the copyrighted sound recordings by providing the title, name of recording artist, names of the files available on the Napster system containing the works, and all variations of file names in connection therewith. Napster was given three days to remove the copyrighted works from its files after the notice. By virtue of the order, Napster was effectively prevented from providing the former service. As of the time of this writing, Napster was taking steps to comply with the order, including providing reimbursement for future services containing copyrighted works.]

CASE QUESTIONS

1. Does downloading of copyright protected music through Napster make everyone who does so liable for copyright infringement?
2. What is to prevent an individual from exchanging music files with friends and acquaintances? With foreign Internet sites?

Napster has been sued for copyright infringement by other parties, including rap artist Dr. Dre and heavy metal band Metallica. Napster has agreed to block access to 317,377 users of the site who were identified by Metallica as wrongfully infringing upon their copyrights. It refused to remove Dr. Dre's music from its site, stating that it would only block access to those users identified as violating his copyrighted music. It also entered into an agreement with certain record companies, settling the lawsuit.

The Napster debate will continue until there is a final, bright-line decision by the Supreme Court or the Copyright Act is amended anew. There are legitimate arguments on both sides of the dispute. Artists rightfully fear that their music or other performances would be compromised unless the copyright laws are enforced. Theoretically, such artists may lose vast sums in royalty fees unless copying is prevented. On the other hand, Napster has a legitimate argument that its service allows a noncommercial use permitted by statute and by prior precedent. In any event, they argue that it has not been demonstrated that artists lose money from such copying. It appears that in some instances the free transmission of recordings encourages users to make purchases of recordings they would not have otherwise made. Also, in recent days, attorneys general from 19 states commenced an antitrust action against the recording industry for its alleged anticompetitive practices, thereby causing an artificial rise in the purchase price of recordings.

In *Religious Technologies Center v. Lerma*, No. 95-1107-A (E.D.Va., 1995), the issue was whether an injunction should be granted impounding alleged copyright protected writings of L. Ron Hubbard, the founder of the Church of Scientology, that were taken by a former member of the church and that were to be published by the *Washington Post.* The court denied the request, stating that the chances of plaintiff succeeding in preventing the publication of the writings was minimal given the newsworthy significance of the documents. The fair use doctrine permits the reasonable use of copyrighted materials and was designed to balance the rights of the copyright holder with the public's interest in ascertaining the information in the documents. Publication of the materials constitutes news reporting, one of the areas exempted under the Copyright Act.

In *Harper & Row v. Nation Enterprises,* 471 U.S. 539 (1985), former President Gerald Ford had contracted with Harper & Row to publish his, as yet unwritten, memoirs. Two years later, Harper & Row negotiated a licensing agreement with *Time* magazine to publish an excerpt of the book. The *Nation* magazine, using an unauthorized copy of the manuscript, published a shortened version (2,250 words) in which it so-called scooped the *Time* article. The issue of fair use was decided in favor of Harper & Row. The Court held that by assuming the right of first publication with generous quotes from the memoirs, Nation Enterprises violated an important marketable subsidiary right of the plaintiff. Such assumption was not a fair use under the Copyright Act.

In *Playboy Enterprises, Inc. v. Webbworld, Inc. et al.,* No. 3-96-CV-3222-DES (N.D.Tex., 1997), the defendant operated a Web site called Neptics. The site made available, for a subscription fee, adult images to subscribing Internet users. A number of the images on the site were taken from *Playboy* magazines. In a lawsuit for copyright infringement, the court held in favor of Playboy, stating that the images shown on the defendant's Web site were so similar as to preclude a finding of independent creation. Also, Neptics was not an Internet service provider protected by law. A person could not gain access to the Internet by using Neptics. A person had to get onto the Internet first before connecting with the Neptics Web site.

Comparative Advertising and Fair Use

Comparative advertising consists of the promotion of one's product or service by displaying its superiority to a comparable product or service of a competitor. Although such advertising is either prohibited or substantially curtailed in other countries, the Federal Trade Commission has given its imprimatur noting that: "Comparative advertising, when truthful and nondeceptive, is a source of important information to consumers and assists them in making rational purchase decisions. Comparative advertising encourages product improvement and innovation, and can lead to lower prices in the marketplace." 16 C.F.R. Section 14.15(c)(1980).

In *Sony Computer Entertainment America, Inc. v. Bleem,* 214 F.3d 1022 (9th Cir. 2000), the defendant, Bleem, developed a "software emulator" that allows the user to divide between console games and personal computer (PC) games. By use of the software, a person can play a Sony PlayStation game on a PC. The results are that the user need not purchase a Sony PlayStation, and the quality of the graphics may be better by use of the defendant's software. The litigation arose when Bleem included comparative screen shots, that is, images from the computer or television screen frozen in isolation during the playing of the video game, of the Sony PlayStation games to demonstrate the comparative advantages by the use of the software. Sony claimed the use of the single image screen shots constituted intellectual property violations.

The court held in favor of the defendant, Bleem, stating that the use of the screen shot came within the bounds of the fair use exception. Reciting the fourfold fair use test, the court stated as follows: (1) purpose and character of use—although Bleem did copy Sony's copyrighted material for commercial purposes, the comparative advertising was of much greater benefit to the public than its corresponding loss to Sony; (2) nature of copyrighted work—both plaintiff and defendant are concerned with commercial video game products and the said factor neither supports nor hurts the defendant's claim of a fair use defense; (3) the amount and substantiality of the portion used—the court found this factor in favor of Bleem "since a screen shot is such an insignificant portion of the complex copyrighted work as a whole"; and (4) the effect of the use on the potential marker—"Bleem's use of a handful of screen shots in its advertising will have no noticeable effect on Sony's ability to do with its screen shots what it chooses. . . . "

Parody as a Fair Use Defense

The U.S. Supreme Court, in a decision entitled *Campbell v. Acuff-Rose Music, Inc.*,[49] decided that *parody* (to make fun of an otherwise serious work) may be protected as a fair use exception under the Copyright Law. In the following case, the court had to decide whether a motion picture company could use a modified version of a well-known copyrighted photograph to advertise a forthcoming comedy.

LEIBOVITZ V. PARAMOUNT PICTURES

137 F.3d 109 (2d Cir. 1998)

FACTS: Annie Leibovitz is a photographer whose works have been published in national magazines and elsewhere. Among the photographs published was one that appeared on the cover of *Vanity Fair* magazine of the pregnant actress, Demi Moore, who was depicted nude in profile with her right hand covering her breasts and her left hand over her stomach. The pose was evocative of Botticelli's *Birth of Venus.* Paramount Pictures, in its promotion of a slapstick comedy featuring Leslie Nielson, used a composite of the photograph with the actor Nielson's face in place of Demi Moore's. The teaser advertisement proclaimed: "DUE THIS MARCH" adjacent to the altered photograph.

ISSUE: Whether the fair use exception is applicable to the alleged parody of the photograph?

DECISION: The Court decided it was fair use and, thus, held in favor of the defendant dismissing the complaint.

REASONING: Judge Jon O. Newman

The fair use doctrine "permits other people to use copyrighted material without the owner's consent in a reasonable manner for certain purposes." . . . Recognized at common law . . . the doctrine is now codified in section 107 of the 1976 Copyright Act. . . . [The court recited the four factors to be considered in applying the fair use defense.]

Although the statute does not specifically list "parodies" among the categories of potentially "fair" uses, we have long afforded such works some measure of protection under this doctrine . . . The [Supreme] Court authoritatively confirmed the applicability of the fair use doctrine to parodies. . . . The Court made clear that all four of the statutory factors "are to be explored, and the results weighed together." The [Supreme] Court cautioned that the quality of the parody is not to be evaluated. . . . The relevant inquiry is "whether a parodic character may reasonably be perceived." A permissible aspect of the inquiry . . . is "whether the parodic element is slight or great, and the copying small or extensive in relation to the parodic element, for a work with slight parodic element and extensive copying will be more likely to merely 'supersede the objects' of the original."

[W]e inquire whether Paramount's advertisement "may reasonably be perceived . . . as a new work" that "at least in part, comments on" Lebovitz's photograph. . . . Plainly the ad adds something new and qualifies as a "transformative" work. Whether it "comments" on the original is a somewhat closer question. Because the smirking face of Nielson contrasts so strikingly with the serious expression on the face of Moore, the ad may reasonably be perceived as commenting on the seriousness, even the pretentiousness, of the original. The contrast achieves the effect of ridicule that . . . would serve as a sufficient "comment" to tip the first factor in a parodist's favor. . . . [T]he ad is not merely different; it differs in a way that may reasonably be perceived as commenting, through ridicule, on what a viewer might reasonably think is the undue self-importance conveyed by the subject of the Leibovitz photograph. A photographer posing a well-known actress in a manner that calls to mind a well-known painting must expect, or at least tolerate, a parodist's deflating ridicule.

B. SECOND FACTOR

Though Paramount concedes the obvious point that Leibovitz's photograph exhibited significant creative expression, *Campbell* [*v. Acuff-Rose Music, Inc.*, 510 U.S. 569 (1994)] instructs that the creative nature of an original will normally not provide much help in determining whether a parody of the original is fair use. . . . The second factor therefore favors Leibovitz, but the weight attributed to it in this case is slight.

C. THIRD FACTOR

In assessing the amount and substantiality of the portion used, we must focus only on the protected elements of the original. Leibovitz is entitled to no protection for the appearance in her photograph of the body of a nude, pregnant female. Only the photographer's particular expression of such a body is entitled to protection. Thus, to whatever extent Leibovitz is contending that the ad takes the "heart" of the original . . . she must limit her contention to the particular way the body of Moore is portrayed, rather than the fact that the ad copies the appearance of a nude, pregnant body. Moreover, in the context of parodies, "the heart is also what most readily conjures up the [original] for parody, and it is the heart at which parody takes aim. . . . Thus, the third-factor inquiry in the parody context concerns "what else the parodist did *besides* go to the heart of the original." . . .

Paramount went to great lengths to have its ad copy protectable aspects of the Leibovitz photograph. Even though the basic pose of a nude, pregnant body and the position of the hands, if ever protectable, were placed into the public domain by painters and sculptors long before Botticelli . . . Leibovitz is entitled to protection for such artistic elements as the particular lighting, the resulting skin tone of the subject, and the camera angle that she selected. . . .

The copying of these elements, carried out to an extreme degree by the technique of digital computer enhancement, took more of the Leibovitz photograph than was minimally necessary to conjure it up, but *Campbell* instructs that a parodist's copying of more of an original than is necessary to conjure it up will not necessarily tip the third factor against fair use. . . . On the contrary, "[o]nce enough has been taken to assure identification" . . . as plainly occurred here, the reasonableness of taking additional aspects of the original depends on the extent to which the "overriding purpose and character" of the copy "is to parody the original," . . . That approach leaves the third factor with little, if any, weight against fair use so long as the first and fourth factors favor the parodist. Since those factors favor fair use in this case, the third factor does not help Leibovitz, even though the degree of copying of protectable elements was extensive.

D. MARKET EFFECTS

Leibovitz all but concedes that the Paramount photograph did not interfere with any potential market for her photograph or for derivative works based upon it. . . . She appears to have conceded as much in her deposition testimony, as well. . . . Her only argument for actual market harm is that the defendant has deprived her of a licensing fee by using the work as an advertisement . . . but she is not entitled to a licensing fee for a work that otherwise qualifies for the fair use defense as a parody. . . . The fourth factor favors the defendant.

E. AGGREGATE ASSESSMENT

The aggregate assessment necessary for an ultimate decision might be difficult in some cases if the relevant weighed heavily on opposite sides of the balance. However, in light of *Campbell,* with its significant depreciation of the second factor where parodies commenting on an original are concerned, we are satisfied that the balance here markedly favors the defendant. Moreover, we are aware of no "generalized equitable considerations" beyond the four statutory factors . . . that are relevant to this dispute.

CASE QUESTIONS

1. What if a person were to copy a song but changed the lyrics as to make it a parody? Would this be a way of copying a song legally without violating the Copyright Act?
2. Are there any limits wherein a parody would violate the intellectual property rights of the owners thereof?

INFRINGEMENT OF A COPYRIGHT

Infringement of a copyright may be *direct, indirect, contributory,* or *vicarious.*[50]

Direct Infringement. The holder of a copyright may establish a *direct* infringement by demonstrating to a court proof of (1) ownership of a valid copyright; and (2) a copying of the original portions of the protected work, that is, an infringement of any of the five exclusive statutory rights (stated previously) possessed by the copyright owner. The intent of the infringer is not an element of proof of infringement. The holder need not prove that the holder possessed any particular state of mind at the time of the infringement.

Indirect Infringement. A person may be found liable for *indirect infringement* by permitting another to use one's facilities for illicit purposes. Internet service providers appear to fall into this category; however, the Communications Decency Act (discussed in Chapter 5) grants immunity to them. In *Randall Stoner v. eBay Inc.,* Civ. No. 305666 (Sup. Ct. Ca., Nov. 7, 2000), eBay was sued under California state law for permitting the sale of copyrighted and bootleg musical recordings by persons using its auction facilities. The California state court held that the Communications Decency Act gives eBay immunity in that it is an interactive service provider, it is not a content provider as to the unlawful activity, and the information originated from outside, third-party sources.

Contributory Infringement. A person may be liable for assisting another to commit a wrong even though such person does not directly commit the wrongful act. Such a person may be liable if he or she, with knowledge of the infringing activity, materially causes, induces, or contributes to the infringing conduct of another. In the criminal law, such person may be designated as an accessory before or after the fact, or a theory of conspiracy may be used in his or her prosecution. One of the theories used in the *Napster* case is that the company was a mere conduit for the exchange of music by persons using the service. After downloading and installing Napster onto one's computer, the home user asks for a particular CD that Napster then seeks from other users of its service. The server becomes the go-between for users of the service. Music companies suggest that such acts as being a medium for direct copyright infringement by others renders Napster liable for contributory infringement if not direct infringement. In the *Intellectual Reserve* case to be discussed, the court distinguishes among the different concepts.

Vicarious Liability. A person may be *vicariously* liable when such a person has the right and ability to supervise the infringing activity coupled with a direct financial interest in the activities. For example, employers may be liable for actions committed by employees within the scope of their employment. As in all defenses, the court will examine the facts of the case to ascertain whether the elements of liability have been established.

INTELLECTUAL RESERVE, INC. V. UTAH LIGHTHOUSE MINISTRY

75 F. Supp. 2d 1290 (D.Utah 1999)

FACTS: Plaintiff published and owned the copyright to the "Church Handbook of Instructions." It alleged that the defendants had directly infringed and contributed to the infringement of its copyright by printing the said Handbook without permission. After the defendants had been enjoined from violating the copyright, they posted, on their website for informational purposes, the names and websites of three persons who also had posted the Handbook in violation of the plaintiff's copyright.

ISSUES: (1) "Did the defendants induce, cause or wrongfully contribute to the infringement?"

(2) "Can the defendants be liable under a theory of contributory infringement for the actions of those who browse the three infringing websites?"

(3) "Do those who browse the websites infringe plaintiff's copyright?"

DECISION: (1) Yes

(2) Yes

(3) Yes

REASONING: Judge Campbell

A. DIRECT INFRINGEMENT

To prevail on this claim of direct copyright infringement, "plaintiff must establish both: (1) that it possesses a valid copyright and (2) that defendants copied protectable elements of the copyrighted work." . . . Defendants initially conceded in a hearing, for purposes of the temporary restraining order and preliminary injunction, that plaintiff has a valid copyright in the Handbook, and that defendants directly infringed plaintiff's copyright by posting substantial portions of the copyrighted material. Defendants changed their position, in a motion to dismiss, claiming that plaintiff has failed to allege facts necessary to show ownership of a valid copyright. Despite the defendants' newly-raised argument, the court finds, for purposes of this motion, that the plaintiff owns a valid copyright on the material defendants posted on their website. Plaintiff has provided evidence of a copyright registration certificate . . . and the certificate "constitutes prima facie evidence of the validity of the copyright." . . . Defendants have not advanced any additional affirmative defenses to the claim of direct infringement. Therefore, the court finds that there is a substantial likelihood that plaintiff will prevail on its claim of direct infringement.

B. CONTRIBUTORY INFRINGEMENT

According to plaintiff, after the defendants were ordered to remove the Handbook from their website, the defendants began infringing plaintiff's copyright by inducing, causing, or materially contributing to the infringing conduct of others. It is undisputed that defendants placed a notice on their website that the Handbook was online, and gave three website addresses of websites containing the material defendants were ordered to remove from their website. Defendants also posted e-mails on their website that encouraged browsing those websites, printing copies of the Handbook and sending the Handbook to others.

Although the copyright statute does not expressly impose liability for contributory infringement,

> The absence of such express language in the copyright statute does not preclude the imposition of liability for copyright infringements on certain parties who have not themselves engaged in the infringing activity. For vicarious liability is imposed in virtually all areas of the law, and the concept of contributory infringement is merely a species of the broader problem of identifying the circumstances in which it is just to hold one accountable.

Sony Corp. v. Universal City Studios, Inc. . . . Even though "the lines between direct infringement, contributory infringement and vicarious liability are not clearly drawn" distinctions can be made between them. . . . Vicarious liability is grounded in the tort concept of respondeat superior, and contributory infringement is founded in the tort concept of enterprise liability. . . . "Benefit and control are the signposts of vicarious liability, [whereas] knowledge and participation [are] the touchstones of contributory infringement." . . .

Liability for contributory infringement is imposed when "one who, with knowledge of the infringing activity, induces, causes or materially contributes to the infringing conduct of another." . . . Thus, to prevail on its claim of contributory infringement, plaintiff must first be able to establish that the conduct defendants allegedly aided or encouraged could amount to infringement. . . . Defendants argue that they have not contributed to copyright infringement by those who posted the Handbook on websites nor by those who browsed the websites on their computers.

[The court found that those who posted the material on the three Web sites are directly infringing plaintiff's copyright. With respect to the defendant's contributory infringement, the court stated:] The evidence now before the court indicates that there is no direct relationship between the defendants and the people who operate the three websites. The defendants did not provide the website operators with the plaintiff's copyrighted material, nor are the defendants receiving any kind of compensation from them. The only connection between the defendants and those who operate the three websites appears to be the information defendants have posted on their website concerning the infringing sites. Based on this scant evidence, the court concludes that plaintiff has not shown that defendants contributed to the infringing action of those who operate the infringing websites.

[With respect to whether those who browse the Web sites infringe plaintiff's copyright, the court said:] Central to this inquiry is whether the persons browsing are merely viewing the Handbook (which is not a copyright infringement), or whether they are making a copy of the Handbook (which is a copyright infringement). . . .

"Copy" is defined in the Copyright Act as "material objects . . . in which a work is fixed by any method now known or later developed, and from which the work can be perceived, reproduced, or otherwise communicated, either directly or with the aid of a machine or device." 17 U.S.C. Section 101. "A work is 'fixed' . . . when its embodiment in a copy or phonorecord, by and under the authority of the author, is sufficiently permanent or stable to permit it to be perceived, reproduced, or otherwise communicated for a period of more than transitory duration. . . . "

When a person browses a website, and by doing so displays the Handbook, a copy of the Handbook is made in the computer's random access memory (RAM) to permit viewing of the material. And in making a copy, even a temporary one, the person who browsed infringes the copyright. . . . Additionally, a person making a printout or re-posting a copy of the Handbook on another website would infringe plaintiff's copyright.

[The court found that the defendants actively encouraged the infringement of plaintiff's Web site after they had been ordered to remove the Handbook from their own Web site. They listed the three Web site addresses, gave instruction on how to browse the three Web sites, and encouraged the copying and posting of copies of the infringing material. Accordingly, the court issued an order compelling the defendants from posting the infringing material and removing the referral to the three directly infringing websites.]

CASE QUESTIONS

1. Do you agree with the court in finding the defendant liable for contributory infringement for referring others to Web sites in which it was not otherwise monetarily or contractually connected?
2. Does anyone who refers others to sites containing unauthorized copies of works become liable for the referral? What if you were to refer someone to the Napster site? Does that make you liable for contributory infringement?

LICENSING AGREEMENTS

One of the rights of a holder of a copyright is to market and distribute one's work. This is generally accomplished by licensing it. A *license* is an agreement by the holder-*licensor* to permit another person, the *licensee,* to use the work as specified in their understanding. The agreement is generally nonexclusive, that is, the licensee may use, incorporate, or derive other benefit from the work, but such right does not prevent the holder-licensor from entering into license agreements with other persons. For example, the author of a novel may grant permission to a publisher to print and distribute the work, give movie rights to a motion picture company, and market the work as a Broadway play. Such rights, however, may be granted on an exclusive basis to a particular licensee. The law of contracts applies to licensing agreements. Many disputes occur and are litigated with respect to licensing agreements. Following is a sampling of the types of disputes that may occur as a result of licensing endeavors.

In *Walthal v. Corey Rusk,* 172 F.3d 481 (7th Cir. 1998), the plaintiffs are members of a musical group known as the Butthole Surfers. They entered into an oral agreement with Corey Rusk, who owned a record and distribution company known as Touch and Go Records. Under the agreement, Touch and Go was given a nonexclusive right to manufacture and sell copies of the Butthole Surfers' musical performances. The net profits from the sales were to be divided equally between the parties. The oral agreement had no termination date nor did the agreement specify how termination might take place. Under ordinary circumstances, any agreement without a termination date is *at will,* which means that any party to the transaction may terminate it. The issue here was whether the Copyright Act mandates a minimum fixed period for such license grant.

Section 203 of the act states that "the exclusive or nonexclusive grant of a transfer or license of copyright or of any right under a copyright . . . is subject to termination" under certain conditions. Subsection 3 states: "Termination of the grant may be effected at any time during a period of five years beginning at the end of thirty-five years from the date of execution of the grant. . . . " The Ninth Circuit Court of Appeals, in a highly controversial decision, *Rano v. Sipa Press,* 987 F.2d 580 (1993), said that the statute prevents termination of a license before the expiration of 35 years. The Court of Appeals for the Seventh Circuit, in the within case, decided that the oral license was to be determined in accordance with the general principles of contract law. Reviewing the congressional reports and the commentaries by scholars, the court held that the oral license was terminable at will. The contract was terminated. Noting that the statute is unclear, the court stated:

> The term of a copyright is the life of the author plus 50 [now 70] years. 17 U.S.C. Section 302(a). The ownership of a copyright vests in the author, who, of course, may transfer his rights as he sees fit. 17 U.S.C. Section 201(a). A "transfer of copyright ownership" is an assignment, mortgage, exclusive license, or any other conveyance, alienation, or hypothecation of a copyright or of any of the exclusive rights comprised in a copyright, whether or not it is limited in time or place of effect, but not including a nonexclusive license." 17 U.S.C. Section 101. Transfers of ownership must be in writing. 17 U.S.C. Section 204(a). Therefore, nonexclusive licenses are excluded from the definition of "transfer of copyright ownership." Therefore, nonexclusive licenses such as the one we are considering here may be granted orally, but they do not transfer ownership of the copyright. . . . "

Accordingly, the law of contracts prevails and the result, as indicated, follows such principles.

In *EPL, Inc. v. USA Federal Credit Union,* 173 F.3d 1356 (11th Cir. 1999), the issue arose concerning whether the licensor, EPL, had breached a software license agreement. USA had entered into a 10-year software license agreement with Norell Financial Services (NFS) that allowed USA to use, translate, and modify a specialized type of computer banking software owned by NSF called VISION. The software ran only on one kind of computer system, namely, Unisys Series V. USA was given a nonexclusive license to translate VISION to operate on the newer Unisys Series A computer system. The agreement allowed USA to translate the VISION source code to A-Series-architecture computer systems and to retain a copy of the source code and all object code compilations thereof. NFS could not sell or market the translated and modified VISION without consent of USA. Thereafter, EPL contracted with the Progeni Corporation to create its own translated version of VISION to operate on the Unisys Series A architecture.

The court of appeals reversed the trial court's grant of summary judgment (decision and judgment without a trial) in favor of EPL and remanded the case for a plenary trial. The lower court interpreted the agreement to mean that EPL could not sell or market the VISION A product *created by USA* but it could sell any other VISION A product. There were conflicting expert reports as to whether EPL was making the USA version of the software or some other version. Accordingly, the case was returned for further disposition.

UNFAIR COMPETITION AND PREEMPTION OF STATE LAW

States also may regulate to a limited degree conduct concerning violations of intellectual property rights. One of the theories attorneys have used successfully is that of unfair competition. It is a common-law theory that is incorporated into the Uniform Deceptive Trade Practices Act of many states. The concept involves selling a good or service of one's creation passed off under the name or mark of another. *Web Printing Controls Co. Inc. v. Oxy-Dry Corp.*, 906 F.2d 1202, 1203 (7th Cir. 1990). States have enacted such laws to protect consumers from deceitful practices of competitors of legitimate companies. The difficulty with state laws is that they may be preempted by the federal statute. A federal statute may be exclusive, that is, no state law may be enacted that covers the same subject matter as the federal law. Section 301(a) of the Copyright Act provides:

> On or after January 1, 1978, all legal or equitable rights that are equivalent to any of the exclusive rights within the general scope of copyright as specified in section 106 in works of authorship that are fixed in a tangible medium of expression and come within the subject matter of copyright as specified by sections 102 and 103, whether created before or after that date and whether published or unpublished, are governed exclusively by this title. Thereafter, no person is entitled to any such right or equivalent right in any such work under the common law or statutes of any State.

The House Report discussing Section 301 makes it clear that misappropriation is not necessarily synonymous with federal copyright statutes. The Report stated:[51]

> "Misappropriation" is not necessarily synonymous with copyright infringement, and thus a cause of action labeled as "misappropriation" is not preempted if it is in fact based neither on a right within the general scope of copyright as specified by section 106 nor on a right equivalent thereto. For example, state law should have the flexibility to afford a remedy (under traditional principles of equity) against a consistent pattern of unauthorized appropriation by a competitor of the facts (i.e., not the literary expression) constituting "hot" news, whether in the traditional mode of *International News Service v. Associated Press,* 248 U.S. 215 . . . , or in the newer form of data updates from scientific, business, or financial data bases.

In *Fred Wehrenberg Circuit of Theatres, Inc. v. Moviefone, Inc.,* 73 F. Supp. 2d 1044 (E.D.Mo. 1999), the plaintiff owns and operates a number of movie theaters in the St. Louis area and elsewhere. Defendant is a Delaware corporation with its principal place of business in New York. Plaintiff maintains an automated phone system and ticketing system through which persons wishing to see a movie may purchase tickets by credit card up to five days in advance. It also generates and publicizes movie show-time schedules as well as having a Web site. Defendant provides movie listings for about 20,000 movie screens of numerous theaters in 34 geographical areas. It also listed movie times for plaintiff's theaters although it did not sell tickets for the movies. Plaintiff claimed that some of the listings and times were inaccurate. Defendant derives its income from advertising revenue on its Web site.

Plaintiff alleges that defendant engaged in common-law unfair competition by free riding on its costly efforts.

In a lawsuit charging copyright infringement, the court found in favor of the defendant, holding that plaintiff failed to prove an essential element of misappropriation. The elements necessary to prove a case of misappropriation of "hot news" are:

(1) the plaintiff generates or collects information at some cost or expense; (2) the value of the information is highly time sensitive; (3) the defendant's use of the information constitutes free-riding on the plaintiff's costly efforts to generate or collect it; (4) the defendant is in direct competition with a product or service offered by the plaintiff; and (5) the ability of other parties to free-ride on the efforts of the plaintiff would so reduce the incentive to produce the product or service that its existence or quality would be substantially threatened.

The defendant, by listing plaintiff's movie schedules and times would not reduce plaintiff's incentive to generate or publicize movie schedules. Plaintiff's core business is to exhibit movies and make a profit from ticket and concession sales rather than from exhibiting schedules.

The two conditions for preemption of state law are: (1) the work is fixed in a tangible form and comes within the subject matter of copyright; and (2) the right must be one specified in the Copyright Act (reproduction, preparation of derivative works, etc.). If a state statute covers the same ground, then it is not enforceable. The state law will be enforceable if it affords protection of a right that is qualitatively different from a copyright infringement claim.[52]

In *KNB Enterprises v. Matthews,* 78 Cal. App. 4th 362 (Cal. App., 2d Dist., Feb. 17, 2000), a state appellate court upheld a state statute against a claim of preemption that allowed persons to prevent an unauthorized third party from using photographs of the likeness of persons without their consent. The defendant had copied and displayed some 400 copyrighted photographs belonging to the plaintiff of models in erotic poses. The court emphasized that a human likeness was not copyrightable. Thus, the two conditions of subject matter and the specified rights were not met. The claim asserted herein of right of publicity is not within the list of rights protected by the federal Copyright Act.

CONCLUSION

In this chapter, we reviewed the essential provisions of the Copyright Act of 1976 as amended. The advent of the Internet has caused a great deal of controversy and danger to holders of copyright protected works. U.S. enforcement has been relatively strict in this regard. In the next chapter, we will continue our discussion of copyright principles by reviewing the president's efforts concerning fair use. Thereafter, we will see how Congress has attempted to come to terms with the technological breakthroughs. We will conclude with the review of international efforts in the protection of copyrights.

Questions and Problems

1. Can one copy the white pages of a local telephone directory without consent of the company that published and holds the copyright to such a publication? At what point does such copying constitute an infringement?
2. A professor writes a book at his or her university using the school's facilities for all of the research, writing, and photocopying for such work. Is it a work for hire? Does the university have any right to the royalties that may emanate from the publication?
3. Many persons have downloaded Napster for copying the music of others. Is every such person in violation of the Copyright Act?
4. Is parody a way of getting around the restrictions of a copyright? Does making fun of any protected work, no matter how trivial the commentary, render such copying lawful?
5. Compare and contrast *direct, indirect, contributory,* and *vicarious* infringement of a copyright.
6. Kapes operated a coin business. In response to requests from customers concerning prices for his coins, he developed "The Fair Market Coin Pricer," which was listed on his Web page and which contained the retail prices of many coins. To ascertain the accuracy of the retail price list, he developed a computer program that enabled him to create retail prices

from wholesale prices. In developing the program, he used the plaintiff's wholesale price lists. The plaintiff publishes both a weekly and a monthly newsletter containing the prices of collectible coins. Plaintiff sued claiming copyright infringement. Defendant responded that the prices listed in plaintiff's wholesale coin price guides are not protected under the copyright laws. Decide. *CDN Inc. v. Kapes,* 197 F.3d 1256 (9th Cir. 1999).

7. In 1995 the defendant, Washington Mint, contracted with Medallic Art Company to use Medallic as its sole and exclusive manufacturer of all its custom-minted products. Thereafter, Washington told Medallic to replicate selected Treasury notes and coins, which replicas Washington would sell through its catalogs. The products produced by Medallic were three-dimensional representations of the said notes and coins. In giving final approval of the finished product, Washington made a few minor suggestions. After the three-year contract period ended, Washington sent samples of its product line to other manufacturers. These manufacturers began producing duplicates of the samples given to them, which were then for sale by Washington. Medallic sued for copyright infringement. Decide. *Medallic Art Company, Inc. v. Novus Marketing, Inc.,* No. 99 Civ. 502, 1999 U.S. Dist. LEXIS 12605 (S.D.N.Y. 1999).
8. Victor H. Vroom is a professor at the Yale University School of Organization and Management. In 1972, he entered into a licensing agreement with Kepner-Tregoe, Inc. (K-T), an international management training company. The agreement gave K-T exclusive worldwide rights to copyrighted materials of which Vroom was a coauthor. The materials, known as the Vroom-Yetton model, were used by the company to instruct managers on how to make better business decisions. K-T agreed to pay Vroom and his coauthor royalties for exclusive use of the materials but did allow Vroom to retain nonassignable rights to use the materials for his "own teaching and private consultation work." Thereafter, Vroom created a more sophisticated software program that overlapped with the materials licensed to K-T. Vroom used the materials to conduct management-training seminars for corporate executives at Yale as well as on other college campuses. K-T sued for breach of contract and copyright infringement. Your decision? *Kepner-Tregoe, Inc. v. Vroom,* 186 F.3d 283 (2d Cir. 1999).
9. The plaintiff is a Nevada corporation that produced and distributed videos, calendars, postcards, and novelty items to Las Vegas-area vendors. Plaintiff retained a photographer to take aerial photographs of the Las Vegas Strip, which photos were then used as the basis for the creation of an artistic depiction of the Strip and environs. The artist released all copyrights to the plaintiff, and the registration thereof was filed by plaintiff. Defendant produces similar products for sale throughout Nevada. It also produced digitally altered photographic images of the Las Vegas Strip. A number of plaintiff's images were scanned into defendant's computer and were cut and otherwise manipulated to form the defendant's desired images. Plaintiff claims that the scanning and alteration of its images constituted a violation of plaintiff's rights to *derivative works* that are protected rights under the Copyright Act. Defendant alleged that the contents or constituent elements of the computer-enhanced photograph is not protected under the act. Decision? Is the scanning of a protected image onto the defendant's computer random access memory "copying" under the act? *Tiffany Design, Inc. v. Reno-Tahoe Specialty, Inc.,* 55 F. Supp. 2d 1113 (D. Nev. 1999).
10. Ticketmaster (TM) operates the largest ticket-brokerage business in the country. It maintains exclusive arrangements with many entertainment and athletic events, selling tickets for such events through some 2,900 retail ticket windows, by telephone, and through the Internet. It maintains a homepage, *www.ticketmaster.com,* through which seats for events are sold. The defendant, T.Com, also sells tickets for certain events, but its main business is to act as a clearinghouse to provide users of its service with information as to where tickets to any event may be purchased. For many events to which tickets are sold exclusively by other brokers, it provides a hyperlink to the site where the

purchases may be made. Its earnings in the latter cases are from advertising. It receives no commission from TM for purchases by users of the T.Com site who are directed to the TM site. T.Com's computers enter into the TM computers electronically through the homepage and make note of the URLs of the interior homepages. T.Com extracts the information from TM's event page, copies it temporarily onto its own computers, extracts the facts contained therein, and places the facts on T.Com's own Web pages. The TM Web page is then discarded from T.Com's computer system. TM claims violation of its copyright. T.Com claims it is merely copying facts from TM and thus comes within the *Feist* decision that permits such copying of facts alone. Decide. See *Ticketmaster Corp. v. Tickets.Com, Inc.,* 2000 U.S. Dist. 12987 (C.D. Ca. Aug. 11, 2000).

Endnotes

1. Statement of Q. Todd Dickinson, Under Secretary of Commerce and Director of the U.S. Patent and Trademark Office, "The Costs of Internet Privacy for the Music and Software Industries," before the Subcommittee on Economic Policy and Trade, Committee on International Relations, July 19, 2000, *www.ogc.doc.gov/ogc/legreg/testimon/106s /dickinson0719.htm.*
2. Public Law 94-553, 90 Stat. 2541. The statute as amended may be found in Title 17, United States Code.
3. 17 U.S.C. Section 102(a).
4. Section 101 of the Copyright Act.
5. Final Act Embodying the Results of the Uruguay Round of Multilateral Trade Negotiations, Marakesh, April 15, 1994. Article 14(1) provides protection to performers against the unauthorized fixation and/or the reproduction of their unfixed performance, including the broadcasting and communication of a live performance.
6. Section 102 of the Copyright Act.
7. Id. Section 101.
8. 17 U.S.C. Section 102(b). In *Feist Publications Inc. v. Rural Tel. Ser. Co.,* 499 U.S. 340, 349–50 (1991), the U.S. Supreme Court stated that the objective sought by the Copyright laws according to the Constitution [Article 1, Section 8] is to "promote the Progress of Science and Useful Arts . . ." rather than to reward the labor of authors.
9. For example, see *Kirk v. Harter,* 188 F.3d 1005, 1007 (8th Cir. 1999).
10. An example of a *derivative work* is George Bernard Shaw's play *Pygmalion,* which was transformed into a movie by the same name, and was adapted as the Broadway musical extravaganza *My Fair Lady* and a very successful movie by the same name.
11. *Perform* means to recite, play, dance, act, show images or make sounds (17 U.S.C. Section 101).
12. 17 U.S.C. Section 106.
13. Pub. L. 101-650, 104 Stat. 5128.
14. The Visual Rights Act of 1990 became effective on June 1, 1991. It extended the protection to copyrighted works prior to said date, which the author had not transferred, and to works created on or after June 1, 1991. Moral rights did not extend to works that had been destroyed or mutilated before the said date (see footnote to Section 106A of the Copyright Act).
15. 17 U.S.C. Section 106A.
16. The right is subject to id. Sections 113(d), 106, and 107.
17. Id. Section 106A(c). A *work of visual art* is defined under Section 101 of the Copyright Act as a single painting, drawing, print, a sculpture, or still photographic image for exhibition purposes and up to 200 signed and consecutively numbered such works. It does not include works for hire, U.S. government works, posters, maps, globes, charts, diagrams, models, magazines, newspapers, and the like (these are covered by other copyright provisions).
18. Id. Section 401.
19. Id. Section 302(a)(b)(c).
20. Id. Section 303.
21. Pub. L. No. 105-147, 111 Stat. 2678, amending 17 U.S.C. Section 506(a).
22. 17 U.S.C. Section 502.
23. Id. Section 503.
24. Id. Section 504.
25. Id. Section 505.
26. 18 U.S.C. Section 2319.
27. 17 U.S.C. Section 506.
28. Id. Section 511.
29. *Mitek Holdings, Inc. v. Arce Eng'g Co.,* 198 F.3d 840, 842 (11th Cir. 1999).
30. 17 U.S.C. Section 507.
31. Id. Sections 107–112.
32. Section 102(b) of the Copyright Act of 1976 as amended.
33. 37 C.F.R. 202.1(a) (1994).
34. See 17 U.S.C. Section 105. Another exception may be found in 15 U.S.C. Section 290(e), which permits the secretary of commerce to seek copyright protection for certain standard reference data prepared by the secretary or by his or her department representatives.
35. 17 U.S.C. Section 302(a).

36. See *Ty, Inc. v. West Highland Publishing, Inc.,* 1998 U.S. Dist. LEXIS 15869 (N.D.Ill. 1998) at 32–33.
37. Ibid.
38. See *Tiffany Design, Inc. v. Reno-Tahoe Specialty, Inc.,* 55 F. Supp. 2d 1113, 1122 (D.Nev. 1999).
39. 17 U.S.C. Section 107.
40. For a comprehensive examination of the fair use issue, see Needham J. Boddie II, Thomas C. McThenis Jr., Fred B. Amos II and Douglas W. Kim, *A Review of Copyright and the Internet,* 20 Campbell L. Rev. 193 (Spring 1998), pp. 193–272.
41. See, e.g., *Marcus v. Rowley,* 695 F.2d 1171 (9th Cir. 1983) and *Basic Books, Inc. v. Kinko's Graphics Corp.,* 758 F. Supp. 1522 (S.D.N.Y. 1991).
42. See Robert N. Diotalevi, *Copyright Law: A Guide for the New Millennium,* Syllabus vol. 5 (April 1999), pp. 48–50.
43. For a detailed discussion, see Stepnana I. Colbert and Oren R. Griffin, *The Impact of "Fair Use" in the Higher Education Community: A Necessary Exception,* 62 Alb. L. Rev. 437, pp. 437–65 at 444–47. See *Harper & Row, Publishers, Inc. v. Nation Enterprises,* 471 U.S. 539 (1985), which set forth the said four-prong test. An additional useful discussion of the fair use doctrine can be seen in Dan Thu Thi Phan, *Will Fair Use Function on the Internet?* 98 Colum. L. Rev. 169–215.
44. 758 F. Supp. 1522 (S.D.N.Y. 1991).
45. 1996 Fed App. 0357P (6th Cir. 1996).
46. *A&M Records, Inc. v. Napster, Inc.* , 239 F.3d 1004, 1011 (9th Cir. 2001).
47. *UMG Recordings, Inc. v. MP3.com, Inc.,* No. 00 Civ. 0472 (JSR), 2000 U.S. Dist. LEXIS 17907 (S.D.N.Y. Nov. 14, 2000).
48. *UMG Recordings, Inc. v. MP3.com, Inc.,* 109 F. Supp. 2d 223 (S.D.N.Y. 2000).
49. 510 U.S. 569 (1994).
50. For a discussion of each of the types of infringement as well as the many supporting cases in connection therewith, see *Marobie-FL, Inc. v. National Association of Fire Equipment Distributors,* 983 F. Supp. 1167 (N.D.Ill. 1997).
51. H.R. Rep. No. 94-1476 at 132 (1976) printed in *Fred Wehrenberg Circuit of Theatres, Inc. v. Moviefone, Inc.,* 73 F. Supp. 2d 1044, 1049 (E.D.Mo. 1999).
52. Id. at 1180.

CHAPTER

7

COPYRIGHT ISSUES RAISED BY THE INTERNET

Section 2: Recent National and International Developments

Chapter Outline

In the preceding chapter, we discussed the essential principles of the U.S. Copyright Act. We continue with the discussion by reviewing the president's initiative concerning fair use. Educational institutions are particularly concerned with their right of fair use of copyright protected materials in the classroom. In this digital age, transmitting such materials to distant places presents a totally new series of difficulties wherein the balance between the rights of the educational institution come into conflict with those of authors. Following the review, we will examine recent statutory changes affecting the new technology. Included in the discussion is the Digital Millennium Copyright Act of 1998 and other statutory enactments. We will also review important international developments in this field of study.

EDUCATIONAL CONCERNS AND THE FAIR USE EXCEPTION

Distance learning is an outgrowth of the newly available technologies. It permits students globally to communicate with an instructor located a great distance away, thereby able to gain knowledge previously available only in a classroom setting. This is accomplished by use of electronic or other means. As a result of the rise of telecommunication, including both group and desktop videoconferencing, the classroom experience can be simulated, albeit with less interaction among peers. It is generally a closed system, that is, between the institution and the recipient. Some of the methods used are cable television, fiber optic networks, satellite computer networks, audio and video teleconferences, and other types.

Most universities offer one or more distance learning courses. For example, Pace University offers a number of courses in diverse fields of study. New York University (NYU On.line Inc) has training and courses for working adults to compete with those at the University of Phoenix and other schools.[1] Ohio University, among other universities, offers an online M.B.A. program to students in a number of states.[2] Other distance learning programs are offered by Duke and Purdue Universities. Of course, many educators have had negative reactions to the transmission of educational materials to remote areas,[3] but it is clear that the trend is here to remain in the foreseeable future.

The problem, however, concerns issues such as whether an instructor may use copyright protected media to enhance instruction to students. There is little question that an instructor may show a film in class to broaden the learning experience in a given area. The right to do so in the use of videoconferencing, however, may give rise to legally impermissible results. Violations of copyright law may result in litigation and penalties for the professor and his or her teaching institution. There is no problem, of course, with the instructor placing syllabi, class notes, biography, chapter summaries, and assignments on the Web; however, the use of films, copies of copyrighted articles, books, or summaries thereof leads to enormous potential legal difficulties.

The President's Initiative Concerning Fair Use

The need for rethinking the concept of fair use and other intellectual property issues became evident in the highest reaches of government. Accordingly, President Clinton convened an Information Infrastructure Task Force in 1993, together with the U.S. Advisory Council on the National Information Infrastructure within the Department of Commerce, to investigate and report on a proposed plan for the development of the said infrastructure.[4] The task force met, solicited written and public comments, and released a preliminary draft report on July 7, 1994. A Conference on Fair Use was thereafter convened to review fair use issues and to make recommendations concerning guidelines for fair uses. About 100 organizations representing libraries, publishers, museums, colleges and universities, musical interests, copyright groups, the entire spectrum of the media, and many other groups participated over the next three years in the discussions, formulating suggestions and otherwise assisting to prepare the guidelines to be discussed in this section.[5] Inasmuch as different issues arise concerning digital matters, distance learning, electronic multimedia, electronic reserve systems, and other areas of technological developments, each of the areas was investigated and reported on by different working groups. The Distance Learning Group convened in order "to provide guidance on the application of the performance and display of copyrighted works in . . . distance learning environments. . . . "[6]

The significance of the guidelines is that they will help prevent potential litigation with the participating organizations and may operate as persuasive evidence in a copyright infringement action arising out of the areas covered therein. It would also appear that the more one breaches the guidelines, the more potential liability that person will face. Thus, we will set forth the provisions therein in considerable detail. The guidelines on fair use concern only copyrights. The guidance set forth is for use by noncommercial entities, specifically "educational institutions, educators, scholars and students" using distance learning without first attempting to receive permission from the multitude of possible copyright owners.[7] The guidelines address in particular the provisions of Section 110 of the Copyright Act. Section 110 makes an exception to the grant in Section 106 of exclusive rights in copyrighted works. It declares that it is not an infringement to:

1. Perform or display a work by an instructor or pupil in *face-to-face* teaching activities in a classroom or similar place in a nonprofit educational institution unless an unlawful copy of the work is used and the person using it knew or had reason to know of the unlawful use;
2. Perform or display a nondramatic literary or musical work if it is part of the regular, systematic instructional activity, is directly related or materially assists in the teaching of it; and it is transmitted primarily for reception in classrooms or similar places, or to disabled persons who cannot attend classrooms or is received by employees or officers of government bodies for governmental purposes;
3. Perform a nondramatic literary or musical work or a dramatic-musical religious work for religious services at a religious place;
4. Perform a nondramatic literary or musical work for no fee or other payment or advantage to anyone involved and no fee for admission is charged and the proceeds after costs are used exclusively for religious, educational or charitable purposes unless the copy-

right owner objects in writing is served at least 7 days before the performance and the notice complies with regulatory requirements [if performed for a nonprofit veterans' or fraternal organization not opened to the public, a fee can be charged provided it accrues entirely for charitable purposes];

5. Perform for noncommercial use for one occasion to the blind or other handicapped people; and
6. For sales promotion purposes to the public for purposes of selling copies of the work and the performance takes place solely within the promotion area without admission charge.

Fair use in distance learning is addressed in the first two categories.[8] The distance learning guidelines concern lawfully acquired copyrighted works not covered by the said Section 110(2) that are used for live interactive distance learning classes and prerecorded instruction for use by students in a later transmission. The guidelines provide:

1. The eligible institutions are those engaged in nonprofit education and their focus is to engage in nonprofit research and educational instruction;
2. Students must be officially enrolled for the distance learning course with an eligible educational institution or be government employees taking the course as part of governmental purposes.

The performed works must be a part of the course and directly related to the subject matter and not for entertainment purposes. The transmission must be over a secure system requiring a means of identification such as a password, personal identification number (PIN) and so on. The transmission must be received in a classroom or place devoted to instructional purposes at an educational institution. The use of the copyrighted work must be for one time only or else permission would have to be obtained. The receiving institution may copy or record the transmission and retain it for up to 15 consecutive days for student viewing in a controlled environment such as a library, classroom, or media center. The institution must prevent copying of the work by students or other persons and must delete the copyrighted portion of the transmission unless permission is obtained from the copyright owner.

The transmitting institution may make up to 30 copies of the copyrighted work but cannot make further copies and must destroy all copies within seven years, except that one copy may be kept for archival purposes.[9] If the copyrighted multimedia work was received by means of a license, then the provisions of the license agreement will apply. Permission will be required in all situations where there is commercial use of the work, including when the nonprofit educational institution is using the work for courses for a for-profit corporation for a fee; for further dissemination of the copyrighted work for instructional purposes; where nonemployees may take a course within an agency or institution offering the program; and any use beyond the 15-day period.[10]

Educational Fair Use Guidelines for Digital Images

The guidelines in this section concern the conversion of visual images into digital images. "A digital image is a visual work stored in binary code (bits and bytes)."[11] Included in the definition of such images are *bitmapped images,* which are a series of bits and bytes representing a specific pixel or part of an image, and *vector graphics,* which are encoded equations or algorithms representing lines and curves. An *analog image collection* is a collection of analog visual images in the form of slides, photographs, and other visual media. An educational institution is permitted lawfully to digitize analog visual images for educational purposes, provided such images are not available for purchase or license at a fair price.[12] The institution may also create thumbnail images for placement in a visual catalog for use by the institution. It may display and give access to the images, provided controls are placed to protect copyright owners and give notice that the images may not be downloaded or copied in any manner.[13] The visual online catalog may be placed on the institution's secure electronic network for access by educators, scholars, and students connected with the institution.[14] The educational institution may displaced such images on the secure electronic network for classroom use or for after-class review, provided they are transmitted only to enrolled students of the course and that said students have exclusive access. Access beyond the secure electronic network is not permitted.[15]

The time limitation for digitized images is one academic term unless the holder of the right to the copyright is unknown, in which case the limit is three years.[16] The educator may use the images for face-to-face instruction or over a secure electronic network as well as for peer conferences (seminars, workshops, and related conferences). Students may use the digital images for term papers, for critique, and for use in portfolios for graduate school or for employment applications.[17]

Limitations include the need for reasonable inquiry by educational institutions to ascertain the rightful owner of the images if unknown, for making appropriate attribute and acknowledgment for credit purposes, for ascertaining whether the images are subject to licensing, and for maintaining the integrity of the images (except that they may be altered for scholarship purposes with appropriate notations).[18]

Educational Multimedia Guidelines

The permitted uses of educational multimedia projects, as set forth by the president's task force, are as follows: Students are permitted to incorporate portions of copyrighted works when preparing multimedia projects for a specific course and may further use the projects for personal uses such as, for example, job and graduate school interviews.[19] Educators may also incorporate parts of copyrighted works in educational multimedia projects when used for purposes of teaching in "curriculum-based instructional activities at educational institutions." They may also perform and display such projects to students as part of a curriculum-based instruction when doing so face-to-face, or when the projects are assigned to students for self-study or for remote instruction under the same conditions, provided it is done over a secure electronic network wherein access is secure and copies are prevented. If access cannot be made secure by the educational institution, then the use of the copyrighted portion may be made for a 15-day period, after which one copy may be kept in a learning resource center, library, or similar facility with the proviso that students may not make copies of the work. Educators may also use the multimedia projects for presentations to other professors, for example, in workshops and the like as well as for tenure review or job interviews.[20]

There are limitations in the time, portion, copying, and distribution of the copyrighted works. Instructors may use their multimedia projects for instructional use for up to two years after first instructional use, after which time permission from the copyright owner will be required. Portion limitations for motion media is up to 10 percent or three minutes, whichever is less; for text material, up to 10 percent or 1,000 words, whichever is less, as well as an entire poem of 250 words or less, but no more than three poems by one author or five poems from different authors from an anthology; for longer poems, 250 words but no more than three excerpts or five excerpts from an anthology; for music, lyrics, and music videos, up to 10 percent but no more than 30 seconds from an individual work; for illustrations and photographs, no more than five images by an artist and not more than 10 percent or 15 images, whichever is less, from a published collective work; and for numerical data sets, up to 10 percent or 2,500 fields or cell entries, whichever is less, from a copyrighted database or data table. Up to two copies may be made of the educator's educational multimedia project, one of which may be placed on reserve as previously indicated.[21]

Permission from the owner of the copyright is necessary when the use of the projects is for commercial reproduction and distribution or exceeds the limitations, or the use of the projects is for other than the stated uses.[22] Other limitations and requirements include the attribution and acknowledgment of the copyright owner and author; the inclusion of a notice that certain materials in the multimedia project were prepared in accordance with these guidelines; the maintenance of integrity of the copyrighted works or, when altered, that such alterations be in accordance with specific objectives; and that copying of the works is not permitted.[23]

THE DIGITAL MILLENNIUM COPYRIGHT ACT OF 1998

The Digital Millennium Copyright Act (DMCA) is a response to new technologies,[24] but the types of issues it addresses have been of concern for a long time. Owners of copyrights in the musical and theatrical entertainment industries for decades have greatly feared the development of a technology that would be able to duplicate movies and sound recordings. It was believed that such devices would cause consumers to refrain from purchasing tickets to theaters and to disseminate multiple copies of musical recordings from one purchased copy. The reality appears to be that such devices enhanced rather than detracted from consumer interest. The argument of whether duplication of copyrighted materials poses a threat to copyright holders is perennial in nature and will continue to be debated as technology becomes increasingly sophisticated. It is inconceivable today to realize that the use of video cassette recorders (VCRs) was almost forbidden. The seminal case that placed the judiciary on the side of VCR legality was the following decision that was decided by a bare (5–4) decision.

SONY CORP. OF AMERICA V. UNIVERSAL CITY STUDIOS, INC.

464 U.S. 417 (1984)

FACTS: Sony manufactured and sold Betamax home video tape recorders. It was sued by movie studios and other copyright holding entities alleging that the devices permitted unlawful copying of their protected works. The claim is that Sony was liable for the copyright infringement committed by Betamax consumers because of their marketing of the said product. The Court found that the average person used the device to record a television program that could not be viewed as it was being televised but then watched it at a later time ["time-shifting"].

ISSUE: (1) Whether the sale of Sony's copying equipment to the general public violates any of the rights conferred upon respondents Universal and other copyright parties by the Copyright Act?

(2) Whether the Betamax is capable of commercially significant noninfringing uses?

DECISION: The U.S. Supreme Court decided (1) that the recorders did not violate the Act and (2) it was capable of significant noninfringing uses. The Court upheld the decision of the U.S. District dismissing the lawsuit (reversing the court of Appeals that had ruled in favor of Universal).

REASONING: Justice Stevens

The District Court found:

"Even if it were deemed that home-use recording of copyrighted material constituted infringement, the Betamax could still legally be used to record noncopyrighted material or material whose owners consented to the copying. An injunction would deprive the public of the ability to use the Betamax for this noninfringing off-the-air recording. " . . .

[T]he fact that other copyright holders may welcome the practice of time-shifting does not mean that respondents should be deemed to have granted a license to copy their programs. Third party conduct would be wholly irrelevant in an action for direct infringement of respondents' copyrights. But in an action for *contributory* infringement against the seller of copying equipment, the copyright holder may not prevail unless the relief that he seeks affects only his programs, or unless he speaks for virtually all copyright holders with an interest in the outcome. In this case, the record makes it perfectly clear that there are many important producers of national and local television programs who find nothing objectionable about the enlargement in the size of the television audience that results from the practice of time-shifting for private home use. The seller of the equipment that expanded those producers' audiences cannot be a contributory infringer if, as is true in this case, it has had no direct involvement with any infringing activity. . . .

In summary, the record and findings of the District Court lead us to two conclusions. First, Sony demonstrated a significant likelihood that substantial numbers of copyright holders who license their works for broadcast on free television would not object to having their broadcasts time-shifted by private viewers. And second, respondents [Universal et al.] failed to demonstrate that time-shifting would cause any likelihood of non-minimal harm to the potential market for, or the value of, their copyrighted works. The Betamax is, therefore, capable of substantial noninfringing uses. Sony's sale of such equipment to the general public does not constitute contributory infringement of respondent's copyrights.

The direction of Art. I is that *Congress* shall have the power to promote the progress of science and the useful arts. When, as here, the Constitution is permissive, the sign as of how far Congress has chosen to go can come only from Congress. . . .

One may search the Copyright in vain for any sign that the elected representatives of the millions of people who watch television every day have made it unlawful to copy a program for later viewing at home, or have enacted a flat prohibition against the sale of machines that make such copying possible.

It may well be that Congress will take a fresh look at this new technology, just as it so often has examined other innovations in the past. But it is not our job to apply laws that have not yet been written. Applying the copyright statute, as it now reads, to the facts as they have been developed in this case, the judgment of the Court of Appeals must be reversed.

CASE QUESTIONS

1. Universal alleged that Sony should pay it and other companies who brought suit for money damages, accounting of profits, and an injunction prohibiting Sony from manufacturing the Betamax. After the suit and the continued manufacture of the Sony Betamax and of VCRs by other companies, the dangers alleged by the copyright holders appeared to have no basis in fact. Should the experience in this case negate the claims of potential losses by copyright holders in today's development of copying technology?
2. To what extent must there be noninfringing uses for a court to find a company that manufactures copy devices not liable?

Purpose of the DMCA

The major purpose of the DMCA, which was enacted on October 28, 1998, was to bring U.S. law in compliance with the World Intellectual Property Organization's (WIPO) Copyright Treaty and the Performances and Phonograms Treaty, both of which were concluded on December 20, 1996. Congress sought to balance the claims by persons opposed to anticircumvention measures and those who claim the need to extend copyright protection to the new technologies. We will discuss the provisions thereto inasmuch as they reflect current U.S. law, including measures affecting computer technology.

Copyright Protection and Management Systems Under the DMCA

The DMCA includes Title 1, entitled the WIPO Copyright and Performances and Phonograms Treaty Implementation Act of 1998, which changes a number of sections of the Copyright Act so as to incorporate treaty obligations. It also adds a new Chapter 12, "Copyright Protection and Management Systems." Commencing October 28, 2000, the statute prohibits the circumventing of technological measures controlling access to a copyright protected work.[25] The prohibition is in accordance with treaty mandates upon all signatory parties. No person may manufacture, import, or otherwise engage in the transfer of any technology, product, or service that is primarily designed to circumvent technological measures *protecting access to* or *preventing copying of* protected works.[26] Included in the prohibition are products or services that have limited nonprohibited uses. Such statute may override U.S. Supreme Court decisions permitting copy-type machines having legitimate uses in addition to uses that may be used to violate intellectual property statutes. The statute specifically excepts fair use copying and any other defenses ordinarily permitted in copyright infringement actions.

The relevant provisions of the statute are:

Section 1201: Circumvention of Copyright Protection Systems

(a) Violations Regarding Circumvention of Technological Measures.—(1)(A) No person shall circumvent a technological measure that effectively controls access to a work protected under this title. The prohibition contained in the preceding sentence shall take effect [on October 28, 2000]. . . .
   (2) No person shall manufacture, import, offer to the public, provide, or otherwise traffic in any technology, product, service, device, component, or part thereof, that—
      (A) is primarily designed or produced for the purpose of circumventing a technological measure that effectively controls access to a work protected under this title;
      (B) has only limited commercially significant purpose or use other than to circumvent a technological measure that effectively controls access to a work protected under this title; or
      (C) is marketed by that person or another acting in concert with that person with that person's knowledge for use in circumventing a technological measure that effectively controls access to a work protected under this title.
   (3) As used in this subsection—
      (A) to "circumvent a technological measure" means to descramble a scrambled work, to decrypt an

encrypted work, or otherwise to avoid, bypass, remove, deactivate, or impair a technological measure, without the authority of the copyright owner; and

(B) a technological measure "effectively controls access to a work" if the measure, in the ordinary course of its operation, requires the application of information, or a process or a treatment, with the authority of the copyright owner, to gain access to the work.

The ramifications of the act are discussed in the decision of the following case wherein the plaintiff alleged that the defendant manufactured a product that allowed customers to make unauthorized modifications to a software program copyrighted by the plaintiff.

REALNETWORKS, INC. V. STREAMBOX, INC.

2000 U.S. Dist. LEXIS 1889 (W.D.Wa. 2000)

FACTS: The plaintiff develops and markets software products that allow owners with video, audio, and other multimedia content to send it to other computer users. It also makes products that allow consumers to access video and audio content by means of a process known as "streaming." By streaming in the transmission of an audio or video clip, no trace of the clip remains on the consumer's computer unless the transmitter wishes to permit the user to download the file. It differs from downloading in that in downloading a user can access the downloaded file at will and transmit copies of the file to other persons. By streaming, the content owner may encode the digital content of the work for retransmission to consumers without fear of unauthorized copying.

The defendant, Streambox, enabled end-users to access and download copies of plaintiff's files that are streamed over the Internet. Through its VCR, it enables end-users to download and descramble plaintiff's files and make digital copies thereof. The plaintiff's business is harmed because of its ineffectiveness against defendant's overriding capability.

ISSUE: Whether the defendant violated the Digital Millennium Copyright Act which prohibits the manufacture of a device that is designed primarily to circumvent a technological device to protect the right of a copyright owner?

DECISION: The Court decided in the affirmative, enjoining the defendant from manufacturing, importing, licensing, and offering for sale of the Streambox VCR and products designed to modify plaintiff's programs designed to prevent unauthorized copying.

REASONING: Judge Pechman

6. The DMCA prohibits the manufacture, import, offer to the public, or trafficking in any technology, product, service, component, or part thereof that: (1) is primarily designed or produced for the purpose of circumventing a technological measure that effectively "controls access to" a copyrighted work or "protects a right of a copyright owner;" (2) has only limited commercially significant purpose or use other than to circumvent such technological protection measures; or (3) is marketed for use in circumventing such technological protection measures. 17 U.S.C. Sections 1201(a)(2), 1201(b).

PARTS OF THE VCR ARE LIKELY TO VIOLATE SECTIONS 1201(a)(2) AND 1201(b)

7. Under the DMCA, the Secret Handshake that must take place between a RealServer and a RealPlayer before the RealServer will begin streaming content to an end-user appears to constitute a "technological measure" that "effectively controls access" to copyrighted works. *See* 17 U.S.C. Section 1201(a)(3)(B) (measure "effectively controls access" if it "requires the application of information or a process or a treatment, with the authority of the copyright holder, to gain access to the work"). To gain access to a work protected by the Secret Handshake, a user must employ a RealPlayer, which will supply the requisite information to the RealServer in a proprietary authentication sequence.

8. In conjunction with the Secret Handshake, the Copy Switch is a "technological measure" that effectively protects the right of a copyright owner to control the unauthorized copying of its work. *See* 17 U.S.C. Section 1201(b)(2)(B) (measure "effectively protects" right of copyright holder if it "prevents, restricts or otherwise limits the exercise of a right of a copyright owner"); 17 U.S.C. Section 106(a) (granting copyright holder exclusive right to make copies of its work). To access a RealMedia file distributed by a RealServer, a user must use a RealPlayer. The RealPlayer reads the Copy Switch in the file. If the Copy Switch in the file is turned off, the RealPlayer will not permit the user to record a copy as the file is streamed. Thus, the Copy Switch may restrict others from exercising a copyright holder's exclusive right to copy its work.

9. Under the DMCA, a product or part thereof "circumvents" protections afforded a technological measure by "avoiding bypassing, removing, deactivating or otherwise impairing" the operation of that technological measure. 17 U.S.C. Sections 1201(a)(2)(A), 1201(b)(2)(A). Under that definition, at least a part of the Streambox VCR circumvents the technological measures RealNetworks affords to copyright owners. Where a RealMedia file is stored on a RealServer, the VCR "bypasses" the Secret Handshake to gain access to the file. The VCR then circumvents the Copy Switch, enabling a user to make a copy of a file that the copyright owner has sought to protect.

10. Given the circumvention capabilities of the Streambox VCR, Streambox violates the DMCA if the product or a part thereof: (i) is primarily designed to serve this function; (ii) has only limited commercially significant purposes beyond the circumvention; or (iii) is marketed as a means of circumvention. 17 U.S.C. Sections 1201(a)(2)(A–C), 1201(b)(b)(A–C). These three tests are disjunctive. *Id.* A product that meets only one of the three independent bases for liability is still prohibited. Here, the VCR meets at least the first two.

11. The Streambox VCR meets the first test for liability under the DMCA because at least a part of the Streambox VCR is primarily, if not exclusively, designed to circumvent the access control and copy protection measures that RealNetworks affords to copyright owners. 17 U.S.C. Sections 1201(a)(2)(A).

12. The second basis for liability is met because a portion of the VCR that circumvents the Secret Handshake so as to avoid the Copy Switch has no significant commercial purpose other than to enable users to access and record protected content. 17 U.S.C. Section 1201(a)(2)(B), 1201(b)(d)(B). There does not appear to be any other commercial value that this capability affords.

CASE QUESTIONS

1. Prior to the enactment of the statute, would the results have been different from the decision herein?
2. If the defendant's devices had legitimate use other than the illegitimate use stated in the litigation, would the results be different?

Exceptions to and Constitutionality of the DMCA

In the following action, wherein the court rendered a very lengthy decision, the defendants' claim of falling within the exceptions to the DMCA was reviewed. The case is set forth extensively due to the excellent discussion of the statute and the constitutional issues affecting copyright law.

UNIVERSAL CITY STUDIOS, INC. V. REIMERDES

2000 U.S. Dist. LEXIS 11696 (S.D.N.Y. 2000)

FACTS: The plaintiffs are eight major U.S. motion picture studios who distributed copyrighted motion pictures for home use on digital versatile disks (DVDs). In order to protect against copying, an encryption system called CSS is used. The DVDs are viewable on players and computer drives equipped with licensed technology that allows devices to decrypt and play the files without copying them. Computer hackers thereafter devised a computer program called DeCSS that circumvents the CSS protection system, thereby allowing the unauthorized copying of the motion pictures. The DeCSS was posted by the defendants on their website. Plaintiffs sued for an injunction barring defendants from posting the DeCSS. Defendants claim (a) that their actions did not violate the DMCA; and (b) the DMCA as it is applied to computer programs violates the First Amendment.

ISSUES: (1) Did the defendants' conduct in providing DeCSS violate the provisions of the DMCA?

(2) Are the exceptions to the DMCA applicable to the defendants?

(3) Does the DMCA, as it applies to the public dissemination of DeCSS, violate the First Amendment of the Constitution?

DECISION: (1) The Court held that the defendants' action did violate the statute.

(2) The defendants' actions did not come within the exceptions to the statute.

(3) The Court stated the statute did not violate the Constitution.

REASONING: Judge Kaplan

DeCSS, a computer program, unquestionably is "technology" within the meaning of the statute. "Circumvent a Technological Measure" is defined to mean descrambling a scrambled work, decrypting an encrypting work, or "otherwise to avoid, bypass, remove, deactivate, or impair a technological measure, without the authority of the copyright owner," so DeCSS clearly is a means of circumventing a technological access control measure. In consequence, if CSS otherwise falls within paragraphs (A), (B) or (C) of Section 1201(a)(2), and if none of the statutory exceptions applies to their actions, defendants have violated and, unless enjoined, will continue to violate the DMCA by posting DeCSS.

A. SECTION 1201(a)(2)(A)

1. CSS Effectively Controls Access to Copyrighted Works

First, the statute expressly provides that "a technological measure 'effectively controls access to a work' if the measure, in the ordinary course of its operation, requires the application of information or a process or a treatment, with the authority of the copyright owner, to gain access to a work." One cannot gain access to a CSS-protected work on a DVD without application of the three keys that are required by the software. One cannot lawfully gain access to the keys except by entering into a license with the DVD CCA [Copy Control Association] under authority granted by the copyright owners or by purchasing a DVD player or drive containing the keys pursuant to such a license. In consequence, under the express terms of the statute, CSS "effectively controls access" to copyrighted DVD movies. It does so, within the meaning of the statute, whether or not it is a strong means of protection. . . .

2. DeCSS Was Designed Primarily to Circumvent CSS

As CSS effectively controls access to plaintiffs' copyrighted works, the only remaining question under Section 1201(a)(2)(A) is whether DeCSS was designed primarily to circumvent CSS. The answer is perfectly obvious . . . DeCSS was created solely for the purpose of decrypting CSS—that is all it does. Hence, absent satisfaction of a statutory exception, defendants clearly violated Section 1201(a)(2)(A) by posting DeCSS to their web site.

B. SECTION 1201(a)(2)(B)

As the only purpose or use of DeCSS is to circumvent CSS, the foregoing is sufficient to establish a *prima facie* violation of Section 1201(a)(2)(B) as well.

2. Statutory Exceptions

a. Reverse Engineering Defendants claim to fall under Section 1201(f) of the statute, which provides in substance that one may circumvent, or develop and employ technological means to circumvent, access control measures in order to achieve interoperability with another computer program provided that doing so does not infringe another's copyright and, in addition, that one may make information through such efforts "available to others, if the person [in question] . . . provides such information solely for the purpose of enabling interoperability of an independently created computer program with other programs, and to the extent that doing so does not constitute infringement. . . . " They contend that DeCSS is necessary to achieve interoperability between computers running the Linux operating system and DVDs and that this exception therefore is satisfied. This contention fails.

First, Section 1201(f)(3) permits information acquired through reverse engineering to be made available to others only by the person who acquired the information. But these defendants did not do any reverse engineering. They simply took DeCSS off someone else's web site and posted it on their own.

Defendants would be in no stronger position even if they had authored DeCSS. The right to make the information available extends only to dissemination "solely for the purpose" of achieving interoperability as defined in the statute. It does not apply to public dissemination as means of circumvention, as the legislative history confirms. These defendants, however, did not post DeCSS "solely" to achieve interoperability with Linux or anything else . . . .

Finally, it is important to recognize that even the creators of DeCSS cannot credibly maintain that the "sole" purpose of DeCSS was to create a Linux DVD player. DeCSS concededly was developed on and runs under Windows—a far more widely used operating system.

Accordingly, the reverse engineering exception to the DMCA has no application here.

b. Encryption Research Section 1201(g)(4) provides in relevant part that:

> Notwithstanding the provisions of subsection (a)(2), it is not a violation of that subsection for a person to—
> (A) develop and employ technological means to circumvent a technological measure for the sole purpose of that person performing the acts of good faith encryption research described in paragraph (2); and
> (B) provide the technological means to another person with whom he or she is working collaboratively for the purpose of conducting the acts of good faith encryption research described in paragraph (2) or for the purpose of having that other person verify his or her acts of good faith encryption research described in paragraph (2).

Paragraph (2) in relevant part permits circumvention of technological measures in the course of good faith encryption research if:

> (A) the person lawfully obtained the encrypted copy, phonorecord, performance, or display of the published work;
> (B) such act is necessary to conduct such encryption research;
> (C) the person made a good faith effort to obtain authorization before the circumvention; and
> (D) such act does not constitute infringement under this title. . . .

In determining whether one is engaged in good faith encryption research, the Court is instructed to consider factors including whether the results of the putative encryption research are disseminated in a manner described to advance the state of knowledge of encryption technology versus facilitation of copyright infringement, whether the person in question is engaged in legitimate study of or work in encryption, and whether the results of the research are communicated in a timely fashion to the copyright owner.

Neither of the defendants remaining in this case was or is involved in good faith encryption research. They posted DeCSS for all the world to see. There is no evidence that they made any effort to provide the results of the DeCSS effort to the copyright owners. Surely there is no suggestion that either of them made a good faith effort to obtain authorization from the copyright owners. Accordingly, the defendants are not protected by Section 1201(g).

c. Security Testing Defendants contended earlier that their actions should be considered exempt security testing under Section 1201(j) of the statute. This exception, however, is limited to "assessing a computer, computer system, or computer network, solely for the purpose of good faith testing, investigating, or correcting [of a] security flaw or vulnerability, with the authorization of the owner or operator of such a computer system or computer network."

The record does not indicate that DeCSS has anything to do with testing computers, computer systems, or computer networks. Certainly defendants sought, and plaintiffs' granted, no authorization for defendants' activities. This exception has no bearing in this case.

d. Fair Use Finally, defendants rely on the doctrine of fair use. . . . The doctrine traditionally has facilitated literary and artistic criticism, teaching and scholarship, and other socially useful forms of expression. It has been viewed by courts as a safety valve that accommodates the exclusive rights conferred by copyright with the freedom of expression guaranteed by the First Amendment.

The use of technological means of controlling access to a copyrighted work may affect the ability to make fair uses of the work. Focusing specifically on the factors of this case, the application of CSS to encrypt a copyrighted motion picture requires the use of a compliant DVD player to view or listen to the movie. Perhaps more significantly, it prevents exact copying of either the video or the audio portion of all or any part of the film. This latter point means that certain uses that might qualify as "fair" for purposes of copyright infringement . . . would be difficult or impossible absent circumvention of the CSS encryption. Defendants therefore argue that the DMCA cannot properly be construed to make it difficult or impossible to make any fair use of plaintiffs' copyrighted works and that the statute therefore does not reach their activities, which are simply a means to enable users of DeCSS to make such fair uses.

Defendants have focused on a significant point. Access control measures such as CSS do involve some risk of preventing lawful as well as unlawful uses of copyrighted material. Congress, however, clearly faced up to and dealt with this question in enacting the DMCA.

. . . Section 107 of the Copyright Act provides in critical part that certain uses of copyrighted works that otherwise would be wrongful are "not . . . infringement[s] of copyright." Defendants, however, are not sued for copyright infringement. They are sued for offering and providing technology designed to circumvent technological measures that control access to copyrighted works and otherwise violating Section 1201(a)(2) of the Act. If Congress had meant the fair use defense to apply to such actions, it would have said so. Indeed, as the legislative history demonstrates, the decision not to make fair use a defense to a claim under Section 1201(a) was quite deliberate. . . .

The first element of the balance [of the rights of copyright owners with those of noninfringing users of portions of copyrighted works] was the careful limitation of Section 1201(a)(1)'s prohibition of the act of circumvention to the act itself so as not to "apply to subsequent actions of a person once he or she has obtained authorized access to a copy of a [copyrighted] work. . . . " By doing so, it left "the traditional defenses to copyright infringement, including fair use, . . . fully applicable" provided "the access is authorized." . . .

Third, it created a series of exceptions to aspects of Section 1201(a) for certain uses that Congress thought "fair," including reverse engineering, security testing, good faith encryption research, and certain uses by nonprofit libraries, archives and educational institutions.

[The court goes on to discuss the constitutionality of the DMCA:]

III. THE FIRST AMENDMENT

Defendants argue that the DMCA, at least as applied to prevent the public dissemination of DeCSS, violates the First Amendment of the Constitution. They claim that it does so in two ways. First, they argue that computer code is protected speech and the DMCA's prohibition of dissemination of DeCSS therefore violates defendants' First Amendment rights. Second, they contend that the DMCA is unconstitutionally overbroad, chiefly because its prohibition of the dissemination of decryption technology prevents third parties from making fair use of plaintiffs' encrypted works, and vague. They argue also that a prohibition of their linking to sites that make DeCSS available is unconstitutional for much the same reasons.

A. Computer Code and the First Amendment

The premise of defendants' first position is that computer code, the form in which DeCSS exists, is speech protected by the First Amendment. Examination of that premise is the logical starting point for analysis. And it is important in examining that premise first to define terms.

Defendants' assertion that computer code is "protected" by the First Amendment is quite understandable. Courts often have spoken of certain categories of expression as "not within the area of constitutionally protected speech," so defendants naturally wish to avoid exclusion by an unfavorable categorization of computer code. But such judicial statements in fact are not literally true. All modes of expression are covered by the First Amendment in the sense that the constitutionality of their "regulation must be determined by reference to First Amendment doctrine and analysis." Regulation of different categories of expression, however, is subject to varying levels of judicial scrutiny. Thus, to say that a particular form of expression is "protected" by the First Amendment means that the constitutionality of any regulation of it must be measured by reference to the First Amendment. In some circumstances, however, the phrase connotes also that the standard for measurement is the most exacting level available.

It cannot seriously be argued that any form of computer code may be regulated without reference to First Amendment doctrine. The path from idea to human language to source code object code is a continuum. As one moves from one to the other, the levels of precision and, arguably abstraction increase, as does the level of training necessary to discern the idea from the expression. Not everyone can understand each of these forms. Only English speakers will understand English formulations. Principally those familiar with the particular programming language will understand the source code expression. And only a relatively small number of skilled programmers and computer scientists will understand the machine readable object code. But each form expresses the same idea, albeit in different ways.

There perhaps was a time when the First Amendment was viewed only as a limitation on the ability of government to censor speech in advance. But we have moved far beyond that. All modes by which ideas may be expressed or, perhaps, emotions evoked—including speech, books, movies, art, and music—are within the area of First Amendment concern. As computer code—whether source or object—is a means of expressing ideas, the First Amendment must be considered before its dissemination may be prohibited or regulated. In that sense, computer code is covered or, as sometimes is said, "protected" by the First Amendment. But that conclusion still leaves for determination the level of scrutiny to be applied in determining the constitutionality of regulation of computer code.

B. The Constitutionality of the DMCA's Anti-Trafficking Provision

1. Defendants' Alleged Right to Disseminate DeCSS
Defendants first attack Section 1201(a)(2), the anti-trafficking provision, as applied to them on the theory that DeCSS is constitutionally protected expression and that the statute improperly prevents them from communicating it. Their attack presupposes that a characterization of code as constitutionally protected subjects any regulation of code to the highest level of First Amendment scrutiny. As we have seen, however, this does not necessarily follow.

Just as computer code cannot be excluded from the area of First Amendment concern because it is abstract and, in many cases, arcane, the long history of First Amendment jurisprudence makes equally clear that the fact that words, symbols and even actions convey ideas and evoke an analytical framework by which the permissibility of particular restrictions on the expression of ideas must be determined.

Broadly speaking, restrictions on expression fall into two categories. Some are restrictions on the voicing of particular ideas, which typically are referred to as content based restrictions. Others have nothing to do with the content of the expression—i.e., they are content neutral—but they have the incidental effect of limiting expression.

In general, "government has no power to restrict expression because of its message, its ideas, its subject matter, or its content. . . . " "Subject only to narrow and well-understood exceptions, [the First Amendment] does not countenance governmental control over the content of messages expressed by private individuals." In consequence, content based restrictions on speech are permissible only if they serve compelling state interests by the least restrictive means available.

Content neutral restrictions, in contrast, are measured against a less exacting standard. Because restrictions of this type are not motivated by a desire to limit the message, they will be upheld if they serve a substantial governmental interest and restrict First Amendment freedoms no more than necessary.

Restrictions on the nonspeech elements of expressive conduct fall into the conduct-neutral category. The Supreme Court long has distinguished for First Amendment purposes between pure speech, which ordinarily receives the highest level of protection, and expressive conduct. Even if conduct contains an expressive element, its nonspeech aspect need not be ignored. "When 'speech' and 'nonspeech' elements are combined in the same course of conduct, a sufficiently important governmental interest in regulating the nonspeech element can justify incidental limitations on First Amendment freedoms."

Thus, the starting point for analysis is whether the DMCA, as applied to restrict dissemination of DeCSS and other computer code used to circumvent access control measures, is a content based restriction on speech or a content neutral regulation. Put another way, the question is the level of review that governs the DMCA's anti-trafficking provision as applied to DeCSS—the strict scrutiny standard applicable to content based regulations or the intermediate level applicable to content neutral regulations, including regulations of the nonspeech elements of expressive conduct. . . .

The "principal inquiry in determining content neutrality . . . is whether the government had adopted a regulation of speech because of [agreement or] disagreement with the message it conveys." The computer code at issue in this case, however, does more than express the programmers' concepts. It does more, in other words, than convey a message. DeCSS, like any other computer program, is a series of instructions that uses a computer to perform a particular sequence of tasks which, in the aggregate, decrypt CSS-protected files. Thus, it has a distinctly functional, non-speech aspect in addition to reflecting the thoughts of the programmers. It enables anyone who receives it and who has a modicum of computer skills to circumvent plaintiffs' access control system.

The reason that Congress enacted the anti-trafficking provision of the DMCA had nothing to do with suppressing particular ideas of computer programmers and everything to do with functionality—with preventing people from circumventing technological access control measures—just as laws prohibiting the possession of burglar tools have nothing to do with preventing people from expressing themselves by accumulating what to them may be attractive assortments of implements and everything to do with preventing burglaries. Rather, it is focused squarely upon the effect of the distribution of the functional capability that the code provides. Any impact on the dissemination of programmers' ideas is purely incidental to the overriding concerns of promoting the distribution of copyrighted works in digital form while at the same time protecting those works from piracy and other violations of the exclusive rights of copyright holders. . . .

Congress is not powerless to regulate content neutral regulations that incidentally affect expression, including the dissemination of the functional capabilities of computer code. A sufficiently important governmental interest in seeing to it that computers are not instructed to perform particular functions may justify incidental restrictions on the dissemination of the expressive elements of a program. Such a regulation will be upheld if:

it furthers an important or substantial governmental interest; if the governmental interest is unrelated to the suppression of free expression; and if the incidental restriction on alleged First Amendment freedoms is no greater than is essential to the furtherance of that interest.

Moreover, "to satisfy this standard, a regulation need not be the least speech-restrictive means of advancing the Government's interests." "Rather, the requirement of narrow tailoring is satisfied 'so long as the . . . regulation promotes a substantial government interest that would achieve less effectively absent the regulation'" [citing *Turner Broadcasting System, Inc. v. FCC*, 512 U.S. 622 (1994)].

The anti-trafficking provision of the DMCA furthers an important governmental interest—the protection of copyrighted works stored on digital media from the vastly expanded risk of piracy in this electronic age. The substantiality of that interest is evident both from the fact that the Constitution specifically empowers Congress to provide for copyright protection and from the significance to our economy of trade in copyrighted materials. Indeed, the Supreme Court has made clear that copyright protection is "the engine of free expression." That substantial interest, moreover, is unrelated to the suppression of particular views expressed in means of gaining access to protected copyrighted works. Nor is the incidental restraint on protected expression—the prohibition of trafficking in means that would circumvent controls limiting access to unprotected materials or to copyrighted materials for noninfringing purposes—broader than is necessary to accomplish Congress' goals of preventing infringement and promoting the availability of content in digital form.

Accordingly, this Court holds that the anti-trafficking provision of the DMCA as applied to the posting of computer code that circumvents measures that control access to copyrighted works in digital form is a valid exercise of Congress' authority. It is a content neutral regulation in furtherance of important governmental interests that does not unduly restrict expressive activities. In any case, its particular functional characteristics are such that the Court would apply the same level of scrutiny even if it were viewed as content based. Yet it is important to emphasize that this is a very narrow holding. The restriction the Court here upholds, notwithstanding that computer code is within the area of First Amendment concern, is limited (1) to programs that circumvent access controls to copyrighted works in digital form in circumstances in which (2) there is no other practical means of preventing infringement through use of the programs, and (3) the regulation is motivated by a desire to prevent performance of the function for which the programs exist rather than any message they might convey. One readily might imagine other circumstances in which a governmental attempt to regulate the dissemination of computer code would not similarly be justified.

2. Prior Restraint Defendants argue also that injunctive relief against dissemination of DeCSS is barred by the prior restraint doctrine. The Court disagrees.

Few phrases are as firmly rooted in our constitutional jurisprudence as the maxim "any system of prior restraints of expression comes to [a] Court bearing a heavy presumption against its constitutional validity." Yet there is a significant gap between the rhetoric and the reality. Courts often have upheld restrictions on expression that many would describe as prior restraints, sometimes by characterizing the expression as unprotected and on other occasions finding the restraint justified despite its presumed invalidity. Moreover, the prior restraint doctrine, which has expanded far beyond the Blackstonian model that doubtlessly informed the understanding of the Framers of the First Amendment, has been criticized as filled with "doctrinal ambiguities and inconsistencies resulting from the absence of any detailed judicial analysis of [its] true rationale" and, in one case, even as "fundamentally unintelligible." Nevertheless, the doctrine has a well established core: administrative preclearance requirements for and at least preliminary injunctions against speech as conventionally understood are presumptively unconstitutional. Yet that proposition does not dispose of this case. . . .

In this case, the considerations supporting an injunction are very substantial indeed. Copyright and, more broadly, intellectual property piracy are endemic, as Congress repeatedly has found. The interest served by prohibiting means that facilitate such piracy—the protection of the monopoly granted to owners by the Copyright Act—is of constitutional dimension. There is little room for doubting that broad dissemination of DeCSS threatens ultimately to injure or destroy plaintiffs' ability to distribute their copyrighted materials on DVDs and, for that matter, undermine their ability to sell their products to the home video market in other forms. The potential damages probably are incalculable, and these defendants would be in no position to compensate plaintiffs for them if plaintiffs were remitted only to *post hoc* damage suits.

On the other side of the coin, the First Amendment interests served by the dissemination of DeCSS on the merits are minimal. The presence of some expressive content in the code should not obscure the fact of its predominant functional character—it is first and foremost a means of causing a machine with which it is used to perform particular tasks. Hence, those of the traditional rationales for the prior restraint doctrine that relate to inhibiting the transmission and receipt of ideas are of attenuated relevance here. Indeed, even academic commentators who take the extreme position that most injunctions in intellectual property cases are unconstitutional prior restraints concede that there is no First Amendment obstacle to injunctions barring distribution of copyrighted computer object code or restraining the construction of a new building based on copyrighted architectural drawings because of the functional aspects of these types of information are "sufficiently nonexpressive." . . . Accordingly, the Court holds that the prior restraint does not require denial of an injunction in this case.

CASE QUESTIONS

1. Would the results have differed if the defendant were domiciled exclusively in a European Union country?
2. If the DeCSS had other legitimate uses, would the results be the same?
3. Should the constitutional doctrine of *prior restraint* be set aside to appease copyright owners?

INTERNET SERVICE PROVIDERS AND LIABILITY ISSUES

The courts in the past had been reluctant to extend liability for copyright infringement to ISPs because they were deemed to be analogous to libraries, wherein books are provided to borrowers without liability for defamatory statements or violations of copyright laws that may be present in the texts. They are distributors rather than publishers of information transmitted to millions of users of such services. Courts and the Congress have determined that no liability should accrue to service providers having little or no ability to screen material transmitted over its network. As stated in *Cubby, Inc. v. CompuServe Inc.,* 776 F. Supp. 135 (S.D.N.Y. 1991), the service rendered by CompuServe is that of the maintenance of a large electronic, for-profit library with many publications for access by numerous users who paid a fee for the access therein. It has little or no control over the content of materials appearing by virtue of its provision of access. The user connects to the ultimate source by means of the ISP. Liability, if any, would extend to the source of the defamatory or copyright infringing material.

In any event, Congress has given ISPs immunity by providing statutorily (47 U.S.C. Section 230(c)(1)) that "[n]o provider or user of an interactive computer service shall be treated as the publisher or speaker of any information provided by another information content provider" (see *Zeran v. America Online Inc.,* 129 F.3d 327 (4th Cir. 1997)). The definition of an ISP is not overly broad. The Digital Millennium Copyright Act of 1998 defines an ISP as "an entity offering the transmission, communications, between or among points specified by a user, of material of the user's choosing, without modification to the content of the material as sent or received."

In *Playboy v. Webbworld,* No. 96-CU-3222-DES (N.D.Tex. 1996), the defendant, Webbworld, operated an Internet Web site known as Neptics, Inc. For a subscription fee of $11.95 monthly, it made adult images available to paying customers. Included in the images were those almost identical to images appearing in issues of *Playboy* magazine that had copyright protection. The court said that the defendant was not an Internet service provider and was thus not entitled to protection afforded to ISPs.

Under the DMCA (Section 512(a)(j)), a service provider may not be held liable for monetary relief although a court may issue injunctive relief consisting of a restraining order from providing access to a subscriber, account holder, or network using the service provider in an unlawful manner. The order may also provide for the blocking of access to a specific, identified online location outside of the United States.

THE AUDIO HOME RECORDING ACT OF 1992

The Audio Home Recording Act of 1992 amends the Copyright Act of 1976 by adding a new Chapter 10.[27] Section 1002 prohibits the importation, manufacture, or distribution of any digital audio recording or interface device that does not conform to the Serial Copy Management System or comparable system that prohibits unauthorized copying. It is also unlawful to import, manufacture, or distribute any device, or to offer or perform any service whose primary purpose is to circumvent the Serial Copy Management System or comparable system. Also prohibited is the encoding of a digital musical recording of a sound recording with inaccurate information relating to the category code, copyright status, or the generation status of the source material for the recording.

Section 1003 of the act prohibits the distribution, importation, or manufacture of the said digital audio recording device or recording medium unless such person files a notice with the Register of Copyrights with respect to such device or medium. It will be necessary to file certified quarterly and annual statements of account with the register. Each statement is to be accompanied with a royalty payment of 2 percent of the transfer price for digital audio recording devices and 3 percent for digital audio recording medium. Limitations of the least amount to be paid as royalty is $1.00 and the maximum is $12.00. There are provisions for payment of the royalty to persons whose musical work has been embodied in the recording and to other persons, including a musical works fund for diverse interested persons. A much broader and comprehensive protection mechanism was created by the Digital Millennium Copyright Act (discussed previously). The next case exemplifies the provisions of this act.

RECORDING INDUSTRY ASS'N OF AMERICA V. DIAMOND MULTIMEDIA SYSTEMS, INC.

180 F.3d 1072 (9th Cir. 1999)

FACTS: Plaintiff represents the major record companies and the artists on the labels encompassing some 90 percent of all recorded music distributed in the U.S. Plaintiff sought to enjoin defendant from manufacturing and distributing the Rio portable music player, which is a small device with headphones that allowed a user to download MP3 audio files from a computer and listen to them anywhere s/he desires. It claimed that the Rio did not meet the requirements of the Act because it did not employ a Serial Copyright Management System that "sends, receives, and acts upon information about the generation and copyright status of the files that it plays." In addition, it sought royalties for the defendant manufacturer and distributor of the digital audio recording device.

ISSUE: Whether the Rio portable music player is a digital audio recording device subject to the restrictions of the Audio Home Recording Act of 1992?

DECISION: It is not a digital audio recording device and, therefore, not subject to the Act.

REASONING: Judge O'Scannlain

The initial question presented is whether the Rio falls within the ambit of the Act. The Act does not broadly prohibit digital serial copying of copyright protected audio recordings. Instead, the Act places restrictions only upon a specific type of recording device. Most relevant here, the Act provides that "no person shall import, manufacture, or distribute any *digital audio recording device* ... that does not conform to the Serial Copy Management System [SCMS] [or] a system that has the same functional characteristics." 17 U.S.C. Section 1002(a)(1), (2) (emphasis added). The Act further provides that "no person shall import into and distribute, or manufacture, any *digital audio recording device* ... unless such person records the notice specified by this section and subsequently deposits the statements of account and applicable royalty payments." *Id.* Section 1003(a) (emphasis added). Thus, to fall within the SCMS and royalty requirements in question, the Rio must be a "digital recording device," which the Act defines through a set of nested definitions.

The Act defines a "digital audio recording device" as:

> Any machine or device of a type commonly distributed to individuals for use by individuals, whether or not included with or as part of some other machine or device, the digital recording function of which is designed or marketed for the primary purpose of, and that is capable of, making a *digital copied recording* for private use....

Id. Section 1001(3) (emphasis added).

A "digital audio copied recording" is defined as:

> A reproduction in a digital recording format of a *digital musical recording,* whether that reproduction is made directly from another digital musical recording or indirectly from a transmission.

A "digital musical recording" is defined as:

> *A material object—*
> (i) in which are fixed, in a digital recording format, *only sounds, and material, statements, or instructions incidental to those fixed sounds,* if any, and
> (ii) from which the sounds and material can be perceived, reproduced, or otherwise communicated, either directly or with the aid of a machine or device.

Id. Section 1001(5)(A) (emphasis added).

In sum, to be a digital audio recording device, the Rio must be able to reproduce, either "directly" or "from a transmission," a "digital music recording."

We first consider whether the Rio is able directly to reproduce a digital music recording—which is a specific type of material object in which only sounds are fixed (or material and instructions incidental to those sounds). *See id.* ...

The typical computer hard drive from which a Rio directly records is, of course, a material object. However, hard drives ordinarily contain much more than "only sounds, and material, statements, or instructions incidental to those fixed sounds." *Id.* Indeed, almost all hard drives contain numerous programs (e.g., for word processing, scheduling appointments, etc.) and databases that are not incidental to any sound files that may be stored on the hard drive. Thus, the Rio appears not to make copies from digital music recordings, and thus would not be a digital audio recording device under the Act's basic definition unless it makes copies from transmissions.

Moreover, the Act expressly provides that the term "digital music recording" does not include:

A material object—
(i) in which the fixed sounds consist entirely of spoken word recordings, or
(ii) *in which one or more computer programs are fixed,* except that a digital recording may contain statements or instructions constituting the fixed sounds and incidental material, and statements or instructions to be used directly or indirectly in order to bring about the perception, reproduction, or communication of the fixed sounds and incidental material.

Id. Section 1001(5)(B) (emphasis added). As noted previously, a hard drive is a material object in which one or more programs are fixed; thus, a hard drive is excluded from the definition of digital music recordings. This provides confirmation that the Rio does not record "directly" from "digital music recordings," and therefore could not be a digital audio recording device unless it makes copies "from transmissions." . . .

Under the plain meaning of the Act's definition of digital audio recording devices, computers (and their hard drives) are not digital audio recording devices because their "primary purpose" is not to make digital audio copied recordings. *See* 17 U.S.C. Section 1001(3). Unlike digital audio tape machines, for example, whose primary purpose is to make digital audio copied recordings, the primary purpose of a computer is to run various programs and to record the data necessary to run those programs and perform various tasks. . . .

In turn, because computers are not digital audio recording devices, they are not required to comply with the SCMS requirement and thus need not send, receive, or act upon information regarding copyright and generation status. *See* 17 U.S.C. Section 1002(a)(2) . . . MP3 files generally do not even carry the codes providing information regarding copyright and generation status. . . . Thus, the Act seems designed to allow files to be "laundered" by passage through a computer, because even a device with SCMS would be able to download MP3 files lacking SCMS codes from a computer hard drive, for the simple reason that there would be no codes to prevent the copying. . . .

Even though it cannot directly reproduce a digital music recording, the Rio would nevertheless be a digital audio recording device if it could reproduce a digital music recording "from a transmission." 17 U.S.C. Section 1001(1).

The term "transmission" is not defined in [the] Act, although the use of the term in the Act implies that a transmission is a communication to the public. *See id.* Section 1002(e) (placing restrictions upon "any person who transmits or *otherwise communicates to the public* any sound recording in digital format") (emphasis added). In the context of copyright law (from which the term appears to have been taken), "to 'transmit' a performance or display is to communicate it by any device or process whereby images or sounds are received beyond the place from which they are sent." 17 U.S.C. Section 101 . . . . The parties really do not dispute the definition of transmission, but rather, whether *indirect* reproduction of a transmission of a digital music recording is covered by the Act. . . .

While the Rio can only directly reproduce files from a computer hard drive via a cable linking the two devices (which is obviously not a transmission), the Rio can indirectly reproduce a transmission. For example, if a radio broadcast of a digital audio recording were recorded on a digital audio tape machine or compact disc recorder and then uploaded to a computer hard drive, the Rio could indirectly reproduce the transmission by downloading a copy from the hard drive. Thus, if indirect reproduction of a transmission falls within the statutory definition, the Rio would be a digital audio recording device. . . .

The Senate Report states that "a digital audio recording made from a commercially released compact disc or audio cassette, or *from a radio broadcast* of a commercially released compact disc or audio cassette, would be a 'digital audio copied recording.'" . . . Thus, a device falls within the Act's provisions if it can indirectly copy a digital music recording by making a copy from a transmission of that recording. Because the Rio cannot make copies from transmissions, but instead can only make copies from a computer hard drive, it is not a digital audio recording device.

[The court of appeals thus sustained the holding of the district court denying injunctive relief against the defendant.]

CASE QUESTIONS

1. Isn't a device that downloads audio files within the ambit of a "transmission" under the act?
2. Didn't Rio intend that the audio file be transmitted from its site to the recipient having access capability?
3. Did Congress intend the statute to be so narrowly construed?

ANTITRUST DIMENSIONS OF COPYRIGHT

The Copyright Act grants the holder of a copyright a number of exclusive rights. Does it permit a holder to violate the antitrust statutes? *United States v. Microsoft,* 87 F. Supp. 2d 30 (D.D.C. 2000) (discussed in Chapter 11) presented the court with the claim by Microsoft that as a holder of a valid copyright in software it had the absolute right to prevent licensees from shipping modified versions of its Windows 95 and 98 (without the Internet Explorer program) without its express permission. It had required all Windows programs to install the program and place an icon on the Windows screen. The court disagreed with Microsoft. It stated:

> It is also well settled that a copyright holder is not by reason thereof entitled to employ the perquisites in ways that directly threaten competition. . . . " The court has held many times that power gained through some natural and legal advantage such as a . . . copyright . . . can give rise to liability if a 'seller exploits his dominant position in one market to expand his empire into the next.' " . . . [A] copyright does not exempt its holder from antitrust inquiry where the copyright is used as part of a scheme to monopolize. . . . " Neither the aims of intellectual property law, nor the antitrust laws justify allowing a monopolist to rely upon a pretextual business justification to mask anticompetitive conduct." . . . Even constitutional privileges confer no immunity when they are abused for anticompetitive purposes.

The court found that the true impetus for Microsoft's restrictions concerning the compelled installation and carrying of the Internet Explorer program was not to preserve the integrity of the Windows platform but to prevent the preinstallation of middleware such as the Netscape Navigator program.

INTERNATIONAL DIMENSIONS OF COPYRIGHT

In addition to efforts made in the United States, major world bodies are initiating their own programs to combat international computer crime, including violation of intellectual property laws. These efforts are vitally important because computer crimes know no boundaries. Many hackers have taken advantage of the inability of law enforcement personnel to enforce domestic laws because of the variations in procedural and substantive safeguards attendant to them. These variations, in the past, have prevented extradition of hackers who have caused significant interruptions of business and government activities.

Included among the efforts commenced internationally are those initiated by the World Trade Organization, the Council of Europe, the Organization for Economic Cooperation and Development, the United Nations, and other world bodies. Many international conferences, attended by most of the leading industrial nations, have been convened and are being arranged to address the issues and problems caused by persons using electronic means to circumvent civil and criminal laws protecting intellectual property. Significant discussions of intellectual property rights topics have taken place, especially those arising out of the Uruguay Round of the General Agreement on Tariffs and Trade.

Berne Convention for the Protection of Literary and Artistic Works (1971)

The Berne Convention was originally enacted in 1886. The latest version of the convention is the one adopted in Paris in July 1971, to which over 120 countries are members. The aim of the convention is to protect the rights of authors in their literary and artistic works (Article 1). *Literary and artistic works* are defined as including:

Every production in the literary, scientific and artistic domain, whatever may be the mode or form of its expression, such as books, pamphlets and other writings; lectures, addresses, sermons and other works of the same nature; dramatic or dramatico-musical works; choreographic works and entertainments in dumb show; musical compositions with or without words; cinematographic works to which are assimilated works expressed by a process analogous to cinematography; works of drawing, painting, architecture, sculpture, engraving and lithography; photographic works to which are assimilated works expressed by a process analogous to photography; works of applied art; illustrations, maps, plans, sketches and three-dimensional works relative to geography, topography, architecture or science. (Article 2(1))

Rights Granted to Authors. As stated before, the Berne Convention sets forth a minimum number of rights that member states (a *state* in international law refers to a country) are to accord authors and allows states considerable freedom to decide the general and specific categories of works that are not protected unless fixed in some material form. Rights include the authorization of translation of the works, reproduction, broadcasting of the works, public recitation, adaptations, arrangements and other alterations, cinematographic adaptation and reproduction, and other rights granted by state law. States must extend protection to collections, such as encyclopedias and anthologies (Article 11).

A number of additional areas of possible protection, such as official government publications, applied art, and industrial designs and models are left to the individual states to determine. News of the day, factual data that constitute items of press information, political speeches, works in the public domain, and statements made in legal proceedings are not protected.

Duration. The term of protection is the life of the author plus 50 years commencing the first day of the new year after the date of death. For cinematographic works, the term is 50 years from its initial availability to the public with consent of the author, or 50 years after the making of such a work, whichever is later. For anonymous or pseudoanonymous works, the term is 50 years after lawful availability to the public. U.S. law added 20 more years to the said terms of duration, as the convention permits individual member states to grant a term in excess of the said terms. Joint-ownership works have their terms measured from the life of the death of the last surviving author (Article 7).

Protection to Foreign Authors. The protection of the Berne Convention extends to works of authors of other member states whether such works are or are not published and to authors of nonmember states who have published their works therein. Such protection is available without any formalities and is independent of the rights accorded to authors in the country of origin. Thus, if the author's own country did not afford protection of works covered under the convention, the author would have protection in the countries belonging to the convention, although member states can invoke the principle of reciprocity and limit protection to foreign authors to the degree of protection that the home state affords to the member state's authors. Publication excludes public performance of dramatic or musical works and public recitation of literary and artistic works, as well as exhibition of a work of art. Of course, individual states may give protection to such performances (Article 5).

Moral Rights. An author, irrespective of any economic rights he or she may have, has the right to claim authorship of a work and to object to the distortion or other mutilation of the work that would be prejudicial to the author. Such rights are extended to the copyright holder after the author's death, at least until the cessation of economic rights (Article 6).

Omissions. The Berne Convention does not provide an enforcement mechanism for breach of the rights of authors. It merely provides that member states are to enact "domestic law to give effect to the provisions of this Convention." There is no stated penalty for countries not abiding by the provisions of the convention. Seizures of infringing copies of works are authorized by the convention, but it is left to domestic law for enforcement. In fact, developing countries are given considerable leeway in enacting protective laws in accordance with their social, economic, and cultural situations. The enforcement is apparently left to individual countries, such as the United States, which may impose economic and other sanctions for violations of the intellectual property rights of its nationals.

Agreement of Trade-Related Aspects of Intellectual Property Rights

TRIPS is an annex to the Final Act Embodying the Results of the Uruguay Round of Multilateral Trade Negotiations at Marrakesh on April 15, 1994, which established the World Trade Organization. It is a significant addition to global protection for all forms of intellectual property. Inasmuch as almost all of the major trading nations are members of what was formerly known as the General Agreement of Tariffs and Trade (GATT), the agreement now binds all of these states. It explicitly recognizes the need to have a multilateral solution to the problem of counterfeit goods in international trade and the recognition that intellectual property rights are private rights. The agreement is administered by the World Intellectual Property Organization (WIPO).

The agreement calls for the recognition and enforcement of the following fundamental principles.

National Treatment. Each member state is to accord all other member states treatment no less favorable than that accorded to its own nationals with respect to the protection of intellectual property rights, subject to exceptions if any in other intellectual property rights treaties (Article 3).

Most-Favored Nation Treatment. Every member state is to grant the same advantage, favor, privilege, or immunity to nationals of all other member states that such state accords to the nationals of any other state. There are exceptions for agreements concerning judicial assistance, such as extradition and the like, other intellectual property rights (IPR) agreements, and the rights of performers, producers of phonograms, and broadcasting organizations (Article 4).

Copyright Protections. A number of provisions of TRIPS apply directly to copyrights. Member states are mandated to comply with the major articles of the Berne Convention of 1971, except those relating to moral rights. The latter exception was apparently due to U.S. objection, inasmuch as the United States provides for such rights only with respect to pictorial, graphic, and sculptural works under Section 113 of the U.S. Copyright Act. As in other conventions and statutes, the agreement provides that copyright protection is accorded to expressions of ideas and is not accorded to ideas, processes, methods of operation, or mathematical concepts (Article 9).

Computer programs are to be protected as "literary works" under the Berne Convention of 1971. Compilations of data or other material in machine-readable form or other formats are to be given protection under TRIPS. Such protection does not extend to the data or material itself unless it is otherwise protected (Article 10).

Authors and successors in title shall have the right to authorize or prohibit the commercial rental of their works, whether originals or copies, with exceptions for cinematographic works and computer programs if the program is not the essential part of the rental (Article 11).

Duration. The term of protection, other than for a photographic work or work of applied art, extends to a term no less than life plus 50 years or 50 years from the making if not calculated on the life of a natural person (e.g., a corporation or partnership entity). Countries may extend a greater term of protection (Article 12).

Protection of Performers, Producers of Phonograms (Sound Recordings), and Broadcasting Organizations. Performers may prevent without authorization the fixation of a live performance and its reproduction. Producers of such shows may also authorize or prohibit the direct or indirect reproduction of their sound recordings. Broadcasting organizations may prohibit without permission the reproduction and rebroadcasting of their programs (Article 14).

The North American Free Trade Agreement

The North American Free Trade Agreement (NAFTA) is the free trade agreement among the United States, Canada, and Mexico. It succeeded the prior free trade agreement between the United States and Canada. It entered into force on January 1, 1994. The articles of NAFTA reflect the same terms and conditions as TRIPS. In addition, the parties agree, at a minimum, to the provisions of the Geneva Convention for the Protection of Producers of Phonograms Against Unauthorized Duplication of Their Phonograms of 1971, the Berne Convention for the Protection of Literary and Artistic Works of 1971, the Paris Convention for the Protection of Industrial Property of 1967, and the International Convention for the Protection of New Varieties of Plants of 1978 or the International Convention for the Protection of New Varieties of Plants of 1991.

There appears to be little doubt that the major reason for the addition of Mexico to the newly created NAFTA was the acceptance by Mexico of the obligations to adhere to the protection of intellectual property rights under the agreement.

CONCLUSION

We live in a society where technological advances in communication are more pronounced than since the invention of the printing press. The Internet has made the accessibility of knowledge instantaneous and global. The sources of information are as finite as the number of persons using it. The difficulty is that the use by such vast numbers inevitably leads to abuse by the few persons who would take copyrighted materials and convert them, without financial reward to the owners of the copyright. The laws presently addressing the main issues herein are not adequate because they inevitably create enormous controversy among the users of the Internet. No one wants government intervention, but, unless we eliminate copyright protection, breach of copyrighted material will continue almost unabated. President Clinton's panel took significant first steps to address the issues raised by the new technologies. These are but first steps because the technology is advancing so quickly that when action is taken, the changes will have already created a need for further regulation. The eventual outcome cannot be predicted.

Questions and Problems

1. It is generally considered to be fair use of a copyright for a professor to show a legally acquired movie in class as part of the lecture. If the same professor were to show the movie to students in different parts of the globe through distance learning, would he or she be in violation of the Copyright Act?
2. How did the World Intellectual Property Organization Copyright Treaty cause a change in U.S. law?
3. If an invention is made that allows copying of literary works at almost no cost, would the courts permit the sale of such invention? Discuss in your answer the significance of lawful versus unlawful uses of the machine or process.
4. Compare the duration of a copyright under U.S. law and under international conventions. Do you believe that lawful protection should be given for such extended periods of time?
5. May an Internet service provider violate the copyright laws? What would cause such a provider to become subject to civil and criminal prosecution?
6. Northern Music sued for copyright infringement of a musical composition known as "Tonight He Sailed Again." The music was written in 1942 and later extended into a number of revisions. The words and music were filed with the Copyright Office in 1944. Thereafter, the song "I Love You, Yes I Do" was recorded by the defendants. There was considerable similarity between the two songs. The defendants claim that the plaintiff's song may have incorporated musical sequences used by other songwriters. Is this a valid defense? What elements do you believe are necessary to establish infringement? Does a song with considerable similarity to a copyrighted work but that was written independently without apparent knowledge of the protected work violate the copyright? *Northern Music Corp. v. King Record Distributing Co.,* 105 F. Supp. 393 (S.D.N.Y. 1952).
7. Kelly is a photographer who specialized in photos of the California gold rush country in connection with the works of Laura Ingalls Wilder. The photos are not sold independently but have appeared in a number of books. He also maintains a Web site providing a virtual tour of California's gold rush country that promotes plaintiff's books and a Web site that markets corporate retreats in the said area. In January 1999, some 35 of plaintiff's images were indexed by

the Ditto crawler and placed in defendant's image database. The images were available in thumbnail form to users of defendant's visual search engine. Plaintiff claims copyright infringement as well as violation of the Digital Millennium Copyright Act. Decide. *Kelly v. Arriba Soft Corp.,* 77 F. Supp. 2d 1116 (C.D.Ca. 1999).

8. Plaintiff sued defendants alleging copyright infringement and other claims. Plaintiff was a longtime member, and was later on the board of directors, of the Gay Male S/M Activists (GMSMA). He possessed certificates of registration for a number of photographs depicting exhibits displayed at various GMSMA events. In 1988, plaintiff provided GMSMA with some of the photographs that were used by the organization in its organizational literature over a period of several years. Plaintiff had not been hired to take the photographs by GMSMA, nor did he transfer the copyright to it. In early 1995, two of the photographs were given by one of the individual defendants to a writer for inclusion in a magazine. The transfer was in violation of the organization's policy that limited use of the photographs for the organization's internal use. The writer of the article was not aware of the plaintiff and did not give credit to him for the use of the photographs. The organization also put out fliers using a photograph taken by plaintiff without attribution. In addition, other photographs were posted on the organization's Web site. Decide. *Scanlon v. Gay Male S/M Activists,* 11 F. Supp. 2d 444 (S.D.N.Y. 1998).
9. Tasini and a number of other freelance authors wrote articles for various newspapers and magazines including the *New York Times, Time, Inc.,* and other well-known publications. They were independent contractors for their services and at no time consented to the placement of their articles in an electronic database. The defendant publishers entered into a licensing agreement with LEXIS/NEXIS, permitting the articles to be placed in the LEXIS/NEXIS database. In addition, the New York Times Company permitted University Microfilms to reproduce the *New York Times* articles, including the plaintiffs' works, on two CD-ROMs. The authors of the articles said that their copyrights were infringed under the Copyright Act. The publishers defended the litigation, stating that the works constituted *collective works.* As such, they claimed that they had the exclusive ownership of the collective works of which the authors' products were a part, and that they had the right to reproduce them without said authors' consent. Decide. *New York Times Co., Inc.* [defendants-appellants] *v. Tasini* [plaintiffs-appellees], 533 U.S. ___ (June 25, 2001).
10. As set forth in the Napster case in Chapter 6, the claim was that Napster was liable for contributory and vicarious infringement of the copyrights held by music companies and others for permitting users to exchange music files by use of the MP3 technology. Napster asserted: (1) that the users of its site were protected by the Audio Home Recording Act of 1992; and (2) that its liability was limited by the Digital Millennium Copyright Act. The pertinent portion of the Audio Home Recording Act, Section 1008, states:

    No action may be brought under this title alleging infringement of copyright based on the manufacture, importation, or distribution of a digital audio recording device, a digital audio recording medium, an analog recording device, or an analog recording medium, or based on the noncommercial use by a consumer of such a device or medium for making musical recordings or analog musical recordings.

    The Digital Millennium Copyright Act, Section 512, limits liability for Internet service providers by affording a safe harbor from copyright infringement suits. What is your opinion on each of these defenses asserted by the defendants? *A&M Records, Inc. v. Napster, Inc.,* 239 F. 3d 1004 (9th Cir. 2001).

Endnotes

1. *NYU Starts For Profit Unit to Sell On-line Classes,* The Chronicle of Higher Education (October 16, 1998) p. A32.
2. *Top Business Schools Seek to Ride a Bull Market in On-line M.B.A.'s,* The Chronicle of Higher Education (January 15, 1999) p. A27.

3. See the warning of J. Bernard Machen, President of the University of Utah, who said that online curriculum cannot offer the advantages of a university setting. *U. of Utah President Issues a Pointed Warning About Virtual Universities,* The Chronicle of Higher Education (October 9, 1998) p. A32.
4. Exec. Order No. 12864, 3 C.F.R. 634 (1993), cited in the Conference on Fair Use, *Report to the Commissioner on the Conclusion of the First Phase of the Conference on Fair Use* (September, 1997) p. 1. The Report (referred to as Guidelines) will be cited extensively hereinafter.
5. Id. A complete list of the participating organizations can be found in pp. 23–24 of the Guidelines.
6. Id. at p. 12.
7. Id. at p. 49.
8. See 17 U.S.C. Section 110(1)(2).
9. Conference on Fair Use, Guidelines, pp. 51–53. The copyright section allowing 30 copies is 17 U.S.C. Section 112(b).
10. Conference on Fair Use, Guidelines, p. 53.
11. Id. at p. 40.
12. Defined as "nonprofit organizations whose primary purpose is supporting the nonprofit instructional, research, and scholarly activities of educators, scholars, and students. . . . " Id. at p. 39.
13. Id., 2.1–2.3 at pp. 40–41.
14. Id., 2.3.1. *Educators* are defined as "faculty, teachers, instructors, curators, librarians, archivists, or professional staff who engage in instructional, research, or scholarly activities for educational purposes . . ." at p. 40.
15. Id., 2.3.2–2.3.3 at p. 41.
16. Id., 2.4.1–2.4.2 at p. 42.
17. Id., 3.2 and 3.4 at pp. 42–43.
18. Id., 5.1–5.7 at pp. 43–44.
19. Id. Sections 2.1 and 3.1.
20. Id. Section 3.2–3.4.
21. Id. Section 4.1–4.3.
22. Id. Section 5.1–5.3.
23. Id. Section 6.2–6.6.
24. Pub. L. No. 105-304, 112 Stat. 2860 (Oct. 28, 1998).
25. Section 1201 amending Section 103 of the Copyright Act.
26. To *circumvent technological measures* means "to descramble a scrambled work, to decrypt an encrypted work, or otherwise to avoid, bypass, remove, deactivate, or impair a technological measure, without the authority of the copyright owner" (Section 1201(a)(3)(A)).
27. 17 U.S.C. Section 1001 et seq.

CHAPTER

8 TRADEMARKS, DOMAIN NAMES, AND CYBERSQUATTING

Chapter Contents

A trademark, in addition to copyrights, is another form of intellectual property that the law protects. A trademark differs substantially from a copyright. A *trademark* is a unique sign or symbol representing a product, service, or organization. The term of protection for the different forms in intellectual property rights also differs greatly. Most copyrights have a protective term of life of the creator plus 70 years, but a trademark has a potentially unlimited life, in indefinite 10-year renewable terms.

TRADEMARKS

Purpose

The purpose of trademark protection is to enable a person or organization to use a symbol or other designation to represent it. The Mercedes symbol or the unique configuration of letters of the alphabet, such as those used by McDonald's restaurants or Kellogg's cereals, conveys to most persons a representation of quality, taste, or other special attributes. It is meant also to protect consumers by preventing copycats from discounting look-a-like products of inferior quality with the same or confusingly similar sign or symbol. Many companies spend a great deal of money and effort to create excellent products or to perform services symbolized by a logo. Without legal protection, any other person can bypass such efforts and expenditures by using the logo and mislead purchasers who believe they have purchased the products or services from the original organization. The Trademark Act of 1946, as amended, was passed by Congress to protect consumers from the ensuing confusion and deception. The key provisions governing infringement and unfair competition that set forth the major purpose of the act are:

(Trademark Infringement) Section 1114 (Lanham Act Section 32)

(1) Any person who shall, without the consent of the registrant—

(A) use in commerce any reproduction, counterfeit, copy, or colorable imitation of a registered mark in connection with the sale, offering for sale, distribution, or advertising of any goods or services on or in connection with which such use is likely to cause confusion, or to cause mistake, or to deceive; . . . shall be liable in a civil action by the registrant for the remedies hereinafter provided.

(Unfair Competition) Section 1125 (Lanham Act Section 43)

(a) Civil action

(1) Any person who, on or in connection with any goods or services, or any container for goods, uses in commerce any word, term, name, symbol, or device, or any combination thereof, or any false designation or origin, false or misleading description of fact, or false or misleading representation of fact, which—

(A) is likely to cause confusion, or to cause mistake, or to deceive as to the affiliation, connection, or association of such person with another person, or as to the origin, sponsorship, or approval of his or her goods, services, or commercial activities by another person, or

(B) in commercial advertising or promotion, misrepresents the nature, characteristics, qualities, or geographic origin of his or her or another person's goods, services, or commercial activities,

shall be liable in a civil action by any person who believes that he or she is or is likely to be damaged by such act.

The U.S. Supreme Court, in an oft-quoted passage, described the basic objectives of the Trademark Act as follows:

[T]rademark law, by preventing others from copying a source-identifying mark, 'reduce[s] the customer's costs of shopping and making purchasing decisions,' for it quickly and easily assures a potential customer that this item—the item with this mark—is made by the same producer as other similarly marked items that he or she liked (or disliked) in the past. At the same time, the law helps assure a producer that it (and not an imitating competitor) will reap the financial, reputation-related rewards associated with a desirable product. *Qualitex Co. v. Jacobson Prods. Co.*, 519 U.S. 159, 163–64 (1995)

A trademark is a limited property right. It is not a grant of a quasi monopoly right like a patent or a copyright. It identifies the source of goods or services. A person possessing a trademark uses it to identify and distinguish his or her goods from those manufactured by another. A person can capitalize on a market created by another person holding a trademark provided such action does not result in confusing the public into believing that the product or service is that of the competing person. A trademark holder cannot prevent another person from all use of words on the Internet. A person can use another person's trademark provided it is not used to identify the source of products. Thus, Playboy Enterprises, the holder of the trademarks Playboy and Playmate, does not prevent another person from using the said words. It is only when such usage causes another to believe that products containing the said words emanate from the trademark holder that the use of the trademark protected words or symbols violate the holder's rights.[1] Thus, in one case, a former Playboy Playmate was permitted to use the words *playboy* and *playmate* in her advertising on the Internet because there was no confusion with plaintiff's enterprise caused by such usage.[2]

Definition and Types of Marks

A *mark* is a generic word to signify a trademark, service mark, collective mark, or certification mark. It is governed by the Trademark Act of 1946, more popularly known as the Lanham Act as amended.[3] A *trademark* is defined as including "any word, name, symbol, or device, or any combination thereof—(1) used by a person, or (2) which a person has a bona fide intention to use in commerce . . . to identify and distinguish his or her goods, including a unique product, from those manufactured or sold by others and to indicate the source or the goods, even if that source is unknown."[4]

A *service mark* is one identifying and distinguishing the service of a person, including a unique service, from those of others. A *collective mark* is a trademark or service mark used by members of a cooperative, association, or other organization of members for use in commerce. A *certification mark* is a word, name, symbol, or device or combination thereof, used by a person or designee for use in commerce to certify the origin, material, mode of manufacture, quality, or other features of the goods or services or that the labor used was accomplished by members of a union or other organization.

A mark, upon registration with the Patent and Trademark Office, is prima facie evidence (constitutes proof unless otherwise shown not to be true) of: (1) the validity of the registered mark and of its registration; (2) the registrant's right to use commercially the registered mark; and (3) the exclusive right to use the mark in connection with goods or services stated in the registration (15 U.S.C. Section 1057(b)). Unregistered trademarks or service marks may also be protected when a person "uses in commerce any word, term, name, symbol, or device, or any combination thereof, or any false designation of origin, false or misleading description of fact, or false or misleading representation of fact, which . . . is likely to cause confusion" (Section 1125(a)(1)(A)).[5]

Classes of Marks

Marks may be divided into four classes: (1) fanciful or arbitrary; (2) suggestive; (3) descriptive; and (4) generic. A mark's distinctiveness is important in determining the protection to be given to trademarks. A *fanciful* mark is one composed of invented words such as *Clorox, Exxon,* and other such words. An *arbitrary* mark is one composed of commonly used words but are not suggestive of the quality or characteristic of the mark. Examples are Camel cigarettes and Apple computers. A *suggestive* mark is one that connotes a quality, ingredient, or characteristic of the goods without describing it. Examples are Playboy and Coppertone. It conveys a positive attribute, but a prospective user would not know the product represented by the mark.

A *descriptive* mark is not inherently distinctive but is one identifying a function, use, characteristic, size, or purpose of the product. To be given legal protection, it is necessary for the product to have a secondary meaning. A *secondary meaning* refers to when the primary significance of a product or term in the mind of the public is the identity of the particular source of the product rather than the product itself. Examples are the Yellow Pages telephone directory and After Tan post-tanning lotion.

A *generic* mark is one that identifies a class of product or service, irrespective of its source. It describes the thing itself rather than a feature or aspect of the product.[6] It does not receive protection under the Lanham Act. The following case contains a lengthy discussion of the nature of marks from which much of the prior discussion emanates. In particular, the court reviewed and applied the concept of generic mark to the facts of the case.

AMERICA ONLINE, INC. V. AT&T CORP.

64 F. Supp. 2d 549 (E.D.Va. 1999)

FACTS: America Online (AOL) is the world's largest interactive online service. For a decade, it used the expressions "YOU HAVE MAIL" and "YOU'VE GOT MAIL" in advising e-mail customers of such mail. It also used the logo of a U.S. mailbox with a red flag that pops up when the user has new e-mail. The expression "You've Got Mail," the mailbox logo, the IM mark, and BUDDY LIST were licensed to Warner Bros. for use in the movie "You've Got Mail." AOL also uses a registered service mark "BUDDY LIST" as a brand for real-time chat among persons using the AOL service. The latter service is called "IM." AT&T also provides Internet access and advertised an added feature known as "You Have Mail" and a "I M Here" instant messaging feature. AOL told AT&T to cease using the comparable words because of its usage for nearly a decade. At about the same time, AT&T advertised to potential customers the use of a Buddy List in connection with its I M Here Navigator window. AT&T refused to cease using the identical or similar words to those used by AOL. AOL sued requesting the court to issue an injunction against AT&T for violation of the Federal Trademark Dilution Act, trademark infringement, unfair competition and false designation of origin, and for other relief.

ISSUE: Were the expressions "YOU HAVE MAIL," "IM," "BUDDY LIST®," "YOU'VE GOT MAIL," and the mailbox logo generic?
DECISION: The Court determined that the expressions "YOU HAVE MAIL," "IM," and "BUDDY LIST" were generic and therefore were not protected by law.
REASONING: Judge Hilton
. . . A mark is generic when "it identifies a class of product or service, regardless of source" . . . "A generic term is one that refers, or has come to be understood as referring, to the genus of which the particular product is a species." . . . "A generic term is one commonly used to denote a product or other item or entity, one that indicates the thing itself, rather than any particular feature or exemplification of it." . . . Rather than answering the questions "Who are you?" and "Where do you come from?," generic marks tell the buyer what the product is. . . .

Generic marks never qualify for the protections of the Lanham Act; are not registrable; and a registered mark can be canceled at any time upon a finding that the mark is, or has become, generic. . . . A generic mark cannot receive trademark protection because "generic" and "trademark" are mutually exclusive terms. . . . Trademarks are used to distinguish a producer's goods and services from those of his competitors, while generic terms denote the product and the service itself, rather than the source, so they are in no way distinctive of the goods and services to which they are applied. . . .

Further, even if a producer or provider has achieved secondary meaning in its generic mark through promotion and advertising, the generic mark is still not entitled to protection because to allow protection would "deprive competing manufacturers of the product of the right to call an article by its name." . . .

"The existence of synonyms for a term does not mean the term is not generic. There may be more than one term which the consuming public understands as designating a category of goods." . . . ("Super Glue," "Instant Glue," and "Ten Second Glue" are all generic).

Also, when a common English word is used as a mark for its ordinary meaning, it cannot be appropriated for exclusive use because the mark is generic. . . . Based on plain meaning of the words "blinded" and "veteran," the phrase "Blinded Veterans" is generic for an association of once-sighted persons who served in the military. . . . "Consumer Electronics" is generic for electronic equipment purchased and installed by consumers and, therefore, "Consumers Electronics Monthly" is generic as a mark for a magazine title. . . .

To prevail on a trademark infringement claim under Section 1125 (for unregistered service marks), a plaintiff must both demonstrate "(1) that it has a valid and protectible [mark] and (2) that the defendant's use of the mark in question creates a likelihood of consumer confusion." . . .

The initial issue the Court must consider is into which of the four categories does the mark fit. . . . It has been said that "the lines of demarcation between the four classes . . . are not always bright." . . . To assist the Court in shedding some light on the lines of demarcation and determining whether the marks are generic, the Court is to employ what is known as the "primary significance" test. . . .

Under this test, a plaintiff who is seeking to establish a valid trademark must show "that the primary significance of the term in the minds of the consuming public is not the product but the producer." . . .

For marks which have been registered, Section 1057 provides the registrant with a presumption that the mark is valid, owned by the registrant, and that the registrant has an exclusive right to use the registered mark in commerce on or in connection with the goods or services specified in the certificate. 15 U.S.C. Section 1057(b). Hence, a party seeking cancellation of the mark due to genericness has the burden of establishing that fact by a preponderance of the evidence. . . .

To determine whether the primary significance of the mark is generic, the Court should consider the following: (1) competitor's use of the mark, (2) plaintiff's use of the mark, (3) dictionary definitions, (4) media usage, (5) testimony of persons in the trade, and (6) consumer surveys [citing *McCarthy on Trademarks and Unfair Competition*].

[The court then found each of the expressions to be generic and not protected by the Lanham Act. The one expression, BUDDY LIST, that was registered as a trademark, was ordered by the court to be canceled by the Trademark Office. There was abundant evidence that each of the expressions and words contained therein were used regularly in connection with the services provided irrespective of the Internet service provider utilized.]

CASE QUESTIONS

1. Do you agree with the Court that "IM," "BUDDY LIST," and "YOU'VE GOT MAIL" are generic expressions that are not protected by the Trademark Act? If so, why are letters of the alphabet, such as the *K* in Kelloggs cereals and other letters of the alphabet, protected by the Trademark Act? Should the pink color of a fiberglass company be also protected?
2. What distinguishes a generic word from very popular words, such as *xeroxing* and *jello*?

In *Image Online Design, Inc. v. Core Assc.,* No. CV 99-11347 RJK 2000 U.S. Dist. LEXIS 10259 (C.D.Ca. 2000), the court found *.web* to be generic. In discussing what is generic, the court said: "Generic marks refer to the 'genus of which the particular product or service is a species . . . the name of the product or service itself—what [the product] is, and as such . . . the very antithesis of a mark.' . . . In determining whether a term is generic, courts have often relied upon the 'who-are-you/what-are-you' test: A mark answers the buyer's questions 'Who are you?' 'Where do you come from?' 'Who vouches for you?' But the [generic] name of the product answers the question 'What are you?'" . . .

In *First Jewellery Company of Canada, Inc. v. Internet Shopping Network LLC,* 2000 U.S. Dist. LEXIS 794 (S.D.N.Y. 2000), plaintiffs sought an injunction for the alleged infringement of their registered trademark, FIRST JEWELLERY, by the defendant Internet Shopping Network (ISN). ISN operated a Web site under the domain name *www.firstjewelry.com* for the sale of jewelry to the public. The plaintiff disclaimed the right to use the word *jewellery* other than for the mark and not for any other purpose. With respect to the defense that the mark FIRST JEWELLERY was generic, the court held that it did not refer to the genus of which the particular product is a species and, thus, was not generic. The court discussed the requirements for a plaintiff to succeed in a Lanham Act lawsuit for trademark infringement. The plaintiff must prove that its mark is entitled to protection and that the defendant's use of its mark was likely to cause confusion with the plaintiff's mark.

The factors that a court will use in ascertaining whether there was confusion are:

(1) the strength of the plaintiff's mark; (2) the similarity of plaintiff's and defendant's marks; (3) the competitive proximity of the products; (4) the likelihood that plaintiff will "bridge the gap" and offer a product like defendant's; (5) actual confusion between products; (6) good faith on the defendant's part; (7) the quality of defendant's product; and (8) the sophistication of buyers.

The court decided in favor of the plaintiff by finding that the domain name *www.firstjewelry.com* was substantially the same as the plaintiff's trademark and would cause confusion, thereby causing irreparable injury to it.

Trademark Protection of Titles

In *Sugar Busters LLC v. Brennan,* 177 F.3d 258 (5th Cir. 1999), the issue was raised whether a title to a book can receive trademark protection. Plaintiff had a federally registered service mark, SUGARBUSTERS, and was the author of a best-selling diet book entitled *SUGAR BUSTERS! Cut Sugar to Trim Fat.* Defendants coauthored a cookbook, *SUGAR BUST for Life* and advertised it as a companion to the plaintiff's work.

The court of appeals, after noting that registrations of book titles as trademarks are consistently prohibited, nevertheless stated: "The descriptive nature of a literary title does not mean, however, that such a title cannot receive protection under Section 43(a) [of the Lanham Act]. In fact . . . it is well known that the rights in book titles are afforded appropriate protection under the law of unfair competition. . . . If the title of such a single work has acquired secondary meaning, the holder of the rights to that title may prevent the use of the same or confusingly similar titles by other authors. . . . It is clear that the title to a song cannot be copyrighted as such, or registered as a trademark. However, a title may be protected as a common law trademark if two elements are satisfied: the title has acquired 'secondary meaning,' and the allegedly infringing use of the title creates a substantial likelihood of confusion." The court said that the plaintiff must demonstrate a high degree of proof to establish secondary meaning. In the within case, "Plaintiff must show that its title 'SUGAR BUSTERS! Cut Sugar to Trim Fat' had developed secondary meaning at the time that defendants allegedly violated Section 43(a) by releasing their book, *SUGAR BUST for Life*!"

Application and Exceptions to Grant

The owner of a trademark for use in commerce must register it by filing an application with the Patent and Trademark Office, together with a drawing of the mark and payment of the appropriate fee. The mark must be either currently used in commerce or is to be used within six months from notice of allowance of the mark. The application for a trademark will be granted unless it consists of: (1) immoral, deceptive, or scandalous matters or falsely suggests a connection with another person, institution, or national symbol; (2) the flag or other insignia of the United States or other governmental entity; (3) name, portrait, or signature identifying a living individual or of a deceased president of the United States whose widow survived him and had not given consent; (4) a mark resembling a mark previously used by another person that has not been abandoned and is likely to confuse, mistake or deceive others; or (5) a mark that is merely descriptive or deceptively misdescriptive of the product, service, or is a surname only (Section 1052).

Nature of Protection

The essence of trademark protection is to prevent a likelihood of confusion by users of the products or services of the trademark owners or licensees. A person buying a product such as a particular brand of soda or perfume, may become confused unless he or she is able to distinguish the trademark protected brand from one that looks remarkably similar to the product. A person who travels abroad often encounters look-a-like products, such as alleged Rolex watches or other such products that are cheap imitations of the quality product sold under the brand name. Some of the factors that courts will weigh to determine whether likelihood of confusion exists are the similarity of the marks; the similarity of the goods; the relationship between the parties' channels of trade; the relationship between the parties' advertising; the classes of prospective purchasers; evidence of actual confusion; the defendant's intent in adopting its mark; and the strength of the plaintiff's mark.[7]

In *Digital Equipment Corp. v. Alta Vista Technology, Inc.* [ATI], 960 F. Supp. 456 (D.Mass. 1997), the U.S. district court was presented with the alleged violation of Digital's rights to the trademark by the defendant, which used the trademark AltaVista. Digital had launched a very successful Internet search service and had purchased the right to the said service mark from the defendant. The agreement provided that the defendant could use the name AltaVista as part of ATI's corporate name and as part of its Web site address, but ATI was precluded from using the name as a product or service offering. After the agreement was entered into, ATI changed the appearance of its Web site so as to have an appearance closely resembling that of Digital. The court weighed the factors illustrating confusion and found that the two marks were very similar, that there was an overlap of trade channels, advertisers, and markets, and that there was a high degree of a likelihood of confusion by ATI's use of the mark. Thus, it issued an injunction barring the unlawful usage.

Initial Interest Confusion. In *Checkpoint Systems, Inc. v. Check Point Software Technologies, Inc.*, 104 F. Supp. 2d 427 (D.N.J. 2000), the plaintiff sued for trademark infringement and unfair competition alleging that the defendant used the plaintiff's registered trademark Checkpoint. The plaintiff is a leading company in the field of retail security. It manufactured and distributed products under the mark, which products were designed to aid retailers in preventing losses by theft of merchandise and manage inventory and supply chain of products and merchandise. The defendant is a leading company in Internet-related field of protecting the electronic data flow in computer networks from electronic intrusion and monitoring the flow of data between the Internet and customer private intranets.

The court refused to issue an injunction barring defendant's use of the mark to identify its goods and services. The court said: "To establish likelihood of confusion, a plaintiff must prove that 'consumers viewing the mark would probably assume that the product or service it represents is associated with the source of a different product or service identified by a similar mark.'" Inasmuch as the parties were not in directly competing products, the court applied a 10-factor test to determine the likelihood of confusion (see *Playboy v. Universal,* presented previously) and whether there was liability for infringement and unfair competition. The court decided in favor of the defendant. It acknowledged that there was a similarity of the marks and that the plaintiff's mark was distinctive and strong (factors 1 and 2). The third factor of price of goods, sophistication of purchasers weighed heavily in favor of defendant inasmuch as the consumer who would purchase the high-end products would be very unlikely to confuse the products of the parties.

As to the fourth factor, or the evidence of actual consumer confusion, the court discussed the doctrine of *initial interest confusion.* It stated:

> The doctrine of initial interest confusion, adopted by numerous courts, recognizes that in some instances evidence that consumers initially mistake the source of a product may predict likelihood of confusion under the Lanham Act, even though that confusion is dissipated by the time of purchase. . . . It is acknowledged that, especially among competitors, if there is initial interest confusion, a sophisticated purchaser of expensive goods or services need only be confused at the time it is drawn into doing business with the junior user, for there to be infringement. "A Court may find infringement has occurred based on confusion that created initial customer interest, even if no final sale is completed as a result." . . . Where, however, the companies are non-competitors, initial interest confusion does not have the same consequences, because there is no substituted product from the junior user, and the senior user does not bear the prospect of harm. . . .
>
> A review of cases which have applied the initial interest doctrine indicates that the parties are either direct competitors . . . or strongly interrelated such that it could be expected that plaintiff would expand into defendant's market. . . . Other cases have also pointed out that one element of applicability of the initial interest confusion doctrine is an intent by the defendant to deceive.

The court then found there was some minor initial interest confusion but there was no evidence that anyone was confused in making the purchasing decisions. Also, there was no evidence of intent by the defendant to capitalize on plaintiff's goodwill. Other evidence of such confusion was weak. Thus, the factor was found in favor of the defendant. The court concluded on balancing the remaining factors that there was no likelihood of confusion and, thus, dismissed the action.

In *Northland Insurance Companies v. Blaylock,* Civ. No. 00-308 (DSD/JMM) (D.Minn. Sept. 25, 2000), the defendant, Blaylock, owned a yacht insured with the plaintiff. Unhappy with the result of the insurance company's alleged failure to pay for the full sum due and owing for damage to the yacht, Blaylock created Web sites with domain names *www.northlandinsurance.com* and *www.sailinglegacy.com.* Persons accessing the sites were told of the plaintiff's alleged abuses, including a lengthy recitation of defendant's dispute with the plaintiff concerning the damage claim.

In an action commenced by Northland Insurance under the Anticybersquatting Consumer Protection Act (ACPA) and for trademark infringement, the court refused to enjoin the defendant preliminarily from using the Web sites. The court found no evidence that any reasonable member of the buying public would conclude that the defendant's Web sites were affiliated with the plaintiff. As to the claim of initial interest confusion, the court noted that cases that applied the doctrine did so where the defendant had a commercial motive or incentive. There was no evidence that the defendant stood to gain materially or financially from the initial confusion caused by the sites. There was no trademark dilution or violation of the Anticybersquatting Consumer Protection Act because the use by the defendant was noncommercial and there was no bad faith intent to profit from the sale of the domain name to the plaintiff.

Is the use of a robot in an advertisement dressed to resemble a well-known television personality violative of her mark as a distinctive persona? The following action instituted by Vanna White discussed this issue.

WHITE V. SAMSUNG ELECTRONICS, INC.

971 F.2d 1395 (9th Cir. 1992)

FACTS: This action concerns Vanna White, the hostess of "Wheel of Fortune," a popular television game show. Because of her fame, she has marketed her identity to different advertisers. The defendant, Samsung, ran a series of advertisements prepared by the defendant, David Deutsch Associates, Inc., in a number of national and regional publications depicting a current popular culture item in a Twenty-First Century setting. The advertisements were humorous lampooning of present day culture. The advertisement at issue in this case for Samsung videocassette recorders showed a robot dressed in a wig, gown, and jewelry resembling Vanna White. The robot was posed next to a game board that was a replica of the Wheel of Fortune. The caption of the advertisement read "Longest-running game show. 2012 A.D." White did not consent to the ad and was not paid for it. The District Court dismissed the complaint. On appeal, the decision was reversed.

ISSUES: (1) Did the defendants violate the Trademark Act of 1946 (The "Lanham Act") as amended?

(2) Was parody a defense to the trademark claim?

DECISION: (1) The Court determined there was a violation of the statute.

(2) Parody was not a defense in the within action.

REASONING: Judge Weiner

III. THE LANHAM ACT

. . . The version of section 43(a) [of the Lanham Act] applicable to this case provides, in pertinent part, that "any person who shall . . . use, in connection with any goods or services . . . any false description or representation . . . shall be liable to a civil action . . . by any person who believes that he is or is likely to be damaged by the use of any such false description or designation." . . .

To prevail on her Lanham Act claim, White is required to show that in running the robot ad, Samsung and Deutsch created a likelihood of confusion . . . over whether White was endorsing Samsung's VCRs. . . .

[The court indicated that there were eight factors for determining whether a likelihood of confusion exists.]

1. strength of plaintiff's mark;
2. relatedness of the goods;
3. similarity of the marks;
4. evidence of actual confusion;
5. marketing channels used;
6. likely degree of purchaser care;
7. defendant's intent in selecting the mark;
8. likelihood of expansion of the product lines.

In cases involving confusion over endorsement by a celebrity plaintiff, "mark" means the celebrity's persona. . . . The "strength" of the mark refers to the level of recognition the celebrity enjoys among members of society. . . . If Vanna White is unknown to the segment of the public at whom Samsung's robot ad was directed, then this segment could not be confused as to whether she was endorsing Samsung VCRs. Conversely, if White is well-known, this would allow the possibility of a likelihood of confusion. . . . White's "mark" or celebrity identity, is strong.

[With respect to the remaining factors, the court found that White's "goods" were her televised performances; there was similarity with respect to the robot's resemblance to White; that, although there was no evidence of actual confusion between the robot and Vanna White, there was such a likelihood that White would appear as endorsing the VCRs; and it appears that the defendants did intend to profit by confusing customers as to her endorsement.]

IV. THE PARODY DEFENSE

In defense, defendants cite a number of cases for the proposition that their robot ad constituted protected speech. . . . Those cases involved parodies of advertisements run for the purpose of poking fun at Jerry Falwell and L.L. Bean, respectively. This case involves a true advertisement run for the purpose of selling Samsung VCRs. The ad's primary purpose: "buy Samsung VCRs." Defendants' parody arguments are better addressed to non-commercial parodies. The difference between a "parody" and a "knock-off" is the difference between fun and profit.

Second, even if some forms of expressive activity, such as parody, do rely on identity evocation, the First Amendment hurdle will bar most right of publicity actions against those activities. . . . In the case of commercial advertising, however, the First Amendment hurdle is not so high. . . . Realizing this, Samsung attempts to elevate its ad above the status of garden-variety commercial speech by pointing to the ad's parody of Vanna White, Samsung's argument is unavailing. . . . Unless the First Amendment bars all right of publicity actions—and it does not, . . . then it does not bar this case.

CASE QUESTIONS

1. The purpose of the Trademark Act is to prevent confusion in the minds of the public as to the origin of a particular product. In examining the eight factors stated by the court, do you believe that the average person would confuse the wigged robot for Vanna White? Is this the test for confusion?
2. Was the use of the robot image by Samsung a parody?

Relief for Violation

In the event a person wrongfully infringes upon the trademark rights of a holder, a court may entertain a variety of relief. Included are (1) issuance of an injunction to prevent continued violation of a holder's rights; (2) order for seizure of goods and counterfeit marks for use of a mark already registered with the U.S. Patent and Trademark Office; (3) recovery of defendant's profits; (4) damages incurred by the plaintiff trademark holder; (5) costs of the action; (6) destruction of the labels, signs, prints, and other such goods containing the infringing trademark; and (7) in exceptional cases, reasonable attorney fees of the prevailing party. For use of a counterfeit mark, the court may award treble (triple) damages plus reasonable attorney's fees.[8]

Preliminary Injunction. In trademark cases, a court may also order a preliminary injunction in order to stop an offending abuse of a protected mark. In the following action, the Disney Company found itself in the somewhat unusual position of being accused of trademark infringement rather than pursuing violators of its many trademarks.

GOTO.COM INC. V. WALT DISNEY COMPANY

202 F.3d 1199 (9th Cir. 2000)

FACTS: This case was an appeal of a preliminary injunction issued against Disney that prohibited it from using a logo confusingly similar to that of the plaintiff. GoTo operated a web site containing a pay-for-replacement search engine that allowed consumers to locate items on the Web. The GoTo logo consisted of the words "GO" and "TO" in a white font stacked vertically within a green circle. Disney prepared a web site to be known as the "GO" Network, which interconnected with other Disney sites. Disney commissioned a design firm to come up with a logo. The logo, that was produced and used, was very similar to that of the plaintiff. When the plaintiff complained to the defendant, Disney ignored the complaint and caused plaintiff to commence the within litigation.

ISSUE: Whether the lower court abused its discretion in granting a preliminary injunction barring Disney from using its logo?

DECISION: The Court upheld the lower Court's decision in favor of GOTO in granting the preliminary injunction.

REASONING: J. O'Scannlain

A plaintiff is entitled to a preliminary injunction in a trademark case when it demonstrates either (1) a combination of "probable success on the merits" and "the possibility of irreparable injury" or (2) the existence of "serious questions going to the merits" and that "the balance of hardships tips sharply in his favor." . . . To prevail on a claim under the Lanham Act, GoTo must establish that Disney is using a mark confusingly similar to its own, which it began using a year earlier. . . .

[In a footnote, the court said that Section 1114 (Section 32) of the Lanham Act covers only registered marks while Section 1125 (Section 43) of the Lanham Act protects against infringement of unregistered marks and trade dress as well as registered marks. Both sections are almost identical and require the same elements of proof.]

[The court recited Section 43(a)(1) of the Lanham Act.]

Neither party contests that GoTo is the senior user. The likelihood of confusion is the central element of trademark infringement, and the issue can be recast as the determination of whether "the similarity of the marks is likely to confuse customers about the source of the products." [The court reviewed the factors to determine whether a likelihood of confusion exists.] The first . . . factor—the similarity of the marks—has always been a critical question in the likelihood-of-confusion analysis. . . .

Because the similarity of the marks is such an important question, we must begin our analysis by comparing the allegedly infringing Disney logo to the GoTo mark. Obviously the greater the similarity between the two marks at issue, the greater the likelihood of confusion. We have developed certain axioms to guide this comparison: first, the marks must be considered in their entirety and as they appear in the marketplace; . . . second, similarity is adjudged in terms of appearance, sound, and meaning; . . . and third, similarities are weighed more heavily than differences. . . .

The likelihood of confusion is the central element of trademark confusion, and the issue can be recast as the determination of whether "the similarity of the marks is likely to confuse customers about the source of the products." . . . [The court then found that the logos were almost identical, calling them "glaringly similar."]

[As to the controlling consideration] that "related goods are generally more likely than unrelated goods to confuse the public as to the producers of the goods." . . . [Here,] the services offered by GoTo and Disney are very similar. Both entities operate as search engines and are, therefore, direct competitors on this score. . . . Both GoTo and Disney use the Web as a substantial marketing and advertising channel. . . .

From our analysis of the . . . factors, we conclude that GoTo has demonstrated a likelihood of success on its claim that Disney's use of its logo violates the Lanham Act. From this showing of likelihood of success on the merits in this trademark infringement claim, we may presume irreparable injury.

[The court then affirmed the grant of a preliminary injunction against the defendant, Walt Disney Company.]

CASE QUESTIONS

1. Compare the GoTo case with the earlier AOL case concerning "YOU'VE GOT MAIL." Is there a distinction? Why were the cases decided differently?
2. Was the addition of the similar coloring the deciding factor?

Conflicting Trademarks. In *Jeri-Jo Knitwear, Inc. v. Club Italia, Inc.*, 94 F. Supp. 2d 457 (S.D.N.Y. 2000), the plaintiff possessed a registered trademark ENERGIE in the United States. The defendants were the holders of valid trademarks for the ENERGIE mark in Italy, France, and Germany and had the right to sell ENERGIE apparel in many other countries. Defendants operated three Web sites, *www.misssixty.com, www.sixty.net,* and *www.energie.it.* All three servers are located in Italy but defendants used a U.S. company to register the first two sites in the United States. The *www.energie.it* site in Italy allows users to view its 1999/2000 collection of ENERGIE apparel. The remaining two sites contain a hyperlink to defendants' ENERGIE apparel, but they did not contain a display of defendant's infringing apparel.

On a motion to hold defendants in contempt for violating court orders preventing infringement of plaintiff's marks in the United States, the court held that there was no proof of monetary damage to the plaintiff, although it did award plaintiff counsel fees payable by the defendants. The court further ordered that the defendant de-link its *www.energie.it* site from its *www.misssixty.com* and *www.sixty.net* sites.

DOMAIN NAMES AND THE PROBLEM OF CYBERSQUATTING

The Domain Name System

A computer attached to the Internet is referred to as a *host.* To facilitate communication between hosts, each host has a numerical Internet Protocol (IP) address. The IP address consists of four groups of numbers separated by decimals. The first portion of the address is the *transfer protocol.* It is usually *http,* for hypertext transfer protocol. Each host has a unique domain name that cannot be duplicated in the Internet. A domain name is "any alphanumeric designation which is registered with or assigned by any domain name registrar, domain name registry, or other domain name registration authority as part of an electronic address on the Internet."[9] A fully qualified domain address consists of three elements, namely, a hostname, a domain name (e.g., *deltaairlines*) and a top-level generic domain (e.g., *.com*).[10] Thus, the domain name is an easy name to remember that, when entered into a search engine, becomes translated into a unique Internet Protocol (IP), which is then transmitted across the Internet.

To access the Internet, users apply programs known as Web browsers, such as Netscape and Mosaic. To connect onto a Web page, the user enters the uniform resource locator (URL), such as *http://www.pace.edu,* into a Web browser program. In the example, *http* is the hypertext transfer protocol, *www* is the World Wide Web, and *pace.edu* is the fully qualified domain name. The server then matches the domain name to the IP address of the domain name server and is relayed to the appropriate host computer. The top-level generic domain names (gTLDs) are: *.com* (for commercial users); *.edu* (for educational institutions); *.gov* (for governmental entities); *.biz* (commenced Oct. 1, 2001; *.info* (for ideas, product information and the like); *.org* (for organizations); *.mil* (exclusively for U.S. military); *.int* (for registering organizations established by treaty; and *.net* (for network service providers). Other gTLDs that are being considered for addition to the present ones are *.firm, .shop, .web, .arts, .rec,* and *.nom.*[11] The domain names are filed on a first-come, first-serve basis to anyone having at least two domain name servers (host computers with software capable of responding to domain name inquiries on a full-time basis with other computers on the Internet). The proposed domain names are filed with a domain name registration authority.

Historical Aspects. Initially, the list of assigned Internet numbers and names were maintained at the University of Southern California under contract with the Department of Defense Advanced Research Projects Agency (DARPA). Thereafter, the National Science Foundation (NSF) was given authority by Congress to maintain computer networks for research and educational institutions in the late 1980s. It contracted with IBM, MCI, and Merit to develop NSFNET, a high-speed network based on Internet protocols.

Congress authorized commercial activity on NSFNET in 1992. In the same year, the NSF entered into a cooperative agreement with Network Solutions, Inc. to be the exclusive registrar of Internet *.com, .net,* and *.org* top-level domains. As the Internet expanded exponentially, there was a growing demand for changes, including a demand for establishing competing top-level domain name registries. The call for significant changes in the registration system was due to: the dissatisfaction about the absence of competition in domain name registration; disputes between trademark holders and domain name holders; a demand for an aggressive management structure by commercial interests; demand by foreign Internet users for participation in the registration system; and the desire to keep the U.S. government out of the regulatory framework.[12]

1998 Changes. The present system is the result of an agreement between the U.S. Department of Commerce and Network Solutions, Inc. A Shared Registration System was established that provided for a competing unlimited number of registrars for domain name registration using one shared registry under NSI administration. In November 1998, a new corporation was formed and recognized by the U.S. Government, namely the Internet Corporation for Assigned Names and Numbers (ICANN). In 1999, it began accepting applications for entities that wish to become domain name registrars.[13] To date there are many registrars worldwide. There are no limits as to the number of registrars that may be accredited.

Dispute Resolution. Another major issue is that of dispute resolution. A problem faced by the NSI prior to the new system was the complaint made to it that domain names should be denied to persons seeking to use the names and goodwill of persons and companies. Often, the person filing the registration used names protected by trademarks or that were well-known names, with the express purpose of reselling them for a substantial profit. For example, a private person, Dale Ghent, a computer engineer, owns the Internet address *www.billgates.com.* He receives 70,000 e-mails a year intended for Bill Gates. The NSI practice of unilaterally making decisions, often barring or withdrawing usage of domain names by first filers, was unsatisfactory and often criticized by courts. The new ICANN has in place a new procedure designed to alleviate many of the complaints previously made under the prior system. A person contesting the registration of a domain name must state that:

(i) the domain name is identical or confusingly similar to a trademark or service mark in which the complainant has rights, including being confusingly similar to those activities in which the Complainant intends to pursue; and
(ii) the registrant has no rights or legitimate interests in respect of the domain name; and
(iii) the domain has been registered and is being used in bad faith.

Bad faith may be established by the following:

(i) circumstances indicating that the domain name was registered primarily for the purpose of selling, renting, or otherwise transferring the domain name to the Complainant who is the owner of the trademark or service mark, or to a competitor of that Complainant, for valuable consideration in excess of the costs relating to registering the domain name; or
(ii) the domain name was registered in order to prevent the Complainant from reflecting the mark in a corresponding domain name, provided that there is a pattern of such conduct; or
(iii) the domain name was registered primarily for the purpose of disrupting the business of the Complainant; or
(iv) the Registrant intentionally attempted to attract, for commercial gain, Internet users to his web site or other on-line location, by creating a likelihood of confusion with the Complainant's mark.

A Registrant may defend against a contest by establishing:

(i) the Registrant's use of, or demonstrable preparations to use, the domain name in connection with a bona fide offering of goods and services; or
(ii) the Registrant (as an individual, business, or other organization) has been commonly known by the domain name, even if he has acquired no trademark or service mark rights in the name; or
(iii) the Registrant is making a legitimate noncommercial or fair use of the domain name, without intent of commercial gain, to confuse consumers or to tarnish the trademark or service mark at issue.

Hyperlinks

A holder of a domain name places a Web page within a domain name and is able to receive inquiries. One may also use a *hyperlink,* which is a link on one site (generally in blue) to another site on the Internet. Among legal issues raised by domain names are: Does a person have an exclusive right to one's name especially if a trademark protects it? Does a corporation have a greater right in such an instance than private persons? Is government intrusion and regulation a danger to the free flow of ideas and data?

Users of the World Wide Web can surf other Web sites by use of hyperlinks; however, such surfing can raise legal issues such as:

1. Using another person's trademark or logo as part of the link by clicking onto highlighted text onto the second site
2. Linking of another person's site through the use of *framing* (linked site is brought into original linking site without the advertising or other data annexed to the linked site)
3. Using another person's mark in *metatags,* which is a hidden source code read by search engines in retrieving site per user's request

The problem is that the highlighted site includes trademarks owned by the second site's owners. Such unauthorized use may violate the U.S. Trademark Act (the Lanham Act), which makes unlawful the use of a protected mark when it is likely to cause confusion, mistake, or is deceiving as to the origin, sponsorship, or approval of the defendant's goods. It is subject to a fair use exception, which consists of use of a trademark to identify the plaintiff's (not the defendant's) goods or services.

In *Planned Parenthood v. Bucci,* 97 Civ. 0629 (KMW), 1997 U.S. Dist. LEXIS 3338 (S.D.N.Y. 1997), the defendant, a Catholic Radio host with antiabortion Web sites, registered the domain name plannedparenthood.com with Network Solutions, Inc. The effect of such registration was to permit the defendant to advertise an antiabortion book that was contrary to the plaintiff's program. The court granted the plaintiff's request for a preliminary injunction forbidding the defendant from using plaintiff's mark Planned Parenthood® or offering defendant's services in connection with the plaintiff's mark.

The court held that the Lanham Act was applicable in that the use of the domain name was "in commerce" by virtue of the fact that defendant's actions affected the plaintiff's ability to offer plaintiff's services and such use was conveyed to an international audience. Further, the use of plaintiff's mark created confusion to users seeking Planned Parenthood's services. The connection to defendant's Web site would lead to anger and frustration on the part of the users.

In *Image Online Design, Inc. v. Core Assc.*, No. CV 99-11347 RJK, 2000 U.S. Dist. LEXIS 10259 (C.D.Ca. 2000), plaintiff sued for common-law trademark infringement, claiming that it had exclusive rights to the service mark *.web*. It alleged that the defendants attempted to misappropriate plaintiff's mark by providing computer network addresses and domain name registry services using the *.web* mark. The court dismissed the lawsuit stating that *.web* does not indicate source to a potential registrant or visitor but indicates the type of services. "The Court finds that .web as used here, falls out of the ambit of trademark categorization. Further, even if it could be categorized, .web is simply a generic term for websites related to the World Wide Web."

THE FEDERAL TRADEMARK DILUTION ACT OF 1995

Prior to the passage of the Federal Trademark Dilution Act (FTDA) of 1995,[14] the essence of the protection was to prevent confusion in the minds of consumers as to the nature, ownership, and quality of the product. Thus, if there were no confusion by the use of a name, symbol, or other protection, then the party suing would not prevail. For example, few persons would be misled into believing that Cadillac dog food had any connection with the General Motors Corporation product. Owners of famous marks began petitioning Congress to extend trademark protection even where there was no such confusion. The claim was one of dilution of the trademark. Dilution is "the lessening of the capacity of a famous mark to identify and distinguish goods and services, regardless of the presence or absence of—(1) competition between the owner of the famous mark and other parties, or (2) likelihood of confusion, mistake, or deception."[15] Accordingly, the Trademark Dilution Act of 1995 amended Section 43(c) of the Trademark Act of 1946 as follows:

(c) Remedies for dilution of famous marks.
  (1) The owner of a *famous* [emphasis supplied] mark shall be entitled, subject to the principles of equity and upon such terms as the court deems reasonable, to an injunction against another person's commercial use in commerce of a mark or trade name, if such use begins after the mark has become famous and causes dilution of the distinctive quality of the mark, and to obtain such other relief as is provided in this subsection. In determining whether a mark is distinctive and famous, a court may consider factors such as, but not limited to—
    (A) the degree of inherent or acquired distinctiveness of the mark;
    (B) the duration and extent of use of the mark in connection with the goods or services with which the mark is used;
    (C) the duration and extent of advertising and publicity of the mark;
    (D) the geographical extent of the trading area in which the mark is used;
    (E) the channels of trade for the goods or services with which the mark is used;
    (F) the degree of recognition of the mark in the trading areas and channels of trade used by the mark's owner and the person against whom the injunction is sought;
    (G) the nature and extent of use of the same or similar marks by third parties; and
    (H) whether the mark was registered under the Act of March 3, 1881, or the Act of February 20, 1905, or on the principal register.

Exceptions to liability are for: (1) fair use for comparative advertising or promotional purposes to identify competing goods; (2) noncommercial use of the mark; (3) news reporting and commentary.

Trademark law issues of the ownership, entitlement of domain names, and dilution of the trademark were reviewed extensively in the following case.

INTERMATIC INC. V. TOEPPEN

947 F. Supp. 1227 (N.D.Ill. 1996)

FACTS: Intermatic sued Toeppen concerning the latter's use of the Internet domain name "Intermatic.com." The plaintiff claimed that Toeppen violated the Federal Trademark Infringement, the Federal Unfair Competition, and the Federal Trademark Dilution Act of 1995, which are part of the Lanham Act, as well as Illinois statutes.

Intermatic had been in business since 1892 and had 37 offices throughout the U.S. with sales of close to $1 billion for the past 8 years. Defendant, Toeppen, operated an Internet service provider and had registered 240 Internet domain names, including some the largest and best-known business entities like Delta Airlines and British Air. Toeppen sought to sell or license the domain names to the companies whose names he had registered. In the within action, Intermatic discovered Toeppen's use of its name and attempted to have Toeppen discontinue its use. The request was refused. Thus, Intermatic could not use its registered trademark name as a domain name.

ISSUE: ... [W]hether the owner of the Intermatic trademark may preclude the use of the trademark as an Internet domain name by defendant Toeppen, who had made no prior use of the Intermatic name prior to registering it as an Internet domain name?

DECISION: The Court held in favor of Intermatic, issuing a permanent injunction against the defendant Toeppen, holding that the trademark owner may so preclude such use.

REASONING: Judge Williams

Toeppen is what is commonly referred to as a cybersquatter.... These individuals attempt to profit from the Internet by reserving and later reselling or licensing domain names back to the companies that spent millions of dollars developing the goodwill of the trademark. While many may find patently offensive the practice of reserving the name or mark of a federally registered trademark as a domain name and then attempting to sell the names back to the holder of the trademark, others may view it as a service. Regardless of one's views as to the morality of such conduct, the legal issue is whether such conduct is illegal. Cybersquatters such as Toeppen contend that because they were the first to register the domain name through NSI it is theirs. Intermatic argues that it is entitled to protect its valuable trademark by preventing Toeppen from using "intermatic.com" as a domain name.

The practical effect of Toeppen's conduct is to enjoin Intermatic from using its trademark as its domain name on the Internet....

Intermatic's name and prior rights over Toeppen to use the INTERMATIC name are clear. Intermatic's first use of the INTERMATIC name and mark predates Toeppen's first use of "intermatic.com" by more than fifty years. Also, it is undisputed that Intermatic holds a valid registration for the trademark INTERMATIC.

... [T]he following seven factors should be weighed to determine if there is a likelihood of confusion: (1) the degree of similarity between the marks in appearance and suggestion; (2) the similarity of products or services for which the name is used; (3) the area and manner of concurrent use; (4) the degree of care to be exercised by consumers; (5) the strength of the complainant's mark; (6) actual confusion; and (7) an intent on the part of the alleged infringer to palm off his products as those of another....

[The court found that Toeppen's use of the domain name intermatic.com is similar to the plaintiff's mark, but there was no similarity between the products and services of the parties. Toeppen's page showed a map of the city of Urbana. As to area and manner of use, the court found that the plaintiff had not set up a Web page of its own and, in any event, could use another similar domain name to advertise its products. There was no evidence educed as to consumer behavior on the Internet and, thus, that was an issue to be tried at a later date. There was no question that the plaintiff's trademark was a strong mark, that is, that it coined or invented a word not previously used as a tradename or mark. Inasmuch as Intermatic failed to show actual confusion by consumers and failed to show unlawful intent by the defendant, the facts were left to a trial at a later date.]

. . . [T]he court holds that Toeppen's action in registering and using "intermatic.com" as a domain name violates section 43(c) of the Lanham Act and the Illinois Anti-Dilution Act because it lessens the capacity of a famous mark, Intermatic, to identify and distinguish goods and services as a matter of law. . . .

Section 43(c) of the Lanham Act, also known as the Federal Trademark Dilution Act of 1995 ("ACT"), became effective on January 16, 1996. . . . The new law benefits only "famous" trademarks . . . the Act provides that:

> The owner of a famous mark shall be entitled, subject to the principles of equity and upon such terms as the court deems reasonable, to an injunction against another person's commercial use in commerce of a mark or trade name, if such use begins after the mark has become famous and causes dilution of the distinctive quality of the mark. . . .

In order to state a cause of action under the Act a party must show that the mark is famous and that the complainant's use is commercial and in commerce which is likely to cause dilution. The statute defines "dilution" to mean "the lessening of the capacity of a famous mark to identify and distinguish goods or services, regardless of the presence or absence of (1) competition between the owner of the famous mark and other parties, or (2) likelihood of confusion, mistake, or deception." . . .

E. THE DILUTION STATUTES HAVE BEEN VIOLATED BY TOEPPEN

1. Intermatic Is a Famous Mark.

As a matter of law the Court finds that the Intermatic mark is famous within the meaning of Section 1125(c). Toeppen does not dispute that the Intermatic mark is famous and no evidence has been presented to contradict Intermatic's long history and use of its mark. The Intermatic mark is a strong fanciful federally registered mark, which has been exclusively used by Intermatic for over 50 years. Therefore since Intermatic has established that its mark is famous, it need only show that Toeppen's use is a commercial use in commerce and that by his use dilution will likely occur.

2. Toeppen Is Engaged in a Commercial Use of the Intermatic Trademark.

Toeppen argues that there has been no violation of the Federal Trademark Dilution Act because his use of the Intermatic mark is not a commercial use. . . .

The use of the first level designation ".com" does not in and of itself constitute a commercial use. . . .

[However] Toeppen's intention to arbitrage the "intermatic.com" domain name constitutes a commercial use. . . . Toeppen's desire to resell the domain name is sufficient to meet the "commercial use" requirement of the Lanham Act.

3. Toeppen's Use of the Internet Constitutes Commerce. . . .

The Court held that Toeppen's use was clearly "in commerce" inasmuch as the requirement should be liberally construed.

4. Toeppen is Causing Dilution of the Distinctive Quality of the Mark.

Toeppen's use of "intermatic.com" is likely to cause dilution of its mark. . . . Toeppen's conduct has caused dilution in at least two respects. First, Toeppen's registration of the intermatic.com domain name lessens the capacity of Intermatic to identify and distinguish its goods and services by means of the Internet. Intermatic is not currently free to use its mark as its domain name. This is not a situation where there were competing users of the same name by competing parties and a race to the Internet between them. This case involves one party, Intermatic, with a long history of trademark use, and a second, Toeppen, who has effectively enjoined Intermatic from using its trademark by the payment of $100 to register the "intermatic.com" domain name. This activity clearly violates the Congressional intent of encouraging the registration and development of trademarks to assist the public in differentiating products. . . . It would seriously undermine the trademark policy to prevent a company from exercising its mark by reason of Toeppen's conduct. Such conduct lessens the capacity of Intermatic to identify its goods to potential customers who would expect to locate Intermatic on the Internet through the "intermatic.com" domain name.

Second, Toeppen's conduct dilutes the Intermatic mark by using the Intermatic name on its web page. . . . "The harm caused by dilution is, for example, that the distinctiveness of the name [Intermatic] and the favorable association that accrued to it by virtue of [Intermatic's] commercial success would be undermined by the use of similar names in connection with other non-competing and non-confusing products." . . . If Toeppen were allowed to use "intermatic.com," Intermatic's name and reputation would be at Toeppen's mercy and could be associated with an unimaginable amount of messages on Toeppen's web page. . . .

Dilution of Intermatic's mark is likely to occur because the domain name appears on the web page and is included on every page that is printed from the web page. . . .

The fact that "intermatic.com" will be displayed on every aspect of the web page is sufficient to show that Intermatic's mark will likely be diluted.

CASE QUESTIONS

1. How did the Federal Trademark Dilution Act of 1995 affect the outcome of this case?
2. Prior to the act, there were a number of cases that held that a person could register the trademark name of a holder as a domain name so long as the use thereof did not interfere with such ownership and did not cause confusion as to the origin of the products or services of the holder. Would this case have been decided differently before the passage of the 1995 act?

In *Panavision Int'l. L.P. v. Toeppen,* 141 F.3d 1316 (9th Cir. 1998), the court of appeals applied the trademark dilution theory to enjoined Dennis Toeppen from using the domain name panavision.com and selling it to Panavision Corporation, which owned the Panavision trademark for movie cameras. The court held that Toeppen's squatting on the domain name diluted or lessened the capacity of the Panavision Corporation to identify and distinguish its goods or services. Thus, the requirement of the Federal Dilution Act of 1995 was met.

Playboy Enterprises has been the plaintiff in a number of lawsuits concerning its famous trademarks. The next case is illustrative of the litigation it has commenced against many other parties. The case states the elements necessary to prove (1) trademark infringement; (2) the likelihood of confusion; (3) trademark dilution; (4) counterfeiting; and (5) damages.

PLAYBOY ENTERPRISES, INC. V. UNIVERSAL TEL-A-TALK, INC.

No. 96-6961, 1998 U.S. Dist. LEXIS 17282, (E.D.Pa. 1998)

FACTS: Playboy Enterprises, Inc. ("P.E.I.") owns trademark registrations for the mark PLAYBOY and other marks through which merchandise is sold through licensees to over 50 countries. The trademark is well-known and has developed a secondary meaning. In addition, the plaintiff also owns and uses RABBIT HEAD DESIGN and BUNNY trademarks that appear on the magazine's masthead and on numerous merchandise sold to the public. Plaintiff also has Internet websites that receives some six million hits a day. One of the websites requires payment by users thereto.

The defendant created and maintained a number of websites. Plaintiff discovered that the defendant used the trademarks PLAYBOY and BUNNY to advertise its collection of sexually explicit photos and offered a subscription service called "Playboy's Private Collection." In addition, defendant utilized the plaintiff's trademarks in other capacities. All such usages by the defendant was without permission of the plaintiff, Playboy Enterprises. The decision to use the trademarks by the defendant corporation was made by the defendant, Huberman. Plaintiff did not prove any damages from the plaintiff's use of the trademarks and defendant apparently lost money on its websites.

ISSUE: Whether the defendants violated (1) plaintiff's PLAYBOY trademark; (2) the antidilution pro-

vision of the Lanham Act; and (3) whether defendant's activities constituted counterfeiting of plaintiff's registered trademark?
DECISION: The Court held in favor of the plaintiff as to all three violations.
REASONING: Judge McGlynn
[Plaintiff] PEI has alleged infringement of the PLAYBOY trademark under . . . the Lanham Act. . . . The test for infringement is . . . whether the alleged infringement creates a likelihood of confusion. . . .

(ELEMENTS OF PROOF OF TRADEMARK INFRINGEMENT)

In order to succeed on the merits, a plaintiff must establish that: (1) the marks are valid and legally protectible; (2) the marks are owned by the plaintiff; and (3) the defendants' use of the marks to identify goods or services is likely to create confusion concerning the origin of the goods and services. . . .

The trademark PLAYBOY has attained incontestable status. . . .

(ELEMENTS TO PROVE LIKELIHOOD OF CONFUSION)

In determining whether a likelihood of confusion exists, the court may take into account

> (1) the degree of similarity between the owner's mark and the alleged infringing mark; (2) the strength of owner's mark; (3) the price of the goods and other factors indicative of the care and attention expected of consumers when making a purchase; (4) the length of time the defendant has used the mark without evidence of actual confusion arising; (5) the intent of the defendant in adopting the mark; (6) the evidence of actual confusion; (7) whether the goods, though not competing, are marketed through the same channels of trade and advertised through the same media; (8) the extent to which the targets of the parties' sales efforts are the same; (9) the relationship of the goods in the minds of the public because of the similarity of function; (10) other facts suggesting that the consuming public might expect the prior owner to manufacture a product in the defendant's market.

Defendants' use of the words "Playboy" and "Bunny" in their website and in the identifying directories of defendants' URLs are identical to PEI's duly registered trademarks PLAYBOY and BUNNY. PEI's registered trademarks have previously been adjudicated as very strong. . . . Suggestive marks are entitled to protection without proof of secondary meaning. . . .

Even if secondary meaning were required, PEI has established that the PLAYBOY trademark and the RABBIT HEAD DESIGN trademark for adult entertainment goods and services have become famous, and have acquired significant secondary meaning such that the public has come to associate these trademarks with PEI.

Defendants intentionally adopted PLAYBOY and BUNNY trademarks in an effort to capitalize on PEI's established reputation in the PLAYBOY and RABBIT HEAD DESIGN marks. . . .

(DILUTION FACTORS)

Evidence of actual confusion is not required. . . . The consuming public is likely to believe the PEI is connected with defendants' hard core. . . . With respect to the dilution claim, dilution refers to the lessening of a mark's distinctiveness. Factors to be considered by the Court are: (1) similarity of the marks; (2) similarity of the products covered by the marks; (3) sophistication of customers; (4) predatory intent; (5) renown of senior mark; (6) renown of the junior mark; (7) the duration and extent of advertising of the mark; (8) the geographical extent of the trading area in which the mark is used; and (9) the nature and extent of use of the mark by third parties. . . . Applying the foregoing factors, the Court concludes that PEI has established its dilution claims with respect to the PLAYBOY trademark.

(ELEMENTS OF COUNTERFEITING)

PEI has also alleged that defendants' activities constitute counterfeiting of PEI's registered trademark PLAYBOY in violation of 15 U.S.C. Section 1116(d). In order to prove counterfeiting, a plaintiff must establish that the defendant (1) infringed a registered trademark in violation of 15 U.S.C. Section 1114(1)(a); (2) intentionally used the trademark knowing it was counterfeit or was willfully blind to such use. 15 U.S.C. Sections 1116(d), 1117(b); . . .

"Counterfeiting is the act of producing or selling a product with a sham trademark that is an intentional and calculated reproduction of the genuine trademark." . . .

A "counterfeit" is a "spurious mark which is identical with, or substantially indistinguishable from, a registered mark." 15 U.S.C. Section 1127. . . . [The court held both the defendant corporation and the defendant Huberman liable, the latter because of his decision to use the mark PLAYBOY and BUNNY and his approval of the work done on the Web site.]

(ELEMENTS OF DAMAGES)

The Lanham Act provides that a prevailing plaintiff who establishes infringement of its registered trademark is, subject to the principles of equity, entitled to recover (1) defendant's profits; (2) plaintiff's actual damages; and (3) costs of the action. . . . Nevertheless, when a violation of 15 U.S.C. Section 1116(d) is involved, plaintiff may elect to recover statutory damages. Statutory damages for counterfeiting are (1) not less than $500 or more than $100,000 per counterfeit mark per type of goods or services sold; or (2) if the Court finds that the use of the counterfeit mark was willful, not more than $1,000,000 per counterfeit mark per type of goods or services sold. 15 U.S.C. Section 1117(c).

[The court granted statutory damages of $10,000, reasonable counsel fees and costs, and a permanent injunction enjoining use of the trademark.]

CASE QUESTIONS

1. Compare *PEI* with the *Avery Dennison* and *Hasbro* cases to follow. Are the cases distinguishable?
2. Would the decision be the same if an antipornography group were to use the Playboy trademarks in a campaign to criticize the magazine and its stance concerning nudity?

A contrary result took place in *Avery Dennison Corp. v. Sumpton,* 51 U.S.P.Q. 2d 1801 (9th Cir. 1999), wherein the defendant also registered a number of domain names consisting of common surnames but using the *.net* rather than *.com* suffix. The plaintiff, an office-supply manufacturer, sued the defendant concerning the registration of the domain names Avery and Dennison. The court held in favor of the defendant, distinguishing the Panavision case by indicating that the defendant's use of *.net* showed a noncommercial use of the names under the statutory guidelines. Also, the failure of defendant to try to sell the domain name to Avery Dennison, and the failure of defendant to admit to the fame of plaintiff's trademark all weighed in his favor. The names "AVERY" and "DENNISON" allegedly were not well known outside of the office-products arena and were common surnames.[16]

A defendant's verdict was received also in *Hasbro Inc. v. Clue Computing Inc.*,[17] wherein the defendant registered the name clue.com for use as a network computing consulting firm. The plaintiff claimed the domain name diluted their trademark CLUE used as a board game. The court emphasized the apparent good faith filing by the defendant, its failure to try to sell the name to Hasbro, and the unrelated use of the name for defendant's services. The court recited the many companies worldwide holding the trademark CLUE for a variety of purposes, including for an educational magazine, for chocolate confectionery, for cosmetics, and for a fungicide. The court was very critical of Network Solutions, Inc., saying that its "policy is manifestly unfair, for reasons that are almost too numerous to count." The court agreed with some commentators that NSI imposed a contract on domain name applicants predicated on unequal bargaining power; that such contract was developed secretly and arbitrarily, and that it provided an almost irresistible opportunity for a latecomer seeking a domain name to obtain injunctive relief against the domain name holder.

THE ANTICYBERSQUATTING CONSUMER PROTECTION ACT OF 1999

In response to the continuing abuse of registering and using trademark names particularly in the filing and utilization of domain names, Congress passed the Anticybersquatting Consumer Protection Act. The act makes a person acting in bad faith who takes the name of a person or entity that has a trademark with respect thereto liable to such person civilly for damages incurred as a result of the taking. Section 3002 amends Section 43 of the Trademark Act of 1946[18] by listing the factors establishing bad faith. They are as follows:

(d)(1)(A) A person shall be liable in a civil action by the owner of a mark, including a personal name which is protected as a mark under this section, if, without regard to the goods or services of the parties, that person—

(i) has a bad faith intent to profit from that mark, including a personal name which is protected as a mark under this section; and

(ii) registers, traffics in, or uses a domain name that—

(I) in the case of a mark that is distinctive at the time of registration of the domain name, is identical or confusingly similar to that mark;

(II) in the case of a famous mark that is famous at the time of registration of the domain name, is identical or confusingly similar to or dilutive of that mark; or

(III) is a trademark, word, or name protected by reason of section 706 of title 18, United States code, or section 220506 of title 36, United States Code.

The nonexclusive factors in determining bad faith are:

1. Whether the domain name consists of a trademark or other intellectual property rights
2. The extent to which the domain name is the legal name or commonly used name of the person
3. The prior use of the domain name in connection with a bona fide offer of goods and services
4. The noncommercial or fair use of the mark accessible under the domain name
5. Intent to harm the goodwill represented by the mark for commercial gain, intent to tarnish or disparage the mark, or to create confusion as to the mark
6. The offer to sell or transfer the domain name for financial gain without prior use for bona fide offering for goods and services
7. The submission of material or false information when applying for registration of the domain name
8. The registration of multiple domain names identical to or similar to other marks
9. The extent to which the mark in the domain name is not distinctive and famous

With some exceptions, the statute also imposes civil liability against any person registering a domain name consisting of the name of another living person without consent with the intent to profit by selling the said name for financial gain. Presumably, billgates.com or other such name would fall under this category. The successful plaintiff may elect to recover actual damages and profits for such wrongful use of a domain name or receive statutory damages of no less than $1,000 and no more than $100,000 per domain name as the court may determine.[19]

Whether the latest amendment to the Trademark Act of 1946 would reverse the basis for the *Avery Dennison* and *Hasbro* decisions remains in doubt. Courts may continue to find noncommercial or nonextortionate bases for upholding defendants' rights to domain names that are similar or identical to trademark names. Obviously, an attempted sale of a domain name to a trademark owner may establish bad faith, but cases wherein the defendant registers a common name for purposes not similar to the trademark holder may result in a contrary decision. The statute specifically says that bad faith "shall not be found in any case in which the court determines that the person believed and had reasonable grounds to believe that the use of the domain name was a fair use or otherwise lawful."

In *Virtual Works, Inc. v. Volkswagen of America, Inc.,* 106 F. Supp. 2d 845 (E.D.Va. 2000), the U.S. district court enjoined the plaintiff Internet service provider from using the domain name of VW.NET, which it had registered with Network Solutions, Inc. in 1996. The owners of the site used it for their business and had intended to sell the site to Volkswagen, the owner of the VW trademark, for a substantial sum of money. The district court, as affirmed by the court of appeals, found that the within case violated the statute stated previously. There was a finding of bad faith in the registration of the VW mark. The court found that the filing of the famous mark coupled with an intent to sell the mark at a later date for a substantial sum placed the filing within the protective provisions of the Anticybersquatting Consumer Protection Act. Accordingly, the court ordered that the domain name be transferred to Volkswagen.

In *Electronics Boutique Holding Corp. v. Zuccarini,* (E.D.Pa. Oct. 30, 2000), the plaintiff sued defendant under the ACPA, alleging that the defendant had registered five domain names that were confusingly similar to plaintiff's trademarks EB and Electronics Boutique. The defendant's very similar domain names, *www.electronicboutique.com, www.electronicsboutique.com,* and other similar names caused persons accessing the sites to be subjected to a series of advertisements that could not be avoided in order to access plaintiff's site. Defendant was paid by advertisers for the said commerical announcements. Defendant also owned domain name sites of many other famous persons and companies for which he received a sum of from $800,000 to $1 million annually.

The court found the defendant liable under the ACPA. The marks owned by the plaintiff were distinctive and famous, having been in existence for more than 20 years and which marks were heavily promoted. The defendant's domain name sites were confusingly similar and were designed to give substantial profits to the defendant. Accordingly, the plaintiff was awarded the maximum statutory penalty of $100,000 for each of the defendant's five Web sites plus substantial counsel fees.

Metatags as Violations of ACPA

Filing a domain name of a well-known person or company appears to come within the ACPA. In the following case, cited also in Chapter 4 in another context, the defendants initially filed the domain names of a well-known interior designer but thereafter relinquished the said names. They then procured domain names not conflicting with trademark names containing metatags that led persons seeking information of the famous names to the defendant's sites.

BIHARI V. GROSS

119 F. Supp. 2d 309 (S.D.N.Y. 2000)

FACTS: The District Court was called upon to determine, among other issues, whether a preliminary injunction should be granted against defendants to stop them from using domain names or metatags in violation of the Anticybersquatting Consumer Protection Act. The issue arose as a result of a bitterly fought alleged breach of contract action. Bihari is an interior designer having provided interior design services in New York City and elsewhere for a period in excess of 15 years. The name is well known in the high-end residential interior market and is reliant upon referrals for business. Gross was a former client of Bihari who became engaged in a state court case as a plaintiff alleging fraud and breach of contract by Bihari. Gross then registered the domain names "bihari.com" and "bihariinteriors.com." The site contained derogatory statements about Bihari. Each of the parties previously filed criminal charges against the other, which charges were ultimately not prosecuted. After the within lawsuit was commenced, Gross relinquished the said domain names and returned them to Network Solutions, Inc.

Thereafter, Gross procured the domain names, "designscam.com" and "manhattaninteriordesign.com" that contained the same negative content about Bihari as the former domain names. The name "Bihari Interiors" were metatags embedded within the websites' HTML code. [A *metatag* was defined by the court as "hypertext markup language ("HTML") code, invisible to the Internet user, that permits web designers to describe their webpage. There are two different types of metatags: keyword and description. The keyword metatag permits designers to identify search terms for use by search engines. Description metatags allow designers to briefly describe the contents of their pages. This description appears as sentence fragments beneath the webpage's listing in a search result."] Thus, a person entering the said names would receive highly derogatory comments about the plaintiffs.

ISSUE: Did the use of the common-law service marks of the plaintiffs as metatags violate the Anticybersquatting Consumer Protection Act and Section 43(a) of the Lanham Act?

DECISION: The Court decided in favor of the defendants refusing to grant a preliminary injunction barring such use.
REASONING: Judge Scheindlin
Because of the great potential for harm which may occur from the issuance of a preliminary injunction, the party seeking the injunction must sustain a heavy burden. . . . The party seeking such relief must demonstrate: (1) likelihood of irreparable harm should the injunction be denied; and (2) either (a) likelihood of ultimate success on the merits, or (b) sufficiently serious questions going to the merits and a balance of hardships tipping decidedly toward the party seeking relief. . . .

Irreparable harm is an injury that is not remote or speculative but actual and imminent, and for which a monetary award cannot be adequate compensation. . . . In a trademark infringement case, a presumption of irreparable harm arises where a plaintiff makes a showing of likelihood of confusion. . . . A showing of likelihood of confusion, therefore, will establish the irreparable harm requisite for a preliminary injunction.

2. LIKELIHOOD OF SUCCESS ON THE ACPA CLAIM

On November 29, 1999, Congress adopted the ACPA "to remedy the perceived shortcomings of applying the FTDA in cybersquatting cases." . . . To establish a claim of cybersquatting, a plaintiff must show: (1) that she had a distinctive mark at the time of registration of the domain name; (2) that the defendant "registers, traffics in, or uses a domain name" that is identical or confusingly similar to that mark; and (3) that the defendant has "a bad faith intent to profit from that mark." 15 U.S.C. Section 1125(d)(1). A preliminary injunction is a remedy authorized by the ACPA. See 15 U.S.C. Section 1116(a).

[The court noted that the defendants had abandoned the bihari.com and bihariinteriors.com Web sites. The question, then, is whether the use of "Bihari Interiors" in the metatags violated the ACPA.] Although no court has expressly stated that the ACPA does not apply to metatags, the plain meaning of the statute and its legislative history make this confusion apparent. . . . ACPA provides an action against one who "registers, traffics in, or uses a domain name. . . ." (Congress's purpose in adopting the ACPA was to "protect consumers and American businesses . . . by prohibiting the bad-faith and abusive registration of distinctive marks as Internet domain names . . . "). Therefore, the ACPA is no longer a basis for preliminary injunctive relief as Gross has voluntarily relinquished the Bihari domain name.

3. LIKELIHOOD OF SUCCESS ON THE TRADEMARK INFRINGEMENT CLAIM

. . . Bihari has failed to demonstrate a likelihood of success on the merits of this claim because Gross's use of the "Bihari Interiors" mark in the metatags is not likely to cause confusion and is protected by fair use.

[The court discussed the four judicially-developed categories of trademarks, namely, (1) generic; (2) descriptive; (3) suggestive; and (4) arbitrary or fanciful.]

Generally, personal names used as trademarks are regarded as descriptive terms, protected only if they have acquired distinctive and secondary meaning. . . . However, "Bihari Interiors" is a suggestive rather than a descriptive mark because it suggests Bihari's services. The mark requires an imaginative leap to correctly identify Bihari's services. The work "interiors" does not immediately identify interior design services. It could easily describe a company producing home furnishings, seat covers for automobiles or services such as carpet cleaning or wall painting. As a suggestive mark, "Bihari Interiors" is inherently distinctive and entitled to protection.

b. Commercial Use

The plain language of the Lanham Act makes apparent that Section 43(a) is only applicable to commercial uses of another's mark. First, the statute only applies to actions taken by individuals "in 'connection with any goods or services.'" Second, Section 43(a) is limited to uses likely to cause confusion "as to the origin, sponsorship, or approval of [the defendant's] goods, services, or commercial activities. . . . Third, Section 43(a) is limited by 15 U.S.C. Section 1125(c)(4)(B), which states that "noncommercial use of a mark" is not actionable under the Lanham Act. . . .

[The court stated that the defendants were not interior designers, did not sell to visitors of the site any goods or services, and there was no likelihood of confusion inasmuch as any visitor to the defendants' site would not be misled into believing it was sponsored by Bihari. The court decided that the defendants' use of the Bihari name was a fair use exception under the Lanham Act.]

CASE QUESTIONS

1. Do you believe that the First Amendment should take priority over a person's good name and reputation? Suppose a woman was called a "prostitute" or a business enterprise was defamed as to its honesty and integrity. Should they have the right to prevent libelous comments about them?
2. Is it a simplistic response to say that one may sue for libel or slander. What if the wrongdoer were judgment proof (a judgment holder would not be able to recover money because the person has no assets)?

Liability of Network Solutions, Inc.

Domain names using the suffix *.com,* as previously stated, are established by registering them with Network Solutions, Inc. The role of the NSI was discussed in the following action.

THOMAS V. NETWORK SOLUTIONS, INC.

2 F. Supp. 2d 22 (D.D.C. 1998)

Judge Hogan:

Defendant National Science Foundation ("NSF") is an independent agency of the United States government, organized pursuant to a federal statute. 42 U.S.C. section 1861. NSF's primary function is to support and strengthen scientific research, engineering, and educational activity. . . . With the passage of the Scientific and Advanced Technology Act in 1992, NSF received an expanded mandate to support development of the Internet and to facilitate its use. . . .

Defendant Network Solutions, Inc. ("NSI") is a private company that has been engaged in the registration of domain names since 1991. In 1991, NSI won a subcontract to a procurement contract that Government Services, Inc. (GSI) had been awarded by the Defense Information Services Agency. NSI's duties under that subcontract were to perform domain name registration and to assign Internet Protocol (IP) numbers. In 1992, NSI entered into a cooperative agreement with NSF to perform essentially the same functions. Under the terms of that agreement, which is scheduled to expire later this year [1998], NSI manages and maintains the registry of domain names.

B. THE INTERNET AND DOMAIN NAME SYSTEM

The Internet is a complex network that links computers worldwide. It is the outgrowth of a system known as ARPANET, a network that the military created in 1969 to link its computers with those of defense contractors and universities. . . . While that network no longer exists, it provided a model for a number of similar, civilian networks that eventually coalesced into the backbone of the modern Internet.

Use of the Internet has grown exponentially over the past eighteen years. In 1981, an estimated 300 computers were linked via these networks; by 1996, the number had risen to an estimated 9.4 million computers, and some experts believe that 200 million persons will use the Internet by 1999. Nearly 60% of the computers currently linked to the Internet are located in the United States.

In order to fully access the Internet, a user needs a unique address, called an "Internet Protocol," or "IP," address. It is from this address that a user may post information, access information at other addresses, or exchange information with another user. IP addresses are composed of a long string of numbers;

because of this, however, they are themselves rarely memorable. In order to smooth the transfer of information, a user will often attach an alphanumeric "domain name" to his or her IP address.

Domain names consist of a series of letters and numbers, followed by a period and a specific three-letter designation. The series of letters and numbers to the left of the period is called the "second level domain name," and it is unique to the individual user. This name can be tailored to be easily remembered, and even to convey information about the user—it is often descriptive, catchy, and occasionally clever. In the United States, the three letter designation to the right of the period is one of seven handles: "gov," "org," "com," "net," "edu," "mil," or "int." These seven handles are called "top level domain names."

It is clear that domain names make the Internet much more accessible. Instead of seeking information at a site designated only by a random number, the user can access a site by its descriptive name. If the name is properly registered and linked to an IP address, the user will be conveyed to the site he or she seeks.

The key, of course, is that the name and the IP address must be linked together. In order to prevent confusion—two users with the same name, for example—users must register their second level names with one of the seven top level names. Although there has been discussion of competition in the registration of domain names, at this time a user may register in a top level name only through defendant [since 1998, there are numerous registrars].

B. (*SIC*) SOLICITATION AND AWARD OF COOPERATIVE AGREEMENTS TO NSI

Before 1992, NSF performed many administrative tasks in regard to the non-military aspect of the nascent Internet. Among these tasks were the registration of domain names and the maintenance of the registry of names. However, in March 1992, NSF issued solicitation 92-94 for a Network Information Services Manager for the Internet. NSF considered proposals from three firms that wished to assume the task of providing registration services for the non-military component of the Internet.

NSF chose NSI and on January 3, 1993, the two entered into Cooperative Agreement No. NCR-9218742. The contract specified that, after a three month "phase-in" period, NSI would provide registration services for five years, with a six month "flexibility period" at the end. Therefore, the cooperative agreement that became effective on January 12, 1993, was due to expire March 31, 1998, and has a flexibility period that will expire on September 30, 1998.

In *Lockheed Martin Corp. v. Network Solutions, Inc.*, No. CV 96-7438 DDP (C.D.Ca. 1997), Lockheed owned the service mark Skunk Works and operated an aerospace development and production facility under such mark. In 1996, it learned that NSI had granted domain name registrations for skunkworks.net to two individuals. Lockheed advised the individuals of the alleged infringement of the plaintiff's trademark and requested NSI to cease the registration of the name or similar names. NSI denied the request. Lockheed sued NSI for its denial. The court refused to dismiss the action as against NSI stating that at a trial Lockheed would be given the right to prove whether NSI had committed a tort in knowingly registering names that had trademark law protection. The court stated that "unlike a patent or copyright, a trademark does not confer on its owner any rights in gross or at large. . . . Therefore, the law does not *per se* prohibit the use of trademarks or service marks as domain names. Rather, the law prohibits only uses that infringe or dilute a trademark or service mark owner's mark. . . ."

Congress was called upon to address the issue whether NSI or other registrars of domain names should be liable for registration of names protected by the Trademark Act of 1946. The Anticybersquatting Consumer Protection Act provides for exemption from liability of a domain name registrar. Such registrar will be exempt from monetary relief or injunctive relief regardless of the final court determination of domain name infringement or dilution. Exceptions for injunctive relief would apply in those instances where the registrar fails to provide a court with appropriate documents to enable a court to exercise authority over the domain name; or has transferred, suspended, or otherwise modified a domain name during the pendency of an action; or willfully fails to comply with a court order.[20]

Domain Names and Free Speech

In *CPC International, Inc. v. Skippy Inc.,* No. 99-2318 (4th Cir. 2000), the parties owned two competing trademarks. The plaintiff, CPC, owns the Skippy trademark with respect to peanut butter, and the defendant Skippy Inc. owns the trademark Skippy with respect to its use as a cartoon character in cartoons generated by the company. Previously, in 1986, the defendant, Skippy Inc., was enjoined in a prior lawsuit from using the name Skippy in connection with sale of food products or to license the name for such usage. In 1997, Skippy Inc. acquired the domain name Skippy.com. On the Web site, it proceeded to make statements criticizing the plaintiff for the manner in which it previously acquired its mark. It contained articles entitled: "CPC's Malicious Prosecution" and "CPC's Fraud on the Courts." The defendant, Skippy Inc., did not violate the 1986 injunction other than discussing the earlier litigation. Nevertheless, it was sued by CPC claiming violation of the 1986 injunction.

The district court enjoined the defendants anew and ordered deletions of the critical articles and other statements. On appeal, the injunction was vacated based on the Federal Rules requiring an injunction order to recite the reasons for such an issuance. The appeals court was also concerned that the First Amendment of the Constitution may have been compromised. Speech critical of a corporation and its business practices is not a sufficient basis for the issuance of an injunction. Trademarks should not be used to "transform rights against unfair competition to rights to control language."

In *ACLU of Georgia v. Miller,* 977 F. Supp. 1228 (N.D.Ga. 1997), the constitutionality of a Georgia statute was called into question. The particular act made it a crime for:

> any person . . . knowingly to transmit any data through a computer network . . . for the purpose of setting up, maintaining, operating, or exchanging data with an electronic mailbox, home page, or other electronic information storage bank or point of access to electronic information if such data uses any individual name . . . to falsely identify the person . . . and for
>
> any person . . . knowingly to transmit any data through a computer network . . . if such data uses . . . any trade name, registered trademark, logo, legal or official seal, or copyrighted symbol . . . which would falsely state or imply that such person . . . has permission or is legally authorized to use [it] for such person when such permission or authorization has not been obtained.

The U.S. district court found the statute to be an unconstitutional invasion of freedom of speech in that the statute is overbroad and void for vagueness. It stated:

> On its face, the act prohibits such protected speech as the use of false identification to avoid social ostracism, to prevent discrimination and harassment, and to protect privacy, as well as the use of trade names or logos in non-commercial educational speech, news, and commentary—a prohibition with well-recognized First Amendment problems. Therefore, even if the statute could constitutionally be used to prosecute persons who intentionally 'false identify' themselves in order to deceive or defraud the public, or to persons whose commercial use of trade names and logos creates a substantial likelihood of confusion or the dilution of a famous mark, the statute is nevertheless overbroad because it operates unconstitutionally for a substantial category of the speakers it covers.

The court concludes that plaintiffs are likely to prove that the statute is void for vagueness because it (1) does not give fair notice of the scope of conduct it proscribes; (2) is conducive to arbitrary enforcement; and (3) infringes upon plaintiffs' free expression.

Civil Contempt Orders

When a court issues an order in a particular case, such as an injunction barring a defendant from further violations of a plaintiff's trademark, the order must be obeyed under penalty of contempt. In *Nettis Environment Ltd. v. IWI, Inc.,* 46 F. Supp. 2d 722 (N.D.Oh. 1999), the court considered whether IWI should be held in contempt for allegedly disobeying a court order to purge its Web page of all materials that could cause persons using a Web search engine looking for Nettis Environmental to pull up IWI's Web page. In deciding that the facts did warrant a holding of contempt, the court discussed the considerations in making such a determination as well as the sanctions to be imposed. It stated:

To justify a finding of civil contempt, the complaint must prove that a definite and specific court order has been violated. . . .

The test for determining when an order has been violated is not a subjective good faith standard . . . but rather an objective standard which asks whether the alleged contemnor has "failed to take 'all reasonable steps within [its] power to comply with the court's order.'" . . . There is no requirement of willfulness to establish civil contempt, and "the intent of a party to disobey a court order is 'irrelevant to the validity of [a] contempt finding.'"

The court discussed the failure of the defendant to comply with the restraining order and found that there was a failure to take the reasonable steps necessary for full compliance, although the defendant did partially comply with the said order. With respect to sanctions, the court said:

"Broadly, the purpose of civil contempt is to coerce an individual to perform an act or to compensate an injured complainant." . . . Incarceration of an individual is a valid sanction for civil contempt if it is conditional, so that once the person complies with the court order the person will be released. . . . It is said that such a contemnor carries the jail keys in his or her pocket. A fine is an appropriate sanction, so long as it is either (1) payable to a person harmed by the contempt, based upon evidence of actual loss, or (2) payable to the court if the contemnor does not comply with the court order. . . . In fashioning contempt sanctions, "a court is obliged to use the 'least possible power adequate to the end proposal.'" . . .

The court found insufficient basis for incarceration, daily fine, compensatory fine, or an accounting. It did grant an award of attorney's fees and costs.

INTERNATIONAL PROTECTION OF TRADEMARKS

Paris Convention for the Protection of Industrial Property

For more than a century, under the Paris Convention for the Protection of Industrial Property of March 20, 1883 (amended through July 14, 1967),[21] protection has been given globally to *industrial property,* which is defined as having "as its object patents, utility models, industrial designs, trademarks, service marks, trade names, indications of source or appellations of origin, and the repression of unfair competition." It is a broad-based term that includes not only property of industry in a narrow sense but also includes agriculture and mining, and the production of many agricultural products. Major provisions of the convention are discussed here.

National Treatment. All member states are to accord nationals of other member states the same degree of protection that they accord to their own nationals including the same legal remedies for infringement and without the requirement that such foreign nationals have a domicile or establishment therein (Article 2).

Right of Priority. Any person from a member state who duly files an application for a patent, trademark, utility model, or industrial design shall have a right of priority of filing in the other member states. The periods of priority are 12 months for patents and utility models and 6 months for industrial designs and trademarks (Article 4).

Miscellaneous Provisions: Exceptions to Registration. Member states are to refuse or invalidate registrations of marks that are coats of arms, flags, official signs, or state bearings of member states. Trademark registrations may be denied if they infringe on rights of third parties in the country of registration; are devoid of a distinctive character; are contrary to morality or public order; are deceptive; or simply designate the kind, quality, quantity, intended purpose, value, place of origin, or are customary in the language of the member state (Articles 6 and 6(B)).

Filing of Service and Collective Marks. Member states are required to protect service marks but need not provide for their registration (Article 6). Member states are required to accept for filing and protect collective marks unless they are contrary to the public interest even though the association is not established in the said country. A trade name is to be protected without the requirement for registration (Articles 7 and 8).

Seizure of Contraband Goods. All goods with unlawful trademarks are to be seized both in the country where they are located and at the place of importation. If a seizure is not permitted under the laws of the member state, then laws must be enacted to provide appropriate other remedies for the aggrieved party (Article 9).

Agreement on Trade-Related Aspects of Intellectual Property Rights

In the previous chapter, we discussed TRIPS in connection with the protection of copyrights. The agreement also protects all other forms of such rights including trademarks and patents. The subject matter of trademarks is defined as follows:

[Article 15(1)]. Any sign, or any combination of signs, capable of distinguishing the goods or services of one undertaking from those of other undertakings, shall be capable of constituting a trademark. Such signs, in particular words including personal names, letters, numerals, figurative elements and combinations of colors as well as any combination of such signs, shall be eligible for registration as trademarks. Where signs are not inherently capable of distinguishing the relevant goods or services, Members may make registrability depend on distinctiveness acquired through use. Members may require, as a condition of registration, that signs be visually perceptible.

Rights Conferred. TRIPS provides that the owner of a registered trademark has the exclusive right to prevent others from using identical marks or similar marks that may result in confusion in commercial activity. Provisions of the Paris Convention are incorporated as to services and nonsimilar trademarks (Article 16).

Exceptions. A member state may provide exceptions to the rights conferred such as fair use of descriptive terms (Article 17). Also, they may require use as a condition for maintenance of registration and may cancel a registration for a failure to use the mark for a continuous period of not less than three years. Nevertheless, a state may not have special requirements for use of the mark (Articles 19 and 20).

Term of Protection. TRIPS provides a term of no less than seven years with indefinite renewals (Article 18).

CONCLUSION

A well-known trademark is perhaps the greatest asset of a company. The McDonald's unique *M* symbol causes the saliva glands of many children to overflow in expectancy of the burger, fries, and soda. The Mercedes symbol causes many persons to purchase the vehicle for prestige purposes even though, privately, they would have preferred the appearances of other vehicles. The mark represents the company just as one's name identifies the individual. Protection is potentially forever, provided that legal requirements are fulfilled. The problem to be addressed in the near future is the need to have a central worldwide registry honored by all nations. Requiring individual filings in many countries with race-to-the-register statutes has caused many reputable companies to lose their property rights in favor of a local person who was able to file ahead of the company who created and promulgated the sign or symbol. The advent of the World Trade Organization has given much impetus to a global system.

Questions and Problems

1. What is a *trademark?* Name and describe the types of marks protected by law.
2. How are marks classified?
3. Discuss how domain name disputes are resolved.
4. How does the Anticybersquatting Consumer Protection Act of 1999 affect the utilization of domain names by non-trademark holders?
5. Distinguish trademarks and copyrights in terms of duration.
6. Playboy Enterprises owns registered trademarks for Playboy and Playmate, both of which are used for the sale of products to adult buyers. Netscape and Excite are Internet search engines. Companies wishing to advertise their products or services pay a fee to Netscape, Excite, and other search engines. Netscape and Excite engaged in the practice of *keying,* which permits advertisers to target specific audiences by having their ads shown whenever certain key words are used by prospective users of the Internet. Among the words in a group of some 450 terms Netscape and Excite used in their directory for advertising targeting were *playboy* and *playmate.* Playboy sued for trademark infringement and trademark dilution. Decide. See *Playboy Enterprises, Inc. v. Netscape Communications Corp.,* No. CV 99-320 AHS, 1999 U.S. Dist. LEXIS 9638 (C.D.Ca. 1999).
7. Virtual Works registered the domain vw.net. It sued Volkswagen of America and Volkswagen

AG for tortious interference. Volkswagen counterclaimed for cyberconspiracy, trademark dilution, and trademark infringement. Virtual Works never registered the trademark or other intellectual property rights nor did it conduct business using the initials. Volkswagen has the registered trademark of VW. The domain name vw.net has been used to disparage Volkswagen by references to the company as Nazis using slave labor during World War II. Virtual Works also had previously tried to sell the domain name to Volkswagen. Applying the Anticybersquatting Consumer Protection Act, which party will prevail? See *Virtual Work, Inc. v. Network Solutions, Inc., Volkswagen of America, Inc. et al.,* 106 F. Supp. 2d 845 (E.D.Va. 2000).

8. Epix, Inc. owns the registered trademark EPIX. Interstellar Starship operates under the assumed name of epix.com, which it registered as a domain name with Network Solutions, Inc. Epix, Inc. registered its domain name "epixinc.com." Epix, Inc. initiated a claim with Network Solutions for the domain name epix.com, stating that it held the registered trademark and was thus entitled to the domain name. Interstellar was given the choice to sue Epix, Inc. concerning the issue or deactivate the name. It sued, claiming that the epix.com site was used only for use in publicizing activities of a theatre group including digital images of cast members made by the site. Interstellar contends that Epix, Inc. registered the trademark only for goods that conform to the description "Printed Circuit Boards and Computer Programs for Image Acquisition, Processing, Display and Transmission, in Class 9." Is Interstellar allowed to use its domain name? Did such use violate Epix, Inc.'s trademark? Did Interstellar engage in unfair competition with Epix, Inc.? Will the Anticybersquatting Consumer Protection Act of 1999 change the result? See *Interstellar Starship Services, Limited v. Epix, Inc.,* 983 F. Supp. 1331 (D.Or. 1997).
9. Mattel is a Delaware corporation that is the largest manufacturer of toys in the world. It has numerous trademarks including that of the Barbie doll and the various products connected with the Barbie doll. The doll is world famous and a dominant toy in the industry. Defendant, JCOM, Inc., is a Nevada corporation that began using a Web site located at *www.jcomlive.com/barbie.htm.* It offered so-called adult entertainment services for a fee. Mattel sued JCOM solely on the basis of the Federal Anti-Dilution Act of 1996. Decide. See *Mattel, Inc. v. Jcom, Inc.,* 97 Civ. 7191 (SS), 1998 U.S. Dist. LEXIS 16195 (S.D.N.Y. 1998).
10. In 1994, David Chaum applied for the registration for the trademark Ecash with the Patent and Trademark Office. He then assigned the rights to the mark to Digicash Acquisition Corporation in 1997, which then assigned the mark to the plaintiff Ecash in July 1999. In July 1995, the defendants registered the domain name ecash.com with Network Solutions, Inc. They did not use the mark in any other capacity. Plaintiff had requested the defendant to obtain the ownership or use of the domain name, which defendant refused. Both parties have sued each other concerning the right to use the mark Ecash. Defendants counterclaimed against plaintiff's lawsuit claiming the plaintiff's mark was fraudulently obtained in that the plaintiffs failed to notify the Patent and Trademark Office of the defendant's domain name registration. Does the filing of a domain name constitute a trademark, giving the applicant the sole right to use such name? *Ecash Technologies, Inc. v. Tmark Guagliardo d/b/a Ecash.com,* No. CV 00-03292 ABC (RNBx) (C.D.Ca. Dec. 18, 2000).

Endnotes

1. *Playboy Enterprises, Inc. v. Netscape Communications Corp.,* 55 F. Supp. 2d 1070, 1080, 1081 (C.D.Ca. 1999).
2. *Playboy Enterprises, Inc. v. Welles,* 7 F. Supp. 2d 1098, 1103 (S.D.Ca. 1998).
3. 15 U.S.C. Sections 1051–1127.
4. Section 1127. A color or letter of the alphabet may be protected if the design, manner of usage, or configuration is unique. Examples include the letter *K* in Kellogg's and the color pink for fiberglass. See *In re Owens-Corning Fiberglas Corp.,* 774 F.2d 1116 (Fed. Cir. 1985); and *Qualitex Company v. Jacobson*

Products Company, 514 U.S. 159 (1995). In *Qualitex,* the Supreme Court cited prior trademark protection for the shape of a Coca-Cola bottle, a sound (NBC's three chimes), and a particular scent (plumeria blossoms on sewing thread).

5. For a detailed discussion of the nature, purpose, and types of marks protected by law and from which the text discussion is based in part, see *America Online, Inc. v. AT&T Corp.,* 64 F. Supp. 2d 549 (E.D.Va. 1999).
6. Ibid.
7. *Pignons S. A. de Mecanique de Precision v. Polaroid Corp.,* 657 F.2d 1201, 1205 (1st Cir. 1981).
8. Section 1117 to Section 1118 of the Trademark Act.
9. Section 3005 of the Anticybersquatting Consumer Protection Act of 1999. The statute is entitled "An Act to Provide for the Registration and Protection of Trademarks Used in Commerce, to Carry Out the Provisions of Certain International Conventions, and for Other Purposes." It amended Section 43 of the Trademark Act of 1946 (15 U.S.C. Section 1125).
10. A discussion of the topic from which much of this review is taken may be found in the 1998 white paper of the U.S. Department of Commerce, *Management of Internet Names and Addresses,* Docket No. 980212036-8146-02.
11. See id. at p. 12; and discussion by Ian Jay Kaufman, *ICANN, WIPO Address Domain Names,* New York Law Journal, January 18, 2000, pp. S5, S10–S12.
12. See U.S. Department of Commerce, "The Need for Change," p. 5 of the white paper.
13. ICANN may be accessed through the Internet at *www.icann.org.* The site includes the history of the shared registration system as well as the registrar accreditation agreement that proposed registrars are to sign.
14. Pub. L. No. 104-98, 109 Stat. 985 (1996).
15. 15 U.S.C. Section 1127.
16. For a discussion of cybersquatting, see Richard Lehv, *Cybersquatting in Focus: Are New Rules Needed or Will Existing Laws Suffice?* New York Law Journal: Intellectual Property (Jan. 18, 2000) pp. S4, S7–S8.
17. 1999 U.S. Dist. LEXIS 13848 (D.Mass. 1999).
18. 15 U.S.C. Section 1125.
19. Section 3003 of the statute.
20. Section 3004 of the statute.
21. U.N.T.S. No. 11851, vol. 828, pp. 305–88.

CHAPTER

PATENTS AND TRADE SECRETS

Chapter Outline

- Constitutional and Legislative Basis for Patents
- Utility Patents
- Design Patents
- Plant Patents
- Patent Infringement
- State Exemption
- Duration
- Remedies
- International Protection of Patents
- Protection of Trade Secrets
- Definition of Trade Secret
- The Tort of Misappropriation
- Trade Secrets and the Exercise of the First Amendment
- Calculation of Damages
- Criminal Violations
- International Protection of Trade Secrets
- Conclusion

We have previously discussed two types of intellectual property rights that are protected by law. In this chapter, we will review the remaining forms of such rights that the law has included within its scope of protection. We will begin the chapter by addressing issues regarding patents. A *patent* is an invention or process that is novel, useful, and nonobvious. A patent has the least duration of protection by law, namely 20 years. In the second part of the chapter, we will discuss trade secrets. A *trade secret* is the protection that the law gives to confidential information relating to a person's business, usually generated at considerable expense and effort by the concern. There is no time limit to its protection so long as it remains a secret as defined by law.

CONSTITUTIONAL AND LEGISLATIVE BASIS FOR PATENTS

Patents have been protected since the founding of the republic. The U.S. Constitution, Article 1, Section 8, clause 8 states that Congress shall have the power to "promote the Progress of Science and useful Arts, by securing for limited Times to Authors and Inventors the exclusive Right to their respective Writings and Discoveries." Congress enacted the first Patent Act in 1790. Thomas Jefferson was an administrator of the then patent system and the author of the Patent Act of 1793. The present statute is based on the 1952 Patent Act and its amendment in 1995. The Patent Act sets forth three types of patents that are afforded protection, namely, (1) utility patents; (2) design patents; and (3) plant patents.

UTILITY PATENTS

A utility patent will be granted under the U.S. Patent Act (Title 35 of the U.S. Code) as follows:

Sec. 101. Inventions Patentable

> Whoever invents or discovers any *new* and *useful* process, machine, manufacture, or composition of matter, or any new and useful improvement thereof, may obtain a patent therefor, subject to the conditions and requirements of this title [emphasis added].

Process is defined by the statute (Sec. 100(b)) as a "process, art or method, and includes a new use of a known process, machine, manufacture, composition of matter, or material."

Elements of a Utility Patent

There are three elements necessary for the validity of a patent, namely (1) it must be novel; (2) it must be useful; and (3) it must not be obvious.

Novel. Section 102 of the Patent Act states that a person is entitled to a patent unless (1) the invention was known or used previously in the United States; (2) it was patented or described in a printed publication in the United States or abroad before filing; (3) it was in public use or for sale in the United States more than one year prior to filing; (4) it was abandoned; (5) another person previously filed for the patent; (6) it was not invented by the applicant; or (7) another person had created the invention and had not abandoned, suppressed, or concealed it.

Public Use. In *Mitsubishi Electric Corp. v. Ampex Corp.,* 190 F.3d 1300 (Fed. Cir. 1999), Mitsubishi appealed a jury verdict against it that held Ampex not liable for alleged infringement of a patent concerning "Error Correction Encoding and Decoding System." The jury apparently accepted Ampex's defenses that included an invalidating public use based on Mitsubishi's demonstration of the invention at an Audio Engineering Convention prior to the filing of the application for a patent. The court of appeals concurred with the following district court's instruction to the injury concerning the law affecting prior public use:

> A public use for the purpose of barring access to the patent system is a use for more than a year before the patent's earliest effective filing date, whereby [the] completed "invention" is used in public, without restriction and in circumstances other than substantially for the purpose of experiment. The test is not whether the invention was present at a public place but whether it was actually used in public as recited in the claims of the patent.

Useful. The Constitution refers to the promotion of the useful arts in its grant of legislative authority. The Patent Act requires that the invention or process be useful. Creating a machine that does not work or one that operates for no ostensible purpose will result in the denial of a patent.

Nonobvious. Congress intended to reward a person with a patent monopoly only for such inventions that were not "obvious to a person at the time the invention was made to a person having ordinary skill in the art to which the subject matter pertains" (Section 103(a)). In *Custom Accessories, Inc. v. Jeffrey-Allan Indus., Inc.,* 807 F.2d 955, 962 (Fed. Cir. 1986), the court discussed the characteristics of such person.

> The person of ordinary skill is a hypothetical person who is presumed to be aware of all the pertinent prior art. The actual inventor's skill is not determinative. Factors that may be considered in determining level of skill include: type of problems encountered in art; prior art solutions to those problems; rapidity with which innovations are made; sophistication of the technology; and educational level of active workers in the field.

It stated approvingly the following lower court's instruction to the jury concerning how to analyze a combination of prior art references cited in *Mitsubishi Electric Corp. v. Ampex Corp.*, 190 F.3d 1300 (Fed. Cir. 1999):

The mere existence in the prior art of individual features of a patented invention does not without more invalidate the patent under the obviousness test. There must be evidence that the bringing together of such features or steps would have been obvious to an ordinarily skilled person. It is improper to combine prior art references solely because the inventor's patent itself suggests the new combination of old elements. Thus, to combine any of the teachings of the prior art there must be some teaching or suggestion supporting the combination.

Further, you may not combine the features of prior products where the prior art itself teaches against the combination.

In the following *Amazon.com* case the defense of obviousness was raised in a patent infringement action against Barnes and Noble. In addition, the defense that prior applications had anticipated the plaintiff's patent was also discussed.

AMAZON.COM, INC. V. BARNESANDNOBLE.COM, INC.

73 F. Supp. 2d 1228 (W.D.Wash. 1999)

FACTS: Plaintiff sued for patent infringement of its '411 patent [The number consists of the last three digits of the U.S. Patent Number. Thus, '411 refers to U.S. Patent No. 5,960,411] that describes a Method and System for Placing a Purchase Order Via a Communications Network. It is a method by which potential customers can place an order for merchandise through the Internet using only a single action or mouse click once certain identifying information is displayed to the customer. The method is applicable only after a retailer has on file information about the purchaser such as address and credit card number or other identifier. This "Express Lane" feature was used by Amazon's competitor, Barnes and Noble.
ISSUE: Whether the patent is invalid on the basis of obviousness and anticipation?
DECISION: The Court found the patent to be valid and granted the injunction against the named defendants.
REASONING: Judge Pechman
[The court summarized the testimony of a number of witnesses that allegedly showed that a number of prior patents and systems anticipated the filed patent.]

27. There are key differences between each of the prior art references cited by Defendants and the method and system described in the claims of the '411 patent. The Court finds that none of the prior art references offered by Defendant anticipate the claims of the '411 patent. On the question of obviousness, the Court finds that the differences between the prior art references submitted by Defendants and the '411 patent claims are significant. Moreover, there is insufficient evidence in the record regarding a teaching, suggestion, or motivation in the prior art that would lead one of ordinary skill in the art of e-commerce to combine the references. . . .

29. Barnesandnoble.com's Express Lane allows customers who have registered for the feature to purchase items by simply clicking on the Express Lane button shown on the detail or product page that describes and identifies the book or other item to be purchased. . . .

30. Throughout its web site, Barnesandnoble.com consistently describes Express Lane as a one-click ordering method. . . .

33. The strong similarities between the Amazon.com 1-click feature and the Express Lane feature subsequently adopted by Barnesandnoble.com suggest that Barnesandnoble.com copied Amazon.com's feature. . . .

III. CONCLUSIONS OF LAW

Validity

5. The statutory presumption of validity, 35 U.S.C. Section 282, applies to all patents and is meant "to contribute stability to the grant of patent rights." . . . This presumption operates at every stage of the litigation, including a motion for preliminary injunction against an alleged infringer. . . . A defendant may overcome this presumption, however, if he raises a "substantial question" concerning the validity of a patent and if the party seeking the injunction fails to show that this defendant lacks "substantial merit." . . .

Anticipation

4. Anticipation is a question of fact . . . and is a defense only if "all of the same elements are found in exactly the same situation and united in the same way . . . in a single prior art reference" . . . [The court found that none of the many cited claims of anticipation were valid. Each of the methodologies for making purchases required a several-step process.]

Obviousness

19. "Included within the presumption of validity mandated by 35 U.S.C. Section 282 is a presumption of nonobviousness which the patent challenger must overcome by proving facts with clear and convincing evidence. The presumption remains intact even upon proof of prior art not cited by the Patent and Trademark Office (PTO), though such art, if more relevant than that cited, may enable the challenger to sustain its burden." . . .

20. The issue of obviousness is a mixed question of law and fact. The ultimate question is one of law, but it is based on several factual inquiries, including: (1) the scope and content of the prior art; (2) the differences between the prior art and the claims; (3) the level of ordinary skill in the pertinent art; and (4) applicable secondary considerations. . . .

22. . . . The law is clear that the time period for any obviousness determination is "at the time the invention was made" 35 U.S.C. Section 103(a). . . .

23. "Objective indicia 'may often be the most probative and cogent evidence of nonobviousness in the record.'" . . .

24. "Such secondary considerations as commercial success, long felt but unsolved needs, [and] failures of others" are relevant as evidence of obviousness. . . .

25. Copying of the invention by Barnesandnoble.com and others is additional evidence of nonobviousness. "It gives the tribute of its praise to the prior art; it gives the [invention] the tribute of its imitation, as others have done. . . . "

26. The adoption of single-action ordering by other e-commerce retailers following Amazon.com's introduction of the feature, coupled with the need to solve the problem of abandoned shopping carts [users of the Internet often start to make a purchase but abandon it after one or more clicks of the mouse] by e-commerce customers, is additional evidence of nonobviousness. . . .

27. In light of its consideration of the factors and evidence related to the question of obviousness, the Court finds Barnesandnoble.com is unlikely to succeed in showing by clear and convincing evidence that the claims of the '411 patent were obvious. Barnesandnoble.com's reliance on the simplicity of the invention is unavailing. "Defining the problem in terms of its solution reveals improper hindsight in the selection of the prior art relevant to obviousness." . . .

SUMMARY

50. Based on the foregoing, the Court finds that Plaintiff has demonstrated a reasonable likelihood of success on the merits at trial.

[The court noted that Barnesandnoble.com can easily avoid infringement "by simply requiring users to take an additional action to confirm orders placed by using Express Lane." On appeal, the court of appeals reversed the grant of a preliminary injunction in favor of Amazon, although it did agree that Amazon would most likely prevail. Nevertheless, it sent the case back to the trial court for a full trial on the merits of the action. 239 F.3d 1343 (Fed. Cir. 2001).]

CASE QUESTIONS

1. Do you believe that a method enabling retailers to sell via a one-click method should be patentable?
2. Why would a two-step method survive a patent infringement attack?
3. Was the method of operation herein *obvious*?

The Defense of Anticipation. In the *Amazon.com* case, the defense of anticipation was raised. In *United States Filter Corp. v. Ionics, Inc.,* 68 F. Supp. 2d 48, 53 (D.Mass. 1999), the court discussed the defense in a patent infringement claim involving an electrodeionization apparatus. The defense is a claim for lack of novelty of the invention. The court said:

> A determination of anticipation involves two steps: "First in construing the claim, a question of law for the court, followed by . . . a comparison of the construed claim to the prior art." . . . Invalidity by anticipation requires that the party arguing for invalidity prove by clear and convincing evidence "that each and every limitation of the claimed invention be disclosed in a single prior art reference." . . . This means that if a prior art reference lacks any claimed element, then as a matter of law a decisionmaker (whether in the patent office or in a court) cannot find anticipation. . . . "In addition, the reference must be enabling and describe the applicant's claimed invention sufficiently to have placed it in possession of a person of ordinary skill in the field of the invention."

The court then indicated that to defend against such a claim, the patent holder "need only show that not every element of every allegedly anticipated claim is disclosed by the prior art" (at p. 58).

Subject Matter of a Utility Patent

Not every discovery is patentable. The statute, cited previously, permits obtaining a patent for a "new and useful process, machine, manufacture, or composition of matter." Even though the U.S. Supreme Court has given a broad scope to the definition of the protectable subject matter, there are categories of subject matter that are not patentable. Included are the laws of nature, natural phenomena, and abstract ideas. The court of appeals, in the following case, reviews the nature of patentable subject matter. In doing so, it had to determine whether a process that had as its basis a mathematical algorithm, was patentable subject matter. The district court had determined that the filed patent was invalid.

AT&T CORP. V. EXCEL COMMUNICATIONS, INC.

172 F.3d 1352 (Fed. Cir. 1999)

FACTS: AT&T filed its '184 patent, entitled "Call Message Recording for Telephone Systems," in 1994. The system is designed to operate in a telecommunications system involving a number of long-distance service carriers, such as Sprint, Excel and others. When a caller dials a long distance number, it is transmitted over the local exchange carrier's [LEC] network to a switch that identifies the caller's primary long-distance service carrier (PIC). The call is then automatically routed to the PIC, which then carries the call to the LEC of the call recipient. As the call is made, the switch monitors and records data concerning the call which is then sent to a message accumulation system for processing and billing. The District Court said that such a process was not patentable because the '184 patent implicitly recited a mathematical algorithm. The entire process allegedly was one only of data-gathering for the algorithm.

ISSUE: Whether the claims asserted by AT&T were invalid because they involved unpatentable subject matter?

DECISION: The Court of Appeals found in favor of AT&T, holding that the process was patentable, thereby reversing the decision of the District Court.

REASONING: Judge Plager

A mathematical formula alone, sometimes referred to as a mathematical algorithm, viewed in the abstract, is considered unpatentable subject matter. . . . Courts have used the terms "mathematical algorithm," "mathematical formula," and "mathematical equation," to describe types of nonstatutory mathematical subject matter without explaining whether the terms are interchangeable or different. Even assuming the words connote the same concept, there is considerable question as to exactly what the concept encompasses. . . . This court recently pointed out that any step-by-step process, be it electronic, chemical, or mechanical, involves an "algorithm" in the broad sense of the term. . . . Because Section 101 includes processes as a category of patentable subject matter, the judicially-defined proscription against patenting of a "mathematical algorithm," to the extent such a proscription still exists, is narrowly limited to mathematical algorithms in the abstract. . . .

Since the process of manipulation of numbers is a fundamental part of computer technology, we have had to reexamine the rules that govern the patentability of such technology. The sea-changes in both law and technology stand as a testament to the ability of law to adapt to new and innovative concepts, while remaining true to basic principles. In an earlier era, the PTO published guidelines essentially rejecting the notion that computer programs were patentable. As the technology progressed, our predecessor court disagreed, and, overturning some of the earlier principles regarding Section 101, announced more expansive principles formulated with computer technology in mind.

. . . The Supreme Court . . . explained that although the process used a well-known mathematical equation, the applicants did not "pre-exempt the use of that equation." Thus, even though a mathematical algorithm is not patentable in isolation, a process that applies an equation to a new and useful end "is at the very least not barred at the threshold by Section 101." . . .

Thus, the . . . inquiry simply requires an examination of the contested claims to see if the claimed subject matter as a whole is a disembodied mathematical concept representing nothing more than a "law of nature" or an "abstract idea," or if the mathematical concept has been reduced to some practical application rendering it "useful." . . . As previously explained, AT&T's claimed process employs subscribers' and call recipients' PIC as data, applies Boolean algebra to those data to determine the value of the PIC indicator, and applies that value through switching and recording mechanisms to create a signal useful for billing purposes. . . . Because the claimed process applies the Boolean principle, on its face the claimed process comfortably falls within the scope of Section 101. . . .

CASE QUESTIONS

1. At what juncture does a mathematical algorithm or formula become patentable?
2. What additional steps must take place for the transition to a patented right?
3. Would the result in this case have been different a decade ago? Two decades ago?

The Business Method Exception. In *State Street Bank & Trust Co. v. Signature Financial Group Inc.,* 149 F.3d 1268 (Fed. Cir. 1999), Signature held a patent entitled "Data Processing System for Hub and Spoke Financial Services Configuration" that allows an administrator of a financial services organization to monitor and record the system's information flow and make calculations for the maintenance of a partner fund financial services configuration. A partner fund consisted of a number of mutual funds, or Spokes, which pool their funds into a single portfolio known as a Hub. The system provides means for a daily allocation of assets for a number of Spokes invested in the same Hub. The system then determines the percentage share each Spoke maintains in the Hub and other calculations. In determining whether the process was patentable, the court of appeals adopted reasoning similar to the *AT&T* case.

The district court said that the patent failed because of two exceptions to the claimed subject matter, namely, the "mathematical algorithm" exception and the "business method" exception. The court of appeals, in reversing the lower court's decision, quoted the U.S. Supreme Court's decision in *Diamond v. Diehr,* 450 U.S. 175, 192 (1981):

When a claim containing a mathematical formula implements or applies that formula in a structure or process which, when considered as a whole, is performing a function which the patent laws were designed to protect (e.g., transforming or reducing an article to a different state or thing), then the claim satisfies the requirements of Section 101.

The focus should not be on which of the four categories of subject matter a claim is concerned with (process, machine, manufacture, or composition), but rather the practical utility of the subject matter. The Hub and Spoke software does produce a "useful, concrete, and tangible" result. It satisfies the Patent Act "even if the useful result is expressed in numbers, such as price, profit, percentage, cost, or loss."

With respect to the so-called business method exception, the court in the *State Street Bank* case, said that it was eliminated by Section 103 of the Patent Act. Some courts had indicated the exception to patentability by stating that: "The claimed accounting method [requires] no more than the entering, sorting, debiting and totaling of expenditures as necessary preliminary steps to issuing an expense analysis statement . . ." and thus was not novel and nonobvious.[1] Business methods are subject to the same legal requirements for patentability as any other process or method. Was *business method* eliminated by the Patent Act? In the following recent case, the U.S. Court of Appeals for the Federal Circuit disagreed with the trial court in its limitation of the right of the persons' creation as a business method from claiming infringement of its patent right.

INTERACTIVE GIFT EXPRESS, INC. V. COMPUSERVE, INC.

231 F.3d 859 (Fed. Cir. 2000)

FACTS: Interactive claimed that its 643 patent was infringed by major software users and distributors including CompuServe, Broderbund Software, Inc., Intuit, Inc. and other such companies. Interactive's patent, known as the "Freeny patent," is a method for reproducing information in material objects utilizing information manufacturing machines at point of sale locations. It included a central control station and a number of remotely located manufacturing stations whereby, upon receiving a consumer demand for a recording, book etc., the desired selected information is copied onto a blank material object (such as cassettes, paper and so on) and sold locally to the consumer. Prior thereto, the manufacturer had to produce the material at a location and shipped out to the consumer in distant areas.

The method permits the manufacturer, at great cost savings, to manufacture and distribute the desired object at the distant locations. The defendants allegedly infringed on the Freeny patent by selling software or documents online using the method, including the use of a CD-Rom containing encrypted computer applications requiring use of passwords.

ISSUE: Whether the activities of the defendants violated the Freeny business method patent?

DECISION: The court reversed the lower Court's decision in dismissing the patent claim, holding that it erred in denying the patent's validity.

REASONING: Judge Linn

[The court addressed five disputed claim limitations.]

I. POINT OF SALE LOCATION

. . . [A] point of sale location is "a location where a consumer goes to purchase material objects embodying predetermined or preselected information." . . . [The court said the lower court was in error in saying that the point of sale could not be the consumer's home.] [W]e find nothing precluding a home from being a point of sale location. . . . We construe a point of sale to be a location where a consumer goes to purchase material objects embodying predetermined or preselected information. This construction permits a home to be a point of sale location. A point of sale location need not have more than one blank material object and it need not have any material objects separately for sale as blanks. . . .

[W]e construe a material object to be a tangible medium or device in which information can be embodied, fixed, or stored, other than temporarily, and from which the information embodied therein can be perceived, reproduced, used or otherwise communicated, either directly or with the aid of another machine or device. A material object must be offered for sale, and be purchasable, at point of sale locations where at least one IMM [information manufacturing machine] is located. Further, a material object must be separate and distinct from the IMM, removed from the IMM after purchase, and intended for use on a device separate from the IMM either at the point of sale location or elsewhere. "Material object" does not encompass the hard disk component of a home personal computer. Finally, a material object need not be offered for sale independently from the information that may be reproduced onto the material object, that is, as a blank. . . .

[The appeals court disagreed with the district court that held that the invention had to cover real-time transactions in which the requested item of the consumer is transmitted to the IMM at the time it is requested. Accordingly, the case was remanded to the district court to reexamine and redetermine the merits of the patent claim.]

There is no clear definition of *business method.* In a bill introduced in the House of Representatives by Congressmen Howard Berman and Rick Boucher, known as the Business Method Improvement Act of 2000 (HR 5364), but which has not been enacted to date into law, a definition was stated that may be of assistance in arriving at uniform meaning. In Section 2, the bill defines a *business method* as

(1) a method of:
    (A) administering, managing, or otherwise operating an enterprise or organization, including a technique used in doing or conducting business; or
    (B) processing financial data;
(2) any technique used in athletics, instruction, or personal skills; and
(3) any computer-assisted implementation of a systematic means described in (1) or a technique described in (2).

A *business method invention* is defined as

(1) any invention which is a business method (including any software or other apparatus); and
(2) any invention which is comprised of any claim that is a business method.

The bill would require the director of the Patent and Trademark Office, on application of a proposed business method patent, to determine whether the invention does in fact constitute a business method invention, give notice to the applicant of the determination, and allow the applicant 60 days to respond. The application is to be published 18 months after filing and allow the public to contest the application as prior art, as known or used previously, or as in public use or sold previously. Panels of opposition judges are to be convened in order to hear contested cases.

Business method patents have generated a great deal of controversy and potentially could harm entrepreneurs, especially in the high tech arena. There has been an enormous increase in the so-called Class 705 filings, with triple the number of filings from 1999 to 2000. Whether the alleged abusive filings will be allowed to continue will remain the province of Congress to make such determination.

The *State Street* and the *Interactive* cases make it quite clear that the business method exception will have a significant effect on electronic commerce. The decisions have led the Patent and Trademark Office to issue a number of patents such as one relating to an electronic payment system for ordering merchandise (No. 5,715,314), one for viewing online advertisements (No. 5,794,2310), and other business method filings.[2]

DESIGN PATENTS

Section 171 of the Patent Act defines *patents for design* as follows:

Whoever invents any new, original and ornamental design for an article of manufacture may obtain a patent therefor, subject to the conditions and requirements of this title. The provisions of this title relating to patents for inventions shall apply to patents for design, except as otherwise provided.

The term of protection is 14 years (6 years less than that of a utility patent). In *Seiko Epson Corp. v. Nu-Kote Int'l, Inc.,* 190 F.3d 1360 (Fed. Cir. 1999), the issue arose concerning the validity of the design and shape of ink cartridges that were not in view after installation and during use in a printer. The trial court said that the consumer was not concerned with the design of the cartridge and, thus, it was not a valid design patent. The U.S. court of appeals reversed the district court's decision stating that "The validity of a design patent does not require that the article be visible throughout its use; it requires only that the design of an article of manufacture and that the design meets the requirements of Title 35 [the Patent Act]." The court cited a case involving a design patent for a hip prosthesis that was no longer in view after implementation that also was found to be protected.[3] The court further noted that the ornamental design need not be aesthetically pleasing, and although a design is for a useful article, the patentability is to be based on the article's design rather than its use.

PLANT PATENTS

The third type of patents protected under the Patent Act is that given to the invention or discovery and asexual reproduction of any new and distinct variety of plants, including hybrids, mutants, cultivated spores, and newly found seedlings other than those found in an uncultivated state.

PATENT INFRINGEMENT

The Patent Act states that a person infringes a patent if he or she "without authority makes, uses, offers to sell, or sells any patented invention, within the United States or imports into the United States any patented invention during the term of the patent . . ." An infringer includes a person who "actively induces infringement" or who offers to sell or sells a component of a protected invention or process knowing it will be adopted in an endeavor to infringe a patent. There are a number of exceptions relating to importation of biological products for review by federal agencies or where a product has been materially altered by later processes or is a trivial and nonessential component of another product.

The Doctrine of Equivalents

A patent may be infringed even if the original invention or process was not duplicated in totality. Under the doctrine of equivalents if the differences between the claim that is asserted by the patent holder and the alleged infringing device are insubstantial, then such claim may be recognized. In *WMS Gaming Inc. v. International Game Technology,* 184 F.3d 1339 (Fed. Cir. 1999), the court cited the lower court's holding with approval that the defendant's slot machine infringed on plaintiff's patent under the said doctrine. The patent concerned a slot machine that decreases the probability of a player winning while still maintaining the appearance of a standard slot machine. The defendant's machine used a multiple random numbering system in a multistep process instead of the plaintiff-patent holder's more direct selection of stopping positions. Such difference was found to be insignificant and, thus, a violation of the patent.

The U.S. Supreme Court cautioned, however, that "the doctrine of equivalents must be applied to individual elements of the claim, not to the invention as a whole" and "application of the doctrine, even as to an individual element, is not allowed such broad play as to effectively eliminate that element in its entirety."[4]

Defenses to an Infringement Claim

The Patent Act (Section 273) permits an otherwise wrongful infringer to allege and prove that the said person, acting in good faith, had reduced the subject matter of the patent to practice at least one year before the effective filing date of the patent, or to establish that the holder of the patent had abandoned its use, for example, not using the patent for an extended period of years (some decisions use a six-year-plus criteria).

STATE EXEMPTION

The Patent Act, Section 296, explicitly states that any state, instrumentality of a state, and any officer thereunder, is not immune under the Eleventh Amendment of the U.S. Constitution, nor under a doctrine of sovereign immunity from a lawsuit in a federal court by any person alleging patent infringement by such governmental entities. The issue of whether such a statute was constitutional was raised in the following case.

FLORIDA PREPAID POST SECONDARY EDUCATION EXPENSE BOARD V. COLLEGE SAVINGS BANK

527 U.S. 627 (1999)

FACTS: College Savings Bank, a New Jersey Bank, sued Florida Prepaid, an entity created by the State of Florida, for patent infringement with respect to a patent for its financing methodology for certificates of deposit guaranteeing investors sufficient funds to cover tuition expenses for their children. Florida Prepaid administered tuition prepaid contracts similar to those of the College Savings Bank.
ISSUE: Whether the Patent Act's provision was an unconstitutional attempt by Congress to abrogate state sovereign immunity?
DECISION: In a 5–4 decision, the U.S. Supreme Court decided in favor of the State of Florida holding that the attempt by Congress to place states on the same footing as private persons was an unconstitutional exercise of its Article I powers.
REASONING: Justice Rehnquist
The Eleventh Amendment provides:

The Judicial Power of the United States shall not be construed to extend to any suit in law or equity, commenced or prosecuted against one of the United States by citizens of another State, or by citizens or Subjects of a Foreign State.

As the [Supreme] Court recently explained in *Seminole Tribe [of Fla. v. Florida,* 517 U.S. 44 (1996)] . . .

Although the text of the Amendment would appear to restrict only the Article III diversity jurisdiction of the federal courts, 'we have understood the Eleventh Amendment to stand not so much for what it says, but for the presupposition . . . which it confirms.' That presupposition, first observed over a century ago . . . has two parts: first, that each State is a sovereign entity in our federal system; and second, that "it is inherent in the nature of sovereignty not to be amenable to the suit of an individual without its consent." . . . For over a century we have reaffirmed that federal jurisdiction over suits against unconsenting States 'was not contemplated by the Constitution when establishing the judicial power of the United States.' . . .

Here, College Savings sued the State of Florida in federal court and it is undisputed that Florida has not expressly consented to suit. . . . We agree with the parties and the Federal Circuit that in enacting the Patent Remedy Act, Congress has made its intention to abrogate the States' immunity "unmistakenly clear in the language of the statute." . . .

Whether Congress had the power to compel States to surrender their sovereign immunity for these purposes, however, is another matter. Congress justified the Patent Remedy Act under three sources of constitutional authority: the Patent Clause, Art. I, Section 8, cl. 8 ["Congress shall have Power . . . to Promote the Progress of Science and useful Arts, by securing for limited Times to authors and Inventors the exclusive Right to their respective Writings and Discoveries."]; the Interstate Commerce Clause, Art. I, Section 8, cl. 3 ["Congress shall have Power . . . to regulate Commerce with foreign Nations, and among the Several States, and with the Indian Tribes."]; and Section 5 of the Fourteenth Amendment. . . . *Seminole Tribe* makes clear that Congress may not abrogate state sovereign immunity pursuant to its Article I powers; hence the Patent Remedy Act cannot be sustained under either the Commerce Clause or the Patent Clause. . . . The Federal Circuit recognized this, and College Savings and the United States do not contend otherwise.

Instead, College Savings and the United States argue that the Federal Circuit properly concluded that Congress enacted the Patent Remedy Act to secure the Fourteenth Amendment's protections against deprivations of property without due process of law. The Fourteenth Amendment protection provides in relevant part:

Section 1. . . . No State shall . . . deprive any person of life, liberty, or property, without due process of law.
. . . Section 5. The Congress shall have power to enforce, by appropriate legislation, the provisions of

this article." . . . "[T]hrough the Fourteenth Amendment, federal power extended to intrude upon the province of the Eleventh Amendment and therefore that Section 5 of the Fourteenth Amendment allowed Congress to abrogate the immunity from suit guaranteed by that Amendment. . . .

We . . . held that for Congress to invoke Section 5, it must identify conduct transgressing the Fourteenth Amendment's substantive provisions, and must tailor its legislative scheme to remedying or preventing such conduct. . . .

Can the Patent Act be viewed as remedial or preventive legislation aimed at securing the protections of the Fourteenth Amendment for patent owners? . . . The underlying conduct at issue here is state infringement of patents and the use of sovereign immunity to deny patent owners compensation for the invasion of their patent rights. . . . It is this conduct then—unremedied patent infringement by the States—that must give rise to the Fourteenth Amendment violation that Congress sought to redress in the Patent Remedy Act.

In enacting the Patent Remedy Act, however, Congress identified no pattern of patent infringement by the States, let alone a pattern of constitutional violations. Unlike the undisputed record of racial discrimination confronting Congress in the voting rights cases, . . . Congress came up with little evidence of infringing conduct on the part of States. . . .

The historical record and the scope of coverage therefore make it clear that the Patent Remedy Act cannot be sustained under Section 5 of the Fourteenth Amendment. The examples of States avoiding liability for patent infringement by pleading sovereign immunity in a federal-court action are scarce enough, but any plausible argument that such action on the part of the State deprived patentees of property and left them without a remedy under state law is scarcer still. The statute's apparent and more basic aims were to provide a uniform remedy for patent infringement and to place States on the same footing as private parties under that regime. These are proper Article I concerns, but that Article does not give Congress the power to enact such legislation after *Seminole Tribe*.

CASE QUESTIONS

1. Does the decision mean that states can take any intellectual property rights and do as they see fit?
2. If so, how can the United States complain of theft of intellectual property rights by other countries?

It would appear that the same constitutional restraints would apply in other cases involving intellectual property rights, such as in copyright and trademark cases. Inasmuch as the decision was decided by one vote, a future court may distinguish future cases or overrule the *Florida* holding.

DURATION

The holder of a utility or plant patent has a 20-year right of exclusivity from the date of filing of the application. There are provisions for extending the time to the extent that the Patent and Trademark Office has failed to respond or act within the time limitations set forth in the statute (Sections 154–55).

REMEDIES

The Patent Act specifies a variety of remedies that a court may grant to a holder for infringement of a patent right. They include (1) the grant of an injunction to prevent violation of a patent right; (2) damages to compensate for the infringement but no less than a reasonable royalty for the use of the invention by the infringer plus interest and costs; (3) treble damages if the court so determines; and (4) reasonable attorney fees in exceptional cases to the prevailing party. Damages may not be granted for a period beyond six years prior to filing of the complaint or counterclaim for infringement (Sections 283–287).

Effect of Bankruptcy Petition on Remedies

The filing of a bankruptcy petition by a debtor under the Bankruptcy Reform Act of 1978 operates as a stay or hold on any legal proceedings affecting the debtor. Thus, if a person is being sued concerning an alleged indebtedness, the litigation must be suspended pending determination of the bankruptcy court of the petitioner's request for relief. The act provides as follows:

Section 362 Automatic Stay

(a) Except as provided in subsection (b) of this section, a petition filed under section 301, 302, or 303 of this title, or an application filed under section 5(a)(3) of the Securities Investor Protection Act of 1970, operates as a stay, applicable to all entities, of—

(1) the commencement or continuation, including the issuance or employment of process, of a judicial, administrative, or other action or proceeding against the debtor that was or could have been commenced before the commencement of the case under this title, or to recover a claim against the debtor that arose before the commencement of the case under this title.

In the aforementioned *Seiko* case, Seiko sued Nu-Kote and Pelikan Produktions for patent infringement and other relief concerning ink cartridges manufactured by Nu-Kote in violation of plaintiff's patents. Nu-Kote filed a Chapter 11 (reorganization) voluntary petition under the Bankruptcy Code. The issue arose whether the litigation against Pelikan could proceed inasmuch as there was a stay of all proceedings against Nu-Kote. The court held that the patent infringement litigation could proceed against Pelikan inasmuch as "the automatic stay does not apply to non-bankrupt co-defendants of a debtor 'even if they are in a similar legal or factual nexus with the debtor.' . . . The rule also permits claims by the debtor, and counterclaims, to proceed. . . . 'Within one case, actions against a debtor will be suspended even though closely related claims asserted by the debtor may continue.' " The same principles apply to cases on appeal from a lower court's ruling.

INTERNATIONAL PROTECTION OF PATENTS

The Paris Convention for the Protection of Industrial Property

The Paris Convention of March 20, 1883 (as amended) was the first major international convention for protecting the variety of industrial property.[5] As stated in the discussion of trademarks, the convention covers a broad spectrum that includes object patents, utility models as well as the extractive and agricultural sectors. Patents include those of importation, of improvements, certificates of addition, and other recognized forms. The comments regarding the protection of trademarks under the convention are applicable herein.

Agreement on Trade-Related Aspects of Intellectual Property Rights

Section 5, Article 27(1) of TRIPS provides protection "for any inventions, whether products or processes, in all fields of technology, provided that they are new, involve an inventive step and are capable of industrial application." Protection is to be extended without discrimination as to field of technology, place of invention, and whether imported or domestic. Countries may exclude patentability for reasons of morality, protection of human, animal, plant life, health, or serious prejudice to the environment. Also, exclusions may be made for diagnostic, therapeutic, and surgical methods for the treatment of humans or animals and for biological processes (Article 27(2)).

The rights conferred include the prevention of other persons without consent from "making, using, offering for sale, selling, or importing" a patented product or product obtained from a protected process (Article 28). To receive protection the applicant for a patent must disclose the nature of the invention to the extent that a person having skill in the art is able to carry out the invention (Article 29). A member state can make exceptions concerning the use of the subject matter of the patent subject to a number of conditions. These conditions include the requirements that the authorization be made on individual merits, be permitted only if the holder refuses to grant permission on reasonable commercial terms and conditions, that the use be nonexclusive, that it be nonassignable, that it be for domestic market predominantly, that reasonable compensation be granted, that the scope and duration of use be limited, and that the patent holder have access to judicial review (Article 31). The term of protection is 20 years from the filing date (Article 33).

North American Free Trade Agreement

The provisions set forth in Chapter Seventeen of NAFTA are similar to those of TRIPS.

PROTECTION OF TRADE SECRETS

The creative process encompasses innovative modes of thinking that leads to new inventions, processes, and ideas filling the many voids attendant to daily living. Companies engage in vast expenditures for research and development to discover ways to go beyond existing technology to find or increase their niche in the marketplace. Unfortunately, many persons, seeking to avoid the costly enterprise, engage in spying and other illicit activities in order to take advantage of the efforts of others. Governments have from time immemorial sought to ascertain secrets of other nations, both friendly and perceived enemies. With the Cold War at an end, spying has moved from the uncovering of secrets affecting national security to corporate secrets. There have been numerous reports of industrial spying, ranging from efforts of the French government to ascertain business secrets from foreign executives on behalf of French companies to alleged spying by the U.S. Central Intelligence Agency (CIA) and its passing of sensitive business materials to American companies.

Processes, formulas, and other secretive data are closely guarded by companies. The use of patents, trademarks, and copyrights may give only limited protection to registrants. For example, patents have only a limited life span, after which time anyone may copy the invention or process. Even where patents do provide the ostensible protection needed by inventors, nevertheless, many countries permit the blatant violation of such rights. When one files a patent, the secret process or makeup of the invention is necessarily revealed. Also, there are many items of inventiveness that may come within exceptions to patent and trademark protection. Thus, the option of retaining the secrecy of such inventions or processes is often chosen. It is this option that the law seeks to protect. Unlike the other forms of intellectual property, there is no registration process inasmuch as the main reason for having a trade secret is to prevent its disclosure beyond a select few persons.

DEFINITION OF *TRADE SECRET*

The Uniform Trade Secrets Act (UTSA), which has been adopted by most states, defines a *trade secret* as:

information, including a formula, pattern, compilation, program, device, method, technique, or process, that:

i. derives independent economic value, actual or potential, from not being generally known to, and not being readily ascertainable by proper means by, other persons who can obtain economic value from its disclosure or use, and
ii. is the subject of efforts that are reasonable under the circumstances to maintain its secrecy.

In order for protection to accrue to the business concern, it is necessary that significant steps be taken to maintain the secrecy of the information being protected. If the alleged secret is known beyond the scope of a select few persons in the company, then it is highly unlikely that the law will protect it. Courts have emphasized the need to protect company secrets that have accrued as a result of considerable effort and expense. Unlike a filing of a patent, copyright, or trademark wherein the subject matter of protection is made known, a court is giving protection to an idea, formulation, and the like that the holder seeks to prevent from being disseminated.

The revelation of the trade secret to another in confidence does not destroy the element of secrecy. Licensees of the holder must be given the protected information that is a part of the license. Employees who must know the trade secret in order to fulfill their duties are within the limited range of persons who may be told of the confidential data without loss of legal protection. Persons who wrongfully obtain or utilize trade secrets may be liable for the tort of misappropriation.

THE TORT OF MISAPPROPRIATION

The UTSA defines *misappropriation* as

(i) Acquisition of a trade secret of another by a person who knows or has reason to know that the trade secret was acquired by improper means, or
(ii) Disclosure or use of a trade secret of another without express or implied consent by a person who did one or more of the following:
   (A) Used improper means to acquire knowledge of the trade secret.
   (B) At the time of disclosure or use, knew or had reason to know that his or her knowledge of the trade secret was derived from or through a person who had utilized improper means to acquire it, acquired

under circumstances giving rise to a duty to maintain its secrecy or limit its use, or derived from or through a person who owed a duty to the person to maintain its secrecy or limit its use.

(C) Before a material change of his or her position, knew or had reason to know that it was a trade secret and that knowledge of it had been acquired by accident or mistake.

Trade secrets are almost always acquired by senior executives of a company. The difficulty is that most executives will leave the company for which they are employed to seek better, more lucrative positions in companies requiring their unique skills. Such executives bring with them the experience and knowledge gained at their former employer's company. Inevitably, the problem arises that the new company will expect disclosure of secrets acquired previously. In fact, the reason why the new company retains the executive at a higher income is due often to the expectancy of the revelation of such secrets. Litigation by the prior employer to prevent such disclosure may be the end result of the executive's transition. The following action concerns a senior employee allegedly in possession of a number of trade secrets who left his position to join a company in an allied field.

EARTHWEB, INC. V. SCHLACK

71 F. Supp. 2d 299 (1999)

FACTS: EarthWeb, Inc. sued Schlack to prevent him from being employed with International Data Group ("IDG") and to prevent him from disclosing certain trade secrets acquired from EarthWeb which had previously employed him. It sought a preliminary injunction to prevent Schlack from commencing employment and from disclosing trade secrets of the plaintiff. EarthWeb was founded in 1994 to provide online products and services to professionals working in the information technology industry. It possessed a number of websites through which it offered articles, training materials, compilations, a reference library, and online forums for such purposes. The Company hired Schlack, who had extensive experience in the publishing business, as a vice-president in charge of its worldwide websites. After being employed for a year, he resigned to assume a position with ITworld.com, a subsidiary of IDG. IDG was the leading provider of print-based information having over $1 billion in annual revenues.

EarthWeb claimed that Schlack had extensive access to trade secrets and proprietary information concerning strategic content planning, licensing agreements, advertising, and technical knowledge. It was unclear what ITworld.com was going to do given that it was to commence operations after commencement of the lawsuit. At the inception of his employment with EarthWeb, Schlack signed an employment agreement that limited Schlack's right to disclose or use confidential information acquired during his employ with EarthWeb and further prevented him from becoming employed for a year after termination with an employer in essentially the same field as the plaintiff.

ISSUE: (1) Whether EarthWeb established that it would be irreparably harmed by the alleged "inevitable disclosure of trade secrets"?

(2) Whether Schlack breached the non-compete agreement with EarthWeb by becoming employed with a company in a similar business?

DECISION: The Court held in favor of Schlack, refusing to grant a preliminary injunction finding that such harm was not established and that the non-compete agreement was overbroad and unenforceable.

REASONING: Judge Pauley

A. THE PRELIMINARY INJUNCTION STANDARD

Preliminary injunctive relief is "an extraordinary and drastic remedy which should not be routinely granted." . . . Accordingly, the movant has the burden of establishing the following elements: "(1) irreparable harm or injury, and (2) either (a) a likelihood of success on the merits, or (b) sufficiently serious questions going to the merits to make them a fair ground for litigation and a balance of hardships tipping decidedly in favor of the movant" . . .

A demonstration of irreparable harm is the "single most important prerequisite for the issuance of a preliminary injunction." The mere possibility of harm is not sufficient: the harm must be imminent and the movant must show it is likely to suffer irreparable harm if equitable relief is denied. . . . If irreparable harm is remote, speculative, or a mere possibility, the motion must be denied. . . .

B. INEVITABLE DISCLOSURE OF TRADE SECRETS AS IRREPARABLE HARM

In this circuit, irreparable harm may be presumed if a trade secret has been misappropriated. A trade secret, once lost, is lost forever; its loss cannot be measured in money damages. . . .

It is also possible to establish irreparable harm based on the inevitable disclosure of trade secrets, particularly where the movant competes directly with the prospective employer and the transient employee possesses highly confidential or technical knowledge concerning manufacturing processes, marketing strategies, or the like. . . .

Pepsico [*Pepsico, Inc. v. Redmond,* 54 F.3d 1262 (7th Cir. 1995)] is a leading example. In that case the employee, Redmond, signed a confidentiality agreement at the outset of his employment, but he did not sign a non-compete agreement. Redmond worked within the highly competitive sports-drink industry, and he eventually became a general manager for a business unit that had annual revenues of over $500 million per year and accounted for twenty percent of Pepsico's profit for all of the United States. . . . Redmond's position made him privy to information such as Pepsico's national and regional marketing strategies for the upcoming year . . . He was recruited for a similar, high level position with Quaker Oats, a direct competitor of Pepsico in the sports drink industry. Under these circumstances, the court effectively converted Redmond's confidentiality into a non-compete agreement by enjoining him from working for a direct competitor of Pepsico for a sixth month period.

. . . [I]n its purest form, the inevitable disclosure doctrine treads an exceedingly narrow path through judicially unfavored territory. Absent evidence of actual misappropriation by an employee, the doctrine should be applied in only the rarest of cases. Factors to consider in weighing the appropriateness of granting injunctive relief are whether (1) the employers in question are direct competitors providing the same or very similar products or services; (2) the employee's new position is nearly identical to his old one, such that he could not reasonably be expected to fulfill his new job responsibilities without utilizing the trade secrets of his former employer; and (3) the trade secrets are highly valuable to both employers. . . .

C. THE NON-COMPETE PROVISION

. . . In New York, non-compete covenants will be enforced only if reasonably limited in scope and duration and only "to the extent necessary (1) to prevent an employee's solicitation or disclosure of trade secrets, (2) to prevent an employee's release of confidential information regarding the employer's customers, or (3) in those cases where the employee's services to the employer are deemed special or unique." . . .

The policy underlying this strict approach rests on notions of employee mobility and free enterprise. "Once the term of an employment agreement has expired, the general public policy favoring robust and uninhibited competition should not give way merely because a particular employer wishes to insulate himself from competition." . . . "Important, too, are the powerful considerations of public policy which militate against sanctioning the loss of a man's livelihood." . . . On the other hand, "the employer is entitled to protection from unfair or illegal conduct that causes economic injury." . . .

Applying these principles here, EarthWeb's restrictive covenant would fail to pass muster even if Schlack's position at ITworld.com fell within the provision's relatively narrow parameters.

1. Duration

As a threshold matter, this Court finds that the one-year duration of EarthWeb's restrictive covenant is too long given the dynamic nature of the industry, its lack of geographical borders, and Schlack's former cutting-edge position with EarthWeb where his success depended on keeping abreast of daily changes in content on the Internet. . . .

2. Unique and Extraordinary Services

Contrary to EarthWeb's contentions, Schlack's services are not "unique and extraordinary." . . . [M]ore must . . . be shown to establish such a quality than that the employee excels at his work or that his performance is of high value to his employer. It must also appear that his services are of such character as to make his replacement impossible or that the loss of such services would cause the employer irreparable injury.

3. Trade Secrets

Under New York law, a trade secret is defined as "any formula, pattern, device or compilation of information which is used in one's business, and which gives [the owner] an opportunity to obtain an advantage over competitors who do not know or use it." . . .

New York courts consider the following factors in determining whether information constitutes a trade secret: "(1) the extent to which the information is known outside of the business; (2) the extent to which it is known by employees and others involved in the business; (3) the extent of measures taken by the business to guard the secrecy of the information; (4) the value of the information to the business and its competitors; (5) the amount of effort or money expended by the business in developing the information; [and] (6) the ease or difficulty with which the information could be properly acquired or duplicated by others." . . . The most important consideration is whether the information was kept secret. . . . This requires that the owner of a trade secret take reasonable measures to protect its secrecy.

[The court found proof lacking in Schlack's knowledge of trade secrets. He did not routinely communicate with top management; the strategic-thinking trade secret behind the plaintiff's Web sites were revealed once they were launched; there was no proof that knowledge of licensing agreements and acquisitions were secret; Schlack did not misappropriate copies of company contracts and licenses; Schlack was merely an at-will employee and could be discharged at any time; and there was no imminent risk that Schlack would disclose or use EarthWeb's trade secrets. The court then dissolved the temporary restraining order it previously granted and denied the preliminary injunction. On appeal to the U.S. Court of Appeals, (2000 U.S. App. LEXIS 1146, May 18, 2000), the court upheld the district court's decision.]

CASE QUESTIONS

1. Isn't it inevitable that an employee will reveal trade secrets to a competing company that hired him or her so as to enhance the employee's standing in the company?
2. What steps should be taken by a competing company that hires employees from competitors to avoid being sued for conspiracy to steal trade secrets?
3. Why wasn't the noncompete clause enforced by the court? Is there a difference in enforcement against an individual employee and a corporation with respect to such a clause?

In *Mai Systems Corp. v. Peak Computer, Inc.*, 991 F.2d 511 (9th Cir. 1993), the court stated, "To establish a violation under the UTSA, it must be shown that a defendant has been unjustly enriched by the improper appropriation, use or disclosure of a 'trade secret.'" In the said case, the defendant was a licensee of the plaintiff manufacturer and serviced its computer hardware and software. It employed two former employees of the plaintiff including its service manager and other key employees. The defendant contended that it neither physically took any of the plaintiff's customer database nor was any such information installed into its database. The facts of the case revealed, however, that the defendant's new employees went beyond informing the defendant of the plaintiff's customers but also actively solicited these customers by calling upon them to transfer their business to the defendant. In so doing, a violation of the act appears to have taken place.

Comparison of Patents with Trade Secrets

In the following U.S. Supreme Court case, the issue is whether states are preempted by federal statute from enacting their own trade secret laws. The issue is less important than the discussion of the nature of a trade secret and its relationship to patents.

KEWANEE OIL CO. V. BICRON CORP.

416 U.S. 470 (1974)

FACTS: Harshaw Chemical Co., a division of Kewanee Oil Co., engaged in the research in the development of a synthetic crystal for use in the detection of ionizing radiation. After very considerable expense in 1966, it was able to produce a 17-inch crystal that no other person had accomplished previously. In addition, it developed many other processes that it considered to be trade secrets. Bicron is a company that came into existence in 1969 to compete with Kewanee in the production of the crystals and did, in fact, grow a 17-inch crystal a year later. Bicron was composed in part of former employees of Kewanee who previously had signed non-disclosure confidentiality agreements with Kewanee while in its employ. Kewanee sued for injunction and damages for misappropriation of trade secrets under Ohio's trade secret law.

ISSUE: Whether Ohio's trade secret law protection statute is pre-empted by federal patent law?

DECISION: The Court decided in favor of Kewanee holding that Ohio's trade secrets law is not so preempted. In so doing it sustained the decision of the District Court and reversed the decision of the Court of Appeals that had held in favor of Bicron on the ground of preemption of the patent law.

REASONING: Chief Justice Burger

Ohio has adopted the widely relied-upon definition of a trade secret found at Restatement of Torts Section 757, comment *b* (1939). According to the Restatement,

> a trade secret may consist of any formula, pattern, device or compilation of information which is used in one's business, and which gives him an opportunity to obtain an advantage over competitors who do not know or use it. It may be a formula for a chemical compound, a process of manufacturing, treating or preserving materials, a pattern for a machine or other device, or a list of customers.

The subject of a trade secret must be secret, and must not be of public knowledge or of a general knowledge in the trade or business. This necessary element of secrecy is not lost, however, if the holder of the trade secret reveals the trade secret to another "in confidence, and under an implied obligation not to use or disclose it." . . . These others may include those of the holder's "employees to whom it is necessary to confide it, in order to apply it to the uses for which it is intended." . . . Often the recipient of confidential knowledge of the subject of a trade secret is a licensee of its holder.

The protection accorded the trade secret holder is against the disclosure or unauthorized use of the trade secret by those to whom the secret has been confided under the express or implied restriction of nondisclosure or nonuse. The law also protects the holder of a trade secret against disclosure or use when the knowledge is gained, not by the owner's volition, but by some "improper means," Restatement of Torts Section 757(a), which may include theft, wiretapping, or even aerial reconnaissance. A trade secret law, however, does not offer protection against discovery by fair and honest means, such as by independent invention, accidental disclosure, or by so-called reverse engineering, that is by starting with the known product and working backward to devine the process which aided in its development or manufacture.

Novelty, in the patent law sense, is not required for a trade secret. . . . "Quite clearly discovery is something less than invention." . . . However, some novelty will be required if merely because that which does not possess novelty is usually known; secrecy, in the context of trade secrets, thus implies at least minimal novelty.

The subject matter of a patent is limited to a "process, machine, manufacture, or composition of matter, or . . . improvement thereof," 35 U.S.C.A. Section 101, which fulfills the three conditions of novelty and utility as articulated and defined in 35 U.S.C.A. Sections 101 and 102, and nonobviousness, as set out in 35 U.S.C.A. Section 103. If an invention meets the rigorous statutory tests for the issuance of a patent, the patent is granted, for a period of 17 [now 20] years, giving what has been described as the "right of exclusion," . . . This protection goes not only to copying the subject matter, which is forbidden under the Copyright Act, but also to independent creation.

. . . The patent law does not explicitly endorse or forbid the operation of trade secret law. . . . To determine whether the Ohio law "clashes" with the federal law it is helpful to examine the objectives of both the patent and trade secret laws.

The stated objective of the Constitution in granting the power to Congress to legislate in the area of intellectual property is to "promote the Progress of Science and useful Arts." The patent laws promote this progress by offering a right of exclusion for a limited period as an incentive to inventors to risk the often enormous costs in terms of time, research and development. . . . In return for the right of exclusion—this "reward for inventions,"—the patent laws impose upon the inventor a requirement of disclosure. To insure adequate and full disclosure so that upon the expiration of the 17-year period "the knowledge of the invention enures to the people, who are thus enabled without restriction to practice it and profit by its use." . . .

The maintenance of standards of commercial ethics and the encouragement of invention are the broadly stated policies behind trade secret law. . . .

Having now in mind the objectives of both the patent and trade secret law, we turn to an examination of the interaction of these systems of protection of intellectual property—one established by the Congress and the other by a State. . . .

[T]rade secret law protects items which would not be proper subjects for consideration for patent protection under 35 U.S.C.A. Section 101. . . .

Since no patent is available for a discovery, however useful, novel, and nonobvious, unless it falls within one of the express categories of patentable subject matter of 35 U.S.C.A. Section 101, the holder of such a discovery would have no reason to apply for a patent whether trade secret protection existed or not. . . .

Certainly the patent policy of encouraging invention is not disturbed by the existence of another form of incentive to invention. In this respect the two systems are not and never would be in conflict. Similarly, the policy that matter once in the public domain must remain in the public domain is not incompatible with the existence of trade secret protection. By definition a trade secret has not been placed in the public domain.

Trade secret law provides far weaker protection in many respects than the patent law. While trade secret law does not forbid the discovery of the trade secret by fair and honest means, e.g., independent creation or reverse engineering, patent law operates "against the world," forbidding any use of the invention for whatever purposes for a significant length of time. The holder of a trade secret also takes a substantial risk that the secret will be passed on to his competitors, by theft or by breach of a confidential relationship, in a manner not easily susceptible of discovery or proof. Where patent acts as a barrier, trade secret law functions relatively as a sieve. The possibility that an inventor who believes his invention meets the standards of patentability will sit back, rely on trade secret law, and after one year of use forfeit any right to patent protection . . . is remote indeed.

We conclude that the extension of trade secret protection to clearly patentable inventions does not conflict with the patent policy of disclosure.

. . . Trade secret law and patent law have coexisted in this country for over one hundred years. Each has its particular role to play, and the operation of one does not take away from the need for the other. Trade secret law encourages the development and exploitation of those items of lesser or different invention than might be accorded protection under the patent laws, but which items still have an important part to play in the technological and scientific advancement of the Nation. Trade secret law promotes the sharing of knowledge, and the efficient operation of industry; it permits the individual inventor to reap the rewards of his labor by contracting with a company large enough to develop and exploit it. Congress, by its silence over these many years, has seen the wisdom of allowing the States to enforce trade secret protection. Until Congress takes affirmative action to the contrary, States should be free to grant protection to trade secrets.

CASE QUESTIONS

1. Compare a *trade secret* with a *patent* right. What are the advantages and disadvantages of each right?
2. What is meant by the doctrine of preemption? When is it clear that federal law is exclusive?

In *E. I. du Pont de Nemours & Co. v. Christopher,* 431 F.2d 1012 (5th Cir. 1970), the defendants were photographers who were retained by an unknown third person to take aerial photographs of the construction of a new plant of du Pont. Du Pont was developing a highly secret unpatented process for producing methanol, which was discoverable during the construction of the plant. The 16 photos that were taken were delivered to the third party. The court held that aerial photography is an improper way of discovering trade secrets that were exposed during the construction of the plant. The court added that the trade secret was developed after considerable expense and effort of time. Further, to require du Pont to install a roof over the exposed plant at much expense to prevent such espionage would not be warranted.

TRADE SECRETS AND THE EXERCISE OF THE FIRST AMENDMENT

Trade secrets are subject often to disclosure by key employees who may have complaints against the companies for whom they are employed. The tobacco industry was severely brought to task as a result of trade secret revelations of a scientist in a major tobacco firm that became the focus of a movie and *60 Minutes* television shows. The following case is analogous to the tobacco disclosures and discusses whether a person who receives trade secrets from anonymous sources may publicize it over the Internet.

FORD MOTOR COMPANY V. LANE

67 F. Supp. 2d 745 (E.D.Mich. 1999)

FACTS: Ford developed strategic, marketing, and development plans that are trade secrets known only to certain selected personnel. The plans include program structures, engineering and pricing data, and blueprints for their vehicles. It owns many copyrights and trademarks including "FORD" and the "FORD OVAL" mark. The FORD OVAL mark is a cursive font inside a blue oval. Defendant, Robert Lane, is a student doing business as Warner Publications and publishes a website with the domain name of "blueovalnews.com." The site was previously "fordworldnews.com." The website publishes news and information about Ford products and used the Ford blue oval mark. Prior to the lawsuit, Lane did receive permission from Ford to access its press release website. When Ford learned of the use of the domain name "fordworldnews.com" it objected and blocked Lane's access to the Ford website.

Lane then wrote a letter to Ford saying he had sensitive photographs, including one of the newest not yet revealed photo of the Ford Thunderbird given to him by a Ford employee. He also threatened to reveal so-called disturbing news about Ford and encouraged Ford employees to send him secret information for publication on his website. Thereafter, Lane did post an article critical of the Ford Mustang Cobra that contained confidential material sent by an anonymous source, as well as other confidential material from similar sources. Lane knew that such revelations by Ford employees violated their non-disclosure agreement with Ford. Ford sued for a preliminary injunction to prevent Lane from publishing its trade secrets and for damages for copyright infringement, misappropriation of trade secrets and other claims.

ISSUE: Whether the proposed issuance of an injunction against the defendant restraining him from publishing Ford's trade secrets would constitute an invalid prior restraint of free speech in violation of the First Amendment of the U.S. Constitution?

DECISION: The Court decided in favor of Lane stating it would be an unconstitutional restraint of free speech.

REASONING: Judge Edmunds

Our legislatures have passed trade secret laws to encourage both business ethics and innovation. Such laws enable businesses to enter into good faith transactions, form stable relationships, and share confidential information, which in turn assists in product development. Also, trade secret laws encourage research and development by supplementing the patent system and supporting innovators who seek to retain the value of their discoveries. Further, trade secret laws punish industrial espionage and deny competitors an advantage they have obtained by unfair means [citing *Kewanee Oil Co. v. Bicron Corp.*] . . . Ford alleges that Lane violated [the previously cited misappropriation statute by publishing trade secrets he knew were improperly given to him.] . . .

Although Ford has presented evidence to establish that Lane is likely to have violated the Michigan Uniform Trade Secrets Act, the Act's authorization of an injunction violates the prior restraint doctrine and the First Amendment as applied under these circumstances. The First Amendment protects freedom of speech and freedom of the press by providing, "Congress shall make no law . . . abridging the freedom of speech, or of the press. . . ." The First Amendment applies to speech on the Internet. *Reno v. America Civil Liberties Union*. . . . The primary purpose of the guarantee of freedom of the press is to prevent prior restraints on publication. . . . Even a temporary restraint on pure speech is improper absent the "most compelling circumstances." . . .

[The court cited *Near v. Minnesota,* 283 U.S. 697 (1931), which decided a case involving a newspaper that was prosecuted for publishing anti-Semitic articles concerning local officials. The *Near* court stated:]

> Although the prohibition against prior restraints is by no means absolute, the gagging of publication has been considered acceptable only in "exceptional cases." Even where questions of allegedly urgent national security, or competing constitutional interests, are concerned, we have imposed this "most extraordinary remedy" on where the evil that would result from the reportage is both great and certain and cannot be militated by less intrusive measures.

The Sixth Circuit has recently applied the prior restraint doctrine to overturn an injunction against the publication of trade secrets and other confidential material in *Proctor & Gamble Co. v. Bankers Trust Co.,* 78 F.3d 219 (6th Cir. 1996). Proctor & Gamble and Bankers Trust were parties to civil litigation and had stipulated to the entry of a protective order, which prohibited disclosure of trade secrets and other confidential documents obtained during the discovery process. A journalist from *Business Week* magazine obtained some of those documents. Proctor & Gamble and Bankers Trust sought an injunction prohibiting *Business Week* from publishing or disclosing any information contained in the documents. . . .

[T]he Sixth Circuit held that *Business Week*'s planned publication of the documents did not constitute a grave threat to a critical government interest or to a constitutional right sufficient to justify a prior restraint. To justify a prior restraint on pure speech, "publication must threaten an interest more fundamental that the First Amendment itself." . . .

[With respect to the threats by Lane to use the Internet to extort concessions from Ford, the court found no proof that Lane carried out the threats.] Although the Sixth Circuit in Proctor & Gamble has held that a defendant's improper conduct in obtaining confidential information does not justify a prior restraint, the legal system may yet provide redress through criminal prosecution, if such is found to be warranted by the underlying facts.

CASE QUESTIONS

1. Does Ford or any other company have a right not to have its trade secrets revealed over the Internet?
2. Did Lane commit extortion? Must there be proof of the actual carrying out of an extortion threat for a defendant to be sued successfully?
3. What are the limits to the "prior restraint" doctrine?

CALCULATION OF DAMAGES

In determining the damages to be awarded to the party in an intellectual property violations case, a court will allow either statutory damages or provable sums lost by the holder or a sum by which the defendant was unjustly enriched plus attorneys' fees, costs and other damages as previously stated. When the amount of damages to be awarded is uncertain as to be speculative, the reasonable royalty to be awarded will be based on the "commercial setting of the injury, the likely future consequences of the misappropriation, and the nature and extent of the use the defendant put the trade secret to after misappropriation." The court, with the assumption that the parties had acted in good faith at the time of the misappropriation,

> should consider such factors as the resulting and foreseeable changes in the parties' competitive posture; the prices past purchasers or licensees may have paid; the total value of the secret to the plaintiff, including the plaintiff's development costs and the importance of the secret to the plaintiff's business; the nature and extent of the use the defendant intended for the secret; and finally whatever other unique factors in the particular case which might have affected the parties' agreement, such as the ready availability of alternative processes.[6]

CRIMINAL VIOLATIONS

As a result of extensive spying and theft of industrial secrets, particularly by foreign companies, Congress passed the Economic Espionage Act of 1996 (EEA) (PL 104-294, 18 U.S.C. Sections 1831 et seq.). It is the first federal statute to cover thefts of both government and private sector trade secrets. A prior law, the Trade Secrets Act, 18 U.S.C. Section 1905, forbade the unauthorized disclosure of confidential government information by a government employee. It did not encompass the revealing of trade secrets by a nongovernmental person.

The Act (Section 1832(a)) provides as follows:

> Whoever, with intent to convert a trade secret, that is related to or included in a product that is produced or placed in interstate or foreign commerce, to the economic benefit of anyone other than the owner thereof, and intending that the offense will injure any owner of that trade secret, knowingly—
>
> (1) steals, or without authorization appropriates, takes, carries away, or conceals, or by fraud, artifice, or deception obtains such information;
> (2) without authorization copies, duplicates, sketches, draws, photographs, downloads, uploads, alters, destroys, photocopies, replicates, transmits, delivers, sends, mails, communicates, or conveys such information;
> (3) receives, buys, or possesses such information, knowing the same to have been stolen or appropriated, obtained, or converted without authorization;
> (4) attempts to commit any offense described in paragraphs (1) through (3); or
> (5) conspires with one or more other persons to commit any offense described in paragraph (1) through (3), and one or more of such persons do any act to effect the object of such conspiracy, shall, except as provided in subsection (b), be fined under this article or imprisoned not more than 10 years, or both.

The EEA defines *trade secrets* to cover a wide variety of data.

> The term "trade secret" means all forms and types of financial, business, scientific, technical, economic, or engineering information, including patterns, plans, compilations, program devices, formulas, designs, prototypes, methods, techniques, processes, procedures, programs, or codes, whether tangible or intangible, and whether or how stored, compiled or memorialized physically, electronically, graphically, photographically or in writing, if:
>
> (A) the owner thereof has taken reasonable measures to keep such information secret; and
> (B) the information derives independent economic value, actual or potential, from not being generally known to, and not being generally ascertainable through proper means by, the public.

The statute makes it a felonious crime to knowingly steal trade secrets. The crime is punishable by imprisonment up to 10 to 15 years and a fine up to $500,000 or twice the value of the stolen proprietary information, whichever is greater, for an individual, and up to a $10 million fine or twice the value of the information taken for a corporation. In addition, there are forfeiture penalties, and import-export sanctions. Industrial spying is often aided and abetted by governmental agents. There have been reports within the last several years of CIA involvement with U.S. corporate entities both in preventing industrial espionage and assisting companies in accessing materials from foreign companies.

In one of the first criminal cases arising out of the EEA, the U.S. court of appeals had to determine whether a court must permit the disclosure of trade secrets at a trial to determine if they, indeed, were trade secrets that could be unlawfully taken.

UNITED STATES V. HSU

155 F.3d 189 (3rd Cir. 1998)

FACTS: Hsu and two others were indicted for conspiracy to steal corporate trade secrets on behalf of a Taiwanese company from Bristol-Myers Squibb. They sought to obtain formulas and other data concerning Taxol, an anti-cancer drug produced by the Company and which was a highly valued trade secret. The defendants sought the information from an undercover FBI agent mistakenly believed to be an intermediary with a Bristol-Myers scientist. There were numerous communications between the FBI agent and the defendants over a period of fourteen months, which included discussions of price, core technology data requested, and other discussions. The defendants demanded that the trade secrets be revealed to their attorneys inasmuch as they would be necessary for preparation of defenses with respect to the criminal charges.

ISSUE: (1) Is proof that the information sought was a trade secret a necessary element to establish the crime of conspiracy or attempt to steal a trade secret?

(2) Did the defendants have a constitutional right to the secret documents alleged to have been negotiated for by the defendants and the FBI agent in order to determine whether the "trade secrets" actually existed?

DECISION: (1) The U.S. Court of Appeals stated that proof that the information sought was indeed a trade secret was not an element of the crime.

(2) The Court remanded the case to the trial court to determine in closed chamber *(in camera)* whether the documents were properly excluded from the trial and whether there are documents that must be given to the defendants that are material to the defense of the proceeding.

REASONING: Judge Rendell

The EEA became law in October 1996 against a backdrop of increasing threats to corporate security and a rising tide of international and domestic economic espionage. The end of the Cold War sent government spies scurrying to the private sector to perform illicit work for business and corporations . . . and by 1996, studies revealed that nearly $24 billion of corporate intellectual property was being stolen each year. . . .

The EEA consists of nine sections which protect proprietary information from misappropriation. Three sections are of particular import to our analysis: what acts are penalized by the statute, how the law defines a "trade secret," and when trade secrets are to remain confidential.

A. CRIMINAL ACTIVITIES

The EEA criminalizes two principal categories of corporate espionage, including "Economic espionage" as defined by 18 U.S.C. Section 1831, and the "Theft of trade secrets" as defined by Section 1832. The former provision punishes those who knowingly misappropriate, or attempt or conspire to misappropriate, trade secrets with the intent or knowledge that their offense will benefit a foreign government, foreign instrumentality, or foreign agent. . . . By contrast, Section 1832, the section under which the defendants are charged, is a general criminal trade secrets provision. It applies to anyone who knowingly engages in the theft of trade secrets, or an attempt or conspiracy to do so, "with intent to convert a trade secret, that is related to or included in a product that is produced for or placed in interstate or foreign commerce, to the economic benefit of anyone other than the owner thereof, and intended or knowing that the defense will, injure any owner of that trade secret." Section 1832(a) makes clear that attempt and conspiracy are distinct offenses, and it lists them separately from those acts that constitute completed crimes under the statute.

Section 1832 also contains at least three additional limitations not found in Section 1831. First, a defendant charged under Section 1832 must intend to convert a trade secret "to the economic benefit of anyone other than the owner thereof," including the defendant himself. This "economic benefit" requirement differs from Section 1831, which states merely that the offense "benefit," in any manner, a foreign government, instrumentality, or agent. Therefore, prosecutions under Section 1832 uniquely require that the defendant intend to confer an economic benefit on the defendant or another person or entity. Second, Section 1832 states that the defendant must intend or know that the offense will injure an owner of the trade secret, a restriction not found in Section 1831. The legislative history indicates that this requires "that the actor knew or was aware to a practical certainty that his conduct would cause such a result." . . . Finally, unlike Section 1831, Section 1832 also requires that the trade secret be "related to or included in a product for or placed in interstate or foreign commerce."

B. WHAT CONSTITUTES A "TRADE SECRET"

[The court recited the previously stated definition of trade secret.]

C. PRESERVATION OF CONFIDENTIALITY

The EEA also contains a provision designed to preserve the confidentiality of trade secrets during criminal prosecutions. 18 U.S.C. Section 1835 states that a court:

> Shall enter such orders and take such other action as may be necessary and appropriate to preserve the confidentiality of trade secrets, consistent with the requirements of the Federal Rules of Criminal and Civil Procedure, the Federal Rules of Evidence, and all other applicable laws. . . .

This section does not, of course, abrogate constitutional and statutory protections for criminal defendants. It does, however, represent a clear indication from Congress that trade secrets are to be protected to the fullest extent during EEA litigation. . . .

A. LEGAL IMPOSSIBILITY: THE RELATIONSHIP OF THE EXISTENCE OF TRADE SECRETS TO THE CRIMES CHARGED

[The court concluded that the defendants did not have a constitutional right to access the trade secrets based on the constitutional principles of due process and fair trial guarantees of the Fifth and Sixth Amendments of the U.S. Constitution.] [T]he crimes actually charged do not include the substantive offense of theft of trade secrets. Rather the crimes charged—attempt and conspiracy—do not require proof of the existence of an actual trade secret, but, rather, proof only of one's attempt or conspiracy with intent to steal a trade secret. 18 U.S.C. Section 1832(a). . . .

If we were to hold that legal impossibility [the defense that the attempt to steal a trade secret that factually was not a trade secret] is a defense to the attempted theft of trade secrets, the government would be compelled to use actual trade secrets during undercover operations in order to obtain convictions under Section 1832(a)(4).

Aside from the logistical difficulties this would create, it would also have the bizarre effect of forcing the government to disclose trade secrets to the very persons suspected of trying to steal them, thus gutting enforcement efforts under the EEA. . . .

Accordingly, we hold that legal impossibility is not a defense to a charge of attempted misappropriation of trade secrets in violation of 18 U.S.C. Section 1832(a)(4). We agree with the district court's conclusion that a charge of "attempt" under the EEA requires proof of the same elements used in other modern attempt statutes, including the Model Penal Code. A defendant is guilty of attempting to misappropriate trade secrets if, "acting with the kind of culpability otherwise required for commission of the crime, he . . . purposely does or omits to do anything that, under the circumstances as he believes them to be, is an act or omission constituting a substantial step in a course of conduct planned to culminate in his commission of the crime." . . . Thus, the defendant must (1) have the intent needed to commit a crime defined by the EEA, and must (2) perform an act amounting to a "substantial step" toward the commission of that crime. . . .

It naturally follows that a government need not prove that an actual trade secret was used during an EEA investigation, because a defendant's culpability for a charge of attempt depends only on "the circumstances as he believes them to be," not as they really are. The government can satisfy its burden under Section 1832(a)(4) by proving beyond a reasonable doubt that the defendant sought to acquire information which he or she believed to be a trade secret, regardless of whether the information actually qualified as such. . . .

Conspiracy

We also hold that the defendants have no need for the Taxol documents to defend against the government's charge of conspiracy, because we conclude that legal impossibility is not a defense to conspiracy....

It is ... the conspiratorial agreement itself, and not the underlying substantive acts, that forms the basis for conspiracy charges.... The "illegality of the agreement does not depend on the achievements of its ends," and it is "irrelevant that the ends of the conspiracy were from the very inception of the agreement objectively attainable."

Consequently, it is equally irrelevant that the commission of a substantive offense may have been legally impossible for the conspiracy to achieve all along....

CASE QUESTIONS

1. How could a person be accused of stealing or conspiring to steal trade secrets without determining in open court whether the alleged theft was composed of trade secrets?
2. Can a person be accused of committing a crime that is impossible to commit (for example, shooting a person already dead)?

INTERNATIONAL PROTECTION OF TRADE SECRETS

Agreement on Trade-Related Aspects of Intellectual Property Rights

The world community has acknowledged the need for member states to protect against the disclosure of trade secrets in the Agreement on Trade-Related Aspects of Intellectual Property Rights (TRIPS). Article 39 of TRIPS provides:

1. In the course of ensuring effective protection against unfair competition as provided in Article 10*bis* of the Paris Convention (1967). Members shall protect undisclosed information in accordance with paragraph 2 and data submitted to governments or governmental agencies in accordance with paragraph 3.
2. Natural and legal persons shall have the possibility of preventing information lawfully acquired within their control from being disclosed to, acquired by, or used by others without their consent in a manner contrary to honest commercial practices so long as such information:
   a. Is secret in the sense that it is not, as a body or in the precise configuration and assembly of its components, generally known among or readily accessible to persons within the circles that normally deal with the kind of information in question;
   b. Has commercial value because it is secret; and
   c. Has been subject to reasonable steps under the circumstances, by the person lawfully in control of the information, to keep it secret.
3. Members, when requiring, as a condition of approving the marketing of pharmaceutical or of agricultural chemical products which utilize new chemical entities, the submission of undisclosed test or other data, the origination of which involves a considerable effort, shall protect such data against unfair commercial use. In addition, Members shall protect such data against disclosure, except where necessary to protect the public, or unless steps are taken to ensure that the data are protected against unfair commercial use.

Article 10*bis* of the Paris Convention referred to in TRIPS is the article granting protection against unfair competition.[9] Disclosure of trade secrets comes within the meaning of *unfair competition* in the global community, although it is normally with trademarks in the United States. Article 10*bis* requires members of the Paris Convention "to assure to nationals of [member] countries effective protection against unfair competition.... Any act of competition contrary to honest practices in industrial or commercial matters constitutes an act of unfair competition." Thus, TRIPS explicitly includes trade secrets within the category of practices to be granted protection.

A case that exemplifies the prohibition is *General Motors Corp. v. Jose Ignacio Lopez de Arriotua,* 948 F. Supp. 684 (E.D.Mich. 1996), wherein the federal district court denied defendants' motions to dismiss the General Motors (GM) lawsuit based on alleged theft of trade secrets and unfair competition. Lopez was a senior-level GM executive who left the company to join Volkswagen, a major competitor of GM. The complaint alleged that Lopez and others left GM to obtain higher salaries and took with them some 20 cartons of stolen, confidential documents. The court found sufficient evidence for a plenary trial based on the violation of the Lanham Act that prohibited unfair competition. The court noted the defendants' alleged violation of 10*bis* of the Paris Convention that was incorporated into the Lanham Act. It cited approvingly the comment of a scholar who said:

> Article 10*bis* is not premised upon the narrow meaning of "unfair competition" as it was understood in American common law, but adopts the more liberal construction of the European countries such as France, Germany and Switzerland. . . . The statement that unfair competition is competition "contrary to honest practice" is not a definition; it merely expresses the concept that a particular act of competition is to be condemned as unfair because it is inconsistent with currently accepted standards of honest practice. It impliedly affirms that unfair competition is too broad a concept to be limited to any narrow definition such as for instance, passing off.[10]

CONCLUSION

The new technology has created enormous problems for persons wishing to protect their trademarks, patents, and trade secrets. Particularly with trade secrets, courts are reluctant to permit and enforce restrictive covenant agreements inasmuch as it prevents persons from engaging in the occupation of their choice. Courts will not assume that senior personnel, who transfer to competing companies, will bring with them the trade secrets of their former employer. Whether such holdings are realistic and in accordance with real-world competitive practices may be questioned. Nevertheless, in this brave new world, trade secrets can be ascertained by persons sitting at their computers and downloading such information by a variety of invasive techniques. Even as sophisticated a computer software giant as Microsoft was compelled to call in the Federal Bureau of Investigation to assist in ascertaining and arresting those responsible for invading its source files. Intellectual property protection may be beyond the realm of legal enforcement but may have to be left to technological breakthroughs that will prevent invasive episodes.

The protection of intellectual property rights from the U.S. and industrial nations' perspectives has received significantly added emphasis in the past decade. As nations become more adept at creating their own forms of creative works, the need for such protection will bring about even greater global scrutiny. The advent of the Internet requires global intervention because, without such attention, it would be impossible to control persons desirous of converting the works and ideas of others for their own unlawful gain.

Questions and Problems

1. Compare and contrast the types of patents. How do they differ in degree of protection, duration, and purpose?
2. Why would a company prefer to opt for keeping an invention a trade secret rather than seeking a patent for it?
3. Is there any limit to the number of persons who may have access to an alleged trade secret before it loses such status?
4. How may ownership and use of patents violate the antitrust laws?
5. To what degree may a person in possession of significant trade secrets of a company be barred from working for a competing company?
6. Arrhythmia received a patent for an invention that analyzes electrocardiographic signals in order to determine the characteristics of the heart function. Heart activity is monitored by means of an electrocardiograph device, whereby electrodes attached to the patient's body detect the heart's electrical signals in accordance with the various phases of heart activity. Mathematical formulae are used to configure the computer. In a suit for patent infringement, the defendant stated and the trial court agreed that the patent amounted to a mathematical algorithm. Decide by stating the factors that courts will use in determining whether such devices are protectable statutory subject matter. See *Arrhythmia Research Technology, Inc. v. Corazonix Corp.*, 958 F.2d 1053 (Fed. Cir. 1992).
7. Injection Research Specialists, Inc. and Pacer Industries, Inc. sued Arctic Cat, Inc., Suzuki

Motor Corp., and others for alleged trade secret misappropriation and fraud. Injection claimed that it caused the invention of a prototype EFI system for two-cycle engines used in snowmobiles and other vehicles. The system replaces the engine's carburetor, thereby increasing the engine's efficiency and use under varying temperature conditions. In July 1987, Injection contacted Polaris Industries, in an endeavor to sell its system to the major snowmobile manufacturer. For 15 months, Injection shared trade secrets with Polaris. Polaris rejected the purchase of the plaintiff's system, hired the plaintiff's former employee familiar with the trade secrets, and developed its own EFI-equipped snowmobiles. Injection then contacted Arctic Cat, a major competitor to Polaris, which signed a confidentiality and nondisclosure agreement. After selling prototypes to Arctic and staging field tests, Arctic rejected the offer and collaborated with Suzuki to develop its own EFI system in December 1991. In 1990, Injection sued Polaris, and sued Arctic and Suzuki in 1997. The Statute of Limitations is three years for misappropriation claim and six years for a claim based on fraud. Should the lawsuits be barred by the passage of the Statute of Limitations? *Chasteen v. UNISIA JECS Corp.*, 216 F.3d 1212 (10th Cir. 2000).

8. Berkes began working as a summer intern and later as a full-time employee for Vermont Microsystems, Inc. (VMI), a small company in Vermont that created AutoCAD accessories to increase the functionality of computer-aided design (CAD) software by the company Autodesk. He signed an Invention and Nondisclosure Agreement in which he acknowledged that all trade secrets developed on VMI's time were company property and promised not to disclose trade secrets. He left VMI in the fall of 1991 and joined Autodesk. The VMI CEO sent a letter to Autodesk advising it of the VMI trade secrets that Berkes was privy to and said it should exercise caution in assigning Berkes to certain projects. Berkes worked on noncompeting projects for a number of months but, thereafter, was assigned to projects that implicated VMI trade secrets. Berkes claimed that he had the right to use the Berkes-Pilcher Shading algorithm that bears his name but which was developed at VMI. VMI sued Berkes and Autodesk, alleging misappropriation of trade secrets. Decide. *Vermont Microsystems, Inc. v. Autodesk,* 88 F.3d 142 (2d Cir. 1996).

9. Aronson filed an application in October 1955 for a patent on a new type of key holder. While the patent application was pending, she negotiated a contract with Quick Point Pencil Co. for the manufacture and sale of the key holder. Quick Point agreed to pay Aronson a 5 percent royalty of the selling price in return for exclusive rights to make and sell the key holder. Quick Point did not have to manufacture the key holder. Aronson received a $750 advance on royalties and could rescind the exclusive license if Quick Point failed to sell one million key holders by the end of 1997. Quick Point also could cancel the agreement if the volume of sales did not meet its expectations. A second agreement between the parties stated that if Aronson did not receive the patent within five years, Aronson would receive 2.5 percent of sales made by Quick Point. As of June 1961 Aronson did not receive the patent, and Quick Point reduced the royalty to 2.5 percent. Thereafter, the patent application was rejected. By 1975, Quick Point had made over $7 million in sales off the key holder. Because there was no patent, competitors began selling the key holder, thereby substantially reducing the sales. Quick Point sued in November 1975 for a judgment stating that the royalty agreement was unenforceable and that state law was preempted by federal patent law. Did the patent law preempt state contract law? Was Aronson entitled to continue receiving the 2.5 percent royalty as per contract on an invalid patent? *Aronson v. Quick Point Pencil Co.*, 440 U.S. 257 (1979).

10. Rockwell is a manufacturer of printing presses and parts thereof used by newspapers. It sued DEV Industries, a competing manufacturer, of misappropriation of trade secrets. Some of the parts made by Rockwell are in fact manufactured by independent machine shops. When parts are given by Rockwell to these subvendors, Rockwell gives them a piece part drawing, indicating the materials, dimensions, tolerances, and methods of manufacture. The piece part drawings are

kept secret except from the subvendors. Rockwell had employed two persons in responsible positions allowing them access to the piece part drawings. Both left the company, one to become the president of DEV and the other to become employed by DEV when he was fired by Rockwell for allegedly stealing piece part drawings. Of some 600 piece part drawings possessed by DEV, some 100 were from Rockwell. Although DEV claimed it received the drawings from the said vendors, no proof evidencing the lawful possession was established. The district court dismissed the misappropriation of trade secrets lawsuit, stating that there were thousands of drawings in the hands of vendors. The drawings were not piece part drawings but were assembly drawings that show how the parts of a printing press fit together. On appeal, what is your decision? *Rockwell Graphic Systems, Inc. v. DEV Industries, Inc.,* 925 F.2d 174 (7th Cir. 1991).

Endnotes

1. *Ex Parte Murray,* 9 U.S.P.Q. 2D (BNA) 18 (Section 271) 19, 1820 (Bd. Pat. App. & Interf. 1988).
2. Scott M. Alter, "The Effects of State Street: The Year-and-a-Half in Review" (unpublished paper delivered at the Advanced Computer Law Institute, Georgetown University Law Center, Washington, D.C., 2000).
3. *In re Webb,* 916 F.2d 1553 (Fed. Cir. 1990).
4. *Hilgraeve Corp. v. McAfee Associates, Inc.,* 70 F. Supp. 2d 738, 757 (E.D.Mich. 1999) citing 117 S. Ct. at 1048–49.
5. U.N.T.S. No 11851, Vol. 828, pp. 305–88. Revised at Brussels on December 14, 1900, at Washington on June 2, 1911, at the Hague on November 6, 1925, at London on June 2, 1934, at Lisbon on October, 1958, and at Stockholm on July 14, 1967.
6. *University Computing Co. v. Lykes-Youngstown Corp.,* 504 F.2d 518, 539 (5th Cir. 1974).
7. TRIPS is Annex 1C of the *Final Act Embodying the Results of the Uruguay Round of Multilateral Trade Negotiations,* April 15, 1994.
8. A *manner contrary to honest commercial practices* is defined as "at least practices such as breach of contract, breach of confidence and inducement to breach, and includes the acquisition of undisclosed information by third parties who knew, or were grossly negligent to know, that such practices were involved in the acquisition."
9. Paris Convention for the Protection of Industrial Property of March 20, 1883, as amended through July 14, 1967, U.N.T.S. No. 11851, vol. 828, pp. 305–88.
10. Rudolf Callmann, *The Law of Unfair Competition, Trademarks and Monopolies,* 4th ed. (1994), Section 2610 (Wilmette, Ill., Callaghan).

PART IV

PRIVACY AND SECURITY ISSUES

CHAPTER

10 PRIVACY RIGHTS AND SECURITY ISSUES

Chapter Outline

- What Is *Privacy?*
- The U.S. Constitution and Privacy
- Tort Liability for Privacy Invasion
- Employment Privacy Issues
- Legislative Enactments
- The President's Initiative
- Privacy in the Health Arena
- Federal Trade Commission Initiatives
- Industry Self-Regulation
- International Initiatives on Privacy
- Security Issues
- The President's Framework
- International Initiatives on Security
- Conclusion

At this juncture, it is almost a trite statement to state that the Internet has changed our lives in a fundamental way. The problem is that the technology has led to a significant invasion of what heretofore was privately possessed and guarded information about our needs, tastes, medical conditions, monetary status, and other fundamental data. The concept of privacy is not a recent idea. It has its roots going back to ancient times. In the United States, privacy, as a legal concept, can be traced to a Harvard Law Review article published in 1890. The article, entitled "The Right to Privacy," was written by Samuel D. Warren and his law partner, Louis D. Brandeis (later a famed U.S. Supreme Court justice). The essence of the writing was that an individual had the right not to have one's thoughts, statements, or emotions be made public without consent.[1]

The most cited quote concerning this topic was by Scott McNealy, the CEO of Sun Microsystems, who said: "You have zero privacy anyway. Get over it."[2] As will be detailed hereafter, the statement was premature. There is no right of privacy explicitly stated in the Constitution. In past decades, persons who became subject to privacy invasion used a variety of tort theories, such as defamation, violation of one's intellectual property rights, and statutes such as the New York law that protects a private person from use of one's image without consent for commercial purposes.[3] Later the

Restatement of Torts, Section 867, provided a remedy as follows: "Any person who unreasonably and seriously interferes with another person's interest in not having his affairs known to others or his likeness exhibited to the public is liable to the other." Before we review the legal results and trends in privacy cases, it is necessary to clarify the meaning of privacy.

WHAT IS *PRIVACY*?

Two authors suggested that there are at least four categories of privacy, namely, (1) *information privacy,* that is, rules concerning gathering and using personal data such as credit reports and medical records; (2) *bodily privacy,* that is, protection extended to persons with respect to drug testing and the like; (3) *communications privacy,* or privacy with respect to communications by telephone, e-mail, and other such modes; and (4) *territorial privacy,* which governs invasions, for example, into one's workplace or public space (dressing rooms and the like).[4] Another author suggested that three facets of the constitutional right of privacy have emerged: "the right of the individual to be free in his private affairs from government surveillance and intrusion"; "the right of an individual not to have his private affairs made public by the government"; and a third, the "right of an individual to be free in action, thought, experience, and belief from governmental compulsion."[5]

The discussion of privacy issues appears to be dependent on the context upon which the issue may arise. Governmental intrusion is more constitutionally scrutinized than private conduct. Unreasonable search and seizures by government agents, acting without a search warrant, would run afoul of the Constitution. In the nongovernmental arena in employment-related cases, bodily and communications privacy may be in conflict. For example, many employers require drug testing or lie detector examinations in certain sensitive positions. Recent cases have involved companies that fired employees for alleged abuses in the sending and receipt of e-mails. We will review the development of privacy protection under the Constitution and legislatively. The emphasis in this chapter is on privacy, primarily as affected by computer technology.

THE U.S. CONSTITUTION AND PRIVACY

As stated before, there are no explicit constitutional provisions that grant inhabitants of the United States the right to privacy. There are rights spelled out in the Constitution that are aspects of or imply the right of privacy. There are U.S. Supreme Court precedents that have granted limited privacy rights. Examples are *Griswold v. Connecticut,* 381 U.S. 479 (1965), that nullified a state statute forbidding use of contraceptives, and the pro-choice abortion decision in *Roe v. Wade,* 410 U.S. 113 (1973). In *Roe v. Wade,* the Court addressed the right of privacy. It stated:

> The Constitution does not explicitly mention any right of privacy. In a line of decisions, however, going back perhaps as far as . . . (1881), the Court has recognized that a right of personal privacy, or a guarantee of certain areas or zones of privacy, does exist under the Constitution. In varying contexts, the Court or individual Justices have, indeed, found at least the roots of that right in the First Amendment . . . in the Fourth and Fifth Amendments, . . . or in the concept of liberty guaranteed by the first section of the Fourteenth Amendment. . . . These decisions make it clear that only personal rights that can be deemed "fundamental;" or "implicit in the concept of ordered liberty"; . . . are included in this guarantee of personal privacy.

In the following U.S. Supreme Court decision, the Court had to decide the privacy rights of persons whose names and addresses were recorded in a centralized file when particular types of drugs were prescribed and filled by a pharmacy.

WHALEN V. ROE

429 U.S. 589 (1977)

FACTS: New York, concerned with the diversion of many drugs into unlawful channels, enacted a statute classifying potentially harmful drugs into five schedules. In the first category, a drug, such as heroin, that

has no known medical use is banned. A second category, which is the subject of the within case, includes dangerous drugs that have legitimate purposes (opium, cocaine and the like, that assist in the treatment of a number of disorders). All prescriptions of these drugs require a prescription in triplicate that gives detailed information including the identity of the patient. These forms are filed with the NYS [New York State] Department of Health, where they are sorted, coded, logged, and recorded on a magnetic tape for retention for a five-year period. A group of patients receiving such drugs and two doctors' associations sued alleging an unconstitutional invasion of their right of privacy.
ISSUE: Whether the State of New York may record, in a centralized computer file, the names and addresses of all persons who have obtained, pursuant to a doctor's prescription, certain drugs for which there is both a lawful and an unlawful intent?
DECISION: The Supreme Court held in favor of Whalen, the Health Commissioner of the State of New York, reversing the decision of the trial court, which stated that such recording violated the appellees right of privacy.
REASONING: Justice Stevens
. . . State legislation which has some effect on individual liberty or privacy may not be held unconstitutional simply because a court finds it unnecessary, in whole or in part. For we have frequently recognized that individual States have broad latitude in experimenting with possible solutions to problems of vital local concern.

The New York statute challenged in this case represents a considered attempt to deal with such a problem. It is manifestly the product of an orderly and rational legislative decision. It was recommended by a specially appointed commission, which held extensive hearings on the proposed legislation, and drew on experience with similar programs in other States. There surely was nothing unreasonable in the assumption that the patient-identification requirement might aid in the enforcement of laws designed to minimize the misuse of dangerous drugs. For the requirement could reasonably be expected to have a deterrent effect on potential violators as well as to aid in the detection or investigation of specific instances of apparent abuse. At the very least, it would seem that the State's vital interest in controlling the distribution of dangerous drugs would support a decision to experiment with new techniques for control. For if an experiment fails—if in this case experience teaches that the patient-identification requirement results in the foolish expenditure of funds to acquire a mountain of useless information—the legislative process remains available to terminate the unwise experiment. It follows that the legislature's enactment of the patient-identification requirement was a reasonable exercise of New York's broad police powers. . . .

Unquestionably, some individuals' concern for their own privacy may lead them to avoid or to postpone needed medical attention. Nevertheless, disclosures of private medical information to doctors, to hospital personnel, to insurance companies, and to public health agencies are often an essential part of modern medical practice even when the disclosure may reflect unfavorably on the character of the patient. Requiring such disclosures to representatives of the State, having responsibility for the health of the community, does not automatically amount to an impermissible invasion of privacy. . . .

A final word about issues we have not decided. We are not unaware of the threat to privacy implicit in the accumulation of vast amounts of personal information in computerized data banks or other massive government files. The collection of taxes, the distribution of welfare and social security benefits, the supervision of public health, the direction of our armed forces, and the enforcement of the criminal laws all require the orderly preservation of great quantities of information, much of which is personal in character and potentially embarrassing or harmful if disclosed. The right to collect and use such data for public purposes is typically accompanied by a concomitant statutory or regulatory duty to avoid unwarranted disclosures. Recognizing that in some circumstances that duty arguably has its roots in the Constitution, nevertheless New York's statutory scheme, and its implementing administrative procedures, evidence a proper concern with, and protection of, the individual's interests in privacy. We therefore need not, and do not, decide any question which might be presented by the unwarranted disclosure of accumulated private data—whether intentional—or by a system that did not contain comparable security provisions. We simply hold that this record does not establish an invasion of any right or liberty protected by the Fourteenth Amendment.

CASE QUESTIONS

1. Does the statute violate the Fourth Amendment privilege of unreasonable search and seizure? What about the Fifth Amendment right to remain silent?
2. Inasmuch as drug information and medical diagnosis is known by medical insurers, what steps should be taken to ensure the preservation of privacy?

In *Kallstrom v. City of Columbus,* 136 F.3d 1055 (6th Cir. 1998), three undercover police officers sued the City of Columbus, Ohio, for disclosing their personnel and preemployment file to defense counsel in certain criminal drug cases. The information contained highly personal information, such as officers' addresses and telephone numbers, the names, addresses, and phone numbers of immediate family members and other personal data. The information was passed on by counsel to their criminal clients. The officers had been assured that the information would be held in strict confidence. The court held in favor of the officers, stating that the officers have a constitutionally protected privacy interest under the substantive component of the due process clause of the Fourteenth Amendment.

With respect to the claim of right of privacy, the court of appeals reviewed in detail the many U.S. Supreme Court decisions concerning the right of privacy. It stated:

A. Due Process—Fundamental Privacy Right

The officers contend that the release of the personal information contained in their personnel files infringes upon their right of privacy. Although the Supreme Court first recognized this right over thirty years ago, see *Griswold v. Connecticut,* 381 U.S. 479 . . . (1965) (recognizing married couples' right to privacy with respect to use of contraception), the boundaries of the right to privacy have not been clearly delineated. The privacy cases have developed along two distinct lines. The first line of cases involves the individual's interest in independent decision making in important life-shaping matters, while the second line of cases recognizes the individual's interest in avoiding disclosure of highly personal matters. *See Whalen v. Roe.* . . . Cases concerning an individual's interest in autonomy have extended constitutional protection to activities relating to marriage, *see Griswold,* 381 U.S. at 484–86; *Loving v. Virginia,* 388 U.S. 1 . . . (1967), procreation [reversed state court that mandated the sterilization of habitual criminals], *see Skinner v. Oklahoma ex rel. Williamson,* [316 U.S. 535] . . . (1942), contraception, *see Eisenstadt v. Baird,* 405 U.S. 438 . . . (1972); *Griswold,* 381 U.S. at 485, family relationships, *Moore v. City of East Cleveland,* 431 U.S. 494, (1977), and child rearing, *see Pierce v. Society of Sisters,* 268 U.S. 510 . . . (1925); *Meyer v. Nebraska,* 262 U.S. 390 . . . (1923).

Fourth Amendment Privacy Protection

The Fourth Amendment states, "The right of the people to be secure in their persons, houses, papers, and effects, against unreasonable searches and seizures, shall not be violated. . . ." Every person has the right to privacy from unreasonable intrusion within his or her dwelling place and to be free from bodily searches. The right is not unlimited. The Constitution permits such searches when a warrant is issued by a judge based upon probable cause and a sworn affidavit or affirmation "describing the place to be searched and the person or things to be seized." The penalty for governmental intrusion without a proper search warrant or without justifiable excuse is the invocation of the *exclusionary rule.* The rule provides that evidence elicited as a result of the wrongful search constitutes "fruit of the poisonous tree" and is to be excluded from introduction at a trial of the accused.[6]

There are exceptions and limitations to the exclusionary rule. They include evidence that is obtainable by independent means or evidence that would inevitably have been obtainable without the unlawful intrusion; evidence that was gathered by private means without government instigation; and exceptions for honest mistakes and acting in good faith. Examples of the latter are if officers made a search after obtaining a search warrant that should not have been granted because of legal insufficiency or if officers executed a warrant in an adjacent apartment believed to be the residence described in the warrant.[7]

In the next case, the issue arose whether a Foreign Bureau of Information Services (FBIS) employee had a Fourth Amendment privilege against a warrantless search of his computer at the FBIS office.

UNITED STATES V. SIMONS

206 F.3d 392 (4th Cir. 2000)

FACTS: Simons was employed as an electronic engineer at the FBIS office, a division of the C.I.A. He had an office not shared with anyone with a computer having Internet access. FBIS had a policy concerning Internet usage that prohibited its use for non-Government-related business. Accessing unlawful material was strictly prohibited. The policy included a warning that FBIS would conduct electronic audits to ensure compliance with its policy. FBIS contracted with a company to install a "firewall" that funnels and registers all Internet access flows and acts as a database. When the firewall was tested and the word "sex" entered on the keyboard, it was discovered that a large number of hits emanated from the defendant, Simons', computer. The discovery was reported to Simons' supervisors for further investigation. Pornographic images, including child pornography, were found by investigating police officers. Thereafter, the officers procured search warrants concerning the computer. Simons was arrested for knowingly possessing material containing images of child pornography.

ISSUE: Did the initial warrantless search violate defendant's fourth amendment rights prohibiting unreasonable searches and seizures?

DECISION: The Court held against the defendant, stating that the search was lawful.

REASONING: Judge Wilkins

To establish a violation of his rights under the Fourth Amendment, Simons must first prove that he had a legitimate expectation of privacy in the place searched or the item seized. . . . And, in order to prove a legitimate expectation of privacy, Simons must show that his subjective expectation of privacy is one that society is prepared to accept as objectively reasonable.

Government employees may have a legitimate expectation of privacy in their offices or in parts of their offices as their desks or file cabinets. . . . However, office practices, procedures, or regulations may reduce legitimate privacy expectations. . . .

Simons did not have a legitimate expectation of privacy with regard to the record or fruits of his Internet use in light of the FBIS Internet policy. The policy clearly stated that FBIS would "audit, inspect, and/or monitor" employees' use of the Internet, including all file transfers, all websites visited, and all e-mail messages, "as deemed appropriate." This policy placed employees on notice that they could not reasonably expect that their Internet activity would be private. Therefore, regardless of whether Simons subjectively believed that the files he transferred from the Internet were private, such a belief was not objectively reasonable after FBIS notified him that it would be overseeing his Internet use. . . .

CASE QUESTIONS

1. What if the employer had an announced policy of privacy protection for employees. Would the result be different?
2. If the employer did not announce the inspection policy, would the court have held in favor of Simons?
3. Are private employees subject to the Fourth Amendment privilege of unlawful search and seizure?

Right of Privacy of Convicted Sex Offenders

In the late 1990s, a rash of sex crimes against children by previously convicted sex offenders, who lived in the neighborhood of their victims after release from prison, led to the enactment of federal and state laws known as Megan's law (Megan was a child murdered by one such sex offender). The following case reviews the constitutional aspects of the rights of sex offenders to be free from registration and notification requirements.

AKELLA V. MICHIGAN DEPARTMENT OF STATE POLICE

67 F. Supp. 2d 716 (E.D.Mich. 1999)

FACTS: Two of the plaintiffs, "Doe" and "Roe" pled guilty to statutory rape in that they had sexual relations with their respective girlfriends, both under the age of sixteen years. Under the State of Michigan's Sex Offenders Registration Act, individuals convicted of one of a number of enumerated sex offenses are required to register and update any change of address within ten days of relocation. Failure to register is a felony. The information is stored in a computerized database that contains detailed information concerning the offender including name, address, zip code, physical description, and date of conviction. The public registry is open for inspection by anyone and is accessible on the Internet by identification of the zip code. Plaintiffs claim lack of privacy and that they are subject to harassment, vilification, loss of employment opportunities, and other social benefits.
ISSUES: Whether defendants' right to privacy under the Constitution was violated?
DECISION: The Court rejected the claim of right to privacy.
REASONING: Judge Duggan

B. RIGHT TO PRIVACY

According to the Doe and Roe plaintiffs, the Act infringes on constitutionally protected privacy interests by "subjecting their names and addresses to public scrutiny in massive proportion." . . . The Supreme Court in *Whalen, supra,* delineated a constitutional right to privacy pertaining to disclosure of personal information as follows: "The other principle of privacy . . . protects an individual's right to control the nature and extent of information released about that individual." . . . The Sixth Circuit has "narrowly construed the holdings in *Whalen* . . . to extend the right to information privacy only to interests that implicate a fundamental liberty interest." . . . The Sixth Circuit . . . set forth the following test applicable to alleged deprivations of the right to privacy: (1) the interest at stake must implicate either a fundamental right or one implicit in the concept of ordered liberty; and (2) the government's interest in disseminating the information must be balanced against the individual's interest in keeping the information private. . . . Against this framework, the Court must determine whether the Doe and Roe plaintiffs have alleged a sufficient deprivation of the right to privacy.

To the extent that plaintiffs challenge the dissemination of information concerning their arrests as violative of the right to privacy, the Court rejects such a claim. This Court agrees with prior decisions in our district confronting challenges to Michigan's statute on privacy grounds and concluding that plaintiffs do not have a "legitimate privacy interest in preventing compilation and dissemination of truthful information that is already, albeit less conveniently, a matter of public record." . . . Further, the Ninth Circuit dismissed a similar challenge, on privacy grounds, to the State of Washington's sex offender act stating: "Any right of privacy, to the extent that it exists at all, would protect only personal information. The information collected and disseminated by the Washington statute is already fully available to the public and is not constitutionally protected. . . ." Thus, the Court concludes that dissemination of sex offender registration material does not violate any constitutionally protected privacy interest of plaintiffs.

[Concerning dissemination of plaintiffs' home addresses:] To the extent that plaintiffs desire to limit widespread exposure of that information which is already public, the Court does not conclude that the plaintiffs' interest outweighs the State of Michigan's interest. Accordingly, the Court concludes that plaintiffs have failed to articulate a constitutionally protected privacy interest in the dissemination of their home address.

C. PERSONAL SECURITY

[Plaintiffs claimed that the public dissemination of the information subjected them to threats and other wrongful acts. Plaintiffs cited the *Kallstrom* case.] In *Kallstrom,* the Sixth Circuit noted that "individuals have a 'clearly established right under the substantive component of the Due Process Clause to personal security and to bodily integrity,' and this right is fundamental where 'the magnitude of the liberty deprivation that [the] abuse inflicts upon the victim . . . strips the very essence of personhood.'" . . . The Court continued by noting "it goes without saying that an individual's 'interest in preserving her life is one of constitutional dimension.'" . . . The facts of *Kallstrom* involved the City of Columbus' disclosure of personal information contained in the police officer personnel files to defense counsel during a criminal trial in which the officers testified against the defendants. In finding that the disclosure implicated a due process privacy protection, the Court noted:

> In finding that the City's release of private information concerning the officers to defense counsel . . . rises to constitutional dimensions by threatening the personal security and bodily integrity of the officers and their family members, we do not mean to imply that every governmental act which intrudes upon or threatens upon an individual's body invokes the Fourteenth Amendment. But where the release of private information places an individual at substantial risk of serious bodily harm, possibly even death, from a perceived likely threat, the "magnitude of the liberty deprivation . . . strips the very essence of personhood."

The Court concludes that plaintiffs Roe and Doe have failed to state a claim for a violation of due process rights. First, the due process protection accorded the plaintiffs in *Kallstrom* assumed the disclosure of "private information." Here, the information that plaintiffs allege implicates the privacy right, to wit their sex offender convictions, is already a matter of public record that is available for inspection at a local police station. Further, even viewing the allegations of the complaint in the light most favorable to plaintiffs, the Court cannot conclude that plaintiffs have articulated, with any degree of specificity, a "perceived likely threat" to their personal security and bodily integrity. . . .

CASE QUESTIONS

1. Suppose the statute read that all felons were subject to the same law and revelations. Would the statute be constitutional?
2. What if the crimes for which registration and disclosure were required were misdemeanors; would the statute be constitutional?
3. A number of years ago, persons found with prostitutes were publicized on a New York City government-owned radio station, and the information was given to newspapers. Would such disclosure be actionable as a tort claim by the persons publicized?

TORT LIABILITY FOR PRIVACY INVASION

Invasion of one's privacy is now considered to be a tort in most states. The Restatement, Torts (Second), Section 652A, states that invasion constitutes four torts, namely:

(1) *Section 652B. Intrusion upon Seclusion:* One who intentionally intrudes, physically or otherwise, upon the solitude or seclusion of another or his private affairs or concerns, is subject to liability to the other for invasion of his privacy, if the intrusion would be highly offensive to a reasonable person;

(2) *Section 652C. Appropriation of Name or Likeness.* One who appropriates to his own use or benefit the name or likeness of another is subject to liability to the other for invasion of his privacy.

(3) *Section 652D. Publicity Given to Private Life.* One who gives publicity to a matter concerning the private life of another is subject to liability to the other for invasion of his privacy, if the matter publicized is of a kind that (a) would be highly offensive to a reasonable person, and (b) is not of legitimate concern to the public.

(4) *Section 652E. Publicity Placing Person in False Light.* One who gives publicity to a matter concerning another that places the other before the public in a false light is subject to liability to the other for invasion of his privacy, if (a) the false light in which the other was placed would be highly offensive to a reasonable person, and (b) the actor had knowledge of or acted in reckless disregard as to the falsity of the publicized matter and the false light in which the other would be placed.

The *intrusion upon seclusion* is exemplified by persons committing, without proper authorization, the act of tapping another person's telephone, being a peeping Tom, reading another person's mail, and so on. The *appropriation of name or likeness* is illustrated by a case previously litigated by this author. The client, a model who had a photo portfolio made for use in applying for related jobs, found one of her photos placed without authorization in an advertisement in an unsavory man's magazine. The photo was in an ad soliciting the purchase of a book discussing ways to engage female companionship. Such usage not only was made without consent or monetary reimbursement but also was a source of significant embarrassment to the model.

Publicity given to private life refers to the act of publicizing nonpublic information about a person, such as alleged indebtedness owed by such person, or that such a person has acquired immunodeficiency syndrome (AIDS), or other private data. The fourth tort, *publicity placing person in false light,* is similar to the tort of defamation and requires that wrongful information be publicized about another that is untrue.

The following case discusses at length the application of the Restatement to the alleged invasion of privacy.

HARRIS V. EASTON PUBLISHING CO.

335 Pa. Super. 141, 483 A.2d 1377 (1984)

FACTS: Brigitte Harris was a German national who married a U.S. soldier stationed in Germany and gave birth to their three children. She moved to the U.S., gave birth to a fourth child and made application for medical assistance and food stamps for herself, her pregnant daughter, and for her granddaughter. She withdrew the application because she refused to comply with the demand of the caseworker to photocopy certain legal documents allegedly because the photocopy of such documents was illegal. The Department of Public Welfare prepared a fictionalized account of the case that was sent to a number of newspapers in northeast Pennsylvania for inclusion in a public service column it regularly submitted for publication. The fictionalized account recited the facts of the Harris application. Harris complained that numerous persons recognized Harris as being the person described in the newspaper account thereby causing alleged severe embarrassment. The trial court dismissed the case on motion for summary judgment [without a trial]. On appeal, the decision of the trial court was reversed.

ISSUE: Was such publication an invasion of privacy as a matter of law?

DECISION: The Court held in favor of Harris finding a privacy invasion.

REASONING: Judge Johnson

The gist of privacy is the sense of seclusion, the wish to be obscure and alone, and it is a trespass to abuse these personal sensibilities. . . . The right of privacy is a qualified right to be let alone; but to be actionable, the alleged invasion of that right must be unlawful or unjustifiable. . . .

An action for invasion of privacy is comprised of four distinct torts: (1) intrusion upon seclusion, (2) appropriation of name or likeness, (3) publicity given to private life, and (4) publicity placing the person in a false light. . . . Our state courts have cited with approval the Restatement (Second) of Torts Sections 652B–E for support regarding invasion of privacy matters. . . . We believe that the Restatement most ably defines the elements of invasion of privacy as that tort has developed in Pennsylvania.

[The court recited Section 652B, stated previously.] An action pursuant to this section does not depend upon any publicity given to the person whose interest is invaded or to his affairs. Restatement (Second) of Torts Section 652B, comment a. The invasion may be (1) by physical intrusion into a place where the plaintiff has secluded himself. (2) by use of the defendant's senses to oversee or overhear the plaintiff's private affairs, or (3) some other form of investigator or examination into plaintiff's private concerns. *Id.,* comment b.

The defendant is subject to liability under this section only when he has intruded into a private place, or has otherwise invaded a private seclusion that the plaintiff has thrown about his person or affairs. *Id., comment c.* . . . There is also no liability unless the interference with the plaintiff's seclusion is substantial and would be highly offensive to the ordinary reasonable person. Restatement (Second) of Torts Section 652, comment d.

[The court held that there was no invasion by means of intentional intrusion and dismissed the claimant's first privacy claim.]

[The court then recited Section 652D.] The elements of the tort are: (1) publicity, given to (2) private facts, (3) which would be highly offensive to a reasonable person and (4) is not of legitimate concern to the public. . . .

The element of "publicity" requires that the matter is made public, by communicating it to the public at large, or to so many persons that the matter must be regarded as substantially certain to become one of public knowledge. Restatement (Second) of Torts Section 652D, comment a. . . .

The second element requires that the publicity involve a private fact. A private fact is one that has not already been made public. Liability cannot be based upon that which the plaintiff himself leaves open to the public eye. Restatement (Second) of Torts Section 652D, comment b. It also follows from the use of the term *private* fact that the reader or recipient of the private fact not have prior knowledge of that fact: there can be no liability where the publicity given involves facts with which the recipient is familiar.

The third element requires that a reasonable person of ordinary sensibilities would find such publicity highly offensive . . . committed in such a manner as to outrage or cause mental suffering, shame or humiliation to a person of ordinary sensibilities. . . .

The final element exempts from liability those facts which are of legitimate concern to the public, such as official court records open to public inspection. . . . This also applies to persons who, voluntarily or involuntarily, have become public figures, Restatement (Second) Torts Section 652D, comments e and f, and may also apply to certain private facts relating to those public figures, such as the life history of one accused of a sensational crime, *id,* comment h, and even to the members of that person's family. . . . *Id.,* comment i. . . .

[The court found that although the column did not reveal the identities of the Harris family by use of fictitious names, 17 people were able to so identify them. There was a large enough number to constitute the element of publicity. The revelation of the private facts could be found at a full trial to be highly offensive. There was no legitimate public concern in giving publicity to the intimate facts set forth in the article. Welfare applicants have a legitimate right of privacy of such fact.]

The right of privacy competes with the freedom of the press as well as the interest of the public in the free dissemination of news and information, and these permanent public interests must be considered when placing the necessary limitations upon the right of privacy. . . . An action based on such right must not become a vehicle for establishment of a judicial censorship of the press. . . . However, on balancing the various interests, we hold that the Company was not entitled to judgment as a matter of law.

The right of privacy is intended, inter alia, to protect persons from unwarranted publicity concerning their personal lives. There can be no doubt that the facts publicized in the instant case were of the type which were designed to be protected. . . .

[The court remanded the case to the trial court for a plenary trial on the merits of the case.]

CASE QUESTIONS

1. Do you agree with the decision? If the 17 persons recognized the plaintiff as being the person indicated in the hypothetical question, what invasion of privacy existed?
2. What if the hypothetical person was a blend of two or more persons, would each such person be permitted to sue?

In the following case involving a gay naval officer, America Online became an inadvertent party to the confirmation of private information.

MCVEIGH V. COHEN

983 F. Supp. 215 (D.D.C. 1998)

FACTS: McVeigh is a highly decorated veteran of the U.S. Navy, having served for seventeen years. He was the most senior enlisted man aboard a nuclear submarine. A civilian Navy volunteer received an e-mail message through America Online concerning a toy-drive she was coordinating for the children of the submarine crewmembers. The sender was signed by a "Tim" from a site "boysrch." The volunteer searched the member profile directory of the sender. The directory stated that "boysrch" was an AOL subscriber living in Honolulu, Hawaii, who was a member of the military and who described himself as "gay." The volunteer forwarded the e-mail and profile to her husband, who also was a noncommissioned officer aboard the same submarine.

An investigation was commenced by a Judge Advocate officer on orders from the Commander of the vessel. AOL was again contacted, and by means of a ruse, the full name of the plaintiff was revealed. The investigator stated he was "a third party in receipt of a fax sheet and wanted to confirm the profile sheet, [and] who it belonged to." McVeigh was advised of the charge of having violated the provision governing sodomy and indecent acts and of his rights under the Uniform Code of Military Justice. After an administrative discharge hearing in which the plaintiff was ordered to be separated from the Navy, the within action was commenced.

ISSUE: Whether the plaintiff violated the "Don't Ask, Don't Tell, Don't Pursue" enactment?

DECISION: The Court held in favor of the plaintiff deciding that McVeigh did not violate the statutory policy.

REASONING: The facts as stated above clearly demonstrate that the Plaintiff did not openly express his homosexuality in a way that compromised this "Don't Ask, Don't Tell" policy. Suggestions of sexual orientation in a private, anonymous email account did not give the Navy a sufficient reason to investigate to determine whether to commence discharge proceedings. In its actions, the Navy violated its own regulations. See Guidelines for Fact-Finding Inquiries Into Homosexual Conduct, Department of Defense Directive No. 1332.14 ("Guidelines"). An investigation into sexual orientation may be initiated "only when [a commander] has received credible information that there is a basis for discharge," such as when an officer "has said that he or she is a homosexual or bisexual, or made some other statement that indicates a propensity or intent to engage in homosexual acts." Id. Yet in this case, there was no such credible information that Senior Chief McVeigh had made such a statement. Under the Guidelines, "credible information" requires more than "just a belief or suspicion" that a Service member has engaged in homosexual conduct. Id. In the examples provided, the Guidelines state that "credible information" would exist in this case only if "a reliable person" stated that he or she directly observed or heard a Service member make an oral or written statement that "a reasonable person would believe was intended to convey the fact that he or she engages in or had a propensity or intent to engage in homosexual acts." Id. . . .

The subsequent steps taken by the Navy in its "pursuit" of the Plaintiff were not only unauthorized under its policy, but likely illegal under the Electronic Communications Privacy Act of 1986 ("ECPA"). The ECPA, enacted by Congress to address privacy concerns on the Internet, allows the government to obtain information from an online service provider—as the Navy did in this instance from AOL—but only if a) it obtains a warrant under the Federal Rules of Criminal Procedure or state equivalent; or b) it gives prior notice to the online subscriber and then issues a subpoena or receives a court order authorizing disclosure of the information in questions. See 18 U.S.C. Section 2073 (b)(A)–(B), (c)(1)(B).

In soliciting and obtaining over the phone personal information about the Plaintiff from AOL, his private on-line service provider, the government in this case invoked neither of these provisions and thus failed to comply with the ECPA. . . .

IV. PUBLIC INTEREST

Certainly, the public has an inherent interest in the preservation of privacy rights as advanced by Plaintiff in this case. With literally the entire world on the world-wide web, enforcement of the ECPA is of great concern to those who bare the most personal information about their lives in private accounts through the Internet. In this case in particular, where the government may well have violated a federal statute in its zeal to brand the Plaintiff a homosexual, the actions of the Navy must be more closely scrutinized by this Court. It is disputed in the record exactly as to how the Navy represented itself to AOL when it requested information about the Plaintiff. The Defendants contend that Legalman Kaiser merely asked for confirmation of a fax sheet bearing Plaintiff's account. Plaintiff contends, and AOL confirms, however, that the Naval officer "mislead" AOL's representative by "both failing to disclose the identity and purpose [of his request] and by portraying himself as a friend or acquaintance of Senior Chief McVeigh's."

CASE QUESTIONS

1. Is the "Don't Ask, Don't Tell" policy constitutional?
2. It appears that McVeigh, in his "boysrch," sought the companionship of minors. Do you agree with the court that a person subject to military discipline should not be discharged for such conduct?

The Restatement, Section 652C, makes it an invasion of privacy to appropriate the name or likeness of another person. The following case exemplifies the concept as well as other legal issues discussed elsewhere in the text.

WHITE V. SAMSUNG ELECTRONICS AMERICA, INC.

971 F.2d 1395 (9th Cir. 1992)

FACTS: [The facts of the within case may be found in Chapter 8 and are repeated herein.] This action concerns Vanna White, the hostess of "Wheel of Fortune," a popular television game show. Because of her fame, she has marketed her identity to different advertisers. The defendant, Samsung, ran a series of advertisements prepared by the defendant, David Deutsch Associates, Inc., in a number of national and regional publications depicting a current popular culture item in a Twenty-First Century setting. The advertisements were humorous lampooning of present day culture. The advertisement at issue in this case for Samsung videocassette recorders showed a robot dressed in a wig, gown, and jewelry resembling Vanna White. The robot was posed next to a game board that was a replica of the Wheel of Fortune. The caption of the advertisement read "Longest-running game show. 2012 A.D." White did not consent to the ad and was not paid for it. The District Court dismissed the complaint. On appeal, the decision was reversed.

ISSUES: (1) Did the defendant violate the California right of privacy statute Section 3344 that provides "any person who knowingly uses another's name, voice, signature, photograph, or likeness, in any manner, ... for purposes of advertising or selling, ... without such person's prior consent ... shall be liable for any damages sustained by the person or persons injured as a result thereof"?

(2) Did the defendants violate White's common law right of publicity?

DECISION: (1) The Court dismissed the initial claim of violation of the California statute.

(2) The Court held in favor of White finding a violation of her right of publicity claim.

REASONING: Judge Goodwin

I. SECTION 3344

White argues that the Samsung advertisement used her "likeness" in contravention of Section 3344. In *Midler v. Ford Motor Co.,* 849 F.2d 460 (9th Cir. 1988), this court rejected Bette Midler's Section 3344 claim concerning a Ford television commercial in which a Midler "sound-alike" sang a song which Midler had made famous. In rejecting Midler's claim, this court noted that "the defendants did not use Midler's name or anything else whose use is prohibited by the statute. The voice they used was [another person's], not hers. The term 'likeness' refers to a visual image not a voice imitation." *Id.* at 463.

In this case, Samsung and Deutsch used a robot with mechanical features, and not, for example, a manikin molded to White's precise features. Without deciding for all purposes when a caricature or impressionistic resemblance might become a "likeness," we agree with the district court that the robot at issue here was not White's "likeness" within the meaning of Section 3344. Accordingly, we affirm the court's dismissal of White's Section 3344 claim.

II. RIGHT OF PUBLICITY

... In *Eastwood v. Superior Court* [149 Cal. App. 3d 409 (1983)] ..., the California Court of Appeal stated that the common law right of publicity cause of action "may be pleaded by alleging (1) the defendant's use of the plaintiff's identity; (2) the appropriation of plaintiff's name or likeness to defendant's advantage, commercially or otherwise; (3) lack of consent; and (4) resulting injury." *Id.* at 417 (citing Prosser, Law of Torts ...). The district court dismissed White's claim for failure to satisfy *Eastwood*'s second prong, reasoning that defendants had not appropriated White's "name or likeness" with the robot ad. We agree that the robot ad did not make use of White's name or likeness. However, the common law right of publicity is not so confined. [In a footnote, the court said, "Under Professor Prosser's scheme, the right of publicity is the last of the four categories of the right to privacy. ... "]

In *Midler,* this court held that, even though the defendants had not used Midler's name or likeness, Midler had stated a claim for violation of her California common law right of publicity because "the defendants ... for their own profit in selling their product did appropriate part of her identity by using a Midler sound-alike." ...

In *Carson v. Here's Johnny Portable Toilets, Inc.,* 698 F.2d 831 (6th Cir. 1983), the defendant had marketed portable toilets under the brand name "Here's Johnny"—Johnny Carson's signature "Tonight Show" introduction—without Carson's permission. ... [T]he sixth circuit found ... the defendant had appropriated Carson's identity by using ... the phrase "Here's Johnny."

... It is not important *how* the defendant has appropriated the plaintiff's identity, but *whether* the defendant has done so. ...

Television and other media create marketable celebrity identity value. Considerable energy and ingenuity are expended by those who have achieved celebrity value to exploit it for profit. The law protects the celebrity's sole right to exploit this value whether the celebrity has achieved her fame out of rare ability, dumb luck, or a combination thereof. We decline Samsung and Deutsch's invitation to permit the evisceration of the common law right of publicity through means as facile as those in this case. Because White has alleged facts showing that Samsung and Deutsch has appropriated her identity, the district court erred by rejecting, on summary judgment, White's common law right of publicity claim.

CASE QUESTIONS

1. If the likeness were of a deceased personality, would the decision be the same?
2. Compare the cited Midler case. Should such a distinction be made between visual and voice imitation?

EMPLOYMENT PRIVACY ISSUES

Medical and Prescription Drug Records

The issue of violation of the right of privacy often arises in the context of employer-employee relationships. The leading cases that encompass the public and private employment arenas are *United States v. Westinghouse,* 638 F.2d 570 (3d Cir. 1980) and *Doe v. SEPTA,* 72 F.3d 1133 (3d Cir. 1995). In the *Westinghouse* litigation, the National Institute for Occupational Safety and Health (NIOSH), a federal agency, received a written request for a health hazard evaluation from a union at the Westinghouse plant in Pennsylvania as a result of some cases of alleged illnesses incurred by employees. NIOSH conducted a walk-through inspection of the plant. Thereafter, a NIOSH physician and a hygienist requested medical records of potentially affected employees. When Westinghouse refused, claiming privacy considerations, NIOSH subpoenaed the records. Westinghouse refused to release them without written consent of the persons concerned and written assurance that the records would not be disclosed.

The district court ordered compliance with the subpoena. The court of appeals upheld the lower court's decision. Important to our discussion is the analysis of the factors to be considered in balancing the privacy rights of individuals with the need for disclosure. They are: (1) the type of record requested; (2) the information it does or does not contain; (3) the potential for harm in any subsequent nonconsensual disclosure; (4) the injury from disclosure to the relationship in which the record was generated; (5) the adequacy of safeguards to prevent unauthorized disclosure; (6) the degree of need for access; and (7) whether there is an express statutory mandate, articulated public policy, or some other recognizable public interest favoring access.

The court thereafter found that the government did establish a need for investigating occupational health and safety of workers; that its interest in protecting workers was substantial in justifying some intrusion into an individual's privacy; and that there was no evidence that the limited disclosure would adversely affect the workers. Concerning the security of the maintenance of the records as required in *Whalen,* there appeared to be adequate safeguards assuring nondisclosure of names and addresses of the employees. Accordingly, the court required that NIOSH give prior notice to the employees of the examination of their records and permit them to raise individually the concerns of privacy, if any.

DOE V. SEPTA

72 F.3d 1133 (3d Cir. 1995)

FACTS: John Doe [a fictitious name] is an employee of the Southeastern Pennsylvania Transportation Authority (SEPTA). He sued SEPTA for violation of his right of privacy in that, by monitoring the prescription drug program, the Chief Administrative Officer (C.A.O.) and the Director of Benefits learned that Doe had contracted AIDS. In 1991, Doe was HIV-positive and began to take Retrovir, a prescription drug used solely to treat HIV. Before he filled his prescription, he asked the SEPTA physician if he or anyone reviewed the names of persons using such drugs. He was responded to in the negative. After Doe had switched from the employer's health insurance to Rite-Aid, the Chief Administrative Officer requested and received utilization reports from Rite-Aid as per contract between the two concerns. The report included the names of employees whose drug costs exceed $100. The C.A.O. called the Director of Benefits into her office to review the report. The purpose was to look for signs of fraud and drug abuse due to past practice of employees purchasing drugs for other non-eligible persons. She also examined the report to determine the extent of usage of generic drugs and, the costs thereof, and other related purposes.

The C.A.O. then approached the SEPTA physician and asked about Retrovir. After discussing the report with two physicians, she was told that they were uncomfortable speaking about specific persons taking the drugs. Thereafter, the C.A.O. had Rite-Aid submit future reports without disclosure of the names of persons taking such medication. Doe was informed of the C.A.O.'s inquiries. He then commenced the within litigation. A jury found in favor of Doe and awarded him substantial damages. On appeal, the decision was reversed.

ISSUES: (1) Whether a person has the right of privacy with respect to his/her medical prescription record?

(2) Were such rights violated in the within action?

DECISION: (1) There is a right of privacy under the Constitution.

(2) The Transportation Authority did not violate Doe's right of privacy.

REASONING: Judge Rosenn

As a preliminary matter, this court must decide if a person's medical prescription record is within the ambit of information protected by the Constitution. If there is no right of privacy, our inquiry stops. . . .

Medical records fall within this scope. The Supreme Court, in *Whalen v. Roe . . .*, noted that the right to privacy encompasses two separate spheres. One of these is an individual's interest in independence in making certain decisions. The other is an interest in avoiding disclosure of personal information. . . . Medical records fall within the second category. . . . Therefore, the *[Whalen]* Court held that individuals do have a limited right to privacy in their medical records.

This court reinforced this holding through our decision in *United States v. Westinghouse Elec. Corp.* . . . An individual using prescription drugs has a right to expect that such information will customarily remain private. The district court, therefore, committed no error in its holding that there is a constitutional right to privacy in one's prescription records.

Such a right is not absolute, however. See *Whalen v. Roe* . . . (while individuals have a legitimate expectation of privacy in their prescription purchases of controlled substances, such right must be weighed against the state's interest in monitoring the use of dangerously addictive drugs). . . . As with many individual rights, the right of privacy in one's prescription drug records must be balanced against important competing interests.

[The court then reviewed the *Westinghouse* seven factors in determining whether a given disclosure was an invasion of privacy. After weighing the factors affecting the within case, the court concluded:] We hold that a self-insured employer's need for access to employee prescription records under its health insurance plan, when the information disclosed is only for the purpose of monitoring the plans by those with a need to know, outweighs an employee's interest in keeping his prescription drug purchases confidential. Such minimal intrusion, although an impingement on privacy, is insufficient to constitute a constitutional violation.

CASE QUESTIONS

1. Assuming the Transportation Authority maintained the medical records to ascertain whether an employee was taking drugs that may affect the safety of the general public, would the decision be the same?
2. If an employee were suspected of selling the drugs prescribed to him, would such monitoring be legal?

Employees' Use of E-Mail

Employers have been examining e-mails being sent by employees. They do so for legitimate and illegitimate reasons. Some employers read such e-mails because of their concern that messages may create litigation exposure for their firms. Examples would be messages that would constitute sexual harassment or other abusive activity. Also, employers want to monitor lack of company commitment and waste of company resources. On the other hand, some employers have abused such examination by ascertaining and divulging highly confidential messages. The right of privacy of employees using the employer's equipment is an issue courts are addressing.

An example of the issue raised by reading employee e-mails is *Bourke v. Nissan Motor Corp.*, No. B068705 (C.A., 2d App. Dis. 1993). In the action, plaintiffs were employed by Nissan to assist an Infiniti car dealership to solve problems with its computer system. A coworker of the plaintiffs was conducting a training session demonstrating the use of e-mail at the dealership. She randomly selected a message sent by Bourke to another employee that contained sexually explicit and personal matter. The coworker reported the incident to her supervisor. Nissan then examined e-mail messages of the entire group and found that many personal messages were being sent by employees. Nissan issued warnings to the plaintiffs and prohibited use of the company computer system for personal purposes. After several warnings concerning alleged unsatisfactory performance, the plaintiff Bourke resigned and a second plaintiff was fired. Plaintiffs sued for breach of their privacy rights.

The California court dismissed the action, holding that there was no reasonable expectation of privacy in their use of company computers to send e-mails while employed by Nissan. There was no violation of the Penal Code that forbids intentionally tapping of any telephone wire, line, or cable. Nissan had access to the network without resort of a telephone line tap and did not access messages during transmission. Nissan did not violate the eavesdropping or recording of a confidential nature, because no amplifying or recording device was used to retrieve and read the e-mail messages. Moreover, there was no proof that the plaintiffs were fired or caused to resign as a result of the e-mail activity.

In the following case, the company allegedly told its employees that their e-mails would be confidential. Nevertheless, the plaintiff employee was dismissed from his employment as a result of such use in a manner the company found offensive.

SMYTH V. PILLSBURY

914 F. Supp. 97 (E.D.Pa. 1996)

FACTS: Plaintiff was an at-will employee with the position of regional operations manager for Pillsbury. Defendant maintained an e-mail communication system for use in internal corporate communications among the employees. Pillsbury allegedly assured its employees that all e-mail communications would remain confidential and privileged. They were also told that e-mails would not be intercepted and used by the company for purposes of termination or reprimand. In October 1994, plaintiff received e-mail communications from his supervisor over his computer at home. He responded and exchanged e-mails with his supervisor. At a later date, Pillsbury intercepted Smyth's e-mail messages made in October of 1994 and dismissed him from employment on the ground that the e-mails were inappropriate and unprofessional. It appears that one of the e-mails contained threats to "kill the backstabbing bastards" and said that the planned holiday party was a "Jim Jones Koolaid affair." [Jim Jones was the leader of a cult who caused hundreds of members to consume poison, causing their deaths.]

ISSUE: (1) Under the circumstances of the within case, did the plaintiff, as an at-will employee, have a right not to be terminated from his employment?

(2) Did the defendant violate the plaintiff's privacy right of intrusion upon the solitude or seclusion of another in his private affairs?

DECISION: (1) The Court found in favor of the defendant, Pillsbury, stating that Smyth could be terminated from his employment.

(2) The plaintiff's privacy rights were not violated.

REASONING: Judge Weiner

As a general rule, Pennsylvania law does not provide a common law cause of action for the wrongful discharge of an at-will employee such as plaintiff. . . . Pennsylvania is an employment at-will jurisdiction and an employer "may discharge an employee with or without cause, at pleasure, unless restrained by some contract." . . .

However, in the most limited of circumstances, exceptions have been recognized where discharge of an at-will employee threatens or violates a clear mandate of public policy. . . . A "clear mandate" of public policy must be of a type that "strikes at the heart of a citizen's social right, duties and responsibilities." . . . This recognized public policy exception is an especially narrow one. . . . To date, the Pennsylvania Superior Court has only recognized three such exceptions.

First, an employee may not be fired for serving on jury duty. . . .

Second, an employer may not deny employment to a person with a prior conviction. . . .

And finally, an employee may not be fired for reporting violations of federal regulations to the Nuclear Regulatory Commission. . . .

As evidenced above, a public policy exception must be clearly defined. . . . ("Unless an employee identifies a 'specific' expression of public policy violated by his discharge, it will not be labeled as wrongful and within the sphere of public policy.") The sources of public policy can be found in "legislation, administrative rules, regulation, or decision; and judicial decisions. . . . Absent legislation, the judiciary must define the cause of action in case by case determinations." . . .

Plaintiff claims that his termination was in violation of "public policy which precludes an employer from terminating an employee in violation of the employee's right of privacy as embodied in Pennsylvania common law." . . .

[T]he allegations in the Complaint might suggest that plaintiff is alleging an exception to the at-will employment rule based on estoppel, i.e. that defendant repeatedly assured plaintiff and others that it would not intercept e-mail communications and reprimand or terminate based on the contents thereof and plaintiff relied on these assurances to his detriment when he made the "inappropriate and unprofessional" e-mail communications in October 1994. The law of Pennsylvania is clear, however, that an employer may not be estopped from firing an employee based upon a promise, even when reliance is demonstrated. . . .

The Court of Appeals in *Borse* [*v. Piece Goods Shop, Inc.*, 963 F.2d 611 (3d Cir. 1992)] observed that one of the torts which Pennsylvania recognizes as encompassing an action for invasion of privacy is the tort of "intrusion upon seclusion." [In the *Borse* case, the court decided that an employee could not be fired for refusing to submit to urinalysis screening and personal searches at her work place pursuant to her employer's drug and alcohol policy.] As noted by the Court of Appeals, the Restatement (Second) of Torts defines the tort as follows:

> One who intentionally intrudes, physically or otherwise, upon the solitude or seclusion of another or his private affairs or concerns, is subject to liability to the other for invasion of his privacy, if the intrusion would be highly offensive to a reasonable person.

Restatement (Second) of Torts Section 652B. Liability only attaches when the "intrusion is substantial and would be highly offensive to the 'ordinary reasonable person.'" . . .

Applying the Restatement definition of the tort of intrusion upon seclusion to the facts and circumstances of the case sub judice, we find that plaintiff has failed to state a claim upon which relief can be granted. In the first instance, unlike urinalysis and personal property searches, we do not find a reasonable expectation of privacy in e-mail communications voluntarily made by an employee to his supervisor over the company e-mail system notwithstanding any assurances that such communications would not be intercepted by management. Once plaintiff communicated the alleged unprofessional comments to a second person (his supervisor) over an e-mail system which was apparently utilized by the entire company, any reasonable expectation of privacy was lost. Significantly, the defendant did not require plaintiff, as in the case of an urinalysis or personal property search to disclose any personal information about himself. Rather, plaintiff voluntarily communicated the alleged unprofessional comments over the company e-mail system. We find no privacy in such communications.

In the second instance, even if we found that an employee had a reasonable expectation of privacy in the contents of his e-mail communications over the company e-mail system, we do not find that a reasonable person would consider the defendant's interception of these communications to be a substantial and highly offensive invasion of his privacy. Again, we note that by intercepting such communications, the company is not, as in the case of urinalysis or personal property searches, requiring the employee to disclose any personal information about himself or invading the employee's person or personal effects. Moreover, the company's interest in preventing inappropriate and unprofessional comments or even illegal activity over its e-mail system outweighs any privacy interest the employee may have in these comments. . . . In sum, we find that the defendant's actions did not tortiously invade the plaintiff's privacy and, therefore did not violate public policy. As a result, the motion to dismiss is granted.

CASE QUESTIONS

1. If, as here, an employer violates its own policy of privacy of e-mails, are there any other grounds upon which a claim may be made?
2. What if the employee were a *contract* employee, that is, had a contract specifying a particular term of employment; would the decision have been the same?

In *McLaren v. Microsoft*,[8] plaintiff as an employee of defendant, Microsoft, was given access to its e-mail system by means of a network password. Plaintiff and other employees also were allowed a personal folder for storage of e-mail. The personal folder was accessible only by the employee by means of a second password. The within lawsuit arose when Microsoft read the e-mail stored in the plaintiff's personal folder. The case was dismissed by the Texas court. It held that the plaintiff had no reasonable expectation of privacy as to his e-mail because the e-mail traveled through a number of points in the e-mail system that were accessible by Microsoft. Also, its "interest in preventing inappropriate and unprofessional comments, or even illegal activity, over its e-mail system . . . outweigh[ed] McLaren's claimed privacy interest in those communications."

In *Bohach v. City of Reno,* 932 F. Supp. 1232 (D.Nev. 1996), two police officers of the Reno Police Department sent messages to one another and to a third officer using the department's Alphapage message system. They filed the within lawsuit after they were informed of an internal affairs investigation based on the content of their messages. They claimed that the retrieval of the messages by the investigators violated federal wiretapping statutes and their constitutional right of privacy. The message system is a software program installed on the department's local area network. It is used for transmission of brief alphanumeric messages to visual display pagers.

The court decided that the officers did not have an objectively reasonable right of privacy. All messages were recorded and stored not because someone was tapping the system, but because it was a part of the system. Like most pager systems, the messages are stored in a central computer until retrieved by the intended recipient. In addition, the police chief had notified all users of the fact that all messages were logged onto the network and that certain types of messages (such as the messages sent by the officers) were banned from the system. Alphapage was accessible to anyone with access to the computer system. No special password or clearance was needed. Police departments often record messages for a number of reasons, including to determine that the dispatches were accurate, to verify information, and to keep a log of emergency and nonemergency calls. With respect to the alleged violations of the wiretapping statutes, the court said that inasmuch as the City of Reno is the provider of the service, neither it nor its employees could be liable under the federal statutes.

LEGISLATIVE ENACTMENTS

Congress and the various states have attempted to curb privacy invasion excesses by enacting a number of statutes to give consumers and others some measure of protection. There is no overall statute giving such protection; rather, a number of laws and regulations have been passed focusing on specific rights and obligations in a variety of circumstances. We will review major statutes in this regard.

There were early attempts by Congress to impose some degree of privacy protection. A 1973 Report of the Secretary of Health, Education and Welfare suggested a "Code of Fair Information Practices" that contained basic principles as a model in future legislation. These principles were incorporated in the Privacy Act of 1974. The act provided that individuals had the right to determine what records concerning them were collected, maintained, used, or distributed by federal agencies. The said individual is given the right to prevent the misuse of such records for purposes other than the particular purpose for which they were gathered. Also, copies of the records are to be made available on request to such person, who is also given the right to commence civil litigation for intentional or wrongful misuse of the records. The privacy rights granted under the act, however, were weakened by the numerous exceptions contained therein.

Children's Online Privacy Protection Act

The purposes of the Children's Online Privacy Protection Act of 1998 (COPPA) (15 U.S.C. Section 6501) were to enhance the parental role in protecting the privacy of their children; protect children in cyberspace chat rooms, home pages, and the like wherein they may be requested to post identifying information; maintain security of personal identifying information of children that is collected online; and to limit access and spread of such information without parental consent. A *child* is an individual under the age of 13 years. Identifying information includes the first and last name, home and e-mail addresses, telephone number, social security number, a *persistent identifier* such as an identification number, a cookie, a screen name, or other identifying information that allows possible physical or online contact with the child.

The act makes it unlawful for an operator of a Web site or online service directed to children to knowingly collect personal information from a child unless (1) it provides notice on the Web site of the nature of the information collected; (2) how such information is to be used; and (3) the operator's disclosure practices for the information. In addition, the operator must obtain verifiable parental consent for such collection, use, or disclosure. Upon request and verification of the identity of the parent whose child has given personal information, the operator must provide a description of the information given by the child, an opportunity to refuse further use or collection or maintenance in retrieval form, and a reasonable means for a parent to obtain such information.

It is also forbidden for such Web site or online service to condition a child's participation in a game, the offering of a prize, or other activity on the child giving more information than necessary for participation. The operator must establish and maintain reasonable procedures for compliance with the said restrictions.

There are a number of exceptions for compliance with the statute:

1. Information received to a specific request from a child on a one-time basis and the information is not maintained in retrievable form and not used anew to recontact the child
2. Requesting information for sole purpose of using it to obtain parental consent or for providing notice and is not maintained in retrievable form
3. Responding to a child's contact beyond one occasion, provided reasonable efforts are made to provide the parent with notice and giving the parent a reasonable opportunity to request no further use be made of the information; or, in the absence of notice to the parent, where the benefits to the child of access of information and services outweigh the risks to security and safety to the child's privacy (for example, information regarding abortion services or preventive data regarding sexually transmitted disease)
4. The name of the child and online contact information to protect the safety of a child and such information is not used to recontact the child and is not disclosed on the site
5. The collection, use, or dissemination of the information is necessary for the security or integrity of the Web site, is taken as precaution against liability, is used to respond to judicial process, or is otherwise allowed by law

A safe harbor provision for the Web site or service provider exempts them from liability if they comply with a set of self-regulatory guidelines issued by representatives of the marketing or online industries. The said guidelines must include "an effective mechanism for the independent assessment of subject operators' compliance with the guidelines" and "effective incentives" for compliance, such as disciplinary action, consumer redresss, voluntary payments to the U.S. Treasury for violations, and referral to the Federal Trade Commission (FTC) of operators violating the guidelines. The voluntary guidelines require approval of the FTC. Industry groups must maintain records that are to be available to the FTC containing customer complaints, records of disciplinary actions, the results of independent assessments of members' compliance.[9]

Fair Credit Reporting Act

According to the Fair Credit Reporting Act (FCRA) of 1998 (15 U.S.C. Section 1681), no consumer reporting agency may render a consumer credit report that contains information concerning bankruptcies beyond 10 years, and civil suits, judgments, tax liens, accounts placed for collection, any other adverse items of information, and arrest records more than 7 years old. Exempted are credit transactions with a principal amount of $150,000 or more, underwriting a life insurance policy with a face amount of $150,000 or more, or employment of an individual where the salary is $75,000 or more.

The credit reporting agency must report the fact that a consumer voluntarily closed a credit account and must further report if the consumer disputes the information contained therein. Also, the credit agency must include in a consumer report information concerning the failure of the consumer to pay up to 7-years' overdue child support reported to it by a state or local child-support enforcement agency or by any federal, state, or local agency.

Persons furnishing the information to credit reporting agencies are prohibited from reporting any information with knowledge of errors and shall not report data that is contested by the consumer and is in fact inaccurate. Persons reporting information regularly to credit reporting agencies must promptly correct inaccuracies and keep information updated.

Persons reporting information to credit agencies must investigate disputed sums, review all relevant information, report to the consumer the results of the investigation, and report any inaccuracies to the credit reporting agencies.

The Federal Trade Commission is given the authority to enforce compliance of the statute. The FTC may commence a civil action against violators of the statute and recover civil penalties of $2,500 per violation. Other federal agencies may also enforce the statute as it pertains to matters within their jurisdiction. States may also enforce the act in the federal courts and recover damages on behalf of aggrieved residents.

Gramm-Leach-Biley Act

The Gramm-Leach-Biley Act of 1999, also known as the Financial Services Reform Act (P.L. 106-102 (113 Stat. 1338)), repealed the Glass-Steagall Act and expanded the power of banks to enter into the securities markets, as well as to become affiliated with insurance companies and many other financial services-type enterprises and institutions. With respect to privacy, Title V of the act substantially restricts the disclosure of identifiable financial information received by the financial institutions, either online or offline, and whether it was received from the consumer or from a third party. An exception is if such information is public knowledge. All banking institutions are required to have a privacy policy even if they do not engage in the transfer of such data to third parties.

The information gathered may not be given to a third person without consent of the consumer. The institutions must post a conspicuous notice of its privacy policy, the potential disclosure of such information to third parties, and the right of the consumer to decline the transfer of such information. Banks cannot disclose account numbers or access codes to third parties for use in telemarketing, direct mail marketing, or e-mail marketing programs. The Federal Trade Commission regulates this aspect of the statute. It applies its regulations broadly by including within the definition of *financial institutions* those institutions "closely related to banking." Retailers issuing their own credit, collection agencies, mortgage lenders, and other credit-granting institutions are included within the definition for purposes of privacy protection under the FTC Rule. The protected "personally identifiable financial information" is also broadly defined by the FTC Rule to include all information that such institutions receive from consumers in connection with their financial products or services.

Electronic Communications Privacy Act

Under the Electronic Communications Privacy Act of 1986 (ECPA), 18 U.S.C. Sections 2510–2520, 2701–2709 (1999), it is unlawful for any person to intentionally intercept, attempt to intercept, or hire a person to intercept any wire, oral, or electronic communication. It is also unlawful to use any device to intercept when such device is affixed to or transmits a signal through a wire, cable, or other wire connection, by radio or by mail, or uses the device in a place of business affecting interstate or foreign commerce. It is also unlawful to intentionally disclose or utilize or try to disclose intercepted information that such person knows to be in violation of the ECPA. This includes persons connected with a criminal investigation in which such interception was legally accomplished.

There are numerous exceptions including the following: for legitimate governmental purposes; unscrambled satellite video or radio communications not used for tortious purposes; where such person is a party to the communication or consented to the interception; communications readily accessible to the general public; radio transmissions relating to ships, aircraft, and vehicles; and other legitimate reasons. The following case concerns an alleged violation of the ECPA.

SHERMAN & CO. V. SALTON MAXIM HOUSEWARES, INC.

94 F. Supp. 817 (E.D.Mich. 2000)

FACTS: In 1997, Salton won a multi-year contract to sell kitchen and small household appliances under the mark of "White Westinghouse" to Kmart. The plaintiff entered into a contract with the defendant, Salton, whereby Sherman would act as Salton's representative, as well as representing other companies to Kmart. Salton claimed that Sherman's performance was deficient due to his alleged alienation and antagonism with Kmart buyers and contacts. Sherman stopped working for Salton at Salton's request. Salton claimed that Sherman violated the ECPA and misappropriated a trade secret. Specifically, Salton claims that Sherman, after termination of employment, used a computer access code that Kmart provided him when he worked for Salton. He allegedly used the code in order to gain access to Salton sales data in the Kmart system, which he then gave to another of his clients.

ISSUE: Whether, under the facts as set forth, the plaintiff, Sherman, violated the ECPA?

DECISION: The Court held in favor of Sherman in deciding that the statute did not prohibit the disclosure or use of information obtained without authorization.

REASONING: Judge Pepe

The general purpose of the ECPA was to create a cause of action against "computer hackers (e.g., electronic trespassers)." . . . The provisions of section 2701 of the Act apply to persons or entities in general and prohibit intentional accessing of electronic data without authorization or in excess of authorization. Section 2702 prohibits disclosure of electronic data, but this prohibition is limited to persons or entities that (1) provide an electronic communication service to the public; or (2) provide remote computing service to the public. In this case there is no indication that Sherman falls under either of the two limited categories of covered persons or entities of section 2702. Thus, if Salton has a viable claim against Sherman under the ECPA, it will have to fall under section 2701 of that Act.

Section 2701(a) provides that:

(1) intentionally accesses without authorization a facility through which an electronic communication service is provided; or
(2) intentionally exceeds an authorization to access that facility;

and thereby obtains, alters, or prevents authorized access to a wire or electronic communication while it is in electronic storage in such system shall be punished as provided in subsection (b) of this section.

Salton alleges . . . that Sherman obtained Salton sales information and disclosed it to a competitor, Windmere. Yet, unlike section 2702, section 2701(a) of the ECPA does not prohibit the *disclosure* or *use* of information gained without authorization. . . . Rather, section 2701(a) prohibits the intentional unauthorized *access* of an electronic communication service and the subsequent obtainment, alteration or prevention of authorized access to the service. Because the language of section 2701(a) specifically refers to "access" and not disclosure or use, "a person who does not provide an electronic communication service . . . can disclose or use with impunity the contents of an electronic communication service . . . can disclose or use with impunity the contents of an electronic communication unlawfully obtained from electronic storage." . . .

The ECPA's prohibition on intentional exceeding of authorized access anticipates that a person with authorization to a computer database or certain public portions of a database is not thereby authorized to visit "private" zones of data in the system. . . . Yet, for "intentional" access in excess of authorization to be a crime and actionable civilly, the offender must have obtained the access to private files without authorization (e.g., using a computer he was not to use, or obtaining and using someone else's password or code without authorization). At a minimum, there must be a clearer and more explicit restriction on the authorized access than presented by Salton's proposed counterclaim. Here Sherman's access to the Salton data in the Kmart network system was in no way restricted by technical means or by any express limitation. Because section 2701 of the ECPA prohibits only unauthorized access and not the misappropriation or disclosure of information, there is no violation of section 2701 for a person with authorized access to the database no matter how malicious or larcenous his intended use of that access. Section 2701 outlaws illegal entry, not larceny.

[The court dismissed Salton's counterclaim under ECPA but left it to the trial court to determine the remaining issues and claims presented.]

CASE QUESTIONS

1. After Sherman was no longer employed by Salton, isn't such unauthorized use wrongful? Should he be sued under some other theory?
2. Do you agree that sharing private data with a competitor was not a trade secret violation?

In *Andersen Consulting LLP v. UOP,* 991 F. Supp. 1041 (N.D.Ill. 1998), a corporation that operated an internal e-mail system for intracompany communications was held not to be subject to the ECPA because it was not providing electronic communications service to the public or to the community at large. As a result, the ECPA did not bar defendant from disclosing to a newspaper e-mail messages on its system sent by Andersen employees who were performing services for defendant.

Right to Financial Privacy Act

Section 3402 of the Right to Financial Privacy Act of 1978 (RFPA) (12 U.S.C. 3401) (1999) prohibits government authorities from having access to or obtaining copies of financial records from a financial institution unless such records are: reasonably described and are received with permission of the customer; in response to a subpoena or summons; the result of a search warrant; or abide by certain statutory requirements.

Section 3403 prohibits release of financial records or information contained therein by a financial institution to a government authority unless the said authority certifies in writing that it has complied with the RFPA. Exceptions are release of information in connection with a possible violation of statute or regulation; release of records as incident to the perfection of a security interest (for example, recording a mortgage or other security lien); proving a claim in bankruptcy; collecting a debt; or as incident to a government loan, loan guarantee, or other such agreement.

With certain limited exceptions, the customer has the right to receive a copy of the information given to the government. Authorizations signed by the customer for voluntary release of information to the government may not exceed three months duration, allows the customer to revoke the authorization, and such authorization may not be a condition of doing business with the financial institution.

The act sets forth the requirements for issuance and compliance with an administrative subpoena and summons, for search warrants and judicial subpoenas, and for formal written requests made by a government authority. Customers may challenge government requests by making a motion to quash before the appropriate court. There are limitations in the use and transfer of properly obtained financial records. The act provides a number of exceptions generally concerned with law enforcement inquiries. Civil penalties may be imposed against government agencies and financial institutions for violation of the act.

Video Privacy Protection Act

The Video Privacy Protection Act of 1998 (VPPA) (18 U.S.C. Section 2710) (1999) makes a videotape service provider liable to a consumer for knowingly disclosing to any person the personal identifiable information concerning such consumer. Exceptions are when the information is given to the consumer; to any person with consent of the consumer; in response to a warrant from a federal state or other governmental law enforcement agency; to any person provided the consumer is given the opportunity in a clear and conspicuous manner to prohibit the disclosure and the disclosure does not identify the nature of the videotapes or other audiovisual materials; to any person if the disclosure is incident to the ordinary course of business; pursuant to a court order not accommodated by any other means and the consumer is given reasonable notice and is able to appear and contest the disclosure.

Damages to be awarded for such disclosure is the greater of actual damages or liquidated damages of $2,500 plus punitive damages, reasonable attorneys' fees and court costs, and other preliminary and equitable relief as the court may deem appropriate. There is a two-year Statute of Limitations.

Driver's Privacy Protection Act

The Driver's Privacy Protection Act (DPPA) (18 U.S.C. Sections 2721–2725) renders it unlawful for a state department of motor vehicles or any representative or person connected to it to knowingly disclose or otherwise make available personal information about any individual obtained by the department in connection with a motor vehicle record. The disclosure concerns the open-ended disclosure to anyone wishing such information without a justifiable purpose. There are many exceptions and permissible uses of such record. Such information may be disclosed or used in connection with motor vehicle matters, driver safety and theft, recalls, use by government agencies, market research activities, in the normal course of business to verify accuracy of information given by individuals to a business, for use in civil, criminal, administrative, or arbitral proceedings, for use by insurers, on written consent of the person affected, for use by a public or private investigative agency and other such related purposes.

Penalties for wrongful disclosure include a criminal fine, a civil penalty of $5,000 daily to a state department of motor vehicles refusing to comply with the law, and a civil damage award of not less than $2,500, punitive damages, reasonable attorneys' fees, and other preliminary and equitable relief.

Other Legislative Initiatives

Some of the other laws that incorporate some privacy aspects include Protection of Pupil Rights of 1978 (20 U.S.C. Section 1232(h)) that limits psychological testing without parental consent; the Census Act (13 U.S.C. 9214); the Social Security Act (42 U.S.C. 408(h)); the Family Educational Right and Privacy Act of 1974 (20 U.S.C. 1232(g)); and the Child Abuse Information Act (42 U.S.C. 5103(b)(2)(e)).[10]

THE PRESIDENT'S INITIATIVE

In President Clinton's *Framework for Global Electronic Commerce*,[11] the tension between the desire for personal freedom and well-being comes into conflict with the First Amendment, which protects the free flow of information. It was noted that the Privacy Working Group of the U.S. government Information Infrastructure issued a report calling for the adherence of principles governing privacy.[12] These principles were based on the Organization for Economic Cooperation and Development's "Guidelines Governing the Protection of Privacy and Transborder Data Flow of Personal Data" (to be discussed).

With respect to data protection, the United States has entered into a cooperative arrangement with regional groups such as the Asia Pacific Economic Cooperation forum, NAFTA, the Inter-American Telecommunications Commission, and other regional organizations.

PRIVACY IN THE HEALTH ARENA

The Health Insurance and Portability Accountability Act

The Health Insurance and Portability Accountability Act of 1996 (HIPAA) was a major legislative enactment designed to extend federal privacy protection to medical records and to prevent genetic discrimination in health insurance.[13] It specifically provides that group health plans and health insurers may disallow coverage for preexisting conditions only if: (1) the exclusion related to a condition for which medical advice, care, and the like was given within the preceding 6 months; (2) the exclusion does not extend beyond a 12-month period; and (3) the said period of exclusion is reduced by the aggregate of the period of creditable coverage. Genetic information in the absence of a condition having arisen as a result of the predisposition may not be a basis for denial of insurance coverage.

The exceptions to privacy protection are:

1. Public health activities
2. Disclosure for health oversight purposes
3. Use for judicial and administrative proceedings and for use by coroners and medical examiners
4. Disclosures to law enforcement
5. Government health data systems and health directories
6. Disclosure for banking and payment purposes
7. Medical research

FEDERAL TRADE COMMISSION PRIVACY INITIATIVES

The FTC was created by the Federal Trade Commission Act of 1914. Its mandate initially was to prevent unfair methods of competition in interstate of foreign commerce. Later its jurisdiction was expanded to investigate and prosecute unfair or deceptive acts affecting such commerce. Since the mid-1990s, the commission has been concerned with problems associated with online privacy and the attempts by industry to self-regulate. The May 2000 Report to Congress entitled *Privacy Online: Fair Information Practices in the Electronic Marketplace* sets forth the current state of privacy rights in online commercial activity.

In its 1998 Report to Congress, the FTC summarized and identified core principles with respect to privacy protection that are generally agreed to in model codes, guidelines, and government reports. There are four such principles identified therein. They are:

(1) *NOTICE*—data collectors must disclose their information practices before collecting personal information from consumers.
(2) *CHOICE*—consumers must be given options with respect to whether and how personal information collected from them may be used for purposes beyond those for which the information was provided;
(3) *ACCESS*—consumers should be able to view and contest the accuracy and completeness of data collected from them; and
(4) *SECURITY*—data collectors must take reasonable steps to assure that information collected from consumers is accurate and secure from unauthorized use.[14]

In addition, the FTC believes that a fifth principle should be added to the generally accepted principles, namely, "*ENFORCEMENT*—the use of a reliable mechanism to impose sanctions for noncompliance with these fair information practices." *Notice* is the most basic principle and underlies the remaining principles.

Web Sites Privacy Disclosures

In early 2000, the FTC conducted a survey of the major industry sites (sites with 39,000 or more different visitors) on the Internet to ascertain the consumer-protection privacy policies. Using a random sampling of all sites and an examination of the 100 busiest sites, it found that nearly all sites collected personal identifying information from consumers (97 percent of random sample and 99 percent of the 100 most popular sites). Sixty-eight percent of the sites of the random sample and 77 percent of the most popular sites collected nonidentifying information. From the data, detailed information concerning buying behavior and other data were collected. The commission noted that there was a significant increase (from 14 percent to 66 percent) of at least one privacy disclosure in 1999 in the random sample from the prior year. The percentage was expected to rise to 88 percent in the year 2000. Approximately 97 percent of the most popular sites posted a policy in 1999.

The difficulty perceived by the FTC is that less than half of the most popular sites implemented the four core principles of notice, choice, access, and security. Also, many sites posting a privacy policy contained poorly drafted disclosures. Often, language was contradictory or ambiguous or was confusing to consumers. Sites typically reserved the right to change their policies, thereby undermining consumer confidence in their privacy policy.

The FTC recommended to Congress that these principles be incorporated in legislation to ensure adequate protection of consumer privacy online. With respect to notice, it recommended that Web sites be required to give consumers notice of the information practices in a clear and conspicuous manner. Such information should include what information is being collected; how it is to be collected; how the principles of choice, access, and security are to be provided; whether the information collected will be disclosed to other entities; and whether other entities are using the Web site to collect information. As to choice, the Web sites would be required to offer consumers choices as to how the information is to be used beyond the stated use, including internal secondary uses such as marketing back to consumers, and external secondary uses such as giving the disclosed data to other entities.[15]

The access given to consumers is to include a reasonable opportunity to review the information and to correct inaccuracies or delete information contained therein. Reasonable steps are to be taken to ensure the security of all data collected. The FTC is wary of detailed, specific legislation and desires instead that any legislation be made in general terms and be technologically neutral. It wants flexibility in promulgating rules and regulations in keeping with developments as they may take place.

The FTC has investigated numerous complaints concerning abusive and fraudulent practices taking place over the Internet.[16] GeoCities was one of the most visited sites, providing a variety of services including free e-mail, contests, and the like to almost two million members. To become a member, one had to furnish detailed personal information. Part of the services rendered was a club and a variety of contests for children. The children, as part of their membership application, were asked personal information. The difficulty arose when it was learned that GeoCities misrepresented its privacy policy, alleging that the data would be directed only to the specific advertising that they desired. Information was sold or rented to undisclosed third parties who targeted their advertising to the members, including children. The FTC was able to act because of its statutory mandate of investigating and taking action against unfair and deceptive trade practices.

IN THE MATTER OF GEOCITIES, A CORPORATION

Federal Trade Commission, Docket No. C-3850 (Feb. 5, 1999)

FACTS: The FTC had prepared a complaint against GeoCities, a California corporation that had allegedly violated the Federal Trade Commission Act by committing deceptive acts in its commercial activities. The complaint would have alleged that GeoCities made misrepresentations concerning the collection of personal identifying data from children and its use thereafter. Before the complaint could be served, the matter was settled and an agreement was entered lasting a period of twenty years that illustrates the concerns of the FTC and the manner in which similar cases are being resolved.

DECISION and ORDER: [The parties consented to an order prohibiting GeoCities or its agents or affiliates from misrepresenting the personal identifying information gathered from its Web site, including information to be disclosed to third parties; how such information is to be used; the identity of the parties gathering such information; and the sponsors of any activity on the Web site. It further prohibited the gathering of information from children without parental permission. A key provision of the order is as follows:] IT IS FURTHER ORDERED the respondent [GeoCities] . . . shall provide clear and prominent notice to consumers, including the parents of children, with respect to respondent's practice with regard to its collection and use of personal identifying information. Such notice shall include, but is not limited to, disclosure of:

A. what information is being collected (e.g., "name," "home address," "e-mail address," "age," "interests");
B. its intended use(s);
C. the third parties to whom it will be disclosed (e.g., "advertisers of consumer products," "mailing list companies," "the general public");
D. the consumer's ability to obtain access to or directly access such information and the means by which (s)he may do so;
E. the consumer's ability to remove directly or have the information removed from respondent's databases and the means by which (s)he may do so; and
F. the procedures to delete personal identifying information from respondent's databases and any limitations related to such deletion.

Such notice shall appear on the home page of respondent's Web site(s) and at each location on the site(s) at which such information is collected.

Provided that respondent shall not be required to include the notice at the locations at which information is collected if such information is limited to tracking information and the collection of such information is described in the notice required by this Part.

Provided further that for purposes of this Part, compliance with all of the following shall be deemed adequate notice: (a) placement of a clear and prominent hyperlink or button labeled **PRIVACY NOTICE** on the home page(s), which directly links to the privacy notice screen(s); (b) placement of the information required in this Part clearly and prominently on the privacy notice screen(s), followed on the same screen(s) with a button that must be clicked on to make it disappear; and (c) at each location on the site at which any personal identifying information is collected, placement of a clear and prominent hyperlink on the initial screen on which the collection takes place, which links directly to the privacy notice and which is accompanied by the following statement in bold typeface:

NOTICE: We collect personal information on this site. To learn more about how we use your information click here.

[Additional ordered provisions provided that in order for a child to register with GeoCities, it is necessary to give notice to the child to have express parental consent given for the registration and/or to send a notice to the parent's e-mail address. Also, GeoCities is to give a reasonable means to consumers and to parents of children registered with the site to remove the personal identifying information. The notice for removal must be clear and prominent to each consumer over the age of 12 years and to each parent of a child. The notice is to include the information collected, the right to obtain access to such information, the right to have the information deleted, a statement that third parties are not to have access to the information without express parental approval, and other related information.]

INDUSTRY SELF-REGULATION

Online Privacy Seal Program

Industry historically is wary of governmental intervention. Paradoxically, with the assistance and guidance of government, a number of initiatives have been inaugurated to protect the privacy of consumers. The most prominent are privacy seal programs that require prospective members to abide by certain fair information practices and be subject to inspection procedures by the sponsoring organization. Membership entitles the applicant to display a TRUSTe privacy seal on its Web site, much like the Better Housekeeping seal of approval on quality products over the past half century. TRUSTe is the first online privacy seal program. It encompasses over 1,200 members in diverse industries. The approved Web site must inform what personal information is being gathered from the individual, how such information may be used, and whether and to whom such information will be given. The individual has the right to prevent the sharing of the information, correct inaccuracies, and have security concerning the data collected and stored.[17]

TRUSTe also has a children's privacy seal program. In order for a company to post a seal, it must agree that it will not collect online contact information from a child under the age of 13 without prior parental consent or direct parental notification. It may directly respond to a child's direct inquiry but may not use acquired information to reestablish contact with the child. The company may not collect or distribute to a third party personally identifiable contact information from a child under 13 without parental consent. It cannot allow a child under 13 to publicly post personal identifiable information without such consent nor may the company entice such a child with prizes or other inducements to give more information than necessary to participate in the game, prize, or other activity.[18]

Other programs include the *BBB*Online Privacy Seal, the CPA (Certified Public Accountant) WebTrust program, and the PriceWaterhouse Better Web online privacy seal. Additional privacy programs being formulated include the Entertainment Software Ratings Board (ESRB) for the entertainment software industry and the S.A.F.E. (Secure Assure Faith Entrusted) Dependability Seal Program to block access by advertisers and other persons from tracking a user online. Sites available are Network Advertising Initiative, *www.networkadvertising.org;* DoubleClick: PrivacyChoices, *www.engage.com/privacy/koptout.htm;* Avenue A, *www.avenuea.com/info/optout.asp;* Guidescope, *www.guidescope.com;* and Internet Junkbuster, *www.junkbuster.com.1818.*

Although such programs promise to establish the ability of private industry to regulate itself, there is some question whether these organizations will discipline members who fail to comply with its proposed safeguards. An interesting example is the alleged failure of TRUSTe to audit or discipline Microsoft when it was revealed that Microsoft placed an identification number in its Windows 98 operating system that collected data from customers without their knowledge.[19] The inherent difficulty in disciplining Microsoft is that it is one of the companies (together with IBM, Compaq, Excite, and AT&T) that sponsored the formation and activities of the nonprofit TRUSTe initiative. Other problems with self-regulation is the lack of regulation for the great majority of Web sites. Most programs govern specific industries. Also, there appears to be significant difficulty in monitoring the collection of personal identifiable information from the companies who are members of the seal or other such programs.

Drafting a Privacy Policy Statement. In drafting and adopting a privacy policy, companies should not copy verbatim sample policy statements unless they clearly are suited to their needs. One scholar noted the pitfalls of companies that do not take extreme care in drafting such statements.[20] He suggests that before companies draft a policy statement, they should examine their entire operation (marketing, distribution, and the like), to make sure that the statement covers all aspects of the company's business. Rather than having a one-way obligation wherein the company promises to abide by a particularized code of conduct, it should have the customer also acknowledge consent and incur obligations by virtue of a click-wrap agreement (see Chapter 3). Absolute statements about protecting privacy should be avoided because hackers, disgruntled employees, or mistaken revelations—such as by AOL in the *McVeigh* case—could bring about issues of liability. Experienced in-house or outside counsel should analyze and prepare a policy that would limit litigious exposure and allow customers much of the privacy protection they desire.

INTERNATIONAL INITIATIVES ON PRIVACY

European Union Directive 95/46/EC

The European Union has the strictest privacy protection restrictions in the world. Its Directive 95/46/EC, *On the Protection of Individuals with Regard to the Processing of Personal Data and on the Free Movement of Such Data,* sets forth a mandatory minimum of protection to be given by member states to their inhabitants.[21] The directive sets basic requirements for data protection, allowing member states to enact stricter standards. The effective date for implementation is October 25, 1998. A number of member states had not yet enacted data-protective laws when the directive was issued. Moreover, the laws of member states that did enact such measures differed substantially, thereby causing potential obstacles to the free flow of data and difficulties for the inhabitants therein. The directive was enacted to remove such obstacles, harmonize the national provisions, and guarantee the right of privacy.[22]

Part of the basis for the directive is the provisions of the Treaty on the European Union that provides in Title 1, Article F, that the E.U. "shall respect fundamental rights, as guaranteed by the European Convention for the Protection of Human Rights and Fundamental Freedoms signed in Rome on November 4, 1950." Article 8 of the convention provides:

1. Everyone has the right to respect for his private and family life, his home and his correspondence.
2. There shall be no interference by a public authority with the exercise of this right except such as is in accordance with the law and is necessary in a democratic society in the interests of national security, public safety or the economic well-being of the country, for the prevention of disorder or crime, for the protection of health or morals, or for the protection of the rights and freedoms of others.

Scope (Article 3). The directive concerns "any operation or set of operations which is performed upon personal data." Exceptions include data flowing outside of the European Union and data involving state and public security. *Personal data* is defined as "any information relating to an identified or identifiable natural person ('data subject')." The obligations are imposed upon the "controller" who is any person determining the purposes and means of processing data.

Data Quality Principles (Article 6). The directive provides that member states are to ensure that the personal data is: (1) processed fairly and lawfully; (2) collected for specific and legitimate purposes; (3) relevant and not excessive for the intended purposes; (4) accurate and kept up to date when relevant; and (5) kept for no longer than necessary except when kept for historical, statistical, or scientific use, in which case appropriate safeguards are to be enacted.

Criteria for Legitimacy (Article 7). Personal data may be collected only if:

1. The data subject has consented unambiguously (agreed freely after being adequately informed)
2. It is necessary for contract performance involving the data subject (for example, data for job applicants or for billing purposes)
3. It is necessary for compliance with a legal obligation of the controller
4. It is necessary to protect the vital interests of the data subject
5. It is necessary to carry out a task in the public interest or for exercise of official authority involving the parties (for example, by police or tax authorities)
6. It is necessary for legitimate interests of the controller or third party receiving the disclosure that outweigh the protection of the legitimate interests of the data subject

Prohibited Data (Article 8). Member states may not collect personal data concerning racial or ethnic origin, political opinions, religious or philosophical beliefs, trade-union membership, and data concerning health or sex life. There are exceptions to such prohibitions, including consent from the data subject and legitimate and lawful objectives and persons. For example, health professionals need health data for proper diagnosis, police authorities need data concerning prior convictions, and journalists may require background data.

Information to be given to Data Subject (Articles 10 and 11). The directive provides different criteria of information to be given to the data subject depending on whether the data was obtained from the data subject or from some other source. If the data is derived from a third party, the data subject is entitled to know the identity of the controller and his or her representative; the purposes thereof; and additional information such as categories of the data concerned, the recipients or groups of recipients of the data, and the right of access. If the data is from the data subject, he or she is entitled to the same type of information plus information as to corrections of errors. Exceptions are made for collection of data for historical or scientific research purposes.

Right of Access to Data and Exemptions (Articles 12 and 13). The data subject is entitled to know whether data about him or her is being collected, the purposes thereof, the categories of the data, and the recipients, as well as how to rectify, erase, or block data. There are exemptions for national and public security; defense; and prevention, detection, and prosecution of criminal offenses; and for economic or financial interest of a member state.

Right to Object (Article 16). The data subject has the right to object on compelling legitimate grounds to processing of data about him or her. The subject also has a right to object on request and free of charge any data to be given to direct marketers.

Confidentiality and Security (Article 17). Member states are to ensure that agents of controllers not process data except on instructions from the controller. Measures are to be taken to protect the security of the data from accidental or unlawful destruction, alteration, unauthorized disclosure or access, and all other unlawful uses.

Notification and Exemptions (Article 18). Controllers or representatives thereof are to notify member states of automatic processing operations of their names, addresses, the purposes of data collection, and other such information. Exemptions are permitted where the data are unlikely to adversely affect the data subject.

Remedies (Articles 22–24). There are broad remedies available to the data subject for violation of his or her rights under the directive, including judicial access and claim for damages.

Data Transfer to Non Member States (Articles 25 and 26). Data is not to be transferred to countries outside of the European Union, unless those countries ensure "an adequate level of protection." What is *adequate* depends on all of the attending circumstances of the transfer, including the proposed processing operations, the level of security, its professional rules, and other such qualifications. Nevertheless, data can be sent irrespective of such safeguards if the data subject consents; the transfer is necessary in connection with contract performance between parties of the respective countries; it is on public interest grounds; it is necessary to protect the vital interests of the data subject; and the controller assures protection of privacy concerning the data being sent abroad.

Safe Harbor Provision. The promulgation of the directive created a great deal of concern in the international community whose laws and regulations are not as restrictive as those found in the articles of the directive.[23] The fear was that member states of the E.U. would enjoy unlimited access to data arising with the E.U., but countries outside of the region would be deprived of the data. The basis for the fear was Article 25, which concerns the transfer of data to outside the E.U. It provides in part that "Where the Commission finds . . . that a third country does not ensure an adequate level of protection. . . . Member States shall take the measures necessary to prevent any transfer of data of the same type to the third country in question" (Article 25(5)). There were a number of exceptions to the restrictions, including consent of the data subject, the data pursuant to a contract, and other such exceptions. Negotiations took place between the E.U. and U.S. government representatives that culminated in an agreement on March 15, 2000, that provided for a seven-year window wherein data may be exchanged between E.U. and U.S. companies unless such data is misappropriated or misused by the latter.

In order to qualify for the safe harbor provisions, U.S. organizations that receive personal data from the E.U. have a number of ways in which they may avoid violations of the directive. They may join a self-regulatory privacy program that adheres to the E.U. principles; they may have their own self-imposed regulatory privacy policies that comply with the directive (in which case, a failure to comply with such privacy may run afoul of the Section 5 "unfair and deceptive" practices of the Federal Trade Commission Act); they may be obligated by statutory, regulatory, or other regulatory U.S. body provisions, such as registered securities associations; or they may include the E.U. principles in written agreements with other parties that transfer data from the E.U.[24]

OECD Guidelines

As early as 1980, the Organization for Economic Cooperation and Development adopted rules concerning data protection and privacy. It adopted on September 23, 1980, its Recommendation of the Council Concerning Guidelines Governing the Protection of Privacy and Transborder Flows of Personal Data. The recommendation became the basis for such protection in a number of member states.

Part 2 of the recommendation established limits with respect to the collection of personal data, requiring it be done lawfully and with knowledge and consent of the data subject where appropriate. The personal data had to be relevant for the purpose for which it is gathered and be accurate, complete, and up-to-date. The data should not be disclosed other than for the essential purpose underlying its collection. The data should be protected by the use of reasonable security safeguards against unauthorized access or use. The individual about whom the data is collected should have the right to ascertain whether data has been collected about him or her; have the data communicated to the individual at a reasonable charge in a form that can be understood; be given reasons for denial of such information; and challenge inaccurate data and have it rectified.[25]

Part 3 of the recommendation requires member states to consider the implications of domestic processing and reexport of personal data for other member states. Transborder flows of such data should be uninterrupted and secure. With certain exceptions, a member state should permit unrestricted transborder flows of personal data between it and another member state and avoid passing laws creating obstacles to such transmission. The OECD Principles became the basis for international goals, codes, and statutes.[26]

The guiding principles are:

Collection Limitation Principle—There should be limits to the collection of personal data and any such data should be obtained lawful and fair means and, where appropriate, with the knowledge or consent of the data subject.

Data Quality Principle—Personal data should be relevant to the purposes for which they are to be used, and, to the extent necessary for those purposes, should be accurate, complete and kept up-to-date.

Purpose Specification Principle—The purposes for which personal data are collected should be specified not later than at the time of data collection and the subsequent use limited to the fulfillment of those purposes or such others as are not incompatible with those purposes and as specific on each occasion of change of purpose.

Use Limitation Principle—Personal data should not be disclosed, made available or otherwise used for purposes other than those specified in accordance with (the purpose specification principle] except:

a) with the consent of the data subject; or
b) by the authority of law.

Security Safeguards Principle—Personal data should be protected by reasonable security safeguards against such risks as loss or unauthorized access, destruction, use, modification, or disclosure of data.

Openness Principle—There should be a general policy of openness about developments, practices and policies with respect to personal data, and the main purposes of their use, as well as the identity and usual residence of the data controller.

Individual Participation Principle—An individual should have the right:

a) to obtain from a data controller, or otherwise, confirmation of whether or not the data controller has data relating to him;
b) to have communicated to him, data relating to him
   - within a reasonable time;
   - at a charge, if any, that is not excessive;
   - in a reasonable manner; and
   - in a form that is readily intelligible to him;
c) to be given reasons if a request made under subparagraphs (a) and (b) is denied, and to be able to challenge such denial; and
d) to challenge data relating to him and, if the challenge is successful to have the data erased, rectified, completed or amended.

Accountability Principle—A data controller should be accountable for complying with measures that give effect to the previously stated principles.

The United Nations

The U.N. adopted "Guidelines Concerning Computerized Personal Data Files" on December 14, 1990.[27] While leaving to individual countries to issue and implement regulations concerning computerized personal data, it issued a series of principles that should guide each state's initiative. They are:

1. *Principle of Lawfulness and Fairness*—Information is to be collected lawfully in accordance with the UN Charter.
2. *Principle of Accuracy*—The information collected should be accurate and relevant and be kept complete and up-to-date.
3. *Principle of the Purpose-Specification*—The purpose of the file should be legitimate, publicized, told to the subject person where possible, and all collected data should be relevant and be used or disclosed with the consent of the subject person.
4. *Principle of Interested-Person Access*—Anyone proving his or her identity has the

right to know about the information gathered about such person, to obtain it in an intelligible form, and to correct inaccuracies in the data. The principle applies irrespective of the person's nationality or place of residence.

5. *Principle of Nondiscrimination*—Data that would give rise to discriminatory treatment of a person should not be compiled. Such data would include racial or ethnic origin, color, creed, political opinions, membership in a union, and other such data.
6. *Power to Make Exceptions*—There may be exceptions to the first four principles if necessary to protect the public order, national security, public health and morality, the safety of persons being persecuted, and equivalent important reasons. With respect to the fifth principle, exceptions may be authorized so long as they conform to the limits prescribed by the International Bill of Human Rights and other such documents.[28]
7. *Principle of Security*—Countries should enact measures to protect against dangers such as fraudulent misuse of data, computer viruses, unauthorized access, and accidental loss of the data.
8. *Supervision and Sanctions*—Criminal or other penalties are to be enacted by countries for violations of these principles and assurance given that the persons administering such data be independent of pressures from outside sources.
9. *Transborder Data Flows*—The data should be freely circulated among countries having these safeguards. If a country is lacking in protections of privacy, then transfer of data should be allowed subject to protection of privacy demands.
10. *Field of Application*—The principles should be made applicable to all public and private computerized and manual files. Governmental international organizations also should be made subject to the above guidelines.

The Council of Europe

The Council of Europe adopted the Convention for the Protection of Individuals with Regard to Automatic Processing of Personal Data on October 1, 1985. It also sets forth a series of principles very similar to those later outlined in the Privacy Directive of the European Union. In addition thereto, Article 14 of the convention provides for assistance to data subjects residing abroad. It states that each party to the convention shall give to such persons aid in exercising the right to ascertain the existence of a personal file on him or her and its content, and to make corrections or erasures of data violating privacy rights.

The OECD and U.N. Guidelines and Recommendations, as well as those of the Council of Europe, are thus similar in nature. There appears to be a consensus that computerized personal data must be accurate, fair, limited in scope to need for such data, subject to correction by the subject person, and circulated among nations freely subject to privacy safeguards.

Canada

Among the nations acting in accordance with OECD Principles is Canada. Its provisions concerning privacy of electronic data may be found in the Personal Information Protection and Electronic Documents Act.[29] Canada sought to address three major concerns, namely, fear by consumers of tracking their usage on the Internet, consumers' lack of confidence concerning the security of Internet transactions, and the growing international concerns about data privacy. The statute repeats the principles set forth by the OECD and the U.N. They include accountability, identifiable purposes, consent of the subject person with exceptions, data collection limited to need, accuracy, safeguards, openness, right to correct inaccuracies, and access by the individual. A privacy commissioner will monitor compliance with the principles and will receive, investigate, and resolve complaints of aggrieved individuals.

The perceived problems of the legislation are the lack of requirement of express consent, which can be circumvented by a click-wrap type of consent form generally ignored by the subject persons; the need for a complaint before action is taken by the commissioner; and the lack of awareness by consumers of their rights under the act. The benefits are the greater awareness by consumers of their rights of privacy, the power to file complaints for resolution, and Canada's compliance with the OECD Recommendations and the European Union's 1998 Directive.

Other Global Efforts Concerning the Protection of Data Privacy

Argentina enacted a statute in December 1996 giving data protection ("full protection of personal information") in conformance with another law giving its inhabitants the right to obtain information about data collected on them. In addition, a Bicameral Commission on Monitoring of Data Protection was established to enforce the statute. Australia and Belgium, as members of the OECD, enacted a statute in conformity with its principles. Hong Kong, prior to its takeover by the People's Republic of China, enacted a Personal Data (Privacy) Ordinance that is still in effect and is reflective of the E.U. Directive. The same types of protection may be found in the statutes and ordinances of many other countries.[30]

Japan, and Taiwan, have enacted measures to ensure some degree of protection concerning the accumulation and processing of personal data. Among the measures that have been enacted are: (1) in Japan, the Act for Protection of Computer Processed Personal Data Held by Administrative Organs (December 1988); and (2) in Taiwan, the Law Governing Protection of Personal Data Processed by Computers (July 1995).

Japan, as a member of the OECD, is required to enact measures in accordance with the principles set forth in the text. The 1988 statute is somewhat deficient in that it applies only to federal agencies and does not cover the private sector. Taiwan's statute covers both the public and private domains, but both its law and that of Japan refer only to computer processing systems of personal data. Hong Kong contained the broadest coverage, extending to computer and manual data systems in both the public and private sectors.

SECURITY ISSUES

Closely allied to the issue of privacy is that of the installation and maintenance of security of information systems. It is a vexing issue that has plagued companies, particularly financial institutions, throughout the globe. Newspaper accounts are replete with hackers' intrusions upon data banks, including those containing sensitive national security data. The news accounts contain the tip-of-the-iceberg occurrences. There is little question that far more losses of data and funds have taken place because of lax or unsophisticated security systems. We discussed criminal issues affecting such intrusions in Chapter 5. In the prior discussion, the major concern was the loss of privacy as a result of unauthorized use, destruction, or other inappropriate risks to data. We will now review the legal and technological developments designed to address the problems created by hackers. It is readily apparent that international efforts are required to combat the loss and misuse of data. The OECD, in particular, has been actively engaged in bringing about major changes in the development of security system networks.

The interconnectivity of computers makes them particularly vulnerable to invasion by traceable and, at times, nontraceable sources. Hackers located in less technologically sophisticated countries have been able to overcome investigative and prosecutorial attempts to prevent their unlawful activity. Within hours, a computer virus may seriously affect enormous numbers of computers globally. The more dependent companies and other persons are on computer transactions, the more vulnerable they become to outside or inside insidious occurrences.

Other problems affect such technology. There are system overloads, hardware and software malfunctions, plus the ordinary difficulties brought about by weather, fire, floods, air-conditioning malfunctions, and the many other physical occurrences that all persons are subject to. In the end, computer technology relies on the efforts of human personnel who often are not technically advanced to prevent or overcome data invasions. Loss of passwords, wrongful storage of information, and other such daily occurrences are the norm. A further problem is that whenever a system is in place to prevent data invasion or distortion, new technologies become available to overcome in-place systems. This dependence coupled with vulnerability may lead to minor and major interruptions.

THE PRESIDENT'S FRAMEWORK

The president's *Framework for Global Electronic Commerce* states that the Global Information Infrastructure (GII) "must be secure and reliable." To be secure it must have:

(1) secure and reliable telecommunications networks;
(2) effective means for protecting the information systems attached to those networks;
(3) effective means for authenticating and ensuring confidentiality of electronic information to protect data from unauthorized use; and

(4) well trained GII users who understand how to protect their systems and their data.

Such security will involve a range of technologies including encryption, password controls, and the like. Major emphasis is to be placed on the development of certification services supporting the use of digital signatures by means of cryptographic keys. The president supports a voluntary, market-driven mechanism to accomplish such certification. The report notes that the use of strong encryption, which makes stored data and electronic communication unreadable without a decryption key, may also have undesirable consequences. Criminals and terrorists may deter law enforcement officials from preventing such activity. Some means of addressing the problem may be necessary.

The U.S. government is committed to a policy of developing market-driven standards, public-key management infrastructure services, the liberalization of export controls for commercial encryption products, and the cooperation with international bodies, particularly with the OECD, to accomplish these goals.[31]

INTERNATIONAL INITIATIVES ON SECURITY

Council of Europe Convention

The Council of Europe Convention (Treaty 108 of 1981) set forth basic principles for the protection of individuals.

OECD Guidelines for the Security of Information Systems

After extensive study by experts and scholars in the legal and scientific fields, the council of the OECD adopted the Recommendation of the Council Concerning guidelines for the Security of Information Systems on November 26, 1992. The 24 OECD member states also adopted its "Guidelines for the Security of Information Systems."[32] The Guidelines apply to all information systems in both the public and private sectors.[33] Like the privacy guidelines, the OECD set forth a number of principles that are to be followed in the promulgation of statutory and regulatory enactments in this area. They are:

1. Accountability Principle

The responsibilities and accountability of owners, providers and users of information systems and other parties concerned with the security of information systems should be explicit. [The parties include top management, programmers, system and software managers, and other such persons.]

2. Awareness Principle

In order to foster confidence in information systems, owners, providers and users of information systems and other parties should readily be able, consistent with maintaining security, to gain appropriate knowledge of and be informed about the existence and general extent of measures, practices and procedures for the security of information systems. [The information about security should be open to all those having a legitimate need to know and be conveyed in a manner as to not jeopardize security.]

3. Ethics Principle

Information systems and the security of information systems should be provided and used in such a manner that the rights and legitimate interests of others are respected. [Ethical concepts are to be instilled, particularly in young people, concerning the appropriate use and expectations of information systems.]

4. Multidisciplinary Principle

Measures, practices and procedures for the security of information systems should take account of and address all relevant considerations and viewpoints, including technical, administrative, organisational, operational, commercial, educational and legal. [The various groups all have their own unique perspectives, requirements, and resources that should be taken into account to create and maintain an optimal security system.]

5. Proportionality Principle

Security levels, costs, measures, practices and procedures should be appropriate and proportionate to the value of and degree of reliance on the information systems and to the severity, probability and extent of potential harm, as the requirements for security vary upon the particular information systems. [Not all systems require an optimal security system. The type and sophistication of the security system is dependent upon the extent and probability of harm, the cost to incorporate security measures, and other such considerations. Obviously, governmental organizations concerned with national security and financial institutions would require optimal security apparatus.]

6. Integration Principle

Measures, practices and procedures for the security of information systems should be co-ordinated and integrated with each other and with other measures, practices and procedures of the organisation so as to create a coherent system of security. [All aspects of the information cycle must be integrated, from the collection of the information to its transmission, storage, and deletion.]

7. Timeliness Principle

Public and private parties, at both national and international levels, should act in a timely co-ordinated manner to prevent and to respond to breaches of security of information systems. [The need to act expeditiously and with coordination by all such parties whenever breach of security takes place is mandatory.]

8. Reassessment Principle

The security information systems should be reassessed periodically, as information systems and the requirements for their security vary over time. [As technology advances rapidly, it is necessary that the security system in place be checked to make sure that it is able to withstand assaults from the innovations.]

9. Democracy Principle

The security of information systems should be compatible with the legitimate use and flow of data and information in a democratic society. [There is a need to balance the legitimate expectations of owners, developers, and operators of information systems with the needs and expectations of data availability of the public. Security systems should not be used to restrict the flow of data that opposes the needs and desires of a democratic society.][34]

Implementation of the Guidelines. Governments of member states are to cooperate with each other in promulgating and enforcing the Guidelines. Each of the states are to enact laws, decrees, and the like to harmonize global technical standards, promote expertise and best security procedures, provide for security in the negotiation and consummation of contracts, impose penal sanctions for criminal misuse of information systems, provide jurisdictional capabilities for courts over breaches, give mutual assistance to member states and incorporate extradition measures, and allow exchange of evidentiary data for penal and civil proceedings.

Member states are to provide education and training so as to promote awareness of the need for ethical conduct in the use of information systems; the incorporation of security measures to protect against system invasion or misuse; providing and fostering education to auditors, law enforcement authorities, owners, developers, and other persons about the need and availability of security measures.

CONCLUSION

Computer technology raises serious issues about an individual's privacy to an extent not heretofore known. There were analogous technologies, such as the advent of the telephone, cable, and the like, that the Founding Fathers could not possibly have anticipated. The pressing privacy issue in the eighteenth century was the unwarranted intrusion into one's home by Royal soldiers. Such intrusion was addressed in the Fourth Amendment to the Constitution, which forbade "unreasonable searches and seizure" with respect to persons, their homes, papers, and effects. The U.S. Supreme Court has alternately extended and retracted protection under the Fourth Amendment.

The Constitution is a living document, one that is organic in nature. As the new technology enters into the daily lives of a nation's inhabitants, it remains to be seen in future judicial decisions to what degree intrusion upon their privacy will be constitutionally permissible. The legislative branches of federal and state governments are struggling to balance the accessibility of information with the criminal and tortious misuse of data. Their efforts often enter into the realm of constitutional conflict. Courts increasingly will examine the conflict of governmental conduct with the right of privacy. Although not specifically mentioned in the Constitution as an explicit right, civil liberty advocates look to the Ninth Amendment, which states, "The enumeration in the Constitution of certain rights shall not be construed to deny or disparage others retained by the people." The right of privacy would appear to be embodied into its ambit.

The desire to protect individual privacy is now a worldwide phenomenon. Almost all countries have enacted laws dovetailing the principles of the OECD, the Council of Europe, and the European Union. It is anticipated that the issue of privacy, particularly in data accumulation and other new technological innovations, will continue to cause concern and enactment of legislation to protect individuals from injury to their person or property.

Questions and Problems

1. In February 1997, U.S. customs agents, engaged in an undercover investigation, monitored a chat room on the Internet from which they received a number of images featuring child pornography. The Internet service provider's records showed that the site from which the images emanated was owned by a Kathi Morrissey in Maine. Acting with a search warrant, a number of items were seized, including diskettes and 1,400 images of minors engaged in sexually explicit conduct that had been deleted but were undeleted by the agents. Further investigation revealed that the primary user of the computer was the defendant, Troy Upham, who had sent the pornographic images. Upham moved to suppress the evidence, alleging wrongful search. He alleged that he was abused as a child and that the pornographic communications were made in connection with a serious book he was writing concerning child abuse. He was tried and convicted. The search warrant permitted a search of "[a]ny and all computer software and hardware . . . computer disks, disk drive. Any and all visual depictions, in any format or media, of minors engaging in sexually explicit conduct. . . ." On appeal, the court had to determine whether the search warrant was too general and whether the recovery of previously deleted information on the hard drive and diskettes was outside the scope of the warrant. Decide. *United States v. Upham,* 168 F.3d 532 (1st Cir. 1999).
2. Plaintiffs were intercollegiate athletes who were videotaped in various stages of undress in their locker rooms, restrooms, or showers without their knowledge or consent. The videotapes were sold and displayed in various Web sites, including those of two Internet service providers, GTE (GTE Corporation and GTE Internetworking) and PSINet. The Internet service providers requested the district court to dismiss the case on the basis of the exemption found in the Communications Decency Act of 1996. Decide. *John Does v. Franco Productions,* No. 99 C 7885, 2000 U.S. Dist. LEXIS 8645 (N.D.Ill. 2000).
3. McKamey and Jett sued Roach under Title 3 of the Omnibus Crime Control and Safe Streets Act of 1968 as amended by the Electronics Communications Privacy Act of 1986. They complained that the defendants intercepted and recorded telephone conversations between McKamey and Jett and disseminated them to other defendants who were also sued. The district court dismissed that lawsuit because Jett had used a cordless telephone in his conversations with McKamey, which the defendants intercepted and recorded with a scanner capable of doing so. The plaintiffs and Roach were neighbors. Roach intercepted and recorded some 12 to 30 telephone conversations between the plaintiffs. The statute, which is both a criminal statute and a civil statute allowing victims to sue, forbids the nonconsensual interception of wire, oral, and electronic communications, as well as the intentional disclosure or use of the contents of such messages. The statute as stated at the time of the litigation defined an *electronic communication* as "any transfer of signs, signals, writing, images, sounds, data, or intelligence of any nature transmitted in whole or in part by a wire, radio, electromagnetic, photoelectronic or photooptical system . . . but does but include—(A) the radio portion of a cordless telephone communication that is transmitted between the cordless telephone handset and the base unit." The plaintiffs claim that the statute did not apply because McKamey used a traditional land-based telephone and was unaware that Jett was using a cordless telephone. Decide. *McKamey v. Roach,* 55 F.3d 1236 (6th Cir. 1995).
4. The plaintiff, Connection, publishes and distributes a dozen so-called swingers magazines. These magazines contain stories, photographs, letters, and other related materials in connection with its philosophy of catering to persons believing in an alternate lifestyle of nonmonogamous relationships. The Child Protection and Obscenity Enforcement Act of 1988 as amended in 1990 requires all producers of matter having sexual depictions of "actual sexually explicit

conduct" to prepare and maintain records of the names and dates of birth of all performers portrayed in the magazines. The records are to be maintained at the business premises of the magazines and made available at reasonable times for inspection. Connection sued, alleging that its constitutional rights were violated and that "privacy and confidentiality are fundamental to the 'swinging' lifestyle because the participants fear that their employers, communities, and families will reject them upon learning of their controversial lifestyle." Decide. *Connection Distributing Co. v. Reno,* 154 F.3d 281 (6th Cir. 1998).

5. Arias and Albero sued the Mutual Central Alarm Company, claiming a violation of Title 3 of the Omnibus Control and Safe Streets Act of 1968 as amended by the Electronic Communications Privacy Act, in that their employer unlawfully intercepted private telephone conversations by use of a Dictaphone 9102 machine that was attached to the company's telephone system. Mutual is a provider of central-station alarm services by monitoring burglar and fire alarms and when activated alerts the respective fire and other emergency services departments. The Dictaphone complies with industry practice of monitoring and recording all telephone conversations to the central station. New York City Fire Department requires the installation by such companies of automatic recording equipment on all lines used in communicating with the department. The plaintiffs began hearing bleeps on their telephones, indicating a recording of conversations, and when they complained, they were assured by company executives that their conversations were not being recorded. Thereafter, in somewhat convoluted personal relationships between the plaintiffs and the company's president, it was learned that the conversations were overheard and recorded. Did the company violate the Electronic Communications Privacy Act? *Arias v. Mutual Central Alarm Service, Inc.,* 202 F.3d 553 (2d Cir. 2000).

6. First Union is a bank within the FedWire Fund Transfer System. It uses electronic storage to maintain the contents of electronic wire transfers. On September 2, 1993, and November 30, 1993, First Union received electronic wire transfer of funds to the account of Patricia Lopez. Based on verbal instructions of federal law enforcement officials, First Union provided access to the contents of the wire transfers to U.S. law enforcement officers. On February 3, 1994, a U.S. magistrate issued a search warrant directing First Union to freeze Lopez's account and to conduct an inventory of the said account. First Union complied. On June 6, 1995, First Union surrendered some $270,000 of the account to the United States. In a later civil forfeiture case against Lopez, the government and Lopez settled the action by the forfeiture of $108,000 to the U.S. and Lopez received back $162,000. After the case was ended, Lopez sued First Union, claiming violations under the Electronic Communications Privacy Act and the Right to Financial Privacy Act. First Union asked the district court to dismiss the claim, based on the theory that the Annunzio-Wylie Anti-Money Laundering Act immunized First Union from liability.

   The ECPA provides "protection against the unauthorized interception of electronic communications." It further provides that "a person or entity providing an electronic communication service to the public shall not knowingly divulge to any person or entity the contents of a communication while in electronic storage by that service." An exception is made for disclosure pursuant to a federal or state warrant. The RFPA provides individuals with privacy rights as to financial records in the hands of third parties. The act excepts a disclosure of information to law enforcement authorities to the extent of stating the name of the account and "the nature of any suspected illegal activity." The Annunzio-Wylie Act provides for a safe harbor (immunization from liability) to financial institutions for disclosures of any possible violation of law or regulation. Did Lopez state a cause of action that, if proven, would render First Union liable? *Lopez v. First Union National Bank,* 129 F.3d 1186 (11th Cir. 1997).

7. John Williams is a Vietnam veteran who incurred a post-traumatic stress disorder. He received treatment at a Veteran's Administration hospital in Virginia. In February 1993, he

phoned and wrote to the hospital's director concerning the conduct of his psychologist therein. Dr. Sherod Williams (no relation) was assigned to investigate the complaint. He wrote a summary of his review, and drafted a letter to John Williams that contained his conclusions and a recommended course of future treatment. The letter was never sent because his supervisors refused to allow him to do so, apparently because the letter was critical of the hospital. When John Williams sought to obtain copies of the material prepared by Dr. Williams, under the Freedom of Information Act and the Privacy Act, he was rebuffed. The hospital claimed that the letter could not be found and that the review of Dr. Williams had been destroyed. It was later discovered that Dr. Williams had retained the materials as computer files. When he was informed of the files, John Williams was denied access because the records sought were not "retrievable by your name or other identifier assigned to you, [and] your appeal is not subject to consideration under the Privacy Act of 1974."

The Privacy Act provides in part:

(d) Access to records.—Each agency that maintains a system of records shall—
  (1) upon request by any individual to gain access to his record or to any information pertaining to him which is contained in the system, permit him . . . to review the record and have a copy made of all or any portion thereof in a form comprehensible to him
  (2) the term "record" means any item, collection, or grouping of information about an individual that is maintained by an agency, including, but not limited to, his education, financial transactions, medical history, and criminal or employment history and that contains his name, or the identifying number, symbol, or other identifying particular assigned to the individual, such as a finger or voice print or a photograph.

The district court dismissed the case because the materials sought were not *records* within the meaning of the Privacy Act. On appeal, what is your decision? *Williams v. Department of Veterans Affairs,* 104 F.3d 670 (4th Cir. 1997).

8. Russell was convicted of first degree robbery and second degree rape in 1989 in the state of Washington. A year later, Washington passed the Community Protection Act, which required sex offenders to register with local law enforcement authorities and required community notification that included the offender's photograph and residential location. The law applied differently with respect to minor infractions and major infractions. If it was a Level Two (serious sex crime), notification was given to local law enforcement agencies, to schools within the area of residence, and to Block Watch Captains. A Level Three (most serious sex crimes) infraction caused the information to be given to local news media. Russell was a Level Three offender. Russell and others filed a civil rights lawsuit claiming that the act violated the ex post facto clause of the U.S. Constitution and abridged his right of privacy and due process.

   The ex post facto clause in the U.S. Constitution provides: "No State shall . . . pass any . . . ex post facto Law. . . ." It forbids states from enacting any law that imposes a punishment for an act that was not punishable when the act was committed or to increase the punishment after the commission of the act." Decide whether any or all of the claims of civil rights violation were valid. *Russell v. Gregoire,* 124 F.3d 1079 (9th Cir. 1997).
9. Six professors were employed by diverse public colleges and universities in Virginia. They sued, challenging the constitutionality of a Virginia law that restricted access of state employees from accessing sexually explicit materials on computers owned or leased by the state. The term *sexually explicit material* is defined as "content having as a dominant theme (i) any lascivious description of or (ii) any lascivious picture, photograph, drawing, motion picture film, digital image or similar visual representation depicting sexual bestiality, a lewd exhibition of nudity, . . . sexual excitement, sexual conduct or sadomasochistic abuse . . . , coprophilia, urophilia, or fetishism." The U.S. district court held in favor of the professors,

stating that the statute was an unconstitutional violation of the First Amendment. On appeal, what is your decision? *Urofsky v. Gilmore,* 216 F.3d 401 (4th Cir. 2000).

10. The Grand Central Partnership (GCP) sued the U.S. Department of Housing and Urban Development (HUD), alleging that HUD wrongfully refused to give GCP certain documents requested under the Freedom of Information Act. In early 1995, a number of newspapers had reported that GCP employees had used abusive and violent tactics to remove homeless persons from public spaces in and around Grand Central Station in New York. GCP was denied access to HUD programs for one year, which order was rescinded on appeal. While the appeal was pending, GCP asked for all documents held by HUD concerning the allegations. After an initial refusal to turn over copies of the documents, HUD did give copies of most documents but denied access to certain other documents on the ground that information was given to it by informants whose privacy would be invaded if the documents were released. There was no showing that the documents contained the exact identity of the informants. Was the denial of the documents to GCP appropriate? Decide. *Grand Central Partnership v. Cuomo,* 166 F.3d 473 (2d Cir. 1999).
11. Davis operated a computer bulletin board in Oklahoma city. He sold a number of obscene CD-ROMs to an undercover officer who then used the sale as a basis for obtaining a search warrant to search Davis's business premises. After police officers entered the premises pursuant to the warrant, they determined that CD-ROM files could be accessed through the bulletin board and seized the computer equipment used to operate it. Davis was convicted in state court wherein there was also a civil forfeiture of the equipment. Davis, his other related businesses, and a number of users of his e-mail bulletin board sued the said police officers in federal court, claiming that the seizure of the computer equipment constituted a violation of their constitutional and statutory rights. Specifically, the claim was that the officers violated the claimants' Fourth Amendment (unlawful search and seizure) rights, and their rights under the Privacy Protection Act and under the Electronic Communications Privacy Act. Decide. *Davis v. Gracey,* 111 F.3d 1472 (10th Cir. 1997).

Endnotes

1. Alpheus Thomas Mason, *Brandeis: A Free Man's Life* (New York: Viking Press, 1946), p. 70. The article may be found in 4 Harv. L. Rev. 193 (1890).
2. P. Sprenger, *Sun on Privacy: 'Get Over It,'* Wired News, Jan. 26, 1999, *www.wired.com/news/politics/0,1283,17538,00.html.*
3. *McKinney's Civil Rights Law of New York,* Sections 50–51.
4. David Banisar and Simon Davies, *Global Trend in Privacy Protection: An International Survey of Privacy, Data Protection, and Surveillance Laws and Developments,* 18 J. Marshall J. Computer & Info. L. 1.
5. Professor Kurland, quoted in *Whalen v. Roe,* 429 U.S. 589 (1977).
6. See, for example, *Fahy v. Connecticut,* 375 U.S. 85 (1963), wherein a police officer who had stopped a driver in a car and found paint and a paintbrush in the vehicle, later made a warrantless search of the driver's home after he learned of the unlawful painting of a swastika on a synagogue. The search was deemed in violation of the defendant's constitutional rights.
7. See *United States v. Leon,* 468 U.S. 897 (1984), and *Maryland v. Garrison,* 107 S. Ct. 1013 (1987).
8. Case No. 05-97-00824, 1999 LEXIS. App. LEXIS 4103 (Tex. Crt. of App. May 28, 1999).
9. Federal Trade Commission, 16 CFR Part 312, *Children's Online Privacy Protection Rule.*
10. For a review of ethical issues in conjunction with privacy issues, see Deborah G. Johnson, *Computer Ethics,* 2d ed. (Upper Saddle River, NJ: Prentice Hall, 1994).
11. The *Framework* can be found at *www.ecommerce.gov/framewrk.htm.*
12. See report, *Privacy and the National Information Infrastructure: Principles for Providing and Using Personal Information* (June 1995).
13. 42 U.S.C.A. 1320d to 1320d-8. For a discussion of this topic, see Marisa Anne Pignattaro, "Genetic Discrimination and the Workplace: Employee's Right to Privacy v. Employer's Right to Know" (unpublished paper delivered to the Academy of Legal Studies in Business, Baltimore, MD, August 2000).
14. See FTC Report, p. 4.
15. FTC Report, p. 23.
16. For a list of some of the actions taken, see Appendix 3 of the Federal Trade Commission Report of

December 1999, *The FTC's First Five Years: Protecting Consumers Online.*

17. See TRUSTe Web site at *www.truste.org/partners/users_faqs.html.*
18. *www.truste.org/webpublishers/pub_child.html.*
19. For a discussion of the ability of industry to regulate itself, see Jonathan P. Cody, *Protecting Privacy over the Internet: Has the Time Come to Abandon Self-Regulation?* 48 Cath. U.L. Rev. 1183 (Summer 1999). The Microsoft discussion is found at p. 1227.
20. Eric Goldman, *Drafting a Policy Statement? Beware! members.theglobe.com/ericgoldman/privacy.html?nfhp=936388150.*
21. A copy of the directive can be found at *europa.eu.int/eur-lex/en/lif/dat/1995/en_#95L0046.html.* A *directive* in the European Union imposes obligations upon member states to conform their laws to the policies and provisions stated therein.
22. See European Commission, *Data Protection: Background Information, europa.eu.int/comm/internal_... en/media/dataprot/backinfo/info.htm.*
23. See, for example, *E.U. Directive on Privacy May Hinder E-Commerce,* National Law Journal, *www.ljx.com/practice/internat/0629euecomm.html.*
24. November 15, 1999, *Draft International Safe Harbor Privacy Principles Issued by the U.S. Department of Commerce, www.ita.doc.gov/td/ecom/Principles1199.htm.*
25. The Recommendation can be found at *europa.eu.int/comm/internal_market/en/media/dataprot/inter/priv.htm.*
26. See, for example, *Framework,* pp. 11–13.
27. The Guidelines may be found at *europa.eu.int/comm/internal_mark/en/media/dataprot/inter/un.htm.*
28. The 1948 U.N. Universal Declaration of Human Rights, Article 12, declares: "No one should be subjected to arbitrary interference with his privacy, family, home or correspondence, nor to attacks on his honor or reputation. Everyone has the right to the protection of the law against such interference or attacks."
29. Statutes of Canada 2000, Chapter 5 passed on April 13, 2000, effective January 1, 2001. See *www.parl.gc.ca.* The discussion is based on an unpublished article by Steven R. Enman, "Does Electronic Commerce Need Privacy Law?" (Academy of Legal Studies in Business Annual Conference, Baltimore, MD, August 2000).
30. For an extensive discussion of the efforts made in some 51 countries concerning data privacy, see Global Internet Liberty Campaign, *Privacy and Human Rights: An International Survey of Privacy Laws and Practice, www.gilc.org/privacy/survey/.*
31. See *Framework,* pp. 13–14.
32. The "Guidelines for the Security of Information Systems," may be found at *europa.eu.int/comm/internal_... t/en/media/dataprot/inter/secur.htm.*
33. The OECD definition of *information systems* is quite extensive. It states that they include:

    computer hardware; interconnected peripheral equipment; software, firmware and other means of expressing computer programs; algorithms and other specifications either embedded within or accessed by such computer programs; manuals and documentation on paper, magnetic, optical and other media; communication facilities, such as terminal/customer premises equipment and multiplexers, on the information system side of the network termination point of public telecommunication transport networks as well as equipment for private telecommunications networks not offered to the public generally; security control parameters; storage, processing, retrieval, transmission and communication data, such as check digits and packet switching codes, and procedures; data and information about parties accessing information systems; and user identification and verification measures (whether knowledge-based, token-based, biometric, behavioural or other).

34. The need for security versus the public's need for data availability was the subject of a news article by Leslie Chiang in the Wall Street Journal on September 14, 2000, entitled *Web Firms' China Units Face Limits* (p. A21). The article indicated that the People's Republic of China is considering "draconian restrictions on who can operate in the country's promising Internet sector." Such measures by the use of highly abusive licensing regulations would eliminate foreign business from competing in and delivering Internet and multimedia network services. The obvious reason is the desire of the autocratic regime to control the free flow of data to and from China.

PART V

ANTITRUST, SECURITIES REGULATION, AND TAXATION

CHAPTER

11 ANTITRUST ISSUES IN CYBER ACTIVITIES

Chapter Outline

The recent commencement and prosecution of a civil antitrust action against the Microsoft Corporation illustrates the application of the antitrust statutes to the domination of one company that is a maker of the personal computer operating system. As the computer marketplace becomes more integrated, it appears that the antitrust laws will have greater application. The Federal Trade Commission will also have a greater role in investigating and prosecuting the many scams and deceptive acts being perpetrated against consumers and others. In this chapter, we will review the basic principles of antitrust law and proceed with their application to cyberspace issues.

PURPOSE OF ANTITRUST LAWS

The purpose of the antitrust laws is to enhance and preserve the free marketplace wherein goods and services are bought and sold in accordance with the existing supply and demand. In a free market, as demand for goods increase, the supply diminishes, which, in turn, causes the price of those goods to rise, leading to greater profit. As the profit increases, the supply of goods increases, and the price drops accordingly. The entry of diverse persons into the marketplace leads to increased competition, which then leads to better quality goods at lower prices.

Prior to the 1960s, automobiles were manufactured by a small number of U.S. manufacturers. Although the autos were differentiated by the unique styles of each company, none made automobiles designed to last for an extended period of time. New-car warranties extended for only 90 days, after which time the buyer was responsible for any repairs or replacements. When the German manufacturers, followed by Japanese auto companies, began to compete by making quality small vehicles, U.S. companies were placed in near bankrupt condition because they failed to manufacture quality automobiles. The U.S. consumer, with the increased competition, was able to purchase inexpensive vehicles that lasted significantly longer than their American counterparts. After the initial shock that lasted several years, the quality of American cars improved greatly and became priced competitively. Without competition, it is likely that U.S. vehicles would have remained poorly made.

In recent times, control of the oil market supply by the Organization of Petroleum Exporting Countries (OPEC) cartel led to price increases as determined by the cartel rather than by the marketplace. Without pressure to let the market determine the price and supply of goods, the supplier can act as it sees fit. It is this factor and other types of artificial control interference that the antitrust laws are designed to prevent. The downfall of the Soviet Union was due in large part to its inability to meet consumer demands. Its planned economy led to a scarce supply of consumer goods of poor quality, and choice was almost nonexistent. In turn, there was a great deal of black-market and other forms of corruption that carried over in the country's transitional period. Competition is designed to overcome such difficulties.

EARLY HISTORY OF ANTITRUST REGULATION

In the late 1800s, Congress was called upon to pass legislation to curb the abuses of monopolists who possessed a stranglehold over major industries, especially the railroads. States, in theory, could have taken action against monopolistic activity by virtue of state common-law prohibitions having precedents going back several centuries. The problem is that state regulation ends at the borders of the individual states. Subpoenas issued by state courts have no effect beyond a state's boundary. Monopolists could easily move from one state to another whenever regulation threatened their position. In addition, the vast amount of money accumulated by these monopolists enabled them to purchase political influence in particular states so that regulation became a remote circumstance. Farmers and others, who were at the mercy of the monopolists, demanded action by Congress.

In 1890, the Sherman Act was passed making it a crime to engage in certain forbidden practices. The statute forbade contracts, combinations, and conspiracies that interfered with competition and also forbade actions that caused and retained monopolies. Initially the law was applied to existing monopolistic practices; however, the statute was severely curtailed by the ability of corporate attorneys to make the statute work in *favor* of monopolists. They did so by having unions prosecuted as *combinations* in restraint of trade as stated in Section 1 of the act. As a result, the Clayton Act of 1914 and the Federal Trade Commission Act of 1914 were passed to fill in the gaps of the earlier legislation and provide exemptions from the antitrust laws, including labor unions and farmers. Later amendments further refined the application and prosecution of violators of the acts.

THE SHERMAN ANTITRUST ACT

Sherman Antitrust Act (15 U.S.C. Sections 1–2)

Sec. 1. Every contract, combination in the form of trust or otherwise, or conspiracy, in restraint of trade or commerce among the several States, or with foreign nations, is hereby declared to be illegal. Every person who shall make any contract or engage in any combination or conspiracy hereby declared to be illegal shall be deemed guilty of a felony, and, on conviction thereof, shall be punished by a fine not exceeding ten million dollars if a corporation, or, if any other person, three hundred fifty thousand dollars, or by imprisonment not exceeding three years, or by both said punishments, in the discretion of the court.

Sec. 2. Every person who shall monopolize or attempt to monopolize, or combine or conspire with any other person or persons, to monopolize any part of the trade or commerce among the several States, or with foreign nations, shall be deemed guilty of a felony, and, on conviction thereof, shall be punished by fine not exceeding one million if a corporation, or, if any other person, one hundred thousand dollars, or by imprisonment not exceeding three years, or by both said punishments, in the discretion of the court.

The Sherman Act was enacted in 1890 and was the first federal statute designed to curb the abuses by the so-called robber barons who formed trusts among the competitors to eliminate competition and control their respective industries. In addition to the criminal penalties, a civil action may be instituted by the U.S. government and by injured parties who may recover treble damages, reasonable legal expenses, and other relief.

Section 1: Contracts, Combinations, and Conspiracies in Restraint of Trade

The Sherman Act had two main provisions as stated previously. The first section forbids any contract, combination, or conspiracy in restraint of trade. The agreement must be between two or more parties. An agreement between a company and its wholly-owned subsidiary does not come within the statute.[1] The key element is that there must be an unreasonable restraint of trade. Courts have determined that certain conduct is a *per se* violation, that is, it is wrong irrespective of the motivation behind the conduct. In most cases, courts will use the *rule of reason* approach, that is, the court, in a particular case, will analyze the facts to determine whether on balance the conduct should be restrained.

Per Se Rule. The nature and purpose of the per se rule was discussed in an oft-cited U.S. Supreme Court decision, *Northern Pacific Railway Co. v. United States,* 356 U.S. 1, 1958:

> [T]here are certain agreements or practices which because of their pernicious effect on competition and lack of any redeeming virtue are conclusively presumed to be unreasonable and therefore illegal without elaborate inquiry as to the precise harm they have caused or the business excuse for their use. This principle of *per se* unreasonableness not only makes the type of restraints which are proscribed by the Sherman Act more certain to the benefit of everyone concerned, but it also avoids the necessity for an incredibly complicated and prolonged economic investigation into the entire history of the industry involved, as well as related industries, in an effort to determine at large whether a particular restraint has been unreasonable—an inquiry so often wholly fruitless when undertaken. Among the practices which the courts have heretofore deemed to be unlawful in and of themselves are price fixing, . . . division of markets, . . . group boycotts, . . . and tying arrangements.

Tying Arrangements. In *Northern Pacific,* the Court discussed tying as forbidden conduct. It stated:

> [A] tying arrangement may be defined as an agreement by a party to sell one product but only on the condition that the buyer also purchase a different (or tied) product, or at least agrees that he will not purchase that product from any other supplier. Where such conditions are successfully exacted competition on the merits with respect to the tied product is inevitably curbed. Indeed "tying arrangements serve hardly any purpose beyond the suppression of competition." They deny competitors free access to the market for the tied product, not because the party imposing the tying arrangements has a better product or a lower price but because of his power or leverage in another market. At the same time buyers are forced to forego their free choice between competing products. For these reasons "tying agreements fare harshly under the laws forbidding restraints of trade." They are unreasonable in and of themselves whenever a party has sufficient economic power with respect to the tying product to appreciably restrain free competition in the market for the tied product and a "not insubstantial" amount of interstate commerce is affected. Of course where the seller has no control or dominance over the tying product so that it does not represent an effectual weapon to pressure buyers into taking the tied item any restraint of trade attributable to such tying arrangements would obviously be insignificant at most.

The classic cases concerning tying, cited in almost every court decision affecting tying, are *International Salt Co. v. United States,* 332 U.S. 392 (1947), wherein the Court declared illegal the requirement by the company, as a condition to leasing of its patented machines to process salt, that the lessees also purchase all unpatented salt and salt tablets from it; and *International Business Machines Corp. v. United States,* 298 U.S. 131 (1936), wherein IBM unlawfully required lessees of its punching machines to also purchase cards used in the machines from the company. Tying arrangements may be illegal under both Section 1 of the Sherman Act and Section 3 of the Clayton Act.

Boycotts. Ordinarily, a person may transact business or elect not to transact business with anyone he or she may decide. The nature of a market economy is this freedom of choice given to every person. The problem arises when two or more companies with sufficient economic power agree among themselves to refuse to deal with a particular company. In an early case, *Eastern States Retail Lumber Dealers' Ass'n v. United States,* 234 U.S. 600 (1914), the Court declared illegal an agreement among lumber associations composed of retail lumber dealers to boycott wholesale dealers that sold its products directly to consumers, thereby bypassing them. The Court said that the Sherman Act forbids the restraint of interstate commerce whether it be by unlawful contracts, pooling arrangements, blacklists, threats, coercion, intimidation, trusts, contracts, or otherwise.

In *Klor's, Inc. v. Broadway-Hale Stores, Inc.,* 359 U.S. 207 (1959), the defendant required major manufacturers, such as General Electric, RCA, Admiral, Zenith, Emerson, and other companies, as a condition of purchase of their products for its chain of stores, to refuse to sell to the plaintiff, Klor's. The Court held that such group boycotts are forbidden. The boycott prevented manufacturers from possessing the freedom to sell to Klor's at the same prices and conditions available to the defendant. "It interferes with the natural flow of interstate commerce." It clearly has, by its "nature" and "character," a "monopolistic tendency."

In *United States v. Park, Davis and Co.,* 362 U.S. 29, 1960, the U.S. Supreme Court found the conduct of a pharmaceutical company in boycotting stores that sold its drugs at a discount in opposition to its minimum pricing policy was illegal per se under Section 1 of the Sherman Act. Similarly, in *United States v. General Motors Corp.,* 384 U.S. 127 (1966), the Court declared illegal the prohibition of Chevrolet dealers from establishing "a new or different location, branch sales office, branch service station, or place of business including any used car lot or location without the prior written approval of Chevrolet."

Whether boycotts will continue to have a per se prohibition is in doubt due to later U.S. Supreme Court decisions in *Monsanto v. Spray-Rite Service Corp.,* 465 U.S. 752 (1984) and *Business Electronics Corp. v. Sharp Electronics Corp.,* 485 U.S. 108 (1988). In the said cases, the Court appeared to hesitate about invoking the per se rule in cases involving the termination by a manufacturer or distributor that discounted the price of its product in the absence of proof of a conspiracy between the manufacturer and dealers who were not so terminated. In *Monsanto,* the Court did uphold an award of $10.5 million against Monsanto for terminating a dealer that refused to end its discount practice of Monsanto's products. The Court, however, noted that a manufacturer has a right to deal with whomever it pleases as long as it does so independently. It "can announce its resale prices in advance and refuse to deal with those who comply. And a distributor is free to acquiesce in the manufacturer's demand in order to avoid termination." The illegality is when the manufacturer agrees with other distributors who complain about discounting retailers causing the latter to be terminated.

Price Fixing. The extent to which a per se rule will be applied may be found in *United States v. Socony-Vacuum Oil Co.,* 310 U.S. 150 (1940). Beginning in 1926, there was overproduction of crude oil that caused prices to drop below the costs of production. The result was the wasteful abandonment of wells that could not be reused should the need for crude oil again arise. In the 1930s, the Great Depression took place, lessening the need for oil and dropping the price to as low as $.022 a gallon. In order to stabilize the industry, refiners entered into informal agreements with major oil companies whereby purchases would be made at the "fair going market price." The issue thus arose whether reasonableness of the agreement would be considered in determining the alleged violation of the Sherman Act. The Court held that an agreement to raise prices by the combination was illegal irrespective of the circumstances.

> Under the Sherman Act a combination formed for the purpose and with the effect of raising, depressing, fixing, pegging, or stabilizing the price of a commodity in interstate or foreign commerce is illegal per se. Where the machinery for price-fixing is an agreement on the prices to be charged or paid for the commodity in the interstate or foreign channels of trade, the power to fix prices exists if the combination has control of a substantial part of the commerce in that commodity. . . . Proof that a combination was formed for the purpose of fixing prices and that it caused them to be fixed or contributed to that result is proof of the completion of a price-fixing conspiracy under section 1 of the Act.

Both *horizontal* (between competing companies) and *vertical* (between the manufacturer and distributor) price-fixing arrangements may be unlawful *per se.* The Sherman Act is violated when manufacturers or wholesalers attempt to compel distributors to sell their product at a particular price or to set a minimum or maximum price for the retail sale of the product. Competitors who come together to set prices for their products or services run afoul of the act. For example, if major competing airlines were to set the fares at a particular price between certain destinations, such agreement would be unlawful per se. It would not be illegal to raise or lower one's fares after a competitor has done so, so long as there has not been an agreement to do so. Courts have applied the doctrine of *conscious parallelism* where no such conspiracy or agreement could be proven but it is obvious that a concerted effort to fix the price of the product or service had taken place.

Rule of Reason. Conduct not deemed illegal per se may be illegal depending upon the circumstances and facts of a given case. The definition of the *rule of reason* is discussed in another oft-cited case, *Chicago Board of Trade v. United States,* 246 U.S. 231 (1918), wherein Justice Louis Brandeis stated:

The true test of legality is whether the restraint imposed is such as merely regulates and perhaps thereby promotes competition or whether it is such as may suppress or even destroy competition. To determine that question the court must ordinarily consider the facts peculiar to the business to which the restraint is applied; its condition before and after the restraint was imposed; the nature of the restraint and its effect, actual or probable. The history of the restraint, the evil believed to exist, the reason for adopting the particular remedy, the purpose or end sought to be attained, are all relevant facts. This is not because a good intention will save an otherwise objectionable regulation or the reverse; but because knowledge of intent may help the court to interpret and to predict consequences.

In *National Society of Professional Engineers v. United States,* 435 U.S. 679 (1978), the Court elaborated on the rule of reason:

Contrary to its name, the Rule does not open the field of antitrust inquiry to any argument in favor of a challenged restraint that may fall within the realm of reason. Instead, it focuses directly on the challenged restraint's impact on competitive conditions.

The test prescribed in *Standard Oil Co. v. United States* [221 U.S. 1 (1911)] is whether the challenged contracts or acts "were unreasonably restrictive of competitive conditions." Unreasonableness under that test could be based either (1) on the nature or character of the contracts, or (2) on surrounding circumstances giving rise to the inference or presumption that they are intended to restrain trade and enhance prices. Under either branch of the test, the inquiry is confined to a consideration of impact on competitive conditions.

The rule of reason is applied to all none per se cases, such as horizontal and vertical mergers and division of markets.

Section 2: Monopolies

Section 2 of the Sherman Act forbids conduct of companies with significant market power to engage in conduct that tends to promote the formation and maintenance of a monopoly. Monopolies are not in themselves illegal. It is the act of monopolizing that may be illegal. For example, there are many one-newspaper towns due to the fact that former competing newspapers were not able to satisfy the demands of the reading public. As long as the remaining newspaper does not take steps to destroy its competitors, as by threatening and compelling advertisers to deal with it exclusively, no illegality takes place. The marketplace once contained many businesses that have since failed because of their inability to satisfy market demands.

In addition, Section 2 of the Sherman Act forbids "attempt to monopolize or combine or conspire" to monopolize. *Attempt to monopolize* requires proof of "(1) a specific intent to monopolize, that is, the defendant engaged in exclusionary conduct; (2) an overt act or acts; and (3) a dangerous probability of monopolization of a specific product market in a particular geographic market."[2] An *attempt* is the formation of an illegal plan and the taking of some step towards the execution of that plan. A *conspiracy* is an overt or covert agreement between two or more persons to commit an unlawful act. The *Beverly v. Network Solutions, Inc.* case, to be discussed, has an excellent review of the elements to establish a conspiracy.

The elements necessary to establish an offense under Section 2 of the Sherman Act were stated in *United States v. Grinnell Corp.,* 384 U.S. 563 (1966). They are: "(1) the possession of monopoly power in the relevant market and (2) the willful acquisition or maintenance of that power as distinguished from growth or development as a consequence of a superior product, business acumen, or historic accident."

The court in *Berkey Photo, Inc. v. Eastman Kodak Co.,* 603 F.2d 263 (2d Cir. 1979), amplified the nature of the monopoly offense. It said that Section 2 of the Sherman Act does not prohibit monopoly in the concrete. Quoting Judge Learned Hand, the court said that "Congress did not condone 'good trusts' and condemn 'bad trusts.' The successful competitor, having been urged to compete, must not be turned upon when he wins." It is when there are active attempts to maintain or acquire monopoly power that the law's prohibition may come into effect. "A variety of techniques may be employed to achieve this end-predatory pricing, lease-only policies, and exclusive buying arrangements, to list a few. . . ." It is when these practices emerge that the law's prohibitions may apply.

In order to determine whether monopolistic practices have taken place, the law looks to the relevant geographic and product market. A company may be totally dominant in one sector of the country yet be almost unknown in other parts of the country. If one defines the geographic market to be, for example, New England, a court may find a company's practices to be illegal, but if the geographic market is defined as the entire United States, a very different result may ensue. Similarly, how a court defines the competing product may determine the outcome of the decision. The *relevant product market* has been defined "by the reasonable interchangeability of use or the cross-elasticity of the demand between the product itself and substitutes for it." Factors for determining the relevant product market include the product's peculiar characteristics and uses, distinct customers, distinct prices, functional interchangeability, responsiveness of the sales of one product to the price changes of the other, unique production facilities, and degree of competition from the potential substitute.[3]

The so-called *Cellophane Case* is the most-cited case discussing relevant product market.[4] Du Pont was charged with monopolizing the cellophane market in violation of Section 2 of the Sherman Act. In its defense, du Pont alleged that rather than possessing almost 75 percent of the market if the product was defined as cellophane, the Court should define the market as "flexible packaging material," which would then reduce its dominance to less than 20 percent. The Court agreed with du Pont's contention argument. The geographic market was national in scope. It examined the cross-elasticity of demand in the trade. It held that cellophane was interchangeable with other packaging materials, such as aluminum foil, cling wrap, and other such packaging materials. It did not perceive a monopolistic danger, as required by the statute, inasmuch as buyers of the product could easily substitute other wrappings should du Pont raise its prices substantially or otherwise abuse its dominant position.

The *Microsoft* case exemplifies the type of conduct forbidden by the Sherman Act. The lawsuit caused national and worldwide publicity. Microsoft software is part of almost every computer user's life. Its CEO, Bill Gates, is as well known as motion picture and sports figures. The case presents and tests the provisions of the Sherman Act already cited. The discussion is set forth in detail because it summarizes well the current state of the law, particularly as it applies to the new technology.

UNITED STATES V. MICROSOFT

87 F. Supp. 2d 30 (D.D.C. 2000)

FACTS: The U.S., nineteen States and the District of Columbia instituted a civil action against Microsoft alleging that it violated section 2 of the Sherman Act (15 U.S.C. sections 1 and 2) "by engaging in a series of exclusionary, anticompetitive, and predatory acts to maintain its monopoly power." The essential acts complained of were the attempt by Microsoft to monopolize the Web browser market by the tying of its browser to its operating system and entering into exclusive dealing arrangements.

ISSUES: (1) Did Microsoft maintain its monopoly power by anticompetitive means and attempt to monopolize the Web browser market in violation of section 2 of the Sherman Act?

(2) Did Microsoft violate section 1 of the Sherman Act by unlawful tying its Web browser to its operating system?

(3) Did Microsoft violate section 1 of the Sherman Act by engaging in marketing arrangements with other companies that constituted unlawful exclusive dealing under the Act?

(4) Were states foreclosed by the federal antitrust laws from pursuing their claims of liability under state law?

DECISION: The Court decided:

(1) Microsoft did violate section 2 of the Sherman Act by attempting to monopolize the Web browser market.

(2) Microsoft did violate section 1 of the Sherman Act by unlawfully tying of its Web browser to its operating system.

(3) Microsoft did not engage in unlawful exclusive dealing.

(4) States were not foreclosed from suing under state law.

REASONING: Judge Jackson

I. SECTION TWO OF THE SHERMAN ACT

A. Maintenance of Monopoly Power by Anticompetitive Means

Section 2 of the Sherman Act declares that it is unlawful for a person or firm to "monopolize . . . any part of the trade or commerce among the several States, or with foreign nations. . . ." 15 U.S.C. section 2. This language operates to limit the means by which a firm may lawfully either acquire or perpetuate monopoly power. Specifically, a firm violates section 2 if it attains or preserves monopoly power through anticompetitive acts. . . . ("The offense of monopoly power under section 2 of the Sherman Act has two elements: (1) the possession of monopoly power in the relevant market and (2) the willful acquisition or maintenance of that power as distinguished from growth or development as a consequence of a superior product, business acumen, or historic accident.") . . . ("Our section 2 monopolization doctrines are . . . directed to discrete situations in which a defendant's possession of substantial market power, combined with his exclusionary or anticompetitive behavior, threatens to defeat or forestall the corrective forces of competition and thereby sustain or extend the defendant's agglomeration of power.")

1. Monopoly Power The threshold element of a section 2 monopolization offense being "the possession of monopoly power in the relevant market," . . . the Court must first ascertain the boundaries of the commercial activity that can be termed the "relevant market." . . . Next, the Court must assess the defendant's actual power to control prices in—or to exclude competition from—that market. . . .

In this case, the plaintiffs postulated the relevant market as being the worldwide licensing of Intel-compatible PC operating systems. Whether this zone of commercial activity actually qualifies as a market, "monopolization of which may be illegal," depends on whether it includes all products "reasonably interchangeable by consumers for the same purposes." . . .

The Court has already found, based on the evidence in this record, that there are currently no products—and that there are not likely to be any in the near future—that a significant percentage of computer users worldwide could substitute for Intel-compatible PC operating systems without incurring substantial costs. . . . [The court finds] that the licensing of all Intel-compatible PC operating systems worldwide does in fact constitute the relevant market in the context of the plaintiffs' monopoly maintenance claim. . . .

The plaintiffs proved at trial that Microsoft possesses a dominant, persistent, and increasing share of the relevant market. Microsoft's share of the worldwide market for Intel-compatible PC operating systems currently exceeds ninety-five percent. . . . The plaintiffs also proved that the applications barrier to entry protects Microsoft's dominant market share. . . . This barrier ensures that no Intel-compatible PC operating system other than Windows can attract significant consumer demand, and the barrier would operate to the same effect even if Microsoft held its prices substantially above the competitive level for a protracted period of time. . . . Together, the proof of dominant market share and the existence of a substantial barrier to effective entry create the presumption that Microsoft enjoys monopoly power. . . .

[O]ver the past several years, Microsoft has comported itself in a way that could only be consistent with traditional behavior for a profit-maximizing firm if a firm knew that it possessed monopoly power, and if it was motivated by a desire to preserve the barrier to entry protecting that power. . . .

In short, the proof of Microsoft's dominant, persistent market share protected by a substantial barrier to entry, together with Microsoft's failure to rebut the prima facie showing effectively and the additional indicia of monopoly power, have compelled the Court to find as fact that Microsoft enjoys monopoly power in the relevant market. . . .

2. Maintenance of Monopoly Power by Anticompetitive Means In a section 2 case, once it is proved that the defendant possesses monopoly in a relevant market, liability for monopolization depends on a showing that the defendant used anticompetitive methods to achieve or maintain its position. . . . The threshold question in this analysis is whether the defendant's conduct is "exclusionary"—that is, whether it has restricted significantly, or threatens to restrict significantly, the ability to compete in the relevant market on the merits of what they offer customers. . . .

If the evidence reveals a significant exclusionary impact in the relevant market, the defendant's conduct will be labeled "anticompetitive"—and liability will attach—unless the defendant comes forward with specific, procompetitive business motivations that explain the full extent of its exclusionary conduct. . . .

Proof that a profit-maximizing firm took predatory action should suffice to demonstrate the threat of substantial exclusionary effect; to hold otherwise would be to ascribe irrational behavior . . . to the defendant. Moreover, predatory conduct, by definition as well as by nature, lacks procompetitive business motivation. . . . In other words, predatory behavior is patently anticompetitive. Proof that a firm with monopoly power engaged in such behavior thus necessitates a finding of liability under section 2.

[The court found that Microsoft sought to prevent middleware technologies from developing cross-platform applications that would erode Microsoft's applications barrier. It convinced developers by anticompetitive means to ignore Netscape's Navigator Web and Sun's implementation of the Java technology. It induced Intel, Apple, RealNetworks and IBM to cease making technological innovations that would alter the applications barrier. It sought "to maximize Internet Explorer's share of browser usage at Navigator's expense." It bound Internet Explorer to Windows with diverse "shackles" to ensure Explorer's dominance. It imposed severe limits on the freedom of developers to modify Windows to generate usage for Netscape's Navigator. It gave incentives and made threats to developers to favor Internet Explorer to the exclusion of Netscape. Without any legitimate business objectives, Microsoft refused to license Windows 95 to PC manufacturers without the Internet Explorer nor did it permit the uninstalling of the program. Its efforts successfully ostracized the Netscape Navigator from those channels that would lead most efficiently to its usage.]

c. Microsoft's Conduct Taken as a Whole

. . . Microsoft's campaign to protect the applications barrier from erosion by network-centric middleware can be broken down into discrete categories of activity, several of which on their own independently satisfy the second element of a section 2 monopoly maintenance claim. But only when the separate categories of conduct are viewed, as they should be, as a single well-coordinated course of action does the full extent of the violence that Microsoft has done to the competitive process itself. . . .

Microsoft's campaign must be termed predatory. Since the Court has already found that Microsoft possesses monopoly power, . . . the predatory nature of the firm's conduct compels the Court to hold Microsoft liable under section 2 of the Sherman Act.

B. Attempting to Obtain Monopoly Power in a Second Market by Anticompetitive Means

In addition to condemning actual monopolization, section 2 of the Sherman Act declares that it is unlawful for a person or firm to "attempt to monopolize . . . any part of the trade or commerce among the several States, or with foreign nations. . . .

In order for liability to attach for attempted monopolization, a plaintiff generally must prove "(1) that the defendant has engaged in a predatory or anticompetitive conduct with (2) a specific intent to monopolize," and (3) that there is a "dangerous probability" that the defendant will succeed in achieving monopoly . . . [see *Spectrum Sports v. McQuillan,* 506 U.S. 447, 456 (1993)]. Microsoft's June 1995 proposal that Netscape abandon the field to Microsoft in the market for browsing technology for Windows, and its subsequent, well-documented efforts to overwhelm Navigator's browser usage share with a proliferation of Internet Explorer browsers inextricably attached to Windows, clearly meet the first element of the offense.

The evidence in this record also satisfies the requirement of specific intent. . . .

[A]lthough the dangerous probability [in achieving monopoly] was no longer imminent with Netscape's rejection of Microsoft proposal, "the probability of success at the time the acts occur" is the measure by which liability is determined. . . .

II. SECTION ONE OF THE SHERMAN ACT

Section 1 of the Sherman Act prohibits "every contract, combination . . . , or conspiracy, in restraint of trade or commerce . . ." 15 U.S.C. section 1. Pursuant to this statute, courts have condemned commercial stratagems that constitute unreasonable restraints on competition . . . among them "tying arrangements" and "exclusive dealing" contracts. Tying arrangements have been found unlawful where sellers exploit their market power over one product to force unwilling buyers into acquiring another. . . . Where agreements have been challenged as unlawful exclusive dealing, the courts have condemned only those contractual arrangements that substantially foreclose competition in a relevant market by significantly reducing the number of outlets available to a competitor to reach prospective consumers of the competitor's market. . . .

A. Tying

Liability for tying under section 1 exists where (1) two separate "products" are involved; (2) the defendant affords its customers no choice but to take the tied product in order to obtain the tying product; (3) the arrangements affects a substantial volume of interstate commerce; and (4) the defendant has "market power" in the tying product market. . . . All four elements are required. . . .

[The court found as to the first element that the operating systems and browsers are separate products for which there is separate demand. As to the second element, the evidence establishes that Microsoft prohibited licensees of its Windows program from modifying or deleting the Internet Explorer from Windows. Clearly the Windows program affects almost all computer usage and thus substantially affects interstate commerce. Microsoft's market power is beyond question in the tying market.]

B. Exclusive Dealing Arrangements

. . . [C]ourts have tended to condemn [exclusive dealing arrangements] under the section 1 Rule of Reason only those agreements that have the effect of foreclosing a competing manufacturer's brands from the relevant market. More specifically, courts are concerned with those exclusive dealing arrangements that work to place so much of a market's available distribution outlets in the hands of a single firm as to make it difficult for other firms to continue to compete effectively, or even to exist, in the relevant market. . . .

To evaluate an agreement's likely anticompetitive effects, courts have consistently looked at a variety of factors, including: (1) the degree of exclusivity and the relevant line of commerce implicated by the agreements' terms; (2) whether the percentage of the market foreclosed by the contracts is substantial enough to import that rivals will be largely excluded from competition; (3) the agreements' actual anticompetitive effect in the relevant line of commerce; (4) the existence of any legitimate, procompetitive business justifications offered by the defendant; (5) the length and irrevocability of the agreements; and (6) the availability of any less restrictive means for achieving the same benefits. . . .

[The court held in favor of Microsoft as to this aspect of the case. It concluded that Microsoft's agreements with the computer manufacturers and distributors did not, in the end, prevent Netscape from access to all PC users in order to offer them the installation of the Netscape Navigator. Thus, the factors were not fully met.]

III. THE STATE LAW CLAIMS

[The court held that the acts of Microsoft sufficed to meet the causes of action under the laws of the states that joined in the action herein. There is no conflict with existing statutes, such as the Copyright Act, that prevents such state action.]

CASE QUESTIONS

1. Is a monopoly per se illegal? What conduct by Microsoft was instrumental in causing the court to hold it responsible for violating the antitrust statutes?
2. What arguments can you present on appeal that may cause a reversal of the decision?

Note: The decision and order of the district court was appealed to the U.S. Court of Appeals for the D.C. Circuit. In a decision handed down on June 28, 2001 (No. 00-5212 and 00-5213), the court affirmed in part and reversed in part the lower court's decision. The court agreed with most of the district court's Findings of Fact and Conclusions of Law but remanded the case to conduct an evidentiary hearing with respect to the remedies to be imposed upon Microsoft for its violation of the antitrust laws. The most critical aspect of the decision by the appeals court was the conduct of the trial court judge, who gave press and other media interviews and whose conduct exhibited an extraordinary bias against Microsoft. The appellate court agreed that Microsoft did possess a monopoly and did maintain its power through unlawful anticompetitive means in violation of Section 2 of the Sherman Act. The court repeated the prior findings of unjustifiable licensing restrictions and abuses in connection with Internet access providers. It found other Sherman Act Section 2 violations in connection with Microsoft's agreement with Apple Computer, its modification of Java so as to make it compatible only with its programs, and other unlawful courses of conduct. The lower court's determination of attempted monopolization was reversed. The district court's finding of unlawful tying was reversed and sent back to the trial court so as to permit the government to pursue the claim anew. The district court's remedy of breaking up Microsoft was reversed and sent back to the trial court before a different judge for an evidentiary hearing, after which the court may make a determination as to whether Microsoft should be divided into separate entities as well as other remedial actions. Notwithstanding the postdecision comments of Microsoft, in essence, but for the alleged abuse of the trial judge, the decision would have been sustained almost in its totality.

Trade Associations

Companies engaged in specific industries often come together for the purpose of sharing information on mutual problems or of acting as lobbying groups to promote their concerns before state and national legislatures, as well as meeting persons with common interests. Antitrust problems can arise when such gatherings go beyond such purposes to become a forum for engaging in unlawful conduct. Meetings to engage in price fixing are obviously violative of antitrust laws. The dividing line between lawful and unlawful activities can be obscure. Clearly, a mere sharing of nonprice information rarely results in antitrust scrutiny. It is when members share information concerning prices charged for their products or services that problems may ensue. The need for efficiency vis-à-vis other modes of competition often causes competing entities to join forces in an attempt to counter threats of loss of customers and business.

The newspaper industry has been particularly susceptible to threats by competing communications media. As a result, there has been a tendency for competitors to join together to counter their mutual challenges. In the following action, the court of appeals reviewed a lower court's decision dismissing antitrust allegations against a group of newspapers concerning the delivery of advertising to newspapers.

AD/SAT V. ASSOCIATED PRESS

181 F.3d 216 (2d Cir. 1999)

FACTS: AD/SAT is a company that electronically transmitted advertisements to newspapers for the period of the mid-1980s to 1996. The advantage of such transmissions over delivery by manual delivery services was the significant savings of cost and time inasmuch as the transmission services could send the same advertisement to many newspapers simultaneously. The Associated Press ("AP"), an organization of some 1500 newspapers within the U.S., began the same service in 1994, which service consisted of transmitting ads from the advertisers' computers to newspapers' computers in digital form. The service had been approved by the AP board and was presented to the other newspaper associations through the intervention of mutual association members.

As a result, the plaintiff commenced an antitrust action under Section 2 of the Sherman Act alleging that AP attempted to monopolize the market for such advertisements; that the AP engaged in monopoly leveraging; and that the AP monopolized the wire services' news and photo transmission markets. The plaintiff also sued several newspaper associations and number of newspapers alleging that they, together with the AP, conspired to boycott AD/SAT in violation of Section 1 of the Sherman Act and conspired to monopolize the market of electronic transmission of such advertisements. From a dismissal of the allegations, the plaintiff appealed.

ISSUE: (1) Did the defendants engage in anticompetitive or predatory conduct with the specific intent to monopolize coupled with a dangerous probability of achieving monopoly power?

(2) Did the AP leverage its monopoly power in the wire services news and photograph transmission markets to gain an unlawful advantage in the market for delivery of newspaper advertisements, in violation of section 2 of the Sherman Act?

(3) Did the AP and the remaining defendants unlawfully conspire to boycott plaintiff in violation of the Sherman Act and to monopolize the market for delivery of newspaper advertisements, in violation of section 2 of the Sherman Act?

DECISION: The Court of Appeals affirmed the dismissal of all claims of the plaintiff against the defendants finding that the evidence: (1) did not establish anticompetitive or predatory conduct on the part of the defendants; (2) did not show a leveraging of alleged monopoly power by the defendants; and (3) did not prove that the defendants acted in concert to boycott the plaintiff.

REASONING: Per Curiam decision [No judge was the named author of the opinion.]

II. ATTEMPTED MONOPOLIZATION CLAIM

... [I]n order to determine whether there is a dangerous probability that, left unchecked, the defendant will attain monopoly power, i.e., the ability "(1) to price substantially above the competitive level and (2) to persist in doing so for a significant period without erosion by new entry or expansion." ...

The parties agree that that the relevant geographic market is the United States. Based on its finding that physical and electronic delivery services are reasonably interchangeable, the District Court concluded that the relevant product market is the market for delivery of advertisements to newspapers by any means. ... The relevant market for purposes of antitrust litigation is the "area of effective competition" within which the defendant operates. ... Thus, products or services need not be identical to be part of the same market. ... In economists' terms, two products or services are reasonably interchangeable where there is sufficient cross-elasticity of demand. Cross-elasticity of demand exists if consumers would respond to a slight increase in the price of one product by switching to another product. ...

AP's AdSEND [the competing electronic advertising delivery system] enjoys only a small share of the relevant product market. Competition within the market is substantial. Rapidly developing technology for the transmission of data and low barriers to market entry suggest that the AP will face significant competition from new entrants. In the face of these facts, AD/SAT cannot prove an essential element of its attempted monopolization claim—that there is a dangerous probability that AP's AdSEND will achieve monopoly power. ...

III. MONOPOLY LEVERAGING CLAIM

We have said that a "successful claim of monopoly leveraging requires proof of at least three factors: monopoly power in one market, the use of [that] power, however, lawfully acquired, to foreclose competition, to gain a competitive advantage, or to destroy a competitor in another distinct market, and injury caused by the challenged conduct." ...

[A] claim for monopoly leveraging is properly stated only where the plaintiff can demonstrate that the challenged conduct "threatens the [second] market with higher prices or reduced output or quality associated with the kind of monopoly that is ordinarily accompanied by a large market share." ... Thus,

> a large firm does not violate Section 2 simply by reaping the competitive rewards attributable to its efficient size, nor does an integrated business offend the Sherman Act whenever one of its departments benefits from association with a

division possessing a monopoly in its own market. So long as we allow a firm to compete in several fields, we must expect it to seek the competitive advantages of its broad-based activity—more efficient production, greater ability to develop complimentary products, reduced transaction costs, and so forth. These are gains that accrue to any integrated firm, regardless of its market share, and they cannot by themselves be considered uses of monopoly power. *Berkey Photo,* [*Inc. v. Eastman Kodak Co.,* 603 F.2d 263 (2d Cir. 1979)].

. . . [I]t is not unlawful for an existing firm, entering a new product market, to promote its product by touting the benefits afforded by that products' association with the firm. Nor is it unlawful for employees of one division of a firm to promote products produced by another division. . . . [S]uch conduct is the sort of "normal business development which is to be expected by any competitor entering a new business" . . . AD/SAT did not present evidence that could support a finding of tangible harm to competition, an essential element of the claim. . . . Indeed the evidence submitted reveals that AdSEND's services are priced lower than those of AD/SAT, and that the technology used by AdSEND offers certain advantages over physical delivery and some electronic transmission services. . . .

IV. SHERMAN ACT CONSPIRACY CLAIMS

[Discussion of trade associations.]

AD/SAT claims that the AP and the remaining defendants—the newspaper defendants . . . unlawfully conspired to boycott AD/SAT, in violation of section 1 of the Sherman Act, and to monopolize the market for delivery of newspaper advertisements, in violation of section 2 of the Sherman Act.

Section 1 states that "every contract, combination in the form of trust or otherwise, or conspiracy, in restraint of trade or commerce . . . is hereby declared to be illegal." 15 U.S.C. Section 1. A section 1 boycotting claim requires evidence of an illegal agreement that constitutes an unreasonable restraint of trade, either per se or under the rule of reason. . . . Only after an agreement is established will a court consider whether the agreement constituted an unreasonable restraint of trade. . . .

Section 2 of the Sherman Act prohibits individuals from "combining or conspiring with any other person or persons, to monopolize any part of the trade or commerce among the several States. . . ." 15 U.S.C. Section 2. A successful conspiracy claim under section 2 requires "(1) proof of a concerted action deliberately entered into with the specific intent to achieve an unlawful monopoly, and (2) the commission of an overt act in furtherance of the conspiracy." . . .

[A]lthough the nature of trade associations is such that they are frequently the object of antitrust scrutiny, . . . every action by a trade association is not concerted action by the association's members. Indeed, the varying roles played by trade associations such as the AP call for careful consideration by courts faced with allegations of antitrust conspiracy. As has been properly noted,

> there seems no conceptual difficulty in treating organizations created to serve their member-competitors or to regulate their market behavior as continuing conspiracies of the members. Nor is there any practical problem when we focus on those improprieties reducing competition among the members or with their competitors. But what about the day-to-day operations of the organization? Must we also see the trade association's buying, selling, hiring, renting, or investing decisions as continuing conspiracies among the members? . . . All of these decisions become subject to Sherman Act Section 1 litigation if [trade associations] are conspiracies. . . . One might respond to this concern in three ways: ignore it, adjust the necessary allegations or proofs, or hold such organizations continuing conspiracies for some purposes but single entities for other purposes. . . . [Quoting Philip E. Arceda, *Antitrust Law,* vol. 7, p. 1477 at 347]

Consistent with those [U.S. Supreme Court] decisions, an antitrust plaintiff must present evidence tending to show that association members, in their individual capacities, consciously committed themselves to a common scheme designed to achieve an unlawful objective. Accordingly, we must examine the evidence submitted by AD/SAT pertaining to each defendant to determine whether, viewed in the light most favorable to AD/SAT, this evidence could give rise to a reasonable inference of concerted action by the defendants.

[The court found the evidence lacking of defendants conspiring against the plaintiff and, accordingly, dismissed the action.]

CASE QUESTIONS

1. The Associated Press is as dominant in its field as Microsoft is in computer programs. How are the cases distinguishable?
2. How important is it to antitrust litigation that the cost of entry into a market as a new competitor is low versus the situation (as in automobile or airplane production) where the cost of entry is very expensive?

Who Is a *Person* Under the Sherman Act?

Section 2 states, "Every person who shall monopolize. . . ." There is no question that a *person* includes corporations, partnerships, associations and the like, but does the definition include governments? Initially, the U.S. Supreme Court, after considering "the purpose, the subject matter, the context, the legislative history, and the executive interpretation of the statute," concluded that a federal governmental agency was not qualified as a person to seek treble damages. *United States v. Cooper Corp.,* 312 U.S. 600 (1941). In the following year, however, the Court held that a state could be considered such a person for collection of treble damages. *Georgia v. Evans,* 316 U.S. 159, 162 (1942). In a 1978 case, the Supreme Court stated that the definition of the word *person* was inclusive and included the state of India under the Clayton Act. *Pfizer, Inc. v. Government of India,* 434 U.S. 308 (1978).

In *FTC v. MTK Marketing, Inc.,* 149 F.3d 1036 (9th Cir. 1998), the court of appeals had to decide a case involving California state law. The statute stated that all telephonic sellers were required to maintain a surety bond in the sum of $100,000 "for the benefit of any person suffering pecuniary loss in a transaction commenced during the period of bond coverage with a telephonic seller who violated" the statute. The bond included coverage for payment of judgments entered pursuant to statute. The Federal Trade Commission sued MTK Marketing for unfair and deceptive acts in violation of Section 5 of the FTC Act and recovered a multimillion-dollar judgment against MTK and other defendants. The FTC sought to recover the bond amount. The U.S. district court said that the FTC was not a person under the state law and, thus, could not recover the bond sum. The U.S. court of appeals reversed the decision.

The court cited the given decisions, as well as citing California law that defined a *person* as including the state of California and subdivisions of governments within the state. Inasmuch as the federal government was not excluded, the court reasoned that the federal government also would be considered as a person under state law. The court rejected the argument that the Tenth Amendment to the U.S. Constitution ("The powers not delegated to the United States by the Constitution, nor prohibited by it to the States, are reserved to the States respectively, or to the people.") prohibited the FTC from enforcing the bond. The FTC would assist the state of California by furthering the interests of consumers by safeguarding the public against deceitful marketers.

THE CLAYTON ACT OF 1914

The Sherman Act was not effective in seriously curtailing the rise of monopolistic practices. Almost a quarter of a century later, in 1914, Congress enacted two statutes to meet the challenges presented by corporations, their attorneys, and the probusiness bias of the courts, namely, the Clayton Act (15 U.S.C. Sections 12–27) and the Federal Trade Commission Act. Both acts were later significantly amended. Among the most important sections of the Clayton Act are:

(The Robinson-Patman Act Amendment). Sec. 2

(a) It shall be unlawful for any person engaged in commerce, in the course of such commerce, either directly or indirectly, to discriminate in price between different purchasers of commodities of like grade and quality, where either or any of the purchasers involved in such discrimination are in commerce, where such commodities are sold for use, consumption, or resale with the United States or any Territory thereof . . . and where the effect of such discrimination may be substantially to lessen competition or tend to create a monopoly in any line of commerce, or to injure, destroy, or prevent competition: or with any person who either grants or knowingly receives the benefit of such discrimination, or with customers of either of them:

Provided, That nothing herein contained shall prevent differentials which make only due allowance for differences in the cost of manufacture, sale, or delivery resulting from the differing methods or quantities in which such commodities are to such purchasers sold or delivered;

Provided, however, That the Federal Trade Commission may, after due investigation and hearing to all interested parties, fix and establish quantity limits, and revise the same as it finds necessary, as to particular commodities or classes of commodities, where it finds that available purchasers in greater quantities are so few as to render differentials on account thereof unjustly discriminatory or promotive of monopoly in any line of commerce; and the foregoing shall then not be construed to permit differentials based on differences in quantities greater than those so fixed and established;

And provided further, That nothing herein contained shall prevent persons engaged in selling goods, wares, or merchandise in commerce from selecting their own customers in bona fide transactions and not in restraint of trade:

And provided further, That nothing herein contained shall prevent price changes from time to time where in response to changing conditions affecting the market for or the marketability of the goods concerned, such as but not limited to actual or imminent deterioration of perishable goods, obsolescence of seasonal goods, distress sales under court process, or sales in good faith in discontinuance of business in the goods concerned.

(c) That it shall be unlawful for any person engaged in commerce, in the course of such commerce, to pay or grant, or to receive or accept, anything of value as a commission, brokerage, or other compensation, or any allowance or discount in lieu thereof, except for services rendered in connection with the sale or purchase of goods, wares, or merchandise, either to the other party to such transaction or to an agent, representative, or other intermediary therein where such intermediary is acting in fact for or in behalf, or is subject to the direct or indirect control, of any party to such transaction other than the person by whom such compensation is so granted or paid.

(d) That it shall be unlawful for any person engaged in commerce to pay or contract for the payment of anything of value to or for the benefit of a customer of such person in the course of such commerce as compensation or in connection for any services or facilities furnished by or through such customer in connection with the processing, handling, sale, or offering for sale of any products or commodities manufactured, sold, or offered for sale by such person, unless such payment or consideration is available on proportionally equal terms to all other customers competing in the distribution of such products or commodities.

(e) That it shall be unlawful for any person to discriminate in favor of one purchaser against another purchaser or purchasers of a commodity bought for resale, with or without processing, by contracting to furnish or furnishing, or by contributing to the furnishing of, any service or facilities connected with the processing, handling, sale or offering for sale of such commodity so purchased upon terms not accorded to all purchasers on proportionately equal terms.

(f) That it shall be unlawful for any person engaged in commerce, in the course of such commerce, knowingly to induce or receive discrimination in price which is prohibited by this section.

The Robinson-Patman Act of 1936 was designed to give some protection against the predatory pricing and other policies of sellers and also buyers of goods. A manufacturer that sells its goods to one buyer at a price substantially below the price it charges other buyers may cause the latter buyers to be unable to compete successfully with the favored buyer. In an endeavor to afford some protection to the injured parties in the midst of the Great Depression, Congress passed the Robinson-Patman Act, most of which is an amendment to Section 2 of the Clayton Act. Section 2(a) makes it unlawful for a person engaged in commerce to engage in price discrimination between different buyers of commodities (not services) where the effect is to substantially lessen competition or tend to create a monopoly or injure or destroy competition. To prove a price discrimination case the plaintiff must allege and prove:

(1) That the defendant is engaged in commerce;
(2) that, in the course of such commerce, the defendant has discriminated in price between different purchasers of commodities of like grade and quality;

(3) that "*either or any of the purchases involved in such discrimination are in commerce*"; and
(4) that there is likely to be a severe, adverse effect on competition.[5]

The exceptions are to meet (not beat) in good faith the lower prices of a competitor; the imminent deterioration of perishable goods, obsolescence of seasonal goods, sales in good faith for discontinuance of business, court ordered distress sales, and the actual savings passed on to buyer by reason of large purchases.

(Exclusive Dealing). Sec. 3.

It shall be unlawful for any person engaged in commerce, in the course of such commerce, to lease or make a sale or contract for sale of goods, wares, merchandise, machinery, supplies or other commodities, whether patented or unpatented, for use, consumption or resale within the [U.S., Territory, D.C., or possessions] or fix a price charged therefor, or discount from or rebate upon, such price, on the condition, agreement or understanding that the lessee or purchaser thereof shall not use or deal in the goods, wares, merchandise, machinery, supplies, or other commodities of a competitor or competitors of the lessor or seller, where the effect of such lease, sale, or contract of sale or such condition, agreement or understanding may be to substantially lessen competition or tend to create a monopoly in any line of commerce.

Tying falls under this section of the Clayton Act as well as agreements between a supplier and a retailer that prohibits either party from selling to a competitor.

(Mergers). Sec. 7.

No corporation engaged in commerce shall acquire, directly or indirectly, the whole or any part of the stock or other share capital and no corporation subject to the jurisdiction of the Federal Trade Commission shall acquire the whole or any part of the assets of another corporation engaged also in commerce, where in any line of commerce in any section of the country, the effect of such acquisition may be substantially to lessen competition or to tend to create a monopoly.

There are three types of mergers: *Horizontal mergers* are mergers between competing firms. Examples might be two airlines or automobile companies merging. *Vertical mergers* are mergers between buyers and sellers, such as between a manufacturer and its distribution channel. Examples include when a shoe manufacturer merges with the wholesaler or retailer. Many oil companies produce the oil and distribute the product through retail stations owned by them. *Conglomerate mergers* are mergers that are not of the types already stated and, generally, relate to mergers between a manufacturer and a company that is not a direct competitor but is potentially a competitor *(product extension mergers)* or where the firms manufacture the same product but do not compete with one another because they are located in different geographical areas *(market extension mergers)*. The major example of a conglomerate merger that was disallowed was in *FTC v. Proctor & Gamble Co.,* 386 U.S. 568 (1967), wherein the defendant sought to merge with Clorox so as to gain entry into the bleach market. Proctor & Gamble (P&G) had not previously made bleach and, thus, was not a direct competitor. The Court, noting the immense size of P&G, disallowed the merger and stated that P&G should make bleach on its own and become a competitor rather than attempting to gain entry by merger.

Factors that are considered in determining whether Section 7 of the Clayton Act has been violated are:

(1) the size of the industry in comparison to the size of the economy of the nation; (2) concentration ratios in various lines and phases of the industry . . . and in various geographic markets of the industry; (3) the elasticity of the demand . . . and the effect of the elasticity on the market power . . . given their market shares; (4) barriers to the entry of new participants in the industry; (5) the conduct of members of the industry respecting joint ventures and exchange agreements at the exploration, production, transportation, refining and marketing stages of the industry; and (6) the possibility of increased economic efficiency and other benefits that could arise from the consummation of the merger.[6]

Standing

Not all persons may sue under the antitrust laws. It is necessary that a *proper* plaintiff be the litigant. A proper plaintiff is one who "obtains services in the threatened market or a competitor who seeks to serve that market."[7] Antitrust statutes have as their objective to protect "the competitive process that brings to consumers the benefits of lower prices, better products, and more efficient production methods."[8]

Injury

In addition to establishing proof of violation of the antitrust laws and standing, a plaintiff must plead and prove antitrust injury. Failure to allege injury will require a dismissal of the action. Antitrust injury is an "injury of the type the antitrust laws were intended to prevent and that flows from that which makes the defendants' conduct unlawful."[9]

THE FEDERAL TRADE COMMISSION ACT

The major section of the Federal Trade Commission Act (15 U.S.C. Sections 41–58) that applies to our discussion is the following:

Sec. 5.

(a) (1) Unfair methods of competition in commerce, and unfair or deceptive acts or practices in or affecting commerce, are hereby declared unlawful.
(2) The Commission is empowered and directed to prevent persons . . . from using unfair methods of competition in or affecting commerce and unfair or deceptive acts in or affecting commerce.

(b) Whenever the Commission shall have reason to believe that any such person, partnership, or corporation has been or is using any unfair method of competition or unfair or deceptive act or practice in or affecting commerce, and if it shall appear to the Commission that a proceeding by it in respect thereof would be to the interest of the public, it shall issue and serve upon such person, partnership, or corporation a complaint stating its charges in that respect and containing a notice of a hearing upon a day and at a place therein fixed at least thirty days after the service of said complaint. The person, partnership, or corporation so complained of shall have the right to appear at the place and time so fixed and show cause why an order should not be entered by the Commission requiring such person, partnership, or corporation to cease and desist from the violation of the law so charged in said complaint. Any person, partnership, or corporation may make application, and upon good cause shown may be allowed by the Commission to intervene and appear in said proceeding by counsel or in person. The testimony in any such proceeding shall be reduced to writing and filed in the office of the Commission.

The Federal Trade Commission is empowered by Congress to prosecute and prevent unfair methods of competition. The statute was later amended so as to empower the FTC to prosecute cases concerning unfair or deceptive practices. As to the meaning of "unfair competition," the Supreme Court said in a famous decision, *FTC v. Brown Shoe Co., Inc.,* 384 U.S. 316 (1965), that "the Federal Trade Commission Act was designed to supplement and bolster the Sherman Act and the Clayton Act" to stop at their infancy those acts that would eventually violate both statutes and to prosecute present acts that are unfair in the competitive marketplace. In *FTC v. Sperry & Hutchinson Co.,* 405 U.S. 233 (1972), the Supreme Court said that the act permitted the FTC to define the meaning of "unfair methods of competition" even if the alleged unfair acts do not violate "either the letter or the spirit" of the Sherman or Clayton Acts.

The FTC does not have unlimited power to define the meaning of "unfair methods of competition." In *E. I. du Pont de Nemours & Co. v. FTC,* 729 F.2d 128 (2d Cir. 1984), the court of appeals said that the word *unfair* is an elusive concept. A line had to be drawn between conduct that is anticompetitive and conduct that impacts on competition. The fact that competition is lessened by the acts of an entrepreneur does not mean that it is unfair. A competitor may strive diligently and legally to defeat competitors, such as by a more efficient operation, expanding capacity, and the like. "[S]ome indicia of oppressiveness must exist [for the FTC to assert jurisdiction] such as (1) evidence of anti-competitive intent or purpose on the part of the producer charged, or (2) the absence of an independent legitimate business reason for its conduct."

The latter provision is a significant part of the law of advertising inasmuch as the commission's mandate is to prevent false and misleading advertising. As to what is "unfair or deceptive acts or practices," the FTC has identified a number of factors when consumers are involved: "(1) whether the practice injures consumers; (2) whether it violates established public policy; (3) whether it is unethical or unscrupulous."[10]

When the Federal Trade Commission Act was first created, the focus was the protection of the honest entrepreneur who was victimized by the unscrupulous competitor. For example, in an early case, two manufacturers placed the label "wool" on their garments. One company manufactured the product entirely of wool but the second company's garment was only 10 percent wool and was able to charge a lower price. Such tactics were deemed unfair to the first manufacturer. The emphasis in the last three decades has been the protection of the consumer. Thus, the statute was amended to reflect FTC jurisdiction over unfair or deceptive acts or practices. With respect to the injury to consumers, the FTC requires that it be substantial rather than trivial or speculative. The injury must not be outweighed by competing consumer or competitive benefits. Also the injury must be one that the consumer could not have reasonably avoided. As to the second criterion (the violation of public policy), the FTC looks to the statute, common law, the industry practice, and other factors in making the determination of such violation. As to the third criterion, the FTC examines whether the conduct was "immoral, unethical, oppressive, or unscrupulous."

The law of advertising arose from the FTC mandate to prosecute unfair or deceptive acts or practices. *False advertisement* is defined as (15 U.S.C. Section 55(a)(1)):

> An advertisement, other than labeling, which is misleading in a material respect, and in determining whether any advertisement is misleading, there shall be taken into account (among other things) not only representations made or suggested by statement, word, design, device, sound or any combination thereof, but also the extent to which the advertisement fails to reveal facts material in the light of such representations or material with respect to consequences which may result from the use of the commodity to which the advertisement relates under the conditions prescribed in said advertisement; or under such conditions as are customary or usual.

Whereas only the Federal Trade Commission may prosecute false advertising offenses under the Federal Trade Commission Act, private enforcement may take place under the Lanham Act (the Trademark Act of 1946, 15 U.S.C. Section 1125(a)). In the following case, the court reviewed the elements to establish a claim under the act.

State Unfair Competition Statutes: The Sun Microsystems-Microsoft Litigation

Unfair competition in its original formulation in the Federal Trade Commission Act of 1914 concerned acts that arose out of antitrust activities. Although there may not have been sufficient evidence to prove a criminal violation, the Federal Trade Commission was enabled to sue companies that acted in a manner that was unfair to legitimate businesses. Later, the statute was amended to permit the FTC to prosecute unfair and deceptive practices. Individual states also enacted statutes forbidding unfair competition. In the following case that was widely publicized, Sun Microsystems sued Microsoft for allegedly distributing incompatible versions of its Java Technology.

SUN MICROSYSTEMS, INC. V. MICROSOFT CORP.

87 F. Supp. 2d 992 (N.D.Ca. 2000)

FACTS: Sun sued Microsoft seeking an injunction based on Microsoft's alleged unfair competition. Sun and Microsoft had entered into a Technology Licensing and Distribution Agreement ("TLDA") in March 1996, wherein Sun granted Microsoft a nonexclusive development license "under the Intellectual Property Rights of Sun to make, access, use, copy, view, display, modify, adapt, and create Derivative Works of the Technology in source Code form for the purposes of developing, compiling to binary form and supporting Products." Sun also granted Microsoft a limited distribution license to "make, use, import, reproduce, license, rent, lease, offer to sell, sell or otherwise distribute to end users as part of a Product or an upgrade to a Product, the Technology and Derivative Works thereof in binary form." The agreement also imposed compatibility requirements on Microsoft. Sun sued Microsoft for unfair competition in its endeavor to "embrace" Sun's Java technology and then extending the Java platform by developing Java related products that were incompatible with non-Microsoft programming and environment.

As a result of the incompatibility, developers were forced to write different programs for the two Java versions. Microsoft's intentional incompatibility usage discouraged developers from creating applications that were applicable for compatible versions of Java. Microsoft then used its market power to license the technology with the non-compliant technology to software developers, tools vendors, and other companies. Sun also complained that Microsoft made misrepresentations about its software products and made misleading references of the Java technology as the "official reference implementation" for Win32-based systems.

ISSUE: Whether the actions of Microsoft constituted unfair competition under California law thereby warranting the grant of an injunction against such conduct by the Court?

DECISION: The Court granted the injunction, finding Microsoft's action to constitute unfair competition.

REASONING: Judge Whyte

B. UNFAIR COMPETITION: LIKELIHOOD OF SUCCESS ON THE MERITS

California law defines unfair competition as, in part, "any unlawful, unfair or fraudulent business act or practice." Cal. Bus. & Prof. Code Section 17200. In the past, California courts have construed section 17200 broadly to embrace "anything that can properly be called a business practice and at the same time is forbidden by law." . . . However, the California Supreme Court recently clarified what constitutes an "unfair" business act or practice in suits between competitors. See *Cel-Tech Communications, Inc. v. Los Angeles Cellular Telephone Co.,* 20 Cal. 4th 163, 178–87, 973 P.2d 527 (1999). Cel-Tech requires

> when a plaintiff who claims to have suffered injury from a direct competitor's "unfair" act or practice invokes section 17200, the word "unfair" in that section means conduct that threatens an incipient violation of an antitrust law, or violates the policy or spirit of one of those laws because its effects are comparable to or the same as a violation of the law, or otherwise significantly threatens or harms competition. . . .

In determining whether a challenged act or practice is unfair within the meaning of section 17200 of the California Business and Professions, Cel-Tech endorses looking at federal authorities interpreting the prohibition against "unfair methods of competition" in section 5 of the Federal Trade Commission Act. . . . According to the Supreme Court, "the Federal Trade Commission Act was designed to supplement and bolster the Sherman Act and the Clayton Act . . . to stop in their incipiency acts and practices which, when full blown, would violate those Acts . . . as well as to condemn as 'unfair methods of competition' existing violations of them." . . . Accordingly, "unfair methods of competition" under section 5 of the Federal Trade Commission Act covers business practices "which conflict with the basic policies of the Sherman and Clayton Acts even though such practices may not violate those laws." . . .

1. Distribution of Non-Compliant Java Technology

Preliminarily, Sun has established a reasonable likelihood of success in demonstrating that Microsoft's distribution of non-compliant Java technology violates the compatibility of the TLDA. In addition, Sun has also demonstrated reasonably likely success in establishing that Microsoft's alleged violations of the TLDA were committed as part of a concerted effort to devalue the cross-platform and cross-implementation promise of the Java technology it licensed and, ultimately, to gain control of the Java programming environment. . . . Sun has raised a serious question as to whether the incompatibilities introduced by Microsoft into its commercially distributed versions of the Java Technology harm competition.

Sun has demonstrated that Microsoft introduced strategic incompatibilities in its implementation of the Java Technology and relied on its unparalleled market power and distribution channels in computer operating systems to unfairly impede competition in the Java development tools market. Without apparent technological or pro-competitive justification and in contravention of the TLDA, Microsoft excluded Sun's JNI native method interface from commercially distributed versions of its Java Virtual Machine implementation. In place of JNI, Microsoft created its own native method interfaces, such as RNI, Java/COM and J/Direct, which are supported by its Java development tools products. Furthermore, Microsoft's wide array of distribution channels and overwhelming market share in operating systems ensured that its Java Virtual Machine omitting JNI enjoyed a large installed base. . . .

3. Microsoft's Representations Concerning Sun's Java Technology

According to Sun, as part of an effort to confuse and induce developers to use its nonconforming language extensions, Microsoft has falsely advertised that its implementation of the Java Technology is the "official reference implementation" for Win32-based systems and that its "@com" compiler directive is authorized by Sun and complies with the specifications for the Java Technology. . . .

Here, Sun has raised a reasonable likelihood of success or, at a minimum, a serious question going to the merits on its claim that Microsoft's representations concerning Microsoft's implementation of Sun's Java Technology are false or misleading. Microsoft's representations are likely to confuse or mislead developers into thinking that (1) Sun approves of Microsoft's extended Java programming technology, (2) the such extended Java programming technology complies with Sun's specifications, and therefore, (3) is a compatible addition to the standard Java programming and runtime environment. . . .

In addition, Sun has also shown reasonably likely success in establishing that Microsoft's @com compiler directive technology does not comply with Sun's specifications and that, therefore, Microsoft's statements to the contrary are false. . . .

[The court found Microsoft's acts of unfair competition to be sufficiently likely to recur and, therefore, issued an injunction prohibiting Microsoft from using Java technology in incompatible form in violation of the TLDA, advertising its Java technology as the official Java reference implementation, and other related relief.]

CASE QUESTIONS

1. Discuss *exclusive* versus *concurrent* jurisdiction with respect to unfair competition claims. Could the Federal Trade Commission have prosecuted the within case?
2. Why did Sun use a tort theory of unfair competition when there appeared to be a simple case of breach of contract?

ANTITRUST IMPLICATIONS OF PATENTS AND COPYRIGHTS

A patent is inherently anticompetitive. The law gives the patent holder an exclusive right to use, license, or otherwise do as he or she sees fit with the invention or process. Antitrust law is in opposition to monopolistic practices. Nevertheless, the antitrust laws do not prevent the holder of a patent from excluding others from using the patent. The holder is given the right to take commercial advantage of the newly created invention or process for a period of twenty years. Nevertheless, a conflict may arise when the patent holder or other intellectual property rights owners abuse the right given under the respective statutes. Such abuses may take place in a variety of ways. For example, owners of patents may not couple their inventions in concert with holders of other related inventions so as to create a monopolistic stranglehold in the marketplace. As set forth in the *Intergraph* case (to be discussed) at 1362, "market power does not 'impose on the intellectual property owner an obligation to license the use of that property to other.'"

Unlike in many of the countries worldwide, a U.S. patent owner may refuse to sell or license a patent. The Patent Act, Section 271(d) states that "no patent owner otherwise entitled to relief . . . shall be denied relief or deemed guilty of misuse or illegal extension of the patent right by reason of his having . . . (4) refused to license or use any rights to the patent. . . ." Nevertheless, a patent holder may become subject to antitrust claims if the patent was procured through knowing and willful fraud or if the holder institutes a patent-infringement suit in order to interrupt a competitor's business relationships with its customers.[11] Where a suit is a mere sham, the holder can lose patent protection. Also, if a holder attempts to gain an advantage through a patent to exploit its dominant position in that market in order to gain monopolistic advantage beyond the market power gained from the patent, then the protection will be in jeopardy. In the *International Salt Co.* case mentioned previously, the tying of the licensing of salt-processing machines to the purchase of salt was unlawful. Similarly, the tying of the leasing of patented computers by IBM to the purchase of the cards used by the machines was also deemed to be unlawful.

In re Independent Service Organizations Antitrust Litigation v. Xerox Org., 203 F.3d 1322 (Fed. Cir. 2000), the numerous plaintiffs sued Xerox, claiming that it violated the antitrust laws by refusing to sell patented parts and copyrighted manuals and to license copyrighted software. The U.S. court of appeals affirmed the district court's dismissal of the lawsuit on the ground that "if a patent or copyright is lawfully acquired, the patent or copyright holder's unilateral refusal to sell or license its patented invention or copyrighted expression is not unlawful exclusionary conduct under the antitrust laws, even if its refusal to deal impacts competition in more than one market." The plaintiffs claimed that Xerox refused to sell parts to its patented copiers to independent service organizations unless they were also end users of the copiers. The court stated that a holder's intent in refusing to deal and other exclusionary conduct are irrelevant to the antitrust laws.

Addressing the copyright claims, the court reviewed the antitrust implications of a copyright owners refusal to license. The court noted that the Copyright Act gives a copyright owner the exclusive right to distribute the protected work by "transfer of ownership, or by rental, lease, or lending" (17 U.S.C. Section 106(3)(1996)). Thus, the owner of a copyright may refuse to sell or license the work and exclude others from using it. There are some limitations, such as the U.S. Supreme Court's holding in *United States v. Loew's, Inc.*, 371 U.S. 38 (1962), whereby it stated that Loew's policy of compelling block booking (forcing owners of theaters to show unwanted films as a condition to showing desired films) was illegal tying, in violation of the Sherman Act. The various courts of appeals have been divided as to the standards to be used in determining whether a copyright owner has abused the protections given by the Copyright Act vis-à-vis the antitrust laws.

In the *Xerox* case, the Court of Appeals for the Federal Circuit (Washington, D.C.), agreed with the First Circuit Court of Appeals in the imposition of a strong presumption in favor of a copyright holder to refuse to license a copyright. It cited the latter's decision in *Data General Corp. v. Grumman Systems Support Corp.*, 36 F.3d 1147 (1st Cir. 199), which noted that Congress assumed the right of a copyright holder "to exclude others from using their works creates a system of incentives that promotes consumer welfare in the long terms by encouraging investment in the creation of desirable artistic and functional works of expression. . . . [W]hile exclusionary conduct can include a monopolist's unilateral refusal to license a copyright, an author's desire to exclude others from use of its copyrighted work is a presumptively valid business justification for any immediate harm to consumers."

The following case contains an excellent review of a number of legal theories upon which to establish that a defendant is a monopolist. The decision was rendered by the same court of appeals that decided the *Microsoft* appeal.

INTERGRAPH V. INTEL

195 F.3d 1346 (D.C.Cir. 1999)

FACTS: Intel manufactures high performance computer microprocessors that are sold to producers of computer-based devices. One of these producers is the plaintiff, Intergraph Corporation, which develops, makes, and sells computer workstations utilized in the production of computer-aided devices. Prior to contracting with Intel, the plaintiff's workstations were based on microprocessors made by National Semiconductor containing "Clipper" technology. In 1993, Intergraph switched to Intel who, in turn, designated Intergraph as a "strategic customer." Such designation gave Intergraph special benefits such as proprietary information and products under non-disclosure agreements. In 1996, Intergraph sued a number of Intel producer customers claiming infringement of the Clipper patents based on their use of Intel microprocessors. The defendants sought indemnification from Intel.

In November 1997, after protracted settlement discussions, Intergraph sued Intel for infringement of the Clipper patents and upon other legal theories. It requested and received from the District Court an injunction enjoining Intel from cutting off the special benefits received from Intel. Intergraph charged Intel with violations of Sections 1 and 2 of the Sherman Act. On appeal, Intel claims that there is no law requiring it to give special benefits to the plaintiff, including trade secrets, proprietary information, and other preferences. Intergraph claims that it cannot survive without such benefits.

ISSUE: Whether the facts give rise to a violation of the Sherman Act thereby allowing the District Court to grant a preliminary injunction?

DECISION: The Court of Appeals decided in favor of Intel, thereby reversing the decision of the District Court and vacating the preliminary injunction, stating that there was little likelihood of success in the plaintiff's antitrust claims.

REASONING: Judge Newman

The district court ruled that Intergraph is likely to succeed in showing that Intel is a "monopolist," whereby Intel's withdrawal of the benefits it had previously accorded to Intergraph and other actions were deemed to violate sections 1 and 2 of the Sherman Act. . . . The court relied on several legal theories, viz.: (1) the essential facility theory and the corollary theory of refusal to deal, (2) leveraging and tying, (3) coercive reciprocity, (4) conspiracy and other acts in restraint of trade, (5) improper use of intellectual property, and (6) retaliatory enforcement of the non-disclosure agreements. The court alternatively ruled that Intergraph is likely to succeed on its contract claims, including the claim that the mutual at-will termination provision of the non-disclosure agreements is unconscionable. . . .

Intel states that unlawful monopolization was not shown, as a matter of law, because Intergraph and Intel are not competitors. Unlawful monopolization requires both the existence of monopoly power and anticompetitive power. . . . Monopoly power is generally defined as the power to control prices or exclude competition in a relevant market; anticompetitive conduct is generally defined as conduct whose purpose is to acquire or preserve the power to control prices or exclude competition. . . . The prohibited conduct must be directed toward competitors and must be intended to injure competition. . . .

Such conduct must affect the relevant product market, that is, the "area of effective competition" between the defendant and plaintiff. . . . [T]he relevant market has two dimensions: first, the relevant product market, which identifies the products or services that compete with each other; and second, the geographic market, which may be relevant when the competition is geographically confined. Thus, 'the market' which one must study to determine when a producer has monopoly power will vary with the part of commerce under consideration." . . .

The antitrust law has consistently recognized that a producer's advantageous or dominant market position based on superiority of a commercial product and ensuing market demand is not the illegal use of monopoly prohibited by the Sherman Act. . . . Product superiority and the ensuing market position, flowing from a company's research, talents, commercial efforts, and financial commitments, do not convert the successful enterprise into an illegal monopolist under the Sherman Act. [The district court found that Intel's 60 percent to 65 percent market share of high-performance microprocessors established a prima facie case of market power that created a genuine issue of dangerous probability of monopolization. The court of appeals stated, however, that] Intel's market power in the microprocessor market is irrelevant to the issues of this case, all of which relate to the effect of Intel's actions on Intergraph's position in its own market. . . .

The conduct complained of is Intel's withdrawal or reduction of technical assistance and special benefits, particularly pre-release access to Intel's new products, in reaction to Intergraph's suit for patent infringement. However, the Sherman Act does not convert all harsh commercial actions into antitrust violations. Unilateral conduct that may adversely affect another's business situation, but is not intended to monopolize that business, does not violate the Sherman Act. . . .

Defining the relevant market is an indispensable element of any monopolization or attempt case . . . for it is the market in which competition is affected by the asserted predatory or anticompetitive acts. It is the market in which sellers compete, based on products that are in competition with each other. . . .

The district court found that Intel possessed monopoly power in two "relevant markets": (1) the market for high-end microprocessors, and (2) the submarket of Intel's microprocessors. Neither one is a market in which Intergraph and Intel are in competition with each other. Intergraph states that it competes in the microprocessor market by virtue of its Clipper patents. However, the patent grant is a legal right to exclude, not a commercial product in a competitive market. Intergraph abandoned the production of Clipper microprocessors in 1993, and states no intention to return to it. Firms do not compete in the same market unless, because of the reasonable interchangeability of their products, they have the actual or potential ability to take significant business away from each other. . . .

[The court of appeals found that] Intel's conduct with respect to Intergraph did not constitute the offense of monopolization or the threat thereof in any market relevant to competition with Intergraph.

THE "ESSENTIAL FACILITY" THEORY

. . . The district court found that "[Intel's] Advance Chips Samples and advance design and technical information are essential products and information essential for Intergraph to compete in its markets." Reasoning that "the antitrust laws impose on firms controlling an essential facility the obligation to make the facility available on non-discriminatory terms," the court held that Intel's action in withdrawing these benefits violated the Sherman Act. . . . However, precedent is quite clear that the essential facility theory does not depart from the need for a competitive relationship in order to incur Sherman Act liability and remedy. . . .

In *MCI Communications* [*Corp. v. American Telephone & Telegraph Co.,* 708 F.2d 1081 (7th Cir. 1983)], 708 F.2d at 1132–33, the court enumerated the elements of liability under the "essential facilities" theory as (1) control of the essential facility by a monopolist; (2) a competitor's inability practically or reasonably to duplicate the essential facility; (3) the denial of the use of the facility to a competitor; and (4) the feasibility of providing the facility." The courts have well understood that the essential facility theory is not an invitation to demand access to the property or privileges of another, on pain of antitrust penalties and compulsion; thus the courts have required anticompetitive action be a monopolist that is intended to "eliminate competition in the downstream market." . . .

Although the viability and scope of the essential facility theory has occasioned much scholarly commentary, no court has taken it beyond the situation of competition with the controller of the facility, whether the competition is in the field of the facility itself or in a vertically related market that is controlled by the facility. That is, there must be a market in which plaintiff and defendant compete, such that a monopolist extends its monopoly to the downstream market by refusing access to the facility it controls. . . . Absent such a relevant market and competitive relationship, the essential facility theory does not support a Sherman Act violation. . . .

A "refusal to deal" may raise antitrust concerns when the refusal is directed against competition and the purpose is to create, maintain, or enlarge a monopoly. . . . Intergraph provided no support for its charge that Intel's action in withholding "strategic customer" benefits from Intergraph was for the purpose of enhancing Intel's competitive position. . . .

LEVERAGING

. . . Antitrust liability based on leveraging of monopoly power is a concept of imprecise definition, for the courts have varied in their requirements of the nature of the advantage obtained in the assertedly leveraged market. . . . [T]o establish illegal leveraging of monopoly power the challenged conduct must threaten the [second] market with the higher prices or reduced output or quality associated with the kind of monopoly that is ordinarily accompanied by a large market share." . . . Absent an adverse effect in the second market, the Sherman Act would serve to restrain competition rather than promote it. . . .

Intergraph made no proffer to show that Intel possessed market power in either the graphics subsystems market or the workstation market. A manufacturer's plan to enter a downstream market is not a *per se* antitrust violation based on a theory of leveraging. An integrated business does not offend the Sherman Act by drawing on its competitive advantages of efficiency, experience, or reduced transaction costs, in entering new fields. These advantages are not uses of monopoly power. . . . Intergraph provided no evidence or proffer tending to show that "a necessary and direct result" of Intel's planned entry into these markets would have a prohibited effect within the meaning of the Sherman Act. . . . It is an enlargement of antitrust theory and policy to prohibit downstream integration by a "monopolist" into new markets. The specter of Intel's resources and talent is not evidence of future Sherman Act violation. . . .

COERCIVE RECIPROCITY AND TYING

The district court found that Intel engaged in unlawful "coercive reciprocity," defined by the court as "the practice of using economic leverage in one market coercively to secure economic advantage in another," by its proposals to settle the patent dispute. . . .

To violate the Sherman Act the entity that coerces reciprocal dealing must be a monopolist in one product and thus be positioned to require dealing in the coerced product, which but for the monopolist's coercion could be acquired elsewhere. . . . In contrast, Intel's various licensing proposals furthered no illegal relationship. It is Intergraph, not Intel, that owns the Clipper patents. To the extent that the record mentions these negotiations, it appears that Intergraph is interested in selling or licensing the Clipper patents, but has deemed Intel's various offers to be inadequate. Intel did not demand that Intergraph buy its products, and the record describes no market in which Intel's licensing proposals were shown to have distorted competition. . . . No threat or actual monopolization is asserted to flow from the various rejected patent license proposals. Commercial negotiations to trade patent property rights for other consideration in order to settle a patent dispute is neither tying nor coercive reciprocity in violation of the Sherman Act. . . .

USE OF INTELLECTUAL PROPERTY TO RESTRAIN TRADE

In response to Intel's argument that its proprietary information and pre-release products are subject to copyright and patents, the district court observed that Intel's intellectual property "does not confer upon it a privilege or immunity to violate the antitrust laws." That is of course correct. But it is also correct that the antitrust laws do not negate the patentee's right to exclude others from patent property . . . the patent and antitrust laws are complementary, the patent system serving to encourage invention and the bringing of new products to market by adjusting investment-based risk, and the antitrust laws serving to foster industrial competition. . . .

[M]arket power does not "impose on the intellectual property owner an obligation to license the use of that property to others." . . . See 35 U.S.C. Section '271(d)(4) ("No patent owner otherwise entitled to relief for infringement or contributory infringement of a patent shall be denied relief or deemed guilty of misuse or illegal extension of the patent right by reason of his having done one or more of the following: . . . (4) refusing to license or use any rights to the patent"). . . . Precedent makes clear that a customer who is dependent on a manufacturer's supply of a component can not on that ground force the producer to provide it; there must be an anticompetitive aspect invoking the Sherman Act. . . .

THE CONSPIRACY THEORY

[Intergraph claims that Intel engaged in an unlawful boycott of Intergraph by conspiring with and giving assistance to its competitors.] To establish a boycott under section 1 there must be an illegal agreement in restraint of trade; we have been directed to no showing where a customer was required to agree not to deal with Intergraph in order to receive Intel's presentation. . . . The record states that Intergraph's market contains many competitors, with no significant entry barriers. Absent illegal conduct or an adverse effect on competition, Intel's customer presentations are devoid of antitrust significance. . . . The events here complained of do not state an antitrust claim. . . .

[The court found the termination of the at-will agreement by Intel with Intergraph was not unconscionable as found by the district court.] "[R]escission of a contract for unconscionability is an extraordinary remedy usually reserved for the protection of the unsophisticated and the uneducated." . . . Although Intergraph is a much smaller company than Intel, it is one of the Fortune 1000, and does not plead inadequate legal advice in its commercial dealings. . . .

CASE QUESTIONS

1. When does patent abuse become anticompetitive conduct?
2. If Intergraph were a competitor of Intel, would the decision have differed?

In a case that extensively discussed the *Intergraph* decision, *In re Papst Licensing, GmbH Patent Litigation,* 2000 U.S. Dist. LEXIS 12076 (E.D.La. 2000), Minebea sued Papst with respect to a joint venture between the parties for the research and development, engineering, manufacture, and sale of computer hard disk drive motors. As part of the agreement, Minebea paid Papst $14 million for the transfer of the Papst patent portfolio to the joint venture. Minebea alleged that eight months thereafter, the CEO of Papst claimed that certain of the company's patents had not been licensed to Minebea. The parties entered into a number of agreements thereafter. A dispute then arose over Papst's assertions that Minebea had no licensing rights to certain of its patents. Minebea then asserted that Papst violated Sections 1 and 2 of the Sherman Act. The Section 1 claim was that Papst forced customers to enter into a package license covering both the sale of the customer's hard disk drives incorporating the Minebea Motor and the sale of the customer's hard disk drives incorporating other manufacturer's motors where the right to enforce the Papst patents against a Minebea Motor customer has been exhausted.

In a motion to dismiss by Papst, it claimed that the *Intergraph* case governs the within case inasmuch as it was alleged that Papst and Minebea were not competitors in any relevant market. Papst owns and licenses patents. Minebea manufactures motors incorporating the Papst patents. Thus, allegedly the products were not interchangeable in a market. The court decided that Minebea pled sufficient facts to warrant a trial on the merits. The court stated:

> Monopoly power, often referred to as market power, is "the power to control prices or exclude competition." . . . It may be proven by evidence of the control of prices or the exclusion from competition. Minebea has alleged that Papst's patents cover "virtually all" of the HDDs [hard disk drives] and HDD motors in the United States, and that there are no products reasonably interchangeable with HDDs and HDD motors. It is further alleged that it has conditioned the granting of a patent license on the taking of a package license requiring the payment of a royalty for the sake of customers' hard disk drives incorporating a Minebea Motor and the sale of the customers' hard disk drives incorporating other manufacturer's motors. This alleges the control of, prices. Minebea has adequately alleged Papst's market power.

SPAM AND ANTITRUST

Previously we discussed the problem of *spam,* or the use of the Internet by marketers to send thousands and even millions of e-mail advertisements without the consent of the Internet service provider. In the following action, there were two decisions by the U.S. district court involving the same parties. Initially, as set forth in Chapter 4, the court rejected the argument of Cyber Promotions that it had a First Amendment right to use AOL freely, without its consent, to engage in advertising. When Cyber lost the argument, it petitioned the court two days after the first decision to overturn its decision based on an antitrust argument. The decision of the court reviews in depth the argument raised therein.

AMERICA ONLINE, INC. V. CYBER PROMOTIONS, INC.

948 F. Supp. 456 (E.D.Pa. 1996)

FACTS: Two days after the decision of this court denying Cyber the right to use AOL for the sending of unsolicited e-mail advertisements to AOL's customers, Cyber petitioned the Court for permission to serve an amended complaint that states another legal theory upon which it bases its right. Cyber alleges that AOL has attained a monopoly status for providing direct marketing advertising material to its subscribers in violation of Section 2 of the Sherman Act. The Court recited the stipulated facts namely that AOL is a private online company that invested substantial sums of money for equipment, name, software, and reputation. AOL subscribers pay prescribed fees for the use of its service. Its e-mail system operates through dedicated computers known as servers and that the servers have a finite, though expandable, capacity to handle e-mail. Non-AOL members sending e-mail messages to AOL customers have to utilize AOL's computer hardware and software.

Cyber is an advertising agency providing advertising services to companies wishing to advertise by e-mail. Cyber sends its advertisements by means of AOL and other Internet service providers. During the period September 18 through October 21, 1996, Cyber sent an average of 1.5 million e-mail messages per day using AOL. After the said date it averaged one million messages daily and almost two million messages daily from November 4 through November 11, 1996. AOL implemented a "tool" that allows access to Cyber's e-mail advertisements to subscribers who wish to receive them. Subscribers may check a box captioned "I want junk e-mail." The implementation of the "tool" led to the Cyber request herein.

ISSUE: Did AOL violate Section 2 of the Sherman Act by its refusal to permit unfettered e-mail advertisements to be sent through its service facilities?

DECISION: The Court held again in favor of AOL.

REASONING: Judge Wiener

Cyber contends that the ability to advertise to AOL's subscribers over the Internet via Electronic mail is an "essential facility" and that AOL has "refused to deal" with Cyber in violation of Section 2 of the Sherman Act. The irony of this contention is that AOL has *not* actually excluded Cyber from having access to AOL's system. Cyber is continuing to send its e-mail advertisements to AOL's servers. By implementing its PreferredMail system, AOL has given its own subscribers the option of viewing Cyber's e-mail without them having to pay to erase the e-mail every time they go online. Thus, Cyber is only being denied the access to AOL's system in a manner which *it prefers,* i.e., that AOL's customers should be able to view Cyber's e-mail without having to take affirmative steps to view the e-mail.

In any event, under the "essential facilities" or "bottleneck" doctrine, "a business or group of businesses which controls a scarce facility has an obligation to give competitors reasonable access to it." [T]he doctrine should "at most" extend to "facilities that are a natural monopoly, facilities whose duplication is forbidden by law, and perhaps those that are publicly subsidized and thus could not practicably be built privately. . . .

In order to make out a claim under the essential facilities doctrine, Cyber must show "(1) Control of the essential facility by a monopolist; (2) the competitor's inability practicably or reasonably to duplicate the essential facility; (3) denial of the use of the facility to a competitor; and (4) the feasibility of providing the facility." . . .

With regard to the first factor, there is little likelihood that Cyber will be able to demonstrate that AOL is a monopolist. In order to show AOL is a monopolist, Cyber must show that AOL possessed monopoly power in a relevant market and "the willful acquisition or maintenance of that power as distinguished from growth or development as a consequence of a superior product, business acumen, or historic accident." . . . Monopoly power is the power to control prices and exclude competition with respect to a particular product and within a particular geographic market. . . . The determination of a well-defined market, both geographically and by product, is essentially one of fact, turning on the unique market situation of each case. . . .

Cyber alleges that the relevant market to be "the market for providing direct marketing advertising material via electronic transmission to AOL's subscribers." . . . [and] defines the product market as the service of transmitting commercial advertising by electronic means to AOL's subscribers and defines the geographic market as AOL's subscribers themselves, a type of "electronic island to which AOL controls the only bridge." . . .

The first problem with Cyber's definition of the market is that AOL and Cyber are not competitors. . . .

The record reveals, however, that AOL is not a business competitor of Cyber. AOL's business is that of a private commercial online service. Cyber, on the other hand, is not in the business of providing private commercial online service but instead is an advertising agency which provides advertising services for companies and individuals wishing to advertise their products and services via e-mail. . . .

AOL has no problem accepting advertisements from advertisers as long as these advertisers pay AOL and therefore provide AOL with a source of revenue. Cyber, however, refuses to pay AOL for sending approximately 1.9 million e-mail advertisements to AOL servers each day. In short, the federal antitrust laws simply do not forbid AOL from excluding from its system advertisers like Cyber who refuse to pay AOL any fee (as opposed to those advertisers who do pay a fee) for their advertising on AOL's system. . . .

Even if Cyber could prove AOL is a monopolist in the relevant market, there is little likelihood that Cyber could prove that AOL monopolizes an "essential facility."

"An 'essential facility' is one which is not merely helpful but vital to the claimant's competitive viability." . . . The essential facility Cyber contends that AOL monopolizes is advertising to AOL's own subscribers via electronic mail. We believe there is little likelihood that Cyber will be able to show that the ability to advertise to AOL's subscribers is vital to Cyber's competitive ability.

. . . AOL has not even completely excluded Cyber from the AOL system. AOL's PreferredMail simply gives the AOL subscriber the option to choose whether he wishes to view Cyber's e-mail advertisements. In addition AOL currently has approximately seven million members who constitute no more than one-sixth to one-seventh of the current total e-mail population of 40 to 50 million and approximately one-half of the current total online population of 12 million. Cyber also has many other means of disseminating its advertising to Internet users in general and to AOL subscribers in particular besides electronic mail. Cyber can send its advertisements to the subscribers of the many other online services which compete with AOL, including CompuServe, the Microsoft Network and Prodigy. Cyber can send its advertisements to AOL members over the Internet through the World Wide Web which would allow access by AOL subscribers who want to receive Cyber's advertisements. Cyber, as an advertising agency, can disseminate its advertisements to AOL subscribers and others by non-Internet means including the United States mail, telemarketing, television, cable, newspapers, magazines, billboards and leaflets. And, of course, Cyber could attempt to lure AOL subscribers away from AOL by developing its own commercial online system or advertising web and charging a competitive rate.

CASE QUESTIONS

1. Was Cyber precluded from advertising through AOL?
2. Was Cyber denied any constitutional rights by AOL's refusal to allow open-ended use of the server for advertising purposes? Do advertisers have the same constitutional rights as non-commercial persons?

DOMAIN NAME ANTITRUST LITIGATION

Prior to the change transferring the right to assign domain names from Network Solutions, Inc. to the Internet Corporation for Assigned Names and Numbers, the issue arose of whether NSI could be sued for its alleged monopolistic practices in the award and removal of domain names. There were a number of cases in which NSI was a party in litigation by holders of trademarks who claimed that NSI had wrongfully registered and refused to remove domain names from persons using the trademark names as domain names. On several occasions, the issue was raised as to NSI monopoly in granting such registration. In the following case, the status of NSI was clarified.

BEVERLY V. NETWORK SOLUTIONS, INC.

1998 U.S. Dist. LEXIS 20453 (N.D.Ca. 1998)

FACTS: Beverly sued NSI concerning the latter's dispute policy. The policy requires persons registering a domain name represent and warrant that such name does not violate the intellectual property rights of holders thereof. If there is a violation of the policy there are procedures allowing the domain name holder to submit proof of the filing of a prior trademark registration to the complainant, choose a new domain name temporarily until the issue is resolved, file suit against the complainant, refuse the said options wherein NSI will suspend the use of the domain name; or sue the complainant for a declaratory judgment concerning the registration of the domain name.

Beverly registered the domain name, "whoswhointheworld.com." The defendant, Reed Publishing, notified NSI of its trademark dispute with Beverly alleging that it held the trademark "WHO'S WHO IN THE WORLD." NSI advised Beverly of the complainant and told the plaintiff of the said options. Plaintiff refused to accept any of the options. As a result the domain name was put on hold and the plaintiff sued alleging a series of complaints that were later dismissed by the Court. In an amended complaint the plaintiff alleged a civil conspiracy between Reed and NSI in violation of Section 1 of the Sherman Act.

ISSUE: Does the dispute policy of NSI establish a violation of Sherman Act Section 1?

DECISION: The Court dismissed the complaint finding no such conspiracy.

REASONING: Judge Walker

Although plaintiff asserts that defendants' conduct is a violation of the Sherman Act Section 1, he has not alleged a per se violation of the antitrust laws. Consequently, plaintiff's claim for civil conspiracy must be judged against the "rule of reason" standard. . . . To establish a violation of the Sherman Act Section 1 under the rule of reason, a plaintiff must demonstrate three elements: (1) an agreement, conspiracy, or combination among two or more persons or distinct business entities; (2) which is intended to harm or unreasonably restrain competition; and (3) which actually causes injury to competition, beyond the impact on the claimant, within a field of commerce in which the claimant is engaged. . . .

In order to establish a conspiracy claim under Section 1, plaintiff must establish than an agreement existed between the defendants, the nature of the agreement, and that the agreement was to accomplish either some unlawful purpose, or a lawful purpose by an unlawful means. . . . Plaintiff has alleged that an agreement exists but has provided no evidence of such an agreement. Rather, the record indicates that communications between defendants NSI and Reed were a direct result of the procedures spelled out in plaintiff's domain name registration agreement. . . . And, defendant Reed communicated with defendant NSI merely to protect its perceived trademark rights. . . . Defendant NSI neither received nor expected anything of value from defendant Reed for invoking the dispute policy. . . .

Viewing the facts in the light most favorable to the plaintiff, the court finds that defendants Reed and NSI were not engaged in a civil conspiracy. There is no evidence of an agreement. Even if there was an agreement, the agreement was for the purpose of accomplishing a lawful purpose, protection of defendant Reed's trademark. Moreover, the means which defendant NSI undertook to accomplish this purpose, through NSI's dispute policy, has already been determined by this court to be lawful. . . .

Additionally, plaintiff has not established injury to competition. An antitrust complaint must allege a relevant market in which the anticompetitive effect of a challenged activity can be assessed and an antitrust injury, or injury to competition. . . . Antitrust injury requires "proof of actual detrimental competitive effects such as output decreases or price increases." . . . Injury to a competitor is not sufficient. . . .

CASE QUESTIONS

1. What arguments can you raise that would contradict the assertion by the court that NSI is not a government entity?
2. Is NSI the sole registrar today? Assuming it was found to be monopolistic, would that finding be relevant at this juncture?

In *Thomas v. Network Solutions, Inc.*, 2 F. Supp. 2d 22 (D.D.C. 1998), in another alleged conspiracy claim against NSI, the court said that the alleged co-conspirator, National Science Foundation, was immune from suit under the Sherman Act because it is an agency of the federal government. "Under the federal instrumentality doctrine, private parties [such as NSI] acting in compliance with a clearly articulated government program are immunized to the same extent as the government entity." NSI was acting as the registrar of domain names in accordance with a compliance agreement with the U.S. government.

In *PGMedia, Inc. v. Network Solutions, Inc.,* 51 F. Supp. 2d 389 (S.D.N.Y. 1999), the plaintiff established a competing network of 13 name servers in its own domain name registry. It accepted many registrations under 530 new gTLDs. The name servers were allegedly in compliance with industry standards. For the domain names to be registered under the new gTLDs, NSI would have to amend its root zone files on the other root servers for them to be universally resolvable. Without the amendment to the root servers, persons typing in a domain name would not be able to connect to the site. In March, 1997, PGMedia (PGM) wrote to NSI, requesting that it add PGM registered domain names to its configuration file *named.root* on NSI root name servers. NSI responded that it could not do so because it was only one of a number of root name server administrations who, together with other root server administrators in the United States and Sweden, receive their direction from the Internet Assigned Numbers Authority (IANA) in California.

Both NSI and IANA were sued. IANA denied it had authority over NSI and placed the onus upon NSI's decision to refuse PGM's request. PGM claimed that NSI was liable under Section 2 of the Sherman Act because it had monopolistic control of an essential facility that could not be duplicated and had denied use of the facility although it could have permitted it. The court decided in favor of NSI under the "federal instrumentality immunity" doctrine, which gives it immunity from antitrust liability. Even though NSI is a private concern, when it acts "in compliance with a clearly articulated government program," it is entitled to immunity. The court stated:

> The gravamen of the federal instrumentality immunity, as applied to non-Government entities, is that a party to whom an agency of the Federal Government delegates or contracts to perform a function or provide a service is entitled to the same protections against antitrust liability as the Government agency itself. Whether the Government's immunity will also apply to the contracting party, however, depends on the extent to which the Government is acting pursuant to a clearly articulated policy or program. . . . At least two courts have stated the proposition more broadly: "Private parties, to the extent they are acting at the direction or with the consent of federal agencies, also fall outside the pale of the act's prohibition." . . .
>
> NSI operates the root server pursuant to a valid contract with the Government. The basic contract is the Cooperative Agreement, entered into with NSF [National Science Foundation]. . . . [T]he Cooperative Agreement was a valid exercise of the NSF's authority under the National Science Foundation Act . . . and the Federal Grant and Cooperative Agreement Act. . . .
>
> The Cooperative Agreement is a partnership between NSF and NSI that is valid under the Federal Grant and Cooperative Agreement Act.

APPLICATION OF ANTITRUST LAWS TO FOREIGN COMMERCIAL ACTIVITIES

As was stated previously, attempts by the United States to enforce its antitrust laws abroad created a great deal of antagonism with foreign jurisdictions. As a result, the United States passed the Foreign Trade Antitrust Improvements Act of 1982. The act states that the Sherman and Clayton Antitrust Acts will not apply to trade or commerce with foreign states unless the conduct has a direct, substantial, and reasonably foreseeable effect "(a) on trade or commerce which is not trade or commerce with foreign nations, or on import trade or import commerce with foreign nations; or (b) on export trade or export commerce with foreign nations, of a person engaged in such trade or commerce in the U.S.," and the effect is to give rise to a claim under the Sherman Act or Federal Trade Commission Act.

The act reaches activity of foreign enterprises that consist of cartels or monopolies, where their conduct has a substantial, direct, and reasonably foreseeable effect on the United States. In order to enforce its anticompetitive enactments against foreign enterprises, the United States would have to gain jurisdiction over the foreign entities. It may do so by prosecuting the companies that have a presence within the United States or where other nations have entered into cooperative arrangements with the United States concerning such exercise of enforcement jurisdiction.[12]

International Enforcement of Antitrust Activities

Historically, the United States, as a descendant of English common-law tradition, took the leadership role in the promulgation and enforcement of the antitrust laws. For the past century, there has been a prolific amount of antitrust litigation, both criminally and civilly. The difficulty arose, however, when the United States sought to enforce its antitrust legislation to companies abroad, whose activities affected the United States. Such enforcement was seen as a sign of America's attempt to exert domination and (to left-leaning regimes) as imperialistic tendencies. As Western European states became more integrated into the global economy, however, the value of protecting the free marketplace became apparent. With the Treaty of Rome's creation of what is today the European Union, antitrust enforcement has occurred to a degree exceeding that of the United States.

European Union. The Treaty of Rome of 1957, which created the European Economic Community (now the European Union), contained two articles, 85 and 86, that, in essence, reflect the same antitrust prohibitions as U.S. legislation.[13] Enforcement has been vigorous, unlike in the United States, where public enforcement often reflects ideological preferences of the political party in power. An example is the refusal by the European Union in 2001 to approve the proposed merger of General Electric with Honeywell International, albeit it would have been permitted under U.S. antitrust laws.

CONCLUSION

The *Microsoft* case presents a scenario wherein the alleged monopolistic policies of a major competitor could injure seriously the enormous efforts of competing companies to play a major role in the electronic marketplace. It is the opinion of this author that the decision will be upheld on appeal when the U.S. Supreme Court renders its decision. At best for Microsoft, the Court may concur with the court of appeals to lessen the punitive action taken by Judge Jackson. The district court's decision, however, appears to be in accord with past statutory and decisional authority.

A factor to be considered is the makeup of the Supreme Court. At present, the Court appears to be split between liberal justices and their more conservative colleagues. President Bush may have the opportunity to appoint several new members of the court in accordance with his ideology, although the new Democrat majority may impede his selections. Thus, the makeup of the Court in future years will determine whether the Court will be more aggressive in deciding if the antitrust laws have been violated. Adherents to the "Chicago school" (University of Chicago) are rather vehement in their opposition to the determination and enforcement of the antitrust laws, whereas those following the "Harvard," or more liberal, school of economic thought will be more likely to find violations of the antitrust laws. It is unlikely that new statutes will be passed given the current makeup of Congress.

Questions and Problems

1. How did the Clayton Antitrust Act correct the deficiencies of the Sherman Act of 1914?
2. What is the difference and the significance of the *per se* versus the *rule of reason* rules in connection with the antitrust laws?
3. Does a boycott of meat products by vegetarian group advocates violate the Clayton Act? What about a major competitor causing major supermarkets to boycott a competitor's products?
4. Is a monopoly illegal in and of itself? What may cause a company to become subject to the monopoly prohibitions of the Sherman Act?
5. Should Microsoft be the subject to antitrust litigation? Were consumers injured by its competitive practices?
6. Can one subsidiary of a corporation conspire to fix prices with another subsidiary of the same corporation?
7. Can a maker of very sophisticated patented machinery make it a condition of its purchase or lease that all servicing be done by the manufacturer?
8. May a private person or company injured by anticompetitive or unfair competitive practices of another company sue under the Federal Trade Commission Act? What remedies are available to such a company if its grievance does not come within the Sherman or Clayton Antitrust Acts?
9. It has been said that the Federal Trade Commission Act created the law of advertising. In what manner did the statute affect advertising industry practices?
10. Do you agree that U.S. antitrust laws should be applied to foreign companies who enter into agreements that are legal within their

countries but that may have a deleterious effect upon U.S. consumers?

11. Consider the following case that involved Microsoft during its litigation with the U.S. government. In its action against Microsoft, the government sought to prove, among other acts of monopolistic practices, that Microsoft illegally tied its Internet Explorer browser to its Windows operating system in order to undermine Netscape Navigator, which had a large percentage of the Web browser market. During the proceeding, Microsoft learned of two tenured full professors at Harvard and M.I.T., respectively, who had written a forthcoming book entitled *Competing on Internet Time: Lessons from Netscape and the Battle with Microsoft.* As part of the book, the professors interviewed some 40 current and former employees of Microsoft. During their interviews, they signed a nondisclosure agreement with Netscape wherein the professors agreed not to disclose proprietary information given to them during their interviews and related investigation except if required by court order and, if so required, to give Netscape advance warning so it could oppose the court order. The professors also recorded the interviews and provided that each interviewee had the right to correct errors in the quotes stated therein. Microsoft subpoenaed the professors' notes, tapes, or transcripts. After the professors declined to release them, Microsoft sought a court order to require submission of the said documents. Do the professors have a First Amendment right to prevent such disclosure? Are they in the same position as news reporters who seek to prevent disclosure of their confidential sources? *In re Cusamano v. Microsoft Corp.*, 162 F.3d 708 (1st Cir. 1998).

Endnotes

1. *Copperweld Corp. v. Independence Tube Corp.*, 467 U.S. 752 (1984).
2. *The Morning Pioneer v. The Bismark Tribune Company*, 493 F.2d 383 (8th Cir. 1974); *Hewlett-Packard Company v. Boston Scientific Corp.*, 77 F. Supp. 2d 189, 197 (D.Mass. 1999).
3. *Brown Shoe Co., Inc. v. United States*, 370 U.S. 294, 325 (1962).
4. *United States v. E. I. du Pont de Nemours & Co.*, 351 U.S. 377 (1956).
5. *Hampton v. Graff Vending Co.*, 516 F.2d 100 (5th Cir. 1975).
6. *Marathon Oil Co. v. Mobil Corp.*, 669 F.2d 378 (6th Cir. 1981).
7. *SAS Puerto v. Puerto Tel. Co.*, 48 F.3d 39, 44 (1st Cir. 1995).
8. *Clamps-All Corp. v. Cast Iron Soil Pipe Inst.*, 851 F.2d 478, 486 (1st Cir. 1988), cited in *Hewlett-Packard v. Boston Scientific*, 77 F. Supp. 2d 189, 198 (D.Mass. 1999).
9. *Brunswick Corp. v. Pueblo Bowl-O-Mat, Inc.*, 429 U.S. 477, 489 (1977), cited in *Hewlett-Packard supra*.
10. Letter from the Federal Trade Commission to the Senate Committee on Commerce, Science & Transportation, December 17, 1980.
11. *Walker Process Equipment, Inc. v. Food Machinery & Chemical Corp.*, 382 U.S. 172, 177 (1965).
12. See U.S. Department of Justice, "Antitrust Enforcement Guidelines for International Operations" (1994).
13. Article 85 states:

    1. The following shall be permitted as incompatible with the common market: all agreements between undertakings, decisions by associations of undertakings and concerted practices which may affect trade between Member States and which have as their object or effect the prevention, restriction or distortion of competition within the common market, and in particular those which:
        (a) directly or indirectly fix purchase or selling prices or any other trading conditions;
        (b) limit or control production, markets, technical development, or investment;
        (c) share markets or sources of supply;
        (d) apply dissimilar conditions to equivalent transactions with other trading parties, thereby placing them at a competitive disadvantage;
        (e) make the conclusion of contracts subject to acceptance by the other parties of supplementary obligations which, by their nature or according to commercial usage, have no connection with the subject of such contracts.

    2. Any agreements or decisions prohibited pursuant to this Article shall be automatically void.

3. The provision of paragraph 1 may, however, be declared inapplicable in the case of:

— any agreement or category of agreements between undertakings;
— any decision or category of decisions by association of undertakings;
— any concerted practice or category of concerted practices;

which contributes to improving the production or distribution of goods or to promoting technical or economic progress, while allowing consumers a fair share of the resulting benefit, and which does not:

(a) impose on the undertakings concerned restrictions which are not indispensable to the attainment of these objectives;
(b) afford such undertakings the possibility of eliminating competition in respect of a substantial part of the products in question.

Article 86 states:

> Any abuse by one or more undertakings of a dominant position within the common market or in a substantial part of it shall be prohibited as incompatible with the common market in so far as it may affect trade between Member States.
>
> Such abuse may, in particular, consist in:
>
> (a) directly or indirectly imposing unfair purchase or selling prices or other unfair trading conditions;
> (b) limiting production, markets or technical development to the prejudice of consumers;
> (c) applying dissimilar conditions to equivalent transactions with other trading parties, thereby placing them at a competitive disadvantage;
> (d) making the conclusion of contracts subject to acceptance by the other parties of supplementary obligations which, by their nature or according to commercial usage, have no connection with the subject of such contracts.

CHAPTER

12 SECURITIES REGULATION AND THE INTERNET

Chapter Outline

- The Securities Act of 1933
- The Securities Exchange Act of 1934
- Jurisdictional Issues in Securities Cases
- Abuses in Litigation: Amendments to the Securities Acts
- Insider Trading
- Commodities Futures
- The Foreign Corrupt Practices Act
- Electronic Records and Signatures under Federal Securities Law
- Conclusion

One of the causes of the Great Depression was the enormous degree of fraud perpetrated during the 1920s upon purchasers of securities. Many stocks were sold in companies that had false and misleading earnings reports and tangible assets, or indebtedness. There was little or no regulation of the marketplace. With the accession of the new president, two laws were passed that imposed stringent regulations upon the issuance and distribution of securities. The laws that were enacted were the Securities Act of 1933 and the Securities Exchange Act of 1934. These laws, as modified and amended thereafter, remain as the principal legislative forays in the securities marketplace. In addition, there are state laws, known as *blue sky laws,* that regulate securities issued within the individual state domain.[1]

The Internet presents new dimensions to the formulation and trading of securities. The legal issues arising as a result of the technological development are as momentous as those occurring in the post-1929 era. Trading no longer is restricted to the limited hours of the major exchanges. Firms are and will be working on a 24-hour basis. The events in one part of the globe may affect exchanges elsewhere. Securities may be bought and sold through a variety of securities forums. Sales and purchases are concluded globally in seconds. Companies are able to sell new offerings without the necessity of intermediary brokerages through the Internet. Traditional brokerage firms, such as Merrill Lynch, have been compelled to adapt to the new realities by offering online services in order to compete with Internet-based firms. The possibility of fraud and other unlawful or unethical activity becomes exacerbated. In this chapter, we will review classical securities legal principles and relate the Internet to later changes in regulatory permutations.

The main regulatory mechanisms are derived from a variety of legislative efforts emanating almost 70 years ago. They are the Securities Act of 1933 (15

U.S.C. Section 77a-17mna); the Securities Exchange Act of 1934 (15 U.S.C. Section 79l-78mm); the Investment Advisers Act of 1940 (15 U.S.C. Section 80b-1 to 80b-21); and the Investment Company Act of 1940 (15 U.S.C. Section 80a-1 to 80a-64).[2]

THE SECURITIES ACT OF 1933

Security Defined

The Securities Act of 1933 regulates the issuance of securities as well as creating the federal Securities and Exchange Commission to regulate and supervise the enforcement of federal laws governing the field. The word *security* is very broadly defined. Section 2(1) defines it as:

> any note, stock, treasury stock, bond, indenture, evidence of indebtedness, certificate of interest or participation in any profit-sharing agreement, collateral-trust certificate, preorganization certificate or subscription, transferable share, investment contract, voting-trust certificate, certificate of deposit for a security, fractional undivided interest in oil, gas, or other mineral rights, any put, call, straddle, option, or privilege on any security.

Thus, virtually any investment wherein a person gives something of value with a reasonable expectation of profit through the efforts of others may fall within the definition. The issue of whether the investment is a security was raised in the following case.

S.E.C. V. ALLIANCE LEASING CORP.

No. 98-CV-1810-J (CGA), 2000 U.S. Dist. LEXIS 5227 (S.D.Ca. 2000)

FACTS: Alliance was a San Diego-based equipment leasing company. From December 1997 to October 1998, it caused some 1,500 persons throughout the U.S. to invest in an enterprise wherein the investor gave money to the company to purchase commercial or kitchen equipment that was then leased out to third parties. The lease payments were to be paid by the lessees monthly over a two-year period at the end of which a balloon payment [the entire principal] balance would be due and owing. Alliance represented that investors would earn a 14% rate of return on their investment and that the investment was low risk. The SEC alleged that the investment contracts offered by the defendant were unregistered securities and that the company and its principals violated the securities laws by failing to register them as well as making misrepresentations to the prospective investors. In addition, there was a failure by principals to disclose a 30% commission taken with respect to the leasing program. The defendants claimed the investment contracts were not securities under the relevant statutes.
ISSUE: Were the investment contracts "securities" under the Securities Act of 1933 and under other securities statutes?

DECISION: The Court decided in favor of the SEC, holding that they were securities.
REASONING: Judge Jones

DEFINITION OF A SECURITY

A "security" is defined in both 15 U.S.C. section 77b(1) and 15 U.S.C. Section 78c(a)(10) to include "investment contracts" and "notes." In *SEC v. W. J. Howey Co.*, . . . the Supreme Court set forth the framework for analyzing whether transactions such as those involved in the Alliance Leasing Program are investment contracts that may be characterized as securities. Under Howey, an investment contract exists if the following three part test is met: (1) there is an investment of money, (2) in a common enterprise, and (3) with an expectation of profits produced by the efforts of others. . . .

1. "Investment of Money"

It is undisputed that there is an investment of money. Over 1,500 investors nationwide contributed at least $54 million to the venture. . . . Hence, the first element of the Howey test is clearly satisfied.

2. "A Common Enterprise"

The Ninth Circuit has determined that "common enterprise" can be demonstrated by a showing of *either* horizontal or vertical commonality. . . . Horizontal commonality is illustrated when the enterprise is common to a group of investors; this is illustrated most easily by a showing that there is a pooling of interests amongst the investors. . . . Vertical commonality, on the other hand, is defined as an enterprise to an investor and the seller, promoter, or some third party; this is established by showing "that the fortunes of the investors are linked with those of the promoters." . . .

With respect to horizontal commonality, the Court finds that there is no dispute of material fact that the Alliance Leasing Program exhibited horizontal commonality. According to the terms of the Joint Venture Agreement, the investors would provide the investment capital for Alliance to purchase commercial equipment to lease to third parties. . . . Alliance promotional materials disclose that in some cases "it bundled the leases together in packages of several million dollars each which [were] purchased by institutional investors." . . . This disclosure makes it apparent that investor funds were pooled together to purchase leases. Horizontal commonality is therefore satisfied since investor interests were pooled in the endeavor. Accordingly, the Alliance Leasing Program is an enterprise common to a group of investors as required under the second prong of Howey.

. . . [T]he Court . . . also finds that the Leasing Agreement exhibited vertical commonality . . . that the "fortunes of the investor are interwoven and dependent upon the efforts and success of those seeking the investment." [T]he investors and Defendant Alliance actually do share in the percentage of the returns from the leasing agreements. . . .

3. "Profit by Effort of Others"

The third prong of the Howey test is met when there is an "expectation of profits produced by the efforts of others." . . . This expectation is created when "the efforts made by those other than the investor are the undeniably significant ones, those essential managerial efforts which affect the failure or success of the enterprise." . . . This third factor can be shown by the following examples:

(1) an agreement among the parties leaves so little power in the hands of the partner or venturer that the arrangement in fact distributes power as would a limited partnership; or (2) the partner or venturer is so inexperienced and unknowledgeable in business affairs that he is incapable of intelligently exercising his partnership or venture powers; or (3) the partner or venturer is so dependent on some unique entrepreneurial or managerial ability of the promoter or manager that he cannot replace the manager of the enterprise or otherwise exercise meaningful partnership or venture powers. . . .

Here, the terms of the Joint Venture Agreement and the Equipment Management Agreement show that the structure of the relationship between the Alliance and the investors ("principals") was one in which Alliance held most of the responsibility and the principals' role was pro forma. . . . The third prong of the Howey test is therefore met.

CASE QUESTIONS

1. How do the facts differ from a person investing money in some trucks and leasing them to whomever may need them for transport?
2. If all of the investors and the enterprise were solely within a state, do the Securities Act provisions apply?

The act, in essence, requires that the issuer of an interstate security file a registration statement with the SEC containing essential information concerning the security. Such information includes the names of all participants, including the issuer, officers, directors, underwriters, attorneys, and other participants. The statement must describe the nature of the business, the management, certified financial statements by independent accountants, risks, and other pertinent information. A prospectus is also filed with the SEC, which will eventually be given to all initial investors after the filing period has lapsed. The prospectus is designed to convey all appropriate information regarding the security so that an investor can gauge the nature of the company, its history, the type of management that will run the company, the risks presented, and so on. The SEC does not guarantee that the company is a sound investment. It only ensures that the information contained in the registration statement and the prospectus is accurate under penalties of criminal and civil prosecution.

In the *S.E.C. v. Alliance* case, the court found that Alliance violated Sections 5(a) and 5(c) of the Securities Act in using interstate commerce or using the mail to offer or sell the security. The statute does not require evidence of intent to violate the said sections of the statute, merely that the registration statement was not filed if the security meets the said two conditions.

Is a pyramid promotion enterprise a security for purposes of the Securities Acts? In *SEC v. Koscot Interplanetary, Inc.*, 497 F.2d 473 (5th Cir. 1974), Koscot engaged in selling cosmetics by means of a multilevel network of independent distributors. At the lowest level are beauty advisors who are engaged in selling Koscot products available to them at a 45 percent discount. There are progressive levels with higher discounts for sales made to the lower levels of distribution. The main effort is to solicit prospective salespersons to attend so-called Opportunity Meetings, wherein they become subject to intense efforts of recruitments by displays of affluence and sales pitches. Persons could purchase supervisor and distributorship levels by increasing expenditures of money. The SEC's position is that the scheme qualified as a profit-sharing arrangement and as an investment contract. The court of appeals found such an arrangement to be an investment contract. The three *Howey* elements were present, to wit, an investment of money, a scheme in which a person invests money in a common enterprise, and an expectation of profits solely from the efforts of persons other than the investors.

The court found indisputably that the purchasers of supervisorships and distributorships were made by an investment of money. The second element of a *common enterprise,* defined as "one in which fortunes of the investor are interwoven with and dependent upon the efforts and success of those seeking the investment or of third parties. . . . [T]he fact that an investor's return is independent of that of other investors in the scheme is not decisive. Rather, the requisite commonality is evidenced by the fact that the fortunes of all investors are inextricably tied to the efficacy of the Koscot meetings and guidelines on recruiting prospects and consummating a sale."

The third element of the expectation of profits from the efforts of individuals other than the investor created the most difficulty in the case. The investor did partake in meetings and in the sale of products to lower-level persons. The court said that the critical test is not whether there was some effort made in the enterprise by the investor but rather "whether the efforts made by those other than the investor are the undeniably significant ones, those essential managerial efforts which affect the failure or success of the enterprise." This was a scheme in which the promoters retained immediate control over the most important managerial aspects of the enterprise and where the profits to be realized by the investors were "inextricably tied to the success of the promotional scheme."

The act exempts certain securities and certain transactions from some or all of the statutory requirements. Exempt securities include those of governments, banks, railroads, nonprofit organizations, insurance companies, and farmers' cooperatives. Generally, exempted groups are regulated by other government agencies. Exempt transactions include purely intrastate securities (state blue sky laws would apply); small issues up to $1.5 million within a 12-month period, although the issuer must file a notification with the SEC; private placement of securities up to $5 million in a 12-month period to accredited investors (sophisticated high-income individuals, or banks, and other knowledgeable persons) and up to 35 other purchasers; short-term (nine months) commercial paper; and casual sales.

After a filing of the registration statement, the SEC has 20 days within which to reject the filing. Generally, it requires amendments and clarifications of the statement. If there are inaccuracies in the statement, civil and criminal penalties may be applicable. Civil liability may accrue in favor of the investor who incurred a loss as a result of the issuance of the security. Liability may be imposed for a false statement of material omission upon every person connected with the statement, including all those preparing and signing the statement as well as experts whose input was false or misleading and underwriters up to the amount underwritten. Criminal liability may accrue, including significant fines and imprisonment against persons intentionally making false statements or omissions in connection with the security.

Exempted Securities

Although the definition of a security is extremely broad, not all securities need be registered under the Securities Act of 1933.

Intrastate Issues. Congress derives its power to regulate securities under the commerce clause of the U.S. Constitution, Article 1, Section 8, cl. 3, which gives it the power "[t]o regulate commerce with foreign nations, and among the several States. . . ." Accordingly, it would be constitutionally impermissible for Congress to regulate purely intrastate commercial activity. Thus, securities may be sold, subject to the state's blue sky laws, to residents within the state. All purchasers must be located within the state, resale of the securities can be made only to residents of the same state for a period of nine months, the issuer must be a resident of the same state, and 80 percent of the issuer's business and of the proceeds from the sales of the securities must take place within the state.

Regulation A: Small Public Offerings. *Small issues,* defined as issues of up to $5 million, within a one-year period may be exempted if the corporation files an offering circular with unaudited financial data with the SEC and is given to the potential investors. Persons other than issuers may sell up to $1.5 million in a one-year period.

Miscellaneous Exempt Securities. Other securities that are exempt are insurance and annuity contracts, securities issued by nonprofit, religious, educational, and charitable institutions, securities of governments, banks, savings and loan associations, farmers, and cooperative associations, and commercial paper having a maturity of less than nine months.

Regulation D Transactions Exemptions

Regulation D arose as a result of the passage of the Small Business Investment Incentive Act of 1980.[3] The goals of the enactment were to ease the regulatory restraints imposed upon small business capital formation. Regulation D provides for a number of exemptions from the requirements of the Securities Act of 1933, albeit the antifraud provisions of the statute are still applicable. They are provided for in Rules 504, 505, and 506.

Rule 504. Rule 504, 17 CFR [Code of Federal Regulations] Part 230, provides an exemption, the *seed capital* exemption, from the registration requirements of the Securities Act for securities offerings not exceeding a total amount of $1 million in a one-year period. The rule permits a nonreporting issuer to solicit and advertise offers to potential investors. There are no resale restrictions or restrictions concerning the number and type of investors who may purchase the securities. State blue sky laws must still be obeyed. Thus, the securities laws of the states in which the securities are sold must be complied with. The SEC, concerned with recent fraudulent secondary transactions in over-the-counter markets, modified Rule 504.[4]

According to the SEC, the rule was used to permit fake sales to nominees in states without registrations or prospectus delivery requirements, which securities are then placed with broker-dealers who cold-called investors selling the securities at higher prices that then collapsed. This dump-and-pump scheme caused investors to lose their investments. Accordingly, the amendment to Rule 504 provides that an issuer may issue unrestricted or freely tradable securities and engage in general solicitation or general advertising in two circumstances: (1) if the issuer registers the offering under state law requiring a public filing and delivery of a disclosure document to investors before sale; or (2) if there is a state law exemption that permits general solicitation and general advertising, then sales may be made only to "accredited investors."

An *accredited investor* is one that is a bank, insurance company, investment company, or employee benefit plan; any business development company; any charitable or educational institution with assets of more than $5 million; any director, executive officer, or general partner of the issuer; any person who bought at least $150,000 of the securities offered, provided that the purchase didn't exceed 20 percent of the person's net worth; any person with a net worth of over $1 million; and any person with an annual income of more than $200,000 (Rule 501).

Rule 505. The issuance of securities up to $5 million in a one-year period is exempt from registration requirements to an unlimited number of accredited investors and up to 35 unaccredited investors. The resale of the securities is restricted for a two-year period after issuance. Although it is not necessary to provide accredited investors with disclosures concerning the offered security, nonaccredited investors are entitled to an audited balance sheet and other available financial statements.

Rule 506. Formal registration requirements will be exempt for the sale of an unlimited amount of securities to an unlimited number of accredited investors and up to 35 nonaccredited investors who are or are represented by sophisticated investors (attorneys, accountants, etc.). In practice, the sales are made solely to accredited investors.

Implications for Sales of Securities over the Internet

The Internet permits direct sales of securities to purchasers without the necessity for intermediaries.[5] Thus, the implications are far reaching for securities firms connected with their sale and distribution. Such sales, of course, make fraudulent practices far more likely, as well as taking place without the expertise that brokerage firms possess. The SEC has undertaken extensive investigation and has promulgated rules and regulations affecting such sales.

THE SECURITIES EXCHANGE ACT OF 1934

The Securities Exchange Act of 1934 regulates trading of securities by stock exchanges after the initial offering. The act requires companies whose securities are publicly traded to file periodic financial reports, such as Form 10K annual report, 8K report of significant events, and 10Q quarterly reports. The 10K report must be certified by an independent public accountant. Securities dealers must register with the SEC.

Meaning of *Exchange*

What is a stock exchange? Ordinarily, the answer to the question is quite evident as exemplified by the New York Stock Exchange and Nasdaq. In *Board of Trade v. SEC,* 923 F.2d 1270 (7th Cir. 1991), the court of appeals was called upon to decide "whether a system for trading options on federal government securities that has been put together by RMJ, a broker; Delta, a clearing agency; and SPNTCO," a bank acting only in custodial role; is an *exchange* within the meaning of Section 3(a)(1) of the Securities Exchange Act of 1934. If so, it had to be registered with the SEC. The Board of Trade and the Chicago Mercantile Exchange, fearing competition from the system, had appealed a decision by the SEC that the system for trading options was only a clearing agency and not an exchange. The court found in favor of the SEC.

The court described the Delta system as follows:

> The system specifies the form of option contract that shall be the security traded. Some of the terms are fixed, such as the maximum term of the option and the day of the month on which it expires. Others are left open to be negotiated by the parties, such as the premium, the exercise price, and the month of expiration. The traders, who consist not only of securities dealers but also of banks, pension funds, and other institutional investors, communicate their buy or sell offers to RMJ, which enters the offers in the system's computer. Delta, the clearing agency, monitors the computer and when it sees a matching buy and sell offer it notifies the traders that they have a deal (but doesn't tell them with whom) and it takes the necessary steps to effectuate the completed transaction. The interposition of Delta between the traders protects the anonymity of each from the other as well as guaranteeing to each that the other will honor the terms of the option traded.

The court was persuaded by the fact that the various participants were comprehensively regulated and that the SEC had considerable discretion in determining what is an exchange from a statute that had considerable ambiguity in the definition given to it.

Proxy Solicitations

Proxy solicitations are covered by the Securities Act. In essence, all registered companies must provide shareholders with a proxy statement in advance of shareholders' meeting together with a copy of the annual report of the company if directors are to be voted for at the meeting. All material facts concerning matters to be voted on at the meeting must be furnished. Shareholder proposals are to be included with the proxy statements, and any management opposition to the proposal is to be also included. The proxy statement, together with accompanying materials is to be filed with the SEC.

What are *material facts* that must be furnished to shareholders in proxy statements? In *TSC Industries, Inc. v. Northway, Inc.,* 426 U.S. 438 (1976), the U.S. Supreme Court gave a bright-line rule for courts to follow in making the determination. In an action brought by Northway, a shareholder in TSC, Northway alleged that a joint proxy statement containing a proposal to liquidate and sell all of TSC's assets to National Industries was incomplete and materially misleading. It was alleged that the proxy statement failed to state that the transfer of the interest of a major shareholder would give National control of TSC in contravention of Rule 14a-3(a) of the Securities Exchange Act of 1934.[6]

The Court noted that the purpose of Section 14(a) of the Securities Exchange Act was "intended to promote 'the free exercise of the voting rights of stockholders' by ensuring that proxies would be solicited with 'explanation to the stockholder of the real nature of the questions for which authority to cast his vote is sought.'" The standard of materiality is:

> An omitted fact is material if there is substantial likelihood that a reasonable shareholder would consider it important in deciding how to vote. . . . It does not require proof of a substantial likelihood that disclosure of the omitted fact would have caused the reasonable investor to change his vote. What the standard does contemplate is a showing of a substantial likelihood that, under all the circumstances, the omitted fact would have assumed actual significance in the deliberations of the reasonable shareholder. Put another way, there must be substantial likelihood that the disclosure of the omitted fact would have been viewed by the reasonable investor as having significantly altered the "total mix" of information made available.

Insider Trading and Profits

Insider trading and profits are also to be disclosed. Under the Insider Trading Sanctions Act of 1984, the SEC may seek to enjoin insider trading and recoup up to three times the profits made by the insider for trading with knowledge of nonpublic material information about the company. Insiders include not only officers and directors but also beneficial owners (including shares held by a spouse or children) of more than 10 percent of any class of securities in the company. It also includes accountants, attorneys, and others connected with the security. Criminal penalties may also be applicable. There are exceptions for small trades and odd-lot transactions. A person buying more than 5 percent of a publicly traded security must report such purchase to the issuer, to the exchange in which the trade took place, and to the SEC.

The antifraud provisions of the 1934 act are quite extensive. Section 10(b) states that it is unlawful

> [t]o use or employ, in connection with the purchase or sale of any security . . . any manipulative or deceptive device or contrivance in contravention of such rules and regulations as the [Federal Trade] Commission may prescribe as necessary or appropriate in the public interest or for the protection of investors.

Rule 10b-5 states:

> It shall be unlawful for any person, directly or indirectly, by the use of any means or instrumentality of interstate commerce, or of the mails or of any facility of any national securities exchange, (a) to employ any device, scheme, or artifice to defraud, (b) to make any untrue statement of a material fact necessary in order to make the statements made, in light of the circumstances under which they were made, not misleading, or (c) to engage in any act, practice or course of business which operates as a fraud or deceit upon any person, in connection with the purchase or sale of any security.

In order to establish a claim under the Section and Rule, the plaintiff's complaint must contain the following elements to be proven at a trial:

> (1) a material misstatement or omission, (2) scienter—an intent to deceive or defraud, (3) in connection with the purchase or sale of a security, (4) through the use of interstate commerce or a national securities exchange, (5) upon which plaintiffs rely, and (6) which caused injury to plaintiffs.[7]

It does not matter whether the security is registered under the act, is or is not publicly traded, or is an initial or subsequent issuance of the security. A false statement is material if its disclosure would alter the "total mix" of facts available to an investor and "if there is a substantial likelihood a reasonable shareholder would consider it important."[8] The 1934 act requires that the material misrepresentation or omission was relied upon by the innocent party, unlike the 1933 act, which does not require reliance but only proof that there was material misrepresentation or omission.

Proof of reliance can be established by a plaintiff proving that but for the misleading or false statements or omissions, the purchase of the securities would not have taken place. Reliance can also be shown by use of the fraud on the market doctrine. As stated in *McNamara v. Bre-X Minerals Ltd.*, 57 F. Supp. 2d 396 (E.D.Tex. 1999):

> The premise of this doctrine is that "the market price of the shares traded on well-developed markets reflects all publicly available information, and, hence, all material misrepresentations. . . . Under this doctrine, "where materially misleading statements have been disseminated into an

impersonal, well-developed market for securities, the reliance of individual plaintiffs on the integrity of the market price may be presumed." . . . To satisfy their pleading burden on causation, the Plaintiffs "need only allege facts which show that Defendants omissions and misrepresentations caused the market price of the stock to be artificially inflated, and therefore to appear to be a good risk for investment, so that when the truth came out about the company's condition, the stock lost value and Plaintiffs suffered a loss."

Manipulating the Price of a Security. It appears to be a violation of the Rule 10b-5 if the sole purpose of an investor in purchasing a security is to manipulate the price of the said security. In *United States v. Mulheren,* 938 F.2d 364 (2d Cir. 1991), the defendant was accused of violating Rule 10b-5 in his purchase of 75,000 shares of Gulf & Western (G&W) common stock in 1985. The alleged reason was to raise the price of the stock to the $45 price level so as to enable Ivan Boesky (later, a convicted felon) to sell his shares at an inflated price and for a considerable profit. The court reversed the conviction that had taken place in the district court, finding insufficient evidence to warrant a conviction. The pertinent evidence was a conversation between Boesky and the defendant wherein Boesky told him that the G&W security would be "a good purchase and worth owning." After Mulheren's purchase, Boesky sold his shares for the said $45 sum.

In overturning the conviction, the court discussed what would constitute unlawful manipulation. "One of the hallmarks of manipulation is some profit or personal gain inuring to the alleged manipulator." Other indicia of fraud would be purchasing the shares using "fictitious accounts, matched orders, wash sales, dissemination of false literature," and a strong pecuniary interest in assisting another to profit from the manipulation of the price of the security.

Aiding and Abetting. Aiding and abetting another person to commit fraud is also a violation of Section 10(b) and Rule 10b-5. The elements of the violation are: (1) the existence of the violation or wrong; (2) actual knowledge of the wrong and his/her role in aiding the wrong by the accused of aiding and abetting; and (3) such assistance was substantial. Silence may constitute aiding and abetting if such person had a duty to disclose the wrong to investors if such disclosure would be material to them. In *Roberts v. Peat, Marwick, Mitchell & Co.,* 857 F.2d 646 (9th Cir. 1988), the defendant accounting firm was accused of aiding and abetting the alleged fraud perpetrated against investors who had purchased limited partnerships in an oil and gas concern engaged in the use of oil recovery technology to produce oil and gas from otherwise nonproductive oil-bearing property. The complaint alleged that the value shown for the business concern was overvalued because the oil technology was unproven; that the limited partnerships were considerably over-priced; and that Peat, Marwick knew or should have known of the alleged fraud.

The court of appeals reversed the dismissal of the action by the district court against the defendant, Peat, Marwick, on its motion for summary judgment (the district court dismissed the case without a trial on the merits because it held there was no basis for the claim inasmuch as the investment was made prior to Peat, Marwick's involvement). The court indicated that a trial on the merits had to take place on the basis that if it were proven that Peat, Marwick allowed its name to be placed on reports and memoranda of the business concern known to be fraudulent, it could be held liable for aiding and abetting the fraud.

Rule 9(b) of the Federal Rule of Civil Procedure imposes very stringent requirements upon persons alleging fraud. The rule requires that the parties suing (1) state specifically the time, place, and contents of the false misrepresentations and state who the person was making the false statements; (2) show why the said statements were false and misleading as to constitute fraud; and (3) must state facts showing that the defendant knew the statements were false or acted with extreme reckless and disregard for the truth concerning the false statements. Fraudulent intent can be demonstrated by showing a motive for committing securities fraud, or state the circumstances indicating conscious behavior by the defendants. Motive can be shown by demonstrating the concrete benefits to be gained by the person making such statements or omissions. Such benefits must be more than a financial interest unless it rises to the level of huge potential profit by the said person. The defendant's false statements or omissions rise to the heightened level of proof of severe recklessness "only if they (1) involve an 'extreme departure from the standards of ordinary care' and (2) 'present a danger of misleading buyers and sellers which is either known to the defendant or is so obvious that the defendant must have been aware of it.'"[9]

Does puffery (for example, exaggerating a company's strength in the marketplace) or future predictions as to growth potential constitute fraudulent conduct? In the following case, the issues of puffery and prediction are discussed in connection with Rule 10b-5.

IN RE HI/FN, INC., SECURITIES LITIGATION

No. C 99-4531 SI, 2000 U.S. Dist. LEXIS 11631 (N.D.Ca. 2000)

FACTS: A class action was commenced on behalf of purchasers of the common stock of Hi/fn, Inc. between July 26, 1999 and October 7, 1999. Hi/fn designs and markets semiconductor devices to provide secure, high-bandwidth connections to the Internet and increased data storage. Most of its revenues were dependent on two companies, Quantum Corporation and Lucent Technologies. Hi/fn executives learned from a meeting that Lucent planned to substantially reduce its requirements of Hi/fn's devices. In addition, it allegedly became aware that Quantum would reduce its order due to overstocking. Plaintiffs claimed that Hi/fn made public statements assuring the company's optimistic outlook notwithstanding it knew of the impending substantial decrease in future orders. In interviews with CNBC and with market analysts in September 1999, two of the company's executives said that Hi/fn's outlook was positive and that it expected returns of $65 million for the following year. On October 6, 1999, the company announced that there would be a shortfall causing the price of the shares to substantially decline.
ISSUE: Did the statements communicated to the public projecting revenue forecast constitute a violation of rule 10b-5?
DECISION: The Court found substantial evidence to warrant a trial of Hi/fn and its CEO/Chairman on the merits concerning the issue of alleged violation of rule 10b-5.
REASONING: Judge Illston

A. STATEMENTS OF OPTIMISM

1. The Bespeaks Caution Doctrine

Defendants assert that the disputed statements made by the defendants fall within the scope of the "bespeaks caution" doctrine because in Hi/fn's February, May, and June 1999 forms 10-Q, defendants meaningfully and specifically warned the market of the company's high dependence from Quantum and Lucent....

The judicially-created "bespeaks caution doctrine" "provides a mechanism by which a court can rule as a matter of law ... that defendants' forward-looking representations contained enough cautionary language or risk disclosure to protect the defendant against claims of securities fraud." ... Misleading oral statements are not protected by the general cautionary language "spread out among various documents." ... "Courts are generally reluctant to hold that a forward-looking statement is protected by cautionary language contained in documents other than that which contains the forward-looking statement." ... Although Hi/fn's form 10-Q warned of the risk of a reduction in orders, those statements do not speak directly to the allegedly false statements. Assuming as true plaintiffs' allegations of knowledge regarding the imminent reduction of orders from Hi/fn's two largest customers, this generalized potential risk had become a reality. This court cannot conclude that a prior and generalized cautionary statement was adequate as a matter of law to protect defendants' latest oral statements.

2. Puffery

Defendants also argue that the disputed "general statements of optimism" are not actionable, because they constitute vague and ambiguous "puffery" and "corporate cheerleading." ...

"Projections and general expressions of optimism may be actionable" under federal securities laws.... A forecast may be actionable if any of the following factors are correct: (1) the statement is not genuinely believed, (2) there is not a reasonable foundation for the belief, or (3) the speaker is aware of undisclosed facts that tend to undermine the accuracy of the projection.... [I]t is apparent that plaintiffs have alleged falsity based on the previously detailed undisclosed information. Accordingly, the Court concludes that the forecasts of significant increases in Hi/fn's business and revenues were not puffery and can be actionable.

3. Duty to Make Predictions

Defendants also argue that Hi/fn was under no duty to predict with precision if and when Quantum and Lucent would reduce their orders. . . . A company is not charged with the ability to know "to a certainty" the plans of another entity. . . . The argument would be closer to the mark if Hi/fn's management had made no statements at all concerning the strength of the market for its products. Since Hi/fn chose to make such statements, however, and since their actual statements are alleged to have been false and misleading, their duty to disclose becomes academic. . . .

CASE QUESTIONS

1. At what juncture does *puffery* become the basis for an investor's claim of fraud?
2. Must all negative reports be revealed by a company as they become known?

Corporate Internet Web sites may run afoul of the fraud provisions. Many corporations are now using the Internet to disclose information previously found in their annual reports and in their SEC filings. The difficulty is that the temptation to puff corporate data could lead to civil and criminal prosecutions. Less controversial data, such as current stock prices and past stock price data does not pose any difficulties. It is when the site has incomplete data that emphasizes the positive aspects of the company and omits negative, modifying data that problems may emerge. Merely posting quarterly and annual reports filed with the SEC on the Web entails no difficulties unless, of course, the reports contain fraudulent data. Company CEO speeches and overviews of financial performance may pose significant danger zones that open the door for attorneys to file federal and state lawsuits alleging fraud and other claims.[10]

Companies should, at a minimum, review corporate Web data postings regularly for their accuracy, have disclaimers as to all projections, and divide data into current and historical data so as to lessen confusion by those reading the data.[11] Excessive optimism concerning future earnings should be avoided unless the company executives have documented bases upon which to make such forecasts. When a company does well, no one complains. When a shareholder loses a substantial sum in a particular security, the Pandora's box of company statements and activities may lead to litigation in the hope of recovering all or a substantial part of the losses.

JURISDICTIONAL ISSUES IN SECURITIES CASES

Internet sales of securities present a number of problems that courts must resolve. The United States has the most advanced laws and regulations governing such transactions. Enforcement of such rules and regulations beyond the nation's borders becomes highly problematical. In Chapter 2, the bases for assertion of jurisdiction over foreign entities were discussed. In the following litigation, a number of parties are foreign nationals concerning which the court discusses the issues of jurisdiction, and 10b-5 is discussed.

IN RE THE BAAN COMPANY SECURITIES LITIGATION

103 F. Supp. 2d 1 (D.D.C. 2000)

FACTS: Plaintiffs, who consisted of a number of U.S. and foreign persons, sued the Baan Company, a Netherlands corporation with offices in the Netherlands and in Virginia, as well as a number of Baan officers and directors, alleging that Baan reported fraudulently inflated revenue and earnings, made ma-

terially misleading statements, and omitted material facts, as well as other allegations. The alleged improper inflation of earnings was done through the cooperation of Baan, Vanenburg, and their affiliates and subsidiaries. Vanenburg is a privately held Dutch company controlled by two brothers, Jan and Paul Baan. Baan, through a series of sales to affiliated concerns, reported sales that they knew to be misleading. Its filings with the SEC were supposedly in violation of the Generally Accepted Accounting Principles ("GAAP") for a period of several years.
ISSUES: Whether the Court possesses subject-matter jurisdiction over claims by the foreign parties against the defendants?
DECISIONS: The Court dismissed the action instituted by the foreign plaintiffs.
REASONING: Judge Green

II. SUBJECT MATTER JURISDICTION

Many members of the plaintiff class, including two of the lead plaintiffs, are foreign nationals who purchased Baan stock on foreign exchanges. The defendants contest this Court's jurisdiction over the claims by the foreign plaintiffs. Whether jurisdiction exists "over an action arising under the securities laws of the United States is a question of congressional intent, subject only to the broad limits set by the due process clause." . . . The intent of the Act was to protect American investors and American markets. . . . Courts have employed two tests, the "effects" test and the "conduct" test to determine whether jurisdiction exists over extraterritorial transactions. Plaintiffs allege jurisdiction over both tests. The conduct test may be satisfied by an allegation that fraud committed within the United States directly caused losses outside of the United States. . . . To satisfy the effects test, plaintiffs must allege that conduct outside of the United States has produced a substantial effect within the United States. . . .

Defendants do not draw a distinction between foreign plaintiffs who purchased their shares on foreign markets, and those who purchased their shares on American markets. However, a different analysis applies to these two groups, and they will be addressed separately.

A. The Conduct Test

The conduct test requires that 1) all the elements necessary to establish a violation of section 10(b) and Rule 10b-5 must have occurred within the United States, and 2) those fraudulent actions in the United States must directly cause the plaintiff's harm. . . . [P]laintiffs argue that much of the fraud took place in the United States, including the failure to adhere to GAAP, "deceptive disseminations," and "the channel misbehavior used by Baan to fraudulently boost reported sales and revenues." However, for the most part the complaint fails to specify where the alleged fraud took place. The only fraudulent actions alleged in the complaint to have taken place in the United States are Baan's filing of forms with the SEC, and perhaps Baan's press releases. To establish jurisdiction, plaintiffs must allege that Baan's filings with the SEC or other fraudulent actions in the United States were "a substantial or significant contributing cause of the decision to purchase stock. . . .

The complaint contains no allegations of specific reliance on those fraudulent acts which occurred in the United States. Instead, the complaint shows reliance through the "fraud on the market" doctrine. . . . Defendants do not challenge the plaintiffs' reliance on that doctrine, as applied to American purchasers. However, employing that doctrine to fulfill the requirements of the conduct test would extend the reach of the 1934 Act too far. It would allow a foreign plaintiff to sue a foreign defendant based on an extraterritorial transaction whenever that foreign defendant had filed a fraudulently misleading document with the SEC. . . .

B. The Effects Test

In *Schoenbaum v. Firstbrook* the Second Circuit applied the general rule that jurisdiction exists over "acts done outside a jurisdiction, but intended to produce and producing detrimental effects within it" within the context of the 1934 Act and the international securities markets. 405 F.2d 200, 206 (2d Cir. 1968). . . . In *Schoenbaum,* foreign defendants purchased the stock of a Canadian company in Canada, but the court found that those sales had an effect on the American plaintiffs, who held stock in the Canadian company. There was an effect in the United States because the Canadian company's shares traded on an American exchange, and that was enough to confer jurisdiction.

The Second Circuit later addressed the application of the effects test where some of the plaintiffs were foreign, and some were American. In that case, the court found that where acts within the United

States had not directly caused the plaintiff's losses (i.e., the conduct test had not been satisfied), the federal securities laws applied to losses from sales to American residents in the United States, but not to losses from sales to foreigners outside the United States. . . . In this case, plaintiffs argue that the defendants' acts had an effect in the United States because Baan shares trade in tandem on the world's markets, and therefore the value of Baan's shares owned by United States residents was affected. More specifically, the shares owned by the American plaintiffs were affected. However the *Bersch* court rejected the idea that generalized effects in the United States are sufficient to confer subject matter jurisdiction. The effects test only extends jurisdiction as to those American plaintiffs who are affected. . . . This case is different from *Bersch* in that the securities are traded on an American exchange. However, that fact only indicates there might be greater and more pervasive generalized effects in the United States; it does not show that those effects are related to the claims of the foreign plaintiffs. There is a presumption that Congressional legislation "is meant to apply only within the territorial jurisdiction of the United States." . . .

[The court dismissed the complaint of those plaintiffs who neither resided in the United States nor made their purchases therein.]

CASE QUESTIONS

1. If the foreign defendants alleged fraudulent activities that only moderately impacted investors in the United States, would the decision have been the same?
2. If the case had been decided in the 1940s, would the decision have been the same?

ABUSES IN LITIGATION: AMENDMENTS TO THE SECURITIES ACTS

There are a number of law firms whose specialty includes the initiation of litigation on behalf of alleged defrauded shareholders. Generally, such lawsuits result in a minimal amount of recovery for individual plaintiffs coupled with very sizable legal fees for the successful law firms. Such lawsuits often are extremely questionable, based generally on rosy predictions of future growth, alleged impending large orders, and other such comments. Company executives rarely state negative comments publicly about their companies unless clearly necessary to alert analysts and other interested persons. Congress, in an endeavor to lessen abusive litigation, came to the assistance of companies by the passage of the Private Securities Litigation Reform Act of 1995 (PSLRA)[12] and the Securities Litigation Uniform Standards Act of 1998.[13] The statutes made it much more difficult for attorneys to initiate litigation under the securities laws.

The Private Securities Litigation Reform Act of 1995

The PSLRA provided for safe harbors against *strike-suits,* defined as "shareholder derivative actions begun with [the] hope of winning large attorney fees or private settlements, and with no intention of benefiting [the] corporation on behalf of which [the] suit is theoretically brought."[14] 15 U.S.C. Section 78u-4(b)(1)-2 provides:

(b) Requirements for securities fraud actions
   (1) Misleading statements and omissions
      In any private action arising under this chapter in which the plaintiff alleges that the defendant—
      (A) made an untrue statement of a material fact; or
      (B) omitted to state a material fact necessary in order to make the statements made, in the light of the circumstances in which they were made, not misleading;
      the complaint shall specify each statement alleged to have been misleading, the reason or reasons why the statement is misleading, and, if an allegation regarding the statement or omission is made on information and belief, the complaint shall state with particularity all facts on which that belief is formed.
   (2) Required state of mind
      In any private action arising under this chapter in which the plaintiff may recover

money damages only on proof that the defendant acted with a particular state of mind, the complaint shall, with respect to each act or omission alleged to violate this chapter, state with particularity facts giving rise to a strong inference that the defendant acted with the required state of mind.

The following case is one of the first cases to review the application of the Private Securities Litigation Reform Act of 1995 to such an alleged strikesuit.

GREEBEL V. FTP SOFTWARE, INC.

194 F.3d 185 (1st Cir. 1999)

FACTS: FTP develops, markets and supports Internet and Intranet software for personal computers and networks. Plaintiffs alleged that from July 14, 1995 to January 3, 1996, the demand for the software was diminishing due to increasing competition from other companies entering into the same area of development. It was alleged that, although company executives knew of the company's struggle to keep pace with new technological developments, they engaged in alleged fraudulent schemes to inflate stock prices and failed to disclose the company's difficulties. A number of statements by the company's CEO were cited that claimed his belief that the company was doing well, that sales continued to be strong at home and abroad, that new products were being released, and other comparable comments. Some of the individual defendants connected with the company sold their shares for sizable profits. Thereafter, the company revealed that its fourth quarter earnings for 1995 would be less than expected. The stock declined from a high of $31.75 to $11.87, thereby precipitating the litigation.
ISSUE: Whether the plaintiff met the enhanced standards of pleading and proof under the PSLRA?
DECISION: The Court sustained the trial court's dismissal of the litigation stating that the plaintiffs did not meet the stringent requirements of the PSLRA.
REASONING: Judge Lynch
[The court recited the previously stated sections of the PSLRA.]

A. PLEADING STANDARDS FOR FRAUD ALLEGATIONS

The text of the Act requires now that any complaint alleging that a statement or omission is misleading must:

1. specify each statement alleged to have been misleading,
2. [specify] the reason or reasons why the statement is misleading,
3. and, if an allegation regarding the statement of omission is made on information and belief . . . state with particularity all facts on which the belief is formed. . . .

The effect of this is to embody in the Act itself at least the standards of Rule 9(b), Fed. R. Civ. P.

Before the PSLRA, a securities fraud claim had to meet the standards set by Rule 9(b). . . . Rule 9(b) provides that "in all averments of fraud or mistake, the circumstances constituting fraud or mistake shall be stated with particularity. Malice, intent, knowledge, and other condition of mind of a person may be averred generally." . . . This circuit has interpreted Rule 9(b) to require "specification of the time, place, and content of an alleged false representation." . . . "Even where allegations are based on information and belief, supporting facts on which the belief is founded must be set forth in the complaint. And this holds true even when the fraud relates to matters peculiarly within the knowledge of the opposing party." . . .

The PSLRA's pleading standard is congruent and consistent with the pre-existing standards of this circuit. . . . First, this court had already required a fraud plaintiff to specify each allegedly misleading statement or omission. . . . Second, this court has required a securities fraud plaintiff to explain why the challenged statement or omission is misleading by requiring that "the complaint . . . provide some factual support for the allegations of fraud." . . . This means that the plaintiff must not only allege the time, place, and content of the alleged misrepresentations with specificity, but also the "factual allegations that would support a reasonable inference that adverse circumstances existed at the time of the offering, and were known and deliberately or recklessly disregarded by defendants. . . . Finally, this court has required plaintiffs who bring their claims on information and belief to "set forth the source of the information and the reasons for the belief." . . .

B. PLEADING REQUIRED STATE OF MIND: CHARACTERISTIC FACT PATTERNS

Where a plaintiff can recover money damages on proof that a defendant acted with a particular state of mind, the PSLRA now requires a complaint to "state with particularity facts giving rise to a strong inference that the defendant acted with the required state of mind." . . . The "required state of mind" for liability under section 10(b) and rule 10b-5 is referred to as scienter.

The Supreme Court has defined scienter as "a mental state embracing intent to deceive, manipulate, or defraud." . . . [T]he Court explicitly reserved the issue of whether recklessness sufficed, saying "in certain areas of the law recklessness is considered to be a form of intentional conduct for purposes of imposing liability for some act." . . .

We have used a definition of recklessness articulated by the Seventh Circuit:

> Reckless conduct may be defined as a highly unreasonable omission, involving not merely simple, or even excusable, negligence, but an extreme departure from the standards of ordinary care, and which presents a danger or misleading buyers or sellers that is either known to the defendant or is so obvious the actor must have been aware of it.

The effect of the PSLRA on the standard for scienter has been much disputed. . . . We agree with those courts that hold that the PSLRA did not address the substantive definition of scienter. . . . The PSLRA does in fact discuss the role of "knowing" violations, and thus an aspect of scienter, in two different respects. The first concerns contribution; the second, "safe harbors" for defendants. As to contribution, the Act, through a new Section 21D(g), added a section to "preserve joint and several liability for persons who knowingly commit securities fraud, but otherwise to proportionately limit liability to the 'portion of the judgment that corresponds to the percentage of responsibility of that covered person.'" . . . The PSLRA specifies that:

> Any covered person against whom a final judgment is entered in a private action shall be liable for damages jointly and severally only if the trier of fact specifically determines that such covered person knowingly committed a violation of the securities law.

15 U.S.C. Section 78u-4(f)(2)(A). In turn "knowingly commits a violation of the securities laws" is defined (for 10b-5 purposes) as requiring "actual knowledge" that a representation is false or an omission renders a representation false. . . . The definition specifically excludes "reckless conduct" as a basis for construing a knowing commission of a violation. . . .

The "safe harbor" provisions of the Act similarly buttress the conclusion that the Act did not alter preexisting law defining scienter. The PSLRA adopted a statutory "safe harbor" by adding a new section 27A to the 1933 Act, 15 U.S.C. Section 77z-2, and a new section 21e to the 1934 Act, 15 U.S.C. Section 78u-5. The safe harbor has two alternative inlets: the first shelters forward-looking statements that are accompanied by meaningful cautionary statements. See U.S.C. Section 78u-5(c)(1)(A)(I). The second inlet is of importance here. It focuses on the state of mind of the defendant and precludes liability for a forward-looking statement unless the maker of the statement had actual knowledge it was false or misleading. See 78u-5(c)(1)(B). . . .

[The court then agreed with the trial court that the plaintiff failed to properly state the facts meeting the requirements of the PSLRA, and there was no clear showing of scienter in the evidence submitted by the plaintiffs.]

CASE QUESTIONS

1. How did the PSLRA modify the preexisting law and cases concerning antifraud litigation?
2. Do you agree that companies should be more insulated from liability than other potential defendants?

In *Schnell v. Conseco, Inc.*, 43 F. Supp. 2d 438 (S.D.N.Y. 1999), the U.S. district court dismissed a class action against Conseco and another for failure to meet the standards of the PSLRA. The plaintiff claimed that the defendants manipulated the market by artificially depressing the price of shares of a company in which the defendants owned a substantial amount of convertible debentures. The defendants allegedly made telephone calls to investors and disseminated false opinions of value of the corporation's stock. The court, after reciting the aforementioned sections of the act and Rule 10b-5, said that the PSLRA applies not only to misrepresentations and omissions but also to claims involving market manipulation. In order for the plaintiff to sue on a claim of market manipulation under the PSLRA, it "must allege: (1) damage, (2) caused by reliance on defendants' misrepresentations or omissions of material fact, or on a scheme by the defendants to defraud, (3) scienter, (4) in connection with the purchase or sale of securities, (5) furthered by the defendants' use of the mails or any facility of a national securities exchange."

The court further noted that the plaintiff failed to properly plead scienter, a requirement under the act. Scienter may be shown "by establishing a motive to commit fraud and an opportunity to do so" or, if the motive is not apparent, then a plaintiff can do so by "identifying circumstances indicating conscious fraudulent behavior or recklessness." In the within action, the court held that the plaintiff failed to show a fraudulent motive nor did it show any circumstances evidencing conscious misbehavior or recklessness by the defendants.

Recklessness in securities fraud cases is more than carelessness or gross negligence. It involves a conscious state of mind that is inherently deceptive or is so obvious that the person committing the act had to have been aware of it. In *Miller v. NTN Communications, Inc.* (No. 97-CV-1116 TW (JAH), 1999 U.S. Dist. LEXIS 8968 (S.D.Ca. 1999)) the district court found that NTN's concealment of details of personal loans, compensation agreements with generous benefits to the company's executives, and tax loans, and other failure to report truthfully the state of the defendant's financial affairs were sufficient to find scienter under the requirements of Rule 10b-5.

The Group Pleading Doctrine. Under Section 10(b) as amended, plaintiffs are required to allege that each of the defendants being sued made a material misstatement or omission. Aiding, abetting, or conspiring to make a material misstatement or omission does not satisfy the requirements of the statute.[15] As stated in the *Baan* case, "merely stating that all defendants were responsible for all of the misleading statements or omissions does not satisfy the requirements of the PSLRA".[16] With respect to the group leading, or group published, doctrine, the doctrine permits plaintiffs to rely on a presumption that the various documents either required to be filed by law, such as the prospectus, registration statement, annual and quarterly reports, as well as press releases and other group-published information is the product of all individuals directly involved in their preparation.

The courts are split as to whether such doctrine has been overruled by the PSLRA. Some courts have permitted the doctrine to be used as to those defendants holding a high position within the corporation, such as the directors (but not necessarily outside directors) and major officers who presumably were privy to confidential information and had to have been involved in the preparation and filing or releasing the documents.

Securities Litigation Uniform Standards Act of 1998

After the passage of the PSLRA, attorneys tried alternative methods of suing corporations by initiating proceedings under state blue sky laws. The abuses that the PSLRA sought to lessen simply carried over into state courts. As a result, Congress enacted the Securities Litigation Uniform Standards Act of 1998, which became law on November 3, 1998. It amended the Securities Exchange Act of 1934 to prevent a private party instituting certain covered class actions from suing in federal or state court based on the statutory or common law of any state that alleges "a misrepresentation or omission of a material fact" or the use of "any manipulative device or contrivance" concerning the purchase or sale of a covered security.[17] In the following litigation, the plaintiff sought to avoid the restrictions of the act by commencing a securities lawsuit in the California state court.

ABADA V. CHARLES SCHWAB & CO., INC.

68 F. Supp. 2d 1160 (S.D.Ca. 1999)

FACTS: Abada sued Schwab for himself and on behalf of all others similarly situated alleging violations of trade practices and violations of false and misleading advertising under California law, as well as allegations of fraud, deceit, negligent misrepresentation, and unjust enrichment. He claimed that after opening a securities account with the defendant, the latter delayed in processing certain trades thereby causing him financial injury. He purported to represent all investors having online accounts with the defendant on the day in question when the delayed transaction took place. Defendant filed a notice for removal of the case to federal court under federal law including that of the Securities Litigation Uniform Standards Act.

ISSUE: Whether the state law claims alleged in Plaintiff's complaint are *completely* preempted because they fall within the scope of the Uniform Standard's Act's limitations on class actions. . . .

DECISION: The Court determined that the said statute preempted state law.

REASONING: Judge Keep

A. SECURITIES LITIGATION UNIFORM STANDARDS ACT OF 1998

[The court recited the act as stated previously.] As a generality, covered class actions are those class actions involving common questions of law or fact brought on behalf of more than 50 persons or those actions brought on behalf of one or more unnamed parties. See 15 U.S.C. Section 78bb(f)(5)(B). A "covered security" is a security that satisfies the standards for a covered security specified in paragraph (1) or (2) of section 77r(b) of Title 15 of the United States Code "at the time during which it is alleged that the misrepresentation, omission, or deceptive conduct occurred." 15 U.S.C. Section 78bb(f)(5)(E). Generally speaking, a security is a covered security under 15 U.S.C. Section 77r(b) if it is listed, or authorized for listing, on the New York Stock Exchange, the American Stock Exchange, or on the Nasdaq Stock Market, or if it is a security issued by an investment company that is registered, or that has filed a registration statement, under the Investment Company Act of 1940. See 15 U.S.C. Section 77r(b). The relevant portion of the Uniform Standards Act reads:

> No covered class action based upon the statutory or common law of any State or subdivision thereof may be maintained in any State or Federal court by any private party alleging—
> (A) a misrepresentation or omission of a material fact in connection with the purchase or sale of a covered security; or
> (B) that the defendant used or employed any manipulative or deceptive device or contrivance in connection with the purchase or sale of a covered security. 15 U.S.C. Section 78bb(f)(1).

This limitation on securities fraud class actions is quite sweeping—it governs all "covered class actions" "based upon the statutory or common law of any State" with a few, limited exceptions for "preserved actions." See 15 U.S.C. Section 78bb(f)(1). The Uniform Standards Act further provides for the removal of covered class actions, as set forth in subsection (f)(1), from state court to federal district court:

> Any covered class action brought in any State court involving a covered security, as set forth in paragraph (1), shall be removable to the Federal district court in the district the action is pending, and shall be subject to paragraph (1). 15 U.S.C. Section 78bb(f)(2).

The legislative history shows that Congress sought to establish federal courts as "the *exclusive* venue for most securities class action lawsuits "involving nationally traded securities. . . . According to the House Report, the purpose of the Uniform Standards Act was to "prevent plaintiffs from seeking to evade the protections that Federal law provides against abusive litigation by filing suit in State, rather than Federal, court." . . . The House Report noted that one year after the passage of the Private Securities Litigation Reform Act of 1995 in which procedural and substantive protections against abusive and meritless "strike" suits in federal courts were implemented, the Securities and Exchange Commission reported a significant shift of securities fraud cases from federal to state court. . . . The purpose of these strike suits, according to the House Report, is to "extract a sizable settlement from companies that are forced to settle, regardless of the lack of merits of the suit, simply to avoid the potentially bankrupting expenses of litigating." . . . Thus, "in order to prevent certain State private securities class action lawsuits alleging fraud from being used to frustrate" federal objectives, Congress found it "appropriate to enact national standards for securities class action lawsuits involving nationally traded securities." . . . It appears that Congress's intention, then, with the exception of certain "preserved" actions, was to completely preempt state securities class actions alleging fraud or manipulation relating to covered securities when it enacted the Uniform Standards Act. . . .

C. PREEMPTION

[The court found that under the facts alleged by the plaintiff, the Uniform Standards Act was applicable and state law was preempted.]

CASE QUESTIONS

1. All states have blue sky laws. Does the statute and decision remove the power of states to regulate securities?
2. What was the wrong that Congress sought to correct by its legislation?

INSIDER TRADING

During the course of a company's business, diverse persons are privy to information about the company that may be highly beneficial or detrimental to the value of its stock. Unlike in some other countries globally, the securities acts and regulations in the United States provide civil and criminal penalties on insiders who take advantage of the secret information to gain sizable profits before the information is disclosed to the general public. Section 16(b) of the 1934 act permits a company to demand and recover any *short-swing* profit (defined as a profit received from a purchase and subsequent sale of stock or sale and later purchase at a lower price within a six-month period) by an insider of the company (officer, director, or over-10-percent beneficial owner).

Rule 10b-5 of the 1934 act, as has been stated, makes it unlawful to employ any manipulative or deceptive device in connection with the sale or purchase of securities. It includes the use of confidential insider information to trade in securities. There are both significant civil and criminal ramifications for violations of the act, including recovery of profits gained by the insider, injunctions, and criminal sanctions for provable willful serious violations. Tippees who are subject to sanctions include noninsiders who may have received confidential information from insider relatives, friends, and the like.

In *S.E.C. v. Cherif,* 933 F.2d 403 (7th Cir. 1991), Cherif was employed by the First National Bank of Chicago in its International Financial Department for an eight-year period until December, 1987, when his position was eliminated. When his employment was terminated, he retained his magnetic identification card used to enter the First Chicago building. Using fraudulent means to retain his card, he gained access to the building on nights and weekends and was able to gain insider, confidential information that he used for trading in a number of stocks in which First Chicago was a player. Profits from short-term securities totaled $247,000 for a 10-month period ending in February 1989. The SEC sought a temporary restraining order against Cherif, barring him from further violating the securities laws and for discovery against the said defendant.

With respect to Cherif's claim that the SEC wrongly relied on the misappropriation theory to establish violations of the statute, the court said that the theory was proper under Section 10(b) and Rule 10b-5. *Misappropriation* is defined as "one who misappropriates [material] non-public information in breach of a fiduciary duty and trades on that information." As such it violates the said section and rule.

The court cited the case of *Chiarella v. United States,* 445 U.S. 222, which held that corporate insiders and tippees of insiders come within Rule 10b-5:

> [A] person violates the rule when he or she buys or sells securities on the basis of material, non-public information and at the same time is an insider of the corporation whose securities are traded, . . . or a tippee who knows or should know of the insider's breach of duty. . . . The theory is that an insider owes a fiduciary duty to the corporation's shareholders not to trade on inside information for his personal benefit. . . . A tippee of an insider owes a fiduciary duty which is derivative of the duty owed by the insider. . . . The misappropriation theory extends the reach of Rule 10b-5 to outsiders who would not ordinarily be deemed fiduciaries of the corporate entities in whose stock they trade. The misappropriation theory focuses not on the insider's fiduciary duty to the issuing company or its shareholders but on whether the insider breached a fiduciary duty to any lawful possessor of material non-public information.

Williams Act

Tender offers also come with the 1934 act amended by the Williams Act of 1968. Section 13(d) requires any person who owns or purchases 5 percent or more of a class of stock coming with the Securities Exchange Act of 1934 to file a statement concerning such ownership with the SEC, with the stock exchange in which the transactions take place, and with the issuer, within 10 days of acquisition. The statute requires a person seeking to purchase shares by public invitation to the company's shareholders to file a statement with the SEC stating information including the background of the person making the tender, the source of funds, the reason for the purchase, the number of shares owned, and other related information. The target company may respond to such tender offer by recommendation to accept, reject, or remain neutral.

In *Mates v. North American Vaccine, Inc.,* 53 F. Supp. 2d 814 (D.Md. 1999), the plaintiff, a medical doctor and former director and president of the defendant Canadian corporation, was removed from the board of directors and was terminated from her employment therein. Among the grounds claimed by her in the ensuing litigation was that the defendants violated Section 13(d) of the said act. Defendants alleged that there was no private relief affordable under the act and that the plaintiff did not have standing to sue under the statute. The court decided that the plaintiff, in her individual capacity, did not have standing to bring a private action under Section 13(d). The court stated:

> Section 13(d) is derived from the Williams Act, which was passed in 1968 and subsequently amended in 1970 and 1977. Section 13 was enacted in response to the proliferation of the use of cash tender offers in hostile corporate takeovers. . . . The primary objective and impetus for Congress enacting this provision was to ensure that the investing public was provided full and fair disclosure and access to all pertinent information regarding any attempt to obtain control of a corporation by a cash tender offer or privately negotiated securities offer. . . . Congress believed that Section 13(d) would level the playing field between the shareholder/investor, the tender offeror, and the existing management of the target corporation. However, despite Congress's efforts to protect the shareholder and the potential investor with Section 13(d), it failed to explicitly provide for a private right of action to enforce the provision. . . .
>
> [The court cited the reasoning in *Nowling v. Aero Services International,* 752 F. Supp. 1304 (E.D.La. 1990), that said Section 13(d)] "was not to favor management or its adversaries but to insure that the share owning public, confronted by a cash tender for their stock, would have adequate information about the qualifications and intentions of the offering party before responding to the offer." . . . The Court finds the reasoning and decision in *Nowling* to be sound. Although Mates has attempted to distinguish herself from the third-party plaintiff in *Nowling* on the grounds that she allegedly did not have access to all of the pertinent information regarding the financing deal and that she was prevented from exercising her rights as a board member, the Court is not persuaded. The First Amended complaint indicated that Mates was well aware of the details of the financing deal prior to it being approved. In fact, Mates was present at the meeting where the deal was discussed and voted upon it. . . . The legislative history of Section 13(d) clearly evidences Congress's principal concern in designing the legislation was protecting unsuspecting investors, and not well-informed members of management who can adequately protect their own interests. . . .

What Is a *Tender Offer*?

In *SEC v. Carter Hawley Hale Stores, Inc.*, 760 F.2d 945 (1985), the court of appeals recited the eight-factor test that had been proposed by the SEC and that was adopted in *Wellman v. Dickinson*, 475 F. Supp. 783 (S.D.N.Y. 1979). The court said that the existence of a *tender offer* can be determined by examining the following factors:

(1) active and widespread solicitation of public shareholders for the shares of an issuer; (2) solicitation made for a substantial percentage of the issuer's stock; (3) offer to purchase made at a premium over the prevailing market price; (4) terms of the offer are firm rather than negotiable; (5) offer contingent on the tender of a fixed number of shares, often subject to a fixed maximum number to be purchased; (6) offer open only for a limited period of time; (7) offeree subjected to pressure to sell his stock; [and (8)] public announcements of purchasing program concerning the target company precede or accompany rapid accumulation of a large amount of target company securities.

In the *Carter Hawley* case, The Limited, an Ohio corporation, attempted to take over the defendant company by making a cash tender offer for over 20 million shares (55 percent) of CHH's common stock at $30 per share. It duly filed a schedule 14D-1, disclosing all pertinent information with the SEC. CHH announced its opposition and began a repurchase program shortly thereafter. After purchasing over 50 percent of the outstanding common shares, CHH terminated its purchases. The district court, affirmed by the court of appeals, held that the CHH repurchase program was not a tender offer because the eight-factor test had not been satisfied. There was no direct solicitation of shareholders; the repurchase therefore could not have involved a solicitation of a substantial percentage of the CHH shares; the purchase price offered was not a premium over the prevailing market price; the terms of the offer were not firm but rather constituted the purchase by CHH of shares in a number of transactions at many different market prices; the offer to purchase was not open for a limited time; and there was no overt pressure made upon shareholders to sell their shares to CHH.

COMMODITIES FUTURES

Fraudulent practices are also prevalent in the Internet sales and distributions in the commodities market. Commodities are governed by the Commodity Exchange Act, 7 U.S.C. Sections 1 et seq., and regulations promulgated pursuant to the statute by federal agency, the Commodity Futures Trading Commission (CFTC). Section 6b(a) of the act makes it unlawful "for any person, in or in connection with any order to make, or the making of, any contract of sale of any commodity for future delivery, made, or to be made, for or on behalf of any other person . . . (i) to cheat or defraud or attempt to cheat or defraud such other person." The following case concerns the use of computer software that allegedly analyzed transactions in the futures market.

CFTC V. VARTULI

228 F.3d 94 (2d Cir. 2000)

FACTS: The Commodity Futures Trading Commission ("CFTC") instituted an action against the defendant Vartuli and others claiming that the defendants violated the Commodity Exchange Act ("CEA") by manufacturing, selling, and advertising a computer program titled "Recurrence," that purported to analyze transactions in the futures market and give users "buy" and "sell" signals for the profitable trade of futures contracts. The customers had to pay a licensing fee to the defendant's corporation ("AVCO") in exchange for which they would receive the computer program, a market reporting service and instructions from the system. The system was sold for between $1500–$4500 and was advertised as a system for trading commodities futures. Use of the programs by customers resulted in substantial losses. The CFTC instituted the within action for solicitation fraud, fraud by a commodity trading advisor, and

fraudulent advertising under relevant sections of the Act.
ISSUE: Did the misrepresentations in the advertising by the defendant corporation come within the Act?
DECISION: The Court held that the statute governed the misrepresentations.
REASONING: Judge Sack

I. COUNT I: SOLICITATION FRAUD

. . . Vartuli argues that . . . any misrepresentations that were made in the advertising for Recurrence were made in connection with AVCO's sale of its software, not in connection with transactions in commodity futures engaged in by AVCO customers. We find this argument unpersuasive.

"By its terms, Section [6]b is not restricted . . . to instances of fraud or deceit 'in' orders to make or the making of contracts. Rather, Section [6]b encompasses conduct 'in or in connection with' futures transactions. The plain meaning of such broad language cannot be ignored." . . . And liability under Section 6b explicitly extends beyond "members[s] of the contract market" to "any person" engaging in conduct "in connection with" futures transactions. . . .

Recurrence was sold by the defendants as a system for trading futures contracts, a "currency trading system." The purpose and function of the software was to advise users what futures transactions to execute. AVCO implored users to "follow" signals from Recurrence "with no second-guessing." Purchasers of Recurrence were instructed by the defendants to undertake specific transactions entirely in reliance on it. Thousands of such transactions were in fact undertaken. Misrepresentations about Recurrence, the way it functioned, the risks involved in using it, and the results it would, produce were necessarily misrepresentations about all the trades directed by the recurrence system. The intended and direct link between the advertisements and the currency trading rendered any misrepresentations in the advertising "in connection with" the suggested futures transactions. . . .

II. COUNT II: FRAUD BY A COMMODITY TRADING ADVISOR

A. Statutory and Regulatory Framework

. . . Section 6o(1) [of the CEA] makes it unlawful for CTAs [Commodity Trading Advisors] or their associates:

(A) to employ any device, scheme, or artifice to defraud any client or participant or prospective client or participant; or
(B) to engage in any transaction, practice, or course of business which operates as a fraud or deceit upon any client or participant or prospective client or participant.

Regulation 4.41(a) prohibits CTAs from advertising in a manner that violates Section 6o(1). Regulation 4.41(b) prohibits any person from "present[ing] the performance of any simulated or hypothetical commodities account of a CTA" without a specific disclaimer. . . .

We conclude that AVCO meets the statutory definition of a CTA and affirm the district court's holding that AVCO violated the fraud provisions applicable to CTAs.

B. AVCO Is a Commodity Trading Advisor

A CTA is defined in Section 1a5(A) of the CEA, 7 U.S.C. Section 1a(5)(A).

The term "commodity trading advisor" means any person who—

(i) for compensation or profit, engages in the business of advising others, either directly or through publications, writings, or electronic media, as to the value of or the advisability of trading in—
   (I) any contract of sale of a commodity for future delivery made or to be made on or subject to the rules of a contract market; . . . or
   (II) for compensation or profit, and as part of a regular business, issues or promulgates analyses or reports concerning any of the activities referred to in clause (i).

Sections 1a(5)(B) and (C) combine to exclude certain classes of people and entities from this definition, however. Relevant for, our purposes, they exclude both "any news reporter, news columnist, or news editor of the print or electronic media," Section 1a(5)(B)(ii), and "the publisher or producer of any print or electronic data of general and regular dissemination, including its employees," Section 1a(5)(B)(iv), provided that "the furnishing of such [advisory services as described in Section 1a(5)(A)] . . . is solely incidental to the conduct of their business or profession," Section 1a(5)(C).

There is no dispute that . . . AVCO advised others through the electronic media, for profit, as to "the value or the advisability of trading in" futures contracts for Swiss francs and Japanese yen. . . .

[The court held that AVCO did not come within the said exclusions.]

C. Fraud Under 17 C.F.R. Section 4.41(b)

17 C.F.R. Section 4.41(b)(1) provides that:

> No person may present the performance of any simulated or hypothetical commodity interest account, transaction in a commodity interest or series of transactions in a commodity interest of a commodity pool operator, commodity trading advisor, or any principal thereof, unless such performance is accompanied by [a specific disclaimer].

The regulation further requires that the disclaimer be "prominently disclosed." 17 C.F.R. Section 4.41(b)(2). It applies to "any . . . advertisement . . . including the texts of . . . mass media presentations." 17 C.F.R. Section 4.41(c)(1).

It is undisputed that AVCO presented the performance of hypothetical or simulated accounts in advertisements without including the specific disclaimer. . . .

II. COUNT III: REGISTRATION AS A COMMODITY TRADING ADVISOR

A. Liability for Failure to Register

Count III of the complaint charges AVCO with violating 7 U.S.C. Section 6m(1) by failing to register as a CTA. The relevant provision of the Statute reads:

> It shall be unlawful for any commodity trading advisor or commodity pool operator, unless registered under this chapter, to make use of the mails or any means or instrumentality of interstate commerce in connection with his business as such commodity trading advisor or commodity pool operator.

[The court held that AVCO violated the act by not having registered with the commission and upheld the order of the district court that AVCO had to disgorge its ill-gotten gains.]

CASE QUESTIONS

1. When does a computer game that involves investment strategies become a security regulated by the Securities Acts?
2. Suppose there was a person who opened an office and gave similar advice to invitees, would the statute apply to such person?

THE FOREIGN CORRUPT PRACTICES ACT

For more than two decades, the United States has been acting virtually alone in combating international bribery of government officials by agents of domestic corporations. Twenty years after the enactment of the U.S. Foreign Corrupt Practices Act (FCPA) in 1977,[18] the Organization for Economic Cooperation and Development, under pressure from the United States and other sources, adopted a Convention on Combating Bribery of Foreign Public Officials in International Business Transactions (the OECD Convention). In Latin and South America, the Inter-American Convention Against Corruption was adopted and opened for signature on March 29, 1996 in Caracas, Venezuela (the IA Convention). In addition, there are other efforts to combat international bribery. The extensive treatment of this issue in this chapter is due to the provisions explicitly related to securities. We will review: (1) the major elements of U.S. law concerning bribery for foreign public officials; (2) the provisions of the OECD Convention and the IA Convention; and (3) review the other efforts under way to counteract the climate of dishonesty inherent in the international marketplace.

Background

The passage of the FCPA in 1977 was the result of the major scandals that erupted during and arising from (1) a combination of the large illegal corporate contributions to President Nixon's reelection campaigns; (2) the discovery of and the highly publicized Lockheed bribery of senior Japanese officials to obtain aircraft orders; and (3) the election of a deeply religious president, Jimmy Carter. The Securities and Exchange Commission discovered that over 400 corporations had acknowledged making illegal payments in excess of $300 million to public officials of other countries and to domestic political candidates and parties.[19]

A subsidiary, albeit not unimportant, aspect of U.S. concern was the view of the SEC that shareholders of bribing corporations were uninformed about the accounting processes used by companies to conceal such illegal payments. There was no accountability of the slush funds that, in part, were moneys allegedly paid to agents or so-called consultants.[20]

The Act's Provisions

Congress took a dual approach to address the problem of international bribery. The FCPA makes it unlawful for a U.S. issuer of securities required to be registered with the SEC or any person acting for such issuer, including shareholders or any person acting personally or on behalf of a domestic entity, to bribe a foreign public official, a foreign political party, or political candidate for the purpose of inducing such person to do or omit doing any act or decision in his or her performance of any lawful duty or to induce such person to use such influence to assist the U.S. person to obtain or retain business with the foreign governmental entity.[21] The statute covers both overt, direct bribes and bribes given by intermediaries, such as foreign agents. A *bribe* is any offer, gift, promise, or authorization to give anything of value to the foreign official, political party official, or political party candidate.

Persons Covered by the FCPA

The act is divided into two main sections: (1) "prohibited foreign trade practices by issuer;" and (2) prohibited foreign trade practices by domestic concerns.[22] The first section of covered persons is any issuer of securities within the jurisdiction of the SEC or any person required to file reports under the act, as well as any officer, director, employee, or agent of such issuer or stockholder acting on behalf of the issuer. Each covered person is prohibited from using the mails or other instrumentality of interstate commerce in order to bribe foreign public officials, as will be discussed.[23] The second section of covered persons involves "domestic concerns" and their officers and directors.[24]

Domestic concerns refers to any U.S. person (citizen, national, or resident) or business entity with a principal place of business within the United States or organized in any U.S. territory, possession, or commonwealth.[25] The definition in effect clarifies the restrictive definition given to covered persons in *United States v. McLean,*[26] wherein the court held that in order to convict an employee of a corporation for a violation of the act, the United States must first convict the employer for violation of the act. The prior plea of guilty by the employer (International Harvester Company) to a one-count bill of information charging conspiracy to violate the act did not suffice.

Another clarification of covered persons was noted in *United States v. Blondek, Tull, Castle, and Lowry.*[27] Two of the defendants, Castle and Lowry, charged with violation of the act were Canadian officials who allegedly received a $50,000 bribe from defendants Blondek and Tull to assure the acceptance of a bid for the sale of buses. The issue was whether foreign officials could be prosecuted as conspirators to violate the act, even though they could not be prosecuted for violation of the act because the statute clearly intended to and did exclude prosecution of foreign officials. The court held that the said officials could not be so held liable. In *Dooley v. United Technologies,* the court extended criminal liability to foreign persons by holding that foreign individuals acting as agents or in some other similar capacity for domestic concerns could be prosecuted under the act even though the act did not extend to foreign corporations per se.[28]

Enforcement

The responsibility for the enforcement of the antibribery provisions is given to the SEC with respect to issuers of securities and to the Department of Justice with respect to all other persons. Actual enforcement of the FCPA appears dependent upon the political party of the president. Enforcement was virtually ignored under Presidents Reagan and Bush and was revived substantially under President Clinton. After a decade of ignoring the act, the SEC instituted a civil enforcement action against a U.S. corporation (Triton Energy Corporation) for failure to maintain an adequate system of internal accounting controls to detect improper payments made to its business agent in Indonesia, which allegedly would be passed on to Indonesian government officials for favorable action in the award of contracts.[29]

Penalties

There are criminal and civil penalties for violation of the FCPA. Obviously, the more egregious the violation, the more likely criminal sanctions could be sought and imposed. For *willful violations,* wherein any person willfully and knowingly makes or causes to be made a false or misleading statement as to a material fact, the criminal sanction is up to a $1 million fine or up to 10 years in prison or both, and up to a $2.5 million fine for a non-natural person (such as a corporation, etc.).[30] There is no liability if the accused is able to prove that she, he, or it did not know of the act or regulations thereto.[31] For a willful violation of Section 30A(a), the issuer may be fined up to $2 million and is subject to a civil penalty of up to $10,000. The fine for any officer, director, shareholder, employee, or agent acting on behalf of the issuer is a fine of up to $100,000 and imprisonment of up to 5 years or both. A civil fine of up to $10,000 may also be imposed by the SEC to any officer, director, employee, or agent of an issuer or shareholder acting on behalf of the issuer. All such fines to individuals may not be paid by the issuer.

Comparable penalties may also be imposed upon any domestic concerns that violate the act. The fine is up to $2 million and a civil penalty of up to $10,000 may be imposed by the attorney general.

Determining if a person allegedly injured by the corrupt act may commence private litigation against the violator of the FCPA is somewhat in doubt. It appears that no private litigation may be commenced for violation of the accounting provisions of the act.[32] On the contrary, it may be possible for a private person to sue an offender under the Racketeer Influenced and Corrupt Organizations Act,[33] using the offense as a predicate act or under the Travel Act.[34]

Exceptions

Bribes for *routine governmental actions* do not come within the scope of the act. The definition of such actions refers to a foreign official who engages in:

(i) obtaining permits, licenses, or other official documents to qualify a person to do business in a foreign country;
(ii) processing governmental papers, such as visas and work orders;
(iii) providing police protection, mail pick-up and delivery, or scheduling inspections associated with contract performance or inspections related to transit of goods across country;
(iv) providing phone service, power and water supply, loading and unloading cargo, or protecting perishable products or commodities from deterioration; or
(v) actions of a similar nature.[35]

Not included within routine governmental actions are decisions by a foreign official to award new business or continue to do business or any action by a foreign public official who has discretionary power to encourage such decision making.[36]

Difficulty may arise when determining which acts constitute bribes. U.S. companies have become imaginative in their strategies to create good will without violating the statute. The vice chairman of Chubb Corporation, desiring a license to enter China's insurance market, instituted a $1 million program at Shanghai University to teach insurance, placing government officials as board members who were deciding upon its application. Companies offer junkets to Disney World and Las Vegas, use "facilitation" payments to speed application processing and customs clearance, hire public relations firms to pay journalists the equivalent of a week's pay to attend a company's conference, give allowances to visitors of the companies' plants, and other inducements. All of these, except possibly junkets unless directly tied to a marketing effort, do not appear to be violative of the act. On the contrary, hiring middlepersons to bribe officials would come within the scope of the act. A number of companies have resorted to buying contracts from purchasers of contracts who paid bribes to win the awards. This type of unlawful dealing is almost impossible to detect.[37] Due diligence is mandatory for U.S. firms who form contractual relationships abroad as, for example, with agents, distributors, representatives, and consultants.[38]

Affirmative Defenses

The FCPA was amended in the 1988 Trade Act to permit payments that are lawful under local law, that is, payments that are lawful under the laws and regulations (not merely practice) of the foreign country at issue.

Expenditures are permitted that are associated with product demonstrations or contract performance, that is, payments that are reasonable and bona fide expenditures (travel, lodging expense, etc., for a public official) connected to the execution or performance of a contract, promotion, demonstration, or explanation of products or services to execute a contract of a foreign government.

The burden of proving such defense falls on the person claiming such defense.

Statute of Limitations

The Statute of Limitations for both criminal and civil actions is five years.

1998 Amendments to the FCPA

As a result of the signing of the OECD Convention by the United States, it became necessary to incorporate amendments to the FCPA to expand its scope.[39] It is illegal not only to give bribes for the purpose or doing or omitting to do any act "in order to obtain or retain business" but now also extends the prohibition to the attempt by the supplier to obtain "any improper advantage." The language is somewhat broader that the prior prohibitions.

It is illegal to bribe foreign public officials defined as "any officer or employee of a foreign government or any department, agency, or instrumentality thereof, or any person acting in an official capacity for or on behalf of any such government or department, agency, or instrumentality."[40] The 1998 act expands covered persons to "public international organization" such as the World Bank, the U.N., and the International Monetary Fund (IMF).[41]

The act extended jurisdiction of its prohibitions over issuers of securities as stated before and over domestic concerns or their officers, directors, employees, agents, or shareholders acting on their behalf.[42] The amendments to the statute extend jurisdiction beyond domestic concerns to foreign companies and nationals engaged in foreign bribery some aspect of which took place within the United States.[43]

Foreign nations in the past have been wary of the United States extending its jurisdiction to acts committed by foreign nationals abroad but having an effect within the United States. These countries, particularly Western European states, not only refused to cooperate with the United States in investigative activities abroad but also prohibited their nationals to obey U.S. court mandates. The OECD Convention, however, mandates that each member states shall "to the fullest extent possible under its laws and relevant treaties and arrangements, provide prompt and effective legal assistance" to other states that have signed the convention. This assistance includes the furnishing of documents and information requested as well as the status and results of the request.[44] In addition, the OECD Convention provides the legal basis for the extradition of both nationals and foreign nationals from a member state to another requesting member state for prosecution under the agreement, having made the act of bribery of a foreign official an extraditable offense.[45] If a member state refuses to extradite its own national to a foreign member state, then it must take steps to prosecute the individual or business entity within its own country for the said violations.[46]

Amendments to the FCPA removed the unequal penalties assessed against U.S. nationals that were substantially greater than those assessed against foreign nationals acting as employees or agents of a U.S. concern. Before the amendments, only civil penalties could be asserted against such foreign nations; now all employees (foreign or U.S. citizens) are subject to the criminal and civil penalties of the statute.[47]

ELECTRONIC RECORDS AND SIGNATURES UNDER FEDERAL SECURITIES LAW

The Electronic Signatures in Global and National Commerce Act that went into effect on October 1, 2000, modified Section 3 of the Securities Exchange Act of 1934 by adding a section concerning electronic records and signatures. It states that a contract, agreement, or record and/or signature required by the securities law of the federal government or by any state to be in writing shall not be denied legal effect if it is an electronic record or signature. The validity also applies to electronic signatures on agreements between a broker, dealer, investment advisers, and customers.[48] The Federal Securities and Exchange Commission may prescribe regulations in accordance with these provisions, but such regulations may not favor or discriminate against any specific technology, method, or technique for the storage and maintenance of such records and signatures. The SEC may require that the records be filed or maintained in a specified manner and may require that contracts, agreements, or records relating to purchases and sales be manually signed. This provision of the law does not supersede and securities rule or regulation in effect on or before the effective date of the act.[49]

CONCLUSION

The securities laws enacted by Congress and later amendments and additional legislation have made the securities markets much more open and straightforward. A surprising amount of information can be garnered by a reading of the prospectus. The difficulty is that initial buyers often fail to become knowledgeable of their investments but rather succumb to a feeding frenzy like that recently experienced in Internet securities. The legislation does not guaranty or suggest that particular securities are good investments. It only seeks to make potential buyers knowledgeable of the facts stated in the investment circulars. Fraud does occur and will continue to take place. The former reliance upon the SEC, the U.S. Attorney General, and civil litigation to prevent such fraud becomes somewhat more dubious when the Internet becomes part of the mix in such transactions. The laws of the United States end at the borders. Prosecutions and civil litigation are as feasible in other countries as the degree of legal infrastructures that are in place. Internet investments will continue to have greater risk potential than domestic securities, where federal and state laws offer some degree of assistance.

The National Securities Markets Improvement Act of 1996 is concerned with incorporating the technological developments into the securities markets. A number of changes have taken place that will have a significant impact upon securities' transactions. According to the SEC's Report to Congress,[50] most domestic companies are now making their filings with the SEC electronically on the commission's EDGAR (Electronic Data Gathering, Analysis, and Retrieval) system. These companies publicize their business and financial information on the Internet. These developments will make capital markets more efficient by allowing participants almost instantaneous means of exchanging information and to effectuate trades. Electronic trading in secondary markets will become the norm. Information to individual investors will become as available as to institutional investors. The outlook for the future is extremely pronounced as to its beneficial aspects, but to maximize the benefits to investors it will be necessary to coordinate activities with foreign securities regulators.

Questions and Problems

1. A promoter seeks investors to pool their moneys to build a race car and have an expert driver compete in the NASCAR meets. Earnings, if any, from successful meets would be shared by the investors. Is this considered a *security*?
2. Does the acceptance of a filing by the SEC give potential investors any assurance that the security is a good investment? What assurances does the SEC seek to provide investors?
3. Why are banks, railroads, nonprofit organizations, and farmers' cooperatives exempt from the SEC mandates?
4. Are the securities laws under the exclusive jurisdiction of the federal government? Explain.
5. Compare the antifraud provisions of the Securities Act of 1933 with the Securities Exchange Act of 1934. Which act makes it more difficult for an alleged defrauded investor to prevail?
6. The SEC sued the Chinese Consolidated Benevolent Association, Inc. to prevent it from using the mails or instruments of interstate commerce to sell unregistered Chinese government bonds. The association is a New York not-for-profit corporation with a membership of 25,000 Chinese. In 1937, the Republic of China had authorized the issuance of $.5 billion of 4 percent Liberty Bonds. The association set up a committee not officially associated with the Chinese government, which engaged in mass meetings, newspaper advertising, and extensive mailings to purchase the Chinese government bonds, and it offered to act as agent for the transmission of money to Hong Kong and the delivery of bonds to the U.S. purchasers. The committee did not charge any sums for its services and did not receive a commission. The SEC objected and sought to prevent the sale of such securities through the mail. It did not object to the solicitation of contributions to the Chinese government or its citizens. The U.S. district court held in favor of the association, dismissing the action. The dismissal was appealed to the U.S. court of appeals. Decide whether the committee should have been prevented from engaging in such services without having registered as an issuer, underwriter, or dealer. *SEC v. Chinese Consolidated Benevolent Association,* 120 F.2d 738 (2d Cir. 1941).
7. Plaintiffs sued the defendant corporation and its individual officers, alleging Section 10(b) and 20(a) securities violations. Vantive sells and services customer relationship management software that enables field personnel to deliver service across the Internet and other channels. The company went public in 1995 at $6 per share, rising to $35 per share and dropping to $14.75 per share when the suit was commenced. The plaintiffs alleged fraud for knowingly issuing false and misleading statements about the company's competitive prospects and the growth of its work force. In addition, its forecast of revenues for 1998 and 1999 were

falsely stated. The company allegedly reported financial results by prematurely recognizing millions in revenues based on software licenses that would not be revenue producing until they were sublicensed. It also claimed it was hiring a sizable work force although in fact it was losing many of the hirees. When the stock began declining substantially in 1998 and 1999, the lawsuit was commenced. The corporation requested the court to dismiss the case, alleging that there was no proof of deliberate recklessness on the part of the corporation or its officers as required by the Private Securities Litigation Reform Act. Decide. *In re the Vantive Corporation Securities Litigation,* 110 F. Supp. 2d 1209 (N.D.Ca. 2000).

8. De Quijas and others sued Shearson/American Express, Inc., alleging violations of the Securities Act of 1933. The investors signed a customer agreement with the defendant broker that included a clause wherein they agreed that any dispute relating to the accounts between the parties would be resolved by arbitration unless it was found to be contrary to federal or state law. The plaintiffs sued in federal district court. Defendant claimed that any dispute arising between them concerning the accounts between the parties had to be submitted to arbitration. Decide whether the court must dismiss the case and have the parties resort to arbitration. *Rodriguez De Quijas v. Shearson/American Express, Inc.,* 490 U.S. 477 (1989).
9. Winans was a coauthor of a *Wall Street Journal* investment advice column, which influenced the market price of securities after the column was printed. The journal required that the information contained in the column was confidential prior to publication. Winans schemed with certain stockbrokers who were given advanced information concerning the column and purchased securities in anticipation of the impact the information would receive when the column was published. The brokers shared profits of $690,000 from gains made with Winans. The Journal was not a buyer or seller of the stocks traded. The issue is whether Winans and the stockbrokers violated Section 10(b) of the Securities Exchange Act of 1934 and Rule 10b-5, which make it a crime of fraud "in connection with" a purchase or sale of securities, as well as violating the federal mail and wire fraud statutes discussed in Chapter 5. Did Winans and the brokers violate the SEC Act of 1934? Did they violate the federal mail and wire fraud statute? *Carpenter v. United States,* 484 U.S. 19 (1987).
10. Turner Enterprises engaged in a promotional scheme called Dare to Be Great. It offered five plans in a self-improvement program, three of which would allow investors to earn money for inducing other persons to become part of the program. A purchaser of the plan had to pay $2,000 for which he or she received a tutelage of sales promotion and sales ability and which further entitled the person to sell three additional programs to other persons. For each sale, the said person would receive from $100–$900, depending on the program sold. There were additional such programs at higher investment costs. The main task of the investor was to lure people to Adventure Meetings, wherein they would be subject to intense sales pitches from the promoters. Is the scheme an *investment contract* coming within the Securities Act of 1933? *SEC v. Glen W. Turner Enterprises, Inc.,* 474 F.2d 476 (9th Cir. 1973).

Endnotes

1. The expression *blue sky* refers to the fraudulent sales of securities that had no assets or that had no potential value other than the blue sky above.
2. Other related statutes include the Securities Investor Protection Act of 1970, 15 U.S.C. Section 78aaa-77lll; the Trust Indenture Act of 1939, 15 U.S.C. Section 77aaa-77bbbb; and the Public Utility Holding Act of 1935, 15 U.S.C. Section 79-79z-6.
3. Pub. L. No. 96-477, 944 Stat. 2275.
4. Release No. 33-7644, July 14, 1998, which can be found at *www.sec.gov/rules/final/33-7644.txt.*
5. For a discussion of the within topic, see Lisa A. Mondschein, *The Solicitation and Marketing of Securities Offerings Through the Internet,* 65 Brooklyn L. Rev. 185 (Spring 1999); Robert A. Prentice, Vernon J. Richardson, and Susan Scholz, *Corporate Web Site Disclosure and Rule 10b-5: An Empirical Evaluation,* 36 A. Bus. L.J. 531 (Summer 1999); and Alyssa Hall

and Adam M. Schoeberlein, *Securities Fraud,* 37 Am. Crim. L. Rev. 941 (Spring 2000).
6. Rule 14a-3(a) provides: "No solicitation subject to this regulation shall be made unless each person solicited is concurrently furnished or has previously been furnished with a written proxy statement containing the information specified in Schedule 14A." Schedule 14A, Item 5(e) requires: "If to the knowledge of the person on whose behalf the solicitation is made a change in control of the issuer has occurred since the beginning of its fiscal year, state the name of the person or persons who acquired such control, the basis of such control, the date and a description of the transaction or transactions in which control was acquired and the percentage of voting securities of the issuer now owned by such person or persons."
7. *In Re Newbridge Networks Securities Litigation,* 767 F. Supp. 275, 281 (D.D.C. 1991).
8. *Basic Inc. v. Levinson,* 485 U.S. 224, 231–32 (1998).
9. *Lovelace v. Software Spectrum, Inc.,* 78 F.3d 1015, 1018 (5th Cir. 1996), cited in *McNamara v. Bre-X Minerals LTD,* 57 F. Supp. 2d 396, 404 (E.D.Tex. 1999).
10. See Prentice, Richardson, and Scholz, *Corporate,* p. 550.
11. Id. at p. 554.
12. Pub. L. No. 104-67, 109 Stat. 737 (1995).
13. 15 U.S.C. Section 77p and 15 U.S.C. 78bb(f) (Supp. 1996).
14. Henry Campbell Black, *Black's Law Dictionary: Definitions of the Terms and Phrases of American and English Jurisprudence,* 6th ed. (1990).
15. *Central Bank of Denver, N.A. v. First Interstate Bank of Denver, N.A.,* 511 U.S. 164, 177 (1994), cited in *In re The Baan Company Securities Litigation,* 103 F. Supp. 2d 1, 43 (D.D.C. 2000).
16. *In re The Baan Company Securities Litigation,* 103 F. Supp. 2d 1, 43 (D.D.C. 2000).
17. 15 U.S.C. Section 78bb(f)(1).
18. *The Foreign Corrupt Practices Act of 1977,* P.L. No. 95-213, 91 Stat. 1494, 15 U.S.C. Sections 78m(b), Id-1, Id-2, ff (1977), as amended 15 U.S.C. Sections 78m, 78dd-1, 78dd-2, 78ff (1988).
19. H. R. Rep. No. 640, 95th Cong., 1st Sess. 4 (1977).
20. Timmeny, *An Overview of the FCPA,* 9 Syracuse J. Int'l L & Com. 235 (1982), cited in Ralph H. Folsom, Michael Wallace Gordon, and John A Spanogle Jr., *International Business Transactions: A Problem-Oriented Coursebook,* 3d ed. (St. Paul: West, 1995), p. 669.
21. 15 U.S.C. Sections 78dd-1(a)(b) and dd-2(a)(1)(2)(3).
22. Id. Sections 78dd-1 and dd-2.
23. Id. Section 78dd-1(a).
24. Id. Section 78dd-2(a).
25. Id. Section 78dd-2(h)(1)(A)(B).
26. 738 F.2d 655 (5th Cir. 1984).
27. 741 F. Supp. 116 (D.N.D. 1990).
28. 803 F. Supp. 428 (D.D.C. 1992).
29. For a discussion of the case and the statute, see John F. X. Peloso, *SEC Rejuvenates Foreign Corrupt Practices Act,* New York Law Journal (May 2, 1997), *www.ljx.com/practice/intrade/0521fcpa.html.*
30. 15 U.S.C. Section 78ff(a).
31. Ibid.
32. See *Eisenberger v. Spectex Industries, Inc.,* 644 F. Supp. 48 (E.D.N.Y. 1986) and *Lewis v. Sporck,* 612 F. Supp. 1316 (N.D.Ca. 1985).
33. 18 U.S.C. Sections 1962–1968.
34. Id. Section 952(a)(3). See *United States v. Young & Rubicam, Inc.,* 741 F. Supp. 334 (D.Conn. 1990).
35. 15 U.S.C. Section 78dd-1(f)(3)(A)(i-v) and Section 78dd-2(h)(4)(A)(i-v).
36. Id. Section 78dd-1(f)(3)(B) and Section 78dd-2(h)(4)(B).
37. For a discussion of these and other practices, see Dana Milbank and Marcus W. Brauchli, *Greasing Wheels: How U.S. Competes in Countries Where Bribes Flourish,* The Wall Street Journal, September 29, 1995, p. 1.
38. For a discussion of due diligence, see Carl A. Valenstein and Rebecca S. Hartley, *The Foreign Corrupt Practices Act: International Due Diligence,* Arent Fox, *www.arentfox.com/features/international/duedil.html.*
39. For a discussion of the amendments, see Stanley S. Arkin, *Amendments to Foreign Corrupt Practices Act,* New York Law Journal, February 11, 1999, pp. 3, 7; and Reed Smith Bulletin 98-45, *International Anti-Bribery and Fair Competition Act of 1998,* December 1998, *www.rssm.com/pubs/client/bull9845.html.*
40. 15 U.S.C. Sections 78dd-1(f)(1) and Section 78dd-2(h)(2).
41. Id. Sections 78dd-1(f)(1)(A) 2(h)(2)(A) and 78dd-3(f)(2)(A).
42. Id. Sections 78dd-1(a) and 78dd-2(a).
43. Id. Section 78dd-3(a).
44. OECD Convention, Article 9.
45. Id. Article 10.
46. Id. Article 10(3).
47. 15 U.S.C. Section 78dd-3(a).
48. Section 301 of the act. Other enactments affecting securities law include the Public Utility Holding Company Act of 1935 and the Trust Indenture Act of 1939.
49. Id. Section 301(2)–(5).
50. *www.sec.gov/news/studies/techrp97.htm.*

CHAPTER

13 TAXATION OF INTERNET SALES

Chapter Outline

- Internet's Challenge to State Tax Revenue
- Types of Internet Taxes
- Electronic Commerce
- Power of States to Tax Interstate and Foreign Commerce
- Debate Concerning Sales Tax on Internet Sales
- The Internet Tax Freedom Act
- Alternative Measures for Congress to Enact
- U.S. Taxation of International Persons and Transactions
- International Taxation of Electronic Commerce: OECD Report
- Conclusion

The right of a country to tax its inhabitants and business enterprises is an inherent aspect of national sovereignty. Tax revenues provide the financial underpinnings for governmental services at the national, state, and local levels. In the early days of the new republic, tariffs formed the basis for federal expenditures. With the enactment of the Fourteenth Amendment to the Constitution in 1913, Congress was given the "power to lay and collect taxes on incomes, from whatever source derived, without apportionment among the several states." The primary basis of tax receipts is the income tax.

Individual states were left to their own devices to gain the money needed to pay for their expenditures. States could derive taxes from the *income* of its residents or from nonresidents doing business within a state. County, town, city, and village expenditures are most often based upon the taxation of *property* within their jurisdictions. A major area of taxation is the *consumption tax,* that is, a tax collected for the purchase or use of goods or services. Until recently, the imposition of a tax on the purchase of goods, which was collected by the merchant selling the goods, proceeded rather smoothly, resulting in few disputes concerning the legality thereof. Problems arose mainly in the collection of taxes from merchants who attempted to retain unlawfully a part or all of the sales taxes received from consumers. Jurisdictional issues did arise when individual states attempted to collect income taxes from companies doing business within the states on their worldwide income. Nevertheless, in the main, the right of states to collect taxes has proceeded unabated. In this chapter, the focus is on the right and ability of states to tax receipts that are derived from Internet transactions.

INTERNET'S CHALLENGE TO STATE TAX REVENUE

Internet sales are being conducted on a massive level in an almost boundless global environment. Subject to a country's customs laws and regulations, home shopping permits consumers to purchase virtually anything from the almost endless assortment of goods and services available worldwide. Internet merchants can discount goods because of the avoidance of the middleperson, storage and warehouse savings, the collection and transmittal of state and local taxes, and other factors. Systems have been instituted to provide payments by means of electronic cash. Money can be transferred from bank accounts to suppliers, just as credit cards, automatic teller machines, and wire transfers are utilized today for the similar purposes. The essence of the problem for state and local governments is the anticipated loss of revenue from such transactions.

State and local governments require the collection of taxes to fund the many programs they administer. Taxes account for police protection, education, services for the poor and disabled, transportation, and many other programs. The anticipated and actual loss of tax revenue, especially sales tax revenue, is causing great concern among the governors of the 50 states. The fear is manifold. It is not just the loss of revenue that governors fear but also the loss of control over their ability to promulgate and carry out the enforcement of laws, such as privacy laws, Internet regulations, and tax policy.

TYPES OF INTERNET TAXES

Internet taxes may be imposed as: (1) *access charges,* which are taxes paid by Internet service providers or telecommunications companies and charged to their users; (2) *sales or use taxes* for purchases of goods and services over the Internet; and (3) taxes charged for the downloading of software from the provider of such service. Prior to the passage of the Internet Freedom Act of 1998 (to be discussed), approximately 9 states had taxed Internet access charges, 45 states imposed a tax for sales of goods over the Internet, and about a third of the states taxed the downloading of information.[1]

A *sales tax* is defined as a tax that is levied on the sale of goods and services. There are three types of sales tax: a *vendor tax,* which is one imposed on the person doing business who is required to pay a tax based on the goods sold; a *consumer tax,* whereby the buyer pays the tax to the vendor who then transmits the tax to the governmental taxing authority; and a *combination vendor-consumer tax system,* wherein the vendor pays the sales tax to the governmental authority and passes it on to the purchaser of goods or services. In most cases, the buyer purchases the goods from the vendor, who adds the appropriate sales tax to the goods or services and pays the taxing authority. It is far easier to collect the tax from the relatively stationary vendor than from the far more numerous and less traceable consumer purchasers. A sales tax imposed on an out-of-state merchant for sales or services provided to the forum state is known as a *use* tax.[2]

Sales tax revenues constitute some one-quarter of all state tax revenues. It is a regressive tax because it is not based on the annual earnings of a person but rather on the purchases made by the consumer. Inasmuch as poorer persons spend a higher percentage of their earnings on purchases, they contribute more in taxes in relative terms than their wealthier counterparts. At least until the year 2002, out-of-state Internet sales will not be subject to sales or use taxes. The U.S. Department of Commerce estimated that online retail sales of tangible goods were in excess of $5.3 billion for the fourth quarter of 1999. Retail sales over the Internet are expected to rise from 2 percent in the late 1990s to 20 percent or more in the first decade of the new century.[3] Loss of sales tax revenue from such sales would likely have a significant impact upon state programs.

There is no general consensus as to what policies states should adopt to replace the anticipated loss of such revenue within the states. There is substantial disagreement as to which policies the federal government should promulgate. For example, Governor James S. Gilmore III of Virginia, a Republican and the chairman of the Advisory Commission on Electronic Commerce, wants the federal government to retain the tax-free Internet policy and increase grants to states to cope with the anticipated loss of revenue.[4] Other legislators, particularly state and local officials, are vehemently opposed to the prohibition of taxes on Internet transactions.

ELECTRONIC COMMERCE

The Internet, especially the World Wide Web, has created a new environment for marketing and sales of goods and services globally. *Electronic commerce* is the use of the new technologies for such activities.[5] It differs from other media because consumers are now able to communicate instantaneously to all sectors of the world at virtually no cost. Whereas consumer transactions in the past have been almost exclusively local or national in nature, the new medium enables consumers to buy virtually anything by accessing merchants internationally by means of a modem in a home computer. Companies like Amazon.com, have enabled purchasers of reading materials to buy almost any book at a discount from home without payment of a sales or use tax. The advantages to the consumer are obvious. A busy person can avoid the time to travel to a bookstore and can shop at any hour of the day or night from sellers globally, generally at a lesser cost, from an almost unlimited selection. Medical, legal, architectural, and an almost infinite variety of services are now available online. Stock trades, banking, and visual communications are accessible. Managers of shopping malls are so frightened by the new technologies that many of them have placed restrictions and prohibitions of selling goods online upon their retail stores.

Internet sales at this juncture, as stated previously, are not subject to sales or use taxes. Such taxes generally range from 0.875 percent to 11 percent of the cost of the goods. There are many variations not only among the states but also in local jurisdictions within the state. In New York State, for example, the sales tax varies from county to county and from city to city. A major issue that arises is whether states may impose such taxes upon merchants who sell from out-of-state to a local area. This issue and other related attempts by states to regulate interstate activity has given rise to numerous cases that the U.S. Supreme Court and other courts have had to resolve. A further issue is whether the Internet, in general, should remain free from state and local taxation. In the discussion that follows, we will examine the right of states to tax in-state sales of goods and services emanating from without the state, and we will follow that with a discussion of the current debate and status of Congressional enactments concerning the taxation of Internet sales.

POWER OF STATES TO TAX INTERSTATE AND FOREIGN COMMERCE

The major U.S. Constitutional provisions applicable to our discussion are given here.

Article 1, Section 8 specifically grants Congress the power "[t]o regulate Commerce with Foreign Nations, and among the several States, and with the Indian Tribes."

The Fifth Amendment provides: "No person shall . . . be deprived of life, liberty, or property, without due process of law."

The Fourteenth Amendment, Section 1 states, "nor shall any State deprive any person of life, liberty, or property, without due process of law."

Sales and Use Taxes

Approximately 45 states and some 7,600 local governments have enacted sales and/or use taxes.[6] Whether states could impose taxes on interstate commerce was left to Congressional enactments and to judicial interpretations based upon the previously cited Article 1, Section 8 of the Constitution. Earlier decisions by the U.S. Supreme Court appeared to give the federal government exclusive domain to tax interstate commercial activities but, gradually, the Court left it to Congress to determine whether such taxing authority was to be exclusively federal or shared with the states.[7] In the past, businesses had specific physical locations. State and local governments could tax such entities if they were either located within the borders of the governments or did business substantially in the locality. The Internet, however, presents governments with an almost borderless universe. The old test of making the right to tax by state and local governments based upon the substantial or actual presence of the seller of goods or services no longer applies to the new technology.

Survey of Cases Concerning Taxes in Interstate Commerce

Previously, in Chapter 2, we discussed the constitutional issues, particularly the due process clause of the Fifth and Fourteenth Amendments, concerning the jurisdiction of state courts to hear and determine cases involving out-of-state parties. In order for a tax to meet constitutional mandates, the out-of-state person must have a substantial nexus with the taxing state to avoid violating the commerce (Article 1, Section 8) and the due process clauses (Fifth and Fourteenth Amendments). Earlier decisions of the U.S. Supreme Court placed major restrictions on the power of state and local governments to tax interstate commercial activity. As stated in *Freeman v. Hewit*, 329 U.S. 249 (1946) at 252:

> [T]he Commerce Clause was not merely an authorization to Congress to enact laws for the protection and encouragement of commerce among the States, but by its own force created an area of trade free from interference by the States. In short, the Commerce Clause even without implementing legislation by Congress is a limitation upon the power of the States. . . . This limitation on State power . . . does not merely forbid a State to single out interstate commerce for hostile action. A State is also precluded from taking any action which may fairly be deemed to have the effect of impeding the free flow of trade between States. It is immaterial that local commerce is subjected to a similar interference.

Thus, the rule of the Court through the 1950s was that a state could tax: (1) local commercial activity; (2) persons having a residence within the state; and (3) income derived by residents from interstate activity. A state could not impose a direct tax on interstate sales even if the tax was fairly apportioned and was nondiscriminatory. Gradually, the Court began to modify the rigid analysis to one that examined a number of factors in determining whether a state sales tax or use tax was lawful. The modification, while allowing a broader expanse of states' power to tax interstate activity, did not permit open-ended taxation. There are parameters beyond which the attempts by states will be found unconstitutional. The following case illustrates the then-clear boundaries of constitutional prohibition.

NATIONAL BELLAS HESS, INC. V. DEP'T OF REVENUE

386 U.S. 753 (1967)

FACTS: National is a mail order house having its principal place of business in North Kansas City, Missouri, and is licensed to do business solely in Missouri and in Delaware where it was incorporated. The State of Illinois, Department of Revenue, sued and received a court judgment requiring National to collect and pay use taxes to the State. National had no office, distribution or sales house, warehouse, or other place of business in Illinois. It did not have an agent, salesperson, canvasser or other representative in the State to sell or take orders, receive payments or service the sold merchandise. It had no tangible property within the State, no telephone listing, and did not advertise in Illinois. All contacts were made by mail or by common carrier. Its sole activity in Illinois was to send bi-annual catalogues and mailing flyers to past and potential customers throughout the nation, including Illinois. Orders were mailed by the customers and accepted in Missouri.

The Illinois statute imposed the use tax upon a "retailer maintaining a place of business in this State." A retailer was defined as any retailer "Engaging in soliciting orders within this State from users by means of catalogues or other advertising, whether such orders are received or accepted within or without this State."

ISSUE: Whether the user tax violated the Due Process Clause of the Fourteenth Amendment of the Constitution and created an unconstitutional burden upon interstate commerce?

DECISION: The U.S. Supreme Court held that the tax was unconstitutional.

REASONING: Justice Stewart

[The Court discussed the relationship between the commerce clause (Article 1, Section 8) and the Fourteenth Amendment of the Constitution.] These two claims are closely related. For the test whether a particular state exaction is such as to invade the exclusive authority of Congress to regulate trade between the States, and the test for a State's compliance with the requirements of due process in this area are similar. . . . As to the former, the Court has held that "State taxation falling in interstate commerce . . . can only be justified as designed to make such commerce bear a fair share of the cost of the local government whose protection it enjoys." . . . And in determining whether a state tax falls within the confines of the Due Process Clause, the Court has said that the "simple but controlling question is whether the state has given anything for which it can ask return. . . . The same principles have been held applicable in determining the power of a State to impose the burdens of collecting use taxes upon interstate sales. Here, too, the Constitution requires "some definite link, some minimum connection, between a state and the person, property or transaction it seeks to tax. . . ."

In applying these principles the Court has upheld the power of a State to impose liability upon an out-of-state seller to collect a local use tax in a variety of circumstances. Where the sales were arranged by local agents in the taxing State, we have upheld such power. . . . We have reached the same result where the mail order seller maintained local retail stores. . . . In those situations the out-of-state seller was plainly accorded the protection and services of the taxing State. . . . [The Court's furthest constitutional reach allowing a state to collect a use tax was] *Scripto, Inc. v. Carson,* 362 U.S. 207. There we held that Florida could constitutionally impose a Georgia seller the duty of collecting a state use tax upon the sale of goods shipped to customers in Florida. In that case the seller has "10 wholesalers, jobbers, or 'salesmen' conducting continuous local solicitation in Florida and forwarding the resulting orders from the State to Atlanta for shipment of the ordered goods." . . .

But the Court has never held that a State may impose the duty of use tax collection and payment upon a seller whose only connection with customers in the State is by common carrier or the United States mail. . . .

Indeed, it is difficult to conceive of commercial transactions more exclusively interstate in character than the mail order transactions here involved. And if the power of Illinois to impose tax burdens upon National were upheld, the resulting impediments upon the free conduct of its interstate business would be neither imaginary nor remote. For if Illinois can impose such burdens, so can every other State, and so, indeed can every municipality, every school district, and every other political subdivision throughout the Nation with power to impose sales and use taxes. . . . The many variations in rates of tax . . . in allowable exemptions, and in administrative and record-keeping requirements . . . could entangle National's interstate business in a virtual welter of complicated obligations to local jurisdictions with no legitimate claim to impose "a fair share of the cost of the . . . local government."

The very purpose of the Commerce Clause was to ensure a national economy free from such unjustifiable local entanglements. Under the Constitution, this is a domain where Congress alone has the power of regulation and control.

CASE QUESTIONS

1. Could the federal government tax the entity and give the proportionate share to the state?
2. What business events must take place within Illinois before it could tax National?

A decade later in 1977, in *Complete Auto Transit, Inc. v. Brady,* 430 U.S. 274 (1977), the U.S. Supreme Court had occasion to decide whether the state of Mississippi could tax a Michigan motor carrier for General Motors Corporation. The vehicles were sent by railroad to Jackson, Mississippi, where they were loaded onto Complete Auto Transit's trucks for delivery to Mississippi dealers. Complete claimed that the in-state transportation was part of an interstate movement and, therefore, it could not be required to pay a tax on its in-state gross income.

The Court held unanimously that the tax was constitutional. There is no absolute immunity for interstate commerce. "It was not the purpose of the commerce clause to relieve those engaged in interstate commerce from their just share of state tax burden even though it increases the cost of doing business." The Court announced a bright-line four-prong test to determine the validity of a state tax with respect to the commerce clause, namely, whether the tax (1) is applied to an activity with a substantial nexus with the taxing state; (2) is fairly apportioned; (3) does not discriminate against interstate commerce; and (4) is fairly related to the services provided by the state.[8]

After the *Complete Auto* case, there were significant changes in the commercial landscape, including the increasing use of computer technology to engage in business. The question then arose whether the decision in the *National Bellas Hess* case was obsolete. In the following action, the U.S. Supreme Court was presented with a state tax issue having a great resemblance to the *National* litigation. Note the discussion of the difference between the application of the due process clause and the commerce clause.

QUILL CORP. V. NORTH DAKOTA

504 U.S. 298 (1992)

FACTS: Quill is a Delaware corporation engaged in selling office equipment and supplies with offices and warehouses in Illinois, Georgia, and California. It had no employees in North Dakota, little or no property in the State, and solicited business through catalogs, flyers, and advertisements in national publications and by telephone calls. It had $200 million in sales, $1 million of which was made to 3,000 customers in North Dakota. Quill is the sixth largest seller of office supplies in the State and delivered all merchandise by mail or common carrier. North Dakota imposed a use tax on property purchased for storage, use, or consumption in the State. The retailer, defined as "every person who engages in regular or systematic solicitation of a consumer market in the state," was required to collect the tax from purchasers in North Dakota and remit to the State. The North Dakota Supreme Court said that Quill was subject to the law because the mail order business had gone from an inconsequential market niche in 1967 (the year of the National decision) to a "staggering figure of $183.3 billion in 1989." Moreover, Quill licensed a computer software program to some of the State's customers that enabled them to check on Quill's inventories and prices and place orders.
ISSUE: Whether in light of the *Complete* decision, the Illinois statute violated the Due Process Clause of the Fourteenth Amendment and/or the Commerce Clause of the Constitution?
DECISION: The Court held in favor of Quill finding the statute did violate the Constitution.
REASONING: Justice Stevens
[Applying the *Complete Auto* test, *Bellas Hess* was held to be an unconstitutional infringement because of the lack of a sufficient nexus with the state of Illinois. Similarly, in the within case, there was also a lack of sufficient nexus with the state of North Dakota. The Court sought to clarify the difference between the nexus requirements of the due process and commerce clauses of the U.S. Constitution. It stated:]

Due process centrally concerns the fundamental fairness of governmental activity. Thus, at the most general level, the due process nexus analysis requires that we ask whether an individual's connections with a State are substantial enough to legitimate the State's exercise of power over him. We have, therefore, often identified "notice" or "fair warning" as the analytic touchstone of due process nexus analysis. In contrast, the Commerce Clause and its nexus requirement are informed not so much by concerns about fairness for the individual defendant as by structural concerns about the effects of state regulation on the national economy. Under the Articles of Confederation, state taxes and duties hindered and suppressed interstate commerce; the Framers intended the Commerce Clause as a cure for these structural ills. . . . It is in this light that we have interpreted the negative implications of the Commerce Clause. Accordingly, we have ruled that that Clause prohibits discrimination against interstate commerce . . . and bars state regulations that unduly burden interstate commerce. . . .

The *Complete Auto* analysis reflects these concerns about the national economy. The second and third parts of that analysis, which require fair apportionment and non-discrimination, prohibit taxes that pass an unfair share of the tax burden unto interstate commerce. The first and fourth prongs, which require a substantial nexus and a relationship between the tax and state-provided services limit the reach of state taxing authority so as to ensure that state taxation does not unduly burden interstate commerce. . . . Thus, the "substantial nexus" requirement is not, like due process "minimum contacts" requirement, a proxy for notice, but rather a means for limiting state burdens on interstate commerce. Accordingly, contrary to the State's suggestion, a corporation may have the "minimum contacts" with a taxing State as required by the Due Process Clause, and yet lack the "substantial nexus" with that State as required by the Commerce Clause.

. . . "[W]e expressly rejected a 'slightest presence' standard of constitutional nexus." We therefore conclude that Quill's licensing of software in this case does not meet the "substantial Nexus" requirement of the Commerce Clause.

CASE QUESTIONS

1. What is meant by *substantial nexus*?
2. What if salespersons were sent into the state to solicit business? Would such activity suffice to allow North Dakota to tax the entity?

In a case heard on the same day as the *Quill* case, *Wisconsin Department of Revenue v. William Wrigley, Jr., Co.*, 505 U.S. 214 (1992), a manufacturer of chewing gum, based in Chicago, sold gum nationwide through a marketing system that divided the country into districts, regions, and territories. Included among the regions was Milwaukee, Wisconsin. The state of Wisconsin sought to impose a tax on Wrigley's income derived therein. The U.S. Supreme Court held in favor of Wisconsin even though Wrigley did not own or lease real property in Wisconsin; did not operate any manufacturing, training, or warehouse facility; had no telephone or bank account therein; and all orders were filled by common carrier outside Wisconsin. Wrigley, however, did replace stale gum by sales representatives in the latter's possession, stored gum, had display racks and promotional literature, rented space in Wisconsin for such storage, conducted regional manager's recruitment, and trained and evaluated employees in Wisconsin, and the regional manager located in Wisconsin intervened in credit disputes. The Court held there was a sufficient nexus beyond mere solicitation of orders to permit the taxation of the in-state income.

A decade later, the Supreme Court was called upon to determine whether the imposition by the state of Illinois of a 5 percent tax on interstate telecommunications violated the commerce clause of the Constitution. The analysis, as stated in the following case, appears to be reflecting the current view that the Court has moved away from a due process examination to one that is factual in nature. According to such view, the Court will examine the facts in a given case to determine whether the commerce clause of the Constitution has been violated.

GOLDBERG V. SWEET

488 U.S. 252 (1989)

FACTS: In 1985, Illinois enacted the Telecommunications Excise Tax Act wherein a five percent tax was imposed on the gross charge of interstate telecommunications that originated in Illinois and was charged to an Illinois service address, irrespective of where the telephone call was billed or paid. It also imposed an identical tax on intrastate telecommunications. It also allowed a credit to any taxpayer that could prove that s/he paid a tax in another state for the identical call. The credit was inserted in the Act to prevent double taxation for the same telephone call.

ISSUE: Whether the Illinois tax on interstate telecommunications violated the commerce Clause of the U.S. Constitution?

DECISION: The Court found the tax to be constitutional.

REASONING: Justice Marshall

This Court has frequently had occasion to consider whether state taxes violate the Commerce Clause. The wavering doctrinal lines of our pre-*Complete Auto* cases reflect the tension between two competing concepts: the view that interstate commerce enjoys a "free trade" immunity from state taxation; and the view that businesses engaged in interstate commerce may be required to pay their own way. . . . *Complete Auto* sought to resolve this tension by specifically rejecting the view that the States cannot tax interstate commerce, while at the same time placing limits on state taxation of interstate commerce. . . . Since the *Complete Auto* decision we have applied its four-pronged test on numerous occasions. We now apply it to the Illinois tax.

As all parties agree that Illinois has a substantial nexus with the interstate telecommunications reached by the Tax Act, we begin our inquiry with apportionment, the second prong of the *Complete Auto* test....

[W]e are mindful that the central purpose behind the apportionment requirement is to ensure that each State taxes only its fair share of an interstate transaction.... But "we have long held that the Constitution imposes no single [apportionment] formula on the States...." Instead, we determine whether a tax is fairly apportioned by examining whether it is internally and externally consistent....

To be internally consistent, a tax must be structured so that if every State were to impose an identical tax, no multiple taxation would result.... We conclude that the Tax Act is internally consistent, for if every State taxed only those interstate phone calls which are charged to an in-state service address, only one State would tax each interstate telephone call....

The external consistency test ask whether the State has taxed only that portion of the revenues from the interstate activity which reasonably reflects the in-state component of the activity being taxed....

[The Court held that the tax did meet the test.] The tax at issue has many of the characteristics of a sales tax. It is assessed on the individual consumer, collected by the retailer, and accompanies the retail purchase of an interstate telephone call. Even though such a retail purchase is not a purely local event since it triggers simultaneous activity in several States ... the Tax Act reasonably reflects the way that consumers purchase interstate telephone calls.

We believe that only two States have a nexus substantial enough to tax a consumer's purchase of an interstate telephone call. The first is a State like Illinois which taxes the origination or termination of an interstate telephone call charged to a service address within that State. The second is a State which taxes the origination or termination of an interstate telephone call billed or paid within that State....

[The Court found only a limited possibility of multiple taxation.] To the extent that other States' telecommunications taxes pose a risk of multiple taxation, the credit provision contained in the Tax Act operates to avoid actual multiple taxation....

In sum, we hold that the Tax Act is fairly apportioned. Its economic effect is like that of a sales tax, the risk of multiple taxation is low, and actual multiple taxation is precluded by the credit provision....

We next turn to the third prong of the *Complete Auto* test, which prohibits a State from imposing a discriminatory tax on interstate commerce.... [T]he economic burden of the Illinois telecommunications tax falls on the Illinois telecommunications consumer, the insider who presumably is able to complain about and change the tax through the Illinois political process. It is not the purpose of the Commerce Clause to protect residents from their own state taxes.

Finally, we reach the fourth prong of the *Complete Auto* test, namely, whether the Illinois tax is fairly related to the presence and activities of the taxpayer within the State.... The purpose of this test is to ensure that a State's tax burden is not placed upon persons who do not benefit from services provided by the State....

The tax, which may be imposed on a particular interstate transaction, need not be limited to the cost of the services incurred by the State on account of that particular activity.... On the contrary, "interstate commerce may be required to contribute to the cost of providing *all* government services, including those services from which it arguably receives no direct benefit." ... Indeed ... we noted that a taxpayer's receipt of police and fire protection, the use of public roads and mass transit, and other advantages of civilized society satisfied the requirement that the tax be fairly related to the benefits provided by the State to the taxpayer.

In summary, in order for a state to impose a sale or use tax upon goods or services from outside the state, there has to be a sufficient nexus that satisfies both the Due Process and Commerce clauses of the Constitution. Once it is determined that a state may impose such a tax, the next issue is whether Internet sales should be taxed?

CASE QUESTIONS

1. If a state cannot tax interstate commerce activities, why was the tax permitted in the within case?
2. Should there be a national sales tax that becomes proportionately divided among the states?

Unlike sales taxes, corporations have a safe harbor statute, P.L. 86-272, 15 U.S.C. 381(a) (1959), wherein a state may not subject a foreign corporation to a tax on or measured by net income derived within the state from interstate commerce if the only business activities within the state by or on behalf of such foreign corporations are the solicitations of orders for sales of tangible personal property, where the orders are sent out of state for approval or rejection, and are filled by shipment or delivered from outside the state. The statute protects only tangible personal property, not intangible property, including electronic commerce.

DEBATE CONCERNING SALES TAX ON INTERNET SALES

Arguments in Favor of a Sales Tax

There are sound arguments both for and against the Internet sales tax. Legislators, businesspeople, and local administrators offer the following reasons that Internet sales should be taxed.

- Sales taxes account for about one-fourth of the income of state and local governments ($150 billion). The elimination or extensive diminution of such taxes will seriously jeopardize necessary governmental programs such as police, fire, and other public programs.
- Failures to impose a tax on Internet sales and services will seriously jeopardize local merchants who are required to collect the tax on in-state sales. The tax moratorium is "a disguised subsidy that favors one type of business over another."[9]
- A major fear of antitax proponents is the enormous burden that the many taxing jurisdictions, with their multiple types of taxation, may have on e-commerce. Such argument may have little merit if a system could be set up whereby intermediaries collect taxes from customers at the point of sale, which would be transmitted to the appropriate taxing agency.

Arguments Against Imposition of Sales Tax

Others are against taxing Internet sales.[10]

- There is a serious risk that the various governmental authorities may apply inconsistent taxes leading to quixotic taxation, including the problem of double taxation. With over 7,600 taxing authorities in the United States alone, the potential burden on multistate sellers could seriously endanger electronic commerce. Sellers receive little or no money for collection of the taxes and have to be aware of the rates, exemptions, and requirements of each taxing entity.
- There is a serious question whether the use of the Internet diminishes or *increases* sales tax collection. The claim made is that the Internet is opening new markets for brick-and-mortar businesses, leading to more jobs, better wages, and a stronger economy.[11]
- Government does not need the added income from the imposition of sales tax. Electronic commerce will increase tax revenues through the expansion of the economy. Added taxes will cause companies to relocate to markets in a more favorable tax forum.
- State and local governments will more than make up the loss of sales tax revenues (estimated at $10 billion annually) by the increase in income and corporate taxes from increased economic activity.[12]
- The expansion of electronic commerce and information technologies will benefit Americans more than programs funded by the added taxes.
- The imposition of sales and use taxes will hinder the growth of electronic commerce, thereby limiting job creation.
- Freeing Internet sales to consumers abroad from taxation will disproportionately benefit U.S. merchants inasmuch as the United States is the leader in the use of the new technologies. This would apply particularly to foreigners whose governments tax domestic electronic sales.[13]
- If sales taxes are imposed on electronic commerce, they should be easy for the local retailer to collect.
- The added taxes should be treated equally among similarly situated competitors.
- Sales and use taxes are regressive rather than the more progressive income tax system.
- Requiring out-of-state sellers to report all transactions to the purchasers' states may be contrary to privacy statutes in some states.

THE INTERNET TAX FREEDOM ACT

Congress made a determination that the Internet should be free from taxation. It was believed that information should not be taxed. By granting the new medium special status, it was felt that it would continue to develop and grow and benefit all of the users worldwide. It was also believed that the Internet was susceptible to the vagaries of the multiples of tax jurisdictions to a degree other commercial activities have not been subjected to. If e-commerce were left open to taxation and other local regulations, its growth could be hindered significantly.[14] The result of these views was the passage of the Internet Tax Freedom Act.[15]

Provisions of the Statute

Section 1101 of Title 11 prohibits states or political subdivisions thereof from imposing taxes on Internet access and upon multiple or discriminatory taxes of electronic commerce for a period of three years commencing October 1, 1998. It excepts taxes that were imposed and actually enforced prior to the said date. Another exception to the tax exemptions are persons or entities who knowingly transmit nonrestricted access materials that are "harmful to minors" (Section 1101(e)). Telecommunications carriers, Internet access service providers, and similar persons are not subject to the exception. Whether such exception is constitutional, in light of *ACLU v. Reno,* is left for future judicial determination.

Section 1102 creates an Advisory Commission on Electronic Commerce for a term of 18 months, composed of 11 members from the federal, state, and local governments, and 8 representatives from the electronic commerce industry, telecommunications carriers, local retail businesses, and consumer groups. The duty of the commission is to "conduct a thorough study of Federal, State, and local, and international taxation and tariff treatment of transactions using the Internet and Internet access and other comparable intrastate, interstate or international sales activities." Included in the topics to be studied was an examination of foreign barriers erected against U.S. persons engaged in e-commerce and how such barriers affect U.S. consumers; the competitiveness of U.S. persons providing services, goods, or information in foreign markets; and the expansion of the Internet. Other issues to be studied are how taxes on e-commerce are accomplished in foreign markets, the impact of the Internet on U.S. taxes, model state legislation with respect to sales and use taxes in relation to the Internet, and the effects of taxation on Internet transactions.

The statute provided that in order for the commission to issue a finding or recommendation, at least two-thirds of the commission members had to consent. Any recommendation issued had to be tax and technologically neutral and apply to all forms of remote commerce (Section 1103). The act further stated that it is the sense of Congress that no new federal taxes affecting the Internet should be enacted as to the Internet and Internet access (Section 1201) and that the president is to seek agreements from world organizations to remove barriers to global e-commerce (Section 1203).

The advisory commission did render its report in April 2000. The commission, while reflecting the fear that the increase in Internet commerce will result in decreased state and local tax income, nevertheless said that the amount of sales and use tax loss is difficult to calculate. Studies undertaken by the commission projected possible revenue losses from Internet sales of $3.5 billion for the year 2003, which is less than 2 percent of state sales and use taxes. The commission also noted that the Internet might actually increase sales for traditional brick-and-mortar retailers. It said that the current sales and use tax system was too complex and burdensome, requiring simplification and uniformity. None of the proposals passed for want of the two-thirds majority required under the act. The 19-member commission voted 10–8 to send its majority views.

Proposals considered by the commission included an additional five-year moratorium barring multiple and discriminatory taxation of e-commerce; those factors that would or would not establish a seller's physical presence in the state to determine sufficient nexus for tax purposes; and a simplification of the sales and use tax system by creation of a uniform mode of such taxation. With respect to factors that would not provide a nexus so as to enable a state to tax Internet transactions include the seller's use of an Internet provided that has a physical presence within the state, the placement of the seller's digital data on a server located in the state, and the seller's ownership of intangible property that is used or is present in the state. With respect to Internet access, the present moratorium expires on October 21, 2001. Eight states have assessed sales tax on Internet access. The commission's majority suggested that the current moratorium be made permanent on such access charges.

The commission also voted 10–8 to repeal the current 3 percent federal telecommunications excise tax and permanently ban any tax on accessing the Internet.

The commission did possess a more than two-thirds majority in three areas: (1) *Digital Divide.* By a vote of 15–0 (3 abstentions), it recommended that federal welfare guidelines be clarified so as to allow states to spend certain surpluses to provide needy families with computer training and access to the Internet. It also encouraged states and localities, with federal government assistance, to make the Internet accessible to schools, libraries, families, and community centers, as well as providing training for the use thereof. (2) *Privacy.* By a vote of 16–0 (1 abstention) the commission recommended that Congress explore privacy issues in the collection and administration of taxes on e-commerce so as to safeguard and secure personal information derived therefrom. (3) *International Tax Issues and Tariffs.* By a vote of 18–1, the commission recommended the administration take a leadership role with respect to the issue of tariffs on Internet commerce. The tariff system should facilitate and continue the growth of e-commerce, not discriminate against the U.S. The administration should "support implementing and making permanent a standstill on tariffs at the earliest possible date."

Notwithstanding the affirmative recommendation on international tax issues, the commission was divided by a vote of 11–0 in favor (7 abstentions, thus, not meeting the two-thirds requirement for a recommendation) concerning the issue of supporting the extension of the current moratorium on tariffs and duties by the World Trade Organization for electronic transmissions. Similarly, a two-thirds majority could not be achieved (11–0 in favor with 7 abstentions) for the recommendations to the OECD that no new taxes be applied to e-commerce, and that tax rules be modified to achieve neutrality and not distort, discriminate against, or hinder e-commerce.

ALTERNATIVE MEASURES FOR CONGRESS TO ENACT

Those opposed to taxation of electronic commerce advocate the following actions by Congress: (1) abolition of state and local taxation of Internet access; (2) prevention of the imposition of taxation by state and local governments on electronic sales and services; and (3) definition of *nexus* for purposes of taxation to require a physical presence within a state so as to exclude electronic sales and services.[16]

The National Tax Association, concerned with the multitude of taxing jurisdictions, has suggested that should taxation of electronic commerce take place, then:

> [t]here should be one tax rate per state, which would apply to all commerce involving goods or services that are taxable in that state. Provision must be made to ensure protection and equitable distribution of revenues to local jurisdictions. The details of how to encourage or require states, local governments, and businesses to participate in this new system need further study.[17]

There is general agreement that requiring multistate vendors to know and comply with the almost infinite variety of tax laws would be an intolerable burden on interstate commerce. Thus, there should be a consensus both nationally and internationally as to the products or services that are taxable, the methodology of the determination as to which jurisdiction will tax, and other related issues. Accordingly, the association further recommended concerning the sourcing of transactions that they be sourced at the state level only, thereby eliminating the myriad of local taxation rules; that adequate information be made available by the state concerning its regulations; and that appropriate procedures for auditing and recordkeeping be developed.

Whenever there was a need for uniformity in the law, legislatures have enacted model laws to satisfy that need. An example is the Uniform Commercial Code, created to meet the needs of interstate sales, leasing, and other cross-border transactions. Similarly, it appears that a uniform mode of taxation of sales will have to be enacted to allow states to have their tax income while dispensing with the great variety of possible tax programs that could cripple e-commerce.

Another alternative is to have a single national sales tax administered by a federal taxing authority that has the mandate to determine and divide the proportionate share of sales taxes to the individual states. The states, thereafter, would divide the revenue among the local jurisdictions or provide some other method for revenue reimbursement. Also, retaining the present variable sales taxes may not be as difficult to administer by local merchants because there are or will be software tax programs that can determine and allocate taxes to the appropriate jurisdictions. Accountants today can determine taxes due and owing by clients to the different states within seconds after determining the federal tax return.

As of this writing, Congress is considering extending the exemption of Internet sales tax to the year 2005 and thereafter either mandating a federal sales tax, with proceeds portionately to the states, or providing for a uniform state sales tax in place of the many varieties currently in existence.

U.S. TAXATION OF INTERNATIONAL PERSONS AND TRANSACTIONS

All nations impose taxes upon their citizens to pay for their social and other programs. Taxes provide the revenues for a nation's progress as well as serving as a means of achieving its economic, political, and social goals. All countries have laws that provide for the collection of taxes from their nationals and from foreign persons doing business within their borders. Major questions arise, however, as to what extent a country may tax nationals for the conduct of business outside of its borders or tax foreign entities or persons that are affiliated with local companies or engage in domestic transactions.

Jurisdiction

As said in Chapter 2, jurisdiction is the right of a governmental entity to exercise power or control over persons or property. Jurisdiction may be inherent in one governmental unit, or there may be concurrent jurisdiction shared among two or more such units. For example, a U.S. citizen working abroad is subject to the jurisdiction of both the United States and the foreign state. The problem that immediately arises is whether a person is subject to double taxation, that is, by both the host and the home country of the employee. In theory, such a person would be liable for a dual tax, but almost all countries have provided for protection against such results by entering into a series of reciprocal treaties that delineate the respective jurisdictional responsibilities of signatory states.

The possibility of dual liability was clearly enunciated by the U.S. Supreme Court in *Cook v. Tait,* 265 U.S. 47 (1924), when it upheld the power of Congress to impose a tax upon income of a U.S. citizen permanently residing in and domiciled in Mexico from real and personal property located in Mexico. It stated that the power to tax does not depend on the site of the property but rather is found in the relation of a citizen to his or her country, irrespective of where that person may reside. The United States is one of the few countries to tax its citizens for all income generated whether foreign or domestic. U.S. citizens who renounce their citizenship to escape U.S. tax consequences may nevertheless be liable for taxes if they maintain a substantial presence within the United States (defined as 31 days or more in the current year and 183 days or more for the past three years).[18]

There are multiple considerations that affect a country's decision to tax earnings of domestic and foreign persons within its borders. Taxation is a method not only of attaining income for the host state but may also be used to promote the export of goods abroad. Conflicting policies dominate Congressional action in their realm. Political as well as economic factors ally to create the tax programs of a particular state. These factors explain why the United States forgives a significant percentage of earnings of foreign service corporations and gives free trade status to Canada, Mexico, Israel, the Caribbean Basin countries, and other favored states.

Sources of Income

Nations assert the right to tax both nationals and foreigners where appropriate on the basis of their *status* or the *source* of their income. By *status,* we mean the relationship of such person to the government. By *source,* we refer to where the income was generated, which includes both foreign and U.S. generated income.

A U.S. person (citizens, residents, corporations, or other legal entities) is taxed on its worldwide income, subject to various deductions including credit for taxes paid abroad. The United States may tax a foreign person, generally a corporation, if its activities encompass those set forth in the Internal Revenue Code (I.R.C.) and Regulations. The basis of the tax is dependent on the sources of its income as well as its activities in a U.S. trade or business. It may be subject to the same taxes as a U.S. corporation if it is effectively connected with a U.S. trade or business but, unlike U.S. companies, it need not report nor is it taxed on non-U.S. connected income. Thus, it is important to determine the source of its income.

Foreign Corporations. In order to tax a foreign corporation, it is necessary to determine (1) the source of its income and (2) whether the foreign corporation was involved in a U.S. trade or business. Foreign source income received by a foreign corporation can be taxed in the United States only if the corporation was engaged in a trade or business within the United States. I.R.C. Section 864, in defining *trade or business within the United States,* specifically omits trading in securities or commodities except for dealers or companies whose principal business is in such trading or the taxpayer has an office or place of business in the United States through which the transactions are carried out.

Except as stated, all other foreign corporate income that is derived from sources within the United States that is effectively connected with the conduct of trade or business within the United States, and all income/gain or loss outside the United States, is taxable if the corporation has an office or other fixed place of business within the United States to which the income is attributable and that consists of rent or royalties for use of intangible property, dividends, interest, or gains or losses by corporations in the banking or securities businesses derived from the sale or exchange of personal property as defined by the I.R.C.

"Effectively Connected Income" and "Trade or Business Within the United States." The elements that have a major bearing in the determination of whether a foreign corporation has a "fixed place of business" within the United States are: (1) fixed facilities—an office or other fixed place of business through which it conducts business, such as a factory, store, or workshop; (2) management activity—does not include mere occasional visits or temporary conduct of business, however; (3) agent activity—if such agent has the authority to negotiate and conclude contracts on behalf of the foreign corporation or possesses stock for sale belonging to the foreign corporation (activities of independent agents, i.e., commission agents or brokers, are excluded); (4) employee activity—carrying on the trade or business of the foreign corporation in or through a fixed facility within the United States; and (5) office or other fixed place of business of a related person—provided such related person has the authority to negotiate and conclude contractual arrangements on behalf of the foreign corporation as agents within the United States (Regulations 1.864-7).

Excluded foreign source income, and therefore not taxable income, are dividends, interest, or royalties paid by a related foreign corporation or from sales of stock or securities, rents, or royalties unless the gain or loss thereof is attributable to an office or other fixed place of business within the United States to which such income or gain is attributable in the ordinary course of business therein. The net result of these regulations is to distinguish between business and investment income. Only the former is "effectively connected" for tax purposes.

The trend in taxation is to focus increasingly on residence-based principles. The determination is one of ascertaining whether the taxed person is permanently residing or based in a particular country. Such residence-based principles will most likely have increasing importance in computer-related business because determining the source of income is more difficult than deciding where a business is located. Persons, including corporations, are born, reside, or are established in a particular location.

Income Connected with U.S. Business. A foreign corporation engaged in a U.S. trade or business is fully taxed like a domestic corporation on all income, from whatever source it is derived, if it is effectively connected to U.S. trade or business, subject, however, to a foreign tax credit for foreign source income. All income (U.S. or foreign source) that is effectively connected with a U.S. trade or business will be fully taxable.

When is a foreign corporation so engaged? There are complex rules established to determine whether a company is deriving income from a U.S. trade or business. The problem with computer-related businesses is that the location of the seller may be difficult to ascertain because physical location has less importance than in established, rooted enterprises. Foreign companies need not enter the United States to do extensive business therein. If the business dealings are accomplished from abroad via the computer, then it would be equivalent to selling from abroad without U.S. tax consequences for the foreign person. Does the use of a U.S.-based computer server change the tax consequences? Such transactions generally require no employees located within the United States, no warehouse, sales office, or other permanent or semi-permanent physical facilities within the United States. At this juncture, it is difficult to determine the answer. Factors to be considered are the extent of activity directed to U.S. customers, use of U.S. credit facilities, royalty income derived from U.S. activities, amount of time spent within the United States soliciting sales, licensing of software within the United States, ownership or use of computer terminals within the United States, post-sale activities, and other such factors.[19]

Controlled Foreign Corporations. Inasmuch as U.S. corporations pay taxes on their worldwide income and foreign corporations pay taxes only on such income that is U.S. sourced or is effectively connected to a U.S. trade or business, various devices have been utilized to minimize such tax by creating foreign subsidiaries. The foreign subsidiary often would be located in a *tax haven* country (one imposing little or no tax on earning derived therein). Goods would be sold at no gain to the foreign subsidiary, which then resold the goods to the ultimate buyer at a substantial gain. The profit was not taxable in the tax haven country, thereby eliminating the taxation thereof until the money was returned to the parent company either by way of dividends or when the foreign company became dissolved.

To remove the abuse of transfer pricing, the United States has a provision whereby the U.S. company is taxed on such earnings if the foreign corporation is a controlled foreign corporation, that is, one wherein more than 50 percent of the total voting power of all classes of stock is owned by U.S. shareholders on any day during the taxable year. Voting power is determined by an examination of facts and circumstances in the specific cases and includes the power to elect, appoint, or replace a majority of the board of directors; the power to elect persons who have the power of such a board; and other factors. There are a number of technical rules that may be found in the I.R.C. and are beyond the scope of this chapter.

Foreign Sales Corporations

In order to encourage U.S. businesses to initiate and expand their exports abroad, Congress created the Foreign Sales Corporation (FSC) in 1984. The law was created after a prior law, the Domestic International Sales Corporation (DISC) program, became subject to sanctions by the General Agreement on Tariffs and Trade. In essence, about 15 percent to 30 percent of the federal tax is forgiven on export sales, provided certain conditions are met. These conditions include the establishment of a foreign presence, a foreign management, and meeting certain foreign economic process requirements. The legality of the FSC has been called into question by the World Trade Organization and, thus, may not be viable in the near future.

Tax Treaties. The United States has entered into a number of treaties with about 50 countries relating to the taxation of foreign nationals. It would be necessary to examine the appropriate treaty, if any, to determine the effect upon the tax scheme, particularly as to whether certain income is taxable and the rate of taxation thereof.

INTERNATIONAL TAXATION OF ELECTRONIC COMMERCE: OECD REPORT

European nations, being as close to each other as U.S. states are to one another, have engaged in interborder commercial activity for centuries. The growth of the European Union and the Internet has made it much easier for consumers to make purchases throughout the region. As a result, the Organization for Economic Cooperation and Development examined the issue of taxation of electronic commerce. A discussion paper was prepared and a report was rendered stating the views of the organization and a proposed plan for implementation.[20]

The OECD Report affirmed that electronic commerce potentially would be one of the great economic developments in the new century. It recognized the need for governments to provide a climate wherein such commerce would flourish. The report sought to balance the need to encourage electronic commerce with the need for governments to gain revenues for providing services to the public. Accordingly, the report offered a number of conclusions that the OECD had reached for governments to adopt:

1. The new technologies offer tax authorities new opportunities in which to improve taxpayer service.
2. Conventional taxation principles should act as a guide for taxing electronic commerce.
3. Use of conventional principles should not deter enactment of new administrative or legislative measures as long as the new measures

do not impose a discriminatory tax on electronic transactions.

4. Any application of the said principles both domestically and internationally should be structured in such a way as to achieve a fair sharing of the electronic commerce tax base so as to avoid double taxation or no taxation.
5. There should be intensified cooperation and consultation with businesses in the implementation of the said principles.

A critical issue is which national authority should be able to impose a consumption (use or sales) tax. The discussion paper examined the issue in relation to supplies of physical goods to business and private consumers, supplies from business to business, and supplies from business to private consumers of services and intangible property. The paper cited the need to avoid double taxation and nontaxation, the protection of tax revenue, the prevention of tax fraud, the minimization of cost of compliance for businesses, and the prevention of hindrance in the development of electronic commerce. It stated the view of collectors of revenues that "consumption taxation of cross-border trade should result in taxation in the jurisdiction where consumption takes place."[21] The paper noted that a consensus of the different nation-states will be required to prevent double taxation or non-taxation of such transaction. A common set of definitions of services and intangible property is necessary as well as a consensus as the circumstances necessary to establish a showing of the place of consumption.

The paper emphasized that the supply of digitized products (services and intangible property) should not be treated as a supply of goods for consumption tax purposes. Such products are received directly by the customer from the supplier without customs control. Countries should ensure that systems are developed to collect taxes on the importation of physical goods and that such systems do not impede tax collection and the efficient delivery of such goods to consumers.[22] It concludes with a discussion of the need to clarify and modify the OECD Model Tax Convention so as to provide for the changes recommended in the paper and the report.

It appears, therefore, that the OECD, while desirous of promoting electronic commerce, is not adverse to the taxation of electronic commerce in whatever form such activity may take. Its recommendations emphasize the need for governments to preserve their tax base to meet the needs of the citizenry while promoting the growth of the new commercial realities.

Both U.S. and OECD policymakers emphasize the same basic principles.[23] As formulated in the OECD Report, they are: (1) *Neutrality*—conventional and electronic commerce should be treated alike without preference to either mode; (2) *Efficiency*—taxation systems should minimize compliance costs for taxpayers and administrative costs; (3) *Certainty and Simplicity*—the tax rules should be clear and easy to understand; (4) *Effectiveness and Fairness*—the tax rules should minimize the opportunity for evasion and avoidance and afford an appropriate amount of tax during a specified interval; and (5) *Flexibility*—taxation systems should be dynamic in nature and adaptable to technological and commercial developments.

As in other tax matters, it is highly likely that there will be tax treaties and conventions that will clarify international tax issues.

CONCLUSION

Governments are aware of the necessity of fostering, rather than hindering, the growth of electronic commerce. In the United States alone, there are two and one-half million people currently employed in the new technologies with $.5 trillion of sales taking place annually. Such transactions are increasing at a multiple rate annually. The tax policies of governments should be one that offers simplicity of compliance, fairness, and balances the needs of governments for revenue and the encouragement of the wondrous opportunities made possible by the new technologies.

There may be a confrontation among the taxing jurisdictions globally. OECD assumes that electronic commerce will be taxed in the same manner as conventional transactions. The United States, by imposing a moratorium on the taxation of such activity, is acting in contravention to other national and regional bodies. Without consensus, the taxation of electronic sales and services will foster confusion in regard to the stated goals.

As in all other issues raised and affected by computer technology, countries and subdivisions therein will have to reorganize and adapt to the changes brought about as a result of the ongoing exponential growth of e-commerce. Physical presence criteria and the concept of *doing business* within a particular locality have little relevance for tax purposes. New tax policies must be implemented that afford governmental entities the money needed for their programs without jeopardizing the unique advantages of doing business by the Internet. Such policies can no longer be only national in scope. Global cooperation is mandatory in order to accomplish the transition to the new economy. Such cooperation, in the end, will foster international policies that are beneficial to the inhabitants who stand to gain from the expansion of goods and services to all sectors of the globe.

Questions and Problems

1. You own and operate a store in a shopping mall. State your arguments in favor of your state being permitted to tax Internet sales.
2. Do you believe the Internet Tax Freedom Act should be extended? Look up the topic on the Internet and ascertain the current debate and prospects for the act's extension.
3. Compare U.S. and European approaches with respect to taxation of Internet sales.
4. State the constitutional basis upon which an out-of-state company may refuse to comply with a state's demand for taxation of sales to consumers within the state.
5. What factors must be present before a company may be required to pay sales or use taxes on its interstate sales?
6. May a state tax in-state merchant sales made over the Internet to out-of-state residents?
7. Is the nexus required to be present to tax a company's activities the same as the nexus required for jurisdictional constitutionality discussed in Chapter 2?
8. Should there be a national sales tax replacing state and local sales taxes? Give arguments for and against such a tax.
9. May a foreign, overseas company be subject to sales taxes for goods sold to U.S. consumers? Would such a tax be enforceable?
10. If sales taxes are abolished, how should the revenue lost therefrom be recovered?

Endnotes

1. Vertax Tax Library, *Internet Taxation Questions & Answers, www.vertaxinc.com/taxcybrary20/CyberTax_Channel/q_n_a_77.html.*
2. The Internet Tax Freedom Act, Section 1104(8) defines *sales or use tax* as "a tax that is imposed on or incident to the sale, purchase, storage, consumption, distribution, or other use of tangible personal property or services as may be defined by laws imposing such tax and which is measured by the amount of the sales price or other charge for such property or service."
3. According to the Christian Science Monitor, February 28, 2000, p. 3, citing projections by Forester Research in Cambridge, MA, Internet retail sales are expected to rise to between $130 billion and $180 billion by 2004, and business-to-business commerce, which totaled $176 billion in 1999, is expected to rise to $1.3 trillion by 2003.
4. Steve Lohr, *States Confronting Challenge of How to Respond to the New World of the Internet,* New York Times, February 26, 2000, p. A.10.
5. The Internet Tax Freedom Act defines *electronic commerce* as "any transaction conducted over the Internet or through Internet access, comprising the sale, lease, license, offer, or delivery of property, goods, services, or information, whether or not for consideration, and includes the provision of Internet access" (Section 1104(3)).
6. National Tax Association, *Executive Summary, www.ntanet.org*. The five states that do not charge a sales tax are: Alaska, Delaware, Montana, New Hampshire and Oregon.
7. For a discussion of the historical derivation of state power to tax interstate commerce, see Lawrence H. Tribe, *American Constitutional Law,* 2d ed. (Mineola, NY: University Textbook Series, 1988), pp. 403–8. Chief Justice Taney's opinion in *The License Case,* 46 U.S. 504 (1847) permitted states to tax interstate sales, provided Congress did not legislate to the contrary.
8. *Complete Auto Transit, Inc. v. Brady* at 279.
9. Robert J. Samuelson, *Why Not Tax the Internet?* Newsweek, March 6, 2000, p. 49.
10. For a summary of the arguments against the sales tax imposition on Internet sales, see Dean F. Andal, *State and Local Taxation of Electronic Commerce: Read My E-mail, No New Taxes,* Paper presented on April 5, 1997, Spring Symposium, Multi-Jurisdictional Taxation of Electronic Commerce, International Tax Program and the Society for Law and Tax Policy, Harvard University, esp. p. 3. For a review of the issues raised by the new technologies, see Department of the

[U.S.] Treasury, Office of Tax Policy, *Selected Tax Policy Implications of Global Electronic Commerce,* November 1996, *jya.com/taxpolicy.htm.*

11. According to a release of a leading congressional proponent of a permanent moratorium on Internet taxation, sales tax collection, at least in California one of whose districts the congressman represents, increased in the fourth quarter of 1999 from the prior year. U.S. Rep. Christopher Cox, *Internet Tax Freedom at One: No Net Taxes, More Sales Tax Revenue,* Los Angeles Times, October 31, 1999, *cox.house.gov/press/columns/1999/internettaxes.htm.*
12. Gov. Gray Davis, Democrat governor of California, quoted in San Francisco Chronicle, March 1, 2000, p. A24.
13. House Policy Committee Policy Perspective, *A Global Free Trade Zone on the Internet,* February 13, 1997, *policy.house.gov/documents/perspectives/global.htm.*
14. See background to the *"Plain English" Summary of the Internet Tax Freedom Act, cox.house.gov/nettax/lawsums.html.*
15. Title 11 of P.L. 105-277, the Omnibus Appropriations Act of 1998. The text of the statute may be found at *www.ecommercecommission.org/ITFA.htm.*
16. Andal, *State and Local Taxation.*
17. National Tax Association, *Executive Summary,* p. ii.
18. Internal Revenue Code, Section 7701(b).
19. Department of the Treasury, Office of Tax Policy, *Selected Tax Policy Implications of Global Electronic Commerce, jya.com/taxpolicy.htm;* and Arthur Andersen, *The Taxation of Commerce, www.caltax.org/andersen/part5.htm.*
20. The OECD Report, dated October 8, 1998, known as *Electronic Commerce: Taxation Framework Conditions,* was presented to the ministers at the OECD Ministerial Conference discussing A Borderless World. The Directorate for Financial, Fiscal, and Enterprise Affairs, Committee on Fiscal Affairs of the OECD, which prepared the Report, also prepared a paper: "Electronic Commerce: A Discussion Paper on Taxation Issues" on September 17, 1998.
21. See Implementation Option 17 of Committee on Fiscal Affairs of the OECD, "Electronic Commerce" (discussion paper), p. 19.
22. Id. Options 18 and 19, pp. 20–21.
23. Compare OECD Report *Electronic Commerce* with Department of the Treasury, *Selected Tax Policy Implications.*

CONCLUDING REMARKS

Throughout history, there have been events that changed forever the manner in which the human enterprise is conducted. In earliest times, the invention of the wheel, the discovery of control of fire, the philosophical strivings of the early Chinese and the later Greek thinkers, the invention of the printing press, the scientific endeavors of the last two centuries, and also the advances in weaponry, have altered for good and bad how human beings interact with each other. The advance in computer technology, particularly access to the Internet, is such a seminal event. As in all major advances, there are winners and losers, benefits and new difficulties.

The Internet is a mode of communication as are the telephone, hand-delivered mail, and the telex and facsimile machines. The difference is the degree to which we can access and communicate with each other. Five centuries ago, few persons were literate. Access to writings was extremely limited. Until the past century, higher education was the province of the wealthy and the few persons who were able to overcome their lesser financial status. Today, access to all avenues of knowledge and culture is open to all but the relatively few persons in the poorest underdeveloped nations. A person can become knowledgeable concerning a specific topic, with few exceptions, in moments or within a few hours from one's home or office.

A person can be living in a remote village yet have available, by means of a computer with modem and telephone linkage, most of the global advances in the pure and social sciences and the fine arts. Such access creates problems for both autocratic and democratic states. It is a truism in political science that those societies of the past that engaged in significant trade (generally, sea-faring nations) tended to be the most democratic states. The more insulated a population and their leaders, the more distrustful and autocratic the government. The Internet knows no physical or human-made boundaries. It is not an accident that nations have become more democratic as communications have advanced. Radio and television have been excellent means of showing the world the many cultures existing therein. Governments desirous of preventing ideas that were perceived as wrongful from entering their domain, however, limited such advances.

The Internet makes blockage of access quite difficult. Persons who are barely teenagers are able to manipulate the new technology almost at will. Governments that attempt to prevent unlimited access find such endeavors almost impossible to accomplish. Even if such efforts bear fruit, their societies will quickly descend to extreme backwardness. The problem, however, is how to prevent unlawful and harmful transmissions. Computer fraud and theft, pornographic enterprises, and violations of intellectual property rights have come to the forefront.

As one becomes more familiar with issues addressed by courts, it becomes evident that, quite often, the issue is not one of right versus wrong but rather the balance to be determined between opposing rights. This is true especially in matters affecting the Internet. To what degree does a society allow pornography in cyberspace in order to promote unlimited freedom of access to all data? Who decides what data should be censored? How does one prevent criminal behavior by persons not within the jurisdiction of a nation? Should a nation grant an extraordinary degree of intellectual property rights that significantly limits the rights of the public to download whatever materials it desires? Is it true today that intellectual rights protection fosters creativity when creativity abounds without such governmental intrusions?

These and many other issues are to be left to future governments and societies to decide. Decisions, however, can no longer take years and decades to determine. The Internet has sped the process to a degree that, heretofore, was unimaginable. It is a brave new world that offers almost unlimited possibilities and fascination as well as the attendant negative consequences.

Appendix I

CASES

The cases set forth in detail are italicized. Cases cited in the text or within the opinions are in normal (roman) type. The number following the cite is the page wherein the case may be found. The italicized number is the page where the case is set forth at length.

Appendix II

SELECTED BIBLIOGRAPHIC REFERENCES

CONTRACTS

Anderson, Ronald A., Ivan Fox, David B. Twomey, and Marianne M. Jennings. *Business Law and the Legal Environment,* 17 ed. St. Paul, MN: West, 1999.

Cannata, Jennifer B. *Time is Running Out for Customized Software: Resolving the Goods Versus Service Controversy for Year 2000 Contractual Disputes.* 21 Cardozo Law Review 283 (October 1999).

Cheeseman, Henry R. *Business Law: Ethical, International, & E-Commerce Environment,* 4th ed. Upper Saddle River, NJ: Prentice Hall, 2001.

Cox, Trevor. *Recent Development: Information and the Internet: Understanding the Emerging Legal Framework for Contract and Copyright Law and Problems with International Enforcement.* 11 Transnational Law 23 (Spring 1998).

Einhorn, David A. *Shrink-Wrap Licenses: The Debate Continues.* IDEA: The Journal of Law and Technology, 38 IDEA 383–401 (1998).

Farnsworth, E. Allan. *Contracts,* 2d ed. Boston: Little, Brown, 1990.

Feeley, Matthew J. *EU Internet Regulation Policy: The Rise of Self-Regulation.* 22 Boston College International and Comparative Law Review 159 (Winter 1999).

Gale, Jody Storm. *Service Over the "Net": Principles of Contract Law in Conflict.* 49 Case Western Reserve 567 (Spring 1999).

Horovitz, Bonna Lynn. *Computer Software as a Good Under the Uniform Commercial Code: Taking a Byte Out of the Intangibility Myth.* 65 Boston University Law Review 129 (1985).

Howard, Nigel, Karen Opp, and Erika Takeuchi. *Proposed Directive Is an Important Step.* New York Law Journal, Supplement pp. S1, S8–S9 (July 26, 1999).

Kania, Edward D. *The ABA's Digital Signature Guidelines: An Imperfect Solution to Digital Signatures on the Internet.* 7 CommLaw Conspectus 297 (Summer 1999).

Lui-Kwan, Kalama M. *VI. Business Law: 1. Electronic Commerce: a) Digital Signatures: Recent Developments in Digital Signature Legislation and Electronic Commerce.* 14 Berkeley Tech. Law Journal 463 (1999).

Pompiian, Shawn. *Is the Statute of Frauds Ready for Electronic Contracting?* 85 Virginia Law Review 1447 (October 1999).

White, Ron. *How It Works: Digital Signatures.* PC Computing (March 2000), 152–53.

COPYRIGHTS

Caviedes, Alexander A. *International Copyright Law: Should the European Union Dictate its Development?* 16 Boston University International Law Journal 165 (Spring 1998).

The Chronicle of Higher Education. *NYU Starts For Profit Unit to Sell On-line Classes* (October 16, 1998), p. A32.

The Chronicle of Higher Education, *Top Business Schools Seek to Ride a Bull Market in On-line M.B.A.'s* (January 15, 1999), p. A27.

The Chronicle of Higher Education, *U. of Utah President Issues a Pointed Warning About Virtual Universities* (October 9, 1998), p. A32.

Cohen, Barbara. *A Proposed Regime for Copyright Protection on the Internet.* 22 Brooklyn Journal of International Law 401 (1996).

Conference on Fair Use, *Report to the Commissioner on the Conclusion of the First Phase of the Conference on Fair Use* (September 1997).

Cox, Trevor. *Information and the Internet: Understanding the Emerging Legal Framework for Contract and Copyright Law and Problems with International Enforcement,* 11 Transnational Law 23 (Spring 1998).

Morano, Michael F. *Legislating in the Face of New Technology: Copyright Laws for the Digital Age.* 20 Fordham International Law Journal 1374 (1997).

CRIMES

Goldstone, David, and Betty-Ellen Shave. *International Dimensions of Crimes in Cyberspace.* 22

Fordham International Law Journal 1924 (June 1999).

American Business Law Association, Baltimore, MD, August 2000.

CYBERLAW GENERAL TOPICS

Krasovec, Jay. *Cyberspace: The Final Frontier, for Regulation.* 31 Akron Law Review 101 (1997).

The Law of Cyberspace. I. Introduction. 112 Harvard Law Review 1574 (May 1999).

The Law of Cyberspace. II. Communities Virtual and Real: Social and Political Dynamics of Law in Cyberspace. 112 Harvard Law Review 1586 (May 1999).

The Law of Cyberspace. III. The Long Reach of Cyber-reach. 112 Harvard Law Review 1610 (May 1999).

The Law of Cyberspace. IV. Internet Regulation Through Architectural Modification: The Property Rule Structure of Code Solutions. 112 Harvard Law Review 1634 (May 1999).

The Law of Cyberspace. V. The Domain Name System: A Case Study of the Significance of Norms to Internet Governance. 112 Harvard Law Review 1657 (May 1999).

DEFAMATION

Kane, Michelle J. *VI. Business Law: 1. Electronic Commerce: b) Internet Service Provider Liability: Blumenthal v. Drudge.* 14 Berkeley Tech. Law Journal 483 (1999).

The Law of Cyberspace. III. The Long Reach of Cyber-reach. 112 Harvard Law Review 1610 (May 1999).

DISPUTE RESOLUTION

Eisen, Joel B. *Are We Ready for Mediation in Cyberspace?* 1998 Brigham Young University Law Review 1305 (1998).

Hart, Christine. *Online Dispute Resolution and Avoidance in Electronic Commerce.* Uniform Law Conference of Canada. *www.law.ualberta.ca/alri/ulc/current/hart.htm.*

Kessedjian, Catherine. *Internet Dispute Resolution Mechanisms and Applicable Law. www.cetp.ipsl.fr/~porteneu/inet98/2e/2e_1.htm.*

Ponte, Lucille M. *Throwing Bad Money after Bad: Can Online Dispute Resolution (ODR) Really Deliver the Goods for the Unhappy Internet Shopper?* Unpublished paper delivered to the

JURISDICTION

Austin, Graeme W. *Domestic Laws and Foreign Rights: Choice of Law in Transnational Copyright Infringement Litigation.* 23 Columbia-VLA Journal of Law & the Arts 1 (Winter 1999).

Biegel, Stuart. *Indictment of CompuServe Official in Germany Brings Volatile Issues of CyberJurisdiction into Focus.* The UCLA Online Institute for Cyberspace Law and Policy. *www.gseis.ucla.edu/iclp/apr97.html.*

Burk, Dan L. *Muddy Rules in Cyberspace.* 21 Cardozo Law Review 121 (October 1999).

European Union. *Comments on the U.S. Regulations Concerning Trade with the U.S.S.R.* 21 International Legal Materials 891 (1982).

Flaming, Todd H. *The Rules of Cyberspace: Informal Law in a New Jurisdiction. www.sw.com/rulescyb.htm.*

Henkin, Louis. *International Law: Cases and Materials.* St. Paul, MN: West, 1980.

Henry, Joan C. *Establishing Personal Jurisdiction for Internet Transactions. www.law.stetson.edu/courses/computerlaw/papers/jhenryf97.htm.*

International Review of Criminal Policy—Nos. 43 and 44. *International Review of Criminal Review of Criminal Policy—United Nations Manual on the Prevention and Control of Computer-Related Crime. www.ifs.univie.ac.at/.*

Janis, Mark W. *An Introduction to International Law,* 2d ed. Boston: Little, Brown, 1993.

Johns, Roger J., Jr., and Anne Keath, *Caught in the Web: Websites and Classic Principles of Long Arm Jurisdiction in Trademark Infringement Cases.* 10 Albany Law Journal of Science & Technology 65 (1999).

Johnson, David R. *Due Process and Cyberjurisdiction. www.ascusc.org/jcmc/vol2/issue1/due.html.*

Johnson, David R., and David G. Post. *Law and Borders—The Rise of Law in Cyberspace.* 48 Stanford Law Review 1367 (1996).

Kuester, Jeffrey R., and Jennifer M. Graves. *Personal Jurisdiction on the Internet: Where is Cyberspace? www.tkhr.com/articles/personal.html.*

Oberding, Juliet M., and Terje Norderhaug. *A Separate Jurisdiction for Cyberspace? www/ascusc.org/jcmc/vol12/issue1/juris.html.*

Renault, Ogilvy. *Jurisdiction and the Internet: Are Traditional Rules Enough?* Uniform Law Conference of Canada. *www.law.ualberta.ca/alri/ulc/current/ejurisd.htm.*

Vartanian, Thomas P. *The Confluence of International, Federal, and State Jurisdiction over E-Commerce (Part II).* Journal of Internet Law (December 1998). *www.gcwf.com/articles/journal/jil_dec98_2.html.*

OBSCENITY

Cole, April Bailey. *Indecency on the Internet: Reno and the Communications Decency Act of 1996.* 27 Capital University Law Review 607 (1999).

Doherty, Kelly M. *Analysis of Obscenity and Indecency Regulation on the Internet.* 32 Akron Law Review 259 (1999).

Rappaport, Kim L. *In the Wake of Reno v. ACLU: The Continued Struggle in Western Constitutional Democracies with Internet Censorship and Freedom of Speech Online.* 13 American University International Review 765 (1998).

PRIVACY AND SECURITY

Banisar, David, and Simon Davies. *Global Trends in Privacy Protection: An International Survey of Privacy, Data Protection, and Surveillance Laws and Developments.* 18 John Marshall Journal of Computer and Information Law 1 (Fall 1999).

Baumer, David, Julia Brande Earp, and Fay Cobb Payton. *Privacy, Computerization of Medical Records, and the Health Insurance Portability and Accountability Act of 1996.* Unpublished paper delivered to Academy of Legal Studies in Business, Baltimore, MD, August 2000.

Chiang, Leslie. *Web Firms: China Units Face Limits.* Wall Street Journal (September 14, 2000), p. A21.

Clinton, William J., and Albert Gore, Jr. *A Framework for Global Electronic Commerce. www.ecommerce.gov/framewrk.htm.*

Cody, Jonathan P. *Protecting Privacy over the Internet: Has the Time Come to Abandon Self-Regulation.* 48 Catholic University Law Review 1183 (Summer 1999).

Enman, Steven R. *Does Electronic Commerce Need Privacy Law?* Unpublished paper delivered to Academy of Legal Studies in Business, Baltimore, MD, August 2000.

European Commission. *Data Protection: Background Information. europa.eu.int/comm/internal_ . . . en/media/dataprot/backinfo/info.htm.*

European Commission. *European Commission Guidelines for the Security of Information Systems. europa.eu.int/comm/internal_ . . . t/en/media/dataprot/inter/secur.htm.*

E.U. Directive on Privacy May Hinder E-Commerce. National Law Journal. *www.ljx.com/practice/internat/0629euecomm.html.*

Federal Trade Commission. *Privacy Online: Fair Information Practices in the Electronic Marketplace: A Report to Congress* (May 2000).

Global Internet Liberty Campaign. *Privacy and Human Rights: An International Survey of Private Laws and Practice. www.gilc.org/priivacy/survey/.*

Goldman, Eric. *Drafting a Policy Statement? Beware! members.theglobe.com/ericgoldman/privacy.html?nfhp=936388150.*

Graubert, John, and Jill Coleman. *The Impact of Technological Change in the Canada/U.S. Context: Consumer Protection and Antitrust Enforcement at the Speed of Light: The FTC Meets the Internet.* 25 Canada-U.S. Law Journal 275 (1999).

Johnson, Deborah G. *Computer Ethics.* Upper Saddle River, NJ: Prentice Hall, 1994.

Mason, Alpheus Thomas. *Brandeis: A Free Man's Life.* New York: Viking, 1946.

Pagnattaro, Marisa Anne. *Genetic Discrimination and the Workplace: Employee's Right to Privacy v. Employer's Need to Know.* Unpublished paper delivered at the Academy of Legal Studies in Business, Baltimore, MD, August 2000.

Pearce, Graham, and Nicholas Platten. *Orchestrating Transatlantic Approaches to Personal Data Protection: A European Perspective.* 22 Fordham International Law Journal 2024 (June 1999).

Pippin, Major R. Ken. *Consumer Privacy on the Internet: It's "Surfer Beware."* 47 Air Force Law Review 125 (1999).

Reidenberg, Joel R. *Restoring Americans' Privacy in Electronic Commerce.* 14 Berkeley Tech. Law Journal 771 (Spring 1999).

Schwartz, Paul M. *Internet Privacy and the State.* 32 Connecticut Law Review 815 (Spring 2000).

Sprenger, P. *Sun on Privacy: "Get Over It."* Wired News (January 26, 1999), *www.wired.com/news/politics/0,1283,17538,00.html.*

U.S. Government. *Privacy and the National Information Infrastructure: Principles for Providing and Using Personal Information* (June 1995).

SECURITIES REGULATION

Arkin, Stanley S. *Amendments to Foreign Corrupt Practices Act.* New York Law Journal (February 11, 1999), pp. 3, 7.

Folsom, Ralph H., Michael Wallace Gordon, and John A. Spanogle, Jr. *International Business Transactions: A Problem-Oriented Coursebook,* 3rd ed. (St. Paul, MN: West, 1995).

Milbank, Dana, and Marcus W. Brauchli. *Greasing Wheels: How U.S. Competes in Countries Where Bribes Flourish.* The Wall Street Journal (September 29, 1995), p. 1.

Peloso, John F. X. *SEC Rejuvenates Foreign Corrupt Practices Act.* New York Law Journal (May 2, 1997). *www.ljx.com/practice/intrade/0521fcpa.html.*

Reed Smith Bulletin 98-45. *International Anti-Bribery and Fair Competition Act of 1998* (December 1998). *www.rssm.com/pubs/client/bull9845.html.*

Timmeny, *An Overview of the FCPA,* 9 Syracuse Journal of International Law and Commerce 235 (1982).

Valenstein, Carl A., and Rebecca S. Hartley. *The Foreign Corrupt Practices Act: International Due Diligence.* Arent Fox. *www.arentfox.com/features/international/duedil.html.*

TAXATION

Andal, Dean F. *Read My E-mail, No New Taxes.* Paper delivered to the Spring Symposium, Multi-Jurisdictional Taxation of Electronic Commerce, International Tax Program and the Society for Law and Tax Policy, Harvard School of Law (April 5, 1997).

Anderson, Arthur. *The Taxation of Commerce. www.caltax.org/andersen/part5.htm.*

Cox, Christopher. *Internet Tax Freedom at One: No Net Taxes, More Sales Tax Revenue.* Los Angeles Times (October 31, 1999). *cox.house.gov/press/columns/1999/internettaxes.htm.*

Cox, Christopher. *Plain English Summary of the Internet Tax Freedom Act. cox.house.gov/nettax/lawsums.html.*

Lohr, Steve. *States Confronting Challenge of How to Respond to the New World of the Internet.* New York Times (February 26, 2000), p. A.10.

Mazerov, Michael. *Should the Internet Remain a Sales Tax Haven* (December 23, 1999). *www.cbpp.org/12-13-99tax.htm.*

Muscovitch, Zak. *Taxation of Internet Commerce* (April 26, 1996). *www.globalserve.net/-zak/Taxation.html.*

National Tax Association. *Executive Summary. www.ntanet.org.*

Organization for Economic Cooperation and Development. *Electronic Commerce: Taxation Framework Conditions.* Report presented at the OECD Ministerial Conference, Ottawa, Canada, October 7–9, 1998.

Organization for Economic Cooperation and Development, Directorate for Financial, Fiscal, and Enterprise Affairs, Committee on Fiscal Affairs. "Electronic Commerce: A Discussion on Taxation Issues." Discussion paper presented at the OECD Ministerial Conference, Ottawa, Canada, October 7–9, 1998 (prepared on September 17, 1998).

Samuelson, Robert J. *Why Not Tax the Internet?* Newsweek (March 6, 2000), p. 49.

The Taxation of Cyberspace. www/caltax.org/andersen/part1.htm, Part 2 et seq.

Tribe, Lawrence H. *American Constitutional Law,* 2d ed. St. Paul, MN: West, 1998.

U.S. Department of the Treasury, Office of Tax Policy. *Selected Tax Policy Implications of Global Electronic Commerce. ustreas.gov.*

U.S. House of Representatives, House Policy Committee Policy Perspective. *A Global Free Trade Zone on the Internet* (February 13, 1997). *policy.house.gov/documents/perspectives/global.htm.*

U.S. Treasury, Office of Tax Policy. *Selected Tax Policy Implications of Global Electronic Commerce* (November 1996). *jya.com/taxpolicy.htm.*

Vertax Tax Library. *Internet Taxation Questions & Answers. www/vertexinc.com/taxcybrary20/CyberTax_Channel/q_n_a_77.html.*

TORTS

Young, Taylor C. *Turning Back the Clock on the Millennium Bug: Trigger of Coverage for "Year 2000" Claims Under CGL Occurrence Policies.* 31 Arizona State Law Journal 259 (Spring 1999).

TRADEMARKS

Kaufman, Ian Jay. *ICANN, WIPO Address Domain Names.* New York Law Journal: Intellectual Property (January 18, 2000), pp. S5, S10–S12.

Lehv, Richard. *Cybersquatting in Focus: Are New Rules Needed or Will Existing Laws Suffice.* New York Law Journal: Intellectual Property (January 18, 2000), pp. S4, S7–S8.

Monseau, Susanna. *Balancing Trademark Rights on the Internet: The Case of Domain Name Disputes.* Unpublished paper delivered to Academy of Legal Studies in Business, Baltimore, MD, August 2000.

Pittman, Jeffrey. *Preparing for the Future: Internet Top Level Domain Name Expansion.* Unpublished paper delivered to Academy of Legal Studies in Business, Baltimore, MD, August 2000.

Appendix III

WEB SITES

CHAPTER 1. INTRODUCTION TO CYBERLAW

History of the Web—*www.w3.org/People/Berners-Lee/ShortHistory.html*

Centers for Cyberlaw Studies (extensive site for history and online national and international resources): UCLA Online Institute for Cyberspace Law and Policy—*www.gseis.ucla.edu/iclp/gen.resourses.html*

Course outlines: Stetson University—*www.law.stetson.edu/fitz/courses/computerlaw;* Professor Eric Goldman at *members.theglobe.com/ericgoldman*

President's Framework for Global Electronic Commerce—*www.ecommerce.gov/framewrk.htm*

Forester Research (statistical and other data concerning Internet usage)—*www.forester.com*

Cornell University's Legal Information Institute's (LII) extensive Internet law site—*www.law.cornell.edu* and a general list of available topics at *www.law.cornell.edu/topics/topic2html*

Emory Law Library (federal courts and other extensive Internet law–related sites)—*www.law.emory.edu/FEDCTS*

U.S. Government Web sites:

House of Representatives—*law.house.gov*

U.S. Senate—*www.senate.gov*

White House—*www.whitehouse.gov*

Federal Trade Commission (Reports on Internet Policy to Congress)—*www.ftc.gov*

U.S. federal courts—*www.uscourts.gov/*

U.S. Supreme Court decisions—*www.law.cornell.edu/supct*

U.S. Court of Appeals and U.S. District Courts—*www.vcilp.org/Fed-Ct/fedcourt.html*

State courts—*www.law.vill.edu/State-Ct/*

Federal Register—*www.access.gpo.gov/su_docs/aces/aces140html*

State laws—*www.findlaw.com/casecode/state.html*

FindLaw—*www.cyber.lp.findlaw.com*

N.Y. Law Journal site for links to federal and state decisions and a variety of law topics—*www.megalaw.com*

Federal Trade Commission Act—*law.cornell.edu/uscode/15/41.html*

www.cyber.lp.findlaw.com

A comprehensive Web site with dictionaries, federal and state sources, law sites, and newsletters—*www.law.law.onu.edu/internet*

International sites—

European Union—*europa.eu.int/*

World Trade Organization (WTO)—*www.wto.org/*

United Nations law sites—*www.un.org/law/*

Internet Legal Resource Guide—*www.ilrg.com*

International multilateral conventions—*www.tufts.edu/departments/fletcher/multi/chrono.html*

CHAPTER 2. JURISDICTION IN CYBERSPACE

American Bar Association—*www.abanet.org*

American Bar Association Global Cyberspace Jurisdiction Project—*www.kentlaw.edu/cyberlaw/docs/foreign*

LII—*www.law.cornell.edu/topics/jurisdiction.html*

Canadian jurisdiction—*www.law.ualberta.ca/alri/ulc/current/ejurisd.htm*

FindLaw—*www.cyber.lp.findlaw.com/jurisdiction*

www.geocities.com/SiliconValley/Bay/6201/index2.html

CHAPTER 3. INTERNET CONTRACTS

American Bar Association's Digital Signature Guidelines tutorial—*www.abanet.org/scitech/ec/isc/dsg-tutorial.html*

Uniform Computer Information Transactions Act and the Uniform Electronic Transaction Act—*www.upenn.edu/bll /ulc/ulc.htm*

UCITA discussion—*www.law.cornell.edu/topics/contracts.html*

American Law Institute, Restatements of the Law—*www.ali.org*

Uniform Commercial Code—*www.law.cornell.edu/ucc/ucc.table.html* (a specific article in the UCC can be found by substituting the numbered article; for example, Article 2 can be found at *www.law.cornell.edu/ucc/2/overview.html*)

Revisions of Uniform state laws—*www.law.penn.edu/library/ulc/ulc.htm*

FindLaw—*www.cyber.lp.findlaw.com/commerce*

Electronic commerce—*www.mbc.com/ecommerce.html*

CHAPTER 4. INTERNET CONTRACTS AND TORTS

UNCITRAL—*www.un.or.at/uncitral/index.html*

U.N. Convention on Contracts for the International Sale of Goods—*www.cisg.pace.edu/* or *cisgw3.law.pace.edu*

LII—*www.law.cornell.edu/topics/contracts.html* and *www.law.cornell.edu/topics/torts.html*

Tort law library of House of Representatives—*law.house.gov/110.html/*

FindLaw—*www.cyber.lp.findlaw.com/expression*

Alternative dispute mechanisms:

American Arbitration Association—*www.adr.org/*

International Chamber of Commerce—*www.iccwbo.org.arb.index.htm*

Rules and procedures—*www.legal.gsa.gov/legal89.htm*

Disability accommodation—*www.eeoc.gov/docs/accommodation.html*

CHAPTER 5. CRIMINAL ASPECTS OF CYBERSPACE

Department of Justice—*www.usdoj.gov/criminal/cyberspace*

LII—*www.law.cornell.edu/topics/criminal.html*

RICO—*www.law.cornell.edu/uscode/18/1961.html*

Scams—*www.digitalcentury.com/encyclo/update/crime.html*

FindLaw—*www.cyber.lp.findlaw.com/criminal*

CHAPTERS 6 AND 7. COPYRIGHT ISSUES RAISED BY THE INTERNET

LII—*www.law.cornell.edu/topics/copyright.html*

Lanham Act—*www.law.cornell.edu/lanham/lanham.table.html*

American Bar Association—*www.abanet.org/intelprop/home.html*

Copyright cases before the U.S. Supreme Court—*supct.law.cornell.edu/supct/cases/copyrt.htm*

Copyright treaties: Berne Convention and related statutes—*www.cornell.edu/topics/copyright.html*

Fair Use: Stanford University extensive site on copyright and fair use that includes statutes, judicial opinions, and related subject-matter—*fairuse.stanford.edu*

George Washington University—*www.nmjc.cc.nm.us/copyrightbay/coprbay.htm*

University of Nebraska, College of Law, Schmid Law Library (contains numerous hyperlinks to intellectual property sites)—*www.unl.edu/lawcoll/library/topic_ip.html*

U.S. Copyright Society—*www.csusa.org*

Findlaw—*www.findlaw.com/01topics/23intellectprop/01copyright/index.html*

Yahoo!—*www.yahoo.com/Government/Law/Intellectual_Property/Copyrights*

Copyright Office—*lcweb.loc.gov/copyright/*

World Intellectual Property Organization (WIPO)—*www.wipo.org/eng/general/copyright/bern.htm;* also, see *www.wipo.org/eng/newindex/intellct.htm*

World Trade Organization Agreement (TRIPS)—*www.wto.org/wto/intellec/intellec.htm*

CHAPTER 8. TRADEMARKS, DOMAIN NAMES, AND CYBERSQUATTING

Findlaw—*www.findlaw.com/01topics/23intellectprop/03trademark/index.html*

LII—*www.law.cornell.edu/topics/trademark.html*

U.S. Patent and Trademark Office—*www.uspto.gov*

Yahoo!—*www.yahoo.com/Government/Law/Intellectual_Property/Trademarks*

International Trademark Association—*www.inta.org*

CHAPTER 9. PATENTS AND TRADE SECRETS

Findlaw—*www.findlaw.com/01topics/23intellectprop/02patent/index.html*

LII—*www.law.cornell.edu/topics/patent.html*

U.S. Patent and Trademark Office—*www.uspto.gov*

Patent database—*www.uspto.gov/patft*

Yahoo!—*www.yahoo.com/Government/Law/Intellectual_Property/Patents*

European Patent Office—*www.european-patent-office.org*

United Kingdom Patent Office—*www.ukpats.org.uk*

CHAPTER 10. PRIVACY RIGHTS AND SECURITY ISSUES

Privacy self-regulating organizations:

TRUSTEE—*www.truste.org*

Better Business Bureau—*www.bbbonline.co*

Privacy Alliance—*www.privacyalliance.org*

Consumer issues—*www.consumer.gov*

Americans with Disabilities Act Center—*janweb.icdi.wvu.edu/kinder/*

Electronic Frontier Foundation—*www.eff.org/pub/Legal/*

Findlaw—*www.cyber.lp.findlaw.com/privacy*

Obscenity and Privacy: American Civil Liberties Union—*www.aclu.org*

U.N. Guidelines—*europa.eu.int/comm/internal_market/en/media/dataprot/inter/un.htm*

OECD Guidelines—*www.cdt.org/privacy/guide/basic/oecdguidelines.html*

E.U. Directive 95/46—*europa.eu.int/eur-lex/en/lif/dat/1995/en_395L0046.html*

CHAPTER 11. ANTITRUST ISSUES IN CYBER ACTIVITIES

Sherman Antitrust Act—*www.law.cornell.edu/uscode/15/1.html*

Clayton Antitrust Act—*www.law.cornell.edu/uscode/15/12.html*

Robinson-Patman Act—*www.law.cornell.edu/uscode/15/13.html*

U.S. Federal Trade Commission—*www.ftc.gov/* and *www.ftc.gov/ftc/antitrust.htm*

CHAPTER 12. SECURITIES REGULATION AND THE INTERNET

Securities and Exchange Commission—*www.sec.gov/*

Securities Act of 1933—*law.uc.edu/CCL/33ACT/*

Securities Act of 1934—*www.law.uc.edu/CCL/34Act/*

Securities fraud—*www.securitieslaw.com*

Foreign Corrupt Practices Act—*www.law.cornell.edu/uscode/15/78dd-2.html*

Federal Reserve Board Regulations—*www.bog.frb.fed.us.frregs.htm*

North American Securities Administrators Association NASAA Internet Resolution—*www.nasaa.org*

New York Stock Exchange—*www.nyse.com*

Nasdaq—*www.nasdaq.com*

Federal Reserve Board—*www.bog.frb.fed.us*

SEC's Electronic Data Gathering Analysis and Retrieval system (EDGAR)—*www.sec.gov/edgarhp.htm*

Transparency International—*www.transparency.org*

CHAPTER 13. TAXATION OF INTERNET SALES

Internal Revenue Service—*www.irs.ustreas.gov*

Internal Revenue Code—*www.law.cornell.edu/uscode*

Vertax Tax Library—*www.vertaxinc.com/taxcybrary20*

National Tax Association—*www.ntanet.org*

House of Representatives Policy Committee Report—*www.policy.house.gov/documents/perspectives/global.htm*

Department of the Treasury, Office of Tax Policy—*www.caltax.org/andersen/part5.htm*

Glossary

absolute sovereign immunity An extreme view of sovereign immunity in which a country as sovereign is immune from any and all litigation without its permission, including public and political actions by the country.

access charges A type of Internet tax paid by Internet service providers or telecommunications companies and charged to their users.

access device Any card, plate, code, account number or other means of account access that can be used, alone or in conjunction with another device, to obtain money, goods, services, or anything of value used to initiate a transfer of funds, other than a transfer originated solely by paper instrument.

accredited investor An investor that is a bank, insurance company, investment company, or an employee benefit plan; any business development company; any charitable or educational institution with assets of more than $5 million; any director, executive officer, or general partner of the issuer; any person who bought at least $150,000 of the securities offered, provided that the purchase didn't exceed 30 percent of the person's net worth; any person with a net worth of over $1 million; and any person with an annual income of more than $200,000.

active Web sites Web sites that convey information and that encourage interaction with or between users of the sites.

actus reus An act or omission forbidden by law.

alternative dispute resolution (ADR) Method of resolving conflicts other than by litigation in a court of law. Examples are arbitration, conciliation, and mediation.

amici curiae Non-party "friends of the court" who file briefs on behalf of one party or another in a legal dispute.

analog image collection A collection of analog visual images in the form of slides, photographs, and other visual media.

antitrust laws Laws created to enhance and preserve the free marketplace wherein goods and services are bought and sold in accordance with the existing supply and demand.

appropriation of name or likeness An invasion of privacy by borrowing, for one's own use or benefit, the name or likeness of another.

arbitrary mark A mark composed of commonly used words that are not suggestive of the quality or characteristic of the mark, such as Apple computers and Tide laundry soap.

arbitration Similar to mediation, arbitration is a method of solving a dispute between two parties with the assistance of a neutral third party. Arbitrations usually consist of a binding determination, but they may be advisory, or conditionally binding.

ARPANET (Advanced Research Projects Agency Network) Early network linking computers and computer networks formerly owned by the military, defense contractors, and university laboratories engaged in defense related research.

assignment Transfer of rights under a prior contract to a third party.

at will An agreement that can be terminated at any time, by any party to the agreement.

attachment jurisdiction Jurisdiction over parties, obtained by permitting the seizure of in-state property belonging to out-of-state persons.

attempt to monopolize The formation of an illegal plan to monopolize and the taking of some step towards the execution of that plan.

automatic stay Suspension of litigation pending determination of the court of a petitioner's request for relief.

bespeaks caution doctrine Mechanism by which a court can rule as a matter of law that the defendants' forward-looking representations contained enough cautionary language or risk disclosure to protect the defendants against claims of securities fraud.

bilateral contract A promise made in exchange for another promise.

bit The smallest unit of memory in a computer, comprised of a single digit, either a one or zero.

bitmapped image A series of bits and bytes representing a specific pixel or part of an image.

blue sky laws State laws regulating the fraudulent sales of securities that have no assets or that have no potential value other than the blue sky above us.

bootlegging Recording of live performances for commercial gain without performers' consent.

boycott When two or more companies with sufficient economic power agree among themselves to refuse to deal with a particular company.

bribe Any offer, gift, promise, or authorization to give anything of value to a foreign official, political party official, or political party candidate.

bright-line policy A type of decision rendered by the Supreme Court that sets specific guidelines for courts to follow.

business method invention Any invention which is a business method (including any software or other apparatus); and any invention which is comprised of any claim that is a business method.

business method A method of (1) administering, managing, or otherwise operating an enterprise or organization, including a technique used in conducting business; or processing financial data; (2) any technique used in athletics, instruction or personal skills; and (3) any computer-assisted implementation of a systematic means described in (1) or techniques described in (2).

byte A group of eight bits that represents a letter or a number.

C.I.F. (costs, insurance, and freight) The responsibility of a seller of goods for all costs of shipments of the goods plus the cost of insurance and freight charges.

certification mark A word, name, symbol, or device or combination thereof, used by a person or designee for use in commerce to certify the origin, material, mode of manufacture, quality, or other features of the goods or services or that the labor used was accomplished by members of a union or other organization.

choice-of-law A provision in a contract that specifies the forum and jurisdiction to be used in the event of a dispute.

circumventing technological measures Descrambling a scrambled work, decrypting an encrypted work, or otherwise avoiding, bypassing, removing, deactivating, or impairing a technological measure, with or without the authority of a copyright owner.

civil law Area of the law that applies to disputes between private parties.

civil RICO action A civil lawsuit filed against a person for damages incurred as a result of the defendant's racketeering activity.

click-wrap agreements Agreements on software programs that compel the user to accept its contents and terms prior to opening the program. The user must "accept" by clicking his or her consent on the computer screen.

closed-ended Past criminal activity extending over a substantial period of time.

coercive reciprocity The practice of using economic leverage in one market to secure economic advantage in another.

collective mark A trademark or service mark used by members of a cooperative, association, or other organization of members for use in commerce.

collective work A collection of separate works, such as anthologies or encyclopedias.

combination vendor-consumer tax system A type of sales tax wherein the vendor pays the sales tax to the governmental authority and passes the cost on to the purchaser of goods or services.

comity A concept of international law holding that courts of one country will extend the discretionary privilege of courtesy and deference to the judgements and private rights accorded to persons under the laws of foreign countries.

commodity trading advisor Any person who, for compensation or profit, engages in the business of advising others, either directly or through publications, writings, or electronic media, as to the value of or the advisability of trading in (1) any contract of sale of a commodity for future delivery made or to be made on or subject to the rules of a contract market; or (2) for compensation or profit, and as part of a regular business, issues or promulgates analyses or reports concerning any of the activities referred to in clause. Excluded from this definition are news reporters, news columnists, or news editors of print or electronic media, and publishers or producers of "any print or electronic data of general and regular dissemination."

common law The body of law developed in England primarily from judicial decisions based on custom and precedent, unwritten in statute or code, and constituting the basis of the English legal system and of the system of law in all the United States except Louisiana.

community In criminal law, the standard of conduct as reflected by the mores of a particular locality.

comparative advertising The promotion of a product or service by displaying its superiority to a comparable product or service of a competitor.

compensatory damages A common law remedy for breach of contract in which the aggrieved party is entitled to recover the moneys required to place the innocent party in a position that that party would have been in had the contract been performed properly.

compilation A work formed by the collection and assembling of preexisting materials or of data that are selected, coordinated, or arranged in such a way that the resulting work as a whole constitutes an original work of authorship.

computer information transaction An agreement or the performance of it to create, modify, transfer, or license computer information or informational rights in computer information.

computer information Information rendered in electronic form obtained from the use of a computer or in a form that is capable of being processed through a computer. This includes a copy of the information as well as any documentation or packaging that comes with the copy.

computer program A set of statements or instructions to be used directly or indirectly in a computer in order to bring about a certain result.

computer An electronic, magnetic, optical, electrochemical, or other high speed processing device performing logical, arithmetic, or storage functions, and includes any data storage facility or communications facility directly related to or operating in conjunction with such device, but such term does not include an automated typewriter or typesetter, a portable held calculator, or other similar device.

concurrent jurisdiction Judicial power shared between federal and state courts.

conflict-of-laws Private international law. The term also refers to the divergent laws and rules from one country to another and from one state to another.

conglomerate mergers Mergers between a manufacturer and a company that is not a direct competitor but is potentially a competitor, or between firms that manufacture the same product but do not compete with one another (due to geographic location).

conscious parallelism A situation in which no conspiracy or agreement can be proven but it is obvious that a concerted effort to fix prices or products or services has taken place.

consequential damages A common law remedy for breach of contract in which the aggrieved party is entitled to recover monies in addition to compensatory damages for the cost of reasonably foreseeable injuries occurring as a result of the breach.

consideration Something of legal value given in exchange for another's promise or performance.

conspiracy to monopolize An overt or covert agreement between two or more parties to commit an act of monopoly.

conspiracy An agreement between two or more people to commit a crime and at least one act committed by a coconspirator in furtherance of the conspiracy.

consultant's privilege The ability of a consultant, or other advisor, to offer good-faith advice to a client without fear of liability should the client act on that advice to the harm of a third person.

consumer tax A type of sales tax; one paid by the buyer to the vendor who then transmits tax to the governmental taxing authority.

consumption tax A tax collected for the purchase or use of goods or services.

content-neutral Having no bearing upon a particular question or topic.

contract law A type of law that rests on obligations imposed by bargain.

contract A legally enforceable agreement between two or more parties.

contributory infringement Assisting another to commit a wrong, even though such person does not directly commit the wrongful act.

cookies Electronic markers implanted into a computer's memory by commercial Web sites that are used to identify potential customers.

copyright infringement The encroachment or trespass on copyrighted material, such as reproducing, publishing or selling the material without permission.

copyright The protection given to a person for the expression of an idea, such as a book, poem, musical composition, dance movements, and other such creations. Most copyrights have a protective term of life of the creator plus 70 years.

corporate espionage A crime with two principal categories: economic espionage and theft of trade secrets.

counterfeit access device Any access device that is counterfeit, fictitious, altered, or forged, or an identifiable component of an access device or a counterfeit access device.

countertrade Barter-type transactions, that is, the transfer of title to goods in exchange for other goods.

counteroffer An acceptance of an offer that states terms that are additional to or different from the original offer.

covered security A security listed or authorized for listing on a stock exchange or issued by a registered investment company. It is a security that satisfies the standards under the U.S. Code.

crime An act or omission forbidden by law, coupled with criminal intent in the commission of the act or omission of the required duty.

cybercrime A generic term, covering the multiplicity of crimes found in penal codes or in legislation having the use of computer technology as a central component. Cybercrimes include criminal trespass, willful destruction of property, theft of intellectual property, forgery, obscenity, child pornography, larceny, and other offenses.

cyberlaw Area of the law that applies to cyberspace.

cyberspace A decentralized, global medium of communications that links people, institutions, corporations and governments around the world through a giant network of computers, allowing for the free exchange of information.

cyber-squatter Persons who attempt to profit from the Internet by reserving and later reselling or licensing domain names back to companies that often spent millions of dollars developing the goodwill of a trademark.

damage As defined in the Computer Fraud and Abuse Act: "Any impairment to the integrity or availability of data, a program, a system, or information that . . . causes loss aggregating at least $5,000 in value during any 1-year period to one or more individuals . . . "

data message Information generated, sent, received, or stored by electronic, optical or similar means including but not limited to, electronic data interchange, electronic mail, telegram, telex, or copy.

data subject An identifiable natural person.

defamation A tort consisting of the making of a false statement about a person that injures that person's reputation in the community. Defenses to defamation actions are truth, fair comment, and privilege. It is unclear whether defamation through the internet is libel or slander.

definite proposal or offer A statement of goods being offered that includes an explicitly or implicitly fixed price and quantity.

derivative work A work based upon one or more preexisting works, such as a translation, reproduction abridgement, condensation, or any other form in which a work may be recast, transformed, or adapted.

descriptive mark A mark that is not inherently distinctive but is one that identifies a function, use, characteristic, size, or purpose of the product, such as Pine-Sol cleanser or Brawny paper towels.

design patent Any new, original and ornamental design for an article of manufacture.

digital audio copied recording device Any machine or device of a type commonly distributed to individuals for use by individuals, whether or not included with or as part of some other machine or device, the digital recording function of which is designed or marketed for the primary purpose of, and is capable of, making a digital copied recording for private use.

digital audio copied recording A reproduction in a digital recording format of a digital musical recording, whether that reproduction is made directly from another digital musical recording or indirectly from transmission.

digital divide The disparity that exists between those who have computer skills and Internet access and those who do not.

digital musical recording A material object—(1) in which are fixed, in a digital recording format, *only sounds, and material, statements, or instructions incidental to those fixed sounds,* if any, and (2) from which the sounds and material can be perceived, reproduced, or otherwise communicated, either directly or with the aid of a machine or device. Not included in this definition are recordings in which the fixed sounds consist entirely of spoken word recordings, or *in which one or more computer programs are fixed.*

digital signatures A form of encoded attachment that permits verification of the authenticity of a document sent through the Internet.

dilution of a famous mark The lessening of the capacity of a famous mark to identify and distinguish goods and services, regardless of the presence or absence of—(1) competition between the owner of the famous mark and other parties, or (2) likelihood of confusion, mistake or deception.

direct infringement Copying, in part or in total, of a copyrighted work.

disability A physical or mental impairment that substantially limits one or more of the major life activities of such individual, a record of such an impairment, or being regarded as having such an impairment.

discrimination An act that screens out individuals with a disability unless such action is necessary for the goods, services, and facilities being offered.

diversity of citizenship Exists between parties who are citizens of different U.S. states or are citizens of different countries.

domain name Any alphanumeric designation which is registered with or assigned by any domain name registrar, domain name registry, or other domain name registration authority as part of an electronic address on the Internet. In http://www.deltaairlines.com, *deltaairlines* is the domain name.

domestic concerns Any U.S. person or business entity with a principal place of business within the United States or organized in any U.S. territory, possession, or commonwealth.

due process A constitutional requirement of "fairness"—fairness in the substance of the law, and fairness in the procedures utilized in the prosecution and enforcement of the law.

duress The state of being threatened into performing an act unwillingly.

economic espionage Knowingly misappropriating, or attempting to or conspiring to misappropriate trade secrets with the intent or knowledge that the offense will benefit a foreign government, foreign instrumentality or foreign agent.

economic loss The diminution in the value of a product because it is inferior in quality and does not work for the general purposes for which it was manufactured and sold.

economic loss doctrine A doctrine that provides that a commercial purchaser of a product cannot recover from a manufacturer, under tort theories, damages that are solely economic losses.

educational institution Nonprofit organizations whose primary purpose is supporting the nonprofit instructional, research, and scholarly activities of educators, scholars, and students.

educators Faculty, teachers, instructors, curators, librarians, archivists, or professional staff who engage in instructional research, or scholarly activities for educational purposes.

effects principle A principle referring to jurisdiction based on the effect that outside conduct has within a nation, such as U.S. courts determining the legality of conduct by a foreign company having a substantial effect within the United States, though the company's conduct may legal in its own country.

electronic commerce (e-commerce) Any transaction conducted over the Internet or through Internet access, comprising the sale, lease, license, offer, or delivery of property, goods, services, or information, whether or not for consideration, and includes the provision of Internet access.

e-mail One-to-one messaging over the Internet, comparable to sending a letter.

employee One engaged by another to work for wages or salary within an established organization or business.

essential facility theory In antitrust law, certain restrictions apply to the exclusive control of a facility essential to the manufacture or distribution of a product.

estoppel A legal bar to alleging or denying a fact because of one's own previous actions or words to the contrary.

ex post facto clause A clause in the Constitution that forbids any law that imposes a punishment for an act that was not punishable when the act was committed or to increase the punishment after the commission of the act.

exclusionary rule Evidence elicited as a result of wrongful search is to be excluded from introduction at the trial of an accused criminal. Exceptions and limitations to this rule are: evidence obtainable by independent means or evidence obtainable without unlawful intrusion; evidence gathered by private means without government instigation; and evidence obtained via honest mistakes made while acting in good faith.

exclusive dealing Occurs when any person engaged in commerce, in the course of such commerce, either directly or indirectly, discriminates in price between different purchasers of commodities of like grade and quality, where either or any of the purchasers involved in such discrimination are in commerce, where such commodities are sold for use, consumption, or resale with the United States or any Territory thereof and where the effect of such discrimination may be substantially to lessen competition or tend to create a monopoly in any line of commerce, or to injure, destroy, or prevent competition: on with any person who either grants or knowingly receives the benefit of such discrimination, or with customers of either of them.

exclusive jurisdiction Judicial power that is reserved solely to specific courts by law.

express warranties Affirmations of fact or promises by sellers to buyers that are part of the basis of the bargaining process, including descriptions of goods and uses of samples or models in the discussions of the purported transaction.

F.A.S. (free alongside) The responsibility of a seller of goods to place goods next to a designated vessel.

F.O.B. (free on board) The responsibility of a seller of goods to place goods on a designated carrier at its cost and expense.

facility All or any portion of buildings, structures, sites, complexes, equipment, rolling stock or other conveyances, roads, walks, passageways, parking lots and other real or personal property, including the site where the building, property, structure or equipment is located.

fair comment A statement of opinion rather than of fact about another person.

fair use Permissible reproduction of copyrighted materials for purposes such as criticism, comment, news reporting, teaching, scholarship, or research.

false advertisement An advertisement, other than labeling, which is misleading in a material respect, not only representations made but also includes suggestions by statement, word, design, device, sound or any combination thereof.

fanciful mark A mark composed of invented words, such as Clorox, Kleenex, or Exxon.

federal question Arises when the court has to determine issues involving federal statutes, matters of constitutional interpretation, or treaties entered into by the U.S.

file transfer protocol (FTP) A method of information retrieval that lists the names of computer files available on a remote computer and allows the transfer of one or more files from the remote computer to an individual's local computer.

financial institutions Institutions closely related to banking, including retailers issuing their own lines of credit, collection agencies, mortgage lenders, and other credit-gaining institutions, as well as banks and credit unions.

fixation The established representation of a work or idea in a medium of expression, such as in a copy that may be seen, reproduced, or communicated in a somewhat permanent form.

force majeure A condition excusing breach of contract due to conditions beyond the contracted parties' control, such as fire, war, and acts of God.

foreign party A person residing outside of the jurisdiction of a given court. This may include out-of-state residents or citizens of other countries.

form non conveniens A doctrine that is the basis for refusing to hear a case if it can be shown that another forum would be more suitable for adjudication of the dispute at hand.

framing Linked site brought into the original linking site without the advertising or other data annexed to the linked site.

fraud A tort rendering an agreement void or voidable.

fraud in the execution The intentional, false representation of a contract by one party to another in the execution or signing of an agreement. An example would be when a person asks a celebrity to sign an autograph on a document that is a negotiable instrument, contract or the like, disguised as an innocent document and which is unknown to the celebrity.

fraud in the inducement The intentional, false representation of material fact by one party to another in order to induce the other party to enter into an agreement that that person would not have entered into without such representation, to the other party's injury.

FTP (file transfer protocol) A type of remote information retrieval listing names of computer files on remote computers for transfer to local computers.

general jurisdiction The exercise of personal jurisdiction over a defendant in a suit *not* arising out of or related to the defendant's contacts with the forum. Also exists when the defendant engages in significant activities within a given state but the lawsuit is not about those activities.

generic mark A mark that identifies a class of product or service, irrespective or its source, describing the thing itself rather than a feature or aspect of the product. Generic marks do not receive trademark protection.

gigabyte 1,024 megabytes.

Global Information Infrastructure (GII) Part of the presidential initiative to provide unfettered global access to all aspects of information and professional services.

gopher A type of remote information retrieval guiding individual search through available remote computer resources.

goods All things (including specially manufactured goods) that are movable at the time of identification to the contract for sale other than the money in which the price is to be paid, investment securities and things in action. This includes the unborn young of animals and growing crops and other identified things attached to realty.

Also included are all things that are movable at the time of identification to the lease contract, or are fixtures, not including money, documents, instruments, accounts, chattel paper, general intangibles, or mineral or the like, including oil and gas, before extraction.

graphic violence Visual depiction or representation of realistic serious injury to a human or human-like being where such serious injury includes amputation, decapitation, dismemberment, blood shed, mutilation, maiming or disfiguration.

hash function A mathematical computation performed on a document to encode or process it in preparation for secure transmission over the Internet.

horizontal commonality Enterprise that is common to a group of investors—a pooling of interest amongst a group of investors.

horizontal mergers Mergers between competing firms.

horizontal price fixing Price fixing that occurs between competing companies.

host A computer attached to the Internet.

hostname The second part of an internet address, such as "www," for World Wide Web.

hyperlink A link or pathway from one Web site to another.

hypertext markup language (HTML) A type of common formatting language used to create documents for the World Wide Web.

illicit roaming The use of a cellular phone that transmits unauthorized and unidentifiable access codes, allowing the user to place calls without being charged for them.

implied warranties Generally accepted indirect or inferred guarantees by sellers to buyers regarding the integrity of goods.

in camera (in closed chambers) A judge may review evidentiary documents in his or her chambers without the presence of the parties or their attorneys in cases concerning trade secrets and espionage cases wherein the maintenance of security is essential.

in personam actions Litigation based on a court's power over a person served with process within the state.

in personam jurisdiction Judicial power that extends to all parties involved in a lawsuit.

in rem A method of obtaining jurisdiction over parties in a lawsuit by assuming authority over property located within the state.

incidental damages A common law remedy for breach of contract in which the aggrieved party is entitled to recover, in addition to compensatory and/or consequential damages, the miscellaneous costs incurred as a result of the breach.

income source The country in which income is generated.

income status The relation of a person and his or her income to the government.

independent contractor One who contracts to perform work or provide supplies, and is not an employee of the party to which he or she is contracted.

indirect infringement Permitting another to use one's facilities to encroach upon the rights of another.

industrial property Property of industry, such as patents, utility models, industrial designs, trademarks, service marks, indications of source or appellations of origin, agriculture, mining, and agricultural products.

information systems Computer hardware; interconnected peripheral equipment; software, firmware and other means of expressing computer programs; algorithms and other specifications either embedded within or accessed by such computer programs; manuals and documentation on paper, magnetic, optical and other media; communication facilities, such as terminal/customer premises equipment and multiplexers, on the information system side of the network termination point of public telecommunication transport networks as well as equipment for private telecommunications networks not offered to the public generally; security control parameters; storage, processing, retrieval, transmission and communication data, such as check digits and packet switching codes, and procedures; data and information about parties accessing information systems; and user identification and verification measures (whether knowledge-based, token-based, biometric, behavioral or other).

injunction A court order either barring a person from performing a specific action, or compelling a person to perform a specific action.

innocent infringement Unintentional encroachment upon a copyrighted idea or work.

intentional tort A wrongful act committed deliberately or with gross carelessness that causes injury to the person or property of another, such as hitting another person without just cause, or committing fraud.

internet relay chat (IRC) Analogous to a telephone party line, IRC allows multiple parties to converse in real time, usually about a specific subject. Some IRC conversations are overseen by moderators or "channel operators."

intrusion upon seclusion Intentional invasion, physical or otherwise, upon the solitude or seclusion of a person or his private affairs or concerns, or any other intrusion that would be found highly offensive to a reasonable person.

joint work A work prepared by two or more authors with the intention that their contributions be merged into inseparable or interdependent parts of a unitary whole.

jurisdiction The power, right, and authority of a court to hear and rule over a legal case.

kilobyte 1,024 bytes.

laches Undue delay in asserting a legal right or privilege.

lease A transfer of the right to possession and use of goods for a term in return for consideration. A sale, including a sale on approval or a sale or return, or retention or creation of a security interest is not a lease.

leveraging Using monopoly power to control a market with higher prices or reduced output or quality.

libel Written defamation that includes all forms of the media, including magazines, radio and television and computer transmissions.

license An agreement that permits another person to use a copyrighted work as specified in the agreement.

licensee The person who is permitted by specific agreement to use a copyrighted work.

licensor The person who holds a copyright, and permits another to use the work by specific agreement.

liquidated damages A remedy for breach of contract wherein the parties agree at the outset what money will be due and owing in the event of a breach.

listserv A one-to-many electronic messaging service that allows communications about particular topics of interest. Messages are submitted to the listserv and forwarded to the mailing list subscribers.

literary and artistic works Every production in the literary, scientific and artistic domain, whatever may be the mode or form of its expression, such as books, pamphlets and other writings; lectures, addresses, sermons and other works of the same nature; dramatic or dramatico-musical works; choreographic works and entertainments in dumb show; musical compositions with or without words; cinematographic works to which are assimilated works expressed by a process analogous to cinematography; works of drawing, painting, architecture, sculpture, engraving and lithography; photographic works to which are assimilated works expressed by a process analogous to photography; works of applied art; illustrations, maps, plans, sketches, and three-dimensional works relative to geography, topography, architecture, or science.

long-arm jurisdiction A court's authority to rule over cases involving a resident and a nonresident party when the nonresident either committed a tort or engaged in business within the state, although it has no actual presence therein.

long-arm statutes Statutes that give state courts authority to have jurisdiction over cases involving a resident and a nonresident party when the nonresident either committed a tort or engaged in business within the state, although it has no actual presence therein.

mail or wire fraud An intentional tort, the elements of which are: (1) a scheme to defraud whose object is the attainment of (2) money or property, and (3) uses the mails or wires to conduct the scheme.

mark A generic word signifying a trademark, service mark, collective mark, or certification mark.

market extension mergers Mergers between companies that manufacture the same product but do so in different geographic locations.

mass market transaction A consumer contract; or any other transaction with an end-user licensee if: the transaction is for information or informational rights directed to the general public as a whole, including consumers, under substantially the same terms for the same information; the licensee acquires the information or informational rights in a retail transaction under terms and in a quantity consistent with an ordinary transaction in a retail market; and the transaction is not a contract for redistribution or for public performance or public display or a copyrighted work; a transaction in which the information is customized or otherwise specially prepared by the licensor for the licensee, other than minor customization using a capability of the information intended for that purpose; a site license; or an access contract.

means of identification Any name or number used to identify an individual, including a name, social security number, driver's license, unique electronic identification number, telecommunication-identifying information, or access device, and other such identifying manifestations.

mediation A method of solving a dispute between parties by inviting a neutral third party to assist in negotiating an agreement. Mediation is not binding on the parties.

megabyte 1,048,576 bytes.

mens rea Criminal intent.

merchant A person who deals in goods of the kind involved in a transaction, or otherwise by his occupation holds himself out as having knowledge or skill peculiar to the practices or goods involved in the transaction or to whom such knowledge or skill may be attributed by his employment of an agent or broker or other intermediary who by his occupation holds himself out has having such knowledge or skill.

message digest A string of code generated by a sender performing a mathematical computation on his or her document (hash function). It is encrypted by use of a private key that is a password or number known only to the sender.

metatag Hypertext markup code, invisible to the Internet user, that permits Web designers to describe their Webpage. The keyword metatag permits designers to identify search terms for search engines. Description metatags allow designers to briefly describe the contents of their pages.

method of operation The means by which a person makes something perform a function.

minimum-contacts A requirement of systematic or continuous contacts, necessary to establish general jurisdiction.

mirror image A type of acceptance of a contract, made in exact accordance with the terms of the offer.

misappropriation A wrongful use or possession of private property.

modem An electronic device used to connect one computer to a larger computer network over a telephone line.

monopoly Exclusive possession or control through legal privilege, command of supply, or concerted action.

moot Hypothetical, deprived of practical significance, made abstract or purely academic.

moral rights Rights assigned to the author of a copyrighted work: to claim authorship of a work and to object to the distortion or other mutilation of the work that would be prejudicial to the author.

MP3 MPEG-3, a type of compressed information format that is used to copy audio compact disks. This format allows for rapid transmission of digital audio files from one computer to another.

nationality principle A principle based on the concept that a nation may apply its laws over its citizens, irrespective of where they may be located.

natural person A human being. (Businesses or corporations are considered non-natural persons.)

negligent tort A wrongful act committed unintentionally but in violation of legal requirement of due care by a reasonable person that causes injury to the person or property of another, such as an accident caused by inattentive driving.

nominal damages Symbolically small sums of money awarded to a person who has a legitimate claim but was not monetarily injured.

non-merchants Persons not possessing or holding themselves out as dealing in goods or services for which they have specific skills.

non-natural person A business or corporation, not a single human being.

obscenity Materials or information that the average person applying "contemporary community standards" would find the work, taken as a whole, appealing to "the prurient interest;" that depicts or describes, in a patently offensive way, sexual conduct specifically defined by applicable state law; and that, the work, taken as a whole, lacks serious literary, artistic, political, or scientific value.

offer A proposal that is addressed to another party and is sufficiently definite, indicating an intention by the offeror to be bound.

offeree The person receiving an offer.

offeror The person making an offer.

ombudsman An elected official who may act as an intermediary between persons or as an advocate for persons generally unable to afford an attorney.

online dispute resolution (ODR) Resolution of disputes between contestants by use of computer technology whereby the hearing or mediation takes place through the said medium.

open-ended Past criminal conduct with a threat of future criminal conduct.

operating system A software program that permits users to perform tasks, as well as allocating disk space, main memory space, and other functions on a computer. The most popular operating system is Microsoft Windows.

original work Work independently created by an author that possesses at least some minimal degree of creativity, no matter how crude, humble or obvious.

parens patria Acting as a surrogate parent.

parody To make fun of an otherwise serious work.

passive personality principle A principle that permits a government to assert jurisdiction over foreign persons whose actions injured the country's citizens.

passive Web sites Web sites that convey information but are not specially directed at any territory or user.

patent infringement The making, using, offering to sell, or selling of any patented invention, without consent of the owner thereof within the United States or importing into the United States any patented invention during the term of the patent.

patent The legal protection given to persons who create an invention or process that is new, useful, and not obvious. The life of a patent is 20 years.

patents for design Any new, original and ornamental design for an article of manufacture.

pattern An established pattern of racketeering consists of at least two acts of racketeering within 10 years.

per curiam decision A judicial opinion that is made without any specific judge being named as author.

per se rule A rule of unreasonableness based on certain agreements or practices which because of their pernicious effect on competition and lack of any redeeming virtue are conclusively presumed to be unreasonable and therefore illegal without elaborate inquiry as to the precise harm they have caused or the business excuse for their use.

per se violation Certain conduct that is wrong irrespective of the motivation behind the conduct.

perfect tender A condition of sale that allows a buyer to initially reject goods that have the slightest defect at time of delivery.

perform To recite, play, dance, act, show images, or make sounds.

persistent identifier Identifying information that allows possible physical or online contact with another specific person, such as an identification number, a cookie, or a screen name.

person In court, the definition of "person" may include individuals, partnerships, corporations, states, or other recognized legal entities.

personal data Any information relating to an identified or identifiable natural person.

place of accommodation A facility operated by a private entity, whose operations affect commerce and fall within a number of categories under the Americans with Disabilities Act.

plant patents Patents given to the invention or discovery and asexual reproduction of any new and distinct variety of plants, including hybrids, mutants, cultivated spores, and newly found seedlings other than those found in an uncultivated state.

post hoc After an occurrence has taken place.

price fixing An agreement among companies in a given industry to set prices at a certain level.

prima facie evidence Evidence that constitutes proof unless otherwise shown not to be true.

prima facie violation A violation that has been alleged to having taken place and will be assumed proven unless contradicted by the opposing party.

prior restraint A doctrine of restriction of or injunction against types of expression made by characterizing the expression as unprotected.

privacy seal programs Online initiatives designed to protect the privacy of Internet users that require prospective members to abide by certain fair information practices and be subject to inspection procedures by the sponsoring organization. TRUSTe is the first online privacy seal program.

privacy The right not to have one's personal data, communications, space, thoughts, statements, or emotions made public without consent. There is no explicit constitutional right to privacy.

privilege The conditional right of a person to be free of liability absent proof of malice.

process Function, operation, art, or method.

product extension mergers Mergers between a manufacturer and a company that is not a direct competitor but is potentially a competitor.

proper plaintiff in an antitrust litigation A plaintiff who obtains services in a threatened market or a competitor who seeks to serve in that market.

property Goods, wares, merchandise, securities or money.

protected computer As defined in the Computer Fraud and Abuse Act: "Any computer which is used in interstate or foreign commerce or communication."

protected speech Speech that is permissible by constitutional standards and cannot be controlled by statutory enactment.

protective principle A principle based on the theory that a state has the power to make a rule of law governing conduct from outside the state that threatens its security or the operation of its government functions.

proxy solicitations A statement provided to shareholders in advance of a shareholders' meeting, including shareholder proposals and all facts concerning matters to be voted on at the meeting.

public accommodations Any facility designed for public use, including inns, motels, restaurants, movie houses, bakeries, grocery stores, shopping centers, museums, libraries, parks, zoos, sports facilities, and places of education.

publicity given to private life An invasion of privacy by making public a matter of another person's private life of a kind that would be highly offensive to a reasonable person and is not of legitimate concern to the public.

publicity placing a person in false light An invasion of privacy by giving publicity to a matter concerning another that places the other before the public in a false light. If the false light in which the other was placed would be highly offensive to a reasonable person, and the actor had knowledge of or acted in reckless disregard as to the falsity of the publicized matter and the false light in which the other would be placed.

puffery Exaggerated statements regarding a company's strength in the marketplace. Under federal securities laws, puffery is a crime if any of the following factors apply: (1) the statement is not genuinely believed, (2) there is not a reasonable foundation for the belief, or (3) the speaker is aware of undisclosed facts that tend to undermine the accuracy of the projection. [I]t is apparent that plaintiffs have alleged falsity based on the previously detailed undisclosed information.

punitive damages Monies awarded over and above the claimant's actual damages for injuries received due to the commission of an intentional tort which the law permits in order to punish the wrongdoer.

purposeful availment The intentional planning or encouragement of interaction by one party toward another.

qualified person having a disability Under the Americans with Disability Act, such person is "an individual with a disability who, with or without reasonable accommodation, can perform the essential functions of the employment position that such individual holds or desires."

racketeering activity A crime whose definition includes violent offenses, dealing in obscene matter, fraud, transmission of gambling information, and criminal infringement of intellectual property.

real time communication A form of communication over the Internet that allows two or more parties to type messages to each other that almost immediately appear on the others' computer screens.

reasonable accommodation Changes made for disabled persons that may include making existing facilities used by employees readily accessible to and usable by individuals with disabilities; job restructuring, part-time or modified work schedules, reassignment to a vacant position, acquisition or modification of equipment or devices, appropriate adjustment or modifications of examinations, training materials or policies, the provision of qualified readers or interpreters, and other similar changes.

recission The act of setting aside a contract and restoring all parties to their position before the contract was entered into.

reformation A court order that modifies a contract in the best interest of justice.

regressive tax A tax not based on the annual earnings of a person but rather on the purchases made by the consumer.

relevant product market A category of products that can be used reasonably interchangeably and have a "cross-elasticity of demand."

remedy A legal consequence or solution that provides a form of compensation to an injured or wronged party.

restrictive immunity A doctrine that permits a person to sue a foreign country or entity in his or her own court for private commercial disputes.

RICO (Racketeer Influenced and Corrupt Organizations Act) A statute that makes it a crime for a person to be involved in a pattern of racketeering activity, and also permits civil lawsuits for persons injured by the activity.

ripeness Requirement that the controversy that is being litigated can result in effective judicial relief. If no relief can be granted, then the case will be dismissed as being moot.

roamer A cellular telephone customer whose cellular carrier permits calls to be placed from foreign geographic cells.

routine governmental actions (i) obtaining permits, licenses, or other official documents to qualify a person to do business in a foreign country; (ii) processing governmental papers, such as visas and work orders; (iii) providing police protection, mail pick-up and delivery, or scheduling inspections associated with contract performance or inspections related to transit of goods across country; (iv) providing phone service, power and water supply, loading and unloading cargo, or protecting perishable products or commodities from deterioration; or (v) actions of a similar nature.

rule of reason A court's analysis of facts to determine whether on balance a certain conduct should be restrained.

sales or use taxes Internet taxes paid for purchases of goods or services over the Internet.

sampling Selecting a representative portion of a product for the purpose of determining whether to purchase that product or not.

security Any note, stock, treasury stock, bond, indenture, evidence of indebtedness, certificate of interest or participation in any profit-sharing agreement, collateral-trust certificate, preorganization certificate or subscription, transferable share, investment contract, voting-trust certificate, certificate of deposit for a security, fractional undivided interest in oil, gas, or other mineral rights, any put, call, straddle, option, or privilege on any security.

seed capital exemption An exemption from SEC registration requirements for securities offerings not exceeding a total of $1 million within a one-year period.

server A computer that permits simultaneous access to data, services, and other information by multiple users.

service mark A mark identifying and distinguishing the service of a person, including a unique service, from those of others.

sexually explicit material Content having as a dominant theme (1) any lascivious description of or (2) any lascivious picture, photograph, drawing, motion picture film, digital image or similar visual representation depicting sexual bestiality, a lewd exhibition of nudity, sexual excitement, sexual conduct or sadomasochistic abuse, coprophilia, urophilia, or fetishism.

short-swing profit A profit received from a purchase and subsequent sale of stock or sale and later purchase at a lower price within a six-month period.

shrink-wrap agreement An agreement placed generally within a sealed package that is opened after the purchase has been made that binds the purchaser to provisions therein unless the purchaser returns the package within a specific period of time.

shrink-wrap license A legal licensing agreement printed on the outer wrapper of a product that is entered into when the product's wrapper is opened.

signature Any symbol, executed or adopted by a party with present intention to authenticate a writing.

slander Oral defamation.

small issues Stock offerings of up to $5 million within a one-year period.

source (for tax purposes) The place where income is generated.

sovereign immunity A doctrine that assumes that a foreign country as sovereign is immune from all lawsuits arising in another country and cannot be compelled to litigate without its permission. This defense may preclude an opposing party from proceeding with litigation to make a country responsible for its conduct.

space shifting Duplication of previously purchased copyrighted material to another location, such as copying an audio file from a compact disk to a computer.

spam Unsolicited commercial bulk email.

specific jurisdiction The exercise of personal jurisdiction in a lawsuit relating to an out-of-state person, based on contacts with the forum.

specific performance A nonmonetary remedy for breach of contract in which the subject matter of the contract is transferred from one party to the other.

standing Right of a person to sue based on injury in fact and the power of a court to address the relief sought.

state actor Person acting on behalf of a governmental authority.

state In international law, the term *state* refers to a country.

status (for tax purposes) Relationship of a person to his or her government.

statute of frauds Legal requirement that certain agreements must be in writing, signed by the party to be charged and containing all of the essential elements of a contract.

streaming Transmission of an audio or video clip that leaves no trace of the clip on the consumer's computer unless the transmitter wishes to permit the user to download the file.

strict liability tort Conduct that is unrelated to intent or carelessness but that is punishable by law, such as failure to post warnings of danger with respect to a product. It includes cases involving animal bites, use of dangerous instrumentalities, and products liability.

strikesuits Shareholder derivative actions begun with [the] hope of winning large attorney fees or private settlements, and with no intention of benefiting [the] corporation of behalf of which [the] suit is theoretically brought.

subject-matter jurisdiction Judicial power that extends to all cases arising under the Constitution; laws of the U.S.; between citizens of different states if the statutory sum is realized; where the U.S. is a party; between citizens of a state and a foreign state or its citizens or subjects.

substantial nexus Requirement that a business concern have more than minimal contact with a state for it to be taxed on its sales therein. It must have a presence within the state such as an office, permanent sales persons therein, or comparable presence.

substantial presence A tax liability regulation—residency of 31 days or more in the current year and 183 days or more for the past three years for U.S. citizens.

suggestive mark A mark that connotes a quality, ingredient, or characteristic of the goods without describing it, such as Playboy and Coppertone.

support contract An agreement to correct performance problems in computer information other than an agreement to cure a defect amounting to a breach of contract.

tamper Any act of interference.

tax haven country A country that imposes little or no tax on earnings derived therein.

telnet Real time remote computer utilization.

tender offer An offer to purchase stock that meets the following requirements: (1) active and widespread solicitation of public shareholders for the shares of an issuer; (2) solicitation made for a substantial percentage of the issuer's stock; (3) offer to purchase made at a premium over the prevailing market price; (4) terms of the offer are firm rather than negotiable; (5) offer contingent on the tender of a fixed number of shares, often subject to a fixed maximum number to be purchased; (6) offer open only for a limited period of time; (7) offeree subjected to pressure to sell his stock; [and] (8) public announcements of purchasing program concerning the target company precede or accompany rapid accumulation of a large amount of target company securities.

territorial principle A principle that provides that every country has a right to make rules concerning persons and property within its territory, and to enforce those rules therein.

theft of trade secrets Knowingly engaging in the misappropriation of trade secrets or conspiring to do so with the intent to convert a trade secret to the economic benefit of anyone other than the owner thereof [and to the injury of the owner thereof].

third-party beneficiary contracts Contracts that name a third party to be the recipient of rights thereunder, such as life-insurance policies.

time-shifting Using a device to record a broadcast program for viewing or listening to at a later time.

tippee A person who receives and capitalizes financially on material, non-public information concerning securities that he or she knows was derived from an insider who wrongfully disclosed such information.

top-level generic domain(gTLD) The final part of an internet address that identifies what type of organization the address belongs to. The gTLDs are:*.com,.edu,.gov, .info, .int, .mil, .net,* and other newly proposed or newly created ones.

tort law A type of law that rests on obligations imposed by law.

tort Wrongful conduct for which the law provides a remedy.

trade secret Any formula, pattern, device or compilation of information used in a business, and that gives an opportunity to obtain an advantage over competitors who do not know or use the information. There is no time limit given to the protection of a trade secret.

trademark A unique word, name, sign or symbol representing a product, service, or organization. Trademarks have a potentially infinite term of protection, in indefinite 10-year renewable terms.

transaction in goods Sale or other commercial exchange with respect to things that are movable at the time of identification to the contract.

transaction An exchange or transfer of goods, services, information, or funds.

transfer protocol The first portion of an internet address, such as "http," for hypertext transfer protocol.

transmission The design, manufacture, creation, distribution, sale, and marketing of a product.

trespass as to chattel Intentionally using or intermeddling with chattel the in possession of another.

tying arrangement Forbidden business conduct defined as an agreement by a party to sell one product but only on the condition that the buyer also purchases a different (or tied) product, or at least agrees that he will not purchase that product from any other supplier.

unclean hands A situation in which a litigant has committed wrongful conduct against the opposing party, and such conduct affects the subject matter of the lawsuit.

unconscionable In all or part shocking to the conscience of the court.

undue influence Having inappropriate or overwhelming control over another party.

unfair competition Competition contrary to honest practices in industrial or commercial matters.

unilateral contract A promise made in exchange for an act.

universality principle A principle that permits a country to assert jurisdiction over universally condemned conduct, such as piracy, slave trading, narcotics trafficking, and war crimes.

unlawful access to stored communications Intentional unauthorized access to a facility through which electronic communication service is provided, or intentional exceeding of authorization to access such a facility; thereby obtaining, altering, or preventing access to a wire or electronic communication while it is in electronic storage.

use tax A sales tax imposed on an out-of-state merchant for sales or services provided to the forum state.

utility patent A patent granted for the invention or discovery of any new and useful process, machine, manufacture, or composition of matter, or any new and useful improvement thereof.

vector graphics Encoded equations or algorithms representing lines and curves.

vendor tax A type of sales tax; one imposed on the person doing business who is required to pay a tax based on goods sold.

venue The place or county for purposes of a trial where the court has jurisdiction and the place is convenient to the parties based on the availability of process and witnesses and is in the interest of the parties.

vertical commonality Enterprise that is common to an investor and the seller, promoter, or some third party—the fortunes of the investors are linked with those of the promoters.

vertical mergers Mergers between buyers and sellers, such as manufacturers and distributors.

vertical price fixing Price fixing that occurs between manufacturers and distributors in a given industry.

vicarious liability Exists when a person has the right and ability to supervise an illegal activity coupled with a direct financial interest in the activity.

voidable Not obligatory, capable of being nullified by the party with the disability.

WAIS Wide Area Information Services.

warranty of fitness for a particular purpose An affirmation of fact or promise by a seller to a buyer who relies on the seller's expertise that the goods selected by the seller will satisfy the buyer's needs.

warranty of merchantability An affirmation of fact or promise by a seller to a buyer that goods are fit for the ordinary purpose for which they are sold; that they be adequately contained, packaged, and labeled as the agreement between the parties requires; and that, in the case of fungible goods, the goods be of fair average quality.

willful violation Willfully and knowingly making or causing to be made a false or misleading statement as to a material fact.

work made for hire A work prepared by an employee within the scope of his or her employment.

work of visual art A single painting, drawing, print, sculpture, or still photographic image for exhibition purposes, and up to 200 signed and consecutively numbered such works.

World Wide Web A platform created for global, online storage of knowledge containing information from many diverse sources that is accessible to Internet users. It makes use of hypertext markup language (HTML) to browse the Web and display HTML documents with text, maps, sound, animation, and moving video.

worm A computer virus hidden in a seemingly normal computer program.

writ of certiorari A type of permission rarely granted by the U.S. Supreme Court, allowing a case to be further appealed to the Supreme Court after an adverse decision by a lower federal court or the highest court of a state.

Index

A

B

D

E

J

K

L

M

N

O

P

Q

R

S

V

W

Z